THE DIVINER
The Art of Brian Friel

D0826956

THE DIVINER
The Art of Brian Friel

Richard Pine

University College Dublin Press
Preas Choláiste Ollscoile Bhaile Átha Cliath

First published as *Brian Friel and Ireland's Drama* by Routledge, 1990
This second edition first published 1999 by
University College Dublin Press
Newman House, St Stephen's Green, Dublin 2

© Richard Pine 1999

ISBN 1 900621 23 1

Cataloguing in Publication data available from the British Library

Typeset in 10/12 Sabon by Elaine Shiels, Bantry, Co. Cork, Ireland
Printed in Ireland by Colour Books, Dublin

CONTENTS

PREFACE to the
SECOND EDITION

There are several reasons for a new edition of this book, which was first published in 1990 as *Brian Friel and Ireland's Drama* under the Routledge imprint. Principally, Brian Friel has written three further plays since the book appeared – *Wonderful Tennessee* (1993), *Molly Sweeney* (1994) and *Give Me Your Answer, Do!* (1997) – and has made two further translations of Russian classics, Turgenev's *A Month in the Country* (1992) and Chekhov's *Uncle Vanya* (1998). Furthermore, the main part of the first edition of this book was prepared before the productions of *Making History* (1988) and *Dancing at Lughnasa* (1990) and was published before that of *The London Vertigo* (1991); as I could therefore give the two former plays less than adequate attention at the time, the opportunity to assess them more thoroughly in the context of their successors has been welcome. Also, in 1998 I fortuitously located a previously unknown radio play by Friel, *The World of Johnny del Pinto* (*circa* 1960), which I have given due attention in Chapter 3.

In addition, the level of scholarly criticism accorded to Friel has increased significantly since 1990. Two new full-length studies of his work, by Elmer Andrews (*The Art of Brian Friel: Neither Reality Nor Dreams*, 1995) and Martine Pelletier (*Le théâtre de Brian Friel: Histoire et histoires*, 1997) have, as their titles indicate, widened both the scope of the attention paid to Friel and the directions it may take, as has a collection of essays edited by Alan Peacock (*The Achievement of Brian Friel*, 1993). Two very significant surveys of modern Irish drama have also added to this sense of a growing corpus of critical literature – Anthony Roche's *Contemporary Irish Drama from Beckett to McGuinness*

(1994), in particular, provides valuable reassessments of *Philadelphia, Here I Come!* and *Faith Healer*, while Christopher Murray's *Twentieth-Century Irish Drama: mirror up to nation* (1997), by acknowledging the presence of such work, and by desisting from joining it, has emphasised instead the need to pursue themes rather than individual playwrights. Again, as publication of my own book approached, work was published by George O'Brien (*Brian Friel*, 1989) and Michael Etherton (*Contemporary Irish Dramatists*, 1989) which I was unable to give due consideration at the time.

George O'Brien has proved to be both the hero and the victim of the formula imposed by his publishers: his five- or six-page summaries of Friel's individual plays are some of the best concentrated analyses one could hope to find, yet the necessary constriction makes it almost impossible for him to establish the vital connections between one play and another, or to give extended consideration to any of the themes which he correctly identifies in Friel's work.

Conversely, in the sixty pages devoted to Friel by Michael Etherton, one never comes to believe that the critic has engaged with his subject – the treatment is perfunctory, episodic and superficial. Yet, as Etherton has demonstrated in a fascinating and insightful programme note for *Dancing at Lughnasa*, there is an affinity with both the playwright and his themes which clearly requires a latitude unavailable in such formulaic writing.

I believe that unless commentators on the work of a dramatist are permitted such latitude in order to pursue their interest in his structures, preoccupations or affiliations, the mindset will be inhibited to the 'who? when? where?' of exegesis which, however necessary, prevents one from approaching the '*why?*' which is the vital issue in any writer's setting out from his first house.

Friel's engagement with the Field Day company, which he founded with Stephen Rea in 1980, ended in 1994, and this, together with the appearance of Marilynn J. Richtarik's survey of Field Day's first five years, *Acting Between the Lines: the Field Day Theatre Company and Irish Cultural Politics 1980–1984* (1994), calls for a reassessment of this period in Friel's career, which has altered the structure of the original Chapters 5 and 6.

In the wider field of drama and related subjects, including the ever broadening vista of post-colonial studies, there have also been significant advances since 1990, the most important of which have been Homi K. Bhabha's *Nation and Narration* (1990) and *The Location of Culture* (1994). I have taken this opportunity of extending the consideration previously given to this aspect of Friel's work, in particular the correspondences between drama and ritual, between culture and the environment, and between history and storytelling, which are such compelling topics in relation to *Translations, Making History* and *Dancing at Lughnasa* among others. In addition, the connections between liminality and the split personality which were central preoccupations of the first edition, have been hugely deepened by what Bhabha has written. Generally speaking, the availability of such applied theory also helps us to understand how the occupation of being a playwright and his *pre*-occupations coincide to an extent perhaps more intense than anything since the examples of Shakespeare or Molière.

Inevitably, as one's work develops and proceeds, one's understanding of a subject as profound and affective as the work of Brian Friel will deepen. Although I have allowed much of this book to remain in its original form, significant changes have been made throughout, and readers of the first edition should not allow themselves to assume that this is simply the same book with a new final section. Clearly, there is a new Introduction, in which I have tried to establish the current status of Friel as a contemporary playwright, in circumstances that are substantially different from those of ten years ago. And, as already mentioned, there is a new final section, taking account of the plays since *Making History*. This in itself indicates a sea-change both in Friel's writing and in my response to it, since the original division of the book into 'Plays of Love', 'Plays of Freedom' and 'Plays of Language' has been radically affected by the addition of this new section, 'Plays of Beyond' – the third section is now entitled 'Plays of Language and Time' to take account of my inclusion of *Making History* in the same context as *Translations*. In particular, my reading of *Translations* itself has changed quite fundamentally over the years, not least as a result of what I perceive Friel to have been doing in his more recent plays, and this has coloured my view of a work which suffered too long from being regarded as 'a national epic'.

Another factor which deepens and enriches one's appreciation of the playtexts is continued exposure to their performance. Many productions of *Translations* have edged me towards an increasingly ambivalent relationship with a play for which initially I had nothing but passionate admiration, but which today tells me that the author was uncomfortable not merely with the outcome of the critical reaction both for and against the transactions of the play but with the process of writing, which revealed the deep dichotomy between one's allegiances to the local and the universal. Nevertheless, great performances carry their own greatness into one's heart, and I will always recall with deep affection the original impersonation of Frank Hardy by Donal McCann, the Maire Chatach of the American actress Kate Ingrams, the Teddy of Ron Cook in the 1990 revival of *Faith Healer* at the Abbey, Seán McGinley as Eamon in *Aristocrats* at the Gate in 1990, Ian McEwen as Fr Jack and Gerard

McSorley as the narrator in *Dancing at Lughnasa*, a brilliant and definitive production of *Philadelphia, Here I Come!* in 1995 with Rosaleen Linehan as Madge and Harry Towb as the father; and T. P. McKenna and Mark Lambert in *Molly Sweeney* with, between them, the alabaster transparency of Catherine Byrne in the title role.

Nothing is static, and Friel's reputation is subject to the mood-swings of critics and audiences – on an increasingly global scale – as well as to his own preoccupations and writing skills. It is also subject to extra-dramatic factors such as the political and social climate in which the playwright lives and to which he responds. As I write, the Northern Ireland Assembly is coming into existence as a measure of cross-community and inter-governmental determination to bring to an end over thirty years of sectarian and internecine fear and violence, and to find a long-term solution to the problems of the region. Concurrently, a new investigation is being conducted into the events of 'Bloody Sunday' 1972, which, although not directly related to the Widgery Tribunal, is bound to revisit the same questions and the same localities. The day of bloodshed and its aftermath which crystallised a work in progress into *The Freedom of the City*, is thus to be retold and rejudged, and while this will do nothing to change the meaning of the playtext, it may well alter our perceptions of the environment which gave rise to it. The map of Ireland, both physi-cally and psychically, may well take on contours and definitions which none of us will recognise, but which may be more easily discerned than those among which we currently live. The drama of Brian Friel has a place both within and around that process.

Readers of both editions may, indeed, detect a more 'political' reading of the texts in this light, but I believe that it is at the same time more introspective and more focused on the privacies. There are two funda-mental aspects to such a work of criticism. The first is accuracy, by which I mean honesty. One cannot write truthfully, one cannot hope to convey one's sense of what the dramatist is 'about', unless one is faithful to the texts and to their ambience. This applies to the small things as well as to the big ones. I do not think anyone can be convincing on the subject of Brian Friel who writes consistently of plays entitled *The Faith Healer* or *The Three Sisters* where none exists, or who thinks that there are *four* sisters in *Dancing at Lughnasa*. One wonders about a critic who can take Owen O'Donnell's jocose gambit about owning nine or ten shops in Dublin as a sign that he genuinely 'has made his fortune'.

One would hope to be sympathetic to one's subject but, as Fintan O'Toole said in reviewing the first edition of this book, not reverential. Hostility to the basic premises or allegiances of the writer will not equip a critic with insight, with the ability to 'translate between privacies' as Friel would have it. This does not mean, however, that a critic must come from the same cadre or locale as his subject, but that he must have the capacity to empathise with what is other, with what is compelling and mysterious beyond himself which he believes he may be able to comprehend.

In the Afterword to the first edition I wrote what I believe still to be apposite to, and true of, my relationship with Brian Friel:

> Ultimately, all Friel's work revolves around the crucial connection between map-making and communication, and this is especially important for an 'extraterritorial' like myself who is intensely conscious that as an Englishman I do indeed speak a *different language* from Brian Friel, one that, as a post-colonialist, he is intent on annexing and subverting. In my case this has only been partly tempered by over twenty [today, thirty] years' residence in Ireland, which has also served to create an awareness of self as a displaced consciousness. This book is a public document, but it has also been an intensely private experience. In recent years I have been involved, both as a public servant and as a private citizen, in examining many of the issues which have been discussed in this book...In doing so I have tried to reconcile my absence from post-imperial England with my strangeness in post-colonial Ireland: and to develop a voice which might adequately serve that predicament. To quote Yeats, I believe 'I have found all myself'. The right gesture in the right language – perhaps.
>
> This has meant a psychological discovery also. There is a George Yolland and an Owen O'Donnell in each of us. Usually, for the Englishman in Ireland, conscience is dominated by the former. But great chunks of awareness, certainty, sensibility, can start to fall around and become as violent as Frank Hardy's innermost tensions. To be free of these 'thugs' of one's psyche, one must recover the power of laughter. One is continually aggravated by the fear of losing and the chance of winning, until ultimately one finds that the qualitative difference between winners and losers is a certain kind of *freedom*; that even when one is powered by a lie, the exhilaration of knowing that no brake can be put on it, that, even though the leap into the dark will be the hour of one's death, one is liberated by the natural fact of the gesture, carries one beyond the logical point of control, to contain and overwhelm the mythos of eternity itself. This is where dream meets reality.
>
> Brian Friel is particularly concerned with the question of loyalty: to one's friends, to one's folk, to one's country, to one's art. This engagement with community, circumstance or context may be difficult to gauge at times of particular tension. Public crises have, up to now, elicited little direct response from a man who nevertheless displays an immense capacity for caring, but all his work is a divining of his constituency, a marking of depths and shallows and a testing of its capacity, against another day of fate. Especially, of its capacity for laughter. And that has also meant a testing of self, a divining of the inner landscape. Studying his work, and knowing him, has helped me to learn that to live, however briefly or disastrously, within our own fictive world, enables us to know that the ultimate necessity is not even betrayal of one's country, but of one's self, and that the ultimate freedom is a self-deriding laughter.

When I wrote that, I was unaware that James Simmons had said of *The Communication Cord* that it resembled Friel 'pissing on his own monument' – a not unreasonable analogy. But it serves to underline the fact that farce, however serious it may be in its intentions, can only go so far in deepening our awareness of that which it satirises. While *Translations* and *The Communication Cord* may be mirror images of one another, their relationship is much more than mocker and mocked. The questions of which is master and which servant, which the provider of status and purpose, which the mapper and negotiator of the terrain, which the perpetrator of the vital action, are the central issues which playwright and critic, like harlequin and pierrot, constantly toss back and forth between them if there is to be a healthy and elastic dialogue.

The fact that I was initially attracted to Brian Friel because of his wordplay, his own fascination with language becoming *my* fascination, makes me continue to see him at the centre of the language debate, not merely or exclusively an Irish writer or an Irish playwright but a figure of global significance in an increasingly global context who nevertheless uses every word at the value of its local currency, its *haeccitas*. That knowledge of Friel of which I spoke in the Afterword of 1990 has deepened considerably, both intellectually and emotionally. I have been immensely privileged in having known two of the greatest writers of the twentieth century (the other was Lawrence Durrell), and having been granted access to their privacy, to their mindscapes, in having been able to write intelligently about them. It is a humbling experience but the sense of excited discovery carries one through.

A note on the title: my original intention was to give the book its present title, *The Diviner: The Art of Brian Friel* since that seems to me to sum up the essence of the playwright's task as discussed in Chapter 1 (The Landscape Painter). However, the original publishers felt that, unless the name of the subject constituted the main title, it was apt to be miscatalogued by its initial market – librarians. Perhaps they feared that it would appear in company with texts on water-sourcing, or even comparative theology: my god is diviner than your god. So 'and Ireland's drama' was chosen, despite my disappointment at losing the thrust of my original intention, and despite my misgivings that the new title did not entirely successfully embody the sense of a country where drama was central to everyday life. Nevertheless, the book has had its career as the bearer of a title suggesting Friel's engagement with Ireland, and this present turn of emphasis will, I hope, increase that sense of engagement as well as restoring the idea of deep exploration.

ACKNOWLEDGEMENTS

In 1990 I said 'this book could not have been written without the active encouragement and support of Seamus Deane and Richard Kearney' – an acknowledgement which I am happy to repeat, not least because Seamus Deane in particular continued to show an interest in the book. When the book was written, Seamus Heaney generously wrote me a letter from which his commendation of the first edition was drawn, and I am most grateful to him for his continued interest and support.

I also acknowledged the valuable opportunity of residence at the Tyrone Guthrie Centre at Annaghmakerrig, where most of the book was originally written. Since then, Annaghmakerrig has been a place of inspiration and fulfilment which I have often revisited, not least in order to undertake much of the revision of the present text.

Others whom I thanked then and wish to thank again are Crissie Poulter, Vincent Mahon, Jim Sheridan and Eugene McCabe, all of whom I met at Annaghmakerrig; Gary McKeone and Ulf Dantanus and the late Ronald Mason. Will York, director of the graduate acting programme at Alabama State Theater (where a remarkable insight into *Translations* was achieved), Brendan Flynn of the Clifden Community School, and Julian Girdham of St Columba's College, Rathfarnham, all gave me the opportunity to discuss the plays with their students. Since then, I have lectured and given seminars on aspects of Friel's work in many arenas. Principal among these was the inaugural lecture ('Brian Friel and the Politics of Failure') at the 1991 McGill Summer School in Glenties, County Donegal, a week dedicated to the work of Friel, for which I am indebted to the then director of the school, Joe Mulholland. But my greatest debt of this kind is to Anthony Roche, whose support and encouragement has been, and continues to be, invaluable, not least for his own often extraordinary insights into the work. He was the most painstaking and perceptive critic of this book when it first appeared, reviewing it for the *Irish Literary Supplement* (of which we were co-editors); as guest editor of the *Colby Quarterly,* he published my lecture 'Brian Friel and Contemporary Irish Drama', and he commissioned a contribution to the 1999 Friel special issue of the *Irish University Review* of which he is now editor. My deepest thanks and admiration.

Brian Friel himself, as will have been evident from the first edition, has been a frank correspondent and conversationalist, and this generosity was never affected or interrupted by the appearance of the book. Indeed, he has been once more forthright and concerned in discussing both the sources and inspirations of his plays and their fortunes. He has allowed me to write programme notes for the premieres of *Molly Sweeney* and *Give Me Your Answer, Do!* and this trust has been much appreciated.

The dedicatee of this book is my daughter, Emilie (*antea* Emily). When the first edition appeared, perceptive though she was as a 'face reader', she was merely a child. Today she has become a scholar and has collaborated with me as a research assistant on two important projects. To paraphrase Heraclitus, you can never talk to the same daughter twice.

Finally, when it became evident that Routledge did not wish to re-publish the book – believing that thematic works were to be preferred to those on single authors – I was most fortunate in finding at the newly established UCD Press two old friends, Stephen and Barbara Mennell, whom I had first encountered as a consultant to the Council of Europe in the 1970s. Something of the flavour of the programmes on cultural development and cultural identity which we undertook then has, I think, rubbed off on the present work. It has been a great pleasure to work with them again.

RICHARD PINE
Emlaghmore – Annaghmakerrig, 1998

ABBREVIATIONS

For ease of reference, all quotations from the published texts of plays or short stories by Brian Friel are followed by the relevant page reference. Reference to other texts and to unpublished material – mainly the type-scripts of radio plays, and communication by Brian Friel to the author – are by means of superscript numbers. The following abbreviations, indicating the editions I have consulted, will be found throughout.

Ar.	*Aristocrats* Dublin: Gallery Press, 1981
Cass	*The Loves of Cass McGuire* Dublin: Gallery Press, 1984
CC	*The Communication Cord* Loughcrew: Gallery Press, 1989
CF	*Crystal and Fox* Dublin: Gallery Press, 1984
Diviner	*The Diviner, the Best Stories of Brian Friel*, with an introduction by Seamus Deane, Dublin: O'Brien Press 1983
DL	*Dancing at Lughnasa* London: Faber & Faber, 1990
EW	*The Enemy Within* Dublin: Gallery Press, 1979
FH	*Faith Healer* Loughcrew: Gallery Press, 1991
Freedom	*The Freedom of the City* Loughcrew: Gallery Press, 1992
FS	*Father and Sons, after the novel by Ivan Turgenev* London: Faber & Faber, 1987
GI	*The Gentle Island* Loughcrew: Gallery Press, 1993
GMYAD	*Give Me Your Answer, Do!* Loughcrew: Gallery Press, 1997
Gold	*The Gold in the Sea* London: Faber & Faber, 1969
Lovers	*Lovers (Winners and Losers)* Loughcrew: Gallery Press, 1984
LQ	*Living Quarters* Loughcrew: Gallery Press, 1992
LV	*The London Vertigo, based on a play The True Born Irishman or The Fine Irish Lady by Charles Macklin* Loughcrew: Gallery Press 1990
MH	*Making History* London: Faber & Faber, 1989

MiC   *A Month in the Country, after Turgenev* Loughcrew:
             Gallery Press, 1992
MS   *Molly Sweeney* Loughcrew: Gallery Press, 1994
Mundy   *The Mundy Scheme* in *Two Plays* New York: Farrar Straus
             & Giroux, 1970
Ph.   *Philadelphia, Here I Come!* London: Faber & Faber, 1965
Saucer   *The Saucer of Larks* London: Gollancz, 1962
Sisters   *Three Sisters by Anton Chekhov, a translation* Dublin:
             Gallery Press, 1981
Tr.   *Translations* London: Faber & Faber, 1981
UV   *Uncle Vanya, a version of the play by Anton Chekhov*
             Loughcrew: Gallery Press, 1998
Vol.   *Volunteers* Loughcrew: Gallery Press, 1989
WT   *Wonderful Tennessee* Loughcrew: Gallery Press, 1993

CHRONOLOGY

1929   Brian Friel born in Omagh, County Tyrone.

1939   Friel family moves to Derry City.
Friel attends St Columb's College, Derry.

1949   BA Degree, St Patrick's College, Maynooth.
Teacher training course at St Joseph's College, Belfast.

1950   Teaches in primary and intermediate schools in Derry.

1952   Starts writing short stories; contract with *New Yorker*.

1958   *A Sort of Freedom* produced by BBC Northern Ireland Home Service; *To This Hard House* (BBC Radio).

1962   *A Doubtful Paradise* (BBC Radio); *The Enemy Within*, Abbey Theatre, Dublin (BBC Radio, 1963); *The Saucer of Larks* (Gollancz).

1963   With Tyrone Guthrie in Minneapolis, USA; *The Blind Mice*, Olympia Theatre, Dublin and BBC Radio.

1964   *Philadelphia, Here I Come!* Gaiety Theatre, Dublin (New York; Lyric Theatre London, 1967). *Three Fathers, Three Sons*, RTÉ television; *The Founder Members*, BBC Radio.

1966   *The Gold in the Sea* (Gollancz); *The Loves of Cass McGuire*, Helen Hayes Theater, New York (Abbey Theatre, Dublin, 1967).

1967   *Lovers*, Gate Theatre, Dublin (Fortune Theatre, London, 1968)

1968   *Crystal and Fox*, Gaiety Theatre, Dublin.

1969   *The Mundy Scheme*, Olympia Theatre, Dublin.

1971   *The Gentle Island*, Olympia Theatre, Dublin.

1973   *The Freedom of the City*, Royal Court Theatre, London: Abbey Theatre, Dublin (New York, 1974).

1975   *Volunteers*, Abbey Theatre, Dublin.

1976   *Farewell to Ardstraw*, BBC NI television; *The Next Parish*, BBC NI television

1977   *Living Quarters*, Abbey Theatre, Dublin.

1979   *Faith Healer* Longacre Theater, New York (Royal Court
        Theatre, London, 1981; Abbey Theatre, Dublin, 1982);
        Aristocrats, Abbey Theatre, Dublin.

1980   Friel and Stephen Rea found Field Day Theatre Company;
        Translations, Guildhall, Derry (Hampstead and Lyttleton
        Theatres, 1981; Manhattan Theatre Club, New York, 1981).

1981   *Three Sisters,* Guildhall, Derry; Gaiety Theatre, Dublin.

1982   *The Communication Cord,* Guildhall, Derry; Gaiety Theatre,
        Dublin; (Hampstead Theatre, London, 1983).

1986   *The Last of the Name* by Charles McGlinchey, edited and with
        an introduction by Brian Friel

1987   Friel is appointed to the Irish Senate (until 1989); *Fathers and
        Sons,* Lyttleton Theatre, London (Long Wharf, New Haven,
        1988).

1988   *Making History,* Guildhall, Derry; Gaiety Theatre, Dublin;
        National Theatre, London.

1989   BBC Radio devotes a six-play season to Friel: the first living
        playwright so to be distinguished.

1990   *Dancing at Lughnasa,* Abbey Theatre, Dublin; National
        Theatre, London (Plymouth Theatre, New York 1991).

1991   *The London Vertigo,* Andrews Lane Theatre/Gate Theatre,
        Dublin; *The Field Day Anthology of Irish Writing* edited by
        Seamus Deane is published.

1992   *A Month in the Country* Gate Theatre, Dublin

1993   *Wonderful Tennessee* Abbey Theatre, Dublin; Plymouth Theatre,
        New York

1994   Brian Friel leaves Field Day. *Molly Sweeney* Gate Theatre,
        Dublin; Almeida Theatre, London (Round House Theatre, New
        York, 1995).

1997   *Give Me Your Answer, Do!* Abbey Theatre, Dublin

1998   *Uncle Vanya* Gate Theatre, Dublin.

1999   Friel Festival at Abbey, Peacock and Gate Theatres, Dublin, to
        celebrate the playwright's seventieth birthday.

for

EMILIE PINE

face reader

who was right about Brian Friel

INTRODUCTION

'In other men . . . life is a series of beginnings'
The Enemy Within, 47

On 11 August 1991 Brian Friel's *Dancing at Lughnasa* was performed in Glenties, County Donegal, the home town of his mother, Christina McLoone, and the imaginative resource for much of his work, to which he has given the name 'Ballybeg' – in Irish, 'Baile Beag', small town or small home. Probably no other performance of any of his plays – not even *Lughnasa*'s prize-winning successes in London or on Broadway – can have had such a significance for the playwright or indeed for his work. The man whose theatre revolves around language and meaning, around memory and homecoming, came 'home' to Ballybeg – if home there be. That event becomes the benchmark from which all subsequent consideration of Friel must depend, because the play's ultimate message – that there is a level of meaning beyond the clumsy fumbling of language – meant more that evening than on any other. The play represented his strongest challenge to language as a vehicle for bringing us home to truth, to self, to the past, and its stagecraft has subsequently become the genre through which he continues to strive towards such a level of meaning.

In *Language and Silence* George Steiner has said: 'Only genius can elaborate a vision so intense and specific that it will come across the intervening barrier of broken syntax or private meaning'.[1] The question is one of metaphor. Friel's genius has created metaphors to make vital connections between past and present, between myth and narrative, creating meanings which have both public and private resonance. But it is also a temporary genius, only valid at the transitory moments at which the metaphor inheres in the imagination. Elsewhere, the people in Friel's plays become, in his words, 'lost, wandering around in a strange land. Strays',[2] and it is in this condition that we shall encounter them most often.

In this introductory chapter, I shall set out the chief grounds on which Brian Friel is to be considered one of the most important playwrights today, and the chief topics under which his work is to be examined.

SURVEY OF THE WORK

Since 1955, when he began writing professionally, Brian Friel has gained an international reputation for Irish writing in the English language. His particular genre, the 'memory' or 'nostalgia' play, and his capacity to address local themes which have universal significance, have earned him comparison with Anton Chekhov, with whose work he has considerable affinity. That his plays have a political dimension is also evident from the critical response which detects a connection between playwriting and other kinds of writing such as history, and other kinds of drama such as politics, especially in the post-colonial context into which modern Ireland seems to fit so comfortably.

Friel's work is therefore the subject of scrutiny for the twin reasons that, firstly, he opens windows both internally and externally for people living in, or trying to make sense of, modern Ireland; and that, secondly, he provides an example of a writer concerned with the meaning and purpose of the word, both as a central problem of modern aesthetics and as a strategy for conducting the business of contemporary society.

We must recall, however, that Friel began as a writer of short stories, producing two collections which might suggest that he was a very different writer at the start of his career. But the next phase of that career, as a writer of radio plays, is related organically to the short stories and leads – not entirely seamlessly – to the early plays for stage. There is, in fact, a quite clear and deliberate series of progressions in his career: first, from the short story 'The Child' (1952) to *Philadelphia, Here I Come!* (1964); secondly, from *The Enemy Within* (1962) to the later history plays, *Translations* (1980) and *Making History* (1988); thirdly, a phase during which the writer of public plays became a public figure as a founder-director of the Field Day company; fourthly, in the author of *Dancing at Lughnasa* – that play dedicated to his own aunts, 'those five brave Glenties women' – we can detect the author of the journalistic colour piece 'A Fine Day at Glenties' (1963) which marks him out as a diviner or 'landscape painter' in Chekhov's terms, a portraitist in miniature of the huge themes which occupy the imaginations and memories of people who are radically local in their knowledge and experience.

Hannah Arendt says 'conscience is the anticipation of the fellow who awaits you if and when you come home'.[3] In some senses Friel is permanently away from home, not even knowing what or where 'home' might be. He has indeed allowed himself to be characterised as 'the man from God knows where'[4] – an allusion to the title of Florence Wilson's ballad about Thomas Russell, which, as we shall see, has interesting connotations. The homecoming, to be followed inexorably by a new leavetaking, and the stories that demand to be told on each crossing of the threshold, constitute a permanent self-examination and redefinition – 'to begin again' has preoccupied Friel's intelligence since *The Enemy Within* (1962) and recurs tellingly in his reflection on metamorphosis in *The London Vertigo* (1990). Collectively, too: in 1972 he wrote that 'we are still too busy with beginnings'.[5] The 'myth of eternal return' as Mircea Eliade has called it – the homecoming and the leavetaking, whether physical or psychic – is at the centre of Friel's concerns. In 1980, the year of *Translations*, he was still observing, and implicitly advocating, that 'for people like ourselves living close to such a fluid situation, definitions of identity have to be developed and analysed much more frequently'.[6] Hence the necessity of exile and uncertainty, the idea, as Martine Pelletier puts it, that *'le foyer devient alors une sorte de sanctuaire interdit'*.[7] In his work as it progresses we discover more and more echoes of Friel's preoccupations, the development of a voice so distinctive that we are always conscious of the urgency of his disquiet, even when it is at its most eloquent and confident. It is as if he is trying to weave all his work into one seamless garment in which each play mirrors and confirms the others, moving towards one final play, one definitive homecoming, answering and resolving the complexities. This is reflected in the fact that Friel has remained faithful to a form of *credo* which he established in three seminal texts at the opening of his career: a lecture on 'The Theatre of Hope and Despair' (1968),[8] a radio talk 'Self-Portrait' (1972)[9] and a piece commissioned by Denis Donoghue for a *Times Literary Supplement* special Irish issue (also 1972) entitled 'Plays Peasant and Unpeasant'[10] which has been described by Christopher Murray as 'the best guide to the directions taken by Irish drama after 1958'.[11]

   Friel is also a man resolutely connected with, and loyal to, locales: his father's home of Derry, the city where he has spent a great portion of his life, and Glenties. To remember place, which is the locus of both personality and culture, is the vital retrospect. The importance of locality, and of the actors who perform their everyday lives in it, is affirmed in the play with which, it is commonly acknowledged, contemporary Irish drama began in 1964: Friel's *Philadelphia, Here I Come!*, directed by Hilton Edwards for the Edwards-MacLiammóir company at the Gaiety Theatre, Dublin, during the Dublin Theatre Festival. Thomas Kilroy, a fellow playwright and a member of the Field Day company for some years, has spoken on several occasions of the significance of *Philadelphia* in the evolution of Irish drama. 'We had had plays set in country kitchens before this, often, as in Friel, located behind "the shop". What was startlingly different about this play was the sensibility behind it, a mind that was unmistakably of the modern world and one with a clear sense of what modern theatre could do.'[12] More than that, *Philadelphia* showed that Friel could divine more about the kitchen – or could certainly represent more of its inner emotions – than previous playwrights. Kilroy again: 'The play . . . divided us from an Irish theatre that was depressingly provincial in its interests and technically very bad . . . What was manifestly different was the quality of mind behind the work; brimming with intelligence and enormously confident in its use of the stage . . . in the presence of a controlling idea, of a highly developed sense of form'.[13] Thus a technical side to the 'use of the stage' became informed by an intelligence not previously available to Irish drama. Certainly, in his ability to craft dramas which employ the full potential of both human and technical resources – often dangerously so – Friel is able at the same time to invest human strengths and frailties, the sense of hope and despair, with a more synoptic view of the world than most of his contemporaries – with the notable exceptions of Tom Murphy, Frank McGuinness and Kilroy himself.

'Friel's importance will be seen in the way he received [the] youthful tradition [of the modern Irish theatre] . . . and opened it up to the enquiry of a mind schooled in modern theatre and literature'.[14] *Philadelphia* itself was a liminal, transformative moment in Irish theatre, and at the same time typified the crucial experience defined by Arnold van Gennep as the *rite de passage*.[15] *Philadelphia* addressed the central problem of the 1960s, emigration, while its sister-play, *The Loves of Cass McGuire*, attended to its reverse image, the 'returned Yank'. *The Freedom of the City* was a response (but only one) to the events of 'Bloody Sunday' (1972–73). *Translations* (1980) portrayed – or remembered – Irish society in the 1830s as the British administration anglicised the maps and introduced the national school system. In a similar vein, *Making History* (1988) caught the last moments of the dying gaelic culture at the close of the sixteenth century. *Dancing at Lughnasa* (1990) photographed a Donegal family on the verge of disintegration as the livelihood of their home knitting is imperilled by industrialisation.

Philadelphia was the result of a study period spent by Friel observing his friend and mentor Sir Tyrone Guthrie, who was preparing the inaugural season at the Guthrie Theatre, Minneapolis, in 1962, directing *Hamlet* and *Three Sisters*. This, Friel has said, was 'my first parole from inbred, claustrophobic Ireland'.[16] The fact that he employed the term 'parole', ambiguously meaning both 'word' and 'promise' ('I give you my word') is significant, since, beginning with *Philadelphia*, Friel's course as a writer has taken him through the minefields of language, personality, discrepancy and mendacity: in one of his earliest plays, *A Doubtful Paradise*, we find someone declaring 'I'm sick and tired of words and words and words'[17] and the same exhausted emotion recurs whenever too great a burden is placed on language. Put more simply, Friel has occupied the 'theatre of hope and despair'.[18] At the close of *Philadelphia*, Gareth O'Donnell asks himself 'Why do you have to leave? Why? Why?' to which he answers stumblingly 'I don't know. I – I – I don't know' (*Ph.* 110). The uncertainty will be resolved at some points in later plays, and re-asserted at others. But the playwright is left with words, silence and music as the means to keep faith (parole) or to become a traitor, which puts him into a liminal position which we shall shortly address.

The 'controlling idea' identified by Kilroy as Friel's distinctive note[19] is thus both specific to the play – the uncertainty or aporia of Gar O'Donnell and his Ballybeg – and universal in the continuing 'themes and concerns' evinced throughout his work: the doubts, anxieties, discontinuities, local pieties and disavowals, the growth and the failures of love.

Joe Dowling, acclaimed as a director of Friel's work, has said, 'I don't know of any other playwright who will go out on a limb as often as he does. He is the one who has most consistently over the last twenty-five years reflected the changes in Ireland'.[20] With Friel's impetus, the 1980s and 1990s have seen a phenomenal engagement by Irish playwrights with the history and evolution of their country. There is no complacent Irish drama. It is as if the emergent Catholic writers, coming out from the shadow of the crumbling Church–State alliance, had taken up the ambitions of the largely Protestant Irish Literary Theatre at the beginning of the century – a Protestant being someone who will not take 'yes' for an answer.

And yet the public nodes of Irish history provide only one pole for Friel's genius. The other is the intensely private, which cannot be defined by calendars. When he was writing *Translations* Friel adverted to this difficulty:

> I don't want to write a play about Irish peasants being suppressed by English sappers. I don't want to write a threnody on the death of the Irish language . . . The play has to do with language and only language . . . The play must concern itself only with the exploration of the dark and private places of individual souls.[21]

Language thus becomes the fulcrum on which balance two crucial elements in all his work: the tension between public issues and 'private souls', and that between freedom (flight) and commitment (responsibility).

The splitting of Gareth O'Donnell into the simultaneous *personae* of Private Gar and Public Gar enabled him to address the interior and exterior worlds, and to maintain a private conversation while conducting a public address.

> *Public Gar is the Gar that people see, talk to, talk about. Private Gar is the unseen man, the man within, the conscience, the alter ego, the secret thoughts, the id. Private Gar, the spirit, is invisible to everybody, always. Nobody except Public Gar hears him talk. But even Public Gar, although he talks to Private Gar occasionally, never sees him and never looks at him. One cannot look at one's alter ego. (Ph. 11–12)*

His subsequent characters have, to a greater or lesser extent, continued this play: two Gars left home on 28 September 1964, and many of their successors have attempted a twin homecoming, to the private and public selves, reuniting the whole, integrated person in a definitive homecoming. Even when a homecoming is impossible, the two forms of speech, internal and external, continue. In the late 1970s this liminality – the playwright (and his characters) standing on the threshold – was demonstrated in the Chekhovian *Aristocrats* (1979) in which a homecoming is almost achieved. But the most advanced and sophisticated occasions on which this occurs in Friel's theatre were the return of 'Private' Gar to Ballybeg in the guise of Frank Hardy in *Faith Healer* (also 1979) while 'Public' came home to Baile Beag as Owen O'Donnell in *Translations* (1980). The latter play was notable for the fact that Owen speaks in a different fashion when addressing his employers, the English sappers, than when speaking with his own family and community. This characteristic was developed in *Making History* (1988) in which leavetaking and exile represent the other side of the coin of homecoming. Friel had become aware that in one production of *Translations* Owen had in fact used different accents – recognisably English and Irish – to represent this division in his interests and loyalties. In *Making History* this strategy is employed in the figure of Hugh O'Donnell who 'always speaks in an upper-class English accent except on those occasions specifically scripted' (*MH* 1) when he speaks in a 'Tyrone accent' (14, 70).[22]

This 'discontinuity of the ego', or 'dismantl[ing] the unified subject', as Elmer Andrews calls it,[23] is a characteristic of Rimbaud's semantic disturbance in which 'I' becomes 'other' (*Je est un autre*), and as such it will see Friel's characters becoming not only split but muted and blind.

In such a process, we can observe an accommodation between theory and practice, as well as an increasing convergence of the physical and the intellectual, in modern drama. In a discontinuous world, disjunction of elements vital to its health becomes a commonplace in the makebelieve as much as in 'real' life, as the two increasingly come to resemble each other. Ironically, the unified field within which these elements combine is an unreal one, and the translation between them is one unknown to conventional languages.

Friel's career thus exhibits three key aspects of modern life and its drama: the status and uses of language; the issues of loyalty and affiliation; and the essentially local nature of a household compared with the larger 'society'. This last aspect, which has been conveniently labelled 'Chekhovian', will be examined in Chapter 1 (The Landscape Painter). We will now turn to the aspects of language and liminality.

LANGUAGE

One of Friel's most compelling achievements is his approximation, in his writing of *Translations*, to the work of George Steiner. Indeed, *Translations* has been regarded as a dramatisation of Steiner's *After Babel*. In Hugh Mor O'Donnell, the master of the hedge-school of Baile Beag, we witness the *dominus* of a senescent culture, and assent to a linguistic illusion in which, without apparent translation, words spoken in one language are comprehended in another; but what we *hear* are words from the first chapter of *After Babel*:[24] 'it can happen . . . that a civilisation can be imprisoned in a linguistic contour which no longer matches the landscape of – fact' (*Tr* 43 – comparisons between the texts of *After Babel* and *In Bluebeard's Castle* and *Translations* are contained in the Appendix).

Yeats said that 'We make of the quarrel with others, rhetoric, but of the quarrel with ourselves, poetry'[25] and in crude terms that distinction between poetry and rhetoric, between the internal discourse and the external (the private and public selves) is a reasonable indication of the levels and types of discourse available to us. But language, as the distinctive form of communication among humans, is so complex that its use by a playwright to convey emotional states, to present the affections, to encode statements with varying degrees of intensity and significance, is strewn with danger. Language as a vehicle of perception becomes the messenger of love, hate, fear, the cause of bonding, violence, alienation.

After Babel, subtitled *Aspects of Language and Translation* (1975), was a milestone in our understanding of the difficulties in communication between the deep structures of opposing or unlike cultures or perceptions. This is especially true when the book is read in conjunction with Steiner's *Extraterritorial: Papers on Literature and the Language Revolution* (1972) and *In Bluebeard's Castle: Some Notes Towards the Re-definition of Culture* (1971). Ironically, in his autobiographical essay *Errata*, Steiner complains that many have borrowed from the thesis of *After*

Babel without acknowledgement[26] – a criticism that cannot be levelled at Friel, who recorded in his published diary the central presence of the book in the process of writing *Translations*.[27] Moreover, it has been amply discussed by commentators on *Translations* who have noted the fertile symbiosis of the two texts.[28]

Indeed, the coincidence, in that diary and that process, of *After Babel* and John Andrews's history of the Ordnance Survey exercise in Ireland, *A Paper Landscape*,[29] makes it clear that the topological aspect of language present in Steiner's text ('a linguistic contour . . . the landscape of fact') is not merely a convenient device for creating a mental image of language. It is in fact a conjunction between the development of language as the bearer of shared meaning and that of understanding the landscape which gives rise to perception: map-making on both the physical and metaphysical levels.[30]

Further fruitful examples of this dramatic topology are Thomas Whitaker's *Fields of Play in Modern Drama* (1977) and Peter Brook's *The Empty Space* (1968), while the political dimension of writing on the issue of identity has been addressed by André Brink in *Mapmakers: Writing in a State of Siege* (1983). In Ireland, from George Moore's *The Untilled Field* through Heaney's analogy of *digging* (*Death of a Naturalist*) and *Field Work* to his more recent *Opened Ground*, the land of Ireland has provided a metaphor for its identity, the land itself, in Estyn Evans's expression, being the personality of Ireland[31] – an identification of its what-ness with its it-ness.

This leads us to the observation that the exploration of culture and psychology which is characteristic of many contemporary Irish dramatists (John B. Keane, Tom Murphy, Thomas Kilroy and Frank McGuinness in particular) has at its back a vast literature in philosophy, anthropology, psychology and sociology. We should recall that the programme for the inaugural production of *Translations* carried, in addition to an epigram from Steiner, the following text from Heidegger (which also prefaces *After Babel*): 'Man acts as though he were the master of language, while it is language which remains mistress of men. When this relation of domination is inverted, man succumbs to strange contrivances'.[32]

Another adaptation from *After Babel* is relevant here: Steiner refers to a pre-existent form of language, the 'Ur-Sprache', which, he says, 'had a congruence with reality . . . Words and objects dovetailed perfectly. As the modern epistemologist might put it, there was a complete point-to-point mapping of language onto the true substance and shape of things'[33] – which Friel 'translates' as: 'Each name a perfect equation with its roots. A perfect congruence with reality' (*Tr.* 45). On occasions it may seem as if there has been a 'point-to-point mapping', an 'equation' between the precedent text and the play. I have already alluded to the extent to which *After Babel* provided one dimension of the argument in *Translations*.

Friel has in fact employed many texts either implicitly or explicitly, either acknowledged or tacitly incorporated, in his plays. Works such as Oscar Lewis's *La Vida* (in *The Freedom of the City*), Sean O'Faolain's *The Great O'Neill* (in *Making History*), and John Andrews's *A Paper Landscape* (in *Translations*) have provided him with pre-texts addressing issues such as the culture of poverty, the versions of historical truth, the inner and outer perceptions, and ritual as drama. In *Molly Sweeney* Friel explicitly acknowledges 'I am particularly indebted to Oliver Sacks's case history "To See and Not See" and the long strange tradition of such case histories' (*MS 9*). Elsewhere, the chapter in Erving Goffman's *Forms of Talk* entitled 'Response Cries' was the impetus for the thesis on 'Discourse Analysis with Particular Reference to Response Cries' in *The Communication Cord* (*CC 18*). These are not the *reasons* for his own plays, but the hinterland into which others, in disciplines organically related to drama, have already quarried, and which enable him to create a framework within which the 'exploration of the dark and private places of individual souls'[34] can take place.

But there are two further senses in which this 'mapping' can be considered, both of which demonstrate the significance of a shared vocabulary within and between the various disciplines under discussion. Firstly, as the work of Erving Goffman demonstrates, there is a language relating to both 'ordinary' and 'normal' people in everyday behaviour and to those in exceptional circumstances, which has a 'performance' or 'acting' aspect. In addition to direct employment of the technical writing in *Forms of Talk*, Friel might be said to have borrowed the *idea* of a book such as Goffman's *Stigma*, with its subtitle – *notes on the management of spoiled identity* – suggestive of the condition of suppression and poverty experienced by the minority population in Northern Ireland, as evidenced in *The Freedom of the City*.

More important, however, is Goffman's study *Asylums*, which categorises five different kinds of 'total institution': homes for the aged or indigent; mental hospitals and sanitaria; prisons; army barracks, compounds, boarding schools and servants' quarters; convents and monasteries.[35] A superficial knowledge of Friel's work would reveal that such 'total institutions' appear frequently in his plays: 'Eden House', the old people's home in *The Loves of Cass McGuire*; the psychiatric wards sheltering Grace's mother in *Faith Healer*, Molly herself in *Molly Sweeney* and the daughter, Bridget, in *Give Me Your Answer, Do!*; the internment camp in *Volunteers*; the army barracks in *Living Quarters*; the monastery

of Columba in *The Enemy Within*. Goffman obviously makes a contrast
between the home environment and that of the 'total institution', but it
could be argued that 'home', as we see it in *Aristocrats, Losers, The
Gentle Island* or *Dancing at Lughnasa*, or the circus in *Crystal and Fox*,
is a form of total institution in that it embraces all its inmates and
imposes certain rules of speech and behaviour upon them. Certainly, in
the case of *Philadelphia* – in which Gar explicitly declares 'Asylum cases,
the whole bloody lot of them! . . . It's a bloody quagmire, a backwater, a
dead-end! And everybody in it goes crazy sooner or later! Everybody!'
(*Ph*. 80–1) – the strict regime of silence interspersed with embarrassed talk
can be seen as a world where duress and tension, whether imposed from
outside or generated within, exercise an affective hold on their victims.[36]

The second sense in which the idea of close coincidence between the
theory and practice of the stage is important to us is that of anthropology,
in which 'social process [is] performative'.[37] Victor Turner's work, in
particular, draws very compelling parallels between ritual and drama,
especially in *The Forest of Symbols: Aspects of Ndembu Ritual* (1967),
Dramas, Fields and Metaphors: Symbolic Action in Human Society (1974)
and *From Ritual to Theatre: The Human Seriousness of Play* (1982),
where he refers specifically to map-making in the exploratory phase of
his work as 'these crude, almost mediaeval maps I have been unrolling of
the obscure liminal and liminoid regions which lie around our
comfortable village of the sociologically known, proven, tried and
tested'.[38] And here we reach a vital shared characteristic of drama and
ritual: that they both involve the concealment and eventual revelation of
a secret. The play, or the social situation in which ritual is transacted, is
liminal (Latin, *limen*: a threshold) in that a dramatic scene or a ritual act
represents a *transitus* from one situation, one state of affairs, one
condition, to another. As Seamus Deane has remarked in discussing
Friel's 'double stage', 'every character has his or her fiction; every fiction
is generated out of the fear of the truth. But the truth is nevertheless
there, hidden in the story which lies at the centre of the play . . . The
function of the hidden story, when it is uncovered, is to transform the
stage as public exhibition area into the stage as private and sacral area'.[39]
As we shall see in the following section, liminality is the crucial condition
in which the culture of a post-modern society, and its predicaments, can
be observed. Before addressing that point, however, I want to explore a
little further the notion of the secret embedded in the play/ritual.

Drama has always contained this essential 'truth' which is approached,
and finally revealed, in the course of the action, and which thereby
involves the spectator in the transitus enacted. It will be one of my major
arguments in the later part of this book (Chapters 7 and 8 particularly)

that Friel's drama in fact includes the participant in the action, making him or her responsible for some element of its resolution – an approval of what is witnessed, or a felt need to resolve, in one's own mind and person, what is not resolved at the play's conclusion. In this way it resembles ritual, in which the 'tribe' or 'community' participates actively rather than as spectators. And of course the parallel must be drawn between the *shaman*, or priest of the tribe, and the playwright-as-story-teller who creates the conditions for that play/ritual to take place. Here we should note Turner's point, that 'play is . . . essentially interstitial, betwixt-and-between all standard taxonomic nodes, essentially "elusive"'.[40]

In the revealing of a secret, the test of the playwright's art is whether he can suggest to the audience that that secret, that truth, is universal. In *Faith Healer*, Teddy recounts one evening when one of those cured by Frank Hardy addresses him:

> 'Mr Hardy, as long as men live in Glamorganshire, you'll be remembered here'. And whatever way he said it, you knew it was true; and whatever way he said Glamorganshire, it sounded like the whole world. (*FH* 39)

It is this Chekhovian ability to connect the smallest place with 'the whole world', to reveal its essentially universal truths, that distinguishes Friel's own drama and makes it so affective, as well as effective, for his audiences.

It is also, of course, one of the reasons why his drama is so well received not only in London and on Broadway but also in societies as disparate as Estonia and Catalonia. The acceptability, the currency, of his work – the familiarity of the situations he depicts and of the transactions within them – is due in no small part to the fact that drama has the capacity to describe, and to draw the audience into the description of, emotions and events which could not be addressed in any other way. This magical process holds the same potent attraction for us as myth, because it is something unbelievable in which, however, we must believe, to which we must acquiesce. When writing *Aristocrats* Friel noted that the essence of the play – one which was 'about *family life*' – was 'the burden of the incommunicable'.[41] Yet this, like myth (indeed, this burden *is* myth) must be communicated and this, too, requires a magical process which can seem anything but magical to the writer at the time of writing. And yet it is this process which, if it is successful, eventually creates a bond between stage and the audience which becomes, in Yeats's phrase, 'like a secret society'.[42]

In a sense, the evolution of post-colonial literature and studies such as those of Goffman and Turner already mentioned, reveal 'truths' which have not previously been voiced. 'Subaltern' studies, articulating the identities of submerged imaginations which the western or 'second' world has been conditioned to think of as 'other', have begun to enter the alternative tapestry of culture which has already seen and accepted the idea of an 'anti-aesthetic' or a 'counter-culture'.[43] Decolonisation, as a period of uncertainty and violence, has been discussed by Frantz Fanon in *The Wretched of the Earth*, which has had a considerable influence on critics such as Declan Kiberd who are concerned with the reassessment and redefinition of post-colonial Ireland. 'Decolonization . . . transforms spectators crushed with their inessentiality into privileged *actors*, with the grandiose glare of *history's floodlights* upon them' [*my emphasis*].[44]

Friel has adverted to this in a typically oblique way in the introduction to the text of *The London Vertigo* (1990), his version of Macklin's *The True-born Irishman* (1761):

> The desire to metamorphose oneself, to change everything utterly – names, beliefs, voice, loyalties, language, ambitions, even one's appearance – secretly excites most people at some stage of their lives and is as old as Adam. It is an element in the dream that charms young people into a career in acting. . . . And of course the desire is a delusion. There are no new beginnings with new identities. (*LV* 9)

The play ironically depicts the manners which 'The Fine Irish Lady' (Macklin's alternative title) acquires after a visit to London. But the transitus which fascinated Friel was that of Charles Macklin himself (né Cathal MacLochlainn in the Inishowen peninsula of County Donegal in the late 1600s), an Irish-speaking peasant who re-invented himself as an Englishman and became a central figure of the London stage (Pope said of his Shylock 'This is the Jew/That Shakespeare drew'). Friel says 'his attempt at transmogrification is interesting for two reasons. The first is that he set about it with calculation and precocious acumen while he was still only a boy, long before he knew the pain of failure as a writer or as an actor. The second is that he pulled it off. Well, almost' (*LV* 9). To invent another identity, to assert – whether surreptitiously, subliminally or explicitly – one's claim on name, language or 'loyalties', is as important as the right to one's initial culture and origins, because the act of transitus, of crossing a threshold into a world different in some degree from one's own – perhaps different in *every* degree – is the act which tests our ability to appear in the world.

In post-colonial terms, Macklin exchanged the lowest of positions and destinies in the British Empire for a role as the maker of plays, of conceits, and as an actor whose pretence could win him the plaudits of that empire. This was the subaltern learning how to turn difference into true otherness, to enter into a different existence and yet ('Well, almost') remaining a 'man from God knows where' and recognisably foreign. (The passage of Sheridan, at the same juncture, from a much more salubrious starting point, to a role not only in the theatre of makebelieve but also in the makebelieve of constitutional politics, is an interesting parallel.)[45] To paraphrase Yeats, we make of the quarrel with others, difference, but of the quarrel with ourselves, otherness.

Every play has a secret waiting to be told, and every playwright has a secret to tell. And every play has one unchanging, emotional element around which the play revolves and which is found to contain the kernel of the playwright's ambitions and fears, the 'controlling idea' which we have already discussed. In the entire corpus of Friel's work, that kernel is performed through the idea of the writer or shaman or conveyer of truths who is himself both in exile and at home, in the 'uncanny' condition known to Freud as the '*unheimlich*' – unhomely. This sense of exile from one's own culture and community – the notion of homecoming and the associated responsibility of telling the story about the journey home – is so powerful an ingredient in Friel's make-up as a writer (my theatrical allusion is deliberate) that he has said on at least one occasion 'There is no home . . . no hearth . . . I acknowledge no community'.[46] There is, of course, a home where one meets one's family and where one lays one's head. But the idea of a hearth (Latin, *focus*: a hearth) as the *focus* of one's life and as the place where meaning is to be found, inevitably sets up tensions between oneself and one's 'community'. Friel has said of Ireland north and south that 'both places are your home, so you are an exile in your home'.[47] Thus 'home' is both the affective place of family and a place of external affiliation. Therefore we also find Friel saying 'There's some kind of instinctive sense of home being central to the life and yet at the same time being a place of great stress and great alienation'.[48] In this sense his role as the writer of his society, as the provider of a critical and creative intelligence, is both political and shamanistic, for Turner has written: 'he who is in communitas is an exile or a stranger, someone who, by his very existence, calls into question the whole normative order'.[49] We shall encounter Friel's consciousness of this dilemma at many stages in this study.

In the same sense that the Chinese believe that we have two birthplaces – the place where one was physically born and the place to which one is travelling[50] – the entire search is *about* 'home' because home is the only place where language can be used successfully, where the story can and must be told. But, because of the internal exile and the simultaneous sense of being outside, or beside, oneself, language remains, in Joyce's words, 'so familiar and so foreign'.[51]

In discussing 'The Irish Writer: Self and Society', Thomas Kilroy remarked on 'the web of secondary circumstances that lie behind the writing', of the point where 'the essentially private activity of writing comes into contact with the shared experience of human beings living in the one culture', of the difference between 'the kinds of roles which writers tend to appropriate for themselves' and 'the roles imposed upon them by the society in which they live'.[52] At the time he wrote this (1982) the ontology of the writer in Irish society had not been explored as thoroughly as it has today; the Irish writer seemed to have a more static relationship with society, derived from experiences since the literary revival in the 1890s and tempered by the era of censorship in the 1930s and 1940s. Today, as we shall see, with exploratory texts such as Robert Welch's *Changing States* (1993) and Declan Kiberd's *Inventing Ireland* (1995), it is possible to see the position and function of the writer as much less polarised between 'self' and 'society' and much more capable of looking critically at our cultural formations and transformations. But Kilroy's identification of the 'web of secondary circumstances' – even if they may be, in Friel's case at least, primary circumstances – does remain valid as a means of discussing the preoccupations which come between the private writer and the publicly written.

This is so not least because there is in fact no strictly delimited space occupied by the 'writer', nor another allotted to 'society'. The space between, often inchoate and usually occupied by confusion, is the place of negotiation, an intimate region from which, once they have been identified, the players can proceed outwards to meet the wider world.

But to do so, in order to both grant himself adequate protection and establish standards of performance, Friel sets up toll-words – counters which must be negotiated by the travellers, the 'strays', in their pursuit of meaning. 'Love' is the most obvious; 'dignity' is equally important. These toll-words dominate the ideas, the syntax and the behaviour of religion, politics and affiliation. Behind each toll-word is a lexicon of experience – joy, grief, despair, madness – and it is in negotiating our path through them that we approximate to successful meaning or to disaster. As Robert Welch has observed, 'there is in Friel a profound distrust of language, because he understands its power'.[53]

In terms of the physical/metaphysical spaces which this drama occupies, some of the most basic toll-words will be: 'boundary', 'gender', 'nation', 'culture' and 'civilisation'. These, as we shall see in Chapter 1, belong among the absolute phenomena of space, time, being and otherness. Others, mediated by experience, are the characteristic qualities of the middle, or between, space I am describing, of which 'translation' and its companions, 'confusion' and 'uncertainty' are paramount. Here, the transformative act and the transformative experience are preceded by attempts – often naïve, fumbling, inarticulate, blind attempts – at homecoming. Friel has written of the desire for metamorphosis as 'the private delirium that middle-aged writers are especially vulnerable to: to obliterate that whole past of botched and failed and embarrassing work and to begin afresh and anonymously with a few simple markings on a white sheet of paper' (*LV* 9). Even though that statement preceded the benchmark I have described (the performance at Glenties of *Dancing at Lughnasa*) there is a sense here that he may have achieved some kind of homecoming in *Lughnasa*, in the recognition and the salutation of 'those five brave Glenties women'.

As we shall see in Chapter 5, 'boundary' and 'march', as both delimiting and ennabling physical and metaphysical concepts, affect both our mindscape and our concrete geography. 'Cultural geography' as an emerging discipline indicates, as Brian Graham suggests, that 'places are invented, a myth of territory being basic to the construction and legitimation of identity'.[54] Here, then, is a further rapprochement between science, art and politics which underpins and expands the work of Steiner on the linguistic level as we have already discussed it, and indicates that 'all knowledge is negotiable, contested through time and across space as social and intellectual circumstances alter'.[55] Thus the toll-words will change over time and according to where they are employed and by whom. Casting one's mind back may evoke a time when one set of words was more powerful than another – may indeed employ such words to effect the evocation – but will not necessarily succeed in once more giving priority to those words. 'Places and landscapes are narrative constructions produced by writers and often more real than reality itself, so powerful and influential is the role of the artist'.[56] In one sense the 'narrative of place' may carry across broken syntax and distracted meaning, may elide time, but in another it can turn both present and past landscapes into killing fields.

The dominant element of *memory* in such a process will be discussed at the close of this Introduction. Here, I will dwell for a moment on the notion of *embarrassment* mentioned by Friel. That notion was central to the transitional play of modern Irish theatre, *Philadelphia, Here I Come!*, in which Private Gar taunts his silent father: '*we embarrass one another*' (*Ph.* 40). Embarrassment is the name we give to a psychic disorder based on the difference between reality and our perception of reality, and exhibited in the conflict between the way we describe how we see the world and the way others describe their own perceptions. We kill, make love, desecrate and rampage in order to protect these visions. We move into strange relationships with history, psychology, mythology, with family, peer groups, foreigners, dependents and providers. We develop concepts of strangeness, normality, inadequacy, which are the prey of fear and lust, and the writer of 'narrative constructions' is no less guilty or vulnerable than any footsoldier in any army, visible or invisible.

Between the father and son in *Philadelphia* we see the rejection of any human relationship: where there is no filiation, there can be no affiliation, and this explains why, because the home is so empty, Gar can have nothing but hollow men for companions.

Another example of the writer in conflict with society was the observation of a Dublin newspaper on the first production of Synge's *Playboy*: 'It is as if we looked into a mirror for the first time and found ourselves hideous. We fear to face the thing'.[57] Master and servant, civilian and barbarian, regard each other in such embarrassment. Friel is 'embarrassed' by some of his earlier works, several of which he will not permit to be reproduced, but which have been his servants and are now, perhaps, his unwanted masters – works which once presented a civil appearance but now are menacing *barbari*. But, however dissatisfied he may be with some of his apprentice pieces, the fact of the embarrassment which each contains – between ideas of dignity and respectability, between unmediated blocks of emotion, between generations, loyalties, genders – is a valuable indication of the route his work has taken.[58]

We should recall that the 'asylum' of 'inbred claustrophobic Ireland' from which he gained (and to which he gave) his 'parole' in 1962 was still the cause of grave embarrassment between the writer and society; and was, due partly to external factors but mainly to the momentum of Irish society itself, increasingly a debating chamber where issues such as conscience, loyalty, faith, and responsibility were opened up as fields of exploration. The domination of society and its agenda by the hegemonies of the Fíanna Fáil party and the Roman Catholic Church was an inhibiting factor on writers whose expression of their frustrations (followed in many cases by the censorship of their expression) was (and is) a mark born by many of his contemporaries and elders.[59] In 1968 Friel said:

> What modern dramatists are saying is . . . that God is dead and that all traditional values died with Him. . . .They say that the Church as a divine institution is an absurdity . . . that the conventions, morals and values of social organism that we know are suspect.[60]

Friel was, perhaps, an 'angry young man' who had every right to be intemperate, however much this may have unbalanced or destabilised his literary output. (We shall find examples of this in the private sphere in the story 'The Child' and in the public arena in *The Blind Mice*.) The fact that there continues to be an interest in a play such as *The Mundy Scheme* (1969),[61] with its ironic focus on the hunger for land and for the profits which land speculation can bring, indicates that, although he will not permit its reproduction, that text remains valuable as a reminder of preoccupations which do not simply disappear with the passage of time.

Friel's theatre has moved away considerably from the atmosphere of the 1960s, yet his most recent output – *Dancing at Lughnasa, Wonderful Tennessee, Molly Sweeney* and *Give Me Your Answer, Do!* – is almost timeless and spaceless in its attention to the inner spirit in a way he had not achieved since *Faith Healer*. In that sense, the question posed in the form of public address to the audience at the opening of *The Mundy Scheme* is both a metaphysical question about the birth and growth of any culture, and a specific interrogation of the fate of modern, post-colonial Ireland:

> Ladies and gentlemen: What happens when a small nation that has been manipulated and abused by a huge colonial power for hundreds of years wrests its freedom by blood and anguish? What happens to an emerging country after it has emerged? Does the transition from dependence to independence induce a fatigue, a mediocrity, an ennui? Or does the clean spirit of idealism that fired the people to freedom augment itself, grow bolder, more generous? The answer to many of these questions can be found in Ireland, a little island in the Atlantic Ocean, 350 miles long, 150 miles broad, and with a population of about four million people. . . . (*Mundy* 157–8)

The subtitle of *The Mundy Scheme* is '*or, may we write your epitaph now, Mr Emmet?*' – a reference to the fact that Robert Emmet had said in his speech in the dock 'When my country takes her place among the nations of the earth, then, and not till then, let my epitaph be written'. The play thus explicitly examines Ireland's effectiveness in becoming an independent, modern nation, and is a not-too-profound reflection on 'what happens when . . . '.[62] Furthermore, the fact that Friel could say in 1973 'Ireland is becoming a shabby imitation of a third-rate American state. This is what *The Mundy Scheme* is about'[63] is, at least superficially, cognate with Frederic Jameson's Marxist critique of modern aesthetics,[64] in Friel's declaration, like an alarm-cry, 'We are rapidly losing our identity as a people . . . we are no longer even West Britons; we are East Americans'.[65]

Ireland has played its part in world affairs: during Friel's childhood Éamon de Valera became President of the League of Nations and subsequently Ireland has become a significant member of both the United Nations and the European Union. Ireland is not, indeed, a country trying to find a stable destiny, but one which is discovering the opportunities and dangers of transition. As a consequence, no one could depict Irish people or their landscape in anything other than a state of flux, an indeterminate state, and the process of map-making must therefore always be provisional – again the 'controlling idea' of Friel's mindscape is echoing here. In addition, at any snapshot moment the image will be true only of one side of the world: for every map there is also an anti-map, and for every map of the external world there is a map of the interior – something which does not become entirely clear in Friel's work until *Molly Sweeney*.

The political import of the prologue to *The Mundy Scheme* is perhaps the best example we have of the often rather facilely expressed connection between literature and politics (even though the play itself is crudely cast as a parable of nationhood). The process of continual redefinition ('revisionism' in the politico-historical context) involves what Kilroy calls 'a kind of shared fiction between writer and society'[66] – not only the writer of 'fiction' but also, as we shall see when discussing *Translations*, all those contributing to the development of what Joseph Lee calls 'the necessary fictions of the new Ireland'[67] – be they historians, political scientists, sociologists or playwrights commenting on the politics and culture of a society conceived by public figures such as Garret FitzGerald (*Towards a New Ireland*, 1972) or – himself both a politician, biographer and playwright – Conor Cruise O'Brien (*States of Ireland*, also 1972).

LITERATURE AND POLITICS

The history of the role of literature in Irish politics is too extensive to allow more than a brief reflection here, but the basic point must be emphasised that the 'syntax opulent with tomorrows' which, in *Translations*, Hugh Mor O'Donnell acknowledges as an Irish strategy to cope with disappointment, and on which energy has been prodigally expended (*Tr.* 42), has been placed at the service of Irish literature and thereby of Irish society as a way of explaining ancient and modern hurts and injustices and of anticipating a return to a more favourable climate. In particular, the centuries-old problem of the colonisation (plantation) of Ulster following the collapse of the Gaelic aristocracy in 1603 has evoked a binary literature of possession, dispossession and mutual siege. In general, many Irish writers, especially since the literary 'renaissance' in the 1890s, and the emergence of the Irish Literary Theatre, have regarded themselves as the custodians of the Irish psyche, as alternate leaders with the revolutionary power to embody the essential qualities that are necessary for such a reflective people to take control of their destiny, especially when that destiny carries within it the continued prospect of grieving and of antagonism to received traditions of authority.

Friel himself has said 'I see no reason why Ireland should not be ruled by its poets and dramatists'[68] but this (said in 1972) should be taken as an indication that he regards the writer as a simultaneous form of government, parallel to that exercising political power. The 'government of the tongue' – to adopt Heaney's expression[69] – is a republic representing the right and capacity of the writer to employ language as a means of self-determination, and echoes Shelley's 'poets are the unacknowledged legislators of the world'.[70] When we come to examine the establishment of Field Day in Chapter 5, we will find that there was a conscious intention among its founders to put in place a republic of letters which could provide its constituency with an alternative source of authority. To 'create a space in which we would try to redefine what being Irish meant in the context of what had happened in the North, the relationship of Irish nationalism and culture'[71] as Heaney put it, was to set up a means and arena of communication – a fifth province – which would inevitably have (as I am sure it has had) political repercussions. Friel's own ambition at that time was that this 'should lead to a cultural state . . . [out of which] a possibility of a political state follows'.[72] This is a transformative moment in a transformative process, one which Homi Bhabha calls the 'hybrid moment'.[73] Serendipity here urges us to reflect that Thomas Kilroy, once again commenting on the timeliness of Irish drama in its relation to social change, has said: 'the typical Irish play of the sixties, the seventies, the eighties, is something of a hybrid, reflecting the suspended condition of the writers themselves.[74] How else could the writers exist except in the vertiginous limbo of the liminal, as the enduring suspension of 'real' life encouraged them to reflect on a society in permanent 'chassis'? Storytelling became the accepted strategy for making sense, because storytelling is inherently personal and yet is capable of giving images to a society in search of identity. The voice of the storyteller is the voice in Friel's drama: what Kilroy (writing of the centrality of the anecdote to Irish fiction) calls 'a voice with a supreme confidence in its own histrionics . . . an unshakeable belief in the value of human actions, a belief that life may be encapsulated into stories that require no reference, no qualification beyond their own selves'.[75]

The use of language, in pamphlets, plays and poetry, to influence politics, to examine received ideology and traditions, to analyse history, to articulate cultural viewpoints which spring from the deep structures and which identify both cultural and political difference, is typical of the process which Declan Kiberd calls 'inventing Ireland'[76] – in the dual sense of invention as both the discovery of extant thought and the proposal of future thought. We have been familiar with this since at least the time of Swift, and as such it marches parallel to the field of political discourse, sometimes of course crossing over into that field. But – and this is the point on which Friel, Heaney and Deane would insist – it is no less important for that, being neither inferior nor subservient in its power and its status to the exercise of political authority.

There is, however, a point at which postmodernist literature has diverged from political behaviour very markedly: the question of authority, which in Northern Ireland in particular – and also to a less visible extent in the Republic – has given way to a sometimes chaotic opposition between the concepts of consensus and conflict. In a salutary account of 'Ireland's *Antigones*: tragedy north and south' (1988) Anthony Roche discussed the continuing relevance of the Antigone crisis to Irish literature and politics, examining the film *Anne Devlin* and three stage versions of Sophocles' play, by Brendan Kennelly, Aidan Carl Matthews and – a production presented by Field Day – Tom Paulin's *The Riot Act* – all taking place in 1984.[77] The crucial point of refusal to countenance an unjust diktat, of withdrawal from an authoritarian space that one cannot accept or respect, is carried by Sophocles to the ultimate conclusion where all five areas of discourse in which the human can engage are refused and closed down: between gods and men, age and youth, men and women, society and the individual, and between the living and the dead. In Friel's plays, as well as in those of many of his contemporaries, those nodes of discourse have been scrupulously analysed: faith (*The Enemy Within, The Blind Mice*); filiation (*Philadelphia, Living Quarters*); marriage (*Making History, Give Me Your Answer, Do!*); individual freedom (*Faith Healer, Molly Sweeney*); and the past (*Translations, Making History*).

Roche's article was timely in that it drew attention to several aspects of subaltern enquiry central to modern Irish society: history and gender (the role of Anne Devlin in the fate of Robert Emmet); the politico-literary exercise of Field Day; and the fact that the broadcasting of the provisions of the controversial Criminal Justice Bill (then before Dáil Éireann) during the performance of Matthews's version was a reflection on political unrest in a Republic which was claiming Northern Ireland to be a 'failed political entity'.[78]

To enquire, in a literary way, rather than a polemical or ideological way, into the issues of historiography, faith, or political science, is not of course new, even in modern times. Joyce set out 'to forge in the smithy of my soul the uncreated conscience of my race'[79] and Yeats attempted much the same. John McGahern's quiet *non serviam* spoke volumes for the individual conscience at the time when Friel was experiencing the inbred claustrophobia of his country both north and south, which in public oratory was being challenged by figures such as Noel Browne and James Dillon.

But in the past two decades, the issue of northern writing in particular – and especially the emergence of northern playwrights capable of addressing the political dimension – has coincided with the acknowledged breakdown of political norms and of even the possibility of dialogue by other means.

On the same principle that 'in the country of the blind the one-eyed man is king',[80] the writer has moved into territory abdicated by political figures unwilling or unable to understand each other, and has claimed the capacity to establish 'a cultural state'.

In the light of political developments, or the lack of them, in the island of Ireland as a whole during the past thirty years, the relations of the Republic of Ireland with its former colonial master, Great Britain, with the province of Northern Ireland, and its changing role in the complex and fractured process of translation between these three entities, all bear a close resemblance to developments in other post-colonial societies which are still in some process of negotiation with neighbours and former masters.

The cases of the playwright Václav Havel and novelist Mario Vargas Llosa, the former becoming President of the Czech Republic and the latter being an unsuccessful candidate in the presidential elections in Peru, are salutary reminders that a writer may indeed make the transitus from the cultural to the political state/field. Havel in particular provides us with an example of someone whose work – and therefore life – was exercised in an alternative, *samizdat* fashion until a moment in his country's history when it was possible for dissenters to 'come out' and be recognised as an anti-culture. Havel had commented severely on the entropy of the modern world, a world without transcendence. His essay 'The Power of the Powerless' is in some ways a rewriting of Fanon's *The Wretched of the Earth*, especially in its exploration of the idea that 'the centre of power is identical with the centre of truth'[81] – if there is no centre, then there can be no truth and, if no power, then no authority. A society lacking truth and authority is alienated from itself and Friel demonstrates this throughout his work, from the short stories and the essentially private radio plays to the drama on major public themes.

An essay on the aesthetic and social conditions of Northern Ireland – which this book is not – could fruitfully explore Havel's essays as well as his deeply allegorical plays. But the connection between literature, or art, and politics is well served by Havel's observation that ideology, as an 'instrument of internal communication which assures . . . inner cohesion' is 'built on lies [and] works only as long as people are willing to live within the lie'.[82] The conjunction, or collision, between literature and politics revolves around Havel's point about lies and truth – the 'emperor's new clothes' syndrome of consensus. If, in order to portray a real situation, we have recourse to drama, then the illusion or make-believe essential to the 'play' automatically requires a suspense of belief and a putting in its place of a readiness to acquiesce in a deceit, however small. Reality or the truth is inverted for the purpose of allowing the audience to believe unconditionally in both truth and lie. The playwright's task, as far as he serves any public at all, is to mine the foundations of the social structure and to expose the lies, or fictions, which hold it together; and to provide the spectator with the means whereby to re-establish life again within that truth.

At the same period in which Friel made the claim for artists to be able to 'rule', he was also dismissing the possibility of drama being able to adequately address the 'troubles' in Northern Ireland, unaware that his own draft attempt to do so, provisionally titled 'John Butt's Bothy', would shortly be catalysed and metamorphosed by Bloody Sunday (30 January 1972) and its aftermath into *The Freedom of the City*.

Friel would, I suspect, maintain that his original projection – that a drama adequate to the condition of the north was many years away – was the more mature, since he has subsequently judged *The Freedom of the City* to have been too heated and too hasty.[83] Eight years after *The Freedom*, when he was in a more assured position to venture into the militancy of Field Day, he would put *Translations* into the field as a vehicle of what might be broadly called 'cultural nationalism', only to find that its reception as a 'national epic' forced him to draw in his horns once more and recant with *The Communication Cord*, a farcical send-up of the 'pieties' of *Translations*. That this self-deprecatory gesture served, in my opinion, not to diminish but to highlight the strengths and weaknesses of *Translations*, to underpin the claims that can be made for the play as an allegory of Irish history, is not as important as the fact that Friel's ambivalence and hesitancy about the nature of political involvement is a necessary part of the anxiety which lies at the heart of the writer's dilemma – is, in fact, that dilemma.

When, however, Friel said in the ensuing debate on the validity of *Translations*, that 'the imperatives of fiction are as exacting as the imperatives of cartography and historiography . . . Drama is first a fiction, with the authority of fiction'[84] he was aligning literature alongside government and its ancillary strategies of control as a parallel form of truth and authority. And he was implicitly identifying the two meanings of 'invention' to which I have already alluded – the function of discovery and that of imagination.

And in making the claim for drama as a necessary fiction in political life, Friel was also affirming the need for a religious sense of life. While I think it is unfair and misleading to say, as Martine Pelletier does, that Friel is 'a Catholic writer',[85] there is a very real sense in which he is a writer in search of faith. In 1972 at the age of 43 he said 'I hope that between now and my death I will have acquired a religion, a philosophy, a sense of life, that will make the end less frightening than it appears to me at this moment'[86] and he says the same today: 'I am still hanging onto the hope that something may emerge, a framework that could support the weight I would put on it'.[87] It echoes the words he puts into the mouth of Columba: 'I am afraid to meet my God' (*EW* 69). This should be seen as an integral element in the 'controlling idea' which permeates his thought and his work, since the alliance between doubt and faith, as strong as that between control and deviance, is the psychomotor that energises the interstitial space where the embarrassment continues.

Whether that energy is measured and calmly projected, or comes unmediated from a continuing sense of rage, is a further dilemma for the playwright. 'In some controlled way the rage increases with time. You can only go so far with some kinds of exploration – it can end up as a kind of self-indulgence which should be done in private'.[88] As we shall see in Part IV, the privacy in which Friel has been conducting recent explorations has in fact given rise to the concentration on 'the secret places of individual souls' in *Dancing at Lughnasa*, *Wonderful Tennessee*, *Molly Sweeney* and *Give Me Your Answer, Do!*. But, as Thomas Kilroy has observed, while 'there are variations in the degree of political urgency between one play and another . . . the general tone of the plays is referential . . . it has a kind of loving attentiveness to the broader fate of the people of Ireland and their culture'[89] and this continues to be a heraldic marker of the *écrivain engagée*. In this sense it may be true that Friel's recent plays are filling the vacuum in a 'post-nationalist' genre, as Fintan O'Toole suggests[90] but it would be wrong, and dangerous, to assume that politically motivated rage is absent from his conscience or consciousness.

Above all, the search for transcendence continues, both in a real, concrete way (attempting to rise above polarised differences) and in a spiritual sense. For any writer this is both a personal project and one which he undertakes on behalf of his 'community' – either narrowly focussed on a locale or more widely motivated by a concept such as the 'nation'.[91] As Elmer Andrews notes of Frank Hardy, the faith healer, 'he was prepared to lay down his life for his faith'.[92] Andrews sees Frank's incantation of place-names as 'expressive of the longing for tran-scendence, for a break with historical reality, a lyric space'.[93] On a more public plane, Witoszek and Sheeran have discussed this quest as the antithesis of 'the appetites of gravity', as 'that which lies beyond experience', 'inscribed in the very image of an action which is no action', a 'suspended energy'.[94] It is a space – or non-space – above and beyond words, but one which can only be reached by negotiating vocabulary and syntax. We shall therefore return to the specific issue of language and Friel's attitude to the uses of English.

The aesthetic question which has to do with language and *therefore* with our relation with both past and future is also inherently political. Oscar Wilde said:

> I do not know anything more wonderful or more characteristic of the Celtic genius, than the quick artistic spirit in which we adapted ourselves to the English tongue. The Saxon took our lands from us and left them desolate – we took their language and added new beauties to it.[95]

Friel has followed this both in his work (*Translations*) and in his own voice:

> We have been pigmented in our theatre with the English experience, with the English language, the use of the English language, the understanding of words, the whole cultural burden that every word in the English language carries.[96]

And, following Wilde, he has asserted: 'We must make them [English language words] distinctive and unique to us . . . We must make English identifiably our own language'.[97] Tom Paulin, in his Field Day pamphlet 'A New Look at the Language Question' (1983), marries this firmly to the issue of identity, both spatially and temporally: 'because no scholar has as yet compiled a *Dictionary of Irish English* many words are literally homeless.[98] . . . The language therefore lives freely and spontaneously as speech but it lacks any institutional existence . . . It is a language without a lexicon, a language without form.' Paulin's conception is that such a language might become 'the flexible written instrument of a complete cultural idea'[99] and as such it is part of the resurgence of cultural nationalism in Northern Ireland to which Friel and the Field Day company were central during the 1980s.

This finds resonances within other post-colonial cultures, of which the Nigerian Chinua Achebe must serve as an exemplar:

> I feel that the English language will be able to carry the weight of my African experience. But it will have to be a new English, still in full communion with its ancestral home but altered to suit new African surroundings.[100]

Thus Macaulay's memorandum on Indian education, contemporaneous with the institution of national education in Ireland, envisaging 'a class of persons, Indian in blood and colour, but English in taste, in opinions in morals and in intellect',[101] is being reversed, as 'the Empire writes back'.[102]

The cautious sense of growth, of acquiring a new language – that of the coloniser – and thereby achieving an extra dimension to one's identity, is an excitement and an anxiety in equal measure. In Friel's case, as Robert Welch succinctly puts it,

> he writes an English cadenced like Burke's, and like his, one attentive to the need for control while at the same time retaining the potential for surprise.

His English is also spare and suspicious, written by someone intensely aware of the presence of a hidden language in modern Ireland: Irish.[103]

Control and surprise: the possibilities of magic. And therewith the political fear of the unknown which, in the age of Burke, made style such a precarious concept.[104] When Seamus Deane said 'in a basic sense the crisis we are passing through is stylistic. That is to say, it is a crisis of language – the ways in which we write it and the ways in which we read it'[105] he was acutely conscious of the suppression which can be exerted, and the violence that can be unleashed, when language becomes the medium in which different perceptions are expressed.

LIMINALITY, SPLITTING AND THE GAP

The perceived need for constant redefinition of the Irish situation – place, time and identity – has also made imperative an examination of the central meaning, or lack of it, in Irish life. While Seamus Deane has said that 'nothing is more monotonous or despairing than the search for the essence which defines a nation',[106] this search has become an integral part of the project of being Irish, one in which Deane himself, as General Editor of the *Field Day Anthology of Irish Writing*, could be said to be a major player.

The important factor for our purposes is the way in which philosophers and poets, politicians and playwrights have circled around this idea of an unknown identity, so much so that they have been accused of concentrating on a 'central vacuity'[107] rather than getting on with the business of being Irish. In conceptual terms, a positive step was indicated with the creation of the *Crane Bag* journal (1977–85) which posited a 'fifth province':

> The [four] provinces were known as 'fifths', *coicead*, as if there were a fifth province . . . Possibly this 'fifth' was less a political area than a symbol of cosmic order.[108]

> Uisneach, the secret centre, was the place where all oppositions were resolved. The constitution of such a place would require that each person discover it for himself within himself.[109]

The Field Day company itself could be said to occupy a zone of similar nature – an experimental field in which the qualities and conditions of being Irish can be examined and discussed. One vital physical property which has metaphysical significance is the fact that the point at the centre of the crossroads, the meeting place of the four provinces, is the *quint-essence* – the fifth place at which the essential secret or truth is buried: it is the location of the final, harrowing scene of *Crystal and Fox*.

But we must now recognise that behind the concept of a fifth or central province is another: that of a gap or discontinuity in experience. Nations or states which pursue a linear, outward-looking, self-confident trajectory do not spend much time examining national characteristics. As Hugh Mor O'Donnell says in *Translations* (adapting Steiner for his purpose[110]), 'certain cultures expend on their vocabularies and syntax acquisitive energies and ostentations entirely lacking in their material lives' (*Tr.* 42). This circularity, constantly reinventing the notion of Irishness, trying to find replies to inevitabilities (I am paraphrasing Friel) is only part of the Irish project, but it is an important part because it acknowledges that the gap in question is a psychic one.

Recent post-colonial theory and practice – most notably that of Homi K. Bhabha and of Gayatri Spivak – has opened up this area of enquiry in a very fruitful way. Bhabha has indicated that when we begin to articulate cultural differences we enter an 'in-between' space[111] which can have three characteristics: it is liminal, because the culture in question is poised on the threshold of a new sense of identity; it is an interstice, or gap, because ideas of cultural difference become displaced or over-lapping;[112] and it is a place where identity becomes 'split' or estranged from itself[113] in the process of being examined and reconstituted. We are taken 'beyond' ourselves 'in order to return . . . to the . . . conditions of the present'.[114]

This is a very exciting and very dangerous space-time, which Peter Brook calls the 'instant of hazard' where new meaning can be generated.[115] In Friel's plays it is often occasioned by a homecoming – Cass McGuire, Chris Carroll in *The Blind Mice*, Owen O'Donnell in *Translations*, the assembly of the O'Donnell family in *Aristocrats*. Ancient time reaches a standstill and duration is suspended while 'something' – indefinable, mysterious – happens which changes their world and their culture forever.

As we shall see in Part IV, which is new to this edition of the book, the concept of 'beyond' will be examined in my discussion of Friel's most recent plays. Here, I shall devote this section to the ideas of liminality, splitting and the gap which Bhabha and others have elucidated, in direct relation to the fashion in which they appear in Friel's work.

The most striking early occurrence of these characteristics – we might almost refer to them as *happenings* or even *characters*, so much do they imbue, and appear immanent in, the society Friel depicts – is in *Philadelphia*: Gar is about to leave home (the threshold experience); he is divided by his author into a split personality (ego and id); and the O'Donnell home is a place without apparent meaning, an 'asylum' or 'quagmire' where identity has been misplaced or abandoned. *Aristocrats* similarly shows us the quadruple liminality of Casimir's and Alice's temporary return, of the father's death, the recorded voice of Anna, and the anticipated wedding of Claire; the split in the consciousness of all the O'Donnell children as they commute between the uncertainty of the present and an ill-remembered and unreliable past; and a gap in their experience as they try to negotiate a way into the future by coming to terms with that past, with memory and the meaning of memory, which might return them safely to 'the conditions of the present'.

Casimir tells us that

> I made a great discovery when I was nine – not even a great discovery but an important, a very important discovery for me. I suddenly realised I was different from other boys.[. . .]What I discovered was that for some reason people found me . . . peculiar. Of course I sensed it first from the boys at boarding-school. But it was father with his usual – his usual directness and honesty who made me face it. I remember the day he said to me: 'Had you been born down there [Ballybeg] you'd have become the village idiot. Fortunately for you, you were born here, and we can absorb you'. Ha-ha. So at nine years of age I knew certain things: that certain kinds of people laughed at me; that the easy relationships that other men would enjoy would always elude me; that – that – that I would never succeed in life, whatever – you know – whatever 'succeed' means (*Ar.* 69–70).

This awareness of 'certain things', this revelation and acceptance of a kind of truth about oneself, about the world to which one relates, was described in 1991 by actress Susan FitzGerald (playing Alice) when she said 'The play is absolutely miraculous in the way it underlines the fact that in the course of change there are poignant losses'.[116] This is true not least because in this vital moment between eternities, personal identity can be lost: as Steiner tells us, 'every act of communication between human beings takes on the shape of an act of translation . . . All dialogue is a proffer of mutual cognizance and a strategic redefinition of self'.[117]

The same factors have driven the people of Baile Beag in *Translations*: a society on the edge of transformation, the dual identity of Owen/Roland, and the 'confusion' and 'uncertainty' which bestride the play, as the land itself surrenders its identity and in doing so imagines both its past and its future. And in *Making History*, the figure of Hugh O'Neill (who is discussed in Chapter 6, in the section entitled 'The Gap') personifies the alterity of an entire civilisation caught on the fulcrum of change, thrown like the villagers of Baile Beag into a 'panic' by their arrival at the brink of history.

A further aspect of this triple condition of liminality is the question of homecoming – both the journey out and the journey back. Friel's reputation as the master of the *nostalgia* play, which addresses, literally, the painfulness of the homeward journey (Greek, *nostos*: homeward journey, *algos*: pain) will be discussed at a later stage, but a factor which needs to be referred to here is Bhabha's description of a 'missing person'[118] in the interstice of experience.

The boy or man who sets out from home in order to return becomes a missing person, a hostage to fortune for the duration of his absence. This limbo is a condition not of suspended animation but of danger, a zone where anything can happen and where the missing person is vulnerable. The idea that there is, 'out there', a person stumbling blindly towards home, towards revelation, is something that threatens the folk at home, which of course includes the audience who also await his return and his story. In this sense, Frank Hardy, throughout the action of *Faith Healer*, is such a missing person, as is Hugh O'Neill in his absence from history in *Making History*. Fox Melarkey in *Crystal and Fox* has gone missing in his inability to put a name to either his dilemma or his desires – 'I want a dream I think I've had to come true' (*CF* 36) is one of the most disturbing lines in all of Friel's work. Any of the characters – and there are many of them – who declare with such decisiveness 'I don't know' are answering the question which, Bhabha indicates,[119] is central to the transitory existence of the man in the gap: *What do you want?* – from which derives anxiety, anomie and alienation.

Another aspect of the liminal or interstitial is the 'time–lag' between two differentiated cultures, which Bhabha calls a 'caesura in the narrative of modernity'[120] – the point at which, in Friel's and Steiner's words, 'ancient time [is] at an end' (*Tr.* 40)[121] and 'new' time has yet to commence. This is a non-place (clearly satisfying Althusser's call not only for time without duration but also space without place[122]), a 'colonial space' which Bhabha calls the 'template' of modernity.[123] As far as this time-lag, or what I would prefer to call a time-warp, concerns Friel's writing, we should note the obvious moments such as the entire duration of *Translations* and *Making History*; but we should also recognise it in the 'flashback' structures of *Faith Healer* and *Dancing at Lughnasa*. In the latter, the situation of the present is contrasted with an 'ancient time' of the 1930s when the five women whose cohesive life is to be separated into various, incoherent lives, is radically re-membered, as they are overtaken by changing times.

Throughout Bhabha's work he refers to the 'split' identity or culture as being simultaneously 'less than one and double' – unable to achieve an integrated whole yet demanding to be seen in both aspects at once.[124] It is not only in Private Gar and Public Gar that we can see two parts of a persona which cannot become whole. As we shall see in *Molly Sweeney*, the attempt to be at one with one's inner self and at one with the self whom the world judges one to be, is a tragic task. In this space, which Bhabha variously calls the 'in-between', a 'middle passage' or a 'third space',[125] the hybridity of the creature born of opposites contains both self and otherness, in an agonistic embrace which Hegel sums up as follows: *Ich bin der Kampf. Ich bin nicht Einer der im Kampf Begriffenen, sondern Ich bin Kampfende under der Kampf selbst* [I am the *agon* – I am not one or other of the antagonists, I am both, and I am the *agon* itself].[126] In similar fashion Derrida says 'it . . . both sows confusion between opposites and stands between the opposites "at once"'.[127]

It is important to note that the hybridity is both spatial and temporal, in that it exists within the actors themselves, representing a caesura in the normative consciousness of everyday life, and is at the same time an interruption of, or deviation from, actual time itself. The 'contour of difference'[128] which we map is thus a real geography of discourse and at the same time a psychic space of discourse. It is unlikely that Bhabha knew of the significance of the Irish 'crossroads' in the concept of the fifth province when he wrote 'it is a form of colonial discourse that is uttered *inter dicta*: a discourse at the crossroads of what is known and permissible and that which though known must be kept concealed; a discourse uttered between the lines and as such both against the rules and within them'.[129] The correspondence of such a discourse with the actions of the Butler family who spend the duration of *Living Quarters* attempting to escape from the lines laid down in the Ledger, or of Hugh O'Neill as he attempts to barter his public history for the story of the whole man, will be obvious. But in the wider sphere of Friel's theatre, there is a search for transcendence of the conditions as there is a discernible search on the part of Irish society for a transcendence of, or delivery from, history. In the latter case, though, it should be emphasised that it is now recognised that the materials and the capacity for such a process are to be found within, rather than from an external *deus ex machina*. Even the vocabulary of this is relevant, since the etymological connection between the 'sublime' and the 'subliminal' indicates the process from inside or beneath this liminal state to a condition of being uplifted.

The ambitions of the Irish Literary Theatre, to find within the allegorical soil 'the deeper thoughts and emotions'[130] of a hidden Ireland is such a project, as was that of Field Day eighty years later. The risks inherent in the undertaking are not unrecognised: as Friel himself acknowledged, employing Joyce's own strategy, the danger of language which is 'familiar and foreign', not fully possessed,[131] can lead to more than cultural death, as we infer from *Volunteers*. As Havel says, 'under the orderly surface of the life of lies . . . there slumbers the hidden sphere of life in its real aims, of its hidden openness to truth'.[132]

It follows that the person who leaves home is not 'at home' in any sense, but it is also clear that one can be, in Seamus Heaney's words,

'lost/Unhappy and at home'.[133] The sense of being ill-at-ease, of something invading the home which is unknown but may become known,
which disturbs the psychic landscape of everyday life in its uncanny
reference to the past, to concealed images, was (as we have already
noted) named by Freud as *unheimlich* – unhomely. We find it throughout
Friel's work in the discomposure of his domestic scenes, which perhaps
explains his otherwise devastating disavowal of 'home' quoted earlier.
The idea that home is an impossibility becomes understandable and
acceptable if we take it that the constant invasion of the home, the threat
to it in the leavetakings and the homecomings, the presence somewhere
'out there' of the 'strays', is a permanent condition of transitus.

Harold Bloom speaks of an intersection between sense and absurdity,
between dream and reason, providence and disaster which creates this
sense of strangeness.[134] This has become the keynote of the cultural
debate which has absorbed the literary and scientific imaginations since
the Romantic era. It is both an individual and a collective concern, since
it occupies not only the identity of the individual artist but also the
discussion which leads to a sense of community among people affected
in common by what happens when they feel this strangeness of not being
at home. It exemplifies Heidegger's argument that literature is 'an attempt
to prepare for a homecoming by accepting the truth that we are no longer
at home in our world'.[135] Thus, Bloom argues, literature has the power
'to be both estranged and at home . . . at once uncanny and natural'.[136]

Freud defines the *unheimlich* as something which 'ought to have
remained hidden and secret and has become visible'[137] and that it refers
to what is 'known of old and long familiar'.[138] The homely becomes
'concealed, kept from sight, so that others do not get to know of or
about it, withheld from others'.[139] The fulcrum *heimlich/unheimlich* thus
becomes an ambivalent space in which the uncanny represents a double
or other self. The uncanny, says Freud, 'is in reality nothing new or alien,
but something which is familiar and of old established in the mind and
which has been alienated from it only through the process of repression'.[140]
The *heimlich*, that which 'belongs to the house', is the 'familiar'[141] and
what is 'uncanny' is what is *not* known and familiar.[142] Freud goes on to
adduce the fact that the *heimlich* and the *unheimlich* are not contrary
and irreconcilable but dual representations of the same truth – again,
Joyce's view of language as simultaneously 'so familiar and so foreign' is
apt. Within the house, the homely, there is secreted a thing withdrawn
from strangers which thereby becomes, in itself, and to itself, a strange
thing.[143] When we read in Freud's essay that 'the subject identifies
himself with someone else' and that there is 'a doubling, dividing and
interchanging of the self'[144] we can understand the Irish preoccupation

with what Joyce called 'invultuation' – the making of images. (As I have argued elsewhere, contemporary Irish theatre might be summarised in three words: *conversations in images*.[145]) And we can make a further connection between what Freud calls the effects of the uncanny – 'silence, darkness and solitude'[146] – and the threefold strategy of Joyce which is so congruent with the themes we have so far identified in Friel: 'silence, exile and cunning'.[147]

A scarce glance at the surface of Friel's work shows us that the domestic *focus* can be distorted, if not permanently unmade, by the revelation of what 'ought to have remained hidden and secret'. The disruption of life in the Butler household in *Living Quarters*, by the disclosure of Anna's affair with her stepson Ben; of the stability of the peripatetic circus life in *Crystal and Fox* by Fox's claim that he had turned informer on his own son; the violence unleashed on an already disoriented community in *The Gentle Island* by publication of the homosexual incident between Shane and Philly – are all instances of the way that the truth, or versions of the truth, can disintegrate the concept of 'home'.

MEMORY AND SPACE

In the 1530s Giulio Camillo devised and constructed a wooden 'Memory Theatre' as a physical epiphany of his treatise on the art of memory, *L'Idea del Theatro*. It was an amphitheatre in which the audience space was divided into seven sections and with seven grades, to be witnessed by a solitary spectator standing in the place of the stage.[148] Its purpose was to illustrate the order of eternal truth, following the classic texts on the art of memory such as that of the *Ad Herennium*,[149] by dividing that truth into its cardinal components. *Image*, the basic strategy of classical memory, is intimately associated with the *word* and conserves 'the things, words and arts which we confide to it'; furthermore, it 'gives us true wisdom from whose founts we come to the knowledge of things from their causes and not from their effects'.[150] Camillo constructed the theatre and placed within it the component literatures (based on the work of Cicero) which underpin the wisdom of memory: his images enable the actor/spectator 'to read off at one glance . . . the whole contents of the universe' and its magic power was contained in the fact that each image possessed a 'talismanic virtue'.[151] Each riser of each grade consisted of cabinets containing this literature of memory. Beyond this, it was also a place of magic, as the basic images took on new and deeper meanings as the actor/spectator progressed up the steps of the amphitheatre to investigate their 'higher' reaches. Insofar as Friel's plays – particularly the 'nostalgia' plays – pursue meaning through memory,

Camillo's Memory Theatre offers us many possibilities of understanding how memory affects meaning. A community living at one with itself, such as Baile Beag supposedly is at the opening of *Translations*, would have an orderly recourse to meaning and cohesion of this kind which would include access, through classical literature, to the wisdom and indeed the acquaintance of the gods. No other manifestation in Friel's work – not even *Making History* with its unstable stability – is so much at peace with itself, but other 'Ballybegs' demonstrate sectors of Camillo's process of putting us in touch with the 'eternal verities' by means of image-based memory.

Frances Yates considered that Camillo's structure was 'a remarkable transformation of the art of memory . . . a building divided into memory places on which are memory images'.[152] The application of such a house of the mind to *The Enemy Within* or *Philadelphia*, with their appeal to specific memories or specific *loci* will be obvious; the lateral expansion of the actor/spectator's imagination from one section of the memory theatre to another, the growing awareness of the connections between different kinds of memory and different kinds of meaning in *Faith Healer*, *Making History*, *Wonderful Tennessee*, and *Molly Sweeney* is awareness of a different order. But the really vital aspect for us to understand is that Camillo conceived the memory theatre 'as representing all that the mind can conceive and all that is hidden in the soul'[153] – thus showing us that the memory theatre is both the home of memory and unhomely – containing what we must know and what we must not know. In this sense it was a Renaissance concept which in time would provide the basis for the Enlightenment and, in turn, the concepts of 'other' and difference which gave rise to modern psychology. In terms of the theatre itself, it provides us with the concept of the secret within the play which is the journey of the actor/spectator towards truth, such as we witness in *Faith Healer* and in Tom Murphy's *Bailegangaire* and *The Gigli Concert*.

The system also offers us the prospect of two kinds of *agon*: firstly, when the Butler family in *Living Quarters* attempt to escape from the events which enfold them, they are merely reorganising the pages of the Ledger contained within the memory theatre, thus demonstrating that there is a certain type of limited freedom within the overall determined universe of fact. Secondly, and more importantly, the situation in *Translations* shows us what happens when two systems, each considered from within to be universally applicable and universally true, collide and the liminal, transformative experience which we have already discussed begins, with the active involvement of, and appeal to, the basic elements of memory and meaning – the earth, air and water, and the mercurial, venereal and vulcanic temperaments.

The fundamental notion which is negated in such an encounter is that 'we endure around truths immemorially posited' (*Tr.* 42). This will be further examined in Chapter 6, but here I want to employ it to illustrate the fact that, as in an 'asylum' or anaesthetic zone which we enter as an initiate, there is a process of 'levelling and stripping', as Goffman calls it, to which we all submit. In entering the space occupied by the actor/spectator in Camillo's memory theatre, we abdicate any claim on, or responsibility for, our inherited baggage, the 'truths immemorially posited', and submit instead to the 'truths' which are to be revealed to us through the imagistic memory contained in this theatre. 'Time immemorial' means time which extends so far back into the human psyche that it cannot be recalled by means of images or memory. The memory theatre demonstrates that such time does not exist. In *Translations* and in *Making History* two types of memory, two types of imagery, two systems of social organisation, confront one another. The fact that both systems claim to be universal demonstrates that *neither* is entitled to such a claim. In entering the space between those systems, Hugh O'Donnell and his son Owen, Hugh O'Neill and his wife Mabel, occupy liminal roles in which they are likely to be destroyed. In entering the memory theatre, the actor/spectator similarly is entering a liminal space in which anything may happen.

In his seminal text *The Empty Space* (1968), Peter Brook refers to 'the true shared territory of theme and concern'[154] between cast and audience. (It is a point shared by Victor Turner.[155]) The notion of a physical space for such a meeting, as well as a metaphysical one, is crucial. Brook's notion of a 'Holy Theatre' or 'Theatre of the Invisible-Made-Visible'[156] is a space in which ritual is enacted in a way that is both threatening and potentially liberating.[157] Brook makes the point that 'today, writers seem unable to make ideas and images collide through words with Elizabethan force . . . We have lost all sense of ritual and ceremony'[158] and it may be that his enthusiasm for the work of Brian Friel, in particular his admiration for *Molly Sweeney*,[159] was generated because he recognised the collision – and collusion – of images and ideas in Friel's memory plays, the significance of which emerged largely since *The Empty Space* was written. Certainly, the strategy by which Friel seduces his audience into the inner journey of characters such as Frank Hardy or Molly Sweeney is imagistic, and in both *Dancing at Lughnasa* and *Molly Sweeney* the coincidence of image, music and text has that same magical Renaissance force which Brook admired in the Elizabethan theatre (he calls it 'a necessary theatre'[160]) and which both Giulio Camillo and Robert Fludd attempted to build in both physical and metaphysical terms.[161]

Brook would have recognised in both *Philadelphia* and *Molly Sweeney* the fusion and yet separation of inner and outer man – 'the outer man whose behaviour is bound by the photographic rule of everyday life . . . and the inner man whose anarchy and poetry is usually expressed only in his words'.[162] (The word 'photographic', meaning literally 'writing with light', gives us, at least etymologically, a congruence between words and images.)

Brook's anxiety about the future of the theatre is echoed, perhaps not fortuitously, by Frances Yates, who states provocatively at the outset of *The Art of Memory* that 'we moderns . . . have no memory at all'[163] – suggesting that the use of memory as a way back to original meaning is no longer relevant to a world which is so future-oriented. If we no longer have memory, then time becomes linear, and we are unable to re-invent because we are at the mercy of the empire.

The two concerns together underline the significance of Friel's theatre in making it possible to re-member, to take apart in order to reconstitute a fragmented integer. For both Brook and Yates, the central process was the combination of images, space and words in order to set in train a transformative experience. Behind this process or concept is the identification of *topos* with topic and of *locus* with locale. In *Translations* Owen O'Donnell taunts his father with the changing landscape of fact, the place-names translated into the newly drawn map of the future:

> OWEN: Do you know where the priest lives?
> HUGH: At Lis na Muc, over near . . .
> OWEN: No he doesn't. Lis na Muc, the Fort of the Pigs, has become Swinefort . . . and the new school isn't at Poll na gCaorach – it's at Sheepsrock. Will you be able to find your way? (*Tr.* 42)

Image, memory and meaning thus all add up or, in the case of an unreadable territory, do not add up, to identity, to the business of survival. The fact that Owen eventually discards the name-book and disowns his involvement in the act of translation, whereas Hugh courageously confronts the ending of ancient time and the commencement of a new age with his agreement to teach the English language, illustrates the fact that the arrival, on the threshold, of the messengers of a new civilisation, capable of disrupting and displacing one's own, is not merely a collision of superior and inferior forces, of constitutional or economic factors, but a psychic meeting point at which the *between* happens and the possibility exists of new meanings being discovered or created.

PART I

Private Conversation

Divining . . . is a gift for being in touch with
what is there, hidden and real, a gift for
mediating between the latent source
and the community.

Seamus Heaney

1

THE LANDSCAPE PAINTER

Vital and living images will reflect the vitality and life of the world . . .
unify the contents of memory and set up magical correspondences between
outer and inner worlds.[1]

MAN, PLACE AND TIME

The diviner stands at the meeting of four roads, and thereby constitutes a
fifth place, the point between. Having taken the road of memory, through
the fourth dimension of time, he now dis-covers the fifth dimension, of
the psyche. Victor Turner, reflecting on the blacker aspects of the divining
role, says:

> Only the diviner, fortified by ritual and protected by ferocious spirits that
> torment him while they endow him with insight, can publicly expose the
> hates that simmer beneath the outward semblance of social peace.[2]

Of course, Friel as diviner exposes more than the 'hates' that Turner
finds in the shaman of the Ndembu: 'passions' would be a more appropriate term, and 'conflict resolution' would be a more contemporary
explanation of his function, as he carries his tribe across the river from
despair to hope, from dreams to realities, and, naturally, back again.
Nevertheless, Turner's description is an uncannily accurate summary of
what 'The Diviner', in Friel's title story, accomplishes and sets in train. He
stands in symbolic relation to his tribe, and is at one and the same time
part of the tribe and outside it; thus he is the necessary 'enemy within' the
tribe and carries his own 'enemy' within himself. The most pungent
quality about his extra-ordinary skill is that it is also an ordinary power,
one that we all carry within us, untapped. Friel's dramatic qualities bring
that skill temporarily to the surface in ourselves, his audience, as he puts
us 'in touch with some otherness' (DL 71) that we already know.

This chapter will explore Brian Friel's mindscape as he acts in the persona of the diviner or 'landscape painter', as Chekhov's Trigorin describes himself in *The Seagull*:

> I've never liked myself. I dislike myself as a writer, and I often don't understand what I'm writing. I love this water here, the trees, the sky. I have a feeling for nature, it arouses a sort of passion in me, an irresistible desire to write. But you see, I'm not a mere landscape painter, I'm also a citizen of my country; I love it, I love its people. As an author, I feel I'm in duty bound to write about the people, their sufferings, their future and about science, the rights of man, and so on.[3]

The relation of culture to psychology, which both Chekhov and Friel explore intensively, depends on locale and the metaphoric capacity to equate landscape with mindscape. Trigorin's view of writing does not dismiss the 'mere' landscape painter – we should take 'mere' in the sense of 'exclusive' – and his mode of 'landscape painting' is astonishingly analogous to that of Thomas Larcom, one of the chief officers of the Ordnance Survey of Ireland in the 1830s who noted:

> Habits of the people. Note the general style of the cottages . . . food; fuel; dress; longevity; usual number in a family; early marriages . . . what are their amusements and recreations; Patrons and patron's days; and traditions respecting them? . . . Nothing more indicates the state of civilisation and intercourse.[4]

The idea that there is more than a surface area to be assessed – that there are depths or 'deep structures' which can open our awareness of people's lives – is, again, the controlling idea of the divining or translation process, of which Steiner has said that it 'translate[s] the underlying metaphysics of a language into its overt or surface grammar'.[5] Victor Turner also acknowledged the role of the 'landscape painter' in the life of a society:

> any society which hopes to be imperishable must whittle out for itself a piece of space and a while of time, in which it can look honestly at itself. This honesty is not that of the scientist, who exchanges the honesty of his ego for the objectivity of his gaze, *son regard*. It is, rather, akin to the supreme honesty of the creative artist who, in his presentations on the stage, in the book, on canvas, in marble, in music, or in towers and houses, reserves to himself the privilege of seeing straight what all cultures build crooked.[6]

Friel's response to his environment has demonstrated that he locates his chief preoccupations such as family life, loyalty and freedom within the physical terrain, and, because he does so in a dramatic representation which so often takes the form of an intimate history lesson, a handing down of local experience, he fulfils Steiner's dictum on the role of genius with which my Introduction opened. Even when he is disaffected by events, attracted elsewhere or simply impeded by a writer's block, he obeys the imperative to be in attendance, as if waiting for voices – as he puts it, 'trying to be available'.[7]

The ability to divine the 'landscape of fact' both physically and psychologically is Friel's particular gift. When we find ourselves, during the dramatic experience, witnessing a universal truth in an undeniably local setting, it is because Friel has touched us definitively, that a statement, however intangible, has been made which is as true of ourselves as it is of his characters, that it somehow concerns and affects us deeply.

As we chart Friel's progress from the young writer of short stories to his present position as one of the most important playwrights of our time, we shall also trace the emergence of modern Ireland, from provincial colonialism to sovereign state, with all the psychic and cultural adjustments that accompany transition and transformation. In the dual careers of writing himself and writing Ireland, Friel has been searching, like Seamus Heaney, for images and symbols adequate both to *his* predicament and to 'ours'. The divining role is dangerous: Victor Turner refers to the shaman as the outsider in a society's rite of passage, precipitating 'actions and relationships which do not flow from a recognised social status but originate outside it'.[8] But in discussing what Friel calls 'concepts of Irishness'[9] he is also on the inside, and this ambivalence places him at risk whenever it appears that he may be not only translating experience into words but also betraying the lode of that experience.

Such a translation has become more evident since I first wrote this book, through the development of an interpretative literature on the subject of Ireland's geographies: further work from John Andrews, *Shapes of Ireland: maps and their makers*, Brian Graham's collection of essays on cultural geography and the late Frank Mitchell's magisterial *Reading the Irish Landscape*, have heightened the relationship of landscape to text – have, in fact, encouraged us to interpret landscape *as* text. In the beginning was the word; and it is the diviner's task to carry the word across the stream of time from one subjective bank to the other. 'Isn't this your job? – to translate?', an hysterical Gar taunts the priest in *Philadelphia* (*Ph.* 96) and in *Translations* the same imperative is repeated to Owen/Roland, the go-between: 'Do your job. Translate' (*Tr.* 61). This is, in Peter Brook's terms, both a rough and a holy theatre.[10]

Furthermore, it is the diviner's job to translate both publicly and privately. Whether it is at all possible to 'interpret between privacies' is not merely a puzzle which Hugh Mor O'Donnell cannot resolve (*Tr.* 67) but one which has engaged the minds of philosophers from Humboldt to Wittgenstein. It is no accident that in *Give Me Your Answer, Do!* Friel quotes Wittgenstein: 'Whereof one cannot speak, thereof one must be silent' (*GMYAD* 70–1). It is a question not only of 'can' speak but of *may* speak: interpretation which fails can become the messenger of misunderstanding and, ultimately, death. To speak where speech cannot be translated (to carry messages between lovers, for example, is an impossibility) is to transgress the median role and power of the messenger. Public translation of public texts may be the furthest we can go, since to interpret or translate a private figure into a public arena is hazardous for both the private man and his translator. 'If one takes art as seriously as the faith healer does', Friel has said, 'as a matter of life and death, that itself is hubristic. You're courting catastrophe'.[11] As diviner, he attempts to translate on two levels: the public stage, on which he reveals the people of Ballybeg to the people of Ireland, and, on the private level, the individual thoughts of men and women to individuals within his audience. The dramatic achievement, when it occurs, is the meeting of public and private, the oneness of the outer behaviour with the inner preoccupations, which melds the actors into an ensemble and presents their various personae as a form of community, thereby bringing together the disparate sensibilities of the audience into a moment of dramatic unity.

In order to understand the man who moves towards this unity, we must understand the man who set out from a particular place at a particular time, and is, in fact, *two* men at the *same* time.

Brian Friel was born in Killyclogher, close to the town of Omagh in County Tyrone, on either 9 or 10 January 1929. His father, Patrick Friel, was a schoolteacher and his mother was a postmistress; he attended the nearby National (Primary) School at Culmore, of which his father was the Principal. Friel has two sisters (also teachers) and had a younger brother who died in infancy. The figure of the schoolmaster appears in many of Friel's stories, radio plays and stage plays, most notably as the central character in *Translations*. More importantly, perhaps, parent and mentor coalesce in two early stories, 'My Father and the Sergeant'[12] and 'The Illusionists'[13] in which Friel discusses the child's relationship with both these figures of authority.

Friel was born into a tradition of nationalism which takes its social and political hue from the context of west Ulster. This fact is also important for an understanding of both Friel's response to the cultural and political history of this part of Ireland and his sense of identity and association within his own place. So too is his consciousness of the fact that all his grandparents were Irish-speaking, and that two, his father's father and his mother's mother, were unlettered; this at times seems paradoxical to the writer working through the *English* language, one of whose principal concerns is the role of language in social communication.

Friel's father's family comes from Derry, in Northern Ireland, where the surname is common, while his mother's family, the McLoones, are from Glenties in the south-west of County Donegal; as we shall see, this is a crucial distinction in Friel's sense of place and in the location of his imaginary world.

Naming, for Friel as for Beckett,[14] is the key to identity, but in his own case it presents a difficulty which typifies the position of the individual in relation to authority, and the problem of communication between two cultures: for, although he is known as *Brian* Friel, his birth certificates bear the names *Bernard* Patrick Friel. At the time of his birth, the Protestant bureaucracy discouraged the registration of 'Gaelic' names, and the anglicisation 'Bernard' was adopted for the purpose of registration. Certificates, because one exists in respect of 9 January and another for 10 January. It is not only Friel's light-heartedness but also a sense of the duality in his background that makes him suggest 'Perhaps I'm twins'.[15] But officially, as far as the record books indicate, there is no such person as Brian Friel. One looks at one's certificate of identity and says 'That is not me' – which is not far from Rimbaud's 'Je est un autre'. When, in *Translations*, Owen O'Donnell's family discover that the English have mistakenly called him 'Roland' he protests: 'It's only a name. It's the same me, isn't it?' (*Tr.* 33) – but translation has made sure that Roland and Owen are different people.

The problem of naming can be extended from Brian/Bernard Friel to the society in which he lives. For while Friel's world, the city of Derry and its hinterland, is known and real and tangible, it is almost impossible to *name* it: known to nationalists as 'Derry' and to unionists as 'Londonderry', the city has become known in the official lexicon as Derry since its nationalist-dominated council voted to change its name, while the county surrounding it remains Londonderry. It was in the days of unionist control of local affairs that Friel's father served three terms on the city council as a nationalist representative.

Derry suffers from its location in the geographical area 'west of the River Bann', which has become a codeword for 'scarcity of resources' from which the region is only now emerging. Distinct from the industrialised east of Ulster, the west is a society divided both from the relative prosperity of the east and from itself. Ulster as a whole, one of the historical provinces of Ireland, was artificially divided by the creation in 1920–25 of a land boundary between the Irish Free State (later to become the Republic of Ireland) and that part of Ulster which remained within the United Kingdom, and became known from then as Northern Ireland – a problematic term which politicians in the south refused to acknowledge for many decades. As Professor M. W. Heslinga points out, 'in the course of one-and-a-half millennia "Ulster" has stood for many territories . . . Historically . . . there is as much or as little justification for the modern Northern definition of "Ulster" . . . as for the pre-partition definition'.[16]

Much more recently, the Deputy First Minister designate of the Northern Ireland Assembly, Seamus Mallon, said

> I could define it [the north of Ireland] in many ways. Northern Ireland? – not quite right. Ulster? – not quite accurate. The north of Ireland? Now don't ask me why I use it. I find it easier to say phonetically, the north of Ireland, rather than 'Norn Iron'. And I don't make any fun in saying that. But I am a product of my environment politically. I am part of a nationalist tradition that would see Northern Ireland as the north of Ireland. I am someone who actually gets a little bit tight at the shoulders when I hear the term Ulster used, when it is not really Ulster. But at the end of the day what does it matter what we call it, if in effect we are all working together to create a new life for us all here?[17]

Three counties of the original province of Ulster (Donegal, Cavan and Monaghan) became part of the southern state. Tyrone Guthrie's mother, at the time of partition, articulated the new orientations when she wrote to him from their home in County Monaghan that instead of going *south* to meet strangers, they would now have to regard *northerners* as alien.[18] A new border was being drawn on the map of the mind as well as in the atlas. As Owen O'Donnell taunts his father: 'Will you be able to find your way?' (*Tr.* 42).

In this transaction, northern Donegal, for which Derry is the natural focus, became restricted in its commerce; the county itself is only linked to the rest of the Republic by a narrow neck of land at its southernmost tip. At its northernmost end, the peninsula of Inishowen, where Friel now lives, is, by definition, only narrowly connected to the rest of the county and, although part of the Republic, is in fact more northerly than almost all of 'Northern' Ireland – as Anthony Roche puts it, 'on the margins of both Irelands'.[19] Without a 'proper' name, a place, like a person, is incapable of fully discussing its identity, conducting its business, knowing its destiny; while it can perceive itself, it can only celebrate itself by subversive means – simile, metaphor and analogue – by pressing imagination into mendacity. In Friel's case, there is a very clear idea of why he would feel cut off from 'Ireland' by reason of where he lives; his engagement with Ireland, as a silent Senator in the years 1987–89, and as an entrepreneur in the Field Day endeavour, was influenced as much by physical location as it was by intellectual preoccupations.

Writing about Ulster has always been problematic for 'southerners' who are largely ignorant of life in Ulster.[20] Few residents of the Republic travel to Northern Ireland, and very few indeed have any regular contact with Ulster folk and their ways. Dervla Murphy, conscious of this lacuna, said that her 'discovery' of Northern Ireland, *A Place Apart*, was 'conceived by shame out of repentance'.[21] The mutual distrust and resentment which persists on both sides of the border (which we shall discuss in Chapter 5) is not, however, the result of that border, although its existence may have intensified the provincial rivalry already fundamental to Irish society. Indeed, Daniel O'Connell found his almost complete ignorance of Ulster a serious political disadvantage, as did Parnell.[22]

The border counties in particular live in a state of bewilderment, as can be experienced vicariously in Colm Toibin's *The Irish Border*.[23] In the drawing of the 1920 border, Derry lost Donegal as a hinterland and Donegal lost Derry as a focus. Friel locates most of his stories in Donegal and most of his plays after 1964 are set in 'Ballybeg', an imaginative realm across the border from the place where he has spent most of his life, the city of Derry. The existence of that border, both physically and metaphysically, is of central interest, because it presents itself both specifically and subliminally as the interstitial space, the place of trial, in many of his works: in his study of the 'extraterritorial' writer, Steiner refers to 'the *a priori* strangeness of the idea of a writer linguistically "unhoused", or displaced or hesitant at the frontier',[24] and Friel's circumstances, as we have rehearsed them in the Introduction and in this chapter, suggest the vertiginous nature of such a border mentality.

Friel's commitment to place is intense and acute. In 1939, when he was ten, his family returned from Omagh to Derry, where his father took up a new teaching post at the Long Tower School. Since then, with two important interludes, he has lived in Derry or on its hinterland. Educated at St Columb's College in the city – the *alma mater* of two Nobel Laureates, Seamus Heaney and John Hume – he then attended for over two years St Patrick's College, the national seminary at Maynooth near Dublin, a constituent college of the National University of Ireland. In these years he explored a possible vocation to the priesthood, and experienced an unsettling introduction to Irish Catholicism which he does not discuss, simply describing it as 'An awful experience. It nearly drove me cracked. It is one thing I want to forget. I never talk about it – the priesthood'.[25] He went instead to St Joseph's College, Belfast, for teacher training, and in 1950 returned to Derry to follow his father into the teaching profession with mathematics as his specialty. He spent seven years at the Christian Brothers' Intermediate School, followed by three at St Patrick's Boys Primary School, Pennyburn, describing the latter as 'happy years'.[26]

There is no integrated picture in such an account of Friel's early life – no sense of a pattern or of a destiny mapped out. Quite the opposite – a restlessness and lack of direction, set against a background in which the nature of authority is both acknowledged and questioned. The way in which the 'landscape painter' would map out and colour the life of the zone in which he lives is permeated by this dualism in Friel's circumstances.

It explains on one side the tension between the artist and his *alter ego* or 'enemy within' and on another between artist and public world; it also encapsulates the sense of a fractured history which characterises that public world in its view of the present and future. Friel has struggled with this tension and dichotomy and, with the phenomenal impetus of *Philadelphia, Here I Come!*, has made them a personal style which can at times be deeply rewarding for his audiences and at the same time deeply disturbing. Friel's activity as a writer is not merely his response to situations but also his involvement in them. He recognises in himself the potential figure of authority whose text takes on an authoritative voice of its own, and the personal risks and possibilities of his own shamanistic role, while working out his own personal preoccupations in parallel with those of Ballybeg.

Displacement and lack of wholeness are both spatial and temporal, physical and metaphysical. In Friel's early plays, this dilemma is expressed in the character of Columba in *The Enemy Within*, who casts out the devils of his private, tribal allegiances thus:

> Get out of my monastery! Get out of my island! Get out of my life! Go back to those damned mountains and seductive hills that have robbed me of my Christ! (*EW* 70).

But he is unable to rid himself of the seduction of the inner man, 'the green wooded earth of Ireland' (*EW* 21). This is a spatial temptation away from his monastery in Iona and a temporal seduction which relies on the affective power of memory. It is a condition of internal exile in which the central image of the Irish historical imagination, the hearth, is known to be unattainable. Because the *community* cannot be collected around the hearth without further violence and disruption, Friel prefers to regard those of whom he writes, and those to whom he responds, as his 'constituency'.[27]

In his short stories Friel has observed – and to that extent has kept faith with – the parishes of his childhood. And he has also done so in editing the memories of Charles McGlinchey, *The Last of the Name* (the title could itself be put at the head of one of Friel's own stories). In his introduction, 'Important Places', Friel points out that McGlinchey does not speak of the epochal events of his lifetime (1861–1954) but overlooks them 'in a manner that is almost Olympian'. Instead, he speaks of

> the everyday, the domestic, the familiar, the nuance of a phrase, the tiny adjustment of a local ritual, the momentous daily trivia of the world of his parish,

which provide

> an exact and lucid picture of profound transition: a rural community in the process of shedding the last vestiges of a Gaelic past and of an old

Christianity that still cohabited with an older paganism, and of that community coming to uneasy accommodation with the world of today, 'the
buses, the cars, the silk stockings'. . . . Meentiagh Glen is an important place,
not of itself but because an astute man observed it, elicited its importance
from it. And that simultaneous bestowing and eliciting is an act of art.[28]

In drawing us into this world, Friel makes McGlinchey the conduit for a
culture which is typical of Europe before Napoleon, and of which mere
vestiges are now available to the anthropologist. In *Making History*,
Translations and *Dancing at Lughnasa* we are re-introduced to aspects of
that world and asked to believe that it can be recreated for the duration
of the dramatic action.

In many ways, therefore, the diviner or translator – whether he be
Charles McGlinchey or Brian Friel – is also an historian. The phenomenon
of Brian Friel is made possible by the combination of two matrices: the
tension between a known, secure but receding and fading past and an
unknown, beckoning, tantalising future which baits and challenges. Thus
each play stands on the fragile moment of the present between these two
matrices, employing memory as the linguistic cord between them. To
continue the landscape analogy, the derivation of topic from *topos*, and
of tropic from trope, emphasises how utterly and irreducibly landscape *is*
text and thus how its representation – whether emotional or social landscape – hangs on the words and cadences of speech. When the diviner's
dowsing rod, with its spasmodic knowledge, brings to the surface what is
hidden but known, then that same spasm happens in the minds of his
audience, and the connection is made between emotion and history.

There is another vital dimension to 'Ballybeg' in our reading of Friel as a
post-colonial writer – its significance as a 'non-place'. Just as Charles
McGlinchey memorialised Meentiagh Glen as a place of no importance,
so Friel's Glenties merges into 'Ballybeg' as a state of mind from which
the new world of modern Ireland can grow.[29] As such – and in a way that
no 'real' *locus* can be – it is emblematic of *all* such places.

This becomes most acute in colonial discourse. The field is known to
the coloniser in one mappable sense, which appears on the cartographer's
drawn or printed page; and it is known to the colonised in an immanent
sense which inheres in the imagination. One is a topic of learning and
discovery, the other, as Bhabha puts it, 'is the site of dreams, images,
fantasies, myths, obsessions and requirements'.[30] To repossess the field,
the post-colonial society must perform two exercises: retain its imaginary
lien on history while taking stock of what is actually there.

Thomas Kilroy underlines this when he refers to 'our jealous insistence
upon minor geography'[31] – the murderous coveting of *the* field, the defence

of 'our own'. But in the post-colonial epoch this takes on an almost paranormal significance: the non-place which is everywhere (equivalent, we might suppose, to a non-entity who is Everyman) is a threatening concept to those who can only conceive of land as visible, tangible territory. To the newly fledged nation, and to the emancipated serf, land is also a metaphysical space. Elmer Andrews makes the exceptional point that 'the diviner opens up a secret space beyond the rational mind'[32] and this, too, is a function of the post-colonial prophet mapping the new land. He transgresses the existing boundaries in order to disturb what is known by means of what is, as yet, unknown.

The principle of indeterminacy or uncertainty, which, as we shall see in Chapter 7 ('Plays of Beyond') becomes central to the argument in *Give Me Your Answer, Do!*, has also become an agent in the post-colonial maelstrom. The idea that one cannot observe a situation without becoming involved in it and taking a role as an agent of change, has its consequences for the diviner. The landscape painter disturbs the landscape, becomes political. Friel, as landscape painter, has observed, anticipated and shaped the events of his parish and his country.

As we see in the case of the eponymous diviner of Friel's short story, the gift of discovery can be employed in any place; it is a connection between one's own power of intuition and the depths of the field in which one stands. When the diviner stands in his own field, surrounded by the familiar and familial, with all the temptation to regard them as 'immemorially posited', the gap between intuition and knowledge is closed and what is divined is revealed as something that has been known and is now recognised by all.

A travelogue piece for *Holiday* magazine in 1963 entitled 'A Fine Day at Glenties' provides a microcosm of this world, identifying the vital elements, human, animal, topographic and meteorological, which constitute the successful operation of a finely balanced set of behaviours and contains within its conservatism a healthy respect for disorder and deviance.[33] It tells us what we need to know about the 'constituency' of this 'Irish Chekhov' – where the people of his stories and plays come from, what social preoccupations they express, and how their dilemmas are resolved. In his portrait of Glenties he presents us with 'The Strawman Shanaghan. the trick-o-the-loop man'; Eddie Doherty, 'farmer, casual labourer . . . a practical hard-working man, not given to daydreams'; Patrick Farrelly, Esq., 'but God and Glenties know him as Pat Tom Nally, that is to say Patrick, son of Thomas, grandson of Eleanor'; Brigid Costigan ('Boston Biddy') who has been to, and returned from, Boston – discontented, 'but that is the way she will always be all her life because she imagines herself an unhappy exile'; and the fair itself, 'an atmosphere, an animation, an aura of adventure' which passes between fact and fiction: 'Glenties is the stage, and the fairgoers are the players. This is the real thing, the superb performance, that wonderful experience of hundreds of people behaving naturally'. It is because performance is 'real', and drama is the natural condition of that social reality, that Friel tells us: 'the events in this piece have happened at one time or another; the people are fictitious and bear no resemblance to anybody, living or dead'. But Shanaghan is the seed-place of Fox Melarkey and his rickety wheel, Biddy is the returned Yank who becomes Cass McGuire, the condition of discontented exile is what characterises the people of Baile Beag at the opening of *Translations* ('Some of you people aren't happy unless you're miserable and you'll not be right content until you're dead' – *Tr.* 21) – and above all it is the convincing trueness of the 'atmosphere' which pervades Friel's most unreal plays and thus gives them the sense of people 'behaving naturally'. This engagement with the 'constituency' thus provides Friel with the types of life sufficient to populate and encompass the largest issues with their essential actors.

These are 'actors' in the sense both of ordinary people carrying out the trans-actions of daily life and of *personae* who carry within them characteristics which they exhibit in ways that we can describe as *drama*. 'The real thing', says Friel, is a 'superb performance'. In executing the job of being a citizen of Glenties, each man or woman also enacts a ritual, both being and belonging, being immanent and at the same time transcendent. Glenties, or Ballybeg, is the thoroughfare of both, and the manner in which its inhabitants negotiate the street is the simplest but also the most telling of *rites de passage* – a dialogue which, in Steiner's terms, is a 'strategic redefinition of self'.

One can easily appreciate the almost natural fit between the observations of anthropology and the way the voices heard by the dramatist arrive in the play-text. Turner says of his work among the Ndembu and other tribes:

> something like 'drama' was constantly emerging, even erupting, from the otherwise fairly even surfaces of social life. For the scientist in me, such social dramas revealed the 'taxonomic' relations among actors (their kinship ties, structural positions, social class, political status and so forth), and their contemporary bonds and oppositions of interest and friendship, their personal network ties, and informal relationships.[34]

In the same way, Friel's description of Glenties on that particular day – a day composite of many observations, of course – encapsulates everything that any drama of the world could say. Yeats, too, had spotted this, even though his preference for the exotic and the paranormal took his attention away from the mundane; in his appreciation of Carleton he wrote:

> The history of a nation is not in parliaments and battle-fields, but in what the people say to each other on fair-days and high days and in how they farm, and quarrel and go on pilgrimage.[35]

The people of Glenties, their history, their homesteads, their livestock, the climate, the landscape – all make up a self-regulating system which is as powerful and dynamic a stage as anything in Yeats's imagination. Here we have the prototypes for all the visionaries and sceptics and domestic exiles of Friel's plays. This 'superb performance' is the cornerstone of his concept of life as play, life with its own internal referent point, its music: outside, the love of country; inside, the love of the unseen life.[36] Everything he has written is a profound meditation upon that idea.

It was Chekhov who said that he discovered his material by looking out of the window, and this was echoed by Susan FitzGerald when she was preparing to play the part of Alice in *Aristocrats*: 'it's just someone looking out of the window, but it breaks your heart'.[37] To observe Ballybeg is no doubt to look out of a window – and not simply in order to break hearts. But one also looks inside, observing the intimacies and tensions of family life. As Peter Brook says of *Three Sisters*, 'any page . . . gives the impression of life unfolding as though a tape-recorder had been left running'.[38] Clearly the way the recording is transcribed will determine whether the mundane speech can be lifted, by the energy and passion within it, to the level of art, but the facts of that life – its loves, fears, hates, aspirations, suspicions, insights and revelations – subsist in every cadence and every inflection.

In some senses politics has nothing to do with this, and in others it has everything to do with the way a family lives its lives and thinks its thoughts. Writing *Aristocrats*, Friel noted:

> the play . . . is about *family life*, its quality, its cohesion, its stultifying effects, its affording of opportunities for what we designate 'love' and 'affection' and 'loyalty'. Class, politics, social aspiration are the qualifying decor but not the core [*emphasis original*].[39]

Yet the 'qualifying decor' is not only a context. It is the set within which the drama is enacted. In *Aristocrats* there is explicit politics (and class) in the references to Judith's earlier involvement with the civil rights movement – something we could hardly anticipate in the 'Ballybeg–Glenties' of 1963, and which is certainly not a moving force in the play. But there is a world of politics (and class) in the current situation of the O'Donnell family, its place in history, and society, marking the almost completed slide from relevance into obscurity.

Politics, as Friel suspected, might be 'irrelevant', but he intuits that 'implicit in their language, attitudes, style, will be all the "politics" I need'.[40] And it is this third, innate political *nous*, the negotiation of the power of corridors, which siblings bear on their inner sleeve. In the same way that Steiner says '"meaning" resides "inside the words"', and that 'the translator must actualize the implicit "sense", the . . . associative range of significations',[41] so the dramatist must make explicit the 'native speaker's at-homeness',[42] the quiddity of what is being lived, so as to make it negotiable, in its turn, by the audience.

It is the family – or the *idea* of family – that creates the decor, and it is in this sense that the landscape painter observes both from within (looking out of the window) and from without (looking in through the window). Thus, the fabric of the plays, the box set which contains the family, takes on a *persona* of its own, and place becomes character, becomes atmosphere, and gives to the play as a whole the presiding context in which love can, or cannot, express itself and be expressed: 'the canvas can be as small as you wish, but the more accurately you write and the more truthful you are, the more validity your play will have for the world', Friel has said.[43]

Homi Bhabha speaks of 'the anxiety of enjoining the global and the local, the dilemma of projecting an international space on the trace of a decentred, fragmented subject'.[44] This may be true of the post-colonial project of bringing global viewpoints to bear on the situation of emergent societies. But in the inverse situation, where the local society-in-transition is moving through a phase which has universal significance, the anxiety experienced is that of meeting the whole world with a tiny grain of truth and finding it acceptable to, and true of, individual souls everywhere. It is Friel's reserve that makes these privacies all the more telling when they reach the public domain. 'What makes Chekhov acceptable to so many different people', says Friel, 'is his suggestion of sadness, of familiar melancholy . . . because sadness and melancholy are finally reasssuring. Tragedy is not reassuring. Tragedy demands completion. Chekhov was afraid to face completion'.[45] The characteristic setting of Chekhov's plays (see Chapter 8) and the ubiquitous unrest of his characters, is symptomatic of the fact that every play is the same, since every actor who enters the empty space begins to observe a common ritual, and this in turn leads to the almost formulaic process in which truth is sculpted. The conditions for this are the almost cliché inertia of the Russian landowners in the late nineteenth century, as if waiting for the barbarians, the middle class, to insert themselves between nobleman and peasant. The obvious affinity between such a play as *The Cherry Orchard* and *Aristocrats* in this connection leads us to reflect on what happens within a society on the brink of change, with all the gaps and discontinuities that this involves.

Friel is very conscious of the passage of time, which invades us from the past by means of memory and from the future by means of anticipation. He is dismissive of past work, insistent that the only reality is the work-in-progress, even when that work is obstructed by some kind of writing block or business commitment. He has an apparently indifferent attitude to his previous work, regarding it as 'finished . . . it is as it is'.[46] We might read this as arrogance: dismissive and at the same time the attitude of a creator – god-like. But this attitude has changed in recent years, and, with the exception of the plays which Friel would want to exclude from his 'canon', he has a more than affectionate interest in the continuing relevance of his more successful works.

This does not mean, however, that he dissociates himself from what he writes. He has said:

> You delve into a particular corner of yourself that's dark and uneasy, and you articulate the confusions and unease of that particular period. When you do that, that's finished and you acquire other corners of unease and discontent.[47]

The past is dealt with at the time, not in retrospect. The writer can only move forward by clearing away the preoccupations. As we have seen, Friel has long hoped for 'a religion, a philosophy, a sense of life',[48] and this embraces vocation as lifework – an outward exploration of concern – and an internal reconciliation of experience with belief. It involves family, which is the most powerful agent of memory. And it involves the question of how we relate, and relate to, the past – the public 'facts of history' and the private remembrances. To quote Friel again:

> What is a fact in the context of autobiography? A fact is something that happened to me or something I experienced. It can also be something I thought happened to me, something I thought I experienced. Or indeed an autobiographical fact can be pure fiction and no less true or reliable for that.[49]

The possibilities are endless, the story that one tells open-ended. To illustrate the point, Friel relates an incident central to his childhood and clear in his memory, which he now realises and acknowledges could not have taken place:

> My father and I used to go fishing on the lakes near the village . . . Although I haven't seen them for twenty-five years I know them with a knowledge that is special and sacred and so private that it is almost apprehensive . . . What I want to talk about is a particular memory of a particular day. There's no doubt in my mind about this – it's here now before my eyes, as I speak. The boy I see is about nine years old and my father would have been in his early forties. We are walking home from a lake with our fishing rods across our shoulders . . . And there we are, singing about how my boat can safely float through the teeth of wind and weather. That's the memory. That's what happened.[50]

This affective memory, which commands the emotive side of our behaviour, is the central agent in Friel's writing. But something can *happen* in memory which did not happen *in fact*. As Friel continues:

> A trivial episode without importance to anyone but me, just a moment of happiness caught in an album. But wait. There's something wrong here. I'm conscious of a dissonance, an unease. What is it? Yes, I know what it is: there is no lake along that muddy road. And since there is no lake my father and I never walked back from it in the rain with our rods across our shoulders. *The fact is a fiction.* Have I imagined the scene then? Or is it a composite of two or three different episodes? The point is – I don't think it matters. What matters is that . . . for some reason this vivid memory is there in the storehouse of the mind. For some reason the mind has shuffled the pieces of verifiable truth and *composed a truth of its own*. For me it is a truth. And because I acknowledge its particular veracity, it becomes a layer of my subsoil; it becomes part of me.[51] [*my emphasis*]

This chasing after the affective becomes the basic ingredient in the harrowing experience at the heart of *Philadelphia*, when Gar tries to establish a line of communication with his father, to coax him into recognising that they had once shared that same experience; the mere details of the 'fact' are immaterial compared with the importance of the shared memory:

PUBLIC: (*quickly*) It doesn't matter who owned it. It doesn't even matter that it was blue. But d'you remember one afternoon in May, we were up there, the two of us, and it must have rained because you put your jacket round my shoulders and gave me your hat –

S.B.: Aye?

PUBLIC: And it wasn't that we were talking or anything, but suddenly, suddenly you sang 'All Round My Hat I'll Wear a Green Coloured Ribbono' –

S.B.: Me?

PUBLIC: – for no reason at all except that we, that you were happy. D'you remember? D'you remember? (*There is a pause while S.B. tries to recall*)

S.B.: No . . . no, then, I don't . . .

PRIVATE: (*quickly*) There! There! There!

S.B.: 'All Round My Hat'? No, I don't think I ever knew that one. It wasn't 'The Flower of Sweet Strabane', was it? That was my song.

PUBLIC: It could have been. It doesn't matter.

PRIVATE: So now you know: it never happened! Ha-ha-ha-ha-ha. (*Ph.* 105)

The same type of memory – the 'wee lakes beyond' – will continue to occupy Friel's 'dark corners' and to provide the contours for the journey back into childhood and into family which he undertook so explicitly in *Dancing at Lughnasa*. It is a poignant illustration of Steiner's point that 'man is a primate who can lie, who can make "impossible" and counterfactual statements'.[52]

The way in which 'reality' or 'the truth' can cause the loss of a treasured memory will occur frequently in Friel's work right up to the present day. In the short story 'Among the Ruins', a man's return to a childhood haunt presents him with a different set of facts from those he carries with him in his memory: 'it had robbed him of a precious thing, his illusions of the past, and in their place now there was nothing – nothing but the truth' (*Diviner* 134). In such circumstances, people tend to insist that there can be two kinds of 'truth': the negligible truth of actual reality and the hermetically possessed truth of memory – 'Our world is real, too – Our world is just as real' (*Cass* 59); 'Doesn't matter if it's true or not – it's part of the Butler lore' (*LQ* 64). And it permits the in-between stage which is neither one thing nor the other: 'Even though it wouldn't have been the truth, it wouldn't have been a lie either' (*LQ* 87).

This in-between space, or gap, is where one can be destroyed by both public History and the private story, since ultimately it is inevitable that this craving for narrative wholeness and integrity will mesh with the greater political will of a people: the landscape painter must include the battle-scenes as well as the pastoral image, since they stand on the same ground – although, in dealing with the Battle of Kinsale and its aftermath in *Making History*, Friel refuses to bow to that greater will, and instead concentrates on the private flight and condition of O'Neill. In Heaney's words, this represents 'a way of reshaping the consciousness of the audience in posterity . . . to engross the present and dominate the memory'.[53] Thus, the broken family, at home perhaps but unable to possess it materially or metaphorically, engages in an interior drama by means of which it 'imposes a truth of its own'. On the physical plane this means simply a *sense* of place; on the metaphysical, an understanding of the *culture* of place, of the freedoms and restraints of boundaries, continuities, loyalty and betrayal, definitions and ambiguities.

One of Friel's chief preoccupations has been the ambi-valence in both Irish and English history of the life of Hugh O'Neill, Earl of Tyrone (1550–1616); his childhood, his exogamy, his dual loyalties to the Gaelic chieftains and the English crown, his exile and the way history has fashioned him into a particular type. Having as a very young man read Sean O'Faolain's biography of O'Neill, Friel was fascinated by O'Faolain's suggestion that 'a talented dramatist might write an informative, entertaining, ironical play on the theme of the living man helplessly watching his translation into a star in the face of all the facts that had reduced him to poverty, exile and defeat'.[54] The significance of these words will not be lost to the reader as we follow Friel's exploration of those themes in Columba, Frank Hardy, and the various manifestations of the O'Donnell family, until we reach his 'creation', Hugh O'Neill himself.

It is relatively easy to state the remaining biographical facts necessary to furnish an introduction to Friel: at the same time as he began teaching he began to explore another 'vocation' (although he disavows the 'rotundity of the expression'[55]) as a writer of short stories, published mainly in *The New Yorker* with whom he had a 'first reading agreement'. He established a substantial reputation in this genre, in which he conducted a 'private conversation' exploring certain areas of his own background and of the Irish psyche. This period of his career, and the transition into the writing of radio plays, is discussed in chapters 2 and 3. From radio plays he moved into the playhouse. He discounts his first and third plays (*A Doubtful Paradise* and *The Blind Mice),* which he has refused to publish, but *The Enemy Within* (1962) marks the beginning of what can now be seen as a conscious line of exploration of the themes of self-discovery, exile, the relationship of time (and distance) to affection, and the problems of communication.

Then came the time with Guthrie in Minneapolis, which encouraged him to hear his own voice more confidently than before. In his 'Self-Portrait' Friel described the time:

> It was an important period in a practical way. I learned about the physical elements of plays, how they are designed, built, *landscaped*. I learned how actors thought, how they approached a text, their various ways of trying to realise it. I learned a great deal about the iron discipline of theatre, and I discovered a nobility and a selflessness that one associates with a theoretical priesthood. But much more important than all these, those months in America gave me a sense of liberation . . . [which] conferred on me a valuable self-confidence and a necessary perspective so that the first play I wrote immediately after I came home, *Philadelphia, Here I Come!*, was a lot more assured than anything I had attempted before [*my emphasis*].[56]

Although married with a young family, he took the risk of writing full time, achieving his first international success with *Philadelphia, Here I Come!* in 1964, first at the Dublin Theatre Festival and subsequently on Broadway. He continues to live close to Derry, for which he maintains a loyal affection, not least because 'it takes its animus and its ethos as much from the twenty-six counties as from the six'.[57] He built a house at Muff, just over the border in Donegal, and later moved to an old house further up the coast at Greencastle, above Moville.

Friel describes the period in his life when he was teaching and writing stories in the evening as:

> the time when I first began to wonder what it was to be an Irish Catholic . . . to survey and analyse the mixed holding I had inherited, the personal, traditional and acquired knowledge that cocooned me, an Irish Catholic teacher with a nationalist background, living in a schizophrenic community . . . What I hope is emerging is . . . a faith, a feeling for life, a way of seeing life

... the patient assembly of a superstructure which imposes a discipline and within which work can be performed in the light of an insight, a group of ideas, a carefully cultivated attitude; or, as Seamus Heaney puts it . . . there are only certain stretches of ground over which the writer's divining rod will come to life.[58]

Heaney refers to 'the discovery of a way of writing that is natural and adequate to your sensibility'.[59] Friel as diviner, however, has no simple task. In his own statement he refers to the 'schizophrenic community' and the 'mixed holding', and the tendency towards what has perhaps been too readily termed 'schizophrenia' is a marked condition of Irish life. 'Displacement from' one's language, land, and citizenship, and ultimately from one's history, is not synonymous with 'loss of' those properties: they continue to exist somewhere in parallel with one's destiny, untouchable but not invisible, at one remove but not finally disappeared. The splitting, or schizoid, aspect of this life is that in attempting to live one's culture one must simultaneously celebrate its strengths without offering another occasion for their loss, sing the old songs, recite the histories, while guarding against their dispersal. Thus one learns to live parallel lives, as shown in what Heaney calls Derry's 'obstinate bilingual determination to live in and through its two names'.[60]

Like Friel, Heaney (who shares much of the same background) believes that language has a life of its own, that 'the poet does not so much master a language as surrender to it'.[61] But the 'landscape painter' is obliged to create two, or perhaps many, simultaneous images, and in Friel's case this surrender has led to a main storyline on which he has worked many variations, as he makes necessary deviations in pursuit of different forms of truth. Place-names are sometimes important, sometimes immaterial, and can be subjected to ruthless action which shatters much more than the management of everyday life. As Heaney tells us, place-names 'lie deep, like some script indelibly written into the nervous system', [62] but when they are bifurcated the writer is faced with difficult choices. There has been an historical muteness of the Irish tongue which gives the writer a 'sense of belonging to a silent ancestry . . . with which he has embarrassed relations'[63] while there is today a corresponding, though not necessarily connected, silence which is the colonised's response to the coloniser; a need to speak but to employ forms of words which negate language and its connotations: 'whatever you say, say nothing'.[64] It is in these circumstances that Friel deploys what Heaney calls, in a brilliant phrase which identifies (and acknowledges) both sides of the problem, 'his subversive intelligence'.[65]

Friel's technique is closely allied to the 'divining' or 'digging' of Heaney's fieldwork. It is a personal construct of reality, a worldview based to a certain extent on the treasure surrendered by the strata of past experience, whether individual or collective. It is territorial, tribal, imaginative; it provides us with the tension between a society and its environment. As Friel half-mockingly said in 1975 in *Volunteers:*

> Archaeology is the scientific study of people and their culture . . . What you have around you is encapsulated history, a tangible précis of the story of Irish man . . . the more practical our information about our ancestors, the more accurate our deductions about his attitudes, the way he thought, what his philosophy was, in other words the more comprehensive our definition of him . . . the more we learn about our ancestors . . . the more we discover about ourselves . . . a thrilling voyage in *self discovery* . . . But the big question is: How many of us want to make that journey? *(Vol.* 35–7)

After the experience of addressing the themes of *Faith Healer* and *Translations,* Friel may very well appreciate even more grimly the distinctions between culture and civility which create the tensions of *Making History,* and which make this Irish Chekhov the fiercer and more forbidding dramatist. O'Faolain, discussing the extinction of Gaelic Ireland, says that:

> nowhere did it so obstinately persist as in the remote Ulster . . . it had conditioned a racial psychosis . . . its racial arrogance, its indiscipline, its rashness, its lack of thought, its impatience, its incogitancy, its hatred of change, its shallow opportunism, its lack of foresight.

In divining this historical experience and creating figures such as Hugh Mor O'Donnell, Friel will have remembered that O'Faolain continues:

> there is in our respect for all such ancient ways of life much more than a veneration for something that in lasting so long seems, by its very endurance, to have established an *a priori* right to our respect. What we venerate, surely in those customs, is their intimations, as yet only half-realized, of a sensible philosophy of life, which those who practice them have no other way of expressing.[66]

In making a simultaneous voyage of self-discovery, Friel therefore finds that in his archaeology he is proving the impermanence, the provisionality, of all our assumptions, and the danger of complacency: in O'Faolain's words, 'wherever life becomes too secure, or too easy, it decays for lack of change';[67] in Hugh O'Donnell's, 'we fossilise' *(Tr.* 66). The diviner or archaeologist stands on the threshold of both past and present, a metaphor we shall meet often in exploring Friel's work.

It becomes important therefore, not so much to research Friel's own personal circumstances as to divine his own divination, to construct a map of 'Ballybeg' in our own minds in order to find it in Friel's. The 'mixed holding' which sometimes bewilders him is the subject of the 'voyage in self-discovery'. It is also a typical ritual of transition from a state of unease and discontent and psychic disorder to one of wholeness. The following pages explore that transition, the states of mind through which it passes, and the condition of liminality which marks the passage.

DRAMA AS RITUAL

Except when (as in *Living Quarters* or *Aristocrats*) he employs stage 'tricks' (see Chapter 8), Friel traffics in ordinary sensations: we see no ghosts, we hear no voices, we are not bewitched by faery. In examining the way in which a society receives and organises the experiences and emotions which are Friel's subject matter – the phenomena of love, courage, tenderness, *dignitas, gravitas,* the private landscape, and the public world, the effect of time, the 'tarot' of the community – we shall provide ourselves with a key to the sensations of the 'mixed holding'.

In order to survive, in order to 'make sense' of experience, we select, organise, classify, ordinate and stratify our knowledge, so that by creating a rationale, developing a sense out of sensation, we may control our environment. This instinct for survival is known as the *will;* it is superior to *being* and *knowing* because future projects must be *willed* in order to activate the otherwise passive memory. The will is therefore the safe-guard, the gatekeeper, of intellect or 'internal vision'.[68]

If we lose that control we may once again become landless, placeless, aglossal, lose our identity, our grip on reality of which the most grievous example is *Molly Sweeney* and her fragile lien on her 'internal vision'. As Steiner says in *After Babel*:

> We speak less than the truth, we fragment in order to reconstruct desired alternatives, we select and elide. It is not 'the things which are' that we say, but those which might be, which we would bring about, which the eye and remembrance compose.[69]

The world, in other words, must be reduced to manageable proportions; we have to create *a* world out of all the *possible* worlds, even including the unpleasant, tragic or puzzling elements of life, so that they can be managed. We must allow the world to tell us that which we need to know, and must forbid it to tell us that which we should not know, even at the risk of losing what we love or crave. In this way, we can 'will' our own tragic fate, as an essential ingredient in the future project. In 1966–8 Friel gave plentiful evidence of how he intended to follow Gar's uncertain exodus with attempts at homecomings (*The Loves of Cass McGuire,* 1966), at the freedom of impetuous flight (*Lovers,* 1967) and at the nature of betrayal (*Crystal and Fox,* 1968). In Fox Melarkey he gives us a crucial portrait of one kind of desperate passion triumphing over, and destroying, a more tender but subservient love. Friel explored this dichotomy with supreme maturity in 1979 in *Faith Healer* and has returned to it in *Fathers and Sons, Making History, Dancing at Lughnasa,* and *Give Me Your Answer, Do!*

The dichotomy illustrates an important and salutary collision between the intellectual and the romantic traditions. Ulf Dantanus refers to 'Friel's basically tragic creative imagination . . . [his] philosophic and artistic stance which is founded on the essential irony of life'.[70] This irony, that man exercises his freedom in obeying the dictates of fate, that a homecoming is essential and yet impossible, that the successful act of love is also one of betrayal, is what most allies Friel to Chekhov. And it exemplifies the chief characteristic of both writers – comparing, for example, *Aristocrats* with *The Cherry Orchard,* or *Translations* with *The Seagull* – that they discover, within the intellectual quest for the 'dark and private places of individual souls',[71] a means of decoding the condition of despair in which the romantic artist, on the outside of society, finds himself.

Steiner suggests that, in order to survive the weight of experience, we live lives based on selected fictions, yet there is a distinction to be made between the capacity for truth and the capacity for fiction, and that distinction is based on the special condition of madness, the inclination to stand outside *(ekstasis)* rather than inside the institutes. Hugh O'Donnell in *Translations* echoes Steiner:[72] 'to remember everything is a form of madness' (*Tr.* 67); but Columba has told us 'I remember everything' *(EW* 18). Some are prepared to set boundaries to the known world, to give it shape, to name their perceptions, to *nominate,* from all the possible ideas, those by which their daily lives can be governed. But others have to jump over the fence, to become barbarians, because that is the only way they can find to embrace their otherness.

A civilisation is a community which has drawn a circle around its identity in order to civilise (to make civil) some barbarians, and yet to exclude more than it embraces. There is a fundamental relationship between culture and *communitas.* But even here we need to distinguish between 'truths immemorially posited' (*Tr.* 42) and the laws by which our society is actually governed, and which give us our boundaries and the rules to play within them. This is clearly established by Friel in *The Gentle Island* in which the biblical device of the two sons is used to show that the role of one in the community is hearth-based and poetic, replacing the lost mother, while the other is outward and manly, deputising for the discommoded father.

Communication translates discrete psychologies into a public culture. This is one of Friel's public tasks. Private psychology provides, public culture authorises. That which is excluded is ignored – (unknown, *ignotus*): *Barbarus hic ego sum quia non intelligor ulli*:[73] I am a barbarian here because no one understands me (cf. *Tr.* 64).

Naming, the *consuetudo nominationum*, as the *Ad Herennium* calls it,[74] or, as Friel calls it, the *caerimonia nominationis* (*Tr.* 23), is central to place and also to time. Places are named *through* time; it is a sensual as well as a temporal process. A thing, a person, or a place initially has no name. Perceiving it, we compare its properties with similar objects, identify its points of congruence and divergence, and name it. *It* can then utter its own name, a catechetic identity, and thus become a subject:

> OWEN: We name a thing and – bang! it leaps into existence!
> YOLLAND: Each name a perfect equation with its roots! (*Tr.* 45)[75]

(Already some of the mocking humour of *The Communication Cord* can be detected here.)

Without a name I cannot function, because I cannot say 'I', I cannot express a psychology, I cannot perceive. To announce one's name is to offer one's most secret life. As Steiner says:

> To falsify or withhold one's real name . . . is to guard one's life from pillage or alien procurement. To pretend to be another, to oneself or at large, is to employ the 'alternative' powers of language in the most thorough, ontologically liberating way. . . . Through the 'make-up' of language, man is able, in part at least, to exit from his own skin, and, where the compulsion to 'otherness' becomes pathological, to splinter his own identity into unrelated or contrastive voices. The speech of schizophrenia is that of extreme 'alternity'.[76]

Similarly, to be given another name is to receive a new identity, something of which we may be justifiably afraid. It affects us superficially, but it also questions our deeper understanding of our identity. It makes that identity provisional, turns 'who we are' into 'who we may be'. It interferes quintessentially with our ability to decide on courses of action. Thus Cass is seduced by the following exchange:

> TRILBE: By the way, m'dear, what *is* your Christian name?
> CASS: Cass.
> TRILBE: Cass? Cass? It's certainly not Cass. (*Cass* 24)

The statement is uncompromising, but it causes the equivocation in Cass's subsequent conduct and relations with both her family and cognate members of 'Eden House'. Cass becomes 'Catherine', and she in her turn renames Mr Ingram (who already has the shadow identity of 'Meurice') as 'Buster'. When she adopts her new identity, accepting Trilbe's re-naming, she con-fuses her past personae, both real and imagined:

CASS: My name is Olsen by the way. My late husband, mebbe
          you heard of him, General Cornelius Olsen; he made
          quite a name for himself in the last war, but you just call
          me Catherine. (*Cass* 67)

And to be given a nickname, or alternative name, is to be denied one's
real existence. Officially, as we have seen, 'Brian Friel' does not exist.
Although we cannot penetrate his privacy, we can speculate on the effect
that the denial and imposition of names can have had on his view of
personality. It is another recipe for Steiner's schizophrenic 'alternity'. Not
only people: within the extended family, places, people, and things
(shipwrecked objects in *The Gentle Island*, or those with personal associations, such as the pieces of furniture in *Aristocrats*) take on special
names according to their role: patronymics, nicknames (according to job,
idiosyncrasy or distinguishing features), size or achievement. In *Making
History* Hugh O'Neill is known as Hugh, as The O'Neill, and as the
Earl of Tyrone, or simply Tyrone.[77] The name as a persona, therefore, is a
function of time, an intricate association of history and secrecy.

Ireland, like Russia, suffers from such schizophrenia. It is recognisable
in R.D. Laing's statement, 'the experience and behaviour that gets
labelled schizophrenia is a special strategy that a person invents in order
to live in an unlivable situation'.[78] Both these peoples suffer from the
inability to say 'I am': there is no expression in the Irish or Russian
language for the present tense of the verb *to be*. Self is perceived as otherness, as someone else to whom things happen, to whom experience
accrues. It comes naturally to writers like Friel and Beckett in putting on
the stage images and symbols of their own predicament.

In this context the 'images for the affection' are also closely felt,
although other, and they can therefore be devalued as easily as they can
be elevated and mystified. We must remember that *Philadelphia* and
Friel's other early plays are the product of his early thirties, and of a
period when Ireland's 'oppressive atmosphere' made many young men
unequivocally and bitterly angry. 'Let me communicate with someone,
that's what they all advise, communicate, pour out your pent-up feelings
into a sympathetic ear' (*Ph.* 42–3). However, the 'Master', the archetypal
pedagogue, becomes a 'sorry wreck . . . arrogant and pathetic' (*Ph.* 44)
and the 'Canon' Mick O'Byrne, that other 'moulder of the mind', is
upbraided for his inability to mediate:

There's an affinity between Screwballs and me that no one, literally, no one
could understand except you Canon (*deadly serious*), because you're warm,
and kind and soft and sympathetic, all things to all men; because you could
translate all this loneliness, this groping, this dreadful bloody buffoonery
into Christian terms that will make life bearable for us all. And yet you

don't say a word. Why Canon? Why arid Canon? Isn't it your job, to translate? (*Ph.* 96)

The outburst that Friel puts into Gar's mouth is surely a loosing of his own frustration:

Look around you for God's sake! Look at Master Boyle! Look at my father! Look at the Canon! Look at the boys! Asylum cases, the whole bloody lot of them! . . . it's a bloody quagmire, a backwater, a dead-end! And everybody in it goes crazy sooner or later! Everybody! (*Ph.* 80–1)

(In *The Enemy Within* Grillaan asks Columba: 'A priest or a politician – which?' [*EW* 33] Within this degraded tarot, the difference hardly seems relevant.)

Within the known permissible world we organise the qualities of life; types of space, of direction, of belief, of sensation, are at first confused and held together in a single aesthetic: *aistheta*, that which is perceived. I perceive a tree, I perceive motion, I perceive a god, are, at first, ideas of equal validity and meaning. But, in order to avoid a metaphysical chaos we soon discover the need to codify, to establish both lateral and vertical hierarchies: the concept of time, as a result of observing motion; the concept of change, as a result of observing the process of time; ultimately, awareness of one's own awareness, and the realisation of self, persuade us that to explore self we must understand otherness and embarrassment. Communication, we discover, is shared, unembarrassed meaning, the social construction of reality. Structures of knowledge, structures of belief, structures of society, are the result of this communication or consensus.

We select that which we *need* to know (*logos*). But, if the will functions badly as gatekeeper, we also allow ourselves to select that which we *want* to know (*mythos*). The confusion of the two results in embarrassment and psychic disorder. Existence, or being, is therefore a membrane or metaphor between myth and logic. This is a mytho-logical present where past and future, known and unknown, seen and unseen meet. As Ernest Fenollosa says, 'metaphor is . . . the very substance of poetry . . . the bridge whereby to cross from the minor truth of the seen to the major truth of the unseen'.[79]

Vision, because it is the quickest sense, is the paradigm of all experience. The way we appear, our epiphany (*epiphanein*), is our first identity. Once we understand what vision is, we realise that that which can see can also be seen. Thus we establish the reciprocity of vision, and therefore of existence. *To know* means *to have seen* (*eidenai* is the past tense of *idein*). All meaning comes from imaging, that is, from picturing to oneself, so that we can think within on that which we have seen without. But the discrepancy between what we see (imagine) and what we think (know) is that while our public world is primarily visual, our interior world is aural. We see ideas, but they are interpreted, controlled and marshalled by voices. This distinction is essential in considering the difference between the world presented to the audience in *Faith Healer* and *Molly Sweeney* and the interior world of their characters. The medium of reception and transmission is the same: I am the threshold, the membrane of cultural exchange. Another potential embarrassment, another source of psychic disorder, arises when we continue to use the visual imperative: demanding that you comprehend, I cry: 'Can't you *see!*'

Map-making becomes a metaphor of the visual and the literal. We explain the world with words, we re-present it with pictures. Our maps, whether they are images of the interior landscape or of the public world, are our way of expressing more than the merely superficial contours. As André Brink puts it in his essay 'Map-makers':

> The writer is not concerned only with 'reproducing' the real. What he does is to perceive, below the line of the map he draws, the contours of another world. And from the interaction between the land as he *perceives* it to be and the land as he knows it *can* be, someone from outside, the 'reader' of the map, watches and aids the emergence of the meaning of the map.[80]

Or as one of Ireland's current cartographers says: 'to fasten my experience of the territory to my expression of it on paper . . . a map will be faithful to more than the measurable'.[81]

A map, like an icon, puts before us a paradigm, something which mediates between an *absolute* and that which we can comprehend. Through maps, icons and myths, the unrealistic concepts of uncontrolled space, being and time are made real. Words, particularly written words, are secondary to all this. As Brink says, truth, 'which is . . . vast and non-verbal, has to assume the form of language', socially acceptable, codified, but also subjectively uttered by 'a relative, uncertain, undependable, disreputable man' who is 'constantly humbled by his encounters with truth and with the world'.[82]

Words themselves become relative, uncertain, undependable, disreputable, and it may be necessary for the writer to dispense with the prevailing conventions, either by inventing new languages, or by abandoning words themselves in favour of new media.

The aesthetic world and its security system might therefore be posited in this way:

ABSOLUTE PHENOMENA

	SPACE	TIME	BEING	OTHERNESS
PARADIGM	World	History	God	Kin
MEDIATION	Place	Myth	Identity	Tarot
PERCEPTION	Vision	Motion	Thinking	Distance
KNOWLEDGE	Omphalos	Present	Persona	Affection
EXPRESSION	Digging	Word	Nomination	Love
INSTITUTE	Boundary	Text	Icon	Tribe

The absolute phenomena, which we cannot perceive or conceive, are represented to us by means of 'paradigms' which make them conceivable but not yet perceptible: world for space, history for absolute time, god for absolute being, kin for 'otherness'. To become the subject of 'perception', however, these paradigmatic concepts must be 'mediated': world by sense of place, which is thus perceived through vision; history by myth which is perceived by temporal motion; God by identity, which is perceived by thought; the paradigm of kin by the tarot, perceived by distance and difference. Perceptions are turned into 'knowledge' and knowledge is thus capable of being 'expressed'. The 'institutes', or boundaries, enable us to distinguish between the permitted and the impermissible, between that which enables life to be lived and that which kills life.

WITHIN	WITHOUT
Communitas	Societas
Simplex	Complex
Ballybeg	Ballymore
Country	Town
Stability	Chaos
Ordered Speech	Babel
Name	Anonymity
Security	Challenge
Religion of Control	Religion of Ecstasy
Mythos	Logos
Unconscious	Conscious
Lived	Learned
Illiterate	Literate
Intuitive	Analytic
Otherness	Difference

Of course, because it is logocentric, such a schema does not sufficiently explain how we become aware of our own existence. Consciousness, or perception of self, depends on being perceived by others. The central importance of the 'esse est percipi' theory is not that *one* is perceived, but that *both* are mutually perceived in a symbiotic relationship.

In such a way we can understand our communal interactions and our relationship, as people, with the real and surreal landscape. It is by becoming conscious of the movement from one condition to another that society, or an individual, can take account not only of the passage of time, but also of the psychic motion which is being undertaken, a carrying across of the psyche from illness to health, from ignorance to knowledge, from incompleteness to fulfilment, from relative barbarism to relative civility. As Victor Turner remarks,

> Practically all rituals of any length and complexity represent a passage from one position to another. In this regard they may be said to possess temporal structure and to be dominated by the notion of time. But in passing from structure to structure many rituals pass through communitas. Communitas is almost always thought of as portrayed by actors as a timeless condition, an eternal now, as a moment in and not of time', or as a state to which the structural view of time is not applicable.[83]

It is when such a state of *liminality* is achieved – standing on the threshold, signifying both arrival and departure – that the artist, or shaman or diviner is at his most vulnerable, and the experience is most painful. To conduct the tribe, or even one's own incomplete self, from one side of the membrane to the other, demands that the artist become membrane himself, establish the threshold, or medium, by which each world can address the other. The *sacerdos liminalis* is therefore a polyglot, able to translate both worlds, but a citizen in neither. Turner's work provides almost a commentary on this stance:

> In this gap between ordered worlds almost anything can happen. In this interim of liminality the possibility exists of standing aside not only from one's own social position but from all social positions and of formulating a potentially unlimited series of alternative social arrangements.[84]

We shall see in *Making History* the especial tragedy that can occur in this 'gap'.

That Turner's theories, based on observation of African tribes, are applicable to Irish drama is clear from his basic theory that drama is the root of all ritual, and that participants are 'released from structure into communitas only to return to structures revitalised by the experience of communitas'.[85] We shall see particularly in the case of *The Freedom of the City* and *Translations* how essential this condition of liminality can be, and how in *Living Quarters* and *Aristocrats* 'almost anything can happen'. As Friel himself said, 'Ritual is part of all drama. Drama without ritual is poetry without rhythm – hence not poetry, not drama . . . Drama is a RITE, and always religious in the purest sense'.[86]

There is a clear indication here of the influence of Tyrone Guthrie, who wrote in 1966:

> The most important rites . . . centred upon human sacrifice. . . Gradually . . . instead of an actual sacrifice, the offering took symbolic form. A *story* of

sacrifice was enacted in honour of the God: a tragedy. All theatrical performances, from *Oedipus* to striptease, are conducted, like war dances, like rain dances, according to age-old formulae. . . The theatre relates itself to God by means of ritual. It does so more consistently than any other activity, except prayer because, like organized prayer, it is the direct descendant of primitive religious ceremonies.[87]

Also, of course, ritual theatre serves as a therapy through role-playing, a psychic release of physical tensions (between man and man) and metaphysical problems (between man and God). But this brings us back to the fact that we must, whether consciously or 'subliminally', achieve some awareness of the fact that the passage-ritual is affecting us, that the therapy is in fact taking effect. And that requires that we are conscious of passage through time *and* space.

To comprehend time *and* place we need to understand place *as* time. This may seem somewhat abstract until we consult the world of writers like Eliot, Heaney, Durrell and Beckett, who in some way mediate in their own work between the myths of sacred history and our everyday cultures. The five senses do not of themselves enable us to understand what 'sense' of place, or 'sense' of time are. Beckett's introduction to *Film* helps to illustrate not only his own concern with his particular brand of metaphysics: it also expressly tackles the problem of what we mean by perception, if 'to be' means 'to be perceived':

> *Esse est percipi.* All extraneous perception suppressed, animal, human, divine, self-perception maintains in being. Search of non-being in flight from extraneous perception breaking down in inescapability of self-perception. . . In order to be figured in this situation the protagonist is sundered into object (O) and eye (E), the former in flight, the latter in pursuit. It will not be clear until end of film that pursuing perception is not extraneous, but self.[88]

Not extraneous, but self. Therein lies the absolute problem of knowing where *I* ends and the rest of the world, other worlds, begin. Although I am created by the eye of another, that other must be me or an affect of me. This is the essence of *communitas*, the ego, the id, the relationship with others, the extension of self into family, into world. In this world, the faces of the tarot are manifestations of my own existence, tribal affects.

Not only do we establish boundaries to our own total civilisation to keep certain things in and certain things out, we also establish boundaries to our personae to make them readily identifiable, since otherwise our personalities would spill over into one another, a situation which can only be accommodated briefly by physical or intellectual intercourse. We therefore develop prototypes or icons of the Tarot whom we invest with unique inherent powers: the father, the mother, the priest, the slave, the farmer, the scholar . . . or as Yeats said,

A country which has no national institutions must show its young men *images for the affections*, although they be but diagrams of what it should be or may be. He [Thomas Davis] and his school *imagined* the Soldier, the Orator, the Patriot, the Poet, the Chieftain, and above all, the Peasant.[89] [*my emphasis*]

What then is the relationship between the Irish landscape and the Irish mind? Is there a specifically Irish psychology which results in a specifically Irish culture? Is there a specially Irish quality of vision, an Irish theory of vision? Heaney says:

although it has long been fashionable to smile indulgently at the Celtic twilight, it has to be remembered that the movement was the beginning of a discovery of confidence in our own ground, in our place, in our speech, English and Irish. And it seems to me undeniable that Yeats's sense of the otherness of his Sligo places led him to seek for a language and an imagery other than the ones which were available to him in the aesthetic modes of literary London.

The result, he affirms, was Synge's expression of 'the life of Aran, in the language of the tribe': 'A new country of the mind was conceived in English, the west that the poets imagined'.[90]

But that new country has not been pursued since Synge's time. The idea that the Irish landscape and its peoples could furnish a dramatic representation of inner states of being still requires the sort of analysis which Friel is mapping. The Irish intellectual tradition, long dismissed or devalued as a twilit irresponsible reverie upon misfortune, has, however, received serious critical attention. For example Richard Kearney writes:

Could it be that the Irish mind, in its various expressions often flew in the face of logocentrism by showing that meaning is not only determined by a logic that centralises and censors but also by a logic which disseminates: a structured dispersal exploring what is *other*, what is irreducibly diverse. In contradistinction to the orthodox dualist logic of *either/or*, the Irish mind may be seen to favour a more didactical logic of *both/and*, an intellectual ability to hold the traditional oppositions of classical reason held together in creative confluence.[91]

Searching for the stable centre, the *omphalos*, the Irish mind casts its imagination back through perhaps four centuries, to rediscover a world such as that evoked by O'Faolain, one which is radically, psychically, different to that which displaced it – medieval as opposed to renaissance, mythopoeic rather than logocentric, observing the 'sacred wood' of its imagination eroded by the exponential growth of the empire of knowledge and logic. We are also asked, as O'Faolain puts it, to place beside 'the Patriot myth': 'each new Hero rising against the ancient Tyrant', an *alternative myth*: 'the ancient Hero rising against the new Tyrant'. On O'Neill's recognition of this alternative myth O'Faolain comments that it was

quite clear to Tyrone. It was beyond the understanding of his Gaelic fol-
lowers because it was outside their experience. And it was equally outside
the experience of all the native annalists who therefore recorded Tyrone's
life in terms of the Patriot Myth without reference to that other myth
which is at the core of so many of Shakespeare's historical and patriotic
plays and about which they knew nothing.[92]

'To remember that', O'Faolain admonishes us, 'is of paramount
importance.' It must have seemed so to Friel when he read it, since the
marrying of those two worlds has so far concerned him that he has abandoned many of the developed conventions of the stage (as Synge did before
him) in elucidating the passage from certainty to doubt, from high ground
to low, from 'quiet depths of the mind' to those charged with maddening
questions and more clamouring answers than can be accommodated into
one familiar pattern. As an example of this he draws our attention to the
fact that the artist John Behan's work, which had previously been rooted
in strength, certainty and security, has come to reflect in its 'flights of
birds, makers of music and uncertain heroes' a complex world of vague
possibilities, in which 'man's mind is on the point of despair', and that
Behan displays 'a new wisdom and a new conviction that the world is one
of necessary doubts'.[93] Friel sees this as clearly in the Ireland of the late
twentieth century as in that of the sixteenth.

　　Words, and all our logocentric thought, are unreliable because, as
Steiner says, 'that which we call fact may well be a veil spun by language
to shroud the mind from reality',[94] from the weight of time. But as he
says also, we are trapped within this unreliability: 'Man is a language
animal . . . What access we have to the life of the mind, to the dynamics
of consciousness, to the metamorphic and innovative capacities of the
imagination, is linguistic.' We might be led to suppose that this imagination is therefore totally strictured by language, but this is not so. As
Steiner also notes, from the example of other forms of non-verbal
communication such as mathematics, 'the experience and perception of
reality [have been divided] into separate domains'.[95]

　　It thus becomes possible to regard the distance between the self that
experiences and the self that describes experience, as the distance also
between experience itself and the description of experience. There is a
fundamental implication here for much of Friel's work, especially *The
Loves of Cass McGuire*, *Crystal and Fox*, *Translations* and *Molly Sweeney*,
as he moves from a problematic relationship between characters and
audience to one where audiences no longer observe action but sense themselves participating in it. This conjuring of perception of a different order
becomes a national drama in its relocation of the Irishman at the centre
of history rather than on its sidelines. We will now examine the application

of such a schema as I have outlined, logocentric though it may be, to Friel's work.

THE PLAYWRIGHT'S COMMITMENT

The city of Derry and its natural hinterland in Donegal constitute a total environment from which Friel draws not just his inspiration but his messages. He sets his stories and plays in 'Ballybeg' (Baile Beag, small town) or in 'Ballymore' (Baile Mór, big town) but the experiences he relates, whether they are fact-as-experience or emotion-as-experience, are translations, into words and images, of 'real' places he has sensed: Glen-na-Fuiseog (the valley, or 'saucer', of larks), Coradinna, Mullaghduff, are composites, extractions and recreations of Glenties, Kincasslagh, Urris; likewise the surnames of people, O'Donnell, Boyle, Sweeney, and their first names, Manus, Sarah, Philly, Nora Dan.

But even within this world there is a tension, epitomised by Derry itself, the last walled city built in Europe, and, even in this, an anachronism, a mediaeval idiom to serve the needs of a modern colonial power. In 1848 Mrs Alexander, wife of the Bishop of Derry, glimpsed 'a green hill far away, without a city wall': it is now the (largely) Catholic Creggan estate, part of the electoral ward once represented by Patrick Friel. This hill outside the city was excluded from the world of the apprentices' protected guilds, for whom Derry was built, and it is almost as if in this social experiment, each element of an equation, town and country, which should have been reciprocally interactive and interdependent, became mutually polarised and exclusive. Perhaps there has always been an implicit failure in the Derry formula, an apprenticeship to the tensions of historical myth. This divorce is another motive force in Friel's psychology, and conditions much of his subject matter.

If, as Professor Estyn Evans argues, the Ulster landscape is representative of the geography of Ireland, then it is in the Ulster mind, representative, in its turn, of that landscape, that the events of history, both *mythos* and *logos*, are best worked out. 'Topographically, Ulster displays the characteristic fragmentation even better than the other three provinces: indeed, when one looks at the full record of habitat, heritage and history, one begins to think of Ulster as the most Irish of all the regions'.[96] Ulster has been called a 'narrow ground': 'the war in Ulster', says A.T.Q Stewart, 'is being fought out on a narrower ground than even the most patient observer might imagine, a ground every inch of which has its own associations and special meaning . . . locality and history are welded together'.[97] And, as F.S.L. Lyons has pointed out:

both sides constantly appeal to history and continue to use sectarian terminology which the world has long discarded. . . . The history and terminology are unavoidable because they relate to unfinished business. They are alive today – and this is pre-eminently the sense in which the seventeenth century lives on in Ulster – because the sequence of events over more than three hundred years has ensured that the issues raised when the different cultures first mingled on that 'narrow ground' should still be crucial issues. The context changes but the issues remain identical.[98]

The issues are those of possession and dispossession, mastery and servility, alienation and exile, crystallised in the stereotypes of the 'Planter' and the 'Gael'. The dispossession of the last Gaelic society by the seventeenth-century plantation was more than a displacement of people from the land. It created a labile people in whose cultural disintegration one can see the original tensions which ultimately led to the civic disturbances, riots and civil war.

Such discovery is, in any case, a tribal as well as a personal knowledge. Heaney refers to:

> My *patria*, my deep design
> To be at home
> In my own place and dwell within
> Its proper name.[99]

And the 'proper' name here implies temporal as well as spiritual connotations – a name, whether it is 'Ulster' or 'Mossbawn', or 'Ballybeg', which has evolved through time, represents the layering of experience. Landscape, Heaney says, is, or was, 'sacramental, instinct with signs, implying a system of reality beyond the visible realities'. And in the same essay he refers to 'that temperate understanding of the relationship between a person and his place, of the way the surface of the earth can be accepted into, and be a steadying influence upon, the quiet depths of the mind'.[100]

This is by no means unique to Ireland or even to the colonised peoples of the imperial West. Indeed, we can legitimately take an anthropological perspective, as Friel himself does in *The Freedom of the City* through the character of Dodds, and state the ubiquity of this form of dispossession and its consequences. As has been written of the Ndembu of Northern Rhodesia, who were the particular subject of Victor Turner:

> Most of the Ndembu's neighbours were suffering in their contact with the white man, with his copper mines and his railways, but the Ndembu . . . seemed to have retained rich cultural and religious traditions. They were obviously a stubborn people. They were also a jealous, individualistic, strife-ridden people, troubled by mischievous spirits, witches and ancestral ghosts who were quick to punish Ndembu who failed to 'remember' them. Symptomatically the weak and powerless were often afflicted with illness and then subjected to elaborate curing rites that gave symbolic expression to

their conflicts and incorporated them into curing cults. Turner says that what little unity existed among the Ndembu was enforced by these rituals. . . . The 'thudding of ritual drums' gave Turner his key to Ndembu society.[101]

If we substitute for the name Ndembu the term 'the people of Ballybeg' we will be able to hear, in most of Friel's work, 'the thudding of ritual drums'. In the curing cult of death in *The Freedom of the City* and *Faith Healer*, in the observance of a ritual of *communitas* in the schoolroom of *Translations* and the confusion of *Aristocrats*, in the hurt of Sarah's muteness as it becomes the catalyst of *Translations*, and in the individual stubbornness of Lily, Columba, Cass and Keeney, we see Friel almost inevitably fulfilling a liminal, shamanistic role as he sets about his task of divining the elements of ritual and translating them into drama.

The tensions which have been concentrated in Ulster have ironically only been contained in 'Northern Ireland' by the artificial boundary of the 1920–25 partition. It has led to the mutation of the *aisling* (dream, vision) culture of loss and poverty of the Gaelic seventeenth-century kingdoms into a Chekhovian dream of national hope focussed on tomorrow, an introspection on the part of the dispossessed, a second-class citizenry, on the glory and wealth of that which they once held, and which they dream of regaining: language, identity, self-respect. That such a demeanour should be servile, and yet eloquent, is a characteristic of depression. As Hugh Mor O'Donnell explains:

certain cultures expend on their vocabularies and syntax acquisitive energies and ostentations entirely lacking in their material lives. . . . A rich language . . . full of the mythologies of fantasy and hope and self-deception, a syntax opulent with tomorrows. It is our response to mud cabins and a diet of potatoes: our only method of replying to . . . inevitabilities. (*Tr.* 42)

Beyond the division of a society which is predominantly agrarian and where largely planter and Gael, Catholic and Protestant (that is, Anglican, Presbyterian, Methodist) live in close and mutual suspicion, there is the specific division of urban sectarian segregation with its own opposing cultures of possession and poverty. Friel's single unequivocal treatment of contemporary disorder and the urban *déclassé* is *The Freedom of the City* (1973). As his sociologist Dodds (whose arguments are derived from Oscar Lewis's *La Vida*) explains in that play:

The subculture of poverty . . . transmitted from generation to generation . . . is the way the poor adapt to their marginal position in society which is capitalistic, stratified into classes and highly individuated; and it is also their method of reacting against society. In other words it is the method they have devised to cope with the hopelessness and despair they experience because they know they'll never be successful in terms of values and goals of the dominant society. . . .They (the poor of the Western world) share a critical attitude to many of the values and institutions of the dominant class; they share a suspicion of government, a detestation of the police, and very often a cynicism to the church . . . any movement, trade union, religious, civil rights, pacifist, revolutionary – any movement which gives them this objectivity, organizes them, gives them real hope, promotes solidarity. Such a movement inevitably smashes the rigid caste which encases their minds and bodies. (*Freedom* 19–21)

Onto this global screen Friel projects, particularly in the character of Lily, the concrete poverty of Derry in the time of the transition from civil rights activities to rioting and death. That in the heat of the moment the incidents of 'Bloody Sunday' (30 January 1972) and the subsequent Widgery Report should have given rise to this play and to Thomas Kinsella's poem 'Butcher's Dozen' is natural;[102] but that nothing else of this literary quality should have followed until the work of Graham Reid and Frank McGuinness's *Carthaginians* (also directly related to Derry and 'Bloody Sunday') as an aesthetic challenge to this or other poignant tragedies is surprising until one realises that in general terms the Irish writer, whether rooted in Ulster or elsewhere, has refused to become engaged in the actual fighting of a war which is taking place today on that narrow ground; preferring (or perhaps finding it impossible not to engage in a dialogue with the past) to rehearse a war in the mind, contrition rather than attrition, imprisoned in its own wordiness.

Only two years before writing *The Freedom of the City*, Friel said that he did not expect a play on the Northern troubles to emerge for some time.[103] He has insisted that he was a spectator, not involved; that this is the appropriate position for the artist,[104] but it is difficult to see his response to those troubles, as shown in *The Freedom*, as a detached view; however much he may wish to remain a cold commentator, no one in Derry, whatever his provenance, could remain uninvolved in the events of the 'war', untouched by the culture of dispossession. One of those injured on Bloody Sunday was Joseph Friel: apparently not a relation of the playwright, but one bearing his name. But Friel argues that while there is 'no Irish writer who is not passionately engaged in our current problems . . . he must maintain a perspective as a writer'.[105]

His strongest plea for the detachment of the artist came in fact in 1972:

In each of us the line between the Irish mind and the creative mind is much too fine. . . . There must be a far greater distinction between the Irishman who suffers and the artist's mind which creates. . . . The intensity of emotion we all feel for our country (and in the present climate, that emotion is heightened) is not of itself the surest foundation for the best drama which, as Eliot says comes from the 'intensity of the artistic process, the pressure, so to speak, under which the fusion takes place'.[106]

Friel here adopts a difficult position, one which will become his most painful, because putting such a distance between himself and the world – *his* world – allows his constituents to accuse him of neglect and betrayal. It makes the writer's own choices that much more painful. It is indeed difficult to make the distinction between the artist-as-citizen and the citizen-as-artist. The difficulty lies in seeing the Irish mind as creative and reflective, expressing *both* thought-as-experience *and* experience-as-thought. Columba, for example, answers the affective call of memory: 'he went because he loved them all . . . every native instinct and inclination tore at him to go to the aid of his friends' (*EW* 27–8); and André Brink, in a very similar society, says 'literature and art are forced back to their very roots, to elemental and rudimentary beginnings. Anything but not silence. *I can't keep silent, because I have lived it*'.[107]

Friel has said that involvement 'means pigmentation and perhaps contamination',[108] but life can also be painful on the sidelines, especially because not to obey the affective rules would amount to an act of betrayal. Writing *Faith Healer* was a betrayal because it concentrated on the privacy of the artist-as-performer rather than the public role of the artist-as-spokesman or saviour. In the same sense, *Making History* betrays the course of Irish history because it asks that the Hero or Saviour described in *The Annals of The Four Masters* be rewritten, re-imagined as a man of private parts, a man whose conscience can be governed by interior as well as communal forces.

Since 1982, when Friel took the drastic step of writing a farce (*The Communication Cord*) to accompany, defuse and subvert the success of *Translations*, he had been exploring, in a number of draft texts, the question of betrayal, something with which he finally came to terms in *Fathers and Sons*. He enters the difficult area which, as Thomas Kilroy says, lies in 'the web of secondary circumstances that lie below the writing . . . where the essentially private activity of writing comes into contact with the shared experience of human beings living in the one culture'.[109] Friel would certainly like to be free to write plays on other themes, but while troubles persist, whether social, intellectual or moral, there remains this Chekhovian compulsion to write about them in terms where the everyday meets the apocalyptic. To take a holiday from Ireland (as he did in writing *Fathers and Sons*) is to betray it by keeping silence. The nearest he can come without frivolity is the catastrophic events of earlier days: the 'Flight of the Earls' which he rubbishes with equal effect in *The Gentle Island* and in *Making History*, or the silencing of the poets. But in doing so he acknowledges the impossibility of keeping silent. Just as André Brink, under the former censorship, was obliged to fictionalise his argument, thus making in *An Instant in the Wind* one of the most beautiful love stories, of the meeting of black and white, finding the gap between cultures, so Friel also 'fictionalises' episodes in Irish history in order to approximate to the intercourse which may have occurred between Hugh O'Neill and Mabel Bagenal in *Making History*, between Maire Chatach and George Yolland in *Translations*: 'Never more than an instant. Perhaps we can't bear more than an instant at a time. . . . This terrible space surrounding us creates the silence in which, so rarely, preciously, I dare to recognise you and be recognised by you'.[110]

An inescapable part of existence is not only perception and consciousness, but also the breaking of silence: to be is to utter. In Friel's context, therefore, that which *matters*, that which is perceived or experienced, must be uttered. Even his 'time out' in the adaptation of *Three Sisters* relates to his concern for wholeness, the integrity of the family as an extension of the self. When writing *Aristocrats* he noticed that

> its true direction is being thwarted by irrelevant 'politics', social issues, class. And an intuition that implicit in their language, attitudes, style, will be all the 'politics' I need.[111]

His loyalty to the tribe and to the particular relationships within the web of affections, is in some ways, therefore, his response to the larger spectacle of the public world.

As we shall see in Chapter 4, the problems of serving one's community and of serving oneself as an artist are equally subject to violence. In order to be engaged, one must be engaged with the past *and* with the future, interpreting each to each. If silence represents privacy, and language approximates to the world, then the paths to silence, to regaining the wholeness of the inner world, lead inevitably through the minefield of language. Privacies have no right to remain privacies. To be the diviner or shaman of a culture exposes the artist not only to the adulation but also the calumny of the tribe.

But there is another more particular sense in which Friel's world is a paradox, and where, as a citizen of that world, he has found it necessary to speak out. This concerns language as a medium of communication and as a metaphor of culture, where it is intimately connected with the provinciality of Ulster both historically and in present politics.

Other northern writers, including John Montague, for example in *The Rough Field* and *The Dead Kingdom*, and Seamus Deane in *Gradual Wars, Rumours* and *History Lessons*, have explored this. Among southerners, also involved in the dilemma of seeking restoration, Thomas Kinsella, in his essay 'The Divided Mind', sets out the problem of writing in one language while culturally pursuing an ideal best asserted in another.[112] Friel is acutely conscious of the fact that 'the language which we speak in

Ireland' is English, but not English as it is spoken or understood by English people. It is a language adopted by Irish people which 'forms us and shapes us in a way that is neither healthy nor valuable to us'. As a result the Irish theatre has barely developed, because 'it is a new and young discipline for us and apart from Synge, all our dramatists have pitched their voice for English acceptance and recognition'. The error of assuming that Ireland and England had a language in common (we should remember that Shaw said they were 'divided by a common language') has therefore led both nations into the mantic *and* semantic errors of thinking that they could provide the metaphor to interpret between privacies. Accordingly, Friel believes 'we must continually look at ourselves, recognize and identify ourselves. We must make English identifiably our own language':[113] this is the realisation which, ultimately, makes Hugh Mor O'Donnell the hero and central character of *Translations*.

Friel's major contribution to this debate has been his 'language plays', particularly *Faith Healer* (1979), *Translations* (1980) and *Making History*. In *Translations* he examines the problem of a civilisation confronted by its own language as a barrier to progress and an instrument of change. He had earlier given us a humorous glimpse into this in the short story 'Mr Sing My Heart's Delight': 'a constant source of fun was Granny's English. Gaelic was her first tongue and she never felt at ease in English which she shouted and spat out as if it were getting in her way' (*Saucer* 60).[114]

Translations is in fact a paradox in that it presents us with a neo-colonial project: to regain its cultural integrity, Ballybeg must not reject, but embrace, the dominant, incursive language in order to make it 'identifiably our own language'. In Genet's *Les Nègres* the blacks, in attempting to reject white civilisation, have to reject white language. Two black lovers find it impossible to communicate without using the language of the whites. In *Translations* the 'blacks' wish neither to reject nor embrace white civilisation. Whichever course they take they will be living a lie; but a lie of great and possibly liberating power. Two lovers, one black one white, demonstrate to us much more than the impossibility of communication, or of translating between privacies: they tell us that the problem of using one language for utterance and another for cultural existentialism is a problem of revolt from both yesterday and tomorrow and that the only real solution lies in silence.

Ultimately the two problems – place and language – merge, because place means who you are and where you come from, and language is the facility by which you express that identity and provenance. A place requires a name, and a tongue to pronounce it. So as Eavan Boland says of 'the northern writers' crisis of conscience', they

cannot continue to accept the confusion of childhood. They must somehow
shape it, order it. The attempt to coax order out of the chaotic experience
of lost community and childhood *could* have produced an inner crisis, in
which either bewilderment is burned away or talent is burned out.[115]

Since that was written, the inner crisis has intensified, and has not been
resolved, because it has not been possible to find the proper way to
dramatise the drama. Tom MacIntyre's almost wordless, balletic drama
has offered one possibility; Friel's antithesis is to pursue words relentlessly,
because he believes that he can thus more satisfactorily approach both the
private and the public – precisely because we cannot abandon that
weapon which has so deeply incised our consciousness. In *Dancing at
Lughnasa*, however, he turns the knife in a different fashion. A play
which is poised between music and vertigo, between the two elements
that make of dance itself the seduction and the ritual that expresses life as
it is both lived and imagined, *Dancing at Lughnasa* attempts to eschew
words in favour of gesture – the logic overtaken by the mythic: 'Dancing
as if language had surrendered to movement. . . . Dancing as if language
no longer existed, because words were no longer necessary' (*DL* 71).
Friel does not in fact make that surrender in the same way that MacIntyre
has done in his gestural theatre – the repetition of the words 'as if' is
salutary – simply because he is not prepared to fumble in the dramatic
interstices, and yet he comes close to acknowledging the claim not only of
silence on the spoken word but also that of movement on thought.

NAMING THINGS

Irish engagement in the present has been conducted as a congruence
between culture and nationalism. This led to the ideological foundation
of the Irish Free State through agencies so apparently disparate as the
Land League, the Irish Literary (later the National) Theatre, the Gaelic
League, the Gaelic Athletic Association, the Irish Republican Brotherhood
and the Irish Volunteers. This congruence was based on the assumption
that there was, in some golden age, a Gaelic race of poet-kings, the reinstatement of which has been the cultural and political quest of the republic.

But the question of identity, of meaning, is the same as that asked by
Shakespeare's MacMorris – 'What ish my nation?'[116] – questions that
appeal not only to kinship and loyalty but which ask what cultural, social
and economic properties are necessary before a community becomes
viable. It is obviously more acute in Ulster, a client province of two
nations, than elsewhere. Declan Kiberd has described the tendency
towards introspection in search of an identity as 'Inventing Irelands',[117] a
discovery within, but one which, in my reading of his essay, has led to

falsification, or a false glorification of an Ireland which could not be reinvented because it had never existed. In this the chief actors in modern times, according to Kiberd, were Yeats, Douglas Hyde and Éamon de Valera. Yeats certainly celebrated a bardic tradition based on 'the oral poetry of unlettered singers'.[118] Yeats claimed:

> In Ireland today the old world that sang and listened is, it may be for the last time in Europe, face to face with the world that reads and writes, and their antagonism is always present under some name or other in Irish imagination and intellect.[119]

The concept of the 'Western Isle', a noble peasant civilisation, is in fact an artificial response to the challenge of change, of which Friel is healthily sceptical: writing *Translations* he noted: 'one aspect that keeps eluding me; the wholeness, the integrity of that Gaelic past. Maybe because I don't believe in it'.[120] The distinctions I have drawn up to this point have been in the field of definitions, the hazards of making statements about situations which, though perhaps perfectly understood, can be only imperfectly expressed, because these all stem from the 'confusions of childhood' of writers like Friel. But a qualitative difference needs to be understood here, between the life we lead, the life we think we lead, and the life we would like to lead. This distinction is vital to the survival of writers and their nations and cultures, both political and aesthetic.

Literature was therefore certain to be obsessed with identity, to confuse form and content, to approach the question of viability by turning, Janus-like, towards both the past which imprisoned it, and the future which contained its best hopes. It is a literature which, however 'opulent with tomorrows', remains wary of the 'nation-once-again' theory, knowing that anthropologists, geographers and historians – those distinguished scientists of the mind – have said that the Irish are a tribal people, not a nation.

In these circumstances, meaning becomes vacuous, and emotion is betrayed when it relies on 'false feeling, false sympathy, and false use of language'.[121] The heart grows brutal in its need to find new means of survival. In the meantime Irish writers feel ambiguously, in Heaney's words 'lost, unhappy and at home'. But overriding this internal debate is what Beckett calls 'the mythological present', a stoical shrinking from the present, from the moment of decision. Beckett might seem a strange bedfellow with Friel, but in discussing the trap of the mythological present he reveals, perhaps because of the spareness of his language, a sensitivity to the imprecision of language and cognition:

> It, say it, not knowing what. . . . The fact would seem to be, if in my situation one may speak of facts, not only that I shall have to speak of things of which I cannot speak, but also that I shall have to, I forget, no matter. And at the same time I am obliged to speak. I shall never be silent. Never.[122]

Echoes, or predictions, of Gareth O'Donnell's 'It doesn't matter'; an immaterialism and an agony of doubt and silence, the man who can not exist because he cannot utter: 'Screwballs, say something! Say something father!' (*Ph.* 83). Silence offers security, but it is also an open prison.

2

THE SHORT STORIES

Silence once broken will never again be whole
Samuel Beckett[1]

DIVINATION

Friel conveys an immediate world. It is not just the quotidian, workaday
continuity of people's actions, but, as Seamus Deane observes, 'that local
intimate detail which emerges out of the author's knowledge of his
society's moral code'.[2] Deane says that 'each story is social in its setting,
moral in its implications' but this takes us only part of the way in
understanding Friel's intentions. Beyond morality, beyond the social
boundaries which the moral code dictates, there is a 'quality of mercy'
which takes the form of a tenderness mediating between the wry and the
grotesque. In the sense that Friel's stories have two dimensions, the
actual and the metaphysical, the important factor is the way in which he
translates each to the other: here he is most Chekhovian because he
unites the reader with his intentions, and *his intention is the subject
itself*, the simple relation of self and society.

While we should take note of Anthony Roche's warning that it is
unwise to regard the short story as idiosyncratically the natural Irish
literary form,[3] the storytelling function, which is essentially *ad hominem*
and episodic, is rooted in the Irish vernacular oral tradition, and, as we
have seen, was discussed compellingly by Thomas Kilroy in 1972: more
recently, he has referred to the figure and mode of the *seanchaí* as 'a
distinctively histrionic artist with his repertoire, his own audience' and
couples this with the statement 'the anecdote resides at the centre of Irish
fiction'.[4] It is also essentially subjunctive, dealing as it does with a sense
of loss and an emotion of hope: as Webster defines it: 'that mood of a
verb used to express supposition, desire, hypothesis, possibility . . .

rather than to state an actual fact, as the mood of *were* in "if I *were* you"'. The possible exchange of identities in that 'if I were you' is fascinating, the idea that by imagining 'what might have been', rather than 'what was', one might become retrospectively 'other'.

Friel's main themes in the stories are: illusion; expectation (and the disillusion which comes with the failure of expectation), and the various types of dignity which interweave among the social and moral dimensions of our lives. His technique in drawing us into his world is to live vicariously through us in the illusion, disillusion, and attempts at dignity, so that when he resolves whatever crisis has been posed – loss of faith, disintegration of the family, failure of memory, displacement of affection – *we* become responsible for that resolution.

In the short stories, as in the piece 'Fine Day at Glenties' and later in the radio plays, many of the stock characters of the later plays are put in place: thus in 'The Diviner' we find a reference to 'the prosperous McLaughlins of the Arcade' and to women who knit for the glove factory, who reappear in *Dancing at Lughnasa* (*Diviner* 19, 48); the Diviner himself presages Frank Hardy, Faith Healer in his appearance: 'faded, too active eyes, fingernails stained with nicotine . . . "A fake! A quack! A charlatan!"' (*Diviner* 27, 28). M. L'Estrange, 'the Illusionist', is another seedy performer like Hardy and indeed the surgeon, Mr Rice in *Molly Sweeney* 'back again to perform his magic on us' (*Diviner* 92); once again, in 'The Illusionists', we meet the notion of the 'trick-of-the-loop man' which is central to *Crystal and Fox* (*Diviner* 93), a failed schoolmaster called Boyle who reappears in *Philadelphia* (*Diviner* 98), a hapless enthusiast for arcane and useless hobbies – 'he had made a study of every detail of it, just as he had studied crop rotation and pig-breeding and Ayrshire cows' (*Diviner* 108) – who becomes Frank Sweeney in *Molly Sweeney*; and even an example of the 'blindsight' from the latter play, in 'Ginger Hero': '"What sort of a stupid bastard are you? What more do you want? Look at her, man! Look at her"' (*Diviner* 114). In 'The Illusionists' we also receive a foretaste of the technique employed in the conclusion of *Making History*, of 'two monologues spoken simultaneously' (*Diviner* 96) and, cognately, the idea of self as other which becomes the split personality, when Friel writes of the childhood memory in 'Among the Ruins' of 'the boy who is I' (*Diviner* 129).

Friel's device is to make us the medium of our own culture by translating us into the *id* of his world; we thus id-entify with the people and psyche of Ballybeg. In this he is divining not only himself and Ballybeg, but also the other participant in this private conversation, the reader. The technique is also applied in the radio plays, which possess the same intimacy of the word spoken directly into the ear. No other Irish writer is so adept at this form of divination except Heaney, whose gift of mediation is as great as Friel's; if Heaney wrote short stories and plays, one feels they would have the same texture and *gravitas* as Friel's.

The Swedish critic Ulf Dantanus refers on several occasions to Friel's 'defining': 'his efforts to define and interpret the Irish psyche'; 'to define its main characteristics'; 'to unearth essential qualities of Irishness and to define the nature of the Irish past'; 'to express and define the Irish identity'; 'an effort to understand and define history and especially the spiritual past and various attitudes to it'; 'these concepts are finally tested and defined'.[5] This is of course the result of mis-hearing a conversation with Friel, which turns 'divine 'into 'define', and which Friel would absolutely disown. The Irish psyche, and the nature of the Irish past, are subject to – and demand – divination, but not definition. Both Friel and Heaney divine and dig below the everyday surface to show us, like a cubist dissecting the inner frames of reference of planes hidden to ordinary view, the tensions which hold some parts of people, and society, together and keep others apart. Eventually, however, they return us to the surface in a closure which often resembles the coda of an archaeologist's exposition.

Friel refers to this as 'the successful invention'. Discussing the accumulation of memory, such as that of the 'fictional' fishing trip already referred to, he says, 'perhaps the important thing is not the accurate memory but the successful invention. And at this stage of my life I no longer know what is invention and what "authentic". The two have merged into one truth for me'. And 'Ballybeg' 'is a village of the mind, more a depository for remembered or invented experience than a geographical location'.[6]

This accounts for the private conception of Ballybeg. The 'public' reason for its existence is, perhaps, more significant, and will become clearer when we turn to the later plays. His emphasis on the parochial has developed,

> perhaps because whatever literary tradition we have here – in the English language – doesn't derive from the confidence of an integrated nation. English authors work from an achieved, complete and continuous tradition. Maybe in lieu of a nation we place our faith in the only alternative we have; the parish.[7]

This helps us to understand why the Irish short story so often strikes English readers as being written in a foreign tongue; although the language is ostensibly the same, it is being used in the service of a quite different set of perceptions, a series of 'successful inventions' predominating over the 'authentic'. As Friel recounts in 'Kelly's Hall':

> I heard the story so often from my mother and I grew so close to the man himself . . . that I can scarcely convince myself that I do not remember the scene although the baptismal water must still have been damp on my head that evening. (*Saucer* 91)

In the fiction, we notice, *the child* is ushered into the family and extended family, the private and the public culture of the tribe, in order to become both a participant in, and a means of relaying, that culture. There are two sides to this awareness of fact, and rejection of its tyranny: one is what Ulf Dantanus calls 'the essentially private nature of truth'.[8] The other is the essentially *public* nature of truth. The difference between them is the difference between language and silence, since private truth is unspoken whilst public truth is a text which must be uttered in order to have existence. One is thought, representing a paradigm of being, the other moves through the paradigm of absolute time, an affect of history.

Between these two, the characters, their author and, by the subtlety of his extension, his audience, move towards a discovery of their faith. Because there are no longer any certainties, either in the secret garden of Irish memory or in the wide world, that movement is bedevilled not only by the unreliability of words and other signals, but by dichotomies in the nature of the world itself, of which we are seeking to make sense by means of description.

'The world of the senses was liable always to sidestep into sinister territories of the mind' says A.N. Jeffares.[9] It is a world which, however much we may resent it, may ultimately expel us into a much more painful and violent exile, the rite of passage in search of home. We feel this insecurity because 'home' can project itself not just as place but as character. This is distinctly Irish as it is essentially Chekhovian, because, in Patrick Kavanagh's words, 'Parochialism is universal; it deals with the fundamentals.'[10] Columba's exclamation, 'what more do you demand of me, damned Ireland? My soul?' (*EW* 71) takes on an extra significance as we see Ireland as a character in the fiction. Friel's 'romantic ideal that we call Cathleen'[11] is not simply a state of mind, but an epiphany of place. The 'mother Ireland', the poor old woman (*shan van vocht*), seeking the restitution of her four green fields, who dominates Yeats's *Cathleen Ni Houlihan* and who haunts modern Irish literature, places Irish men and women at her disposal. The attempt to reunite the modern political states of Ireland is a fictive approach to the greater and deeper mythic needs of the Irish psyche.

If place can have personality, then our response to it cannot be impersonal, it signs to us and we sign to it, in a mythopoeic, rather than a logocentric, language. If we find fault with a place, the fault is similar to that we would detect in another person. In 'The Diviner' this is the essence of Nelly Devenny's resentment of the lake where her husband has drowned; the attraction of the place is the magnetism of a person, as in the silent virginal beauty of 'The Wee Lake Beyond', and the jealousy it engenders between father and son. If we resent place, it is because place to an overwhelming extent gives essence and meaning, forms our perceptions like a teacher, underwrites our earliest sensations like a parent, provides us with name, identity and purpose.

Friel's response in art began in 1952 with the publication in *The Bell* of his first story, 'The Child'.[12] It was an act of courageous faith for a young writer. Friel, however, neither wishes nor permits this story to be republished. It is the seminal work from which flow all his insights into the question of love, language and freedom. But in its bluntness Friel regards it as 'unfiltered' or 'unmediated'[13] as he does the play emanating from his seminarian experience, *The Blind Mice*, and that which followed 'Bloody Sunday' – *The Freedom of the City*. In each case, raw experience was being unloaded into a literary form which was insufficiently strong or flexible to accommodate its violent emotions, its white heat of anger and frustration. *The Blind Mice*, he felt, was 'too solemn, too intense. I wanted to hit at too many things',[14] while in *The Freedom* 'the experience of Bloody Sunday wasn't adequately distilled'.[15] One senses in 'The Child' that he wants to hit at everything in his blind rage, and as such the story stands for a side of Friel's artistic and emotional temperament which emerges at certain points of particular torsion between himself and society, destiny or family: 'on occasion I have lost faith in the fiction and shouted what should have been overheard'.[16] It is also indicative of the fact that many of Friel's most intimate texts are recondite, as if it remains necessary for him to retain control of a secret place, of the secret itself.

A boy ('the child') lies awake at night. He hears the reassuring sounds of his mother at work in the kitchen below. The comfortable world is shattered by the one event which obviously lurks in the child's abiding dread: the entry of the father, a drunkard who can communicate only in the language of familiar hostility. The boy is startled into customary terror. He begs God not to let them fight. But God lets them fight: a ritual, symbiotic captivity of caged animals. He goes almost automatically to the head of the stairs to witness the spectacle: 'the child knew the routine by heart . . . it was the scene he knew so well'. God is implored once more as the intermediary: promise God you will be good if only the beasts below can be separated. 'Down below they were roaring at each other. Quietly he rose, and, blinded with tears, groped his way back to his room.' The summary is, of course, unsatisfactory, and most likely for the reason adduced by D. E. S. Maxwell in his pithy judgement that the stories 'retain within themselves a core of meaning that resists paraphrase'.[19]

This is not 'the reality of rural Ireland' as Dantanus suggests but it is *a* reality.[17] It suggests the personality of a thing called 'home' which, we know, Friel denies. It sets 'pleasant memories of the day' – the Arcadian vision – against the 'waiting black void' of the night, the exit into sleep and our other, subliminal, self. It contrasts the outdoor freedoms with the ferocious domination of the indoors by the father, the fight between mother and father for control of the kitchen, the hearth. The child is outlawed from the adult world in which the tensions of village life are worked out privately; he is blinded both by his own tears and by the darkness.

No clearer proof need be furnished that Friel, by concentrating his vision on rural society and 'Ballybeg', is singing an Arcadian eclogue, to the exclusion of 'reality'. 'Reality' in fact is a mixture of arcadian and infernal, of white and black, dexter and sinister. Friel records:

> One's life in retrospect seems to be defined by precise contours and primary colours: all summers were arcadian, all winters were arctic, pleasures were unqualified, disappointments were total. This remembering, I imagine, is a conscious and deliberate attempt to invest mediocrity with passion and drama.[18]

The art of reconstructing reality lies in qualifying and reducing the absolutes in which children (and some adults) see the world in the light of retrospect, while maintaining the passion and drama of the situation being described. But the description is of course fiction, because it no longer exists. The return to one's past, whether it is purely through time or, as in the case of the revenant exile, also through space, is a *recherche* of a paradise or hell which, because it is no longer real, might never have been real.

Therefore, Friel is at liberty in these stories to construct representations of a reality which may never have been 'authentic'. His travellers carry cardboard suitcases; his father-figures carry authority, usually schoolmasters or those in other positions of guardianship, reaching across *space* to admonish; and grandfathers, irresponsible and attractive, reaching out across *time* to subvert and amaze and reveal; all the stock population of a town like Glenties (Ballybeg) or Omagh (Ballymore). 'Home' is the hearth – literally the *focus* – around which they gather for their rituals. But in the stories and radio plays there is also the wife and mother, fretful, tense, warm, resourceful, beautiful, whose absence in the plays is a continual reproach to Friel's ability to make life whole again.

In reviewing Friel's stories Robert Lacy commented on 'the touching sense of loss, a clearly communicated feeling that something magical and grand has slipped away'.[20] The dangers of such recollection are obvious, but, as I hope I have shown, Friel is not pursuing an arcadian vision. The reconstruction, which places the relation of time and memory at the centre of Friel's stories, is much more than the restitution to the disappointed child of his shattered paradise. Friel knows that the child also numbers hell among his realities, and that he voluntarily throws away the crown of ecstasy. Therefore he seeks to reconstruct not so much what was as *what might have been*.

In this the grandfathers are the perpetrators of a vicious and irresponsible hoax on the boys. In fact there is the suspicion throughout the stories that because of the effective elision of the father-figure where the grandfather is concerned, Friel is describing a world where all the boys are encouraged to grow old and already have an aged psychology. Boys, as if they were old men, are searching back into their own boyhood because they cannot recognise and grasp it as *now*, and are all the time sitting in the waiting room for death.

HOMECOMINGS

One slips back into one's place by the power of memory. 'Baile' means home *and* town. And yet the Irish have never been 'at home' in towns as the English understand them. 'We have always feared towns' says Sean O'Faolain.[21] Yet the search for that powerful focal hearth goes on as surely in the private mind as that for the four green fields occupies, and persists in, the public conscience. In *The Great O'Neill* O'Faolain makes the point more strongly: 'each centre is the centre only of its own *locus*. No hierarchy or predominance has been established. History is still a complete gamble.' Once again the temperament is Chekhovian: Ulster was 'practically bare of town life'; O'Neill and his folk were 'men for whom the outer world existed only as a remote and practically irrelevant detail. Their interests were personal and local.'[22] And they continue to be so when we start to explore the unease we feel with the encroachment of the outer world. Heaney becomes 'Unhappy and at home'; Friel denies the existence of 'home' itself but he encourages sons and fathers to explore what this particular avenue of memory has to offer. Of course they find that memory is only effective if they maintain their faith in history.

In 'Among the Ruins' the child sets about his own mystery, digging at the foot of a tree and declaring 'I'm donging the tower' (*Diviner* 133). (We should recall that in *Secret Gardens* Humphrey Carpenter tells us that 'childhood lies buried at the foot of [a] tree'.)[23] Each reader becomes a party to this mutual act of discovery and mystery, because Friel is translating such experience from private language into public or collective text. But what is 'donging the tower'? Steiner tells us that 'the fracture of words, the maltreatment of grammatical norms which . . . constitute a vital part of childhood, have a rebellious air: by refusing, for a time, to accept the rule of grown-up speech, the child seeks to keep the world open to his own, seemingly unprecedented needs'.[24] We are clearly being prepared for the nonsense talk of the lovers in *Translations*. In one sense it is vital that we know what is meant by 'donging the tower', in another it is vital that we do not.

Thus in 'Among the Ruins', because his own childhood dream of innocence has been lost rather than confirmed, Joe *wills* his son to be a man, because, he now knows, the future at least holds no illusions: 'It's a good thing for a man to cry like that sometimes.' Joe wants the boy to 'grow up', to rush through the misery and disillusion of adolescence, so that he can join his father in a common bond:

> Generations of fathers stretching back and back, all finding magic and sustenance in the brief, quickly destroyed happiness of their children. The past did have meaning. It was neither reality nor dreams, neither today's patchy oaks nor the great woods of his boyhood. It was simply continuance, life repeating itself and surviving. (*Diviner* 136)

If such a Lawrentian resolution appears trite, it is due to the need to reaffirm a life-force in the face of the disintegration Friel sees in the familiar world, a need which endangers the first act of *Translations* in its apparent complacency. (Triteness, encouraged by the *New Yorker* formula, is also a reason for Friel's eventual dissatisfaction with the limiting conventions of the short story in favour of the more open possibilities of the play.) This is particularly evident in the conclusion of 'Everything Neat and Tidy':

> Chilled by the sudden personal disaster, he drove faster and faster, as if he could escape the moment when he would take up the lonely burden of recollection that the dead had fled from and the living had forgotten. (*Diviner* 155)

This fear of taking up 'the lonely burden of recollection' is precisely that fear which persuades the Irish to remember their future rather than their past.[25] And it is one which Friel accosts only imperfectly in his stories. He has not been influenced by Chekhov in story-writing (unlike his play-writing) and this possibly accounts for the fact that his mercy, unlike Chekhov's, is too great, his tenderness mediates too far, in displacing horror with dignity. As a result they ultimately address themselves to the problem of individuation, which, as Seamus Deane notes, 'with its emphasis on internal freedom . . . most often makes a virtue of alienation and a fetish of integrity'.[26] Where Chekhov faced such a challenge by embracing fear, for example in 'A Boring Story', Friel prefers to resolve his crises by rushing into the arms of fate. Seldom in the stories is this technique fully successful, partly because Friel falls into the trap of triteness, and partly because he seems afraid to call the bluff of fate. His greatest success in meeting the challenge is an unjustly neglected story, 'The Flower of Kiltymore', which in many ways announces the ultimate resolution which he achieves in *Faith Healer*. In this story, Sergeant Burke, regarded by his late wife as lacking professional dignity ('she had been a sergeant's daughter herself, and anybody below the rank of superintendent was a nobody'), finds that the 'calm and peace' brought by his wife's death conveys nothing so much as a sense of his own unease, perhaps impending death. He is mocked by his assistant guard, 'a Kerryman, young and keen and cunning', who has outmanoeuvred him socially by his alliance with the Canon; he is taunted by the local pranksters ('the Blue Boys'), bewildered by the clean bill of health from the doctor, which is contradicted by his 'unnatural tranquillity'. Thus excluded from peace, from social position, from professional authority, he asks in a Gethsemane-like appeal, for the 'unnatural tranquillity' to pass:

> So this was peace, this terrible emptiness. So this was what in those odd moments of treachery, when Lily flogged him with her tongue, he had dreamed of, this vacuity that was a pain within him. Sweet God, he prayed, sweet God, if this is what I wanted, take it away from me. (*Gold* 138)

Finally he calls the bluff of 'the Blue Boys' who allege that they have found a mine on the beach. It is no bluff, the mine explodes and the youngsters, 'the flower of Kiltymore', are killed.[27] Now ruined and hated by the community, he faces a commissioner's inquiry which can only restore to him the natural tranquillity he seeks. The events of the tragedy, by making him an outcast, 'assured him that he was still the centre of the pushing stream of life, and not floating, as he had been since Lily's death, in the peace and calm of some stagnant backwater'. Like Frank Hardy, he can face the firing squad of self-betrayal:

> He got up from the bed, put on his Sunday uniform and his good boots, combed his hair, and straightened his tie. As he went down the stairs to meet his judges, the wretchedness of the last four weeks was forgotten, and he knew again the only joy he had ever known. The month of ghostly isolation was over. His prayer in the garden had been answered. Let the Superintendent and the Commissioner do their damnedest to him! He knew now he had the capacity to survive it, because his life had suddenly happily slipped back into its old groove. (*Gold* 144–5)

Perhaps Friel succeeds in this conclusion because he is not afraid of pieties, he does not embrace them simply because they represent some Lawrentian life-force. There comes a point, which becomes clear, particularly in his later plays, where 'piety', in seeking to remain within the borders of the moral code, becomes absurd and grotesque. Here, however,

Friel knows, more maturely than elsewhere in the stories, that the 'enemy within' is a devil, and that homecoming necessitates a death: it predicts the fate of Yolland, the alter ego revenant of *Translations*, and of Bazarov in *Fathers and Sons*, because otherwise the story could not continue.

DIGNITY AND RESPECTABILITY

Friel is at his most suggestive, and his writing exhibits the finest quality, when he combines the descriptive with the emotive. Thus in 'Foundry House' his characterisation of Mrs Hogan: 'She was a tall, ungraceful woman, with a man's shoulders and a wasted body and long thin feet. When she spoke, her mouth and lips worked in excessive movement' (*Diviner* 78).

In fact, Friel's stories reveal a skill not only at characterisation, but also gesture and emphasis, which present quite different challenges in drama, and at which his stage directions are often less successful. Thus his 'private conversation' (confabulation) with the reader sometimes achieves a more affective result than the 'public address' which denies such finesse. In the passage quoted above, the words 'ungraceful', 'worked' and 'excessive' convey a personality and a neurosis which no actor could easily effect. At first the combination of 'long' and 'thin' seems *de trop*, but taken together with the woman's shoulders and her mouth-motion, it suggests a mediaeval effigy which Friel has manipulated into an uneasy recovery, a devilish creation. Similarly with the cadences in which he describes or recreates movement: as Nelly Devenny goes towards her particular Calvary, the divining of her second drunken husband's body in the lake, she 'left the priest's car for the first time that day, and ran to join the watchers. The women gathered protectively around her' (*Diviner* 28–9). *Left, ran, gathered*: a flight towards the fold, in this case the elusive dignity denied to Nelly by a fate she has not found the courage to confront. Another example of Friel's ability to combine the descriptive with the emotive is in the opening pages of 'The Illusionists':

> Once a month Father Shiels, the manager, drove out the twisted five miles from the town, in one breath asked us were we good and told us to say our prayers, shook father's hand firmly, and scuttled away again as if there were someone chasing him. (*Diviner* 91)

Not only is this a comical, clockwork-like figure but we can see how distastefully, almost fearfully, the priest performs his automatic, perfunctory and indifferent task.

It is by means of this emotive descriptiveness that Friel achieves a suggestion of what Seamus Deane calls 'the co-existence of two realms, one clearly stated and social, the other amorphous and imaginative', in which he says 'the author's insistence on the actuality of event and on the reality of imagination is quite impartial'.[28] I would add that the same assumption of the reader's common knowledge and intimacy that greets us in Chekhov's stories is taken a stage further by Friel in inducing a complicity in the moral code and, in his most successful stories, in the transgression of that code in the working out of individual salvation. This was Friel's reply to the situation of displacement of people within a fixed locale. The realisation that it did not go far enough was the reason for eventually abandoning the short story.

We can find that reason clearly spelt out in his approach to the problem of authority. As Deane says, 'Authority in its most basic form grows out of a sense of mystery but in its more quotidian form out of awareness of status.'[29] That degeneracy is best expressed through differing attitudes to, or differing attempts to express, the idea of 'dignity'; those who are 'dignified', who possess dignity, or whose internal explorations result in the repossession of a lost dignity, emerge from the stories as the 'winners', while those who scramble for dignity, for the acquisition of a quality which they imagine can be achieved through an appeal to some external authority, 'respectability', are the 'losers'. Dantanus makes the valuable distinction between *respectability*, an acceptance of agreed communal values, and *dignity*, the individual's response.[30] Tribal pressure to conform is exerted by means of respectability, whereas the divination of the individual seeking dignity can only be achieved by rejecting the collective insistence. Nelly Devenny, through her public humiliation, becomes 'skilled in reticence and fanatically jealous of her dignity' (*Diviner* 20), but in fact she was fanatically jealous of the 'dignity' she sees in others; her second attempt to achieve it, by marrying a second husband (and thus acquiring a new identity in her new name, Nelly Doherty) leaves her the ultimate appeal, to the external authority of her peers – 'the women gathered protectively around her'. The *diviner* discloses more in the waters of the lake than the body of Mr Doherty: he draws up another way of confronting reality, another set of perceptions by which to test our received and time-worn responses to the climate, to land and our 'community'.

It is remarkable that Friel is not especially aware of the pursuit of dignity, or the condition of being dignified in either his stories or plays.[31] Yet Seamus Deane insists that Friel 'never forsakes the notion that human need, however artificially expressed, is rooted in the natural inclination towards dignity'.[32] As we shall see in examining the plays, Friel often explicitly presents us with the fear which inhabits people when that natural inclination is thwarted. Thus in 'Everything Neat and Tidy'

Mrs MacMenamin suffers 'anguish and indignity' at her husband's death; to live with her married daughter is 'the final, crushing indignity'. But her eventual achievement – not acquisition – of peace is in some way a redemption of dignity of a different order (*Diviner* 146–55). This is very effectively expressed in 'The First of My Sins' which also looks at dignity in two ways: 'a slap on the face merely pricks one's pride, but cow-dung on new shoes shatters one's dignity' (*Gold* 157). It would be easy to confuse a superficial tenure on *respectability* with the idea that one must act out the community's perception of oneself. In 'The First of My Sins' that 'slap on the face' is something we all endure every day in social exchange; that which shatters dignity is a breach of the family integer. We are told not of the narrator's boyish 'sins' but of his uncle's petty thieving, a 'crime' which hardly offends the criminal code but inflicts a moral disorder within the family.

Friel is also content to dismiss the search for respectability with wry and disdainful humour, in 'The Queen of Troy Close' (*Gold*: 'We'll put manners on them!') or 'The Fawn Pup' (*Saucer*: 'he managed to carry himself with a shabby dignity, like a down-at-heel military man') or the 'grandfather' whose 'sufficient charity' puts a name to a fatherless child in 'Mr Sing My Heart's Delight' (*Saucer*).

The status of dignity as a *tribal* quality clearly vexes Friel: in *The Enemy Within* there is a distinct relationship between Eoghan's 'gauche dignity' and his 'quiet power' (*EW* 58). There is also a connection between dignity and the exotic as if the ultimate test of dignity is whether or not it can survive the challenge of the external. In 'Kelly's Hall' the debacle of Grandfather's wondrous gramophone as a source of income places his family at the hands of charity:

> This new method of living, 'charity' she called it, imposed a great strain on Grandmother's virtue. She longed for the old days again when he went on binges and when her vanity had to weather only short, well-spaced storms. . . .'God be with the days when he used to be carried home drunk to me'. (*Saucer* 954)

Like Synge, Friel bows to the need for illusion, in Deane's words 'in a society which so severely distorts the psychic life'.[33] This may be the illusion which is simply destroyed by the force of 'reality' as in 'The Illusionists' or an illusion which is reinforced in the flight from reality, as in 'Foundry House': Joe relies on the reality of his memory rather than on what actually is. He knows that Mr Hogan 'was not the image' he carried in his memory but is determined that he shall be made to still fit that image. He insists that Mr Hogan is 'the same as ever . . . no different' (*Diviner* 89–90) which in *Aristocrats* (to which 'Foundry House' is thematically linked) becomes the ironic family motto 'Semper permanemus'

(*Ar.* 53). The exotic, in 'Kelly's Hall', in the form of Grandfather Kelly's gramophone, leads him into the lie or illusion in which the exotic becomes bizarre: 'He never played a disk without first prefacing the performance with an entirely fictitious history of the composer and the music' (*Saucer* 94). In 'The Gold in the Sea' illusion is used as a tool of social engineering: Con, having admitted that the shipwrecked gold has already been salvaged, maintains, in front of the younger fishermen, the pretence that it has *not*: 'It is better for them to think it is still there. They're young men. . . . You see, friend, they never got much out of life, not like me' (*Diviner* 44).

Pigeon fanciers and breeders of fighting cocks are typical, and natural, victims of their own illusions, as in 'The Widowhood System' and 'Ginger Hero' (in *The Diviner*), but Friel's most immediate experience, as the pupil of his own father's national school, provides a most powerful example in the eponymous 'The Illusionists'. In this story there are three illusionists: M. L'Estrange, Prince of the Occult (in reality Barney O'Reilly); the narrator's father, who is refusing to come to terms with the difference between his present circumstances and the image of his former self which he espouses; and the narrator, who expects by becoming an apprentice illusionist to reach some Chekhovian Moscow, and who is eventually forced not only to admit the illusionary nature of M. L'Estrange's past and therefore his own future, but also to embrace, or reclaim, a known, but equally illusory world, offered to him through the affective authority of his mother.

The exotic (in this case M. L'Estrange) is also used as an alternative to familiar disappointment. Friel, and much modern Irish fiction, turns accepted critical theory on its head, since he shows the wisdom of age and authority as a synonym for buffoonery and drunkenness. 'In the analogy of innocence', writes Northrop Frye, 'the divine or spiritual figures are usually paternal wise old men with magical powers'.[34] Irish society tends to smile on, if not to extol, the alchoholic, that genetically disappointed result of psychological and environmental tragedy, in the same way as it invests the associated deficiencies of insanity or mental aberration with healing and magical powers: an illusion – a lie – that guarantees a tender, forgiving smile and recognises those affects in oneself. But the exotic, even though he is also master, and creature, of illusion, can dispel that atmosphere of tolerance and open a door into a more exciting darkness. In 'Segova, The Savage Turk' it is Segova's strength which attracts the child, in contrast to his father's weakness. Segova's thick dark hair symbolises his strength, 'the supreme in manhood . . . the crystallisation of every hope and ambition I would ever have'. Even when he is beaten for trying to be like Segova, the child realises that 'every stroke [was] alienating me more and more from the puny and the feeble and strengthening me in my resolve to join forces with the brawny and the mighty' (*Saucer* 121).

In their treatment of expectation destroyed, or hope deferred, or the assessment of dignity, Friel's stories are more important in a modern reading than his attention to illusion *per se*, which is not in itself as central to his later work as these other elements. The psychic disorders of Irish society are not only served by illusion or illusionism; visually and verbally Irish people are being asked to reassess what they see and what they hear and thus to re-examine the architecture of their minds. Friel's contribution to this process – the German '*Prozess*' or 'trial' seems appropriate here – has been characterised by a concern for tenderness evident in even his overtly violent play, *The Freedom of the City*, and the most covertly fierce, *Crystal and Fox*; while in *The Loves of Cass McGuire* Cass's outbursts are counterpointed by a poignant series of rhapsodies, culminating in Cass's own entry into a dream world. An illusion, yes, but more than that, a way of dealing with time and place rediscovered which reveals the sensibility more attuned to nicety, to tension, to heartache, to panic in the face of the grotesque or bizarre, than to the problems of self-deceit, however disturbing those may be. Friel, particularly in the stories, divines within us the frightened child. With his mixture of strictness and compassion, he exposes the near-brutality to which our psychic disorder has reduced us, and then shows us how to become whole. Through the private conversation of his stories and radio plays, he does this on an intimate level; since the appearance of *The Enemy Within* he has been working out how to achieve this through the public address system. There is a good deal of Eliot's intellectuality and spirituality in Friel's plays, because of his attention to the psyche. These are the stories Eliot might have written.

Friel's psychological techniques are those of recurring visions and appeals to past time. Chekhov's frightened children express the problem thus: Carlotta: 'Where I come from and who I am I don't know'; Yepihodov: 'I can't seem to make out where I'm going, what it is I really want . . . to live or to shoot myself so to speak'; Liubov Andreeyevna: 'What truth? *You* can see where the truth is, and where it isn't, but I seem to have lost my power of vision.'[35] Friel's characters, particularly in the stories, experience the same problem – If I can't speak my name, I can't be a person, so I can't go anywhere among men; if I can't see, I have no moral or aesthetic vision, so I can't find my way in the world; if I can't tell the real from the unreal, I can't discriminate, I lose the power of choice, so I am immobilised. Ordinarily Friel's people have names which delineate their role in society on both its physical and metaphysical levels: Flames Flaherty 'who used to run before the fire brigade in the old days, clearing the street' (*Gold* 80) – we can *see* him *and* his job; 'Mr Sing My Heart's Delight' for the packman Singh, because he fills the lonely woman's fading memories with an exotic richness; and the qualifying names which we meet in 'Sarah Johnny Sally' (*Tr.* 28) telling us seed, breed and generation. Then there are the nicknames – of description: Lobster O'Brien with the injured eye (in 'The Fawn Pup'); of moral value: Anna na mBreag, Anna of the Lies, maker of bad poteen (*Tr.* 27) – and the series of names by which a single body has many personae in the family and extended family: 'at home I was Joe or "Joey boy" or even in his softer moments "Plumb" but in school I was plain Hargan' ('My Father and the Sergeant'). Finally, there are the names that mislead, which give us a mistaken identity: Owen/Roland in *Translations* being the most poignant as well as the most treacherous. Beyond ourselves there are the objective/subjective names we give to places. Once again *Translations* provides us with the mental and physical problem of map-making, but a neglected story, 'The Wee Lake Beyond', tells us not only of the lake whose map-names translate that meaning into topography ('*Lough Fada*, the long lake; *Lough Na Noilean*, the lake with the islands; *Lough Gorm*, the blue lake; *Lough Rower*, the fat lake' *Gold* 69–70) but also of those lakes which 'were nameless and inaccessible'. Nameless and *therefore* inaccessible: naming them would make them accessible, would add to their definition on the map, would open them up for discussion. Ordinarily we locate ourselves by means of *vision*, and only secondarily by other senses. In 'The Gold in the Sea' 'the blackness was so dense that the three fishermen had identity only by their voices' (*Diviner* 37). Their identity, it is suggested, is diminished by their invisibility; in 'The Widowhood System' the bird 'suffered from mental blackouts, like blown fuses, so that it had to fly blind for periods until the psyche righted itself' (*Diviner* 55), in other words it had to relocate itself by reference to the inner, not the outer, world. At the opening of 'The Barney Game' Barney Cole sat on an upturned box in the yard behind the poultry shop, killing chickens with his eyes closed. 'It's the feel of them I know', he explained . . . 'If I looked at what I was doing, I'd only be all thumbs' (*Gold* 103). More than an index to physical contact, vision can also act as a trigger to memory and imagination:

> 'Very poor', she said quietly, adding the detail to the picture she was composing in her mind. 'And the oranges and bananas grow there on trees and there are all classes of fruit and flowers with all the colours of the rainbow on them.'
> 'Yes', he said simply, for he was remembering his own picture. 'It is very beautiful, good lady. Very beau-ti-ful'. (*Saucer* 68)

Finally, there is the use of time as an ordinary technique of story-writing. Friel's stories usually open with a statement of time, rather than of place or person. 'The very day his mother was buried' (*Diviner* 45); 'November frost had starched the flat countryside into silent rigidity' (*Diviner* 65); 'When his father and mother died' (*Diviner* 75); 'I can recall the precise moment in my childhood' (*Gold* 157). This last opening creates a flashback of the kind which triggers memory in the narrator, and imagination of time past in the reader/spectator. It is particularly effective cinematically in its combination of the visual and the temporal dimensions. It is most affective in *Dancing at Lughnasa*: 'When I cast my mind back to that summer . . .' (*DL* 1). The appeal is to a 'state that was', *in illo tempore*, as in 'Among the Ruins': 'We're going to see where Daddy used to play when he was a little boy' (*Diviner* 127); or 'The Wee Lake Beyond' in which the timeless landscape of mountains and lakes holds simultaneously the events of the holiday now and those of the holiday forty-five years earlier. This is partly 'emotion recollected in tranquillity' and partly an attempt to solve the 'crisis recollected from childhood' in the crucible of memory and thus isolate it from contemporary events.

It is of course noticeable that Friel's stories are non-eclectic. As D.E.S. Maxwell comments, 'Friel rarely writes about the city, he writes about Catholics but not Protestants' (even his 'aristocrats in 'Foundry House' and of course in *Aristocrats* itself are Catholics); most of his people are poor, they carry cardboard suitcases. Maxwell says quite rightly that 'he is not an artist of the whole community' and that he could not be, since neither of the two traditions of Ulster 'has any real and natural intimacy with the other'.[36] But while Friel is not a spokesman for Catholic or nationalist viewpoints, and does not attempt to portray anything other than his own folk, the more serious imbalance in his stories is the lack of that intimacy which comes from mutual commerce between town and country. As Raymond Williams says:

> The common image of the country is now an image of the past, and the common image of the city an image of the future. That leaves, if we isolate them, an undefined present. The pull of the idea of the country is towards old ways, human ways, natural ways.[37]

To translate this into the Derry/Donegal context, we can quite distinctly see Friel in his stories addressing one side of the equation in his concentration on the past, on a traditional, Gaelic world, and therefore leaving the 'undefined present' dangerously unresolved. Conscious of writing in a genre that owed too much to the influence of a master like Frank O'Connor, and of being too easily seduced by the demands of the

American market, once Friel had begun to extend the private voice with his radio plays he abandoned the short story form. But at the same time we cannot dismiss the elements of the stories simply because they tend towards the elegiac. (The danger of elegy has been underlined in *The Gentle Island*: 'My God it's beautiful up there, Shane: the sun and the fresh wind from the sea and the sky alive with larks and the smell of heather' *GI* 39–40.) The strengths of the pastoral are present in all his plays, even *Volunteers* and *The Freedom of the City*: the extension lies in the fact that he is now prepared to add into the equation the dynamic of the city, and the future tense. His tone continues to be lyric, but it now looks for external, as well as interior, freedom.

PART II

Public Address

Memoria praeteritorum bonorum –
that must be unpleasant

Samuel Beckett

3

PLAYS OF LOVE

My heart expanded with an immense remembered love for
her, and then at once shrank in terror of her. *Living Quarters*[1]

RADIO DRAMA

With two plays written specifically for radio in 1958, *A Sort of Freedom*
and *To This Hard House*, and a stage play, *A Doubtful Paradise* (1960),
Friel began the progression from the private conversation of the short
stories to the public address of the stage presentation. The Northern
Ireland Home Service, as the BBC's station in Ulster was then called, had
a long and fruitful history of fostering radio drama, initiated by Tyrone
Guthrie himself at the inception of the service in 1924, and continued at
that time by Ronald Mason, who encouraged Friel and commissioned
his first two plays. Radio drama offered a method of developing the
technique of the short story by voicing its various personalities and
making explicit the main preoccupations. MacNeice had found that the
device of 'splitting a mind into different voices' could assist in taking 'the
listener directly into the mind of a complex man',[2] a device which Friel
himself would succeed in putting on the stage in *Philadelphia, Here I
Come!* In his early plays he moves towards that position by experimenting
with the basic short-story form, while (in the radio version of *The Loves
of Cass McGuire*) developing the role of the narrator by aligning it with
the main character in the play.

I will classify the plays in four groups: the 'love' plays in which the
author's main concern is the examination of family and community ties
and allegiances; the 'freedom' plays in which the consequences which
the author has discovered about love are examined; the 'language' plays
in which our means of communicating about love, politics, culture, are
rigorously inspected and largely set aside; and the 'plays of beyond'

which extend the imagination deep into the hinterland of magic. Of course here too there are overlappings: family, for example, runs throughout Friel's work as a major theme, especially in *The Enemy Within*, *Philadelphia*, *Living Quarters*, *Aristocrats*, *Translations*, *Three Sisters*, *Fathers and Sons*, *Dancing at Lughnasa* and *Give Me Your Answer Do!*; while the 'political' element in *The Mundy Scheme*, *The Freedom* and *Volunteers* is also to be found in *Translations*, *Making History* and again in *Fathers and Sons*. It is also tempting to follow the classical formula and to see *Faith Healer* entirely in its own right as a unique statement about the hero and the artist.

All the problems, dichotomies, anxieties latent in Irish society as they are discussed or implied in Friel's short stories are present, and made more explicit, in his first attempts at drama. At first Friel remains in what Northrop Frye calls 'the low mimetic area',[3] using ordinary images of experience to create a set of ideas in, initially, the listener's mind. The transition into drama is thus gradual: the author is extending, rather than exchanging, his original voice, while the reader, who has to create his own voices in the inner ear, becomes the listener for whom the sounds (now external) are provided.

It is perhaps surprising that although Guthrie contributed significantly to the development of radio drama with his own plays *Squirrel's Cage* (1929), *The Flowers Are Not for You to Pick* (1930) and *Matrimonial News* (1932), his influence in this area did not extend particularly to Friel. (Friel's approach to the development of *The Loves of Cass McGuire* from radio to stage is, however, reminiscent of Guthrie's work, and at the time of his death in 1971 Guthrie was preparing to produce *Cass*.) Guthrie regarded the actor's irresistible temptation to create effects as an opportunity to dispense with realism and naturalism and to produce social archetypes – through which to introduce to the listener's ear a series of social and political problems. As in Greek drama, his characters remained masked and 'were wholly dependent upon the word'.[4] In Guthrie's *Matrimonial News* we are introduced to the stream of consciousness of a frustrated and disheartened woman.[5] 'Remember', says the announcer, 'you are overhearing her thoughts. She is alone.' We might easily adopt the same approach to a radio version of *Cass*, but by the time he wrote *Cass* Friel had already moved significantly away from radio, a medium in which he seems to have encountered considerable difficulties, principally because he was approaching it as literature rather than drama. Ronald Mason, however, believed that Friel remains pre-eminently a radio writer, in the sense that not only do his stage plays 'translate' easily and naturally into radio, but also because in those of his plays which are 'short' in action – *Lovers*, *Faith Healer* and *Making History* in particular –

Friel still uses the style and techniques of the radio medium, the 'Come here till I whisper in your ear'.[6]

The stilted language and rhythm of speech in *To This Hard House* indicate that Friel was not yet at ease with the new medium, that he could not confidently convey all the short-story narrator's sense either of the personality of place or of the observations permitted to the narrator himself. Both *A Sort of Freedom* and *To This Hard House* have relatively weak closures because the author had so far failed to adapt the literary closure of the story into a dramatic conclusion: *A Sort of Freedom* closes with Joe Reddin, the recipient of a form of redundancy payment or conscience money from his former employer, Jack Frazer, talking to himself: 'The decentest man in town, in the whole country . . . that's what Joe Frazer is'[7] – a moral statement, resonant of storytelling, such as we find in all the dignity-related stories. In *To This Hard House* a runaway daughter returns to an ineffectual welcome: 'I knew she would be welcome. I'll call her in, Daniel. (*calls off*) Fiona, come on in child; come on in to the room'.[8] The accent in these early plays is predominantly on the nature of *home*. 'A home is an atmosphere' is alleged in *A Sort of Freedom*.[9] The problem of constituting, and maintaining, that atmosphere – or, as we shall see it later, that 'context' – is threatened both within, from the failure of love or affection, and from without by ambition or redundancy. Missing children, or children leaving home, are the hallmark of its failure. 'This is a home' declares one hopeful character in *A Doubtful Paradise;*[10] 'this is your home' insists a bewildered islander in the deserted *Gentle Island* (GI 71). The radio version of *A Doubtful Paradise* (also entitled *The Francophile*) shows us the ineffectual father, disillusioned by his failure to acquire a cosmopolitan culture by taking evening classes in French, fantasising on the 'expression of the brotherhood of man, the one-ness, the family one-ness of creation', and the play ends with his announcement 'Next month I'm going to take up . . . Esperanto!'[11] Short story endings occur within the dialogue also: in *A Sort of Freedom* the doctor tries to persuade Jack Frazer that the death of his adopted child was not due to neglect: 'It was one of those tragic accidents that happen now and again'.[12] That whole sentence could easily, and satisfactorily, provide the 'fateful' conclusion to a story with similar import to 'The Diviner'. But Friel was obviously moving closer to the point where tragic events do take place within the context of, if not necessarily upon, the dramatic stage, and, like a Greek dramatist, he must therefore find a dramatic, rather than a narrative, method. So too he must find ways of expressing emotional conviction. Jack Frazer remonstrates with the doctor, insisting that the dead baby would have grown up in his own image. He has already commissioned new boards for his works' gates – 'Frazer & Son, Haulage Contractors' (the baby is eight months old) – and now he insists 'He was called Jack Frazer after me. He would have been me.'[13] That, too, suits the father in a narrative such as 'Among the Ruins', but is unconvincing as a bald statement which the storyteller has not supported by creating a dramatic emotional context.

Beside the technical problems Friel encountered in these plays, between the stories and the later 'love' plays, they supply one distinctive transitional feature: they are plays in which the hopeful children are a disappointment to their fathers, and in which the mothers mediate the hopes and disappointments. Mary Reddin in *A Sort of Freedom*, Lily Stone in *To This Hard House*, Maggie Logue in *A Doubtful Paradise*, all supply a degree of tenderness and compassion lacking in, for example, *Living Quarters* or *Aristocrats*, in which the children have to work out their own salvation, and their parental relationships, practically unaided. In that sense Friel was still writing in the same frame of mind as in 'The Illusionists' (with which *A Doubtful Paradise*, especially because it is also known as *The Francophile*, has obvious affinities). But he is also changing gear for the bitterness of *Philadelphia:* the mother's intervention, which will be possible in *Philadelphia* only through the surrogate role of the housekeeper, Madge, and impossible thereafter, is here inconclusive and, implicitly, ineffectual.

In another sense Friel is clarifying the elements in his 'family' discussions. The grandfather, who in the stories has been a key figure standing slightly outside the main family circle, but one of 'the child's' key points of reference (as in 'My True Kinsman'), also disappears. Thus the elision of the father, by means of the child-grandfather liaison, is no longer possible and the confrontation so feared in the stories has to begin in *Philadelphia* (*agon*) and to be worked through (*pathos*) until it finds a kind of resolution (*anagnorisis*) in *Translations*.

At the age of thirty Friel was strongly aware of the 'traditional' problems of rural Ireland. He had not yet had the 'first parole from inbred, claustrophobic Ireland', and he presents those problems conceptually, almost symbolically, rather than engagingly. He continues to do this until the transitional *Philadelphia*, where the principal contestants in the *agon*, Private/Public Gar and his father, begin to move from their cardboard effigies into three dimensions. Then in *To This Hard House* Lily Stone mediates not only for her children but between her husband and that other authoritarian figure, the Inspector (who recedes with the stories until he is readmitted obliquely as the offstage Mr George Alexander, Justice of the Peace, and directly in the English sapper Captain Lancey, both in *Translations*). Daniel Stone is 'proud perhaps, and cock-of-the-walk in a transparent sort of way, but for all that, a simple man . . . a good man'.[14] But both fathers and children have feet of clay. Once again in *A Doubtful Paradise*, the mother-wife, Maggie Logue, breaks off from conversation, or remonstration, with her husband to address *us*, the reader/listener, in the third person:

> (*Inexorably*) And when the family was growing up, I hoped that it would be like the father they would turn out. . . . When he said 'Chris is destined for a business career' it sounded the grandest thing in the world. . . . And Kevin, he was to 'grace the legal profession' and Una was to 'care for the sick'. That's what he said, those were his very words. But they were my children as well as his and although I never said it to myself I knew what was happening all along and I done nothing.[15]

The children, like their father, fail to realise their pipe-dreams, and another traditional Irish theme is born. It is left to the mothers to hope. Jack Frazer's wife tells him 'a woman never gives up hope, Jack, never despairs. . . . You will be content to have the vision of what might have been and you will be safe with that. Even you can't destroy a vision'.[16]

A recently discovered, incomplete copy of a previously unknown play for radio by Friel, *The World of Johnny del Pinto*, provides a curious link with the later work. Dating from *circa* 1960, it is autobiographical in that it opens with a maths class and employs the figures of authority and power of the schoolmaster in addition to surgeon, policeman, bully and monster from outer space. It takes place largely in the unconscious mind of the young boy of the title, whose 'world' consists of phantasmagoria similar to Synge's 'Under Ether'[17] which presage the 'rhapsodies' in *The Loves of Cass McGuire*; and it polarises lies and truth and explores the traffic that can take place between them. When it takes actuality speech from one character and attributes it to others in the fantasy episodes, and creates a mixture of half-remembered reality and an other world, it reminds us of the 'impressionist' techniques of Denis Johnston's *The Old Lady Says 'No!'*. In the maths class, Johnny is required to calculate the square footage of an area between the carpet in the centre of the room and the walls: the allegorical nature of the 'space between', which we have already seen as the vital area in the liminal situation, is highlighted by the teacher's ironic comment: 'The shaded area, yes, that's the problem'.[18] The connection between this aspect of drama-as-ritual and the post-colonial situation is also suggested, firstly by the idea of the child regaining consciousness after his dream-under-ether (a pre-echo of 'stirring in our sleep' *Freedom* 63) and secondly by the victory of the underdog in overturning authority in the shape of the 'Dictator of Venus' – the phrase used is 'the power of the powerless'[19] which predicts Havel. A final comment: the child, his father and his siblings have been left by their mother: is it ironic that the last page of the script is missing, and that the final extant line from the nurse to Johnny reads: 'And when you're up and about on your feet again, Mammy'll. . .'?[20]

There is in these plays, though, a new note unrelated to the themes of the stories: not only do we know that 'this is not a world of ideals',[21] but we are made aware for the first time of the consequences of trying to hold to false or unrealistic ideals, of trying to act retrospectively. All at once the search for identity in memory and past time is ruled out of order.

Those who are clearly being left behind are those whose visual impairment is due to a split perspective between the past (which appears clear and certain) and the future (which is turbulent and threatening). In *To This Hard House* Daniel Stone typifies this refusal to accept the 'consequences' of an irreversible demographic trend. His lack of visual acuity is translated into an inability to deal with physical properties, a natural difficulty in coping with one sensual deficiency, given a clever metaphysical twist: 'his eyesight is not as good as it was. . . . Somehow he seems to be losing his grip. . . . He doesn't seem to have the same clear grasp of things.'[22] We encounter the same negative properties in Manus Sweeney in *The Gentle Island* and in Andy Tracey in 'Losers'. 'Losers' is a play with little dramatic content in the conventional sense. Its monologal scheme derives from its origins as a short story ('The Highwayman and the Saint'). In this sense it has more in common with Beckett's work than anything else Friel has written, except *Faith Healer* and *Molly Sweeney*, particularly in the nihilistic visual imagery which he employs in the opening scene: 'He is staring fixedly through a pair of binoculars at the grey stone wall, which is only a few yards from where he is sitting. It becomes obvious that he is watching nothing: there is nothing to watch' (*Lovers* 51).

When Andy begins his monologue, he makes four statements each fixing his position in relation to the wall:

> – I see damn all through these things.
> – Well, I mean there's damn all to see.
> – Anyway, most of the time I sit with my eyes closed. . .
> – These are his glasses. And this is where he was found dead. (*Lovers* 52)

First, Andy perceives nothing, a situation he rapidly rationalises by shifting the initiative for perception, or lack of it, onto an empty backyard; then the lack of perception shifts back to him again, when he makes another attempt to explain his 'blindness', and finally he appeals to his initiation into a tradition of blindness, in which he refers to his father-in-law, his predecessor in the chair. The sightlessness, the lack of any transaction between Andy and his environment, is described as 'a gesture', but it is obviously an empty gesture, a despairing surrender which negates his previous existence as a lively and inventive suitor.

But vision is double, two-faced. The seventeenth-century Irish philosopher William Molyneux suggested that we see things differently by each eye, and that it is the task of the brain to rationalise these two into a single vision.[23] Double vision implies the ability to live by the power of a truth and, simultaneously, by the power of its opposite, a lie. We see Friel hinting at this in *A Sort of Freedom*, when Jack Frazer tries to exercise the individual's rights in the face of authority by persuading the doctor to falsify a certificate of innoculation for his adopted son: 'it's only a matter of signing your name',[24] and in *Making History* Hugh O'Neill offers to verify his biography on the grounds: 'one of the advantages of fading eyesight is that it gives the imagination the edge over reality' (*MH* 66).

THE STRUGGLE OF LOVE

With *Philadelphia* the mothers and wives disappear and remain points of absent reference until *Wonderful Tennessee* and *Give Me Your Answer, Do!*. Suddenly Friel introduces a series of experiments to replace the mother and to create discussion between fathers and sons, between brother and sister: discussion of the mother's role, her relationship with the father, and of the other relationships, mostly between father and son, in which she had previously mediated. The mothers of the stories, pursed, drawn, anxious, determined, grey, real, have become golden-haired memories, more sinned against than sinning.

By this drastic device, and the recession of other characters (grand-fathers, inspectors), Friel literally clears the stage for the expression of his main themes. That the greatest and most pervasive of these themes is 'love' requires some explanation at this point. In the 'love' plays, which correspond closely to the *agon* in Friel's development, he uses the themes and techniques of his stories and radio plays in order to explore the relationships of the ego, the self and the world, to discover for himself, for the hero at the centre of the play, the system of checks and balances which holds the world together, whether it is the family unit, the whole tribe, or the wide world. This is an emotional rather than an intellectual process. Friel takes the psychologies of his zone and translates them into a personal culture: this is what we receive from him as gatekeeper in the texts of these plays, whereas in his next phase we see him attempting to rationalise those emotional findings, a venture which can be equally catastrophic.

These first plays are 'love' plays because they show very clearly not only the relationships of love between fathers and sons, between siblings, within families, but also the 'images for the affection' which transcend direct relationships and represent a 'culture of communitas', or, as Friel might prefer to put it, a culture of constituency. Within this culture we experience the love which affects, and the love by which we affect others. But it need not be the familiar love known as *eros* or *agape*: it may be equally affective in the whole community through the expression of courage, dignity, memory, nomination or the experience of embarrassment – that is, through 'affiliation'. In this sense all Friel's plays are 'love' plays, but the themes he explores explicitly in the earlier plays are tidied (although not put away) in his later writing, in favour of a more clinical approach to language itself. In fact *Dancing at Lughnasa* revisits these questions in exploring the relationships between five sisters and their separate and collective existences.

In *The Enemy Within* and *Philadelphia*, for example, Friel discusses the difficulties of reconciling the inner life, the saving of one's soul, personal integrity, with the competing claims of the public world, one's family, one's external faith. Columba, the Abbot of Iona, is continually plagued by the irresistible interruptions from his old, familiar, tribal life in Ulster which threaten to destroy his search for spiritual salvation in Iona. Rather than curse his own brothers, whose affective call he must answer, he curses Ireland, as a mother, a *femme fatale*, a place which has taken on all the tragedy of human character: 'Damned, damned, damned Ireland! (*his voice breaks*). Soft green Ireland, beautiful green Ireland, my lovely green Ireland. O my Ireland' (*EW* 70).

In *Philadelphia*, the division of private and public is made explicit by the use of two players to represent the one character of Gareth O'Donnell.[25] The division between hope and disappointment lies in the imagined life that awaits him in Philadelphia, in contrast to the silent war between himself and his father in Ballybeg. This stepping out towards an expectation, or vision, is the religion of ecstasy as opposed to that of control, the placing of one's faith on the edge of the known world.

Somewhat controversially, Friel counterpoints Gar's emabarrassment with two repeated motifs, one the corrupted song 'Philadelphia [California] here I come, Right back where I started from', the other a cryptic reference to Burke's *French Revolution*:

> It is now sixteen or seventeen years since I saw the Queen of France, then the Dauphiness, at Versailles. . . . And surely never lighted on this orb, which she hardly seemed to touch, a more delightful vision. I saw her just above the horizon, decorating and cheering the elevated sphere she just began to move in.[26] (*Ph.* 23, 26, 80)

Its purpose is to offer gratuitously another vision, of grace, beauty and splendour which has been dashed by a senseless world; against it, Gar and his father can measure their own memories, presided over by the vanished queen of their own lives: 'it was an afternoon in May – oh, fifteen years ago – I don't, remember every detail but some things are as vivid as can be' (Ph. 89).

The American vision is familiar to Irish men and women dreaming of emigration in order to escape famine, poverty, rural depression or diseases of the affection, failures of affiliation. To be in America in one's mind and yet in Ireland in one's body, 'chained irrevocably to the earth, to the green wooded earth of Ireland' (EW 21), is part of the bifurcation or schizophrenia of the Irish mind, the ability to be in two places at one time, to hold two contradictory thoughts in congruence, to achieve bilocation of the affections. This 'double–vision' gives rise to two ways of perceiving 'reality', subjective and objective, in symbiotic captivity.

In one's roots one thus finds insecurity, 'unhappy and at home'. But one is still compelled to seek those roots, to answer the affective call, in order, one supposes, to confirm uncertainty: we are 'among the ruins' once again. One interpretation of this is Guthrie's view, in 'Theatre as Ritual', that 'we, with our limited vision, by the feeble light of human intelligence, are unable to discern our origin and must proceed blindly towards our darkly incomprehensible destiny',[27] exploring and invoking both 'sight and blindness, light and dark' in order to do so. It is significant that Friel, who knows this essay well, uses so extensively the theory and practice of vision in his stories and plays, as, of course, Beckett does also. (Guthrie continues in that essay to say 'Evil and Good are not, in fact, different ideas, but the same idea viewed from two different standpoints, or considered in two different contexts . . . Dark and light are not in fact opposites, but different degrees of visibility.'[28])

Between The Enemy Within and Philadelphia Friel wrote The Blind Mice, produced at the Eblana Theatre, Dublin, in February 1963 and subsequently in a radio version by BBC Belfast in November of that year. This is a precocious anticipation of some themes in both Philadelphia and Cass. Like The Mundy Scheme, it is out of the ordinary course of Friel's work because, one feels, he intends as far as possible to refrain from representing the principles of Church and State so explicitly on the stage. The Blind Mice is an attempt to exorcise the memory of the years in which he tested the vocation of priesthood and the experience of seminarian Irish Catholicism. It describes the return home to a hero's welcome of an Irish priest who has been imprisoned in China, which turns into calumny and violence when it is revealed that, in order to obtain his 'freedom', he has betrayed his 'faith'. The play is so symbolic that the martyred priest is called 'Chris' (an abbreviation of Christopher, the Christ carrying the sins of the world) and the spokesman of the

Irish hierarchy is 'Father Green'. Chris is subjected to 'the endless questionings'[29] as Frank Hardy will be later; and he, like Columba, has Christ taken away from him, as he slips out of the emotions into the intellect. But apart from crudely pointing out this dichotomy, the play belongs with the works for radio as a transitional piece.

Perhaps the significance of *The Blind Mice* in Friel's overall development is the fact that, like the story 'The Child', he wishes to suppress it. 'It is far too solemn, too intense, I wanted to hit at too many things. It's a play I'm sorry about.'[30] Quite apart from its crude and hostile characterisation and intemperance, however, *The Blind Mice* reveals more than Friel's admitted reaction to the 'priesthood' and 'the kind of catholicism we have in this country':[31] it also tells us of his preoccupation with the themes of failure and betrayal which he has already sketched in the Columba of *The Enemy Within* and which become the psychological platform for almost all his later work. *The Blind Mice*, in all its rawness, exposes the connection between failure and betrayal, one a condition of weakness which we will find in the Casimir of *Aristocrats* and the Frank of *Living Quarters*, the other a condition of strength which characterises the faith healer and both Hugh and Owen O'Donnell. It is, as Friel put it at the time, about how Columba, and after him Frank Hardy and Hugh O'Neill, 'acquired sanctity. Sanctity in the sense of a man having tremendous integrity and the courage to back it up.'[32]

As a further bridge between the stories and the stage plays Chris Carroll discovers the difference between dignity and respectability: 'I will atone . . . for all the years when I have been priestly instead of being a priest.'[33] More than simply regretting 'conceit, pride, jealousies', he now craves understanding and sympathy for his act of apostasy. But he is told by his confessor that they are 'luxuries . . . Never look for them, because once you think you have found them you become righteous again.'[34] Chris committed an act of despair because God had stopped coming to him: 'I was abandoned! He had forgotten me! He had abandoned me; I abandoned Him. We were quits': the beginning of *deus absconditus*.[35] The fears of the mother are projected forcefully onto the child:

> On the day I saw my straight young man step forward to his bishop and take the yoke on his shoulders I knew then that my prayers weren't ending but beginning. And from then on my heart was torn between pride and fear: pride in the greatest thing God could have done to us; and fear that He would be disappointed. It was like – like carrying you again in my womb, a new mothering.[36]

The death of Chris's faith is also the death of respectability. When the angry crowd cries 'Traitor! Traitor!' we discover that the birth of dignity and individuality is fatal to niceties, to localism and to family loyalty. Chris's brother calls him 'that mask of a man' and exclaims 'don't try to justify treason!',[37] little realising that he has explained the whole play: that we all wear masks, especially when we are most sincere, and that treason needs no apology.

At this stage in his career Friel was no doubt unable, as well as unwilling, to face these tensions any more explicitly than he had in *The Enemy Within*. In this sense *The Blind Mice* was a mistake. *Philadelphia*, with its disloyalty and its description of love-in-an-asylum, had yet to be written, and, as we have seen, he had still to be liberated by the Minneapolis experience with Guthrie. But he continued to pursue two kinds of love which Yeats expressed as 'love of country' and 'love of the unseen life'.[38] One is logocentric, future-oriented, concerned with the public life, full of rhetoric, fraught with exile, ironic and ultimately tragic. The other is mythopoeic, silent, turned towards the past, concentrating on the inner existence, full of poetry, occupied with the sense of 'home'. In the inner life, love is unspoken – 'emotion recollected in tranquillity' perhaps – it is not challenged by Frank Hardy's 'maddening questions' (*FH* 14). But in the outer life love is reduced to mere 'faith' – the submersion of the individual in authority, the extinction of individual vision in favour of the greater vision of the tribe.

But each love is fragile, because neither can live without the other. Love, like the present, like 'I am', is always consigned to transience, it is already passed as soon as uttered; its hand is at its lips, always 'Bidding adieu'; the only permanence on which one can build a reality is where past *and* future are gathered together in a *nunc stans*[39] – the liminality of Janus who looks into both a past-oriented knowledge and a future-oriented desire. From infinite past and infinite future we can thus achieve an infinite present, so long as that equilibrium can be maintained. In that infinite *nunc stans*, as in the case of *Molly Sweeney*, all emotion and all intellect can be contained.

Much of the tension between the individual and the tribe is expressed through the conflict between ecstasy and control. Columba is torn away from the spiritual family of his chosen exile, or ecstasis, by the affective memory of tribal affiliation; Gar O'Donnell doubts the meaning of the journey on which he is about to embark, but the doubts originate in the light of the society he is leaving. In *The Loves of Cass McGuire*, Cass, returning home to 'Ballybeg' after fifty-two years waitressing to 'deadbeats, drags, washouts, living in the past' (*Cass* 19) in the pipe-nightmare of Skid Row, stands outside both memories: those of Skid Row which fixed her mind on the future, and those of the remembered childhood which, until they are proved illusory, provide that future. It is fundamentally important to realise that all her emotions are homeless, because it is in the test-tube of homelessness, when the emotions become restless and start to rampage through the junk-room of memory, that Friel can most effectively explore the nature and – more importantly – the consequences of freedom. Thus in 'Winners' Meg and Joe are leaving their families to commit the tribal offence of exogamy; in 'Losers', Andy Tracey sits downstairs, staring out through binoculars at a blank wall, while upstairs his mother-in-law stares at a plaster saint whose identity is protected by its namelessness. In *Crystal and Fox*, Fox Melarkey, with deliberate courage, dismantles the hierarchy and affiliations of his family, his livelihood and his own identity in order to regain his dream of childhood innocence; and the people of 'the gentle island' cannot come to terms with the 'kingdom' where they have chosen to remain while the rest of their tribe abdicates and goes into exile.

The starting point for understanding all these dilemmas is simple: dreamers and visionaries want to make a better life for themselves. By means of their will they have therefore established a future project in which memory and its affects come into conflict with that which it cannot control. This works on the material and emotional levels, which are interrelated by the sense of family and place. Gar O'Donnell sees neither material prospect nor emotional fulfilment in Ballybeg, but he still doubts that he will find them in the unknown Philadelphia; yet he must go in order to escape the asylum of 'home': it is not just a simple question of flying from the emotional centre in order to make a better life, however stifling that centre may be and however attractive that better life might appear.

The real tension in these plays lies in the fact that in stepping outside one set of rules in order to solve a problem of the affections one sets up new demands and new problems one had not 'imagined'. Love knows neither its own strength nor its own consequences. In this sense each play establishes a heroic stance and each hero faces an inevitable tragedy in failing to silence the 'maddening questions'. There is very little reconciliation or repossession in the early plays which is not contrived and of doubtful validity – the rhapsodies of *Cass*, Columba's 'beginning again' (both Eliotic devices), the deaths of the 'Winners', the nihilism of all the 'Losers' – Andy Tracey, Fox Melarkey, and, in *The Gentle Island*, Manus Sweeney. Possibly *Philadelphia* remains Friel's most outstanding early play simply because he leaves its protagonist in uncertainty:

PRIVATE: God, Boy, why do you have to leave? Why? Why?
PUBLIC: I don't know. I – I – I – don't know. (*Ph.* 110)

– an uncertainty which he partially resolves in the later plays. What Gar doesn't know is the way of answering the maddening questions, making the voices silent, which comes from effective communication. Failure of communication is greatest within the family circle. Neither the mother nor the grandfather is there to carry the child away into an alternative vision, and he cannot speak to his father. Friel's own 'project' is to exercise the will in mediating between the inner 'maddening questions' and the ambivalent visions of the public world, and it is only by establishing a liminality in both worlds that he can gain an equilibrium. But, as we will see in the case of *Making History*, the price of the purchase in each world is to lose the right to live or to love within either, because in order to divine, to civilise, within one, he has to be a peregrine, a barbarian, in the other: always other and between.

Cass McGuire solves this by accepting 'election' (in Eliot's sense) to the otherness of 'Eden House', the 'home' to which her dismayed family consigns her. There, the experiences of the past are transformed into dream, in a rhapsody which is inevitably *verbal* in the telling, but predominantly *visual* in the recollection; it is also of a sensual intensity which suggests that the lost children of Eden House would fight savagely to retain their dream, to retain the right to love.

The rhapsodies in *Cass* from two older inmates and, after her 'election', from Cass herself, are of light, and movement, and touch:

TRILBE: Gordon and I walk hand in hand along the country roads between the poplars . . . in the shafts of golden sun . . . still days of sun and children with golden hair, named after princes and princesses; and we travelled and travelled – Russia, India, Persia, Palestine, never stopping, always moving. (*Cass* 30)

INGRAM: She was eighteen with golden hair as ripe wheat . . . I played the piano and she danced and danced and danced . . . her hair swinging behind her . . . I played faster and faster and faster . . . until her eyes shone with happiness and the room swam with delight and my heart sang with joy (*Cass* 45).

CASS: One Christmas I saw a man on a green sledge in Central Park and he was being pulled along by two beautiful chestnuts . . . a man with a kind face . . . and he looked and he looked at me and he lifted his black hat to me . . . And I stood at the stern of the ship, and two white and green lines spread out and out and out before me (*Cass* 63–4).

'Still days', 'always moving'; Friel has captured here the essence of identity: that is, to know oneself and to be known. He has projected it into an imaginary landscape: to sit in the contrivance of a winged chair in order to deliver oneself of a 'confession' is to take flight into a past which *one can only remember because it never happened*. In his 'Author's Note' Friel emphasises this:

> Each of the three characters who rhapsodize . . . takes the shabby and
> unpromising threads of his or her past life and weaves it into a hymn of
> joy, a gay and rapturous and exaggerated celebration of a beauty that
> might have been (*Cass* 7).

Thus past and future have a fragile meeting point, a feature which we shall
see most clearly in Friel's 'Russian' plays in the constant appeal to hope.

The imprecatory leitmotif, to protect 'our truth', is borrowed from
Yeats:

> But I, being poor have only my dreams,
> I have spread my dreams under your feet,
> Tread softly, because you tread on my dreams.[40]

But into the fragile carapace of these personal treasures Friel makes
savage incisions straight to the heart. The different versions of events in
Cass are killers: Friel avows that the play is a concerto with Cass as
soloist, and Cass fights for her identity by pitting herself against the
memories – and therefore identities – of the others, but eventually
succumbs to the power of the rhapsody. Meanwhile in 'Losers' Andy
Tracey finds himself submitting to the greater truth of the womenfolk –
the worship of plaster saints, conducted by his mother-in-law and Cissiy
Cassidy; Cissy, the spokeswoman for his 'eden' days, says, 'You're
coming closer and closer to us' (*Lovers* 61), but Andy shatters that truth
by smashing the plaster saint. Dreams can be shattered on a much more
mundane level too. In *The Gentle Island* Peter's initial announcement
'My God, it's heavenly' – another pseudo-Eden – has already been
negated by the spectacle of mass emigration. The question of heaven and
hell depends on one's perspective. In *The Gentle Island* Friel uses the
conventional cherishing of the rural way of life, the psychological and
emotional pull of the island, sending up the observance of pieties, as he
does later in *The Communication Cord*. And beyond this he uses the
island as a device for testing out the characters' ideas and fantasies about
themselves.

In *Faith Healer* also we are asked to test memory against time itself.
There is very little corroboration of the alternative truths offered by
Frank, Grace and Teddy; on only two points of 'fact' do they agree: that
they were once in Kinlochbervie, 'in Sutherland, about as far north as
you can go in Scotland' (*FH* 17, 24, 41) and that they crossed to Ireland
'from Stranraer to Lame and drove through the night to County
Donegal' (*FH* 18, 30, 46). But Teddy recalls that Kinlochbervie was
'bathed in sunshine' (*FH* 41), whereas for Grace it rained. In Kinlochbervie
Grace's baby was born and Frank's mother died. No-one is lying. The
details are 'immaterial'. Perceptions are disclosed and thus are shown to

be imprecise, labile, indeterminate. Different ways of seeing love and affiliation, different ways of experiencing love and affiliation, different ways of loving and touching.

Possibly an even more poignant illustration of the failure of memory is given in *Living Quarters*, in Anna's explanation of her affair with her step-son Ben to her husband (Ben's father):

> ANNA (*quickly*): and I tried to keep you, to maintain you in my mind, I tried Frank, I tried. But you kept slipping away from me. I searched Tina for you and Miriam, but you weren't in them. And then I could remember nothing, only your uniform, the colour of your hair, your footstep in the hall, that is all I could remember, a handsome, courteous, considerate man who had once been kind to me and who wrote me all those simple, passionate letters; too simple, too passionate. And then Ben came and I found you in him Frank. (*LQ* 79)

To find a father in a son, to allow a trick of memory and perception to reverse time, is to play not the Oedipal, but the Hippolytan, card, and that is to ask us to look not only at horror and guilt, but also at fantasy, the only-so-slight distortion of ourselves in the world. As we discover in the first scene of *Translations*, a distorted vision, if only slightly at odds with the rest of the world, pulls one's perspective of home, name and means of survival seriously out of kilter. And in the operatic soliloquy in which Hugh O'Neill rhapsodises on his childhood memory of the great Sir Henry Sidney (*MH* 34–5) the one irresistible spur to the intensity of his affections as a Gaelic prince has been put at nought – the time-bomb has ceased ticking. But in these scenes from shattered childhood Friel is not insisting on the re-integration of those worlds – the hedge-school or the island or the Gaelic kingdom: he is, indeed, showing us that, ancient or modern, they represent the island in the heart of everyone who inevitably sets out imperfectly attuned to the greater world.

The most powerful tensions established by Friel in these love plays, therefore, are not those between father and son (private love) but those between the individual and his tribe and place, the 'public faith' of family and extended family. Ballybeg *represents* the affective images of an affiliatory culture moving through both time and place. Everyday Ballybeg, like love itself, is destroyed by violation of its boundaries, and renewed through the rewriting of the texts, its sacred institutes. Sometimes this disintegration is treated with comic sarcasm: at the evacuation of Inishkeen (the Gentle Island) one footless islander asks, 'D'you think the flight of the Earls was anything like this?' (*GI* 14). At others, realistically:

MANUS: Fifty years ago there were two hundred people on this island, our
         own school, our own church, our own doctor. No one ever wanted.
JOE: Scrabbing a mouthful of spuds from the sand, d'you call that a
         living? (*GI* 18)

Homecomings and intrusion, more than departures and exile, highlight
the sense of fragility, the inherent instability, of homes and families: Cass,
Owen O'Donnell, and the family reunions of *Aristocrats* and *Living
Quarters*. In *Philadelphia* it is not Gar's impending departure but the
homecoming of his aunt Lizzie which triggers recognition: up to the
middle of the second episode everyone lives or acts a lie in complicity.
Then Lizzie admits the emptiness of her materially successful life in
Philadelphia:

LIZZIE: And it's all so Gawd-awful because we have no one to share it
          with us. (*Ph.* 63)

Similarly in *Cass* none of the statements about the McGuire family is
'true' until her brother Harry admits in Act 3 that Cass is 'better off' in
Eden House because the family itself has disintegrated: there is no longer
a 'family home', merely a nursing home – one kind of asylum has given
way to another.

Columba in *The Enemy Within* is in a different category, because he is
a displaced person. In his chosen life he is the Abbot of Iona, having
forsaken his Ulster homeland, but the calls of that homeland frequently
make him an exile from Iona. Both families suffer by his absence, and in
a sense he himself is never at home, he is always celebrating or fearing a
homecoming. The community of Iona appears to be fraternal, Columba
'looks for no subservience' (*EW* 16) but in practice when faced with a
dilemma, he acts in one of two ways: either he exercises his authority as
Abbot or he pleads with Grillaan, his prior and confessor, to exercise
authority over *him*. His relations with his siblings vacillate equally
between the authoritative and the submissive: he is either the manipulator or the victim of the lie.

Friel establishes these tenuous relationships and uncertainties in order
to show that 'a man's enemies shall be they of his own household'
(*EW* 20), that the external world is not as dangerous or as precious as
the inner, because it holds neither the same threats and penalties nor the
same hope of reconciliation. Thus a future-oriented love is inevitably at
risk, while a retrospective love must live with all the failures of ecstasy.

The pivotal work which capitalises the earlier experiences of
Philadelphia and *Lovers* and predicts both the later family plays and the
plays of language is *Crystal and Fox* (1968). Fox Melarkey (a clever
linguistic pun combining the restlessness and wildness of the animal with

the insecurity and riddling of the player[41] is a lost cause, a creature who dreams brief glimpses of perfection, and finds it necessary to destroy the world because he cannot grasp paradise. The play is a parody of a play, in which everyone becomes deranged or confirms the original sin of the derangement within them. '"What's my name?" . . . "What am I doing here?"' (CF 12) is the motif of the characters, each of whom is playing some other part in another play. The central impossibility of both action and plot is voiced when one member of the cast denounces Fox: 'I know that character!' Fox's response is non-verbal: *'he hides behind a mask of bland simplicity and vagueness'* (CF 19). The inscrutability hides Fox's desolation because he recognises not only the impossibility of regaining his dream – when he was 'like a king' (CF 22) and Crystal was 'a princess' (CF 24–5) – but also the futility of any kind of action at all. The audiences for his fit-up show pre-echo the hopeless cases who come to the Faith Healer: 'conning people that know they're being conned' (CF 36). It elicits the feral in him: he is 'desperate . . . restless. And a man with a restlessness is a savage bugger' (CF 36). Unlike Manus Sweeney, who is described in similar terms, Fox says this about himself because he has recognised that one cannot measure or balance hope against despair. Crystal says 'We had more courage than sense' (the impetuosity of the lovers) and Fox retorts 'And more hope than courage' (CF 25): if despair, in Friel's terms, is the corollary of hope, then fear is the complement of courage. Fox's revenant son tells him 'you're full of hate' (CF 48), but the only way we can understand that word 'hate', Fox's principal motivation, is by seeing it as the quotient when hope and courage have given way to despair and fear. Fox is left in the fifth province of hate, at 'a signpost pointing in four directions . . . in the middle of nowhere' (CF 55–6), confident of the proof that, in Wilde's words, each man kills the thing he loves. The homecoming that precipitates the final savagery is external: it is nothing compared to Fox's own homecoming to the private void of his central space.

EMBARRASSMENT

Rimbaud and Hannah Arendt suggest that one can understand oneself as another: Rimbaud says *Je est un autre*, and Arendt says that one can only think of, or judge, oneself through a *retour secret sur moi-même*.[42] This we find transcends the father-son relationship. But it also underlines one of the more equivocal themes of Irish fiction, which, if we can learn to read in the interstices of tragedy, tells us that there is no such thing as silent love, even self-love. Friel has managed two significant developments both in his stories and, much more successfully, in his plays. In

Philadelphia, particularly, he has, in conceiving Gar as two personae, expressed the otherness of our conscience and thus used what appears to be a technical innovation as an integral part of his intentions. Secondly, he has, out of his own ingenuity, shifted the traditional emotional balance so as to concentrate on the relation of will to time, a way of dealing with continuity and silence which, due to his peculiar vision, involves following a father into the future, dark indefinite rather than a mother into a golden past pluperfect. 'Say something father!' is, as we have already noted, not only the demand for communication, it is also the imperative which calls into existence, which commands the other to *be*. In order to establish some kind of relationship with his father, Private Gar urges Public Gar to keep talking, if only to coax grudging and embarrassed monosyllables from his father:

> S.B.:   Which tea chest?
> PUBLIC: The one near the window.
> S.B.:   Oh, I see – I see . . .
> PRIVATE: You're doing grand. Keep at it. It's the silence that's the enemy.
>   (*Ph.* 102)

But the initial statement holds good: '*We embarrass one another*' – father and son offend and upset the psychic order of their tribal culture. It is possible, of course, to see *Philadelphia* as 'the tail-end of a bad Irish tradition',[43] rather than opening up new ground. Such a view would see S.B. O'Donnell, and Arthur Carroll in *The Blind Mice*, as successors of the miserable Ulster shop-keeper depicted by George Shiels in *The Passing Day*. (It might also seek to connect Friel's Ballybeg with the 'Bailebeag' which was the setting for 'The Microbe', a rural tragedy which appeared anonymously in *The Leader* in 1940 and contains an explicit but arcadian account of some of the themes explored in *Philadelphia*.[44]) While there is little or no communication between father and son there is, ironically, a sinister form of shared meaning which takes place in the absence of speech. They do in fact have a method of knowing each other, of understanding what is going on, even though neither can define himself to the other. The cry 'Say something father!' is an acknowledgement of a relationship which is no longer totemic, as the father-son nexus was in the radio plays, and S.B.'s gestural communication with his son's jacket, and the antiphonal conversation with Madge about the sailor suit, are both indications of a groping towards that language.

The exile theme is *still* being pursued by Irish writers: Tom Murphy's *A Crucial Week in the Life of a Grocer's Assistant*, premiered after *Philadelphia* in 1969 but in fact written before it, contains the same elements and pathos as *Philadelphia*; it was eventually followed by *The White House* (1972) and, after revision, *Conversations on a*

Homecoming (1985). Murphy's drama, despite the fact that it has taken different paths from Friel's – for example in the violence and anti-intellectualism of what Christopher Murray (after Peter Brook) has called 'rough and holy theatre'[45] – still emanates from the same historical source which makes exile and homecoming also the centre of Friel's drama: dispossession. Spiritual dispossession and emptiness, as a result of physical deprivation in the land clearances in the nineteenth century,[46] fills the cistern of the Irish diaspora and makes Murphy the blatant successor to Eugene O'Neill. But it also makes him a cousin, if not a brother, of Friel. Murphy has said of his *Famine* (1968): '*Famine* to me meant twisted mentalities, poverty of love, tenderness and affection; the natural extravagance of youth wanting to bloom . . . but being stalemated by a nineteenth-century mentality.'[47]

Murphy may write differently about the wounded; certainly he makes little attempt, except in *The Gigli Concert*, to cure them, and he shows them little compassion. But he describes the same creatures. The lost children of *Famine* reappear in Mommo's litany in *Bailegangaire*:

> the wretched and neglected, dilapidated an' forlorn, the forgotten an' tormented, the lonely an' despairing, ragged an' dirty, impoverished, hungry, emaciated and unhealthy, eyes big as saucers ridiculing an' defying of their lot on earth below, glintin' their defiance, their defiance an' rejection, inviting of what else might come or *care* to come! Driving bellows of refusal at the sky through the roof.[48]

Murphy's dispossessed suffer the same embarrassment as Friel's: if there is no yesterday and no tomorrow, there can be no set of shared beliefs, no common cause for social or cultural continuity. There can only be a grinding, self-destructive knowledge of the here-and-now, which makes both Friel and Murphy apocalyptic writers.[49]

We live in a constant state of mutual embarrassment because of our failure to reconcile myth with logic, past with future. We invent the conceit of indifference in order to circumvent, to circumlocute, this embarrassment. Yet just as it seems impossible to keep silence, it also seems impossible to achieve this state of indifference, because the essential condition of our instability is that of *cultural difference.* Just as it is impossible to live without hierarchy, without difference of rank or quality.

Here again, embarrassment is acute in both Friel's and Murphy's work. A community secure in the knowledge of its inner strengths defines itself in relation to its heroes and its heroic myths. In Friel's work the heroes have been deposed: S.B. O'Donnell, because of his failure to speak ritual words of healing, Columba because of his inability to lead, Hugh Mor O'Donnell because his authority and therefore his usefulness have fossilised, District Justice O'Donnell because of the stroke which symbolises the muteness of the tribal tongue. Here Friel, too, shows himself the son of Eugene O'Neill, the author of the afflicted O'Donnells in direct descent from him of 'all the four haunted Tyrones'.[50] Murphy, likewise, shows us the brutal Carneys (*A Whistle in the Dark*), an animal family with no effective, commanding presence; the failure of young men's dreams in the absent father-figure of the publican 'J.J.' (*Conversations on a Homecoming*); and the close parallel of S.B. O'Donnell and Gar in the pathetic father and son in *A Crucial Week*.

When Friel's Gar and Murphy's John Joe (*A Crucial Week*) try to establish a fluency they resort to shouting, trumpeting their failures, their hurt and their unique vision of the non-event: as Murphy says, 'one has to slay one's own town by getting away from it',[51] but one must also return, and Murphy has done this by associating closely with drama in the West of Ireland, as Friel has done in a homecoming to Derry.

But of course Friel and Murphy are both also inheritors of Shaw: Shaw's Larry Doyle dreads his homecoming to Rosscullen, 'that hell of littleness and monotony', because he and his father have nothing in common: 'What am I going to say to him? What is he to say to me?' Below this superficial embarrassment is the shifting ground between two apparently polarised world-views:

> Live in contact with dreams and you will get something of their charm: live in contact with facts and you will get something of their brutality. I wish I could find a country to live in where the facts were not brutal and the dreams were unreal.[52]

In *Translations* Lieutenant Yolland, captivated by that charm, will become a foil to the efficiency of Shaw's Broadbent and to Lancey's 'brutality'; while Murphy sets about much the same business with Betty among the Carneys in *A Whistle in the Dark* and J.P.W. King in *The Gigli Concert*. It is as if they endorse Shaw's, and without a doubt O'Neill's, statement, that Ireland 'produces two kinds of men in strange perfection: saints and traitors'.[53]

The comfortable idea that father and son exert some equal-and-opposite symbiotic force on each other is challenged by silence and strength. Private Gar examines a mythic past relationship:

> On that afternoon a great beauty happened, a beauty that has haunted the boy ever since, because he wonders now did it really take place, or did he imagine it. There are only the two of us, he says; each of us is all the other has; and why can we ever not look at each other? . . . To hell with all strong silent men! (*Ph.* 98)

'Silence', Private declares, 'is the enemy.' He urges Public to keep talking to his father in order to get an admission of complicity in this 'great beauty' that once happened (*Ph.* 102). One cannot survive in symbiotic captivity with a ghost to whom one is also merely spectral.

But it is not only the public discourse which must be maintained, but also the dialogue with self, which is only possible if it tries to evade embarrassment by means of strange, oblique speech:

> An' you just keep a'talkin' to you'self all the time, Mistah, 'cos once you stop a'talkin' to you'self ah reckon then you jist begin to think kinda crazy things'. (*Ph.* 26)

The statement represents an acknowledgement of self, but one in which its inevitable vehicle of language con-fuses the distinction between embarrassment and strangeness. Plain speech would have enabled the embarrassment to survive, whereas this patter fails to resolve it, and simply makes it go away by introducing a new form of strangeness: 'with intimacy', says Steiner, 'the external vulgate and the private mass of language grow more and more concordant . . . Inside or between languages, human communication equals translation.'[54] For Friel, this osmosis between his private and public self is spelt out in the persona(e) of Private Gar and Public Gar; elsewhere, for example in *The Enemy Within*, it is expressed in Columba's self-examination as evident in the title of the play, as well as in his confrontation with himself-when-young in the person of the novice Oswald. Oswald has a preconception of Columba as a saint, 'the man of heroic virtue'. But Columba himself denies this: he says 'young boys need heroes' (*EW* 50–1), an idealised way of projecting themselves onto a public screen. Yet he eventually accepts the need for unity with himself, as revealed through the appearance of Oswald, and a new beginning. But Private Gar bitterly attacks his public self: 'how you stick yourself I'll never know! '(*Ph.* 28).

As we have seen, when Friel was wrestling with the draft of *Translations* he noted in his diary that the play embodied a tension between the public domain and 'the dark and private places of individual souls'.[55] This exploration, which began privately with the stories, through, as we have seen, the techniques of the affection, has at its core the intercourse of the public and private selves. This is exemplified in Columba's inability to identify the eponymous hero of the play, the enemy within, and the impossibility of Gar's *seeing* his alter ego (*Ph.* 12) – in other words the haunting of one's familiar. The development from Columba's attempted dialogue with his hidden enemy to Gar's verbalised encounters with his alter ego exemplifies J.S. Mill's view that 'our internal consciousness tells us that we have a power which the whole outward experience of the human race tells us that we never use.'[56] That power, we might crudely say, is the power of love. In the face of this, some of Friel's characters withdraw so far into the inner hermetic life that the only realities are those of another order. Jimmy Jack Cassie in *Translations* encounters reality only in relation to 'the world of the gods and ancient myths [which] is as real and as immediate as everyday life in the townland of Baile Beag' (*Tr.* 11). Jimmy Jack's commerce is with the sole reality, the mythical. For him life is active but meaningless, whereas for others, such as the inmates of Eden House, it is meaningful but merely contemplative. If love is a fiction, as the whole of *Cass* suggests, then Cass and the other rhapsodists learn to love by coming to terms with their fictive powers.

But the long inward journey of self-realisation of one's alter ego becomes for Friel much more than a retreat to the interior, or even a knowledge of one's intricate relationship with 'Ballybeg'. It rests on the idea that one can in fact become the membrane which separates, but only just, one world from another, and by which those two worlds are mediated into each other. Columba, to his spiritual community, is an 'alter Christus' (*EW* 30), mediating between God and souls, whereas to his earthly family he is an *alter frater*,[57] who mediates between men and God – 'the inner man, the soul, chained irrevocably to the earth' (*EW* 21). It might best be described as 'I live in a world, and another world lives in me.' This is the ecstasy of love in which all time is contained in every moment of time.

Beckett says in *The Unnamable*:

> I feel an outside and an inside and me in the middle, perhaps neither one side nor the other, I'm in the middle, I'm the partition, I've two surfaces and no thickness, perhaps that's what I feel, myself vibrating, I'm the tympanum, *on the one hand the mind, on the other the world*, I don't belong to either.[58] [*my emphasis*]

Remember Hegel. We come back again to the urge to speak, but now it has a more positive, active role – mediation of the *will* – which is, in the Nietzschean terms employed by Arendt, 'to sing the future', not in a quest for truth so much as in a quest for meaning.[59] As Hugh Mor O'Donnell, adding to his son's 'Uncertainty in meaning is incipient poetry' (*Tr.* 32) says, 'confusion is not an ignoble condition' (*Tr.* 67). Thus, in the Irish mind uncertainty and meaning come together in double, or multi-vision, seeing many possibilities rather than one enduring truth. Poetry, rather than rhetoric, is the preferred mode of love.

'I was back there in Tirconaill', says Columba (*EW* 21). *Back* moves him both in time and place, and he imagines, he calls up images from memory. As Steiner says, 'It is not the literal past that rules us . . . it is images of the past . . . Images and symbolic constructs of the past are imprinted almost in the manner of genetic information on our sensibility.'[60] Friel 'translates' this into Hugh Mor O'Donnell as: 'it is not the literal past, the "facts" of history, that shape us, but images of the past embodied in language' (*Tr.* 66).

The 'genetic information' is the power of love, while the images translated into poetry become love itself. There is also an echo of Paul Valéry in all this: like Steiner, Valéry emphasised the problems associated with translating from time into experience: 'the past is a thing entirely mental. It is only images and belief.' *But* Valéry says that we must use the 'time of the mind' – 'the idea of the past takes on a meaning and constitutes a value only for the man who finds in himself a passion for the future'.[61] Friel's future volition, or passion for the future, is contained in the realism of extending Steiner's metaphor: 'we must never cease renewing those images, because once we do, we fossilise'.

It therefore emerges from this reading of Friel's psychology that his 'project' is to translate the mind into the world and the world into the mind; intellect into emotion and emotion into intellect; that the writer's function is not only to celebrate 'Ballybeg' but to transcend the mytho-logical present by judging the past and exercising a will over the future.[62] The pilgrimage he makes from the known centre consists of a journey which in itself has no meaning; it is a journey in which the arrival is all, the homecoming to the transfigured place. This is a uniting of private landscape and public world. In terms of Friel's own craft it is a trans-lation from story-writing to play-writing, to hold the private and public voices 'in one receiving sensibility and craft'. Arendt says that conscience and consciousness are interrelated as thinking and judging, and that this is indispensable to survival. 'The ability to tell right from wrong, beautiful from ugly . . . at the same moment when the stakes are on the table, may indeed prevent catastrophes, at least for the self.'[63] In this process – we come back to that word of healing and humbling – the artist must acquiesce in himself, in anticipation of homecomings which, in Arendt's terms, might otherwise be catastrophic.

4

PLAYS OF FREEDOM

When people have no real life, they live on their illusions
Anton Chekhov[1]

DISPOSSESSION

For Friel, as for Beckett, the compulsion to speak implies the destruction
of the world. For his creatures it means the recognition of their vulner-
ability, the fragility and ambiguity of language itself, the dismemberment
of family and the revoking of affiliation. To be is to fracture, never again
to make whole. To break silence is automatically to begin an odyssey, the
aim of which is to return to silence. Friel marked this odyssey first with a
private conversation, as near to silence as possible, a monologue close to
soliloquy, and then moved, somewhat reluctantly, into a public domain
which the occasion demanded. Now he explores the family and its affects
in more clinical intellectual detail in *Living Quarters* (1977) and
Aristocrats (1979); coming out of the period of the 'love' plays he also
writes his one explicit treatment of the northern troubles, *The Freedom of
the City* (1973), and two others, although widely differing, on 'political'
themes, *The Mundy Scheme* (1970) and *Volunteers* (1975). In *Faith
Healer* he returns to the personal, the monologue, the private discourse,
in an attempt to re-examine the artist's role in, and affiliation to, society,
to find out whether he is a 'civilian' or a 'barbarian'.

Now he discusses *freedom*, the freedom which is known and enjoyed
and that which is simply imagined. Through the concept of freedom he is
able to approach the culture of poverty itself, and thence the issues of
dispossession and repossession. In *The Freedom of the City* Friel sets
about celebrating the type of liberation which marks a release from
poverty, a repossession of wholeness. It is essential to stress that freedom
(*eleutheria*) derives from the concept of movement, free to go as I wish

(*eleuthein opos ero*); clearly, therefore, as Descartes realised,[2] it is not simply a matter of exercising some God-given right; the *will* is central to the idea of freedom, as we see both in this play and in its sequel *Volunteers*.

That one may achieve freedom by an act of will is of course countered by the fact that one may acquiesce in one's own dispossession. The fine balance and distinction between will and acquiescence are examined in both *Living Quarters* and *Aristocrats*, in which Friel shows that the will, and therefore freedom, however absolute they may seem, are in fact hedged about, safeguarded by institutes designed both to translate the inexpressible into reality and to reduce the irreducible. These plays constitute a *pathos* in the sense that the exploration of these boundaries, and the freedom permitted within them, is carried out by the 'volunteers', Lily, Michael and Skinner in *The Freedom*, Keeney, Pyne, Knox and Smiler in *Volunteers*, the Butler family in *Living Quarters*, and the O'Donnell family in *Aristocrats*. It is a struggle against fixed and immovable odds. Within the institutes of boundary, text, icon and tribe they find the measure of their own freedom, the degree to which the will can apprehend space, time, being and otherness, and the extent to which they can acquiesce in the consequences of such an act of will. In *Faith Healer* that exploration is taken further in the *sparagmos* in which Frank Hardy continually hurls himself against the barbed wire of apprehension until, after he has torn himself to shreds, he succeeds in making himself whole for the first time. Once Friel has made some vital homecomings in *Translations* and *Fathers and Sons*, he is able once more to confront this *sparagmos* in the Hugh O'Neill of *Making History*, who fails to achieve or maintain his integrity.

The 'love' plays, with the exception of *Philadelphia*, are not *great* plays: not because they fail to answer any 'great' questions, but because they do not set out to address those questions. They don't rise above, or attempt to rise above, the everyday circumstances which give them life. In this sense they are 'naturalistic' plays in the manner of Chekhov. Naturalism of course gives rise to great drama, and, as I have already indicated, Friel goes beyond some of Chekhov's achievements in taking the normal and regular and ordinary, and uniting it to great themes, rather than addressing those themes directly. This is particularly true of *Fathers and Sons*.

But, in looking at the problem or freedom and poverty as a natural issue of the themes discussed in chapter 3, we are looking specifically at the result of drawing boundaries, of inclusion and exclusion, of delineating 'us' and 'them' in the crudest form, as in the polarisation of the two main 'communities' in Ulster, with a mutual suspicion and antipathy which is much stronger than an antagonism, each with its own omphalos,

text, icons, culture, affections and ways of naming. We are also looking at
the different versions of love, especially the reduction of private *love* to
public *faith*, where it concerns the affiliation of individuals to different
communities and their relations with those communities.

To the Greeks the *barbaros* was a foreigner, a non-Hellene; later the
term was used by any dominant tribe to describe that which was *other* –
rude, wild, uncivilised, uncultured. That the divisions of Ulster should be
seen as 'battle-lines' is a natural result of this polarisation, but the lines
are more recognisable in the mind than on the 'narrow ground', a ground
on which each community is dispossessed by the other, in which it is
impossible for either culture to know its own place with integrity. The
sense of dispossession, although more eloquently and frequently expressed
by the 'Catholic Gael', works both ways, as Louis MacNeice says:

> I was the rector's son, born to the Anglican order,
> Banned for ever from the candles of the Irish poor –[3]

a sense repeated more recently by Longley, Hewitt and Mahon. For
example, John Hewitt's poem 'Once Alien Here':

> as native in my thought as any here
> who now would seek a native mode to tell
> our stubborn wisdom individual
> yet lacking skill in either scale of song,
> the graver English, lyric Irish tongue.[4]

In the 'Gaelic' tradition that dispossession was confirmed in the final
disintegration of the Gaelic order in Ulster in the sixteenth and
seventeenth centuries, a collapse which parallels, and was only partly
caused by, the Elizabethan and Jacobean plantations. The seventeenth-
and eighteenth-century poems of 'the dispossessed' express the loss of
heroes, and also look forward beyond the politically dead present to
redemption in some future age.[5] The achievement of these poets was in
establishing a 'mythological present' in which future hope reflected, and
was kindled by, the lost world. Heaney cleverly expresses the retrospective
vision of this culture in his 'An Open Letter':

> The whole imagined country mourns,
> Its lost erotic
> Aisling life.[6]

Irish poetry seems to have kept alive, through various phases, the
concept and the practice of the homeless mind achieving the cultural
(and eventually political) renaissance of modern Ireland; as Donnacha
Dall Ó Laoghaire's epigram says:

> Loss of our learning brought darkness, weakness and woe
> on me and mine, mid those unrighteous hordes.
> Oafs have entered the place of the poets
> and taken the light of the schools from everyone.[7]

It is worth noting that a century earlier an English poet, with much the same intent, expressed the idea of loss and redemption:

> Of man's First Disobedience and the Fruit
> Of that Forbidden Tree, whose mortal tast
> Brought Death into the World and all our woe,
> With loss of *Eden* till one greater Man
> Restore us and regain the blissful Seat,
> Sing Heav'nly Muse.[8]

One laments the usurpation of hearth-rights and the flight of the philosopher-poets while the other sets about dealing with absolutes – 'to justify the ways of God to men'. Yet although they inevitably use the same paradigms, light and darkness, good and evil, Eden and wilderness, one comes from a culture which accepts the double vision of Janus (*demon est deus inversus*) while the other rationalises out of existence the Satanic proposition 'Evil be thou my Good.'

The flight of the philosopher-poets created the 'hedge-school' atmosphere of continuing an education not only in semantics but in culture and semiology itself. Such schools thus complemented the natural repugnance of colonial subjects towards external authority. We have already seen Friel's humorous side-sweep at this mentality ('D'you think the flight of the Earls was anything like this?' *GI* 14) and we will meet it again in the send-up of his own work, *The Communication Cord*. Here, however, we should note how in *Philadelphia* he uses the image of 'old Ireland' in two perspectives: that of the retrospective Lizzie Sweeney and that of the introspective Gar. America, suggests Boyle, the hopeless schoolmaster, is 'A vast restless place that doesn't give a cuss about the past . . . Impermanence and anonymity, it offers great attractions' (*Ph*. 44). 'Don't keep looking back over your shoulder', he advises Gar. 'Be 100 per cent American . . . Forget Ballybeg and Ireland' (*Ph*. 46–7). Gar accepts this *aisling* of America, because he believes he is 'Free! Free as the bloody wind! Answerable to nobody! All this bloody yap about father and son and all this sentimental rubbish about "homeland" and "birthplace", yap! Bloody yap!' (*Ph*. 81). But there can be no failure, or abridgement, of memory for Gar (such as his father can achieve) because time intrudes too powerfully. As Private says to Public:

> You know what you're doing, don't you, laddybuck? Collecting memories and images and impressions that are going to make you bloody miserable . . .

just the memory of it – that's all you have now – just the memory; and even now, even so soon, it is being distilled of all its coarseness; and what's left is going to be precious, precious gold. (*Ph.* 54, 79)

Friel, through the medium of private discourse, is making an inventory of the affections. The question he poses is whether it is possible to stay outside the sacred circle of those affections without feeling the centrifugal force of their gravity. To have gravity within oneself is quite different from obeying the affective pull of the tribal centre. But to be able to ignore that pull is to become a barbarian, a stranger excluded for his uncouth culture, and worse, a sibling exiled, expelled for his lack of piety, his unwillingness to conform; and worse again, one who is *willing* to leave the tribe, and explore unknown territories. The traditional pattern of Irish emigration to America involved two inter-related elements: sending the young to safe places already established by elder siblings (in this case the aunt), and remitting the next passage money. In both ways the 'old Ireland' is maintained at home and recreated in the new world, a colonisation of its own future.

This works very well on the physical and material level, and to a certain extent on the emotional level, but it ultimately breaks down because it is not enough just to foster and protect a culture: that culture must also be *lived*. The successful encounter between cultures, whether they intend to antagonise each other or not, involves, in semantic terms, a decoding of affects and intentions which is beyond most experience; when this is translated into emotional terms it presents a psychological problem on an acutely embarrassing scale, which throws up inconsistencies that a once homogenous culture no longer has the power to rationalise. As Eugene O'Neill says of Irish America in *Long Day's Journey Into Night*:

none of us can help the things life has done to us. They're done before you realize it, and once they're done they make you do other things until at last everything comes between you and what you'd like to be, and you've lost your true self forever . . . the things life has done to us we cannot excuse or explain.[9]

This is touched on in *The Gentle Island* which Elmer Andrews calls 'a bitterly ironical re-working of certain romantic fictions of the past . . . A demoralised version of the absurdist vision':[10] Manus Sweeney regards himself as 'king' of the almost deserted Inishkeen, and his hero–warrior son, plundering the sea, as 'a prince' (*GI* 20). But to possess, in the light of the family disaffection which is taking place, is not enough. As his other son tells him, 'King of Inishkeen, King of nothing' (*GI* 18). We are left with three choices in order to maintain a precarious grip on freedom: going back completely into the hermetic past, *or* exercising some kind of rational, logical rejection of that past and its myth, *or* (the most extreme choice) a jump into the dark. The first choice is implosive, a negative embrace; the second makes the heart brutal, and calls for painful reconstruction of the incised/excised parts; the third obeys the principle that 'he who hesitates is lost', and demands explosive action, where the jump is 'now or never'.

The underlying factor of all this is the fear of dispossession rather than the desire for freedom, and this is instilled by our knowledge and understanding of the past. Security is only as certain as today's seat by the hearth, today's crop, today's reassuring discourse. Irishmen have traditionally survived by distinguishing a sense of 'the past' from a sense of 'history', by recognising that they are liberated by one and oppressed by the other. If 'the past' is regarded as an empty expanse of time, its potential is immense. It becomes possible to equate 'the past' with 'the future'. The only affects which are 'fixed' are the horizons themselves. But if we look at 'history' as a way of filling up that immeasurable past with quantifiable effects – injustices, inadequacies and failures – then the ideas of self-defeat and oppression, as affective characteristics of time itself, become inescapable. Whether it is military defeat, civil incompetence, lack of juridical or economic prowess, or imponderables such as climate, world wars or the run of the salmon, the notion of time, land and language becomes oppressive, once the events of history are allowed to superimpose themselves on 'the past'. Thus, in the view of history the future, too, becomes impossible. The Irish irony lies in the fact that it is logic, the rational child of history, which offers a course towards freedom, whereas it is the fictive imagination of the past which oppresses by its *embarras de richesses* – a 'precious gold' which denies its own dross.

In order to avoid dispossession and poverty, the people of Friel's plays adopt a variety of stances, but there is little idiosyncracy in their basic behaviour. They make one of those three choices. Few of them, like Meg and Joe in 'Winners', jump into the dark; most remain trapped in the paths of their inescapable consciousness. The 'winners' revel in their loss of sense rather than feel themselves disoriented by it. Meg's wild exuberance, powered by her immensely strong intuition, creates a curious ambivalence – a wounded animal who is yet supreme, on a collision course with fate, welcoming the abdication of status, and the rejection of certainty, embracing risk.[10] Most, however – the 'losers' – find their social currency reduced by blindness, deafness, dumbness, their inability to see the world, to hear the texts, to utter their names. (Meg says, 'I'd rather be deaf than dumb, but I'd rather be dumb than blind', *Lovers* 21.) The eventual redemption of Maire Chatach in *Translations* and that of Cass McGuire is achieved by their acquiring a new vision, a new 'method of replying to inevitabilities' (*Tr.* 42).

LOYALTIES

In his early work Friel's characters escape; *time* regained is in a sense synonymous with *place* regained. In 'Among the Ruins' Joe acknowledges that:

> the past is a mirage, a soft illusion into which one steps in order to escape the present . . .What had he expected to find at Corradinna, a restoration of innocence? A dream confirmed? It had robbed him of a precious thing, his illusions of the past, and in their place now there was nothing, nothing but the truth. (*Diviner* 133–4)

But most of Friel's retrospection is 'golden'; its success lies in the fact that it recreates and therefore, as with Trilbe, renews the images for the affection. The power of 'that time' to command the present images is escaped only by the kind of inner dialogue, close to silence, which eludes most of his characters, but not Frank Hardy or Beckett's Krapp.[11] Beckett captures it in identical terms in *That Time* (1974–5): 'that time you went back that last time to look was the ruin still there where you hid as a child',[12] and in *Endgame*, a few years before the conception of Cass: 'we once went out rowing on Lake Como. One April afternoon.'[13]

Escape into the future is no different; a homecoming has to be a future project of the will. The point of coming home, whether it is physical or metaphysical, is to complete an odyssey which began with leaving home. Chekhov's three sisters want to regain 'Moscow', more a place of the mind than a place on the map; in Friel's case, this was only imperfectly approached until he wrote *The Freedom of the City*, but even here one cannot repossess that which one never possessed. As Eliot says, 'You do not know what hope is, until you have lost it.'[14] For this reason, perhaps, he does not ask us to tread softly on their dreams; the poor of Derry have much more than their dreams, because their dreams are of a state never yet experienced, and beside them they live daily lives of hardship and indignity. They are future-oriented, substituting 'what might be' for 'what might have been'.

These parallel lives of deeply felt indignity, and a dream of an imagined future past, are a form of schizophrenia natural to the 'culture of poverty'. As Oscar Lewis says, 'there is no such "condition" as "schizophrenia", but the label is a social fact and the social fact a *political event*' [*my emphasis*].[15] We must recall Friel's statement that politics is implicit in 'language, attitudes and style'. We thus become aware of two types of despair within the one mind, the despair which energises and the despair which enervates, a struggle to reconcile reality with autism; in the words of the sociologist Dodds, who is adopted from Lewis's *La Vida*, 'the way the poor adapt to their marginal position in society' *and* 'their method of reacting against that society' (*Freedom* 14). It also explains the difference between reality and the perception of reality, which we see in the opening of *Translations*. Lewis calls this the difference 'between what they say and what they do'.[16]

Friel has previously displayed this through Meg in *Lovers* and now particularly in Lily's use of demotic/mandarin vocabulary and syntax. This is Friel's response to the malapropisms of O'Casey's noble citizens, those whose hurt is more than material because through their poverty they have been wounded in their psyche. The ultimate failure is the failure to find any redemptive quality in the death which is inevitable: the failure is as inevitable as death itself, because one cannot stand outside oneself and take the alter id-entity residing in one's schizophrenia: one has renounced that kingdom. R.D. Laing borrows Mallarmé's phrase to explain this, 'l'enfant abdique son extase'.[16] One simply wanders round within the circle of one's inadequate personality, within the ring of one's own enemies, like Columba. There is little hope of the *beau geste*, and one's concentration is limited to the anti-heroic. As we have already noted, Friel has said that 'God is dead', and that the concern of modern drama is with different kinds of conflict.[18] He therefore emphasises the dramatist's concern

> with one man's insignificant place in the here-and-now world . . . to portray that one man's frustrations and hopes and anguishes and joys and miseries and pleasures with all the precision and accuracy and truth that they know; and by so doing help to make a community of individuals.[19]

This is yet another reminder of Friel's artistic determination to remain a spectator, even though it is required of him to participate (cf. *LQ* 16); and therefore yet another instance of schizophrenia. For as he told Eavan Boland in 1970: 'everyone suspects that when the violence does come it will be very short-lived, quite brutal and very ugly and that it will end, and we're keeping ourselves in reserve for the situation which will never evolve'.[20]

The three victims in *The Freedom* (like the sisters in *Living Quarters* and *Aristocrats* and of course in Chekhov's own play) jointly form that 'community of individuals'; in *Volunteers* it is not so much the 'community' of the internees as the solitary figure of Leif, the excavated skeleton, who draws the others together in a community of alternative storytelling – a similar function to that performed by Oileán Draíochta in *Wonderful Tennessee*; while in *Faith Healer* the peregrine figure of Frank Hardy embodies both forms of despair and brings them alive: enervation and energy, that which resigns itself to dispossession and that which goes out to embrace its fate.

The specific form of despair which poverty imposed on the Catholic community of Derry reinforced the connection between religion and

politics. As one of the participants in the civil rights campaign has
recorded, 'nationalist candidates were not selected, they were anointed.
Religion and politics were bound up together, were regarded, indeed, as
being in many ways the same thing.'[21] This was created by two converging elements: the redemptorist martyrdom of Irish nationalism: 'one
learned quite literally at one's mother's knee, that Christ died for the human
race, and Patrick Pearse for the Irish section of it',[22] and the effective
gerrymandering of local elections by the Unionists which disenfranchised
the Catholic majority by denying them houses. The culture of poverty
therefore resulted from the fact that people 'were born into misery and
raised in squalor. They lived from day to day, fighting to tear some
dignity from life.'[23] As O'Neill's James Tyrone would say: 'there was no
damned romance in our poverty',[24] because poverty is the worst kind of
violence. It was made more acute by the fact that they had lost self-
respect through their inability to function as citizens because they did not
have the 'freedom' of the city – midnight's bastards.

Friel has commented on the two aspects of Derry which commanded
his loyalty and coloured his own sense of loss: 'One was of a gentle and
in those days, sleepy town; the other was of a frustrating and frustrated
town in which the majority of people were disinherited.'[25] He was a
member of the Nationalist Party but resigned *circa* 1967 'because I felt
the party had lost its initiative, I felt it was no longer vibrant and I think
this is the reason the conflagration started in Derry'.[26] The Civil Rights
movement became a 'conflagration' because confrontation led to police
and army brutality, to rioting and then to open aggression on the part of
a people determined to win back self-respect by reversing the trend of
exclusion and disinheritance – a desperate, autistic people who inevitably
became, like Manus Sweeney and Fox Melarkey, 'dangerous', prepared to
destroy their own families and affiliates in pursuit of integrity. To destroy
love in the pursuit of freedom is the ultimate tragedy and, perhaps, the
ultimate necessity.

As Eavan Boland has observed, the reaction of northern writers to
political events took the form of a growing awareness 'of a crisis of division
in their communities, and therefore, in them as members of those communities, vulnerable to their incoherences as they had been in childhood
to their values'.[27] 'The earliest play by a leading writer to deal with urban
political violence'[28] was Joseph Tomelty's *The End House* (1944), written
as a response to the Special Powers Act; in the 1960s Maurice Leitch's
The Liberty Land (1965) and *Poor Lazarus* (1969), Sam Thompson's
Over the Bridge and John Boyd's *The Assassin* (1969) were followed by
the latter's *The Flats* (1971). Wilson John Haire wrote *Within Two
Shadows* (1972) and *Bloom of the Diamond Stone* (1973); and Patrick

Galvin's *Nightfall to Belfast* (1973) was the only other significant response at that time to the growing violence, sectarianism and deepening political crisis in Northern Ireland. It seems that the playwrights at that stage were incoherent about the situation, paralysed perhaps by the immediacy and the tragedy of what was happening. (Among novelists, *Proxopera* by Ulsterman Ben Kiely and [dedicated to Brian Friel] *Shadows on Our Skin* by Derry-based Jennifer Johnston, approached the subject, while the cinema has witnessed Neil Jordan's *Angel* and *The Crying Game* and Ken Loach's *Hidden Agenda*.) More recently, work by Dan Magee, Graham Reid, Frank McGuinness, Anne Devlin and her father Paddy Devlin, Martin Lynch, Marie Jones, Christina Reid and the late Stewart Parker have addressed the issue more directly and more successfully (and again, in fiction, work such as Bernard MacLaverty's *Cal*, Brian Moore's *Lies of Silence* and Robert MacLiam Wilson's *Eureka Street*). Gary Mitchell, author of *In a Little World of Our Own* and *Tearing the Loom* (1998), has been particularly identified by Friel as a welcome example of a working-class Protestant playwright emerging to take part in the dramatic debate on the revision of Irish history.[29] The presence of Paddy Devlin's name in this list – or indeed that of Alliance Party politician Robin Glendenning (*Culture Vultures and Politicians*) – reminds us that in the fragmented politics and society of the North (which I discuss in Chapter 5) there is a crossing of boundaries between one discipline and another – the artistic and the social recognising each other as forms and places of behaviour which are both representational and symbolic at the same time. It is surprising, therefore, to find Christopher Murray quoting a line from the play *This is It!* (1984) by Andy Tyrie, Chairman of the Ulster Defence Association and adding 'of all people'.[30] It is also surprising to find a Dublin journalist asking 'Does the ceasefire mean that the writers of Northern Ireland will soon be searching for a theme?'[31] – the inference being that the phenomenon of internecine strife had pushed every other 'theme' off the northern stage, a supposition which Parker's *Pentecost* alone would succeed in dispelling, since it would have succeeded in establishing its own context for its emotional content even if there had been no political background to its actual storyline.

We have already seen how Friel's attitude to the northern troubles changed from that expressed at the beginning of the decade. The focus of, and reason for, that change was the events of 'Bloody Sunday'. In 1971 Friel said that 'I have no objectivity in this situation; I am too involved emotionally to view it with calm.'[32] He also believed that a 'drama' of the north of Ireland was not possible because it required a 'conflict of equals'. In *The Freedom* we can detect a controlled rage which is utterly characteristic of Friel's personal confluence with those events, and yet it further indicates the control he exercises over that part of him which is more citizen than artist. Friel himself has said more recently that, while there has quite clearly evolved a 'drama of the north' which was not in existence in the early 1970s, he wonders 'should it be discussed within about another fifty years', by which time it might be possible to discern 'an aggregate of orthodoxies' – and is 'uneasy about the Good Friday Agreement' in the sense that 'saying "Yes" has become a movement'.[33]

Friel has been silently criticised by the Catholic community in Northern Ireland for his supposed 'failure' to represent their predicament through the medium of the theatre of protest and violence. The implication is that Friel is not engaged in the 'realities' of contemporary Northern Ireland since he locates his plays outside it, in Donegal, and concentrates on relatively private issues rather than the unequivocally public domain which younger writers like Martin Lynch and Graham Reid insist are the proper concern of playwrights.

Like the late Stewart Parker, whose play *Northern Star* (1985) deals with the career of the eighteenth-century United Irishman, Henry Joy McCracken, Friel has preferred to think historically about the problems of Ulster.[34] In only one other play, *The Mundy Scheme* (1969), has Friel paid explicit attention to modern (and in this case *southern*) Irish politics: the play is 'about' the plan to turn Ireland into an international graveyard, by trading on its pastoral, restful image ('France is the recognized home of good food; America is the acknowledged centre of art; Switzerland is the centre of Europe's banking. Let's make the west of Ireland the acknowledged eternal resting place'(*Mundy* 204). But as we have seen, the author's *intention* is to ask: what happens to an emerging country after it has emerged? (*Mundy* 157)

Friel prefers to look at the wider context in order to learn his lessons. As the subtitle to *The Mundy Scheme* emphasises ('May we write your epitaph now Mr Emmet?'), Friel wants to learn whether a nation has emerged, or can in fact emerge, from the collective psychologies of its people: the implications for Derry's search for 'freedom' are obvious.

Moreover, Friel's position as a 'Catholic playwright',[35] a spokesman for the Catholic 'community', as he is perceived by the 'Protestants' in Northern Ireland, and as a 'Derry [and therefore Catholic] playwright' as he is perceived from Belfast and the Republic, makes this doubly difficult. He does not occupy such a position from choice: he disowns it because, as we have seen, he disclaims all loyalty to, and succour from, a 'community' in this sense. But the position has been bestowed on him, however undesired and unjustified, and either to accept it (to follow certain implicit tribal dictates) or to reject it (to step outside the tribe) is a course in which Friel himself is seen to act, to make choices.

Friel's own position, as an artist, is that he must stand aside from the actual events of the conflagration in Derry or Northern Ireland generally, in order to describe the greater freedom of which the Irish psyche is capable. That position, in terms of the implicit criticisms just discussed, becomes his defence. Friel as a supporter of the Civil Rights movement did march against the oppression of the Catholics; his knowledge of the events of Bloody Sunday was gained at first hand. But Friel *the artist* feels he must stand on the sidelines and see himself *as citizen* marching past. It makes him no less conscious of the fact that a war was being waged not only in the North but throughout Ireland. As Seamus Deane says, 'the society he [Friel] had known all his life began to break down, publicly and bloodily'.[36] But in portraying that breakdown in *The Freedom* Friel also tells us of the society which, like that of Ballybeg in *Translations*, had already broken down internally, privately and psychologically. Therefore, it is easy to see why, in 1972, when he was about to meet the first serious challenge of that conflict, by translating the events of 'Bloody Sunday' into *The Freedom*, he was also considering a 'retreat' from the public drama of playwriting to the private fabula of the short story.[37] In the sense that it is a political and military war he has therefore, with one exception, declined to celebrate it or engage in it, whereas to the extent that the same war is cerebral and semantic and cultural he has made it the basis of much he has written since 1969.

There is another sense in which Friel could not wish to involve himself in the drama of sectarianism: that is, the danger that by portraying terrorism one might condone or legitimise it. The IRA death-wish, the use of martyrdom to encourage bloodshed, has historical precedents. The combination of mariolatry, dying for the *femme fatale* and Cathleen ni Houlihan, is a recurrent theme in Irish poetry; the hunger-strike is one political weapon, the ecstasy of the mystical experience ('I see his blood upon the rose'[38]) is another. It thus becomes difficult, perhaps, for Friel to conceive a play as explicit and psychological as Graham Reid's *Callers* (1985) in which the concepts and contexts of both the assassins and their victims are explored, together with their respective views of the central event of the play itself.

Outside the area of terrorism, however, there remains the mutual aggression, distrust and often contempt between the Catholic/Nationalist and Protestant/Unionist communities (if they can be so bluntly polarised) and between predominantly rural Catholic western Ulster and predominantly Protestant eastern Ulster. Both 'sides' of this ideological equation have been in a state of mutual siege. To ease the acute psychological embarrassment which this causes, both sides resort not only to terrorism and covert violence but also to hysterical laughter, to romping about with the evidence of their dis-ease.

In these circumstances it is perhaps not surprising that Friel abandoned attempts at explicit approaches to the 'war' in modern Ulster because he could not confirm any sense of community. If he has a constituency in Derry, or in Ulster generally, he does not believe it to be best served by taking a play out onto the streets like a gun or a petrol bomb. His work is nonetheless political, as we shall see in chapter 6, even though it is oblique: in *Translations* and *Making History* he adopted an archaeological approach, drawing his constituency back to another time – 'that time' – in order to divine something in its present condition. In this way, like Tom Murphy in *Famine* or *Bailegangaire*, or Thomas Kilroy in *Double Cross* and his translations of *The Seagull* and *Ghosts*, his oblique approach to the concrete events of modern Ireland does not prevent him from describing their psychic and moral significance head-on.

Seamus Deane, who has been the principal mouthpiece for the activities of the Field Day venture, refers to the 'disfigurement' of the Derry poor, a psychic disfigurement with an external appearance usually described as eccentricity or nervous affliction, which he only recognised as an abnormality when he left Derry and noticed its absence elsewhere.[39] Friel has commented on the appearance of such disfigurement as one expression of the culture of poverty, a 'divine generosity and energy existing in dilapidation and despair',[40] in which we can recognise some of the symptoms displayed by the *staretsi*, the Russian *idiots* whose serene privacy passes across the tragic landscapes of Tolstoy and Dostoyevsky. Deane himself has addressed the problem of being a dramatist of the Troubles in the following terms:

> Northern Ireland has never been either State or nation, nor has it ever had any consciousness of itself that has not been fundamentally beleaguered by the contrary consciousness that each of the different sects there know the other to possess.[41]

To the extent that Northern Ireland is a polarised society, therefore, it enjoys the double vision of the Irish people, the ability to hold the two sides of the equation in the mind without resolution. This is underlined by Deane's remark:

> our main experience of alienation has been sectarianism; and sectarianism is one of the deepest forms of loyalty. To be alienated from that to which you are most loyal is a complicated fate.[42]

In discussing Friel's own 'response' to the situation Deane therefore sees that

> conscience (derived from one's political and class culture) is always wrestling and often clumsily with an author's elusive tact (derived from his own sense of himself and his language). . . . Brian Friel's problem has

always seemed to me to be the classic one whereby a man must find in a particular crisis its universal implication and is sorely tried by the problem of timing the moment in which he should, in any given play, move from one to the other.[43]

In the sense that *The Freedom* is a play arising from a 'particular crisis' it undoubtedly fails to do this, because although Friel particularises the crisis in each of the three victims, he points the finger of the universal through quite unworthy figureheads: the sociologist, the priest, the balladeer and the television commentator. Lily, Michael and Skinner themselves remain the children of the Bogside, despite their claim for the solidarity of the Civil Rights campaign. It certainly does not serve the cause of a community at war to recapture its name and identity, however eloquently it expresses their predicament. He would no doubt adopt the broader and more dispassionate vision of Conor Cruise O'Brien: 'we are . . . forced to think, in our village, whatever its exact boundaries, about the relation of violence to our prevailing myths, to our past history, and to the condition of our society'.[44]

'Violence is terrible, but it is not inhuman', says Thomas Kinsella. 'In political terms it is the final response to unredressed injustice.'[45] Violence is of course done – inflicted and suffered – in *The Freedom*, but Friel is addressing more far-reaching themes. In this sense, it was a 'Field Day' play before its time. Like an American sheriff he is pursuing the bandits of memory across the border not only of space but also of time, seeking in Donegal the causes and cures of violence done to the Irish psyche much longer ago. For many years he worked on the play about Hugh O'Neill which became *Making History*: 'that was a very significant time for Ulster, that was when the first broad primary colours were splashed on the canvas. And what happened then is still exercising us':[46] it is the fact that those colours are still being splashed – especially the implications of the theme of love versus faith, trust and betrayal – that hindered the fulfilment of that play, at least until *Fathers and Sons* had helped to clear the decks.

The plantation of Ulster turned everything on its head and created, or made explicit, many of the dichotomies in Northern Irish society. It is not therefore surprising that Friel's archaeology, first in *The Freedom* and then *Volunteers*, turns itself upside down, subverts time and place in *Living Quarters* and appearance and perception in *Aristocrats*. The 'victims' of *The Freedom* receive the 'freedom of the city' but they are denied freedom from their poverty; they live and die within its institutes. The whole play demonstrates their servility and therefore the irony of 'freedom'. Friel wrote *The Freedom of the City* and not a play about 'Bloody Sunday'; and he wrote *Volunteers* without telling us for which crime the prisoners had been interned or the nature of their imminent death, because in both cases he was not prepared, either as citizen or artist, to describe such forms of '"institutionalized violence" . . . the more antique and atavistic parts of the repertoire of legitimation', as Conor Cruise O'Brien describes it.[47] Nevertheless the play can, according to one observer, 'so easily reinforce hatred and prejudice',[48] a reference to an uncritical reception of a poor production by an embittered and partisan Derry audience.

The Freedom of the City, like Kinsella's 'Butcher's Dozen', was 'not written in response to the shooting of the thirteen dead in Derry' but 'in response to the Report of the Widgery Tribunal'.[49] Kinsella refers to 'Lord Widgery's cold putting aside of truth . . . with injustice literally wigged out as Justice.'[50] If Friel responded by setting *The Freedom* at a different time (1970), in a different part of the city (the three marchers find their way into the Guildhall, which had been the original objective of the Civil Rights march on Bloody Sunday), it could not have been written without either Bloody Sunday itself or the Widgery Report.

The real life Widgery Report made the following statements:

> – that soldiers could only fire at a person carrying a firearm or similar weapon;
> – that none of the thirteen men shot dead was shot while carrying a firearm (although one of them was later found to have had nail-bombs in his pocket);
> – that although the individual decisions of soldiers as to whether or not to open fire ranged from 'a high degree of responsibility' to action which 'bordered on the reckless' this reflects 'differences in the character and temperament of the soldiers concerned' and did not invalidate the standing order under which they operated.[51]

Friel uses the inherent contradictions in these statements in the fictitious tribunal which dominates the action of *The Freedom*. He thus counterpoints the tribunal's 'objective' approach with the 'subjective' text required in order to make 'sense' out of the whole event and its hinterland of hope and despair. But beyond this he allows us the most valuable spectacle of all, the sight of inconsistencies being hammered into a unity in order to validate our preconceptions. In this sense there is a very compelling connection between the 'inherent contradictions' and the process which has at its centre a search for unity or meaning. This is a liminal condition, epitomised not so much by the marches which culminated in the events of Bloody Sunday as in the symbolic crossing of the threshold into the Guildhall – an action so unthinkable in actuality that its symbolism increases in inverse proportion to its practicality. As Victor Turner wrote of the social process of separation: 'symbolic behaviour signifying the detachment of the individual or the group from either an earlier fixed point in the social structure or from an established set of cultural conditions'.[52] Thus the completely unreal situation in which Lily, Michael and Skinner find themselves cuts them off from their individual backgrounds and from the collectivity of the march (on the relevance of which they cannot, in any case, agree) and places them in a crucible in which they can undergo a transformation of their own. (Turner further observes: 'people have a real need . . . to doff the masks, cloaks, apparel and insignia of status from time to time even if only to don the liberating masks of liminal masquerade'[53] – a telling insight into their use of the mayoral insignia.) As Elizabeth Hale Winkler has pointed out:

> in both cases soldiers and policemen were allowed to give testimony under pseudonyms. And the grotesque results of the paraffin tests, ambiguous at best, are also taken directly from reality . . . As in the Report, Friel's Judge discounts the evidence of photographers and eye witnesses, subtly discrediting [the priest] who told the 'truth as he knew it' (*Freedom* 49) (cf. 'truth as he saw it' *Widgery Report* 13).[54]

Friel makes the judge's opening statement the basis for the different 'versions' or perceptions of 'reality': 'these three people came together, seized possession of a civic building, and openly defied the security forces' (*Freedom* 13). Since in the course of the play we 'know' from the evidence of our own senses that Lily, Michael and Skinner 'came together' only by complete coincidence, that they did not 'seize possession' of the Guildhall but only stumbled into it by the same coincidence that connected them in Guildhall Square, and that they only 'defied' the army's order to leave the building through ignorance and ineptitude at dealing with such situations, it is clear that two separate truths are emerging during the play. The final verdicts represent the two ways of living in Northern Ireland, either for or against authority and its implicit oppression of minorities and the individual.

Friel similarly uses Oscar Lewis's *La Vida* to provide sociological 'evidence' from another figure who appears outside the central drama of the Guildhall. But whereas the Widgery Report enables Friel to subvert an unjust text in order to make a statement about the nature of truth, the subversion of Lewis amounts to an unsuccessful attempt to universalise the condition of poverty: where Lily in her own eloquent way expresses that condition emotionally, the speaker Dodds is expected to do so intellectually.

It is possible, judging by the syntax of the following definition by Lewis, that Friel had already made use of Lewis's central idea in discussing the term 'peasant' as noted earlier:

Throughout recorded history, in literature, in proverbs, and in popular sayings, we find two opposite evaluations of the nature of the poor. Some characterize the poor as blessed, virtuous, upright, serene, independent, honest, kind and happy. Others characterize them as evil, mean, violent, sordid and criminal . . . Most frequently the culture of poverty develops when a stratified social and economic system is breaking down or being replaced by another, as in the case of the transition from feudalism to capitalism or during periods of rapid technological change. Often it results from imperial conquest in which the native social and economic structure is smashed and the natives are maintained in a servile colonial status, sometimes for many generations. It can also occur in the process of detribalization . . . The most likely candidates for the culture of poverty are the people who come from the lower strata of a rapidly changing society and are already partially alienated from it.[55]

Friel tries to incorporate much of Lewis's thesis into Dodds's three main speeches (*Freedom* 14–16, 39–42, 72–3), but to lift the text verbatim would have been an unwarranted interpolation into the action with no dramatic content. It is significant that Lewis's thesis remains implicit in Friel's thinking rather than fully-fledged in his play. This is especially true of his observation that poverty has its own security, a view made explicit in Lily's conversation. Lewis says:

As an anthropologist I have tried to understand poverty and its associated traits as a culture or, more accurately, as a subculture with its own structure and rationale, as a way of life which is passed down from generation to generation along family lines. This view directs attention to the fact that the culture of poverty in modern nations is not only a matter of economic deprivation, or disorganization or of the absence of something. It is also something positive and provides some rewards without which the poor could hardly carry on. The culture of poverty is both an adaptation and a reaction of the poor to their marginal position in a class-stratified, highly individuated, capitalistic society. It represents an effort to cope with feelings of hopelessness and despair which develop from the realization of the improbability of achieving success in terms of the values and goals of the larger society. Indeed, many of the traits of the culture of poverty can be viewed as attempts at local solutions for problems not met by existing Institutions and agencies because the people are not eligible for them, cannot afford them, or are ignorant or suspicious of them . . . The culture of poverty, however, is not only an adaptation of a set of objective conditions of the larger society. Once it comes into existence it tends to perpetuate itself from generation to generation because of its effect on the children. By the time slum children are age six or seven they have usually absorbed the basic values and attitudes of their subculture and are not psychologically geared to take full advantage of changing conditions or increased opportunities which may occur in their lifetime.[56]

Even though Dodds's speeches are monological addresses to the audience, they fit within the mediaeval structure of a play which consists of a number of set tableaux linked by a series of textual catwalks which interpret contemporary events by reference to history lessons.

The Freedom of the City opens with a Kafkaesque setting – a judge high up on the battlements of Europe's last walled city, while various witnesses appear below him. The Judge sets out 'the law', the rules within which 'the play' of the tribunal will be conducted, and against the 'logic' of which the three 'volunteers' argue. In the words of the Widgery Report, the official British Government enquiry into the events of 'Bloody Sunday', 'it was essentially a fact-finding exercise', not a social survey, or concerned with making moral judgements, even though the analysis of poverty provided by the academic foil, Dodds, does indicate the need to consider the events of Bloody Sunday in the light of the moral and material poverty of the Derry minority. The judge sets further limits, not to the facts but to the arguments acceptable to the tribunal: the purpose of being in the Guildhall, and the question of whether or not they were armed, which are, he suggests, 'different aspects of the same question'. Conversely Dodds, the sociologist-ex-machina, provides different arguments from a theoretical viewpoint, to explain what has happened: he points out that the culture of poverty is not just an economic condition, but also 'a social and psychological condition', in which one feels inferior, marginal, helpless, dependent, resulting in 'inability to control impulse'. The impoverished man 'is present-time orientated . . . endures his here and now with resignation and frustration' (*Freedom* 39) which, despite its negative aspects, sharpens 'one's attitude for spontaneity and for excitement, for the appreciation of the sensual, for the indulgence of impulse. To live in the culture of poverty is, in a sense, to live with the reality of the *moment*' (*Freedom* 42).

The humour with which Lily and sometimes Skinner treat their situation is evidence of the spontaneous, excited, impulsive culture described by Dodds. Despite the by now expected plea for 'dignity' which Friel utters through the third, Michael ('this isn't my idea of a dignified peaceful protest', *Freedom* 45), through the priest ('a peaceful, dignified movement', *Freedom* 65), and the RTÉ commentator ('I think the word would be dignified', *Freedom* 78), they live their life, and face their death, in the manner of the *morituri*: as Dodds says of the poor: 'they become more and more estranged from the dominant society. Their position becomes more and more insecure. They have in fact no future. They have only today. And if they fail to cope with today, the only certainty they have is death' (*Freedom* 73).

The priest underlines this disinterested analysis in his role as 'spokesman' for the dead, a function now traditional at funerals of both persuasions in Northern Ireland:

> they died because they could endure no longer the injuries and injustices and indignities that have been their lot for too many years. They sacrificed their lives so that you and I and thousands like us might be rid of that iniquitous yoke and might inherit a decent way of life. And if that is not heroic virtue, then the word sanctity has no meaning. (*Freedom* 31)

In other words, the culture of poverty means that poverty kills. But behind this we can hear the words of Grillaan, Columba's confessor: 'You are a priest not a rallying cry!' (*EW* 32).

Dodds warns that the society in which the poor are marginalised is 'highly individuated' (*Freedom* 14). That provides us with an important key to *The Freedom* because, while ostensibly the three occupants of the Guildhall, the 'nerve-centre of Londonderry' (*Freedom* 57), have a common bond and culture of poverty, they have no common *purpose* or *will* (except in so far as they serve that of the author). In fact the deaths of Lily, Michael and Skinner illustrate the distinction drawn earlier between the choices open to us in facing fate – the mythic, the logical and the impulsive – because each particularises the condition of poverty.

Superficially the three characters want to make a better world for themselves, an ambition they share with many of Friel's earlier heroes, but an ambition which we might find difficult to reconcile with the condition of resigned frustration: one *can* will oneself into submission and failure, for example, in that we may acquiesce in loss in order to experience the thrill of search and recovery. Skinner alleges that the Civil Rights movement in Derry was part of a universal awakening: 'It's about us, the poor, the majority, stirring in our sleep' (*Freedom* 63). So the exhortation 'This is your city! This is your city!' (*Freedom* 15) (which we can imagine in the voice of Bernadette Devlin-McAliskey[57]) can be regarded as a universal call. But the Civil Rights position in Derry in many ways overrides the general characteristics of the 1968 revolution, however typical it may have been of that movement.[58]

Lily's humour, which carries the play, is more than a spontaneous wit, because it is also used to mask the preoccupation with the grimmer side of being poor: survival. Her concern is to fill, or make less empty, the stomachs of her eleven children, to avoid the shopkeeper when credit goes too high, to maintain appearances; she puts on her good coat to go marching. She is full of the culture of protest; she knows how to cope with the effects of gas and rubber bullets, where to stand at meetings and how to respond to speeches. But the Civil Rights marches are not a means to an end; they are part of a culture, a Saturday afternoon out. Long after it has been achieved, she still marches for 'wan man, wan vote' (*Freedom* 62) and an end to gerrymandering. Eventually the truth comes tumbling out, as it has for Lizzie Sweeney and Harry and Alice McGuire and the narrator of 'The Illusionists':

> He's not just shy, our Declan. He's a mongol. And it's for him I go on all the civil rights marches. Isn't that stupid? You and him and everybody else marching and protesting about sensible things like politics and stuff and me in the middle of you all, marching for Declan. Isn't that the stupidest thing you ever heard? Sure I could march and protest from here to Dublin and sure what good would it do Declan? Stupid and all that I am I know that much. (*Freedom* 64)

But she is in fact marching in order to win a kind of freedom for Declan. Lily, like Maire Chatach in *Translations*, is one of Friel's most successful creations, and certainly one of those to whom we feel the greatest sympathy as she assumes the autism of her tribe. In her death, which she tells us she knows 'instinctively, the way an animal knows' (*Freedom* 58) a momentary panic is

> succeeded, overtaken, overwhelmed by a tidal wave of regret, not for myself or my family, but that life had somehow eluded me. And now it was finished; it had all seeped away; and I had never experienced it . . . because never once in my forty-three years had an experience, an event, even a small unimportant happening been isolated, and assessed and articulated. And to feel that this my last experience, was defined by this perception, this was the culmination of sorrow. In a way I died of grief. (*Freedom* 58)

Life, through poverty, has robbed her of meaning. Because Friel has developed his device, first used in *Lovers*, of splitting time to foreshadow death, so that the dead themselves speak, Lily's last two sentences take their place among the most poignant in literature: *The Freedom* in its unfolding is not so much a study of poverty as a tragic attempt to celebrate grieving bewilderment.

Michael, by comparison, is trying to rise above the subsistence level, both mentally and physically. He has lost the insouciance, the spunk of poverty, his frustration has been channelled into orderly protest (he sees it as 'a good, disciplined, responsible march', *Freedom* 35); he respects the symbols of authority, he is confident of the effective way to retain his rights, and that is silence:

> that was really impressive, all those people marching along in silence, rich and poor, high and low, doctors, accountants plumbers, teachers, bricklayers, all shoulder to shoulder, knowing that what they wanted was their rights and knowing that because it was their rights nothing in the world was going to stop them getting them. (*Freedom* 35)

(Skinner's response is 'Shite'.) Michael pities what he considers to be Lily's ignorance of the true aims of civil protest, and he objects to Skinner's manner. He is baffled by Skinner: 'I don't know what you think you are up to. I don't know what sort of game you think this is' (*Freedom* 45), and he never deviates from the belief, the rational belief in the face of the irrational fate which awaits him, that: 'As long as we don't react violently, as long as we don't allow ourselves to be provoked, ultimately, we must win', (*Freedom* 48). Michael 'knows' something which he cannot in fact 'know': 'There is no question of their shooting. I knew they weren't going to shoot. Shooting belonged to a totally different order of things' (*Freedom* 58). As Simon Winchester, a journalist with *The Guardian* who was covering the Bloody Sunday march, said: 'the killing of thirteen civilians by soldiers seemed to belong both to another age and another country'.[59] Conversely, Milton Shulman's verdict on the play, that 'perhaps one has to be an Irishman to believe that this is a credible and just interpretation of events in Ulster'[60] highlights the dichotomy between Ireland being an 'other country' in the imaginative sense and polarised against a British 'interpretation' in the factual sense.

Michael dies in bewilderment, apparently thinking that the 'terrible mistake' was some kind of waste: 'That was how I died, in disbelief, in astonishment, in shock. It was a foolish way for a man to die' (*Freedom* 58). The attempt at reason, at staying within the boundaries, has failed.

Skinner, Lily reckons, 'never had no mother to tan his backside' (*Freedom* 38). He never submits to orthodoxy, respects nothing, fears nothing, mocks all. He is a 'vandal', a 'hooligan', the agent of the 'sacrilege' on this 'holy of holies'. But he is also the agent of repossession. He initiates the others into the 'freedom of the city', he organises the masquerade in the mayoral robes, plays the role of the Lord Mayor, puts on an 'antic disposition', makes the claim 'allow me my gesture' (*Freedom* 73). He, of the three, has nothing to lose, but he recognises, unlike the others, that they cannot win because they are incapable of 'a solemnity as formal as theirs [the army's]' (*Freedom* 58).

In terms of military strategy the three were always in a no-win position:

BRIGADIER: My lord, they emerged firing from the Guildhall. There was no possibility whatever of effecting an arrest operation. And at that point we understood they were the advance guard of a much larger force.

JUDGE: Had you known . . . that there were only three terrorists involved, would you have acted differently?

BRIGADIER: My orders would have been the same my lord. (*Freedom* 41)

Did Friel, or Derry, send them out to be shot? On the surface it would appear that Friel is turning away from the world of naturalism as it has been practised in the 'Irish' theatre by Shaw and O'Casey, avoiding perhaps the inevitable caricature which even in 1973 might have been implied. But in this exchange between judge and brigadier I detect a reading from between the lines of, possibly, *Arms and the Man*, and certainly *Juno and the Paycock*. In fact Friel is not turning away from the genre, but turning it on its head, showing that figures of authority have feet of clay, while those of the gutter have not only dignity but a valuable sense of living. But Friel has discovered that he cannot liberate this world: he cannot, as a dramatist, will it to be free, because finally he cannot involve himself in its laughter.

As a response to inevitability, is Skinner's defensive anarchic flippancy any more effective than Lily's grief or Michael's bewilderment? Probably we will not be able to answer these questions until we have a wider class base in Irish drama generally, and a clearer understanding of the socialist role in the attempts to solve the Northern (and the ubiquitously Irish) crises of identity. We can, however, note the mutual embarrassment of the two communities in Derry, which results from the cultural and economic imbalance in the overall society, and which in itself, because of incomprehension and suspicion, serves to reinforce reciprocal siege mentalities, to which Derry's topography naturally lends itself.

Skinner's masterly caricature of the council meeting (*Freedom* 68–9) is neither mimicry nor travesty: it is more an enactment, symbolic, mimetic, but also *real*. This is not so much 'Skinner' as, to give him his full, 'proper' name, Adrian Casimir Fitzgerald, as he would be called if this were an official occasion, taking over. The only thing 'wrong' is that the wrong people are taking part in the transaction, people who should not be there, but *are* there. There is a certain foundation in history in Skinner's antic gesture. As Eamonn McCann records, the gerrymandered Corporation

> was the living symbol in Derry of the anti-democratic exclusion of Catholics from power . . . After the mayor abandoned his chair and adjourned one Corporation meeting, Finbar Doherty (Derry Housing Action Committee) vaulted from the public gallery into the chamber, installed himself in the mayoral chair, declared himself First Citizen, and issued a number of decrees.[61]

But there is also a pathetic side to their regard of themselves as 'distinguished visitors' – Lily's tipsiness, caused by their use of the mayor's hospitality cabinet, is an alcoholic answer to the fact that they know their dreams are empty.

It would be easy to read *The Freedom* as a metaphor of Northern Ireland (just as *Translations* looks not only forward to the present situation but back to the plantations of the seventeenth century and the aftermath of *Making History*). *The Freedom of the City* is dangerous enough as a play which we know to be 'inspired', energised by the events of Bloody Sunday. It is, however, necessary to infer that the play's *engagement* in Northern Ireland, the mutual embarrassment of the minority and the administration, questions the neutrality of the Irish mind, and, by extension, the neutrality of the Irish state in relations with its neighbours.

In such circumstances its artists cannot be neutral. Ulick O'Connor has drawn attention to Yeats's membership of the Irish Republican Brotherhood, in a lecture which locates Friel's writing of both *The Freedom* and *Translations* in the tradition of the *écrivain engagé* identifying in his characterisation the various forces lined up in a post-colonial struggle.[62] But we cannot rely entirely on the engagement as specifically and exclusively local and temporal, because the artist can never be intrinsically and totally part of the situation he describes. Against the image of the *écrivain engagé* we must in any case juxtapose that of the gunman *malgré lui*, the dilemma posed by O'Casey in *The Shadow of a Gunman*. 'In this play', says Frank McGuinness, 'O'Casey reminds every Irish writer they are present at such talks [with gunmen] whether they like it or not.'[63] And at such talks gunmen and poets become interchangeable, as each tries to see the other side, to adopt, however briefly, the other's stance. The shadow of a gunman is an inadequate member of his country's infantry. The shadow of a poet is worse, for failing to provide the right marching songs, since, as O'Casey reminds us, all confrontation leads to war. The inadequate poet is 'a poltroon',[64] and, again illustrating the dilemma of the artist of a community, 'a poet's claim to greatness depends upon his power to put passion in the common people'.[65] In the case of Friel, this is an unresolved dilemma.

Metaphysically, too, Ireland is in conflict with its conscience in the discrepancy between its experience and its decoding of history. As Victor Turner points out:

> in everyday life people in tribal societies have little time to devote to protophilosophical or theological speculation. But in protracted liminal periods, through which everyone must pass, they become a privileged class . . . with abundant opportunity to learn and speculate about what the tribe considers its 'ultimate things'. Here we have a fruitful alienation of the total individual from the partial persona which must result in the development, at least in principle or potentially, if not always in practice, of a total rather than a partial perspective on the life of society.[66]

LAYING GHOSTS

Friel sends people out to their fate. A few find their way back; most are hostages to fortune. The distinction lies between those whose odyssey is simply a voyage of discovery and those for whom it is a quest of *re-*

discovery, a recovery of a holy grail, a golden fleece, a golden-haired mother, freedom, poetry, time. 'Having set forth from that place, it was only natural I should return to it', says Beckett's 'Unnamable'. This journey from silence to silence is of course an impossible one: the exile, whether or not he is the author of his own expulsion, can never penetrate the *same* centre again. 'The man who returns will have to meet the boy who left.' This journey of self-discovery, to pursue Beckett's thought a little further, 'to know what I am, where I am, and what I should do to stop being it, to stop being there', is a destructive process: 'to depart into life, travel the road, find the door, find the axe'. In dramatic terms 'the search for the means to put an end to things, an end to speech, is what enables the discourse to continue'.[67]

Volunteers pursues what may seem a relentless but remorseful discourse by providing a bridge, for the critic at least, between *The Freedom* and *Faith Healer*. Seamus Heaney has rightly criticised a reviewer who greeted *Volunteers* as a response to 'the great dramatic subject of internment'.[68] While *The Freedom* was a deliberate and risky response to the events, or at least the aftermath, of 'Bloody Sunday', *Volunteers* has little to do with internment. Its metaphor is digging, and its purpose is in sifting the layers of meaning which separate reality from the perception of reality. *Volunteers* may seem a 'problem play', because, as Heaney notes, it 'involves an alienation effect but eschews didactic address',[69] a formula Friel interposed in *The Freedom* as a solution to this particular difficulty.

The key to *Volunteers* is Keeney who, like Skinner, acts the Hamlet in his antic disposition ('the public mask of the joker' *Vol.* 17). He asks 'was Hamlet really mad?' (*Vol.* 83) and ironically sums up his carapace as 'the carefully cultivated armour of a shy man' (*Vol.* 80). Like Skinner he might ask 'Allow me my gesture', but he goes far beyond gesture. Keeney initiates the play-acting which reveals the different perceptions of the 'volunteers' towards the symbolic skeleton of their 'pal', the Viking Leif who bears a striking resemblance to, or affinity with, Heaney's 'Tollund Man'. The explanations of Leif are told through the perennial medium of 'that time':

KEENEY: 'once upon a time', keep up the protection of the myth, (*Vol.* 62)

and they occupy three main 'versions' of personal truth: Leif is a young adventurer who marries outside the tribe; he is a lost child of a merchant prince; and a slave who served other men until, his usefulness exhausted, he was thrown away. In any case, he died a 'ritual victim' and the unchanging element in his biography, as told by the surrogate archaeologists, is that he was a voyager and that, whether knowingly or unwittingly, he acquiesced in his own death.

Keeney, like Skinner, takes no heed, his comedy is black but alive. His poverty is not an impediment but a key to the door into the dark: 'I'm feeling reckless, no, not reckless, wild . . . an almost overwhelming sense of power and control and generosity and liberation . . . anarchic' (*Vol.* 56–7). Heaney saw *Volunteers* as

> a vehicle for Friel's quarrel with himself between his heart and his head . . . more about values and attitudes within the Irish psyche than . . . about the rights and wrongs of the political situation . . . he means, one presumes, to shock. He means that an expert, hurt and shocking laughter is the only adequate response to a calloused condition.[70]

Those words apply even more appositely to the third of Friel's 'problem plays', *Faith Healer*, which succeeded the two plays he wrote after *Volunteers*. If I categorise *The Freedom*, *Volunteers* and *Faith Healer* as 'problem plays' it is because he sets up this inner conversation, the call on the most fearful part of our psyche, in order to engage us in the discourse of the informer. The visual metaphor is that of 'Come here till I whisper in your ear',[71] the genre of the short story, the confessional, the informer, the betrayal of the neighbour or of the self, the destructive ego, bred out of servility and fear, which presages abandonment of the text and the death of the heart; and with betrayal, laughter.

Of course Friel offends and shocks: the spectacle of self-destruction is as seductively dangerous today as it was when *Hamlet* was written. To pursue a little further the Hamlet image which Friel himself has set up in Gar, Skinner and Keeney:

> Let the stricken deer go weep,
> The hart ungallèd play,
> For some must watch, while some must sleep,
> Thus runs the world away.

Friel is about the business of dismantling realms and exposing peacocks;[72] he is self-consciously 'other', the *destroyer* of love, freedom and language in order to know himself as the *creator* of love, freedom and language. His faith healer, his diviner, is the instrument through whom he examines his role as an artist in the public world; and the poetic language he adopts, even in the persona of Hardy's Cockney manager, Teddy, is a device in that he permits himself the luxury of questioning language itself, the tendency inherent in words to slip, the distinction between being and knowing, between knowing and meaning; am I a healer or a destroyer? He cuts, with his mockery, into the conscience of kings and courtiers and peasants; the wounded surgeon plies the steel in his search for wholeness, and silence, and thereby questions the nature of freedom itself.

Friel's intention is to keep stage directions to a minimum (*FH* 9) but the play, because it is so personal, is so highly structured that in fact he interposes himself more than usual between the director and the play, a situation of which he himself appears to be unaware.[73] The three protagonists here are puppets, more so even than in the contrived times and action of *Living Quarters* and *Aristocrats*. We are ushered into a private realm of induced mystery. Nothing in this play is real; Friel dispenses with the tribune and defies us to find the consistencies in his narrative. We acquiesce in his deceit as we listen to the opening incantation, and for the first time in his work we realise that the sacred nature of place-names can be illusory, 'abandoned rituals', as he will show us in *Translations*, but only because he specifically tells us so. We accept, *a priori* the utter freedom of the essential artist – 'a craft without an apprenticeship, a ministry without responsibility, a vocation without a ministry' (*FH* 13). Like Skinner and Keeney, Frank Hardy is effectively an orphan, speaking an orphaned language. We know that it not only does not matter whether Frank Hardy heals or not, it does not matter *one way or the other*. For Hardy, as for the Unnamable, the imperative is to 'become whole in myself, and perfect in myself, and in a manner of speaking, an aristocrat' (*FH* 13), which can only be achieved through silencing 'the questions that undermined my life . . . those nagging, tormenting, maddening questions that rotted my life' (*FH* 13–14). As we have seen, the only way to avoid madness is to select, to exclude, to fracture, to become partial, to individuate. And as we shall see once again in *Fathers and Sons*, the rotten life is something not only specific to the person but endemic in families.

It is not 'the crippled and the blind and the disfigured and the deaf and the barren' (*FH* 16) whom he has to make whole, but himself because, however disfigured, deprived or damaged these cripples are, their disinheritance is of a different order, a lymphatic not a psychic order; they are not destroyed by voices, theirs is not an aural cancer. In exposing his audience to four monologues, Friel is exposing his own 'voices', the kind which sent Jeanne d'Arc and the daughters of Loudun to the pyre, the children of Salem to the gibbet, and Virginia Woolf to her novels.

In this clinical setting, drugged by incantation, poised between divination and Jerome Kern's song 'The Way You Look Tonight', 'between the absurd and the momentous' (*FH* 16), Friel sets out to expose the weaknesses of his inheritance, the impossibility of coming into one's own, and the fact that to acquiesce in one's own destruction is in itself a form of relief, a therapy:

> They were a despairing people. That they came to me, a mountebank, was a measure of their despair . . . they knew in their hearts they had come not

to be cured but for confirmation that they were incurable; not in hope but for the elimination of hope; for the removal of that final, impossible chance, that's why they came, to seal their anguish, for the content of a finality. And they knew that I knew. And so they defied me to endow them with hopelessness. (*FH* 16)

Losers. So afraid of the jump into the dark, so apprehensive lest the Redeemer in fact call their bluff, that they are ready, like Lily, to die of grief, to find a freedom in the extinction of hope, and, by extension, as *legati* (*FH* 17), to let their culture die, to relieve the gatekeeper and let the barbarians in.

For every centrifugal force there is an equal and opposite centripetal force. So just as Frank Hardy says 'If we hadn't come to them, they would have sought us out' (*FH* 17), he, in his turn, comes to Ballybeg, to meet McGarvey, an unreal creature conjured out of the Donegal twilight, who Friel/Hardy paints with sensual realism: 'Saw him and recognised our meeting: an open place, a walled yard, trees, orange skies, warm wind. And knew, knew with cold certainty that nothing was going to happen. Nothing at all' (*FH* 19). Hardy's 'homecoming' sees the dominance of ritual: 'A frenzied excessive Irish night when ritual was consciously and relentlessly debauched' (*FH* 19) – but not mocked; ritual which binds one to the tribe and its icons and texts as fiercely when it is debauched and brutalised as when it is piously observed, because debauch is in itself a form of piety.

Grace, the wife/mistress, and Teddy, the manager, provide commentaries on the diviner's artistry. Despite brilliant characterisation in the word-play, they do not feature in the outcome as anything more than ciphers, because they are bound to him as Rosencrantz and Guildenstern are to Hamlet, except that there is another qualitative difference between Frank and Grace on one side and Teddy on the other. But like Frank Hardy himself, Grace and Teddy are *beyond identity*: Teddy has no other name; Grace has many, according to Hardy's whim – Dodsmith, McClure, O'Connell, McPherson, from Yorkshire or Kerry or London or Scarborough, 'I don't remember, they all sound so alike, it doesn't matter' (*FH* 15). It is the same with places, 'Welsh-Scottish, over the years they became indistinguishable' (*FH* 12).

The ritualistic cadence 'in Kinlochbervie, in Sutherland, in the north of Scotland' (*FH* 24) might be a line from 'Mr Sing My Heart's Delight': 'in the sun, in the Punjab, in the Garden of Eden' (*Saucer* 68). Its quality is not in the names themselves but in the effect of the incantation, a 'mesmerism' or 'sedation' (*FH* 12), as Friel uses them to seduce the audience and dig down into the psyche with this litany of place-names. As places, as names, they do not *matter*, they are immaterial in the metaphysical sense. Grace and Teddy are bound to Frank Hardy in the same ritual of observance and debauchery, because they are the supporting cast of his artistry: 'Me, who tended him, humoured him, nursed him, sustained him, who debauched myself for him' (FH 23). Without him, Grace is nothing: 'O my God I'm one of his fictions too, but I need him to sustain me in that existence – O my God I don't know if I can go on without his sustenance.'(FH 32) Without art he is nothing: 'I couldn't even begin to comprehend it, this gift, this craft, this talent, this art, this magic, whatever it was he possessed that defined him' (FH 28).

Grace sees him as the *performer*, 'crouched, wound up, concentrated, in such mastery that anything is possible' (FH 23), who pursues an almost epicurean critic-as-artist role in recreating people:

> it was some compulsion he had to adjust, to refashion, to recreate everything around him. Even the people who came to him, they weren't just sick people who were confused and frightened and wanted to be cured; no, no, to him they were . . . yes they were real enough, but not real as persons, real as fictions, his fictions, extensions of himself that came into being only because of him . . . he kept remaking people according to some private standard of excellence of his own and as his standards changed, so did the person. But I'm sure it was always an excellence, a perfection, that was the cause of his restlessness and the focus of it. (FH 25)

Teddy, from his position of professional expertise, can analyse 'artists' and their preoccupations:

> they know they have something fantastic, sure, they're not that stupid. But what is it they have, how they do it, how it works, what that sensational talent is, what it all means, believe me, they don't know and they don't care and even if they did care they haven't the brains to analyse it. (FH 34–5)

Hardy is in Teddy's view a 'mediocre artist' castrated by his brains, without ambition (FH 37). Loss of ambition suggests loss of will, and in that sense Teddy is correct, although otherwise I cannot see how 'brains' explains Hardy's madness, his anarchic disposition.

In the 'performance' his skill is intuitive; his actions outside the healing circle, however, can only be explained by his surgical power. This distinguishes his behaviour from the impulsive nature of Skinner's 'gesture' in *The Freedom* and Keeney's 'protest' in *Volunteers;* his is a calculating embrace of the unknown, because, through his divination, he does 'know'. 'There was a killer instinct deep down in that man' (FH 42) says Teddy and there is a coldness in his method, even when he is drawing devils out of the poor, but he is compelled to find an order, to fulfil some pattern which will mark a homecoming – 'Some very important appointment he's got to keep . . . he had to have his own way of facing things' (FH 44). He is like Don Giovanni, anxious to keep his appointment with the Commendatore. And like Don Giovanni, Frank Hardy is of course an anarchist who delights in order, whose sacrifice of his own life is the ultimate act of faith: only a psychopath who realises that the playwright has left him no other avenue of escape could conceive so clearly the need for McGarvey. Hardy's (Friel's) obscene caricature of Jerome Kern ('lovely . . . just the way you look tonight') juxtaposed against 'the crippled and the blind, and the disfigured and the deaf and the barren' (FH 16), is typical of the savagery of which Friel is rarely capable but lethally so when he does it: as Tyrone Guthrie said of the closing scene of Philadelphia, 'infinitely poignant although not one word of sentiment is expressed'.[74] This poignancy is central to Friel's work and typical of him when he is being *least* central, that is, displaying a soul at the end of its tether, both in the intensity of its utterance and in its savage inevitability. It is not so much the tension of son against father, or the confusion of meaning and identity, so much as the fact that in exploring these themes Irish 'classic' drama is more closely definable as *tragic* than anything to be seen, for example, on the British stage. Thomas Kilroy asks:

> How is it that persons of ugly, sordid even depraved character, persons with apparently no redeeming features in their personal lives are capable of creating great redeeming beauty in art, works of sustaining spiritual resource?[75]

– another example being McGuinness's portrayal of Caravaggio in *Innocence*, or the criminal figure of Alain-Fournier's *Le Grand Meaulnes*, who would 'sacrifice everyone to his own self-interest'.[76] The reason for Hardy's particularly vicious character is that it accentuates the fact that completion, homecoming, redemption, can be available to the lowest of sinners. The self-interest of such a character is necessary because, as Seamus Deane observes, 'just before he dies he articulates himself. He authors himself in a final act of authority', thus underlining the awful fact that 'the only true place is that which is coincident with time'.[77]

It is in this respect that Teddy's role is differentiated from that of Frank and Grace. Teddy's function is twofold: to act as our guide, a point of reference, to the statements of Frank and Grace; and to relieve, with his Cockney humour, the tragedy of the narration. The two functions are interrelated: humour is part of Teddy's character rather than an adjunct, part of the culture which keeps him alive and therefore convincing. He places Hardy not in a pantheon of charismatic heroes but in the absurd context of down-market showbiz, equating him (along with Olivier, Houdini, Chaplin and Gracie Fields) with Rob Roy the Piping Dog and Miss Mulatto and Her Pigeons. The essential difference is that Teddy is unimportant and his stories are inconsequential, harmlessly humorous, because they are not his own. He leads his own life simply because *he is alive*. He shows us that *Faith Healer* is *a play about death*, that it is, at its core, stories from the dark angels, telling us of their inevitable death: Frank at the hands of the symbolic McGarvey, the half-brother who has always awaited the moment for which he was created; Grace as Hardy's fiction, at her own hands, a self-strangling puppet. Teddy himself will probably never die, because there is nothing to push him over the edge; he is resigned to the ambition, talent, and brainlessness of his clients in their waiting-room-for-death. It is a play, therefore, which could not succeed without Teddy, because we need the living, those who in the chemical sense retain their humours, in order to decode the unremitting brutality and nihilism of the dead. McGarvey, the cripple whom Hardy knows he cannot cure, is, on the other hand, the unseen but essential other character in this non-play, a 'figure of infinite patience, of profound resignation', not so much because he has come to terms with his disability but because he is waiting for Hardy to come to terms with *him*.

As McGarvey becomes 'real', the 'real' world diminishes:

> and as I walked I became possessed of a strange and trembling intimation; that the whole corporeal world – the cobbles, the trees, the sky, somehow they had shed their physical reality and had become mere imaginings . . . even we had ceased to be physical and existed only in spirit, only in the need we had for each other. (*FH* 54)

The closing sequence of this monologue is distinctly visual rather than verbal. In destroying himself we *see* that Hardy comes home. He has passed beyond identity, beyond words, beyond madness, beyond chance, beyond fear, beyond the voices: 'the maddening questions were silent' (*FH* 55).

In *Faith Healer* Friel meets and sees his alter ego, and lays the ghosts of self-doubt and the problem of self-knowledge first explored in *The Enemy Within* and *Philadelphia*. In *Translations*, which we might subtitle 'A Family Reunion', he goes to confront the public world and the context of affiliation.

In *Living Quarters* Friel gets closest to the idea of time suspended, the frozen action of the body (all the meaningless gestures, exits and entrances of the 'play'), while we experience the *communitas* of mind, and it is to this that he returns successfully in *Translations*. In *Living Quarters* the 'ledger' – which is surely a balance-sheet as well as a list of entries? – is verbalised. 'Sir', the servant and interpreter of the ledger, rather than its author, permits shuffling of the pages, but the interpretation which the participants give to their lines is subtle and frustrating for us who cannot look over Sir's shoulder at the document itself. And the reason, of course, is that 'Sir' himself is a stage direction, one of the author's own distancing tricks.[78] As in all good stories, they only reveal its outcome 'in their own good time'. During the rest of the play they interrupt or forestall revelation, analysis and confidences as it suits them. Friel says, through their untimed and unscripted entrances and exits, that the form given to content is ultimately irrelevant, in the same way that much of the 'plot' is unimportant; it does not seem to matter whether the family of *Aristocrats* assembles for a wedding, as they think, or for a funeral, as brought on by Father's unscripted entry; a giving of a name, as in the offstage christening with which *Translations* opens, or a taking away, as in the baby's wake ('it didn't last long, did it?' *Tr.* 60); a wedding as anticipated in 'Winners' or the drowning which 'in fact' results from Meg's panic spring.

Friel here reaffirms a perennial paradox: that man, by the exercise of his free-will, fulfils a pattern of destiny. It does not in fact matter what is said in *Living Quarters* (or even *Aristocrats*) but it is of 'consequence'. The clearest exposition of this principle is Sir's observation (i.e. the statement): 'no sooner do they conceive me with my authority and my knowledge than they begin flirting with the idea of circumventing me, of outwitting me' (*LQ* 12). And yet Sir tells Anna 'You shuffled the pages a bit, that's all. But nothing's changed' (*LQ* 39). The Butler family are following fate within concentric circles of their own constrained freedom. And not only with the subversion of absolute power and knowledge, but also with impassioned, irrational remonstration, somewhere between energised and enervate despair, against absolute reason:

> FRANK: Yes you did say we could speak our thoughts, that was established at the outset, wasn't it? Well, I wish to protest against my treatment. I wish to say that I consider I have been treated unfairly . . . And I am fully aware that protesting at this stage is pointless – pointless . . . The ledger's the ledger, isn't it? Nothing can be changed now – not a thing. But an injustice has been done to me, Sir, and a protest must be made. (*LQ* 82)

(Cass also appeals, but in her case her derision of the author is directed towards the audience, until she is persuaded that the reality is on the stage, not in the auditorium.) As with the onset of any psychic disorder, it is irrelevant who says what is said, or that it is said at all, because it would have been said, the embarrassments would have been conceived, *in any case*. Ben and Frank re-enact the disorder between Gar and his father; we might expect some resolution of the problem but that possibility is complicated by the fact that the only truth uttered comes *after* Frank's death (as it takes place in *this* version of the play):

What I was going to say was that ever since I was a child I always loved him, and always hated her – he was always my hero. And even though it wouldn't have been the truth, it wouldn't have been a lie either. (*LQ* 87)

This kind of liminality in fact fails in *Living Quarters* because it does not permit final resolution: the creatures of the play are condemned to return to the ledger to search for old possibilities. There is an uncertainty in Friel's writing here which we *must* take into account because he confuses 'dead episodes' (*LQ* 11) with 'those lost possibilities' (*LQ* 43).

This is the most unfortunate, *impossible* type of peregrination, in which we expect to meet wandering Jews and flying Dutchmen: it is not the sort of world where Friel's 'losers' fit in, comfortably or otherwise. Interestingly, it is the same trap which Chekhov falls into, and again with the sons rather than the daughters (Constantin in *The Seagull*, Andrey in *Three Sisters*, for example). And in the 'unfairness' complained of we can recognise a specifically masculine reaction to events, whereas in the feminine roles Friel's creatures create, rather than react to, their own actions, as if they were more in accord or complicity with the original powers which set them in motion. The frightened child is inevitably the boy, whereas women conquer their fear by creating strength; the discourse (*logos*) is between *father* and son, the emotive affinity (*mythos*) is between *mother* and son. In *Living Quarters* Father Tom (another aid to the stage directions who, as a priest, can mediate between the absolute and the real) expresses this liminality: 'The enormous gift that Christ purchased for us – the availability of choice and our freedom to choose' (*LQ* 45).

We might consider this the only fully successful statement of the play, until we realise that it does not express the awfulness of the *necessity* of choosing, the collision of freedom *and* responsibility in which the will continually defeats itself, as we have seen in the 'spectacle' of Andy Tracey, the loser. From the experience of these plays, therefore, we are still looking for a condition in which the liminality of Friel's ritual can be resolved. Ultimately, what 'matters' is the breaking and repairing of silence, and for that Friel requires only a test-tube, and a volunteer audience. But as Thomas Kilroy warns us, the environment of the theatre is more than histrionics and the devices of melodrama or masque. He says that as a language becomes more suspect and brittle there is a word 'compounded of anarchic humour and deadly serious motivation, which cannot describe anything concrete of this theatre; it is merely a signal. The word is Danger.'[79]

The test of Friel's skill is whether or not he succeeds in mediating, by means of the play, between subject and audience, without also interfering in the internal relationship of the *subjects* of the play with the *objects* of the play itself This again returns us to the question of form: Friel is not, ostensibly, concerned with 'form' – a play is shaped by the events imagined within it, as they, and the characters who enact them, grow in the author's mind and use it in their passage towards the 'play'.[80]

As Friel noted in the early stages of writing *Aristocrats:*

> The crux with the new play arises, as usual with me, with its form. Whether to reveal slowly and painstakingly with almost realised tedium the work-ings of the family; or with some kind of supra-realism, epiphanies, in some way to make real the essences of these men and women by side-stepping or leaping across the boredom of their small talk, their trivial chatterings, etc. etc. But I suppose the answer to this will reveal itself when I know/ possess the play. Now I am only laying siege to it.[81]

Dantanus sees this as a preoccupation with *form* whereas in my opinion it is such *only* to the extent that form must serve *content*.[82]

Having finished *Translations*, for example, Friel noted:

> The task of writing the play, the actual job of putting the pattern together, itself generates belief in the pattern. The act and the artifact sustain one another. And now that the play is finished the value of the pattern and the belief in the pattern diminish and lethargy sets in: the life process. But only after the play is produced will I be completely cleansed of my subscription to this particular pattern, this ordering of things. Then a vigour will be summoned. Then a new pattern will have to be forged. The process seems trivial and transient because the patterns are so impermanent. But is there another way? It is a kind of vigilance, keeping the bush from encroaching into the yard. All art is a diary of evolution; markings that seemed true of and for their time; adjustments in stance and disposition; openings to what seemed the persistence of the moment. Map-makings.[83]

Map-making itself would be pointless if we did not accept that it is the content which determines the form. In between writing these two pass-ages, as he moved more quickly and surely towards the completion of *Aristocrats*, he wrote:

> To talk of 'meaning' is inaccurate. We say 'What is the play *about?*' with more accuracy than 'What does the play *mean?*' Because we don't go to art for meaning. We go to it for perceptions of new adjustments and new arrangements.[76] [*my emphasis*]

'What is the play *about?*' orients and approximates the questioner to the 'impermanent' public world, whereas 'What does the play *mean?*' enquires about the playwright and his private intentions. In *Living Quarters* we might think Friel has failed to make the distinctions we ask of him, because we are seduced into receiving impressions which should rightly be regarded as privacies. By seeking to 'interpret between privacies' (*Tr.* 67) Friel coldly exposes, by means of an open text, those affects which keep families or tribes together. He thus destroys form, not with a mechanical flourish, but by using the 'fifth province' – by arguing not from the general to the specific, but from Ballybeg to the world. He solves the political problem by way of language, by posing the perennial question, like Chekhov, in the accents of the province, the zone, and establishing a world of correspondence. The 'tricks' lie in the way he introduces the hallowed effects of melodrama, allegory, naming, into our sub-conscious: thus, by means of ritual seduction, creating an interdependence of words, images and time.

If we ask 'what is the play *about?*' we find that *Living Quarters* is 'about' a *femme fatale* whose intrusion into family life disturbs the memory and affections. It is 'about' the events of a day when, although the public world sees everything going according to plan, the private conscience is caught up in a scheme of subversion. Beyond this the play is not 'about' anything. As Guthrie says: 'meaning is explicit "between the lines" of a text; in silences, in what people are thinking and doing far more than in what they are saying: in the music as much as in the meaning of a phrase'.[85]

In *Aristocrats*, similarly, it would be difficult to say what 'happens', without discussing 'meaning'. *Aristocrats* is 'about' 'incipient decay, an era wilted, people confused and nervous . . . *family life*, its quality, its cohesion, its stultifying effects, its affording of opportunities for what we designate "love" and "affection" and "loyalty"'.[86] But we cannot pursue that idea very far, because, as Friel noted in the middle of the writing, the *core* of the play is 'the burden of the incommunicable'. But *Aristocrats* (originally thought of as 'The Judas Hole') is no more 'about' the incommunicable than *Hamlet* is 'about' self-doubt, courage, or madness. But whereas Shakespeare provides us with a baroque backcloth of murders, wars, ghosts, Friel allows us no respite from his rigorous examinations; we can comprehend the spectacle of hypocrisy, or of greed, or of buffoonery in *Hamlet* without being drawn into the 'meaning' of the play, but Friel in these later works is cutting away anything which stands between him and his meaning. He is going out to meet his play and he is dragging the audience/reader with him. He is solving the problem identified by Frank Ormsby in relation to *Philadelphia*, that 'the maddening complexities of circumstance and human nature constantly thwart the seemingly straightforward possibilities for solution'.[87] He is making it difficult to be a spectator, more likely that we will want to become participants. If *Waiting for Godot* is a play in which 'nothing happens twice',[88] *Faith Healer* is a play in which nothing happens four times; while in *Translations* everything never happens, and it is debatable whether *Making History* happens or not.

In *Dancing at Lughnasa*, the techniques of stagecraft subject the ostensible, and very spare, 'action' to the scrutiny of memory, and in so doing they set up a novel momentum which, as we shall see in Chapter 7 in discussing *Wonderful Tennessee* and *Molly Sweeney*, puts Friel's drama on a new footing: one where the difficulty of distinguishing between what happens and what our memory tells us has happened, is resolved by immersing the audience in the action of memory – a new method of involving the spectator and at the same time advancing the playwright's dramatic purpose.

A problem with *Faith Healer* seems to be the intensity with which Friel has approached his 'subject', to the exclusion of the subordinate characters. Frank Hardy, in fact, becomes inaccessible to Grace and Teddy, locked into his own privacy, simply because Friel has conceived of private despair as a medium of healing itself:

> And when you speak to him he turns his head and looks beyond you with those damn benign eyes of his, looking past you out of his completion, out of that private power, out of that certainty that was accessible only to him. God, how I resented that privacy! (*FH* 23)[85]

As a result of concentrating on Hardy's own psyche, Friel comes close to depriving the 'play' of any dramatic content whatsoever; yet he makes us conscious of the dramatic experience by creating a graphic, visual world out of the elements of ambiguity, chicanery and time itself.

As with *Living Quarters* and *Aristocrats*, Friel's technique is akin to Cubism: cutting the subject open and turning it this way and that to expose planes never normally considered by either the spectator or the subject himself. This leads to a form of psychological investigation which is normally approached only by means of the absurd – Ionesco's apparent *non sequiturs* in *The Bald Prima Donna*, for example – in which extrasensory perceptions take over from the sort of naturalism we expect from a successor to Chekhov. As Stanislavsky said of *The Seagull*, 'he who invents a new ending for a play will usher in a new era! These damned endings are the very limit! The hero has either to marry or to shoot himself; there is no other way.'[90] And of course Frank Hardy 'shoots himself', as clearly as Frank/Theseus in *Living Quarters*. Friel, however, eschews endings in the sense of dramatic closures. Only the contrived postscript to *Living Quarters* rounds off the chaos of the 'anything can happen' syndrome with a conventional 'they lived happily ever after', the sort of conclusion which the drifters in *Aristocrats* might look forward to in their hopeful 'next summer in Hamburg' (*Ar.* 84). But in most cases we are left in the condition of 'anything can happen': in *Translations*, where we are still waiting for something to happen, or for proof that something has happened; in *Fathers and Sons*, where a new cycle of happenings becomes possible; or in *Faith Healer*, where nothing keeps on happening. The place for resolution, we feel, has been created somewhat unfairly by Friel in our own minds, as we carry away from the dramatic experience a new sense of volition in our own lives, a sense of how to answer the question 'to marry or to shoot oneself?', to make sense or nonsense, which he makes explicit in his treatment of *Three Sisters* and *Fathers and Sons*. In *Making History* he makes it no easier for us to decode his intentions, but he does lighten the problem of the play's closure, simply by eliding it.

In his diary Friel noted this passage from Norman Mailer:

> if he did something wrong, they [daughters] being women would grow up around the mistake and somehow convert it to knowledge. But his sons! He had the feeling that because they were men, their egos were more fragile – a serious error might hurt them forever.[91]

One begins to approach a conclusion, perhaps not inescapable but certainly very compelling, that Friel is almost too concerned with pursuing the relationship of father and son, which is the one consistent 'plot' throughout his work. In *Living Quarters* the superiority and authority of a father-figure, whose military bearing echoes the Inspector/teacher status of the father in several short stories, is firmly on the stage; in *Aristocrats* the admonishing figure which so effectively reduces Casimir to weak-kneed fear is mediated through the device of the baby-alarm (the Judas-hole turned around), as if Friel cannot allow physical indisposition to prevent the metaphysical pursuit. This pursuit at times creates an imbalance in the otherwise orderly analysis of affiliation which he approaches elsewhere. The three exceptions to the main theme (affiliation) and its development (filiation),[92] are *The Mundy Scheme*, *Faith Healer* and *The Communication Cord*, two of which have earned themselves the status of satire (which at times is synonymous with critical condemnation) and the third (in which there is only an apocryphal father) has so stunned audiences and critics alike that they find it difficult to accept the substitution of aural for visual theatre.

This facility allows him to give *Living Quarters* the puzzling subtitle 'After Hippolytus'. While Euripides' and Seneca's (and indeed Racine's) versions of *Phaedra* deal with the penalty inflicted on the innocent Hippolytus who refuses his step-mother's love, Friel has Ben (Hippolytus) actually having an affair with his stepmother (Phaedra). The possibility remains in some latent text that Hippolytus was justly punished by his father, the semantic fact being not that he defiled his father's bed, but that his father destroyed him, one way or the other. As explicitly as Friel treats the subject of exogamy in *Translations*, we see him here assessing the politics of an internal exogamy, crossing forbidden boundaries within the tribe.

W.J. Cloonan, writing on Racine, notes that, although Hippolytus does not respond to Phèdre's advances:

> they place themselves in positions where they are in apparent violation of generally accepted social taboos . . . their real fault, which neither grasps until the play's end, and even then imperfectly, lies not in the identity of those they love, but in the very act of *loving* . . . *Phèdre* begins with an awareness that cruel and inhuman powers are toying with a desperate woman . . . The queen's desire to love and be loved is as innocent as Hippolyte's.[93]

In a sense the possibilities are still endless, and the only certainties are the identities of the actors themselves; as for working towards a conclusion, Friel has remarked that, as with Steiner's approach to *Antigone*,[94] 'it depends on which version you use'.[95]

What *is* important is the exploration of those identities of which we can never be sure, so that we can never be free from the exploration: as Crystal says to Fox (as Ben might say to Anna as the archetypes break down): 'What . . . are . . . you . . . I don't know you... Don't know you at all . . . Never knew . . . never . . .' (*CF* 63). Even in his use of 'comic relief' Friel fuses form and content: in *Aristocrats*, for example, the nomination of pieces of furniture as 'Chesterton', 'Yeats', 'O'Casey', 'Newman', carries its own farce within it, as Willie Diver mockingly adds 'Shakespeare', 'Lenin', 'Mickey Mouse' and 'Ben Jonson' to the list (*Ar.* 32). And in *Translations* he does not simply relieve a situation with comedy, but uses it in a tragicomic sense to emphasise one aspect of his main theme. For example:

JIMMY: I'm going to get married.
HUGH: Well!
JIMMY: At Christmas.
HUGH: Splendid.
JIMMY: To Athene.
HUGH: Who?
JIMMY: Pallas Athene.
HUGH: Glaukopis Athene?
JIMMY: Flashing-eyed, Hugh, flashing-eyed.
HUGH: The lady has assented?
JIMMY: She asked me, I assented.
HUGH: Ah, when was this?
JIMMY: Last night.
HUGH: What does her mother say?

JIMMY: Metis from Hellespont? Decent people, good stock.
HUGH: And her father?
JIMMY: I'm meeting Zeus tomorrow. Hugh will you be my best man?

(Tr. 65)

Not only is this as farcical and innovatory as anything in Flann O'Brien's *At Swim-Two-Birds*,[96] it also serves to get across (translate) the idea of two worlds, two cultures, meeting in the tympanum represented by Jimmy Jack: 'the world of the gods and the ancient myths is as real and as immediate as everyday life in the townland of Baile Beag' (*Tr.* 11). It is when the two congress in a supposed reality that we find Jimmy Jack (twice) in a posture of 'pained ecstasy' (*Tr.* 14, 65). And that device, too, is pressed into service as, at the close of the play, Jimmy discusses his own wedding and the fatal attraction of Maire and Yolland: 'Do you know the Greek word endogamein? It means to marry within the tribe. And the word exogamein means to marry outside the tribe. And you don't cross those borders casually – both sides get very angry' (*Tr.* 68).

It is little wonder then, that we read in *After Babel*: 'the history of western drama . . . often reads like a prolonged echo of the doomed informalities (literally the failure to define separate forms) before gods and men in a small number of Greek households.'[97] In this version of many Ballybegs, Friel turns time on its head by reintroducing those gods themselves, underpinning them from tradition by calling up the gods of Irish mythology to create in the mind of at least two characters, Jimmy Jack and George Yolland, a convincing, imaginable world, and one which is not merely illusory, but has commerce with the concrete world, a freedom which can exploit its limitations:

JIMMY: '*Nigra fere et presso pinguis sub vomere terra*' [Virgil, *Georgics* Bk.II]
MANUS: 'Land that is black and rich beneath the pressure of the plough . . .'

[. . .]

JIMMY: 'And with *cui putre*, with crumbly soil, is in the main best for corn.' There you are! . . . 'From no other land will you see more wagons wending homeward behind slow bullocks.' Virgil! There! . . . Isn't that what I am always telling you? Black soil for corn. That's what you should have in that upper field of yours, corn not spuds. (*Tr.* 19)

In a sense Friel is pointing out the divorce between the rational and the intuitive, between *logos* and *mythos*, town and country, as a basic flaw in our psychology. But he is also saying that the setting of his plays is irrelevant: they could be in 'a small number of Irish households', or in a mental hospital. In fact the analogy is apt, for a mental hospital is a place where *nothing happens* but happens slowly, and where *everything* is rehearsed.[98] One cannot be cured of madness or psychic disorder, one can only come to terms with it by understanding it, by establishing a community of meaning with the disorder itself, and inhibiting the motive and incidence of embarrassment and despair. Mental hospitals, like prisons, set boundaries to both freedom and control, but, within those boundaries, allow the condition of ecstasy – standing outside one's normal, social self – and permit the celebration of failure. The Ballybeg of *Living Quarters* and of *Aristocrats* (or at least the houses of the Butler and O'Donnell families) is in this sense an asylum, but perhaps the most significant is the hedge-school itself in *Translations*, in which Friel uses the device as a time-capsule to work out the meaning of meaning itself.

The danger of talking about layers of experience, or of history, which, as I have indicated, encourages one to think in terms of 'levels' of comprehension, has to be faced because we do need some such metaphor to help explain the creation of distance: the many versions of truth, we might say, are moments when time and the fact-finding exercise are arrested. In fact, as in *Volunteers* with its explicit metaphor of digging, we are safer in the arms of several conflicting versions, inconsistencies or ambiguities than we are with plain, unadorned truth. As long as we continue to have the power of recollection, as long as dialogue goes on, life goes on. So for Ned, a minor character in *Philadelphia*, one night of dalliance recollected in bravado ('Mind the night Jimmy and us went down to the caves with them Dublin skivvies') is as valid as Gar's contradiction of it ('so we struggled back home, one behind the other and left the girls dangling their feet in the water', *Ph.* 72–3). In *The Freedom* all four versions of the 'truth' (the RTÉ newsman's 'fifty armed gunmen', the report of the voices 'there's at least a dozen dead', the army's 'a band of terrorists' and the balladeer's 'a hundred Irish heroes') are incorrect, as is the Judge's summing up (rationalisation) of the events.

In this sense there are always *two* plays going on, not just the whole range of possible worlds which *might* be, of which the spectacle before us is one, but the play offstage, relating to the play in progress, its *alter ego*. There is another *Philadelphia* in which Private Screwballs is reviewing his relationship with his son and his dead wife, of which we only get a glimpse in the gesture he (Public Screwballs) makes by touching Gar's jacket and in his brief conversation with Madge (*Ph.* 100).[99] And in *Translations*, when Sarah runs off to announce the only 'action' which the audience is permitted to 'see' (the love scene between Maire and Yolland), she goes to tell it in another theatre, which, like *Rosencrantz and Guildenstern are Dead*, is taking place in the wings.

In *The Gentle Island*, Manus Sweeney, sitting in the aeroplane seat, and Sarah wearing men's boots, are indications of absurdity or incongruity which Friel manipulates in order to suggest the other world beyond the painted stage. That Manus occupies the chair when he is unable to face reality is only part of the story: he absents himself from us, facing upstage as he does so. The recitation of Gray's 'Elegy' in 'Losers' (*Lovers*) is equally 'absurd': the recitation is interrupted by Mrs Wilson's bell, which the 'elegy' is intended to pre-empt, the dramatic irony being Gray's line 'The curfew tolls the knell of parting day.' The ultimate absurdity in Friel's work occurs at the end of Act 1/opening of Act 2 of *The Communication Cord*, which resembles the opening scene of Stoppard's *After Magritte:* a group of apparently rational people posed – caught up – in entirely irrational activities, which they follow through to their conclusions, whether logical or illogical is for us to decide. This is what Friel wants to say about the absurdity of freedom.

There are therefore two senses in which Friel's 'freedom' plays leave the spectator aghast. One is the fact that he has tried to create *total* theatre by involving us in his, and his characters', drama. In this he succeeded with the awfulness of the direct address in *Faith Healer* and again in the judgement of the audience on the various pleas of *Making History*. But he finds it difficult to 'marry two incompatible types of theatre' as Fergus Linehan has remarked,[100] a fact made all the more terrible by the anarchism and total exposure of Frank Hardy's self-knowledge, a way of turning our double vision inside out. The other lies in the fact that, against every freedom identified by Friel, we have to acknowledge an irony. 'Irony tends towards stasis of action' says Northrop Frye (in particular describing the last act of *Three Sisters*).[101] Freedom in the future (what might be) is taken from Michael (in shock), from Skinner (in flippancy), and from Lily (through grief). Freedom in the past (what might have been) is taken from the Butlers through the Greek fates enshrined in the ledger, from the O'Donnells through the disestablishment of time's constructs, their nonexistent family history, their aristocracy. Freedom in the present is achieved only by Frank Hardy who becomes an aristocrat, whose freedom seems to be his prison, the personality ringing him round, which he has to meet coming towards him at the speed of fate. Friel has shown us once again that freedom, like love, is only for those prepared to cast away the crown, to tear themselves to pieces in the pursuit of wholeness.

PART III

Politics

The recesses of the domestic space become sites for
history's most intricate invasions. In that displacement,
the borders between home and world become confused;
and, uncannily, the private and the public become part
of each other, forcing upon us a vision that is
as divided as it is disorienting.

Homi Bhabha

5

A FIELD DAY

Images and symbols adequate to our predicament[1]
Seamus Heaney

Ulster offers us an example of two issues which have run parallel in this study: myth and the *unheimlich*. Myth, as I suggested in my Introduction, is something unbelievable in which we must believe. As A. T. Q. Stewart has observed, the two northern communities are commonly described as being unable to live together, but 'they *do* live together, and have done so for centuries. They share the same homeland and . . . must co-exist on the same narrow ground'.[2] Even this does not state the full irony: the 'two communities' live not together but contiguously – 'co-exist' being the realistic term. The 'marches' of the north celebrate this capacity for a form of neighbourliness which has respect rather than affection as its controlling idea. Thus, what cannot be, *is*. Meanwhile, during the decades in which one side of the map was ignored or excoriated by the other, but was known to exist, suppressed and unspoken, it was beginning to manifest itself in marches which would lift the strengths and ambitions of its offended virtue onto a new plane, unhousing all the ghosts, suspicions and hatreds of the past into a limbo from which they are only just beginning to settle. Northern Ireland is in a state of myth and of unhomeliness because for each 'side' the land itself, and everything that goes with land – culture, agriculture, governance – is disputed and seen in terms of the 'other'; identity depends not only on who you are, but on who you are not, and on who is not you.

The north of Ireland is a particularly striking example of the difficulty of finding equivalence. In his essay 'Brian Friel: The Name of the Game' Seamus Deane explores the coincidence of time and place which is involved in mapping and translation, and the likely occurrence of a warp in either time or place which prevents effective mapping and translation.

The discrepancy between histories and History, between different ideas of time and History, between one person's sense of place and another's, makes it almost impossible to establish a context, thus creating a 'predicament' for which, in Heaney's terms, it is exceptionally difficult to find or create an appropriate symbol, a sign that will be both equivalent and active. Deane says 'the function of . . . language is to nominate, to specify the context in which human love is possible';[3] thus, language is entrusted with the most important of all human functions and cannot fulfil its mission. In *Translations*, says Deane, Friel 'seeks to establish the possibility of a time and a place for which there would be a correspondent language'. That that attempt fails to elicit anything more than a vague and tragi-comic approximation to such a language in the love scene between Maire and Yolland is a sign that everything in such an endeavour will be subjunctive – plagued by myth, unhoused by the visitation of the other, and subject to 'if'.

In the 1990s, the age-old suspicion of Ulster by the other three provinces began to take on a new aspect, as their deeply imbued prejudice of something which had been unidentifiable up to that point started to crystallise into a common understanding of what it might mean to be once again in dialogue, if not accord, with Irishmen of other persuasions. Ulster had been 'known', but not spoken about, as an 'other' place, where people were 'different'. It was the site of the great epics such as the *Táin*, with its paean to land- and cattle-wars as its way of aristocratic life, and it was the site of the greatest and most recent appropriation of that way of life and that land in which today's minority had been dispossessed. Brian Graham comments: 'As Ireland profoundly demonstrates, power cannot be conceived outside a geographical context; social power requires space, its exercise shapes space, and this in turn shapes social power'.[4] This, as we have seen, is true of the 'context' of *The Freedom of the City* and of Friel's 'history' plays, *Making History* and *Translations*.

Thus, while the emergence of a Catholic middle class has been identified as a point of departure for the civil rights movement in Northern Ireland,[5] the deeper structures of the fields of Ulster have been the seed-bed of the resentment and suspicion which came to be articulated on its streets. The moment at which violence becomes overt is a public moment concerning people's rights, but it brings to the surface their quiet enmities and covert hostilities which have to do with place.

In many senses the premature *The Freedom of the City* was a Field Day play before its time, a pre-lude to the way in which Field Day, the Derry-based theatre company and publishing house, would address the public issues and the matter of personal culture which pervade the political and social agenda in Ireland. Friel had, of course, been involved in 'political' theatre for many years, in the sense that he had been signalling the collapse of the public world, whether through greed (*The Mundy Scheme*) or indignity and dispossession (*The Freedom*). He had begun to address broader issues as his divining of the Irish psyche brought him to levels deeper than questions about 'love' could – at least for a time – explore. It is pre-eminently political theatre in the sense that Heaney says 'the imagined place is what politics is all about. Politicians deal in images'.[6] In the Irish context the inference is obvious: republican nationalism outside Northern Ireland 'imagines' the repossession of its fourth, lost field; inside the Six Counties the implications are far more complex. But for the writer himself the paradox lies not so much in the tantalus of the inaccessible as in the powerlessness of the word as an idea: the easy propagation (and manipulation) of freedom as a concept which cannot be reconciled with freedom as exercised. This, too, is a political impasse, and we would be wrong to think of the 14-year period of Friel's association with Field Day as a time when he became a hostage to fortune, or emerged from it unchanged: in fact, the plays he has produced since he began to wind down his association (those from *Dancing at Lughnasa* onwards) bear tell-tale signs of the deepened appreciation of what 'love' and similar emotions might mean which the Field Day experience yielded.

Helping to 'make a community of individuals'[7] and to address 'the collective mind' has long been his presiding interest. In 1972 he predicted Field Day when he wrote:

> The future of Irish drama . . . will shape and be shaped by political events. . . . The revolt in Northern Ireland is going to spread to the Republic; and if you believe that art is an instrument of the revolutionary process, then you can look forward to a spate of committed plays.[8]

But it would also be a personal odyssey and transformation. In the same year Friel also said:

> How difficult it is for an Irish writer to find his faith. . . . We want to know what the word native means, what the word foreign means, we want to know have the words any meaning at all. And persistent considerations like these erode old certainties and help clear the building site.[9]

If that clearance had not taken place, it is doubtful if Friel could have written *Translations*, *Fathers and Sons* or *Making History*. In that case, Friel's public project would therefore have continued to concentrate on the erosion of old certainties in order to come to terms with what he called a 'schizophrenia' in Dublin where 'the urban man and the rural man meet and attempt to mingle'.[10] Instead, he began to ask ''What is it that constitutes an Irish reality?' and, quoting Seamus Deane,

'Everything including our politics and our literature has to be re-written, i.e. re-read'.[11]

There had been precedents: the political role of theatre in Ireland has been intimately connected with cultural renaissance and cultural nationalism. There were clear political implications in the founding of the Irish Literary Theatre (1899), the National Theatre (1904) and the Ulster Literary Theatre (1904), as there were in the drama of J. M. Synge, Seán O'Casey and Denis Johnston.

In 1980, in order to promote more explicitly some of his 'political' ideas – the notion that Ireland might 'be ruled by its poets and dramatists' – Friel participated in the formation of Field Day. His original partner in the venture was the actor Stephen Rea, and their main ambition was to stage Friel's *Translations*, the text of which is dedicated to Rea; Rea acted the part of Owen in the first production and went on to become the interpreter of the main role in many subsequent Field Day productions including Hugh O'Neill in *Making History*, and the mirror-roles of Brendan Bracken and William Joyce in Kilroy's *Double Cross*, and he directed Friel's version of *Three Sisters*.[12] In many of these, Rea was playing a figure crucial to Friel's, and Ireland's, drama: the divided mind, oscillating between public and private, conscious always of the *Doppelgänger* at his shoulder.

The other founder-directors of Field Day were Tom Paulin, a poet and critic of Belfast origin; David Hammond, a folklorist and film-maker, also from Belfast; Seamus Heaney, from rural County Derry and Seamus Deane, from Derry City. All, except Rea, were, or had been, school- or college teachers. They were, in Heaney's words, 'a natural set, one circle of natural acquaintance and interchange'.[13] Three (Friel, Deane and Heaney) were from Catholic backgrounds while three (Hammond, Paulin and Rea) were of Protestant stock. More important, however, is the fact that they described themselves as 'lapsed',[14] the notion of dissent from prevailing orthodoxies being more significant than the idea that they might represent a rapprochement between oppositional ideologies.[15]

It is possible to see the course of Field Day's activities from 1980 to 1994, when Friel definitively disengaged himself from the company, as a reflection of cultural politics and political culture in Northern Ireland, and as a contribution to change in Ireland as a whole. Field Day set out to achieve a number of objectives: to bring to public attention the strengths of Irish, as opposed to British, writing in Northern Ireland, which would be focused in the city of Derry; to promote the concept of Irishness as a valid way of life for the vast minority of people in Northern Ireland; to question the hegemonic authority of unionism; and to open up the cultural and political debate on the island of Ireland by means of a 'fifth province' which it largely shared with the contributors to the *Crane Bag*, where the concept had first been promulgated.[16] Some had much more focussed ideas than others of what Field Day might achieve, or of why it was necessary. Seamus Deane spoke of the venture in terms of translation:

> adaptations, readjustments and reorientations that are required of individuals and groups who have undergone a traumatic cultural and political crisis so fundamental that they must forge for themselves a new speech, a new history or life story that would give it some rational or coherent form.[17]

In such terminology we find the crux of an agenda which, as with Grotowski's theatre company in Poland, would have 'a sacred aim',[18] at first parallel to existing realities and later replacing those realities with its own:[19] new intellectual spaces, new perspectives, new ideas of integrity, all expressive of a social and cultural (and ultimately political) reorganisation. It was, in the words of *The Freedom of the City*, a 'platform of defiance' (*Freedom* 57).

Later, Deane would speak of 'reconciliation [as] the political word for translation', using Stewart Parker's *Pentecost* as a metaphor for 'persuading people to . . . translat[e] out of their native prejudices into some more amenable language, more amenable form than their background has provided them'.[20] In this apparently contradictory or at least multi-lingual project between self-assertion and conciliation, *Translations* was to be Field Day's 'central text'[21] and the *Field Day Anthology of Irish Writing* would be its 'generous and hospitable' symbol.[22]

Field Day defined itself in dictionary terms as 'a day on which troops are drawn up for exercise in field evolution; a military review; a day occupied with brilliant or exciting events; a day spent in the field'.[23] As a military exercise – even if restricted to the intellectual sphere – it thus suggested contestation and a kind of passive militancy which has everything to do with identity and place. But it also suggested 'carnival, a popular festival, a celebration of freedom in the open air' as Tom Paulin put it.[24] Deane also called the company 'a double secession – from the North and from the Republic', thus emphasising its view of itself as a 'fifth province'.[25]

'We believed we could build something of value, a space in which we would try to redefine what being Irish meant in the context of what has happened in the North over the past 20 years, the relationship of Irish nationalism and culture . . . independent of the British influence . . . and the equally strong cultural hegemony of Dublin' said Heaney.[26] 'To build a body of work removed from political action' (as Rea defined its purpose)[27] was one aspect of Field Day's endeavour, but the political dimension of that work was evident in the strategic tours of the company's productions within Ireland and its forays to London. The work was

intended both to demonstrate the dualities (indeed, polarities) of life in
Northern Ireland and to encourage a closer understanding between the
'state of two nations' as Friel put it.[28] The 'fifth province' was a place
beyond these divisions, a 'middle ground between the country's entrenched
positions';[29] Friel called it 'a place for dissenters, traitors to the prevailing mythologies in the other four provinces',[30] and elsewhere he said
that he and Rea 'felt there was some tiny little space we might fill that
we could focus the whole North thing on'.[31] The use of the word
'dissenter', traditionally employed in Ireland to indicate non-establishment
protestants, is significant. When Friel said that 'we are trying to make a
home' which would not be 'the English home [by which] we have been
pigmented',[32] we must read this in the light of his previous remarks on
being an exile while at home (above, p. 13); and when he remarked that
'the rejection of all that, and the rejection into what, is the big problem'[33]
we must take 'dissent' as a dilemma, a place of self-doubt as well as a
place in which the prevailing orthodoxies are denied. What happens to
an emerging country after it has emerged?

As Marilyn Richtarik shrewdly points out, Field Day was 'slotted
into' a familiar political category because 'the only politics that have any
reality in Northern Ireland are the old politics of polarity',[34] whereas in
fact 'Field Day was gesturing in the direction of something for which there
was, as yet, no name'.[35] To put a name on Field Day's activities and
possible achievements is premature if not impossible. When Seamus Deane
called it 'a political gesture, smacking of Northerness'[36] it is doubtful if
'northerness' could have been defined at that time (1981) in terms which
we would recognise today as acceptable to the people of Northern
Ireland generally. Friel is doubtful if any conclusion can be drawn from
the Field Day experience: 'it's too early to know what it achieved – if
anything',[37] but he is alert to the changes that have taken place since
1980, if anything becoming more sceptical in the process. But since
Richtarik wrote in the early 1990s, the position in Northern Ireland has
changed, as the 'old politics' have given way to a new situation, much
more noticeably fragmented. A Women's Coalition has taken a political
role, thus establishing that one need not be merely Catholic or nationalist
to be a member of a minority; the Alliance Party, with the election of its
former leader, Lord Alderdice, as chairman of the new Northern Ireland
Assembly, has reasserted its function as a middle ground. The British
Army, which had had a role somewhere between peacekeeping and the
suppression of terrorism, and had been responsible for segregating and
containing potential and actual pockets of sectarian violence and paramilitary activity, began to withdraw and to deconstruct the symbols of
its control and watchfulness.

But much more importantly, the two main political groupings, of paramilitary and constitutional unionism and republicanism, have splintered into many shades of political will, with results in terms of diplomatic maturity which many would have found surprising in the earlier stages of the 'peace process'.

This has both made the disputative nature of Ulsterness more manifest, and indicated ways in which the splintering effect can more readily identify like minds. Two contrasting examples from the unionist 'side' indicate that presumed monoliths or homogeneities can lose their cohesion in the face of political tension and on the threshold of change. In 'Liberty and Authority in Ireland', one of the Field Day pamphlets devoted to establishing the protestant position culturally and historically within the overall Field Day debate, Robert McCartney QC – one of the most eloquent advocates of the Union – set out with the utmost clarity the most compelling arguments why northern Protestants could not conceive of the possibility of unity with the south, these being primarily Church-State relations as exemplified by the constitutional ban on divorce and the domination of education by Catholic thinking, and the irredentist constitutional claim to Northern Ireland. But with the removal of the divorce ban, and the intended removal of the territorial claim, McCartney, rather than moving towards an *entente* with the Republic, has in fact adopted a more extreme posturing on the fringes of unionism, as founder and leader of the new UK Unionist Party.

Conversely David Irvine, a former unionist paramilitary convict who played a key role in brokering the peace agreement in 1997–8, has spoken movingly of how the experience of drama – specifically, a performance of Frank McGuinness's *Observe the Sons of Ulster Marching towards the Somme* – can effect a change in our perceptions of the 'other side' and, in his case, had a fundamental influence on his move towards peace:

> We have fuelled a sense of hatred, a sense of bitterness, on the refusal to understand what other people are, what other people have wanted . . . [In *Sons of Ulster*] none of the people were all the same, they were all different people, naive, uncomplicated people having to deal with very complicated circumstances. [McGuinness] was saying 'Explore, understand, and in the understanding maybe we appreciate each other a wee bit. Don't talk to me about the celebration of the battle of the Somme, there is nothing to celebrate. Talk to me about the commemoration, the understanding of sacrifice, on all sides, and you begin to realise the futility of war'. Frank McGuinness has created something that other people are now running with – the exploration of what the hell happened, why did it happen, what did people experience? I don't think that'll be let go.[38]

The Freedom of the City and *Volunteers* might be read in the same light, even though Friel himself regards the former as too heated in its response to Bloody Sunday, but *Making History* – perhaps because, like *Sons of Ulster*, it refers to an earlier time – explores what happened, what might have happened, and what did not happen, and thus provides a modern audience with an idea of 'what other people are, what other people have wanted' – the sense of 'other' being the crucial presence in every drama of this kind.

Thus the fragmentation of Ulster politics, however vulnerable it may seem, has served to enrich the quality of dialogue within and between the communities and to weaken the function of stereotyping and labelling. Moreover, the extraordinary diplomatic manoeuvering among all parties and governments in the approach to the peace agreement, and the way it was to a large extent 'stage managed', demonstrates that one may assent to a fiction or a pretence in the interests of acting out a drama which preserves the unities and leads to a successful dénouement. The 'allegorical' or 'open-ended' nature of *Translations*, with its concomitant arguments about its truthfulness and its fictionality, becomes particularly relevant in the context of the Northern Ireland ('Good Friday') Peace Agreement of 1998, although ironically Friel himself demurs at the idea that, in his own words, 'saying "yes" has become a kind of movement'.[39] As Seamus Heaney said in 1984, *Translations* spoke of and to 'the condition of the country',[40] while *Making History*, in D. E. S. Maxwell's words, is 'about the stratagem of transcribing – selecting? shaping? perverting? – historical facts in order to establish a version of reality whose "truth" is verified by its acceptance'[41] – again, a way of reading the Northern Ireland Agreement and the dance around its production.

One difficulty with the Field Day project from its inception was similar to this more recent drama: to avoid labelling and yet to make clear what was being said. 'We had less a position than a disposition' said Heaney.[42] To disfavour one inherited set of inhibitions was a clear starting point (Seamus Deane's agenda was 'the destruction of national shibboleths'[43]). Yet it was impossible to state what the destination might be. Republican, catholic and nationalist ambitions might fuel the energy of the company, but an Irish catholic republic was not its aim. 'There is something intrinsically political about what we are trying to do' said Rea, 'in that we stress our Northern, but also our Irish, identity, and that bothers a lot of people'.[44] A sense of the United Irishmen may have hung over the Field Day deliberations, yet even here the articulation of a new state was problematic. 'I'd love to be preachy, but I'm not sure what the sermon is', Friel said in 1981; 'we can only define afterwards what the sermon is'.[45] Tom Paulin said '[We] are separatists . . . who also hunger for Europe';[46] Seamus Deane spoke of everything in terms of fiction, as if placing life, art and politics under that rubric would rob it of its reality and its everyday application and allow a non-specific experiment to take place:

> almost everything which we believe to be nature or natural is in fact . . . an historical fiction. If Field Day can breed a new fiction of theatre . . . which is sufficiently successful to be believed in as though it were natural and an outgrowth of the past, then it will have succeeded.[47]

It is difficult to know whether this logic could best be called byzantine or labyrinthine, so cleverly does it turn in upon itself while exciting the curiosity of the reader. If Deane meant that he wished Field Day's fictions to be judged on the same terms as the fictions of history, then conversely Field Day's activities could also be seen as being equally as real as that history, with all the authority of the real world. It was thus a piece of mirror-logic by which politics could be subsumed into magic and returned to the external world transformed by the fiction of art. And it attuned with the emblematic figure of the peripatetic mad Sweeney whom Heaney translated in a Field Day publication.[48] 'Sweeney is dispersed throughout the country. Sometimes he's south, sometimes he's north. And Field Day straddles the border uneasily like that: published in Derry, off centre'.[49] And Sweeney himself is symbolic of an unhoused aspect of Irish society generally – again in Heaney's words 'the whole population is adept in the mystery of living in two places at one time. Like all human beings, of course, the people would prefer to live in one, but in the meantime they make do with a constructed destination, an interim place whose foundations straddle the areas of self-division'.[50]

Field Day rapidly attracted its critics, not least on the grounds of fiction-versus-accuracy, with *Translations* providing commentators such as Edna Longley, James Simmons, Lynda Henderson and Seán Connolly with the argument that altering the known facts of history was inadmissible in a play which was widely perceived to be allegorical of more recent dispossessions.[51] Counter-arguments to the volatile ideology of Field Day have come mainly from critics of a 'unionist' persuasion unwilling to accept the 'pretence' of fiction: Simmons once penned an article on Friel entitled 'Catholic Playwright';[52] Henderson spent much of her editorship of *Theatre Ireland* putting down Field Day productions and modus operandi;[53] and Longley's attitude has been a condescendingly patrician mixture of lit-crit *hauteur* and establishment disdain of nebulous nationalism.

Deane, in his 'General Introduction' to the *Field Day Anthology of Irish Writing* gave specific voice to Field Day's self-appointed task in respect of such criticism which, as we shall see, brought art and politics, sect and academe into collision:

In a country like Ireland, where nationalism had to be politically opposed to the prevailing power-systems, there was a serious attempt to create a counter-culture and to define it as authentic to the nation. In doing so, it used historical and archaeological scholarship in a tendentious and polemical fashion. For this, it was rebuked. It distorted the facts of history and reduced literature to propaganda. The rebuke came from groups equally anxious to assert some other position against nationalism – unionism, liberalism, internationalism. The political animus informing all these non-nationalist groups was concealed as much as possible, and the most frequently worn disguise was, in history, the pretence to 'objectivity' and in literature the claim to 'autonomy'. Both words had the magical appeal of not being polemical or political; both were against 'propaganda' which pretended to be either history or art.[54]

The fact that Field Day was articulating a non-specific philosophy or ideology that refused to be nominated as 'nationalist', 'republican' or 'catholic', or to be polarised in opposition to unionism or protestantism, does not prevent us from seeing many of its participants as having natural sympathies with Irish nationalism (and thereby republicanism) as a direct result of their experiences as minority citizens. In any society, an alternative way of life, when it becomes coherent and articulated, is usually seen to have been present but previously unacknowledged or even suppressed, chiefly because it runs parallel, beneath or even counter to the culture which is dominant in society.

Lynda Henderson was particularly critical of Frank McGuinness having prefaced *Carthaginians* with the epigram of Czeslaw Milosz 'It is possible that there is no other memory than the memory of wounds'.[55] It is certain that many of the more defeated and embittered people in Northern Ireland would carry such memories, such emblems of hurt, less lightly than people in more healthy societies where ritual enhances and transcends life rather than debases and inhibits it. That mentality was displayed to me when hostage Brian Keenan was released from captivity in the Lebanon; Patrick McGrory, a leading nationalist lawyer who had won a significant victory in the British legal system in an action relating to the killing of three Irish people in Gibraltar, and who had written a pamphlet for Field Day on 'Law and the Constitution: present discontents',[56] was said to be representing Keenan's interests in respect of publishing his story. A first-class honours graduate from a nationalist background, intimately involved with Irish theatre, told me 'Brian Keenan has been released and Patrick McGrory is defending him'. The notion is so absurd as to be almost unbelievable, but so ingrained is that sense of hurt, of the anticipation that one will always be the victim, the accused, the defendant, that British (in)justice will be used against you, that a man who had done no wrong would need a top lawyer, not to maximise his rights, but to ensure that his wrongs were minimised. We find it expressed also in Deane's *Reading in the Dark* where the narrator (Deane) reports 'Innocence was no guarantee for a Catholic then. Nor is it now'.[57]

The crisis of the civil rights movement in the North, especially in the period 1968–69 and culminating in the political apogee of Bloody Sunday in 1972, in a way substituted for the unrest among students and intellectuals witnessed at that period in Paris, Berkeley and London which also had its militant dimension in figures such as Daniel Cohn-Bendit.

Friel himself referred on at least one occasion to the near-labelling of Field Day as analogous to the SDLP.[58] Others, more suspicious of what Field Day's activities augured for republican attitudes to Protestant culture in Northern Ireland, might have seen its ideology as closer to Sinn Féin. The childhood experiences of Seamus Deane, as recounted in his autobiographical *Reading in the Dark*,[59] and given extra point by the audio recording of the book by Stephen Rea, suggest an empathy with people whose lives have been inhibited by *force majeure* and whose expression of their culture and political viewpoints has therefore found alternative outlets – sometimes violent and always empowered by feelings of frustration and hostility – which have provided a counter-culture to the orthodoxies prevailing in Northern Ireland for so many decades. In particular, the process whereby the secret in the bosom of the family is revealed is a paradigm of the unspoken becoming known.

To understand the elements which combined to make Field Day a significant phenomenon in the Northern Ireland of the 1980s we must appreciate not only the symbolism that had encrusted the polarities of northern life since partition, but the life which had given rise to that symbolism, life that was based largely on the mutual suspicions of two communities, commonly referred to as a 'siege mentality', in which each developed a viewpoint of the other as inherently threatening and potentially destructive. The master-servant nature of this relationship is seldom evident, chiefly because both sides were most often at pains to emphasise that there was, in fact, no relationship other than that of mutual antagonism; yet the symbiosis of coloniser and colonised, on which the original division of 'planter and gael' is predicated, makes the polarity one of attraction as well as repulsion. The passionate attachment to land, and the way that attachment is expressed in language, are twin indicators of the way that people are lived by the land.

That Friel's *Translations* diary could have been published by Tim Pat Coogan under the title 'Race and a Sense of Place' underscores the way that Irish people have been encouraged by history to attach themselves to the land metaphysically in an affective, psychic way, as well as in the basic physical sense of deriving life from the soil. Land has – indeed *is* – both a socio-economic function and an historico-emotional one, valid for both the pasturage and the husbandry with which, respectively, native and immigrant modes of living have been narrowly labelled.

Seamus Heaney has long been articulate on the subject of the local and deep energies derived from the land, and the sexual imagery he employs to denote its uses under different masters is compelling. First, there is where you are, the certainty of it: 'I would begin with the Greek word, *omphalos*, meaning the navel, and hence the stone that marked the centre of the world . . . its blunt and falling music . . . the music of someone pumping water at the pump outside our back door'.[60] The pump 'centred and staked the imagination'.[61] Place is deep-rooted and exercises an affective call on the imagination and the emotions: 'each name was a kind of love made to each acre'[62] – with place-names 'like some script indelibly written into the nervous system'.[63] That this is a non-sectarian emotion is emphasised by Heaney:

> Irrespective of our creed or politics, irrespective of what culture or sub-culture may have coloured our individual sensibilities, our imaginations assent to the stimulus of the names, our sense of the place is enhanced, our sense of ourselves as inhabitants not just of a geographical country but of a country of the mind is cemented.[64]

But it also denoted *difference* – 'if this was the country of community, it was also the realm of division . . . the lines of sectarian antagonism and affiliation followed the boundaries of the land'.[65] In historical terms, the personality of the landscape could be celebrated by the poets in a particular fashion learned from the land itself; but it may be confronted by a new reality with which it has to come to terms, which sees and experiences that landscape in a different vocabulary and with different rhythms:

> There is an indigenous territorial numen, a tutelar of the whole island, call her Mother Ireland, Kathleen Ni Houlihan, the poor old woman, the Shan Van Vocht, whatever; and her sovereignty has been temporarily usurped or infringed by a new male cult whose founding fathers were Cromwell, William of Orange and Edward Carson, and whose godhead is incarnate in a rex or caesar resident in a palace in London. What we have is the tail-end of a struggle in a province between territorial piety and imperial power.[66]

Over twenty years later, in the context of a rapidly increasing *entente* between those sectarian divides, Heaney spoke eloquently and persuasively of his own experience in crossing and recrossing boundaries in his childhood and his growing awareness of the boundary ditch as a 'march' –

not a physical act of protest, intimidation or triumphalism but an inert yet expressive statement of difference, a celebration of land.

In his poem 'Terminus' Heaney had written

> I was the march drain and the march drain's banks
> Suffering the limit of each claim.[67]

Of the word 'march' he said in 1998:

> the land itself did the marching. The verb meant to meet at the boundary, to be bordered by, to me marched up to and yet to be marked off from. One farm marched another farm, one field marched another field, and what divided them was the march drain and the march hedge. The word did not mean to walk in a military manner, but to be close, to lie alongside, to border upon and be bordered upon. It was a word that acknowledged divergence but it also contained a future suggestion of solidarity. If my land marched your land, we were bound by that boundary, as well as separated by it.[68]

One result of this geography is that one recognises the man on 'the other side' as sharing an inseparable bond, even if the only manifestation of that bond is the sign of difference, most usually exhibited in language.[69] In the post-colonial context, we find Heidegger saying much the same: 'a boundary is not that at which something stops but . . . that from which *something begins its presencing*'.[70]

From these contiguous fields, Heaney derives his understanding of landscape as language, or, more precisely, landscape as units of speech. Sinking a well-shaft into the deep structures of home is like finding a language within: with the poem 'Digging', 'I felt I had let down a shaft into real life'.[71] Poetry is 'a point of entry into the buried life of the feelings'.[72] But land both commands, and responds to, those who live on and in it, and our viewpoints, including political views, can be shaped by how we make those responses: 'I think that poetry and politics are, in different ways, an articulation, an ordering, a giving form to inchoate pieties, prejudices, world-views, or whatever . . . emanating from the ground'.[73] And these 'pieties' have a gendered existence: 'I think of the personal and Irish pieties as vowels, and the literary awarenesses nourished on English as consonants' he said in 1972. This he put into poetry in a sexual and territorial way in the contemporaneous 'Traditions':

> Our guttural muse
> was bulled long ago
> by the alliterative tradition.[74]

Poem after poem by Heaney (and indeed by many other 'northern' poets from Ferguson[75] to MacNeice, John Montague, John Hewitt and, to a lesser extent, Derek Mahon) speak of land in this affective,

sexual or referential way, always slightly doubtful of their bearings or of
their tenure:

> Anahorish, soft gradient
> of consonant, vowel-meadow – ('Anahorish').[76]

> But now our river tongues must rise
> From licking deep in native haunts
> To flood, with vowelling embrace,
> Demesnes staked out in consonants ('A New Song').[77]

We can thus understand Marilyn Richtarik's observation that 'when
an Irish playwright talks about language, it has a political edge'.[78] She
quotes Friel as saying 'the problem with the Northern situation is how
you can tip-toe through the minefields of language where language has
become so politicized. . . . You see, where you have a war, language is
always the first casualty'.[79] That there has been a continuing implicit
hostility between two traditions, with explicit eruption of violence at
specific points since the seventeenth century (1601, 1641, 1690, 1798,
1803, 1848, 1867, 1916, 1921–23, 1968–1998) is the background
against which we have to see language as a 'casualty'. 'The language we
have now and what use we make of it',[80] as Friel said on another
occasion, is a wounded language which, if we continue to see language
itself as a partisan quality and condition, is used to combat the wounded
language of the other side. He saw the solution to the political problem
in 'the recognition of what language means for us on this island . . .
marrying two cultures . . . which are ostensibly speaking the same
language but which in fact aren't'.[81] The idea of *what language means*
is so profound, complex and problematic that it signals, as in the order
of semiotics only language can, the possible end of civilisation. Seamus
Deane also referred to the 'uses' of language in an eighteenth-century
fashion: 'In a basic sense, the crisis we are passing through is stylistic.
That is to say, it is a crisis of language – the ways in which we write it
and the ways in which we read it'.[82] In the example I gave earlier of the
recognition by David Irvine of concepts of hurt in McGuinness's *Sons of
Ulster* we have the seeds of linguistic *rapprochement* which is embedded
in the Good Friday Agreement.

The uses of language by Field Day – as propaganda in the sense in
which one English critic interpreted *Translations*[83] – were strategic.
Through the often allegorical medium of drama and in the centuries-old
tradition of pamphleteering, the company addressed the Irish public on
the question of exchange of meaning between cultures, on the loss and
acquisition of identity, on the writing of history, on the meaning and
exercise of authority, and, in Seamus Deane's telling title, the distinction

and the confusion between 'civilians and barbarians'. The *Field Day Anthology of Irish Writing*, published in three volumes in 1991, was its most ambitious and controversial project[84] – attempting a 'definition' while rejecting the notion of a 'canon' of Irish literature – as a collection of diverse and disparate texts which were to be 'accommodating and generous' to the various traditions of writing in Ireland and establish a form of cultural unity. But it was also an unequivocal act of repossession, 'an exercise in renaming, the resituation of many texts, . . . in a renovated landscape or context' as Deane put it.[85]

As far as we are concerned primarily with the career of Brian Friel, we should note that he himself subscribed to, and was in most cases the principal architect of, the dramatic thrust of the company, with Stephen Rea its on-stage interpreter, while Seamus Deane became widely regarded as the apologist and ideologue of the venture. Behind the language plays of the 1980s, with their primary focus on the public and private voices, is Friel's insistence on the need to 'make English identifiably our own' – an act of appropriation and transformation which would see Irishness being mapped onto the English language. If Friel has, with a few notable exceptions, eschewed direct political statement, he has at a more subtle level pushed forward the view that Ireland has needed – and still needs – to be more self-confident in order to allow Emmet's epitaph to be written, and that a new critical space was necessary to establish the conditions for this.

As with Heaney's television broadcast in 1998 on the nature of the boundary, with its emphasis on how poems such as 'The Other Side' could both acknowledge difference and provide stepping stones towards a meeting point, so Friel's *Translations*, performed in the Derry Guildhall which had been the setting for the tragedy of *The Freedom of the City*, was seen as 'a symbol of how two cultures could meet in peace and throw away their cares in front of the footlights'.[86]

Friel was not the only northern writer to have the ambition to effect or influence change in his society. Although Heaney, too, has eschewed explicit political comment in most of his poetry (and has been seriously criticised for it) – 'I'm not a political writer and I don't see literature as a way of solving political problems'[87] – he has, both as a member of Field Day and as an individual voice, spoken of poetry as a way of refining feelings and of re-shaping arrangements. Heaney incorporated in his poem sequence *Station Island* lines by Czeslaw Milosz which might equally apply to Friel: 'I was stretched between contemplation of a motionless point and the command to participate actively in history'.[88]

Stewart Parker said in 1986 that through the 'solace and rigour and passionate rejoinder of great drama . . . there is a whole culture to be achieved'.[89] Derek Mahon said that while the function of the arts 'is not to change maps', it can 'change the expressions on the faces of men and women'.[90] Poetry and playwriting may be non-political but may nevertheless have a 'political effect': the expressions on people's faces may well decide the fate of governments. The appearance of work by each of these writers in the Field Day 'canon' may be taken as a positive subscription to the wider project of creating a space from which neither the writer nor his audience could be dispossessed – in Parker's words, to 'bear witness to an alternative way of carrying on in the field of human relations'.[91]

6

PLAYS OF LANGUAGE AND TIME

To translate is to descend beneath the exterior disparities of two
languages in order to bring into vital play their analogies and,
at the final depths, common principles of being[1]
George Steiner

HISTORY AND FICTION

Language is a casualty of war. But war can often result from language
imperfectly uttered or understood. In *Volunteers* the Viking skeleton,
Leif, was 'a casualty of language' and in both *Translations* and *Making
History*, the plays with which we shall be principally concerned in this
chapter, people, whether they are the minor folk of everyday life or the
great presences of history, suffer from the lack or failure of translation
between one privacy and another or between their innate privacy and the
public world in which they are to be re-presented. These plays saw Friel
returning to the theme of *what language means* and how public and
private significances can be laid on the same words with sometimes
disastrous consequences.

In her study of Brian Friel, Martine Pelletier concentrates on the
distinction between story (*histoires*) and history (*Histoire*)[2] and the way
in which History and fiction intermingle. She quotes Michel de Certeau
to the effect that 'western historiography contests fiction. This visceral
engagement between History and stories goes back very far. It is not only
historiography that can speak the truth'.[3] The confrontation takes place
in the now, in which History is being written, but concerns what
happened 'then'.

By the time he came to write *Translations*, Friel had cleared the way
for the examination of issues which had been lurking in the background
of his previous plays. In *Faith Healer*, for example, he had reconciled the

idea of the artist to the experience of privacy. Homecomings of different kinds had been addressed and resolved, in *Living Quarters* and *Aristocrats*: in the former, Ben and his father are able to embrace, and in the latter the decaying and imprisoning symbols of the family's past are discarded in favour of new worlds and individual destinies.

But neither *Translations* nor *Making History* is exclusively concerned with the external world: it is the significance of what is felt by people *as people*, and how their feelings are expressed and negotiated, that constitutes the 'aboutness' of the play. What happens when these transactions become public is a further purpose of the drama, but until the thoughts and exchanges between people, their private translations, are established, the rest of the play means nothing. Then, and only then, may we endow them with external significance, make them into figures of record.

The title of this chapter has two meanings: firstly, not only are *Translations* and *Making History* plays of language but they are also plays about time, since they explore decisive episodes in the history of Ireland, in one case through the lives of ordinary people and in the other through those of figures who contributed to the changes that took place. And in that sense they have had a certain effect on twentieth-century audiences, both in Ireland and abroad, in relation to those events of the late sixteenth and early nineteenth centuries. But they are also, secondly, plays about language-in-time, in that they indicate how a statement, an emotion or an aspiration can have one meaning the moment it is uttered and another meaning a second later when what is intended is received, decoded and understood or misunderstood – appreciated, assessed – by its intended auditor.

Language changes through time. Meaning changes through time. People change through time. And 'time' may not be of long duration. The moment a word is uttered, it is different. The person who speaks it has changed. The person who hears it is changed by having heard it. Some words travel faster than others; some require longer to be decoded, to be acted upon.

George Steiner characterises man as 'the language animal' (Herder: *ein Geschöpf der Sprache*) and quotes Chomsky's *Language and Mind* to the effect that 'language [among humans] appears to be a unique phenomenon, without significant analogue in the animal world';[4] 'no animal remembers historically';[5] 'man's capacity to articulate a future tense . . . makes him unique'.[6] Leaving aside the entire question of what communication does actually take place between non-linguistic animals, and even how animals do remember or anticipate, we are faced with the fact that men and women are at the same time blessed and cursed with the capacity to render experience into speech which can both reflect their joys and destroy their lives. The break-up of families – as we have witnessed it in Friel's radio plays – is due not so much to behaviour as to the way behaviour and experience are reported. Crises of faith in *The Enemy Within* and *The Blind Mice* are conducted entirely through the medium of rational, or rationalised, thought. The embarrassment at the heart of *Philadelphia* is conveyed through silence, or at least the stuttering attempts at bland pleasantries; only the outbursts of nonsense speech can fend off the rage and the darkness.

Man is thus both animal and linguist: 'down below they were roaring at each other' is the *lingua franca* recalled by the eponymous 'Child'. This is evident in *Translations*, in the barely literate Doalty and Nora Dan and the muteness of Sarah, and in *Making History* where the basic speech of Hugh O'Donnell contrasts sharply with the acquired characteristics of Harry Hoveden, Peter Lombard and Hugh O'Neill.

In many instances, these plays signal the breakdown of discourse and the violence which comes in the wake of the breakdown. The deaths in *The Freedom of the City* and *Volunteers* take place when all the stories have been told, when there is nothing left to say, and when creativity, the construction and enjoyment of meaning and identity, has been exhausted.

Semantically, we must take considerable account of Humboldt's view, quoted by Steiner, that 'language makes men at home in the world, but it also has the power to alienate'.[7] So far as we have seen, throughout this study, the writer-as-exile, and the succession of leavetakings and home-comings as a commentary upon the fragile and questionable concept of 'hope', then *Translations* presents the image of a homecoming and a break-up of home, both transacted through the medium of language, underpinned by the practice and theory of translation, where language is a casualty and casualty is a language.

The late 1970s saw an extraordinary surge of energy in Friel's writing, in which the quick succession of *Faith Healer*, *Aristocrats* and *Translations* marked a trio of works (comparable to that of O'Casey's *The Shadow of a Gunman*, *Juno and the Paycock* and *The Plough and the Stars*, produced between 1923 and 1926) which were assured of their quality and status at the time and which have held the interest of directors and audiences since. *Translations*, like *Philadelphia*, was both a hybrid and a defining moment in Irish theatre. *The Communication Cord* as a 'corrective' farce in 1982 and Friel's adaptation of *Three Sisters* in 1980 continued this creative flow which has not been equalled in his subsequent career.

Translations occupies a place of similar importance in the development of Irish drama to that of *Philadelphia*, to the extent that it was a play which spoke publicly to Irish people about an experience which, in the case of the later play, was still resonant within the acoustic of racial memory. Where, as I have argued, *Faith Healer* shows us Private Gar coming home to Ballybeg, *Translations* puts Public Gar on the route to Baile Beag.

Despite Friel's anxiety that the play should concern itself with private preoccupations, the public elements in the play, which he knew were present but which he wanted to serve merely as the occasion for private exploration, have been seen by some critics as giving the play a 'national' characteristic. Friel has been both fêted and pilloried for this, and the recognition of *Translations* – whether it was intended by its author or not – has been marked by its inclusion in the *Field Day Anthology of Irish Writing* alongside Tom Murphy's *Bailegangaire* and Kilroy's *Double Cross* as the most significant texts of contemporary Irish drama. In placing *Translations* in this context, the section editor of the Anthology, D. E. S. Maxwell, observed that the play was part of a series inaugurated by *The Freedom* and including *Volunteers, Living Quarters, Aristocrats, Faith Healer* and *The Communication Cord*, in which there is 'a persistent strain between a group-enforcing authority and an individual urge, not wholly evasive, to disown it'[8] – a strain also evident, we must note, in *The Enemy Within*.

I have said that *Translations* might be read as a dramatisation of *After Babel*, and in the following pages we shall explore Steiner's thesis. In his opening chapter, 'Understanding as Translation', Steiner says:

> We know little of internal history, of the changing proceedings of consciousness in a civilization. How do different cultures and historical epochs use language, how do they conventionalize or enact the manifold possible relations between word and object, between stated meaning and literal performance?[9]

In *Translations* and *Making History* we are in fact given access to some aspects of internal history, not least because of the fortuitous congruence of Friel's historical imagination with, in addition to Steiner, the account of the Ordnance Survey service by John Andrews and the texts which lie behind it, such as those of Larcom and John O'Donovan. It is here, rather than in any grandiose scheme of allegorising modern Ireland, that Friel may have written 'a national epic'.

But it is also an international epic in the sense in which Steiner says 'our homecomings are those of Odysseus' – that is, while the storehouse of Homer continues to provide us with a 'repertoire for most of the principal postures of Western consciousness',[10] its events in Baile Beag, a place already familiar with those of Homer's world, join up with events in other Ballybegs, which already enjoy similar contours and have similar ways of negotiating them.

In this way *Translations* is more international than national, interglottal in its capacity to speak to other identities and the situations in which the collision of the public and private, the imperial and the local, time and Time, story and History, has occurred or may be happening today.

We must take note of the fact that, if *Translations* is allegorical of a loss of language and hence of identity in modern Ireland, it can also be read as symptomatic of the entropy of modern European culture and civilisation (the two are not necessarily coterminous). Václav Havel calls this 'the loss of metaphysical certainties, of an experience of the transcendental . . . strange, but ultimately quite logical'.[11] Steiner, too, identifies the period 1900–25 as that of both a 'language revolution' and 'a drastic crisis of language'[12] – the point being that modernism embodied both a change in our linguistic consciousness and what Steiner calls a 'failure of nerve' in employing language in its new habitat. For both Havel and Steiner there is a 'lost centre'[13] – a place where man was once at home, in and with language, but from which he has become displaced, a refugee from that which made him at home and made sense of being at home: language. When therefore (as we have seen, above pp. 24–5) Robert Welch identifies a second language, Irish, as haunting a mind like Friel's, he highlights Friel's consciousness of *Translations* as a play 'about the disappearance of the Irish language' both then and now. It gives added point and poignancy to the idea of writing as an exile from the affections which finds us at the border of another country, 'linguistically "unhoused" or displaced or hesitant at the frontier' as we have seen Steiner call the condition.

It makes us unfamiliar with everything that should be familiar. When Steiner says of this crisis of language that at an immediate level 'problems of formal description become a matter of general philosophy and of the images one has of one's relations to the Logos',[14] he could easily be referring to the confusion among the people of Baile Beag about the nature and significance of the 'sweet smell' which the villagers believe to herald a plague.

When Steiner writes that 'the modernist movement can be seen as a strategy of permanent exile'[15] he creates a space in which we can see Friel in the unhoused company of Wilde, Synge and Beckett. When, as we have already observed, he also speaks of all communication being 'an act of translation' and a redefinition of the self (above, p. 27) we can better understand why the ontology of writing is such a crucial issue today – whether the writer means anything, *can* mean anything, and whether readers and audiences have any assured method of understanding what is written or spoken. To this extent, Friel's language plays are both private and public because they concern one man's own responses to what he divines, his responses on behalf of his 'constituency', his way of making public certain things while safeguarding the privacy of other things. In an increasingly autistic world, the retreat from the word signifies in a perversely paradoxical fashion the removal from all that the word can offer – *logos*, *topos*, semantic existence, and ultimately any chance of magic. The magic of discovery, whether it be the secret garden of 'donging the tower' or the knowledge of what to sow in crumbly soil (*Tr.* 19) becomes a world closed to us.

The *logos* with which we come face to face most frequently is that of memory – the 'history' which is uniquely available to the 'language animal'. Steiner makes the distinction that 'our history is made of the past tense . . . Our utopias lie in the future of the verb'.[16] In *Translations* and *Making History* Irish society stands between memory and utopia, past and future, occupying a liminal, between-space in which anything can happen. But the 'syntax opulent with tomorrows' is governed by two principles: one is the continual anticipation of the life to come, replacing the suspended animation of today and yesterday during which we have been denied meaning; the other is the memory of the dead, of the generation of suppression, failure, fear, which makes utopia so necessary. In each condition, the *dramatis personae* of this society wait for a catalyst to shift the action from negative to positive mode, to make choices inevitable, to encourage resolutions.

To the extent that they are allegorical works, *Translations* and *Making History* are illustrative of what Fanon says about writing in a post-colonial world:

> The artist who has decided to illustrate the truths of the nation turns paradoxically towards the past and away from actual events. What he ultimately intends to embrace are in fact the cast-offs of thought, its shells and corpses, a knowledge which has been stabilized once and for all. But the native intellectual who wishes to create an authentic work of art must realize that the truths of a nation are in the first place its realities. He must go on until he has found the seething pot out of which the learning of the future will emerge.[17]

'All identity is active statement' says Steiner.[18] A child is named, and from thenceforward its identity constitutes an organic relationship with place, time and family – an act of affiliation which must be taken further each day in transactions between self and world, unless the child is to fossilise.[19] Friel incorporated this into *Translations*: 'it is not the literal past, the "facts" of history, that shape us, but images of the past embodied in language . . . We must never cease renewing those images; because once we do, we fossilise' (*Tr.* 66). In a presumably unconscious echo, Richard Kearney concludes his Field Day pamphlet, 'Myth and Motherland', with the statement: 'we must never cease to keep our mythological images in dialogue with history; because once we do we fossilise. That is why we go on telling stories, inventing and re-inventing myths, until we have brought history home to itself'.[20]

Whatever Friel's concerns that his plays should present the everyday lives of ordinary folk, and however powerfully the transactions between such folk may expand metaphorically to give meaning to the whole world, there is an inevitable sense in which the scene as we witness it is also political: not merely political in the social implications of what is trans-acted, by means of internal forces and agents, but in the ontological sense in which those transactions are also catalysed from without by the forces and agents of other cultures and presences. It is in this sense that *Translations* and *Making History* are political plays – not because they are 'about' the death of Irish culture, its language, its habits of pasturage, its marriage to past customs – since these are all organic elements of its internal systemic life, but because, like Atahualpa's Inca civilisation or Montezuma's Aztecs, faced with the conquistador power and mentality of a Pizarro or a Cortez, the world of Hugh O'Neill is brought up short in the face of Elizabethan expansion, a confrontation which will be re-enacted two hundred years later in the microcosmic encounter of Hugh Mor O'Donnell and Captain Lancey.

In each case, it is the need to proffer and exchange identities, to *move with the times*, which shifts the action seismically from past to future tense. In *Translations* and *Making History*, the presence of both 'sides' in one *persona* is demonstrated respectively by Owen/Roland O'Donnell and Hugh O'Neill. But it is also in each character, to the greater or lesser extent that he or she advances towards or retreats from the other. In *Making History*, Hugh O'Neill introduces his new wife, Mabel Bagenal, the daughter and sister of successive Queen's Marshals, to his associates Hugh O'Donnell and Peter Lombard, Archbishop of Armagh who, like 'Sir' with his Ledger in *Living Quarters*, is preparing the official nationalist history of O'Neill's defeat in which he will become a messianic hero:

> MABEL: I'm pleased to meet you.
> (*She holds out her hand.* O'DONNELL has *to take it. He does not speak. Pause.*)
> ....
> MABEL: I'm pleased to meet you.
> (*Again she holds out her hand. After a pause* LOMBARD *takes it. He does not speak. Pause.*) (*MH* 15)

Although no words are exchanged, O'Donnell and Lombard become complicit in the exchange between identities which has been initiated, since the mere handshake is more than symbolic if less than a courtesy. It has a semantic significance which admits Mabel to a minimal area in the public history of Ireland and enters O'Donnell and Lombard in the annals of Elizabethan diplomacy.

Steiner quotes Descartes' dictum that 'almost all controversy would cease if there was agreement between philosophers as to the meaning of terms' and infers from this, somewhat predictably, that 'human controversies and confusions are, in essence, a matter of failed communication'.[21] What is understood by the gesture, the trans-action of the held hand, is not to be guessed at, even though we 'know', by means of history, that Mabel's and Hugh's fate is ultimately tragic as, we must presume, is that of those other exogamists, Maire and George in *Translations*. The communication, whether understood or not, is the first step towards love or hate.

In *Translations*, people unknown to History take on a supra-personal burden. In *Making History*, people from the pages of History shrink into their real *personae*. Within each play, History and histories interweave and compete for the affections. It may be said that 'Friel does not write history plays, but plays that mock history'[22] but mockery is also a form of acknowledgement of the *force majeure* of the tide of time which rolls over these insignificant lives. One can live, like Charles McGlinchey, outside History, but not outside time.

What matters to the people we see on the stage is what Mabel Bagenal in *Making History* calls 'the overall thing' (*MH* 39). It means the completeness of the individual lives and of the relationship between those lives. But because History is selective in deciding both what shall be included in the Ledger and in ordering the sequence of events, the 'overall thing' is not achieved. History thus diminishes and fragments the smaller histories. Storytelling gives way to politics. Later, in *Dancing at Lughnasa*, Kate realises that the world of Ballybeg, and the place of the Mundy household within it, is breaking up: 'the whole thing is so fragile it can't be held together much longer. It's all about to collapse' (*DL* 35). Perhaps because it does not, in reality, exist. As Friel noted when writing *Translations*, 'one aspect that keeps eluding me: the wholeness, the integrity, of that Gaelic past. Maybe because I don't believe in it'.[23]

Thus, while Friel may be showing us (in both plays) the disintegration of 'that Gaelic past', he may also be showing us that it never existed as a satisfactory unifying concept. In *Translations* this is suggested by the lack of cohesion, the confused state of mind and the vain hope of being organised, of having a purpose, and a future; in *Making History*, by the divisiveness of the Ulster chiefs counterpointed against the need for order, symbols of a predicament which has discontinuity at its heart.

Friel may not have written a History play, but he has certainly written political plays. The fact that the writing of *Translations* caused him so much trouble is indicative of the pull between the private play and the public play, because the political invades both private and public: it inserts itself into the gap between the innermost emotions of two people and oscillates along their private lines of communication. His own dismay at the success of *Translations* was in fact acutely double-edged: 'nowadays to write a three-act naturalistic play set in the 19th century in the Gaeltacht is a recipe for some kind of instant death, so its success astonished me'.[24] The tension between the two is heightened not because of History but because we already know the destiny of the characters both collectively and individually. They are enacting and drawing us into an elaborate make-believe about History because they themselves *are* make-believe – people who in fact never existed, a fantastic extrapolation of some private expedition into 'the back hills' of personal and racial memory. For this reason, it does not matter that many aspects of the action are, historically speaking, impossible.

Here, 'translation' is not so much between cultures or languages or even between privacies, as from one condition to another: from the incoherent and inchoate fumblings with language, meaning and identity to moments of clarity, cohesion and purpose – and back again. Fintan O'Toole calls it 'a self-conscious historical myth'[25] and as a self-conscious work it carries within it the irony of reflection, acknowledging in every line its awareness of myth as an ingredient, a character, in the play itself. To know that it is 'set in the 19th century in the Gaeltacht' is to be aware of History; to insist on the importance of the local and immediate, equal to or greater than the tide which will wash away both the gaeltacht and the century, is to overcome the difficulty of politics by means of the intellectual beauty and brilliance of its own 'translations' between the two.

Two facets of *Translations* illuminate the interplay between the local and immediate and the universal: the triangulation of the Ordnance Survey and the introduction of the National School system. Both have been seen – correctly – as forms of cultural and political imperialism, an invasion and an eviction of Gaelic culture. But they are both also intensely local events which have to do with the way Doalty and Bridget and Maire read and interpret the landscape of everyday life. The characters may be read as symbolic of the last Irish-speaking communities, but they are also symbolic of themselves. And vice versa.

In *The Last of the Name* McGlinchey records that

at the time of the Ordnance Survey in 1835, two of the sappers stopped in our house when they were mapping this part of the parish. My father went chaining with them whenever they would want him. . . . One day the sappers were out on the face of Bulaba somewhere about Currachbeag, and they lay down to rest and take a smoke. When they went to look again, their whole kit was stolen, with papers and records of their work and instruments that were valued for £50 that could not be got nearer than Dublin. . . . They came home and told my father. He questioned them if they had seen anyone about the place and they said they noticed a young fellow about the rocks before they sat down. From the description, my father knew it to be a fellow from that part who had a bad name. So my father went to his home and asked him if he had noticed any men in Currachbeag that day and he said not. Then my father asked if he had seen a kit of tools belonging to them, and from the way he blushed he gave himself away, and my father knew he had him. So my father told him the sappers knew about him and were going to get a warrant for his arrest, but if the fellow handed the kit and papers over to him that he would stand between him and any other bother. The mother then told the lad who had taken them to give them up. So he took my father over to the rock where he had the lot hidden.[26]

Friel was apparently unaware of this at the time that he set Doalty to move the sappers' measuring instruments – one can hardly imagine Doalty blushing.[27] But it is more than possible that such incidents entered into the folklore of Inishowen and that the idea was therefore in Friel's subconscious for a long time prior to writing *Translations*. One wonders whether the map by which Ireland is today represented can be accurate in anything more than a figurative sense, if the contiguous triangles of which it is constructed are drawn from such variable *topoi*.[28]

Similarly, the haunting memory of the hedge-school, as the last custodian of Gaelic culture on the run, asserts itself in *Translations* in defiance of the basic imperial education available in the new National School. It is a simple irony that Edmund Burke, whose apostrophe to Marie Antoinette provided the refrain for Gar O'Donnell's madness in *Philadelphia*, should have received his first education in such a fugitive environment. Hugh Mor O'Donnell, as the representative of that culture, is a figure of the eighteenth century who confronts and almost turns his back on the future, as Hugh O'Neill does in *Making History*.

Both these ideas are at the same time spatial and temporal: the physical picture of the country available to the mapper changes through time as the markers, the signifiers, take up different positions, giving different signals, and the way the landscape is 'read' or interpreted by means of mental images changes through time as different interpretations are forced on us by external events. We can not survive in hidden valleys.

In a playful piece – 'Brian Friel – the name of the game' – Seamus Deane posits the notion that one can only conceive of an absurdity, a 'fabulous creature' such as a unicorn, if one creates the space within which it can exist. (As we shall see below, p. 306, the idea of 'love' itself depends on a 'context'.) The place is a fictional space ('Ballybeg') which is co-ordinated with a historical world 'and produc[es] out of that a projection that includes both. . . . We are in Ballybeg. After that comes Donegal, Ireland, history'.[29] Here, then, we have the inclusive equation which acknowledges both public and private – the 'Ballybeg' which is hermetic, an enclosed community of affiliates, where time passes rhythmically, and a place of events, where history happens.

Deane makes the crucial point that 'writing is . . . an act of memory, of saying what a thing or place is; it is a subversive gift for in nominating everything that it comes to it reveals its own nature; but that nature can never itself be named'.[30] Writing, in this sense, is the public face of divination, since the diviner detects and demonstrates the qualities and conditions of life where he finds it, but he does not speak it. The diviner is thus cognate with the delphic oracle: it neither speaks the truth nor lies, but signifies (*semanei*; σημανει). Writing makes this semantic state – still problematical, still obscure – into a visible, debatable, manifestation, making it amenable to both truthful and mendacious statements about its nature. It is thus inevitably public, inexorably political, even when it speaks of the most sacred and private things. Steiner gives this a spiritual and deeply emotional dimension when he refers to language as 'this vaulting across one's shadow and attempt to examine the skin of one's shadow from within and without'.[31]

The liminal situations in *Translations* and *Making History* are public and the debate which has centred on the fictional authority of the plays concerns the admissibility of the 'real' to the fictional world and of the fictional into the 'real'. There is no demand, at this stage, and in this age of revisionism, that a play should be totally faithful to the 'facts' of history: both John Andrews and Seán Connolly, the chief critics of *Translations* on grounds of historical accuracy, have revised their original objections and have come to accept the *bona fides* of the drama.[32] But there remains a question of what a play *should* be faithful to, of what pieties it should observe.

The liminal condition of Baile Beag, into which a strange, cathartic element is about to be introduced from beyond, is emphasised by the fact that it is Hugh himself who welcomes the intruder: 'I trust you will find access to us with my son's help' (*Tr.* 43) – echoing and inverting Steiner's quotation of Massignon: 'pour comprendre l'autre, il ne faut pas se l'annexer mais devenir son hôte'.[33]

Liminal also suggests fugitive, and the hedge-school itself is symbolic of a flight from normality, a culture sheltering out of doors from everything which would allow it to be 'civilised'; akin to the allegorical flight of 'mad Sweeney' which was both topographical and conceptual in its exploration of opposites.

Elmer Andrews says:

> Language and fiction inhabit the gap between the real and the ideal,
> mediating between what is and what might be: the great task is to create an
> authentic fiction, a workable model of wholeness.[34]

As in the case of the Northern Ireland Agreement, such mediation takes
on a life of its own, a middle space in which the language employed is
true to neither side, in which the translators are trusted despite the fact
that they will inevitably betray each side to the other. The 'workable
model of wholeness' is both real and ideal: real because it is the goal
towards which negotiation must persist, and ideal because it is a fiction in
search of reality. It has meaning under both identities, the real and the ideal.

The 'authentic fiction' is also a 'necessary fiction', acknowledging the
claims of history. As Joseph Lee has observed, 'memory, actual or
induced, is an integral part of politicisation'.[35] Just as Friel has expressed
his reservations about the culture of saying 'yes' – which is clearly a
necessary fiction, corrective of the traditional unionist slogan 'Ulster says
"No!"' – so there is no single path to freedom because freedom itself is
multiple and discursive.

In the Introduction we explored Homi Bhabha's view of the liminal or
interstitial moment in the transformation of a post-colonial culture. This
is particularly apposite in a consideration of *Translations*, where all
participants are caught in the 'gap' between the real and the imaginary.
From the opening bewilderment in the hedge-school (itself an *unheimlich*
site) first at the activities of the engineers with the theodolite; then the
confusion about the 'sweet smell' of the crops; the ambivalent return of
Owen; the ambiguity of the surveying exercise; the deposition of Hugh as
schoolmaster; the flight of Manus; the lurking absence of the Donnelly
twins; Sarah's entrance into and exit from the world of speech; the short
life of Nellie Ruadh's baby; the exogamy of Maire with George, of Jimmy
Jack with Athene; to the dismay of the otherwise assured Captain Lancey
as he discovers his camp has been torched – all these shifts in consciousness make every character a traveller in his own land, a stray.

In order not to see the play merely as an 'eviction' in colonial terms, it
is essential that we gain access to the privacies of Yolland and, if possible,
of Lancey. It is of course true that the map-making is an act of conquest,
and it is indefensible to maintain that it represents merely a civilian
operation. Every map is a discovery, by the superior power, of the resources
of the native and a marking off of the territory into which it remains
unwise to enter – *hic sunt leones*. Even the map of the emotional hinterland which we may essay is still an attempt to 'conquer the emotions' – to
explore and lay claim to previously unknown areas of the psyche. Thus the

map-making, because it carries the surveyor into uncharted country, is also an act of self-discovery, in which the 'otherness' which is the central image and preoccupation of orientalism is confronted and, perhaps, understood.

The map-making exercise is also symbolic of the exercise of power. Whether or not the events of the first or second acts of the play are supposed to have political import, the stark historical fact is that the Ordnance Survey represented a strategy of control by Whitehall over Ireland. In the programme for *Translations* Field Day quoted Lord Salisbury to the effect that 'The most disagreeable part of the three kingdoms is Ireland; and therefore Ireland has a splendid map'. Domesday Book had been a similar visitation upon England by the incoming William the Conqueror following the Norman victory at Hastings in 1066. Mapping alone would reveal the nature of the terrain; changing the place-names would transform it, as Nietzsche recognised: 'translation [is] a form of conquest'.[36]

More immediately significant in everyday life is the introduction of the new educational system which threatens the flight of indigenous language from those contours. The tension between an ubiquitous empire with a global language and code of behaviour and a worldwide distribution of idiosyncratic societies which have only their difference in common, is that between emperor and peasant, where the language of the latter is rooted, chthonic, and that of the former is the result of many hybrids.

Between the two exercises, one essential element of the culture of Baile Beag becomes endangered: the role of place-names in the symbolic rituals of performance, of social action. For Victor Turner, 'the ritual symbol [is] a factor in social action, a positive force in an activity field . . . crucially involved in situations of societal change . . . associated with human interests, purposes, ends and means, aspirations and ideals, individual and collective'.[37]

Hugh O'Neill and, in *Translations*, the two figures of Hugh Mor O'Donnell and his son Owen, stand as figures representative of their cultures, on the eve of irreversible change in their societies. As such they are both symbolic of the older world and responsive, even receptive, to the new. Each in his own way discovers the truth and the danger of standing at the threshold, in the gap, and what it means to become a divided being.

Friel has given us many instances of the 'split' personality, not necessarily in order to exemplify any post-colonial condition but to indicate the divisions in emotions, loyalties, aspirations and motivations which Everyman will suffer on his journey towards wholeness. However, consciousness of the post-colonial condition, of the experience of coming out from the shadow of a dominant culture by which one has been colonised, creates in its turn a change in the consciousness of actors within a culture which is, by virtue of new freedoms and new responsibilities, finding its own voice and its own sense of direction – *The Mundy Scheme* has indicated Friel's awareness of this condition. To leave aside for an interval the plays which address the individual-as-artist, the question of the lonely conscience and the cry for freedom: in his portrayal of Columba (*The Enemy Within*) and Gar O'Donnell (*Philadelphia*) we see Friel studying people under new dispensations, new forms of awareness, in which there are distinct divisions or splits between their emotional attachment to the 'old' life – *illo tempore* – and their acknowledgement of the changed world into which they are entering; between their loyalties to family and kinship and their attraction to the wider world of opportunity and excitement; between texts which have an established affective resonance within their mindscape and books which have yet to be written; between the known and the unknown; between safety and danger.

When, therefore, Bhabha writes of a split within colonised man, within the context of otherness, we can find his image and his mindset in many of Friel's characters, and in the dramatic effect which their activities exact upon their audience:

> The representative figure . . . is the image of post-Enlightenment man tethered to, *not* confronted by, his dark reflection, the shadow of colonized man, that splits his presence, distorts his outline, breaches his boundaries, repeats his action at a distance, disturbs and divides the very time of his being . . . the idea of man as his alienated image; not Self and Other but the otherness of the Self inscribed in the perverse palimpsest of colonial identity.[38]

Going no further than Baile Beag, we can find in the relationship of Owen O'Donnell and George Yolland, in their joint relationship to the forgotten well, Tobair Vree; in Owen's and his father's response to the new place-names; in the way Doalty mows a circle around Yolland's tent; in the suspended time and animation between Act 2 and Act 3; in the exchange of place-names, and thus of identities, between George's home county and the hinterland of Maire's Baile Beag; in the qualitative difference between the confusion reigning in Act 1 and that of Act 3 – in all these interstitial places and times, people are made, unmade, saved and destroyed, but this always happens in relation to others. No single force enters the space, has its effect and leaves unchanged. No aspect of the home culture is unhoused without at the same time changing and disordering the culture which displaces it.

Nowhere will we find a more explicit example of Bhabha's thesis of the symbiotic bond of identity between 'white' and 'black' than in the re-naming of the landscape as conducted between Owen/Roland and George

Yolland: 'the colonial hybrid is the articulation of the ambivalent space where the rite of power is enacted on the site of desire'[39] – where the 'rite of power' is the anglicisation of the names and where the 'site of desire' is the 'Eden' which Yolland would like to make his own home by going native. In this ambivalent space, he is attracted not only to Maire but also to Owen in a way that is not entirely asexual. To share, with the other, one's life story, to offer a full *apologia*, while sharing in the intimacies of the local, is to be at once immediate and far away, to link Norfolk and Baile Beag in such a way as to become other, to enter into the other's identity.

The essential privacy of the individual soul is the source of the story; the essentially public nature of our actions is the source of History. Translation between privacies, between genders, between generations, the gradual making public or communal of what has remained intimate and silent, however political it may become (with a small 'p'), remains private and local until the attempt is made to combine it with other, cognate narratives of similar households into an 'authentic' – or acceptable – fiction which changes all of their smaller stories in constructing the pattern of the larger History. Thus, while Elmer Andrews is correct to say that for Friel 'history is a frame for individual stories, alternative narratives',[40] it is also the means by which those stories are broadcast and thereby both enlarged and diminished simultaneously by the act of translation.

Time immemorial is a routine in which nothing happens, in which the same small story repeats itself with a circularity that constantly but unquestioningly reaffirms its own authenticity. Time in which something – however small – happens is the time of History and the occasion of the fracturing of stories. In this sense, the split which we have observed as a condition of the liminal situation or gap is an expression of the division in a society which occurs when its rehearsal of its story is interrupted by events from beyond, when 'time' is visited by 'Time'. When Charles McGlinchey travelled to Dublin on the occasion of the Eucharistic Congress, he tells us nothing except that he raked the ashes over the fire and on his return 'the fire was living in the rakings all the time'[41] – *all the time* is a condition which ignores Time, because time and place are congruent. But, as Victor Turner tells us, when norms are breached, or custom is infracted, social drama takes place,[42] and when this happens a society is divided among itself.

At this point such a society requires leadership, which is clearly lacking in Baile Beag and which fails tragically in *Making History*. It seems that Friel is unable or unwilling to abandon a 'private soul' to the area of public responsibility and this may, ultimately, be the torsion which creates the post-colonial predicament. As Archbishop Lombard tries to impress on Hugh O'Neill, at times of stress people need a hero:

Ireland is reduced as it has never been reduced before – we are talking
about a colonized people on the brink of extinction. This isn't the time for
a critical assessment of your 'ploys' and your 'disgraces' and your 'betrayal' –
that's the stuff of another history for another time. Now is the time for a
hero. Now is the time for heroic literature. So I am offering Gaelic Ireland
two things. I'm offering them this narrative that has the elements of myth.
And I'm offering them Hugh O'Neill as a national hero. A hero and the
story of a hero (*MH* 67).

It is ironic that Hugh Mor O'Donnell holds the position of authority
traditionally invested in the schoolmaster, since it is the void in that
authority which creates the vortex around which *Translations* spins. If
Translations has been accused of abdicating responsibility for historical
truth, then the question arises of where such responsibility has resided
during the century in which Ireland has written itself a History alternative
to that with which it had previously been provided. *Making History* may
very well be Friel's own corrective propaganda to the cult of *Translations*
as a necessary fiction within this larger narrative.

If Friel had prefaced *Translations* or *Making History* with a disclaimer
such as that preceding *The Enemy Within* – 'neither a history nor a
biography but an imaginative account, told in dramatic form' (*EW* 7) –
his approach to the 'events' of each play would have been less controversial. But there would nonetheless have been grounds for regarding
the plays as 'corrective propaganda' (see below, p. 207), and as such
disputatious, not least because they were Field Day productions. It lay to
Seamus Deane to state: 'The voice of power tells one kind of fiction – the
lie . . . The voice of powerlessness tells another kind of fiction – the
illusion'.[43] One is trying to maintain the status quo, the other to subvert
it. Both engage in pretence, because both depend on not telling the literal
truth to achieve their aim. The outcome – who will win or lose – is not as
important as the effectiveness of the engagement between the two kinds
of fiction, the drama. In that moment of revelation, each side menda-
ciously discloses its 'negotiating position' of which the other tries to
gauge the truthfulness. In this sense, Field Day disclosed to Whitehall
its capacity to enact a lie that could be believed and, by releasing its
core secrets from the lien of history, could be made the basis of the
future tense.

It is instructive to note that the Ordnance Survey exercise and the
introduction of the national primary school system into Ireland were
contemporaneous with Macaulay's minute on Indian education (to which
I referred in my Introduction). Indeed, the mutual attraction between
Ireland and India as post-colonial societies is underlined by Bhabha's
point: 'India [Ireland] is the perpetual generation of a past-present which
is the disturbing, uncertain time of the colonial intervention and the

ambivalent truth of its enunciation'.[44] In Ireland, children were taught to sing 'The English Child':

> I thank the goodness and the grace
> That on my birth have smiled
> And make me in these Christian days
> A happy English child.[45]

It would be sixty years before Douglas Hyde would propose 'the necessity of de-anglicising the Irish people' and almost a century before Gandhi would signal that India was stirring in its sleep. While acknowledging the difference and the intrinsic interest of the colonial 'other', it was the mission of London to send out civilising forces which were assumed to be innately superior in kind and value to the 'native', wherever it might be found and whatever it might constitute. That Ireland, as England's first colony, was on the same verge of assimilation into that superior world as India and most of Africa, is not so much an accident of history as an extension of the imperial logic into the unknown. Once the arrow was loosed on its trajectory the unknown and unspoken would begin to be known and articulated in a language into which it had not yet been translated. As Fanon says, 'a national culture under colonial domination is a contested culture whose destruction is sought in systematic fashion. It very quickly becomes a culture condemned to secrecy'.[46] In the figure of Manus the culture of Baile Beag is carried away to the secrecy of Inis Meadhon as he flees the consequences of Lancey's eviction. It would be almost a century and a half before the people of Derry would start 'stirring in [their] sleep' to give voice to its aspirations once more, by which time, again in Fanon's words, it is emaciated, 'a set of automatic habits, some traditions of dress and a few broken-down institutions' with 'little movement', 'no real creativity and no overflowing life': 'the poverty of the people, national oppression and the inhibition of culture are one and the same thing'.[47]

The post-colonial condition of any emergent state requires not only that it establish a satisfactory brand of autonomy in both governance and culture, but also that it restore to itself whatever cultural values and practices existed prior to colonisation. The first process sees the servant or subaltern becoming master of the present and of the future, making laws and deciding destinies; the second, repossession of a lost or underground heritage, is more complex because it involves an ambivalent attitude to what has been lost and a heart-searching about how it became lost. Making value-judgements about a heritage which has proved to be less than durable, but of which one wishes to prove the permanence, can be a painful experience.

In Ireland the 'celebration' of events such as the 1798 risings, which in themselves were painful experiences, adds even today to the burden of remembrance. '1798', as a rallying cry in modern nationalism, celebrates a defeat which has nevertheless provided a touchstone for determined self-renewal. In this way, the roles of master and servant are merged: one, decisive and authoritarian, the other submissive and subordinate, discover that neither possesses sufficiently convincing characteristics to enable then to act their parts, to establish an 'authentic fiction'. Thus thrown together as a double-act, master and servant exchange qualities and conditions, becoming in the process a hybrid fiction in which the capacity for determination is diminished by that for subservience and the role of leader is inhibited by there being no one to lead; the servant becomes craftier and more realistic than his master, more familiar with the scenes of power which will never be enacted, and the stage Irishman, at once truculent and deferent, whingeing and menacing, is born.

Friel uses 1789 as an emblem of the future, an arrow speeding towards change and expansion, the virile straight line of a rebellion which became a revolution; the circularity by which the French Revolution had been signalled and put aside in *Philadelphia* by means of the recitation of Burke's apostrophe is thus punctured and its energies allowed to explode into the real world. 1798, by contrast,[48] is employed as a symbol of Hugh's and Jimmy Jack's circularity, their god-like stance of the morning march towards destiny evaporating under the influence of a few pints in Phelan's pub in Glenties,[49] bringing them home by nightfall after a great day's heroism in which nothing was achieved. In a further – sarcastic – echo of Steiner he recalls 'Everything seemed to find definition that spring – a congruence, a miraculous matching of hope and past and present and possibility' (*Tr.* 67).

In similar vein, Friel addresses the question of how to keep faith not with the major events of History but with the insignificant histories of forgotten folk. The business between Owen and Yolland about Tobair Vree, the well mis-placed in both time and space, typifies the question: how insignificant must a person or a person's life be to us before we are entitled to forget him, to erase him from History? How long can a mere name, or a corrupted form of that name, continue to command respect or remembrance? The key for Yolland, who wants to maintain that memory of Tobair Vree, is 'tradition' – as long as one person (Owen) can re-call that long-lost Brian and his circumstances, then a slim thread connects past and future and 'Vree' can be encoded in the new map which represents that future, thus engrossed into its greater History.[50] It is the insistence that at some point in time a place or an object had some particular significance for a person or a class of people that sends us to the maps, urges us to rediscover that significance, to identify the point so that time and place can once more coincide, and perhaps understand why that significant coincidence failed subsequently to affect us.[51]

In these two cases we have private and public examples of how the past is both the master and the servant of the future. Lancey's threat to ravish the parish is a violent reminder of the burnings and evictions of 1798 and earlier ('when my grandfather was a boy they did the same thing' says Doalty, *Tr.* 63) and Yolland's insistence that to retain 'Tobair Vree' is to hold back the 'erosion' of local pieties is a pacific attempt to give the place an 'equation with its roots' which transcends time.

The former indicates the strength of memory in political situations: *The Freedom of the City* enables audiences to experience the resonance of two Bloody Sundays – 1972 (Derry) and 1920 (Dublin) and, stretching beyond them, innumerable occasions when innocence was debauched by power. The latter is the playwright's more pathetic appeal for faith to be kept with the mere soil in which such great events are grown. Moving between and connecting the two is the slogan of Irish history, 'The Memory of the Dead'. The master-servant relationship is crucial in such a context because playwright and historian are both master and servant: master of their material but servant of their project, whether it be the construction of a public narrative for an emerging nation or the private whisperings of boy and girl. This has been evident throughout Friel's work: on the public plane, the figures of authority unable to command the disparate energies of their 'subjects'; on the private, their failure to control the emotional tug between duty and freedom; and in an area that is both public and private, the danger of son succeeding or supplanting father as the local *dominus* – it began in *To This Hard House* with the role of the school-master and recurs in *Living Quarters* with son as adulterer and in *Translations* again in the role of master.

Without Friel intending that any such reading should attach to his work,[52] there is a profoundly symbolic spirit of this post-colonial dilemma present in most of his work, whether it is explicit, as in *The Mundy Scheme*, or implied and subliminal in *Aristocrats*. And it is all the more valuable for an understanding of Irish history in its relation to both place and time when we see the chronology of his work moving in and out of the stream of recorded history: Columba in the sixth century, Hugh O'Neill on the threshold of the seventeenth, Murrough and Nancy O'Doherty in the eighteenth (in *The London Vertigo*), Hugh Mor O'Donnell and his Russian cousins in the nineteenth, the Mundy sisters in 1936, the Taoiseach, F. X. Ryan in *The Mundy Scheme* on the threshold of economic transformation in the mid-twentieth, and, at various stages in the timetable of modern Ireland – 'the present' – a succession of figures on whom we can

look back from the eve of the twenty-first, as curiously aged and out-
moded since their fate was first written in the 1960s, 70s, 80s and 90s.

All of these are 'translated' in both temporal and spatial terms – both
language and culture, domus and the location of authority, are changed
by the stranger's knock on the door. Michael Cronin says 'metaphors
become refugees seeking asylum'[53] – in other words, the means of establishing meaning, the bridges from one signifier to another, are themselves
on the run, or, in Friel's killing term, 'strays'. The simplest fact is that the
liminal situation is caused by nothing more serious than a knock on the
door, an announcement ('It's me – I'm back') and an admission ('Come
in'). Then, the Other.

'If', says Cronin, 'the condition of Ireland is the condition of modernity –
discontinuity, fragmentation, self-doubt – then it is only to be expected
that translation will emerge as a dominant feature of contemporary Irish
culture'.[54] *Making History* and *Translations* show us that such a condition
both existed, embedded, in Irish history as a resident characteristic and
can be projected back from our discontinuous present into that past.
Nowhere is that more evident than in *Making History*, where Lombard,
O'Neill and Harry Hoveden exchange roles. become each other's masters
and servants, because it is no longer possible (perhaps it has never been
possible) for any one of them to satisfactorily embody, impersonate, the
definitive master or the unequivocal servant.

LANGUAGE AND SOCIETY

Tom Paulin (one of the members of Field Day) says:

> The history of language is often a story of possession and dispossession,
> territorial struggle and the establishment or imposition of a culture . . .
> spoken Irish English . . . lives freely and spontaneously as speech but it
> lacks any institutional existence . . . a language without a lexicon, a
> language without form . . . A language that lives lithely on the tongue
> ought to be capable of becoming the flexible written instrument of a
> complete cultural idea.[55]

This was written with the hindsight experience of *Translations* and it
embodies much of Friel's intention; the political dispossession that
provided the *mise-en-scène* for *The Freedom* here becomes a text parallel
to the narrative of an impoverished culture threatened by the imposition
of a strange and more confident culture, an invasion and implantation.
This is a 'fact-finding exercise', a map-making which changes the identity
of the region. But Friel is anxious that the political implications of his
storyline should be brought out expressly by the characters themselves,
rather than imposed as a structure of the play. As he wrote at the time:

I don't want to write a play about Irish peasants being suppressed by English sappers. I don't want to write a threnody on the death of the Irish language. I don't want to write a play about naming places . . . *The play has to do with language and only language.*[56] (*my emphasis*)

Language would, however, remain the vital link between public and private which, as we have seen, is the central tension of *Translations* and it is arguable whether Friel has in fact satisfactorily resolved this difficulty. He comes close in spirit, if not in technique, to the absurdist drama of Pirandello and Pinter in his use of the non-sequitur, the mutual incomprehension of his speakers in *Aristocrats*, where the inconsequentiality of conversation is at its most Chekhovian,[57] or in *Translations* which is inherently political in the sense that, commanded by our aesthetic and social security system, we choose to hear, comprehend and respond to, only those offers or messages which neither offend nor challenge our identity. As Pinter says: 'the speech we hear is an indication of that we don't hear. It is a necessary avoidance, a violent, sly, anguished or mocking smokescreen which keeps the other in its place.'[58]

There are two sets of speech, in fact: that which we receive and return in the public, possible world, and that which we employ as internal discourse, the discrete method of relating to private psychology. The dialogue which transforms that private psychology into public culture can never do better than fail (as it fails in *Living Quarters*), to communicate not only between privacies but also between a specific privacy and its public expression: this is the inevitable failure of metaphor.

In *Translations* as we receive it Friel is, at least ostensibly, addressing public themes. And as he himself says: 'If it is not political what is it? Inaccurate history? Social drama?'[59] Friel's characteristic distaste for open politics reinforces this difficulty, because it makes him more aware of his own need to explore the 'dark and private places'. The final form of *Translations* is due to his eventual realisation that the 'political' issues were inescapable, at least in the broadest sense, because for the first time in his work the 'inevitability' of change is presented in the form of a cultural encounter. While therefore he succeeds in reducing the specific implications of a military eviction, he cannot eradicate from his text the damage caused by the breakdown of communication implicit in the form of the play itself. Even more than in *The Freedom of the City*, Friel is writing for his own 'community' or 'constituency', because by this act of faith he can bring into existence the Ballybeg/Baile Beag which represents his hearth.

In this regard the figure of Doalty takes on an extra significance. Doalty is the 'antic' of this play, and yet he is commonly perceived in production as a figure of fun, of light relief. But Doalty's immune system rests in his ignorance: he knows nothing and wishes to know nothing. The opposite, as Lady Bracknell might say, is disaster. To know everything is a form of madness (*Tr.* 67). Frank Hardy knows everything, and therefore he is dead. Doalty, like Teddy, survives. Even in tragedy we need our figures of fun. As a political animal he makes an extremely important statement in the closing scene: 'if we'd all stick together. If we knew how to defend ourselves' (*Tr.* 64). Linking this to the aptitude of the Donnelly twins for survival, Doalty thus unites two kinds of refusal, in saying 'yes' to revolt and 'no' to death. He thus redeems his own imcompetence in the opening scene and earns the sobriquet bestowed on him by Hugh – 'Sophocles from Colonus would agree with Doalty Dan Doalty from Tulach Alainn: "To know nothing is the sweetest life"' (*Tr.* 24).

Friel also succeeds, therefore, in establishing a private and very simple world, in looking at its inner activity and tensions. It would be wrong, for example, to regard Sarah Johnny Sally's muteness merely as a symbol of a people who had lost their tongue, especially in the midst of such loquacity. Her silence is a private question of identity, not a public issue. Similarly Hugh's ambivalent relationship with each of his sons allows Friel the opportunity to look once more at the concept of the dead mother and the role of the revenant, while his camaraderie with Jimmy allows him to bring together the thread of affiliation (which began with Screwballs, Boyle and the Canon) with the appeal to 'that time':

> Everything seemed to find definition that spring, a congruence, a miraculous matching of hope and past and present and possibility. Striding across the fresh, green land. The rhythms of perception heightened. The whole enterprise of consciousness accelerated. We were gods that morning James. (*Tr.* 67)

Thus while Friel is equivocally private in this marriage of the particular with the absolute, he is also equivocally public in looking beyond the bounds of familiarity: '*Barbarus hic ego sum quia non intelligor ulli*' (*Tr.* 64).

As D. E. S. Maxwell has noted, this poses the by now well-rehearsed problem of 'being in two places at the one time' which we first met in Columba:

> being in reality, and being in the world of art, and establishing a contour between the two. And within that secondary world to authenticate its happening as events which occur only there. They will not persuade us because something exactly the same happened yesterday. These problems are at their most acute with political matter, for ideology, dogma, is most favourably placed to subvert the allegiance to language.[60]

Let us therefore examine this subversive ideology, one which subverts as it seduces.

In 1851, 1½ million people spoke Irish, about one quarter of the total population. In County Londonderry there were 5,400, or less than 3 per cent of the population, while in County Donegal there were 73,000, or about 30 per cent of the total population. In the country as a whole 20 per cent of all Irish speakers were monoglot, a proportion which reduced in the following half-century to less than 3 per cent: in Donegal, monoglots in 1851 numbered, according to the census, 34,882 (almost half the total of Irish speakers), while in 1911 there were 4,733 or 8 per cent of the Irish speakers.[61]

Against this factual background we can artificially polarise two contemporaneous attitudes to the Irish language, one of which – Daniel O'Connell's – finds expression in *Translations* ('the old language is a barrier to modern progress' [*Tr.* 25]). In 1835 O'Connell said:

Although the Irish language is connected with many recollections that twine round the hearts of Irishmen, yet the superior utility of the English tongue, as the medium of all modern communication, is so great that I can witness without a sigh the gradual disuse of the Irish.[62]

Meanwhile Thomas Davis, the founder of 'Young Ireland', declared:

A people without a language of its own is only half a nation. A nation should guard a language more than its territories. 'Tis a surer barrier and more important frontier than fortress or river. Nothing can make us believe that it is natural or honourable for the Irish to speak the speech of an alien, the invader, the Sassenach tyrant, and to abandon the language of our kings and heroes. . . . To impose another language on such a people is to send their history adrift among the accidents of translation – 'tis to tear their identity from all places.[63]

The Young Ireland definition of nationalism is also at the heart of *Translations*:

It is the summary name for many things. It seeks a literature made by Irishmen and coloured by our scenery, manners and character. It desires to see art applied to express Irish thought and belief. It would make our music sound in every parish at twilight, our picture sprinkle the wall of every house and our poetry and history sit at every hearth. It would thus create a race of men full of a more intensely Irish character and knowledge and to that race it would give Ireland.[64]

Thus the man who restored to the Irish people their religious freedom and gave them the franchise was also the agent of one form of cultural suicide, while the author of the Young Ireland movement swore fealty to a means of communicating in the 'precious gold' of the past. This ambiguity and tension of modern Irish nationalism becomes the ground on which *Translations* and *Making History* are played out, both publicly and privately.

The significance of this shift, whether or not it was inevitable, from predominantly Gaelic-speaking to predominantly English-speaking, lies in the fact that it encompassed the question of identity. The fact that English is the language Maire needs to know is the central fact of *Translations*, the central reality in which Hugh O'Donnell ultimately acquiesces. One's changing identity (which hangs upon one's ability to speak, on the language in which one chooses, or is compelled, to speak, on one's attitude to one's name, rank and affiliation) thus becomes more important than what one does with the identity by way of social action. One world-view relishes an identity which can no longer be enacted, the other embraces a new meaning which is not yet clear. By 1922 the enunciation of the new State continued in this contradiction as it insisted that the key to the dynamic identity and culture of modern Ireland lay in its language and customs, that is, in an intimate relation of speech to the land, despite the statistical realities already evident from the facts quoted above.

In this sense the seduction of the two world-views, one past, one future, caught in the present which cannot decide whether to follow *mythos* or *logos*, crystallises all the contradictions elaborated in Chapter 3. As an *historical* play, therefore, *Translations* explores the dark and *public* places; the individual souls mass up into a community (*communitas*) threatened by the choice between the rush to English or the retreat to silence. The validity of *silence* depends on whether it is employed as a means of escape or of resolution. With Friel, as with Heaney and Beckett, the claims and character of silence – silence as a living force in the life of society – are as real and effective as babel. Monoglot and polyglot have at least one common language, which is liberated from silence by laughter. Silence is *agelast*, a condition without laughter. The ice of silence is broken by the axe of laughter. In translating between privacies, therefore, the *public* issues are made fictive in a way that history cannot touch.

This brings us back to the point, that Friel enables us to accommodate these parallel texts by a fusion of form and content. The land itself (narrow ground) provides the metaphors – naming, crop failure, invasion and evacuation – for carrying over or translating (Greek: *metaphorein*, Latin: *transferre*) the absolute into the particular.

As we have seen, the original Ordnance Survey was concerned with the movement of people through *time* as well as *space*. Friel reduces this to a 'triangulation'; the use of 'section' for 'parish' is not a translation but a diminution of a three-dimensional concept to two dimensions, a denial of a social and cultural function in the interest of a political and scientific one, the elevation of form over content. At the same time Friel reduces the community to the definition of the hedge-school within which the off-stage action is discussed: a definition which likewise has a temporal dimension as its function shifts in the light of the community's subjective drift into decay and desuetude and of its role as *object* of incursion.

In *Translations* Friel provides a congruence of semantics and history within the framework of fiction. It is instructive to note how both Friel and John Andrews were drawn into a subsequent debate on the subject of map-making. Andrews said that in experiencing the play of *Translations* he realised 'that there can be more than one kind of historical fiction'[65] (just as Baudelaire commented at the Salon of 1846, 'there are two ways of understanding portraiture, either as history or as fiction'). Within such realisations there lurk two kinds of playing with time and language: one which says, as we shall see in the case of *Making History*, that it is possible to have different kinds of simultaneous truth; and another which allows that for whatever truth is being portrayed, there is one (or more) equal and opposite fiction(s).

This has not, however, absolved Friel from severe criticism both in regard to the 'poetic licence' which he has exercised with the 'facts' of history and in the interpretation he has put on them – the 'uses of history'. In this there is an inevitable, and perhaps unresolvable, collision of playwright and historian, poet and critic, about the nature of truth and portraiture. To take one example: Seán Connolly argues that *Translations* 'is written in a tone that seems to make clear that Friel believes he is depicting a real experience' and that the programme notes 'vouch for the authenticity of the version of the past which it sets out'.[66] How can we here divorce the integrity of the act of playwriting from the need to be faithful to history? How to allow the writer sufficient liberty to construct a credible fiction while maintaining the 'version' of the past which has been handed down to us in the long tradition of veracity? How to measure one kind of truth, one way of perceiving (aesthetic), against another?

In order to find even tentative answers to such questions, which Friel himself baulks at in *Making History*, we must look at his intentions in writing *Translations* in the first place. In bearing in mind texts like Dowling's *The Hedge-Schools of Ireland* and Colby's *Memoir* of the Survey,[67] he was working over the idea of

> a play about the nineteenth century, somewhere between the Act of Union and the Great Famine, a play about Daniel O'Connell and Catholic eman-
> cipation; a play about colonialism; and the one constant – a play about the
> death of the Irish language and the acquisition of English and the profound
> effect that that change-over would have on a people.[68]

These 'fugitive notions of a play about language' gradually developed into an interest in hedge-schools and the Ordnance Survey until, with the appearance of *A Paper Landscape* in 1975, 'suddenly here was the confluence, the aggregate, of all those notions . . . here was the perfect metaphor to accommodate and realise all those shadowy notions – map-making'.[69] He set out to dramatise Andrews's book, but, failing to capture the essence of its main characters, and obviously subconsciously putting the idea of John O'Donovan as a quisling to the back of his mind, he 'embarked on a play about a drunken hedge-schoolmaster', since he had discovered that his own great-great-grandfather had been a hedge-schoolmaster from Mayo who settled in Donegal.

The hedge-school story in Ireland is sentimentally linked to the notion that 'every Kerry ploughboy has a copy of Homer in his breeches pocket', a notion which is substantiated, though not certified, by Dowling's *The Hedge-Schools of Ireland*. Friel studied this history to assimilate the background to his chosen theme, and thereby reduced Dowling's subject to suit his particular needs. Friel creates a composite school, Ballybeg, from the many instances cited by Dowling: the strength of the classical tradition is transported from Kerry; the 'poor scholar' is transformed into Jimmy Jack Cassie, 'the Infant Prodigy'; and the level of excellence, usually in mathematics and classics, is reduced to a poor and precarious proficiency. The archetypal master, according to one of Dowling's sources, was a

> pure Milesian, short of stature, fiery in temper, with features exhibiting a strange combination of cunning, thought and humour. He swore at his pupils roundly, and taught them to swear. But he was a good scholar and a successful teacher. Like many of his countrymen his love of classical literature amounted almost to a passion and he had the rare talent of inspiring favourite pupils with his own enthusiasm. Among Latin authors he delighted in Horace[70]

– whose odes he rendered quaintly, one supposes in the same way that Hugh refashions Ovid (*Tr.* 41). The children of the hedge-schools become young adults, but the lessons are the same: copying headlines, arithmetic, geography. Hugh becomes the author of 'the Pentaglot Preceptor or Elementary Institute' (*Tr.* 42), a version of a standard textbook of the time, 'the Hibernian Preceptor', by George Wall of Birr, County Offaly. The schoolmaster was often in an ambivalent position regarding the two languages, English which was 'used in business affairs' and Irish, 'the language of home and the fields'. Hugh calls English 'particularly suited to the purposes of commerce' (*Tr.* 25).[71] Nevertheless:

> the hedge schoolmaster was often proud of his English. In the home parents were particularly careless of imparting a knowledge of Irish to their children; in fact, they sometimes looked upon the ignorance of the younger generation in this respect as an advantage when they wished to discuss private affairs in their hearing. Yet the schoolmaster must have deplored what was happening, for every now and then we find him either defiantly singing the praises of the language or regretting its decay. He has been instrumental, however, in the preservation of thousands of legends, songs and poems, and in helping to perpetuate his native tongue.[72]

And although the master was poorly paid – Friel alters the amounts payable to Hugh from those suggested by Dowling but maintains the same general level of income[73] – his social status was high:

> his knowledge and his very status constituted him the leading authority on all matters of moment to the community. His advice and help were sought and generally paid for in money or kind, and where neither of these were forthcoming he invariably managed to gain in prestige. His social standing in the parish was of considerable importance to him, for the higher it was, the more the people looked to him as guide and counsellor. 'A hedge schoolmaster' writes Carleton 'was the general scribe of the parish, to whom all who wanted letters or petitions written, uniformly applied – and these were glorious opportunities for the pompous display of pedantry.'[74]

We can see in Hugh Mor O'Donnell the relics of 'a leading authority' among the relics of his parish.

Friel also presses into service the fact that while this was a literate culture it was predominantly verbal rather than written. Gaelic society had texts which provided it with the pillars and adjuncts of learning, safeguarded by the *filí*, those native men of learning with the 'responsibility and corporate interest . . . to maintain the traditional integrity of social organisation and the traditional concepts on which it depended'.[75] But these 'texts' were of course oral: the strengths of a patriarchal and traditional society lie in its verbal culture, not enshrined in books which can be stolen but preserved in the secret runes which have all 'the magic associated with solemn oral pronouncement'[76] – a power which invests the *seanchaí* with social importance to this day: why else would the secret-ary of a government department be titled 'An Rúnaí'? With the advent of written texts, the same authority suggests, scholars continued to conform to oral tradition, and we are led to suppose that in Ireland (where content has always been regarded as more important than form, the superiority of the spoken to the written, the aural to the visual, the obedience to inner, heard voices rather than the evidence of our own eyes) the appeal to a text that is more easily uttered than it is read will be a superior appeal.

We turn now to another 'department' in Friel's play-construction, the place-name methods of the Ordnance Survey. (In the same way, of course, Friel 'collects' his place-names such as Termon and Burnfoot and Swinefort, from Derry, Donegal and Mayo. Similarly he brings together the relatively distant Norfolk villages of Winfarthing, Little Walsingham, Saxingham Nethergate and Barton Bendish to make up Yolland's own world.) As Andrews notes, although the policy in anglicising the place-names was to adopt whatever version was recommended by the majority of sources, 'Irish place-names had been too variously mangled by generations of English-speaking settlers for any such assumption to be valid.'[77]

Larcom, one of the directors of the survey, decided

to adopt not necessarily the commonest version but the version which came nearest to the original Irish form of the name. This was an attractive compromise between the empirical and the antiquarian. It was rational, scholarly and practical. It also showed a well-intentioned deference to the Irishness of Irish place-names.[78]

In *Translations* this difficulty is evidenced in the versions given to, for example, Bun na hAbhann: in the church registry 'Banowen'; in the list of freeholders, 'Owenmore'; in the grand jury lists, 'Binhone'. Owen says, 'I suppose we could Anglicise it to 'Bunowen".' Similarly Druim Dubh: Dramduff, Drimdoo, Dramduffy, Dromduff. But, like Larcom, Owen and Yolland set about finding the original meaning:

Bun is the Irish word for bottom. And Abha means river. So it's literally the mouth of the river . . . We are trying to denominate and at the same time describe that tiny area of soggy, rocky, sandy ground where that little stream enters the sea, an area known locally as Bun na hAbhann . . . Burnfoot! (*Tr.* 35)

We are therefore provided with a framework within which a psychological drama can be worked out: the physical shape, personnel and accoutrements of the hedge-school, and the occupation which disturbs both the daily life and the orientation of the village. Into this framework Friel inserts the 'ontological project' discussed by Richard Kearney.

This framework and the 'ontological project', taken together, become deeply divisive of the modern Irish mind. In 1987 Seán Connolly asserted that *Translations* 'represents a distortion of the real nature and causes of cultural change in nineteenth-century Ireland so extreme as to go beyond mere factual error', which includes 'a picture of traditional Hibernophone culture, prior to the coming of the English, so unrealistic and idealised as to cast doubt, not only on his history, but also on his art'.[79] Let us turn again to Friel, who makes two assertions: first, that 'the imperatives of fiction are as exacting as the imperatives of cartography and historiography', and, second, that equal to the advantages of using established facts or ideas is the responsibility 'to acknowledge those facts or ideas but not to defer to them. Drama is first a fiction, with the authority of fiction.'[80] The issue seems to turn on a *political view of culture* as opposed to *a cultural view of politics*. The political view argues that the writing of history, and the acting out of its events in dramas, poetry and novels, maintains the dominance of the recorded fact at the expense of poetic licence; that the dramatic function is to enhance and illuminate, but not to subvert and distort. The cultural view argues that history has still to be written, that distortion, the provision of other versions and subversions, of received 'fact', are equally valid. The distinction rests on the location of the act of judgement: are actors, playwrights and audience to receive and transmit the immutable experiences of known and documented historical figures, or are they able to participate in the act of history itself? Maps can be false, whether conceptual, moral or cartographical. Therefore, the 'imperatives' are related to the right to falsity as well as to truth. 'History', says Paul Ricoeur, 'begins and ends with the reciting of a tale.' He insists that 'narrative is a redefining of what is already defined, a reinterpretation of what is already interpreted', and that 'our future is guaranteed . . . by our ability to possess a narrative identity, to recollect the past in historical or fictive form'.[81]

The proximity of history to fiction, the narrative properties of both, are only beginning to be explored by writers like Barthes and Ricoeur[82] Another aspect of the problem is the conceptual difference between *logos* and *mythos*, which we shall see in discussing *Making History*. Ricoeur puts the emphasis on *mythos*, which 'is the bearer of something which exceeds its own frontiers; it is the bearer of other *possible* worlds'.[83] In putting forward a cultural view of politics Friel falls inevitably into the problem of nicety: language can not bear the weight of both interpretation and reinterpretation. As if he wished to demonstrate even further Steiner's thesis, Friel shows us that there can be no satisfactory translation between the rational and non-rational: in his approach to the criticism his plays have provoked, he is prepared to go only so far as 'to acknowledge . . . but not to defer'.

Possibly the most serious of Friel's subversions is to deny the English sappers in *Translations* a capacity to discourse in Latin, presumably in order to suggest that the otherwise inferior society of Ballybeg might have some cultural values unavailable to the colonists. It has caused an English drama critic to call the play 'a vigorous example of corrective propaganda: immensely enjoyable as theatre if, like much else in Ireland, gleamingly tendentious'.[84] That there can be two opposing and apparently exclusive ways of seeing underlines that there are two ways of observing, and commenting on, the events which occupy the course of time in Ireland: law as order or tyranny, popular movement or revolt, dissent as denial. As Andrew Carpenter observes, 'certain terms have double interpretations: loyalist, big house, patriot, perhaps even the word "border"'.[85] One can become tendentious about both the effects and the affects of time, the ways in which we experience the past and the ways in which we react to it. 'Versions' of *Phèdre* (as in *Living Quarters*) can be regarded as tendentious or simply bemusing. Friel has taken liberties with the 'facts' of Bloody Sunday, of the Ordnance Survey and, in *Making History*, of the Battle of Kinsale and the Flight of the Earls.

But, to paraphrase Steiner, it is not so much the literal facts that become subverted, as (and this is what lies behind Connolly's criticism) the cultural environment, the psychic hinterland. The *effect* of time is that the Battle of Kinsale, like that of the Boyne, decided the course of Irish history; the *affect* of time is that the Irish cannot accept this. The act of betrayal becomes the central metaphor for escaping from collective responsibility for, and interpretation of, the past. It is generally considered, for example, that at Kinsale the Irish/Spanish strategy was sold to the English commander by Brian McHugh Og MacMahon for a bottle of whiskey,[86] and Friel incorporates this into his play. But in adding the rider (expressed by Hugh O'Donnell) that 'we never had a chance',[87] Friel puts forward the inevitability of that betrayal. Furthermore, by emphasising the effect on Hugh O'Neill's character of his nine formative years in English society, and utilising the facts of his continual vacillation, inactivity and diplomatic exploitation of his dual loyalties, Friel suggests that it could as easily have been Hugh O'Neill himself who sold out the Irish future and the Counter-Reformation. It is often overlooked by Friel's critics that he identifies himself in *Translations* not only with the revenant Owen but also with Hugh, not as a precious retrospective but as a man resigned to the future. Friel puts his own words – 'we must make English identifiably our own language'[88] – into the text of *Translations*, thus lining himself up with these agents of erosion and eviction. But the real turning points of history are achieved more subtly than winning or losing either military or cultural wars. Hugh O'Neill's strength, as we shall see, lies in inaction, and in subtlety, but of a kind which inevitably traduces both cultures. In this sense he was/is truly the great *sacerdos liminalis* of Irish history. Thus, for example, he makes 'a gesture of loyalty' to the English crown, and appears to aid the erosion by 'bringing in' his peers and vassals: 'and I assure you, it means nothing, nothing. And in return for that symbolic courtesy London offers you formal acknowledgement and recognition of what you already are, leader of your own people! Politically quaint, isn't it?'(*MH* 26)[89] The comparison with Éamon de Valera's approach to the 'oath of allegiance', and his access to power, by declaring it 'an empty political formula',[90] will be obvious. So the true critical argument, which has yet to be engaged, is more truly located within the question of the relation of time to language than it is in the area of faithfulness to fact.

In the words of Dan H. Laurence, therefore, Friel is illustrating that the playwright's task (he is speaking of Shaw) is 'not to reproduce history but to shape it into credible drama, thus changing us from bewildered spectators of a monstrous confusion into men intelligently conscious of the world and its destinies'.[91] Shaw himself, when asked whether an historical play should be substantially accurate as to the facts – the play in question was *Arms and the Man* – replied:

> not more so than any other sort of play – historical facts are not a bit more sacred than any other class of facts. In making a play out of them you *must* adapt them to the stage and that alters them at once, more or less. Why, you cannot even write a history without adapting the facts to the conditions of representation on the stage. Things do not happen in the form of stories and dramas, and since they must all be told in some form, all reports, even by eye witnesses, all histories, all stories, all dramatic representations, are only attempts to arrange the facts in a faithful, intelligent, interesting form. That is, when they are not intentional efforts to hide the truth, as they very often are.[92]

Obviously the victims of *The Freedom of the City* and of *Living Quarters* are cast by their author into such narrative roles but, more than this, they take on an importance in excess of their own personalities. As Dan H. Laurence noted, speaking of *Saint Joan* and *Antony and Cleopatra*, 'Shaw endowed his characters with sufficient self-consciousness to explain themselves to an audience that was, for the most part, historically misinformed.' Nowhere in Friel's work will we find a more blatant case of this self-consciousness than in the fabrication called *Faith Healer*, which, as far as the audience or reader can tell, is an almost total tissue of lies and incomprehensions, told and experienced across the barrier of death. (In this sense we must once again note the possible importance of Teddy, simply because he is alive and therefore available to verify or discount the stories of the dead.) The adaptation of historical 'facts' in *Translations* scarcely amounts to such a fabrication, in the sense of amounting to 'intentional efforts to hide the truth'. Friel has in fact utilised the already artificial histories of others (O'Donovan's letters for example) in order to create, out of all the available versions, a *possible* world in which the exercise in understanding and expression can take place.

TRANSLATING

In 'Word against Object' Steiner says:

> Our languages simultaneously structure and are structured by time, by the syntax of past, present and future . . . Language is in part physical, in part mental. Its grammar is temporal and also seems to invite and inform our sense of time. A third polarity is that of private and public. It is worth looking at closely because it poses the question of translation in its present form. In what ways can language, which is by operative definition a shared code of exchange, be regarded as private? To what degree is the verbal expression, the semiotic field in which an individual functions, a unique idiom or idiolect? How does this personal 'privacy' relate to the larger 'privacy of context' in the speech of a given community or national language?[93]

Thus to particularise, to individuate a common culture, is to stress the difficulties of adapting absolute feelings such as 'love', 'fear', 'meaning', to real situations where one might need to express some concrete instance of such feelings.

In *Faith Healer*, as Richard Kearney points out, Hardy's attempt at self-analysis, at an understanding of his 'power' or 'gift', is a series of equivocations which 'amount to the fundamental question: Am I the manipulative master or the obedient servant of the healing word?'[94] In the ontological sense this parodox can never be resolved. It is therefore a rational gesture, if a solution can be both rational (i.e. logocentric) and gestic (i.e. impulsive), can embrace irresolution and turn it into 'meaning'.

But here again we run into problems, because, as Lévi-Strauss points out,

> it is absolutely impossible to conceive of meaning without order. There is something very curious in semantics, that the word 'meaning' is probably in the whole language, the word the meaning of which is the most difficult to find. What does 'to mean' mean? It seems to me that the only answer we can give is that 'to mean' means the ability of any kind of data to be translated into a different language.[95]

In translation, therefore, we are looking for meaning, the ability to carry over, to translate, to metaphorise, the integrity of sense, the wholeness of the signal by which perception is expressed and community is established. And this in itself 'means' that there are two subjective meanings to every crossing, one on each bank of the objective river of apprehension. The idea of a language as an entity over which we have temporary logical mastery, but which exercises continuing affective mastery over *us*, suggests that in order to establish and extend control we must define and distinguish on one hand the irresponsible use of language, which allows it to predetermine its use and to run away from us, and, on another, the calculated use, within prescribed limitations, of language, fully realising the risks that its imprecision and fickleness impose: the civilised institute of the text and the barbaric chaos of babel.

In the theatre this requires that we make a difficult adjustment to distinguish between the direct communication of the verbal dramas with our inner aural senses, and the formal communication with our sensual perceptions. For Friel this means that language can become an instrument of either servility or liberation, and that one can exist in a limbo of meaning in which one is deliciously uncertain about significance. Steiner: 'languages are wholly arbitrary sets of signals and conventionalized counters' (*After Babel* 21). Friel: 'words are signals, counters. They are not immortal' (*Tr.* 43). But they *are* promiscuous, and a translation is not only a release or liberation of a word/concept from one language to another, it is also an act of betrayal, a carrying across from the camp of the true to that of the false, from dexter to sinister, adroit to gauche. Such a tradition, or 'handing *over*' (*tradere*), is a subversion or perversion of tradition conceived as continuity, or 'handing *down*'.[96]

This is what Maxwell calls a subversion of 'the allegiance of language'. It also, of course, by extension deals a blow to our allegiance to history. If truth is the daughter of time, chaos and betrayal are the bastards of history. Under the sliding weight of babel, our sense of meaning is abolished, because we lose the power of 'faith' or the 'willing suspension of disbelief'; our behaviour becomes as depraved as the polyglot himself: the retreat into silence may be more a resolution than an escape. This, as the Anglo-Irish writer Lawrence Durrell points out, is a dialectical problem: 'how to convey a state for which words are inadequate? How to name a reality which is no longer itself once you qualify it with a name? How to state something which is beyond opposites in a language which is based on opposites?'[97]

Translation is spatial because it consists in the movement of meaning from one *topos* to another. This is demonstrated in both *Translations* and *Making History* by the existence of a controlling book – the book of place-names in *Translations* and Lombard's life of Hugh O'Neill in *Making History*. But in *Translations* there are in fact many texts purporting to exercise authority: in addition to the highly ambivalent book of names there are Hugh's multilingual lexicon and the classical texts of Homer, Ovid and Virgil. And while Homer particularly provides a universal metaphor in the *Odyssey*, Virgil, in his *Georgics*, is local and immediate as far as the people of Baile Beag are concerned. Jimmy Jack, in his fearful approach to Athene, has access not to any generalised type of god but to a family of highly personalised theophanies. For him, therefore, the texts – or more especially the identities disclosed by the texts – are as immediate as Camillo's Memory Theatre in bringing images from abstraction to meaning.

This serves to explain to us that translation, or transferral, is by its nature always liminal. Movement into, out of and between languages, mindscapes and identities permits or impedes the creation of meaning: the space between may or may not be a place of identification, the place where meaning is created, where metaphor happens. In every case, one actor is the agent of the ensuing change, initiates the process by which people take up different positions. Jimmy Jack is the medium by which Virgil's wisdom on the subject of crumbly soil is transferred to Doalty; Owen is the conduit by which, publicly, the sappers enter the hedge-school and, privately, Yolland enters 'Eden' ('with my son's help', *Tr.* 43); Manus is the channel through whose coaxing Sarah enters the killing fields of speech.

We recall Steiner's simultaneous equations: (a) all communication is a form of translation and (b) all dialogue is a strategic redefinition of the self. When Jimmy Jack puzzles over the issue of whether or not he is sufficiently godlike – or Athene sufficiently human – for union to succeed, he is also asking the fundamental question about how we determine our own identity. In speaking of one's identity, in revealing oneself, one is inevitably sharing that identity, that self, with the other, and thus entering into the identity of the other. When mute Sarah succeeds in making the statement 'My name is Sarah' (*Tr.* 12) she not only enters the world but allows the world to enter, and alter, her. Similarly, the return of Owen, so symbolic of the reentry into Ballybeg of Gar O'Donnell, causes the eviction of his brother Manus – one homecoming occasioning a new leavetaking, confirming the cyclic nature of both memory and translation, spatial as well as temporal.

Yolland's response to his superior officer – 'you can't rename a whole country overnight' (*Tr.* 36) – might be taken as a metaphor for the conquest of Ireland by England and, in the post-colonial context, as a warning that Ireland cannot repossess itself, re-Irish itself, at the instant of independence. But while *Translations* can of course sustain such readings, it is not its principal purpose. It is in this intimacy between place and memory that Friel achieves his stated aim of 'the exploration of the dark and private places of individual souls'.[98] Bearing in mind his anxiety that the play should not be 'political' ('are the characters only mouthpieces for certain predetermined concepts?')[99] we should note that the 'private places' of the memory theatre are the means whereby one speaks to oneself and thereafter to the world.

A further aspect of *Translations* which has been largely overlooked is the example it offers us of the relationship between place and memory. Manus taunts his father – 'will you be able to find your way?' – meaning that, when the place-names have been changed from Irish to English, the landscape will take on different contours and life itself will change; to which Hugh responds that a new life must be learned, a new identity of man-in-the-landscape must be assumed.

The relationship is so profound that the author of the *Ad Herennium* (cf. above, p. 31) speaks of the 'memory places' by which we fix on the inner mind images whose meaning depends on location.[100] Later, Giordano Bruno would speak of '*atria*, fields and cubicles' as the *loci* of memory and its images.[101] When Yolland expresses his surprise that the place 'Termon' is named after the god of boundaries (*Tr.* 42) he is saying that his own world has lost that power of association, has cut itself off from ancient time. So sure is the empire of its linear time, its forward momentum, that it need not continually renew its relationship with the past; its images become those of the future. Similarly, he implicitly acknowledges that to dissociate topic from *topos* is to lose the power of remembering or recalling the topic: Hugh and Jimmy Jack are able to speak of 'Apollo and Cuchulainn and Paris and Ferdia – as if they lived down the road' (*Tr.* 40), the point being that, for Jimmy Jack at least, they *do* live down the road, and have all the immediate presence of living images where memory (the past) and place (the present) are identical.[102] For Friel, when writing *Translations*, the spatial and temporal were the two dominant elements which eventually came together after a great deal of shy manoeuvering – his references to 'unrealized territories', to 'the terrain', are telling, especially his visit to Urris, 'the setting of the hedge-school in the play-in-the-head', 'this remote, bleak, desolate strip of land attenuated between mountain and sea', and his feeling that 'everything is so subtly wrong, just so slightly off-key, just so slightly out of focus'.[103]

Richard Kearney argues that in modern Irish theatre 'words tend to predetermine character, action and plot',[104] as a deliberate response to this condition. History as trader, it appears, is trustworthy while it is on your side, but anathema, traducer, when it crosses over. 'We like to think we endure around truths immemorially posited', says Hugh O'Donnell (*Tr.* 42) whereas we discover that we endure beneath the offensive pressure of the dolmens which ring us round.[105]

In *Translations* Friel attempts to re-establish this situation in order to re-establish the primacy of language as *content* over language as *form*. As Seamus Deane comments on *The Communication Cord*, 'A colony always wants to escape from history. It longs for its own authenticity, the element it had before history came to disfigure it.'[106] If there is any symbolism in *Translations* it lies in the fact that, apart from an irrelevant phrase which amounts only to doggerel ('in Norfolk we besport ourselves around the maypole'), Maire's only original knowledge of English consists of the elemental words 'water', 'fire', 'earth'; and in the process in which she becomes bewildered and debauched by the traitorous word 'always'. Here again is our 'embarrassment', brought about by the confluence of two incompatible matrices, which leads either to tragedy or comedy.

Friel's whole endeavour here is kept in the balance by the fact that he found it difficult in the writing to propel his characters either forward or back. It would be too easy to regard *Translations* simply as a 'powerful metaphor' of modern Ireland, 'bulled' by multinational and multicultural influences, a senescent, hopeless, incapacity; the failure of the new race to rise against the *urbs antiqua* (*Tr.* 68); a parable of Derry's poor. *Translations* does far more than that; it is not just the transparent 'satire' of *The Mundy Scheme*. But we can see how easy it is for both author and critics to take such a view.

Robert Hogan's general view of *Translations* was that 'the language device also underlines the broad theme of the play, about the gulf between cultures . . . So Friel may also more broadly be saying that the failure of language is a symptom of the failure of sympathy.'[107] This analysis confuses what the play is 'about' with what the playwright intends or 'means', and it also allows the devices in the plays to come between the critic and the meaning. Hogan regarded it as a flaw that:

> the most arresting character, the hedge-schoolmaster, is not the main character, and has little to do with the plot. The three young men who impel the plot are not really memorable. Also, some critical developments of the plot occur between scenes, and the conclusion of the plot is really only implied.[108]

I fundamentally disagree with this interpretation of *Translations* because I read, and see, and hear, a different play. This is not a way of politely differing from Robert Hogan: it means that I take an alternative course towards the author's intentions. I do not see the failure of language as a symptom of the failure of sympathy. It is not symptomatic: it is central, it is chemical, it is the disease itself; there is a fusion of form and content here, not a confusion. The fact that the characterisation of three actors, Manus, Owen and Yolland, is not 'memorable' (i.e. that we cannot carry away in our reproductive imagination an image of their achievements) or that the play follows the Greek and Chekhovian pattern of keeping its action firmly off stage, or that the 'plot' seems to have no conclusion, is irrelevant. It is a quibble with the *story*, when that story is only a device to set a distance, to mediate, between ourselves and the images of the absolute. One could argue endlessly but fruitlessly whether the plot demands conclusion, when it hardly has a beginning or a middle.

The original Field Day production in 1980 established a considerable *gravitas* not alone for Hugh O'Donnell but also for Jimmy Jack, whereas the production at the Abbey Theatre in 1983 explored more extensively the play's capacity for humour, which at times bordered on buffoonery in the character of Doalty and greatly detracted from his contribution in the final scene (discussed above). I have seen Hugh and Jimmy Jack played with an almost total lack of *gravitas* which made nonsense of the first scene and especially of Owen's line 'back here with you all again, *civilised* people' (*Tr.* 28).

But this is to worry about the crisis of form when the real issue is to look at the failure not alone of language and sympathy but also of the mediating effects of tenderness, as the dominant characteristic of the diviner. As Friel says:

> the cultural climate is a dying climate, no longer quickened by its past, about to be plunged almost overnight into an alien future. The victims in

this situation are the transitional generation. The old can retreat into and find immunity in the past. The young require some facility with the new cultural implements. The in-between ages become lost, wandering around in a strange land. Strays.[109]

It would be easier in fact to think of modern Ireland as a cultural metaphor for some of the problems of history – what Beckett also expressed through the character of Malone:

> Then he was sorry he had not learnt the art of thinking . . . sorry he could make no meaning of the babel raging in his head, the doubts, the desires, imaginings and dreads. And a little less well endowed with strength and courage he too would have abandoned and despaired of even learning what manner of being he was, and how he was going to live, and lived vanquished, blindly in a mad world, in the midst of strangers.[110]

It is therefore about all the problems of *Faith Healer*, projected onto the screen of *communitas*. And it is about the non-historical problem of indignity. The strays are those for whom the poet, the playwright, the shaman or diviner, essays an alternative mapmaking, a new clutching towards a dimly perceived identity. It is *the coincidence of madness with indignity*, in the sense expressed by Beckett, which has characterised much of Friel's concern with alienation of one's own culture and despair at one's 'political' condition. Madness leads to dream, a dream of continuity and wholeness which may turn to grief or nervous distress when contrasted with reality, when a society realises that it has enjoyed no living past or wholeness in its history. As the psychiatrist R.D. Laing says:

> If we can begin to understand madness and sanity in existential terms, we shall be more able to see clearly the extent to which we all confront common problems and share common dilemmas . . . When a person goes mad, a profound transposition of his position in relation to all domains of being occurs. His centre of experience moves from ego to Self. Mundane time becomes merely anecdotal, only the eternal matters. The madman is however confused. He muddles ego with self, inner with outer, natural with supernatural. Nevertheless, he often can be to us, even through his profound wretchedness and disintegration, the hierophant of the sacred.[111]

It needs no quotation to underline the application of such a view to *Translations*, where 'mundane time becomes merely anecdotal'.

A NATIONAL EPIC?

If Steiner did not directly influence the bending of historical fact in *Translations* (or at least, if his words were not transferred into the playtext) it is certainly the case that his argument that human speech can '"alternate" on reality' or '"say otherwise"', can be redeemed 'from the . . .

confines of truth to the freedom of fiction'[112] supported Friel's response to criticisms of historical inaccuracy from John Andrews and Seán Connolly. Connolly has shifted his position significantly since his original objections to the play. The very fact that in 1994 he was saying 'nor . . . is it easy to say how the departure from historical reality can be said to serve Friel's artistic purpose'[113] indicates that the presence of at least two kinds of reality – historical, fictional and perhaps emotional – has brought historians to the recognition that different kinds of *time* can be present simultaneously in the one text.

Connolly even goes so far as to see in Friel's preface to the programme for *Making History* – that it is 'a dramatic fiction' and that 'history and fiction are related and comparable forms of discourse' – 'an attempt to head off the sort of criticism directed at the handling of historical fact in *Translations* with mock contrition', a 'disingenuous attempt to reduce the issue to self-evidently trivial matters such as dating'.[114]

Connolly's new stance appears to have been influenced by the argument of *Making History*, that there are Histories and histories, public and private narratives. Writing of the latter play, Connolly recognises that 'Friel has deliberately chosen to confuse the picture: partly, one assumes, to advertise even more clearly his liberation from the constraints of the historical record; partly, perhaps, to reinforce the play's satirical treatment of the pretensions of history, by means of a subtle practical joke at the expense of the hapless academic fact checker'.[115]

Connected to this discussion, but of much greater significance, is the issue of the status of such plays. In suggesting that *Translations* might be 'a national epic' we should bear in mind that it was seen by one English critic as 'corrective propaganda'[116] – that is, having a political bias, whether or not that was manifest in historical falsity. Connolly himself has asserted that the play 'has in fact become the basis for a widely-received view of Ireland'.[117] This is a severe judgement, limiting the play to one particular reading, and making it clear that Friel's fear of producing a play that is merely public was very real. An English critic who suggested that the play was not propagandist but was metaphorical was nearer the mark.[118] Characteristically, Seamus Heaney made a more effective critical connection between the play's public and private connotations when he said:

> *Translations* was a moment in theatre when you could feel a relationship between the activity of a single dramatist exploring a theme, and the condition of the country. That play went intravenously into the consciousness of the audiences and the country.[119]

The idea that a member of the audience could find, within the dramatic experience, resonances which were both particular to his or her condition and also revelatory of a wider truth or knowledge is vital to Friel's success as a playwright, as we shall discover in addressing his stagecraft (Chapter 8). The link between the personal and the collective consciousness is suggested effectively by Elmer Andrews who says of *Faith Healer* that Friel 'dramatises the abolition of a centre, of a given and accepted authority'.[120]

The English critic whose review of *Translations* was headed 'Ireland: Destruction of an Idyll'[121] clearly saw the play as an attempt to restore a prediluvian condition to a country whose innocence had been continually and systematically raped by England. Martine Pelletier has called *Translations* 'an elegy in memory of a great civilisation which has disappeared and an attack on those who caused its loss' [*my translation*] and asserts that it is indisputable that to Friel this represents a colonial conflict.[122] It is easy to see why this view would prevail in the years fol-lowing Bloody Sunday and the intensification of both the 'Troubles' and Anglo-Irish diplomacy. Victor Turner refers to *communitas* as appearing 'culturally in the guise of an Edenic, paradisiacal, utopian or millennial state of affairs, to the attainment of which religious or political action, personal or collective, should be directed'.[123] Fanon refers to a 'passionate search for a national culture which existed before the colonial era' which is 'directed by the secret hope of discovery beyond the misery of today, beyond self-contempt, resignation and abjuration, some very beautiful and splendid era whose existence rehabilitates us both in regard to ourselves and in regard to others'.[124]

This circularity is in fact the inhibitor of development. David Harvey has drawn attention to the fact that 'place-bound nostalgias' represent Heidegger's 'land of Motionless Childhood'[125] while Turner makes the crucial point that 'ceremony' is a confirmatory process whereas 'ritual' is transformative – the straight line of the male invading the periodicity of the female.

In this connection it is highly significant that it is Yolland, rather than any of the Irish characters, who calls Baile Beag 'heavenly' – to which Owen retorts: 'The first hot summer in fifty years and you think it's Eden. Don't be such a bloody romantic' (*Tr*. 38). Friel himself has said that 'I have no nostalgia for that time . . . Several people commented that the opening scenes of the play were a portrait of some sort of idyllic, Forest of Arden life. But this is a complete illusion, since you have on stage the representatives of a certain community – one is dumb, one is lame and one is alcoholic, a physical maiming which is a public repre-sentation of their spiritual deprivation'.[126] But what we must remember about this 'deprivation' is that it is personal before it is communal, that although a society may, in Fanon's terms, become resigned and miserable, its motor force remains at the grass-roots, and in the figures of Doalty,

Maire and Bridget, and even Jimmy Jack, in that same scene we have ample evidence of humour, energy and the capacity for self-determination.

But if Friel has no nostalgia for *that* time, we must still acknowledge that 'that time' – the place constantly revisited by memory – exercises an affective command over the imagination. Buried in the grass-roots of memory is the source of all wonder, as surely as it is at the foot of a tree for the small boy in 'Among the Ruins' and in the Mundy house and yard for the child narrator of *Lughnasa*.

In *Translations* the appeal is constantly made to the eighteenth century, itself a period of immense change. Taken together, *Making History* and *Translations* refer like a constantly receding corridor of tableaux to a time before time began, to a place which is Ireland transformed by the elision of History – a state of mind rather than a concrete vulnerable reality.

LANGUAGE AND IDENTITY

One of the identities which the 'volunteers' bestow on Leif is 'the only child of a merchant prince'; 'all young Leif could say was "I own a well-trained falcon" in seven languages' (*Vol.* 57), like a polyglot version of Mervyn Peake's Titus – a baroque conception who belies the fact that time has made him a skeleton while history has robbed him of all identity. Underlying this imagery is the fact that one can change one's identity with one's language – the carapace which both protects and inhibits.

But further beneath this superficial statement we find that language is dependent on sense, since it is the expression of composite sense. Comprehension depends on vision ('Can't you *see!*') and it also depends, perhaps to a lesser extent, on the other ways of perceiving: 'Are you deaf? Are you stupid? Don't you understand simple words?' (*LQ* 78). And it depends very definitely on an aggregated sense of *being*: in Mozart's *Le nozze di Figaro* Count Almaviva begins to make love to his wife *because* she resembles someone else. People are not who they seem, our reasons for doing things are not what they seem, and our interpretation of what we do can also be dangerously ambiguous. The possession of two languages by which to decode a single text or icon is a common psychological feature even among monoglots: we think in one language and we speak in another. We are called 'Skinner' in one and Adrian Casimir Fitzgerald in the other. We think demotic but we speak mandarin – like Lily 'phoning from the Mayor's parlour (*Freedom* 53), or the subtle changes in Hugh Mor O'Donnell's syntax and the blatant changes in the actual tongue he uses, when he is at home or abroad ('outside the parish'). He puts his house in order when Englishmen arrive (*Tr.* 29) just as Manus Sweeney, paradoxically, begins to speak English when Shane and Peter come to the gentle island. We can be deprived of an essential part of our identity by having our name, or one of our names, removed from us – like Leif, or like 'Smiler', the imbecilic victim of police brutality: 'he hardly knows his own name' (*Vol.* 51).

Changing identity with language, or losing identity through lack of language, is made explicitly tragical in *Making History*, where, depending on the context of circumstance and affiliation, Hugh O'Neill employs either an 'Upper-class English' or a 'Tyrone' accent to express his meaning. *Making History* (like the short story 'My Father and the Sergeant') shows us the inflections possible with the use of different names: O'Neill's circumstances differ according to whether he is 'Hugh', 'The O'Neill', 'Earl of Tyrone', or 'Tyrone', or even 'Fox O'Neill' – and so of course do our reactions to, and perceptions of, him.

Under such conditions, communication, meaning and identity begin to disintegrate, and it becomes increasingly difficult to maintain an equilibrium between the inner and the outer voice. Ways of doing things – responses to the perceptible world – become caricatures: the actual difference between English and Irish miles provides a basis for a distinction between efficient and inefficient ways of measuring, and therefore expressing, the world. The English language becomes subverted by its Irish users. Irish nomenclature is 'bulled' by the Englishman because the ambiguity of sense and meaning is resolved by anglicisation.

MANUS: What's 'incorrect' about the place names we have here?
OWEN: Nothing at all. They're just going to be standardised.
MANUS: You mean changed into English?
OWEN: *Where there's ambiguity*, they'll be Anglicized (*Tr.* 32, *my emphasis*)

With the collapse of orientation, community falters:

OWEN: Do you know where the priest lives?
HUGH: At Lis na Muc, over near . . .
OWEN: No he doesn't. Lis na Muc, the Fort of the Pigs, has become Swinefort . . . And to get to Swinefort you pass through Greencastle and Fair Head and Strandhill and Gort and Whiteplains. And the new school isn't at Poll na gCaorach – it's at Sheepsrock. Will you be able to find your way? (*Tr.* 42)

The 'sense' which this condition appeals to, and indeed engenders, lies between 'consternation' and 'melancholy', the key elements of despair which Friel identified in writing *Aristocrats*.[127] The Irish mind is left in Janus-like desolation between the shock of the future and the emptiness of the past. When one does not know whether one's life is a tragedy or a comedy, the only *frisson* possible is that of despair – as Hugh, the enervate, hands over the baton of hope to Maire, the energised. At first we don't realise how serious the position is. There is no experience. The mind cannot will us towards either pole. It is exhilarating to find oneself in 'uncertainties, mysteries, doubts', a condition we often dignify with the name of 'love'. We live within the perimeter of a world which offers security, but one which we would like to escape, if only from curiosity. Then we know the thrill of discovery; the commanding texts are wrong, they therefore lose their authority; the maps are incorrectly drawn, the territory ceases to be closed and becomes open; we turn the icons to the wall. 'The chart's wrong . . . The museum's wrong' (Vol. 41). Then we discover that, however wrong the text may be (the Widgery Report, Sir's Ledger, Lombard's 'History'), the discovery coincides with the hour of our death. The result is grief, bewilderment, 'a casualty of language' (Vol. 28).

We adopt language as a means of communication in order to avoid, or prevent, tragedy and violence, in order to ensure some kind of survival. In the hour of our death, as Heaney says, 'whispering morse',[128] we abandon language as a false god. That is the public world. The inner state is even more consternated and melancholic, because *it* experiences a breakdown in the process of rationalisation:

MAIRE: Never! There never was blight here. Never. Never. But we're always sniffing about for it, aren't we . . . Honest to God, some of you people aren't happy unless you're miserable and you'll not be right content until you're dead!

DOALTY: Bloody right, Maire. And sure St Columcille prophesied there'd never be blight here. He said

> The spuds will bloom in Baile Beag
> Till rabbits grow an extra lug.

And sure that'll never be. So we're alright. (*Tr.* 21–2)

Maire uses 'never' as she later uses 'always'; we know that both are impossible, seductive concepts of *absolute* time which break down in the face of *relative* time. To wish the conjugation of the temporal and the eternal without being able to live it, is to act the fool without cause; to abandon reason is the step immediately before the flight from language: first irrationality, then silence. Perhaps only Jimmy Jack, because of his removal from the rational, quotidian plane, is closest to reality: events as such do not concern him; he has become 'immemorial', part of the fabric of time itself.

The most obvious example of the flight from language in modern Irish literature is of course Joyce. His strategy, in the face of the affective breakdown of Ireland, was 'silence, exile and cunning'. The result, in literary terms, was the renewal of myth and metaphor in the creation of a new language in *Finnegans Wake*. Friel does not attempt to approach Joyce's drastic remedy, but he is acutely conscious of the need for a linguistic revolt: 'we have not yet discovered a language appropriate to the theatre in this country – as singularly appropriate as Synge's invention',[129] and one, we might therefore think, as radical in its own way as Joyce's. What Friel envisaged, but could not at that time feel his way towards, was a 'language' that would encompass the social-political *and* the emotional-familial modes, a dual-purpose method of expressing both opportunities/possibilities and inevitabilities, without double-crossing either. In one sense he needed to move towards a balletic, non-verbal theatre such as that developed by Tom MacIntyre in plays such as *The Great Hunger* and *Rise Up Lovely Sweeney;* in another he required words more than ever before. The idea is compellingly explored in *Dancing at Lughnasa* which, because it is a 'memory play', counterpoints the way we use words with the way they have been used; and because words are re-interpreted through the central metaphor of the play, the spectacle of the dance.

Friel's earlier work contains distilled emotional lessons: those explorations of individual and collective consciousness as we have seen them expressed in the stories, the 'love' plays and the plays of freedom. In *Faith Healer* we were offered some form of resolution to the artist's inner problems, a homecoming to the self. We also saw a steady erosion of the concept of *communitas* in the face of inevitable social change, and a growing awareness of the paucity of dramatic invention where it is needed to meet a 'crisis of form'. In *Translations* most of these lessons were repeated in a way which suggests that the author was using some form of emotional shorthand as an *aide-mémoire*, in pursuit of a further project – that of language itself – and a further resolution. First, therefore, we look at his psychological approach. We realise immediately that the hedge-school pupils, anticipating the entry of the Master, represent a community of doubt and anxiety. A lame man is coaxing an apparently mute girl into the confidence of self-expression, opening the play with the catechetic 'what is your name?' The 'Infant Prodigy' recites Homer's account of the transfiguration of Ulysses by 'flashing-eyed' Athene. The intimacy of the modern and ancient worlds is reinforced by Jimmy's familiarity, and the idea of naming is reinforced by the question of the paternity of Nellie Ruadh's baby: 'she was threatening she was going to call it after its father' (*Tr.* 18).

Perception is faulty: they fear the 'sweet smell' even though they are not sure whether or not the smell is the cause or the effect of crop failure. The failure of perception can be fatal: if memory is the link with the past, then the failure of memory (a breakdown in the recollection of past perceptions) cuts us off from history; Beckett, in particular, explores this through the principle 'esse est percipi': since 'to be' is 'to be perceived', then to remember also depends on being perceived. Memory cannot have an independent existence, since it requires a person to operate it and a perceiver to create that person. If imperception or imperfect perception can be futuristically fatal, Beckett suggests that the imperfect perception of the past, or non-perception, can be equally damaging to one's past:

> Instead of resuming me at the point where I was left oft they pick me up at a much later stage, perhaps thereby hoping to induce in me the illusion that I had got through the interval all on my own, lived without help of any kind for quite some time.[130]

The message for the broken traditions of Irish history is clear.

Sarah's slow progress towards utterance begins with the most basic and personal announcement: 'my name is Sarah'; she accomplishes four further holds on the public world: 'Flowers' (compare this with Maire's three words of English), 'Sarah Johnny Sally' (her full patronymic, marking her place in the world), and, as she witnesses the embrace of Maire and Yolland, the name of her fellow-cripple, 'Manus!' – a 'response cry blurted out as an involuntary reaction to what you've just heard' (CC 19); her final statement is of place, 'I live in Bun na hAbhann'.

Hugh's appearance is intricately connected with his role in the Tarot of the community, a catalogue which Friel has concentrated into this one personage, the *dominus*, surrounded by Yeats's noble peasants, the *ignari*, *stulti*, *rustici*. Hugh has 'residual dignity' (*Tr.* 23); he interprets the events of the parish – the baptism or *caerimonia nominationis* of the baby, the arrival of the sappers, the opening of the new national school; and he draws his pupils closer again to the classical world and its people: 'Sophocles from Colonus would agree with Doalty Dan Doalty from Tulach Alainn: "To know nothing is the sweetest life"' (*Tr.* 24). As Kearney observes: 'he is an inquisitor of origins and etymologies who speaks in the past tense. He is backward looking for the simple reason that the future holds no hope for his language.'[131] He therefore ignores Daniel O'Connell's challenge thrown out by Maire, who insists 'I don't want Greek, I don't want Latin. I want English. I want to be able to speak English because I'm going to America' (*Tr.* 25–6). The ultimate irony is of course that the *dead* languages, which should be meaningless, paradoxically *live* in Baile Beag.[132]

The text maintained by this community and protected by its *dominus* is unwritten. It is the essence of an orally transmitted culture; folklore would hardly describe it, since it is not entirely a matter of custom nor even a simple conjugation of custom and knowledge. It is, as the passage quoted from Larcom (above, p. 38) suggests, both the temporal dimension of habitude and the daily way of going about things, and the interaction and interdependence of the two.

Within this text, however, there are secrets, inner truths. In Baile Beag these are at stake. As Sarah succeeds in saying her name Manus declares 'this is our secret . . . soon you'll be telling me all the secrets that have been in that head of yours all these years' (*Tr.* 12): her private imaginings which are now to be broadcast to a wise and sceptical community. Simultaneously Manus encourages Sarah: 'Nothing'll stop us now! Nothing in the wide world!', but we know that experience stops us, we cannot embrace the wide world because we are enclosed by the limits of the known world, the narrow ground. Manus betrays Sarah, by making public the mute secrets of her privacy. In the public world she is destroyed.

To look to America is to look at a colony, a diaspora – 'the passage money came last Friday' (*Tr.* 20) – and, although Friel uses Jimmy's impending marriage to Athene as a foil to Maire's love for Yolland, even Jimmy's union is across a border vitiated by customary commerce between Baile Beag and 'the parish of Athens'. But to look beyond that world is to contemplate exogamy, and, as Jimmy Jack says:

> Do you know the Greek word *endogamein*? It means to marry within the tribe. And the word *exogamein* means to marry outside the tribe. And you don't cross those borders casually – both sides get very angry. Now, the problem is this: is Athene sufficiently mortal or am I sufficiently godlike for the marriage to be acceptable to her people and to my people? You think about that. (*Tr.* 68)

There is an obvious analogy between this dilemma and that in *The Enemy Within* where Columba's nephew Aedh has married a Pict – a pagan – with resulting suspicion on both sides: the connection between *faith* and *place* is explicit: 'Let it grow up a heathen, a stranger to the soft lands of Gartan' (*EW* 65). As Eliade observes, union between gods and goddesses takes place in sacred time, whereas that between humans occurs in profane time:[133] the dilemma for Jimmy Jack is obvious, since his union with Athene is not only a matter of whether or not he can become godlike or she human, but a matter of crossing the border, of becoming unhoused. 'Every marriage implies a tension and a danger and hence precipitates a crisis; this is why it is performed by a rite of passage' says Eliade.[134] Jimmy Jack and Athene, the atempted wedding in *Aristocrats*, the courtship of Maire and Yolland in *Translations*, the exogamy of Mabel and Hugh O'Neill in *Making History*, are, despite the huge differences in their social significance, all equal parts of the same generic paradox – that in order to survive the most ordinary of emotions and realities one must cross a threshold and in so doing be annihilated. And as *Translations* ends, it is the turn of Hugh to intone, invoking the protection of a text he has by now admitted has no authority:[135] '*urbs antiqua fuit* . . . '(*Tr.* 69). Friel continues his examination of the role of

the revenant by combining elements which we have previously seen in
Gar O'Donnell, Cass McGuire and Ben Butler: a disruption, an evaluation
of the old ways, and a failure of communication. But he also conducts
this visitation in two ways: through Owen O'Donnell, the ambivalent son
of the house who doubles as 'Roland', the cartographer's scout; and
George Yolland, *his* doppelgänger, who is rediscovering or inventing
himself, and coming home for the first time (they congress as 'Rowen' or
'Oland', *Tr.* 45). For Owen, 'everything's just as it was! Nothing's
changed! Not a thing!' (*Tr.* 27), he is back within the tribe, *'civilised
people'* (*Tr.* 28), but he realises, in an echo of *The Gentle Island*, that
permanence is false and civilisation dead:

YOLLAND: It's really heavenly.
OWEN: For God's sake! the first hot summer in fifty years and you
                think it's Eden. (*Tr.* 38)

He taunts his father with the new topography (*Tr.* 42) and asks 'Is it
astute not to be able to adjust for survival?'(*Tr.* 43). Owen is the go-
between, the traducer of cultures who inserts himself between the worlds
of past and future. For Yolland the 'homecoming' is perhaps even more
acute, because, like Private Gar, he is aware of the *inner* tensions which
his 'crude intrusion' (*Tr.* 32) sets up. He realises the problem of translation:
that one must live *within* a culture, the dark and private places of pre-
verbal life, rather than seek a transference: 'Let's leave it alone. There's no
English equivalent for a sound like that' (*Tr.* 35). But he also realises the
impossibility of living within the culture of Baile Beag, even though he
has experienced 'a momentary sense of discovery – not quite a sense of
discovery – a sense of recognition, of confirmation of something I half
knew instinctively' (*Tr.* 40). He acknowledges that 'I may learn the
password but the language of the tribe will always elude me . . . The
private core will always be hermetic' (*Tr.* 40).

For Yolland there can be no going back, however: 'I couldn't face
father' (*Tr.* 39): he is exiled from both worlds and he cannot live up to
his father's aspirations for a new world. For his father (again echoing
Steiner[136]) 'ancient time was at an end . . . There were no longer any frontiers to man's potential. Possibilities were endless and exciting' (*Tr.* 40).
Once again, a world without boundaries is, as we already know, an
explosive culture without immunity, a prey to the bacteria of the unknown.
And Yolland knows that to live in the world one needs 'energy –
coherence – belief' and believes that he has found it in the calm possession with which Baile Beag conducts its daily life, whether it be the
pastoral, hallowed by consuetude, or the appeals to the classical world
which it has made familiar – 'a totally different order, a consciousness

that wasn't striving nor agitated, but at ease with its own conviction and assurance' (*Tr.* 40).

The *dominus*, the *paterfamilias*, extends symbolic welcome to this adopted son: 'I understand your sense of exclusion, of being cut off from life here; and I trust you will find access to us with my son's help' (*Tr.* 43). Hugh has coherence and belief and knows that 'to remember everything is a form of madness'. This is one key to Hugh's character, to the fact that the play revolves around him, as its central persona. He and Rowen/Oland/George are accomplices in the fate of Baile Beag, this 'erosion' or 'eviction' (*Tr.* 43) of one culture by another. O'Faolain calls it an 'infiltration' and comments: 'today we have sometimes disguised our outposts as tourists; then, they disguised them as traders; in either case they ended up as soldiers'.[137] The inference being that, however civilised the infiltration may be, it ends in armed confrontation: the map-making evolves inevitably into what it always contained, a military exercise.

There is also a fierce reaction to this process, not from Hugh but from the lame son, Manus, from the unseen villains whom he protects and excuses, the Donnelly twins, and an ineffective response from Doalty. For Hugh and his cohort, Jimmy Jack, the real eviction excites only a verbal, nostalgic response in a dead tongue ('ignari, stulti, rustici') and an appeal to an heroic engagement in which they did not fight – the 'Thermopylae' of 1798, when they returned to their undefended omphalos before the battle was joined (*Tr.* 58, 67). Manus O'Donnell wants to maintain *communitas* when it is obvious that a larger society is in the wings. Like Manus Sweeney in *The Gentle Island*, he is 'the lame scholar turned violent' (*Tr.* 55) when the secrets are penetrated and laid bare and the language is 'bulled'. But he is only capable of 'the wrong gesture in the wrong language'.

Therefore, Friel addresses the problem of possibilities, not only inconsistencies between different versions of the same event or perception (as we have seen in *Philadelphia, Cass, Living Quarters, Aristocrats, The Freedom*) but also the meanings which lurk within the words themselves, the range of ambiguities which stretch from blatant falsehood and traduction to misplaced or uncomprehended tenderness.

There is a blissful state in which one can be in 'uncertainties' without reaching for meaning; this immaterialism comes out at several points in *Translations*: 'I don't know a word they're saying, nor they me, but sure that doesn't matter does it?' (*Tr.* 17); 'Owen/Roland – what the hell. It's only a name. It's the same me, isn't it? Well, isn't it?' (*Tr.* 33). But communication depends on shared meaning, and between languages there must be a common code. In *Translations* we see that in language, as a gesture of discourse, this commonalty cannot be found, because the symbolic points of contact represent different cultures, different ways of looking at the world. Owen calls Irish 'archaic' and English 'good' (*Tr.* 29); Hugh sums up the difference between Irish and English as that between the aristocratic and the plebeian (*Tr.* 41).

In the scene of *Translations* where this incapacity for communion is expressed most poignantly, Friel creates a tragi-comic situation which he manipulates into a post-verbal exchange based on the nonsense-talk of lovers – the place-names of Baile Beag and Norfolk. This scene is difficult to encompass because it has many elements: the comedy (Maire: 'The grass must be wet. My feet are soaking.' Yolland: 'Your feet must be wet. The grass is soaking.' *Tr.* 49); the pathetic attempts at communication, grasping at wisps of meaning ('if you could understand me . . . I would tell you how beautiful you are', *Tr.* 52); the induction of Maire into English speech, like Manus coaxing Sarah ('Water. Water. Oh yes – water – water – very good – water – good – good . . . fire – indeed – wonderful – fire, fire,' *Tr.* 50) and the use of the traitorous 'always'.[138]

As the Englishman and the Irishwoman come together in a tenderly orchestrated movement towards union in exogamy, they adopt signals, meaningless but not inappropriate, in order to avoid the failure of meaning, but which convey ideas of which they themselves are not capable. They are limited by the same difficulties as Frank Butler ('he wants to smother her, wash her in words of love, but he can't, because he has no fluency in love words', *LQ* 61). And in recompense for the appropriation of the place-names George offers Maire the topography of his own world – a mental map of an imaginary world, an otherness ('Aren't they odd names? Sure they make no sense to me at all', *Tr.* 60) which replaces the invaded ground in her secret memory ('strange sounds . . . nice sounds, like Jimmy Jack reciting his Homer', *Tr.* 60).

So we see a further turn in the language-play, as meaning is twisted for the purpose of betrayal. In his role as Roland, Owen deliberately mistranslates the explanation of the map-making exercise (*Tr.* 31–2); it is significant that Manus, *but not Hugh*, draws attention to this. Owen's version is a sub-version of the militaristic intention. He is, in fact, the instrument of his own tribe's destruction, working through the medium of linguistic distortion.

The disposal of Yolland is not merely the dramatist's inevitable response to the situation he creates in the love scene. In the symbolic metaphorical embrace of Owen and Yolland in Act 2, Friel replicates the welcome dreamed of by all those who fear and yet desire their own destruction – a gnostic death-wish to embrace my-brother-my-executioner. Moreover, Yolland rushes to meet this fate: his exit with Maire from the dance is a 'sudden and impetuous escape' (*Tr.* 49) and their leap into the dark makes him, like Meg in *Lovers*, a winner, whereas Maire is repossessed by the tribe, a relict of ecstasy. So, in addition to Hugh's masterly surrender to fate, power in quiescence, a tragedy without heroism, we have Yolland's paradoxical renunciation of life and love.

In the figure of Hugh O'Donnell, however, Friel has drawn his most convincing and impressive male character to date – only equalled by that of Molly Sweeney. Although, following Dowling's caricature of the typical hedge-schoolmaster, he espouses the dead and dying tongues, he possesses, and can use, the inner strength to resolve their crises. He admits the situation, and while for himself he prefers to favour a detumescent culture, he is willing to aid – he bestows his will upon – those frightened children like Maire who need to learn a new song, in order to recapture faith.

It is Yolland, the usurper of this Eden, who notices this. While Owen taunts his father – 'will you be able to find your way?' – Yolland quietly states: 'He knows what's happening' (*Tr.* 43). And Hugh confirms it by accepting the need for new place-names, for a new way of seeing the familiar. Here once again Friel has borrowed from his O'Neill project, by giving the schoolmaster some of the stature of the Earl. As O'Faolain tells us, 'it is because he did understand what was at stake that he was of such size in his own day and of such interest in ours'. Later, describing O'Neill's recognition of impending catastrophe, O'Faolain says 'the decisions of such a man are real decisions where every hesitation is to be honoured for its courage and humanity in that it springs from a profound knowledge of the consequences of the final choice'.[139] To give, as O'Faolain's O'Neill and Friel's O'Donnell, 'a speech that it could understand and which made it realize itself intelligently',[140] is both a form of salvation and an act of treachery.

Hugh, from a position of historic but wavering strength, that of crepuscular myth, also rewrites the local past, by admitting that he and Jimmy Jack never went to Sligo in 1798, but, fortified by drink, retreated to repossess those familiars whom in their heroism they had deserted. He realises that he is one of a dying race, because 'ancient time [is] at an end', and yet when he says '*we* must learn where we live, we must make there our new home' he speaks for his people but not for himself: he intends to fossilise. In his line 'Yes, I will teach you English, Maire Chatach' there is an operatic quality because, as he moves towards the stairs and ascends from the room he has been regarding 'as if he were about to leave it forever' (*Tr.* 62), he begins to sing the threnody of his own life. Hugh is the complete realist, because he *knows* what is happening. He makes the final statement: 'I will provide you with the available words and the available grammar. But will that help you to interpret between privacies?

I have no idea. But it's all we have . . . As for "always" – it's a silly word, girl' (*Tr.* 67).

In Hugh, the drunken schoolmaster/father is repatriated, restored to dignity. The way in which Manus nurses him is indicative of this restoration. Friel, having come to terms with the artist's responsibilities, perfidies, inherent anarchy, finds a way of rehabilitating the figure who has been most defiled and assaulted, the patrician, the father of the aristocrats. Through the necessary conceit of the Latin tongue he salutes him as 'Dominus'. In the conjunction of Owen and Hugh, Friel finds himself. From the silent S. B. O'Donnell, to the eloquent Hugh Mor O'Donnell, via the stricken Judge O'Donnell of *Aristocrats* is a strange odyssey, but a homecoming nonetheless.

Translations closes with a triologue which repays close attention: Maire says 'When he comes back, this is where he'll come to. He told me this is where he was happiest' (*Tr.* 68). George in a new epiphany will revisit his new home, he will redeem the waiting girl, who represents that which made him most happy, but least fortunate. Jimmy pronounces on the difficulties of becoming a god. And Hugh's threnody, uttered in confusion and forgetfulness, looks back at an uprising, a search for civil rights, for freedom against the ancient city. As he speaks, the lights come down, and, in his own version of Ovid, 'evening comes with its sacred song'.[141]

VERTIGO

Making History is allegorical of the Irish experience to a far more significant extent than *Translations*, chiefly because it insists more strongly on the relationship between the private and the public *personae*. The snapshot image of a culture on the verge of eviction, or extinction, is never fully developed – it exists in the background of Hugh O'Neill's consciousness, in this very cerebral play, but it is an element in 'the overall thing' (*MH* 68) which he carries on his back as well as in his heart. (Only once does O'Neill advert openly to that 'age-old civilisation', to 'the life they knew before they were overrun' [*MH* 40], in contrast to the length at which he discusses his own personal dilemma.)

But in depicting a man – *the* man – of Irish destiny caught in the between-space of decisions, emotional ambivalence and personal dignity, the play typifies the linguistic and semantic dilemma which is at the heart of all post-colonial discourse. In theoretical terms, it brings together, and gives voice to, the dissertations of Steiner and Bhabha in, respectively, the use and meaning of language and the *locus* of cultural authority.

Ostensibly, the situations in *Making History* and *Translations* are very similar: a society – a culture – on the threshold of change, a man indecisive in his choices between past and future, for self and for society – and a possibility of judging and recording the transitional moment subjectively or objectively, for the greater good or the inner truth. That the events of *Making History* predate those of *Translations* by over two hundred years is immaterial – Irish history, especially in its relations to England, habitually repeats itself. And perhaps the mere fact that in each case that way of life stands on the edge of oblivion is a way of reminding us that the rite of passage recurs as often as the sun rises and sets.

The internationalism of *Making History* would be merely trite if it served only to highlight certain points of reference in Anglo-Irish relations. But its allegorical value is more far-reaching. As Peter Brook noted in 1968 – a time when, as we have seen, events in Ireland were starting to take the downward spiral which has led to the 'Good Friday' Agreement of 1998 – a change in human culture, as radical as that of the Renaissance itself, is taking place which continues to determine how people will live in relation to each other, their governments and themselves:

> The role of the individual in the society, his duties and his needs, the issues of what belongs to him and what belongs to the state, are in question again. Again, as in Elizabethan times, man is asking why he has a life and against what we can measure it.[142]

The liminality of modern Ireland during the past half century, in its decision to open itself to external influences, to enter a fiscal and increasingly socio-political pan-European framework, has been dramatic. A very cogent reason for the immediate presence and impact of Irish theatre in so many venues overseas is the centrality of such liminal issues in a society which is otherwise regarded as being at the blunter edge of contemporary affairs. The textbook relevance of Ireland as a country still emerging from its centuries of eternally debatable history makes what the playwrights have to say of import to other societies where the harshness of decision-making is either wallowing in post-imperial stupor or yet to be confronted.

But it would be excessive to load *Making History*, or any of Friel's plays, with extra-textual significance unless the direct analogies suggest themselves. Thus Christopher Murray's 1992 judgement that *Making History* 'is clearly a political allegory for the current situation in Northern Ireland'[143] is critically far-fetched. One might suggest that the play *can be read metaphorically* as such, but the dramatic content does not yield to this kind of analysis.

If I look beyond the simple drama of Hugh O'Neill and Mabel Bagenal, and the incursion into their lives of the force of history, then I see something equally simple: Heaney's 'search for images and symbols adequate to our predicament' – the need to construct a version of the intersection between people and political forces which will make acceptable fictions out of the conflict composed of individual stories which are more true to their authors' idiosyncrasies than to the whims of history. 'We are all revisionists now' said Roy Foster in the inaugural issue of *The Irish Review*, intended to set the cultural standards and agenda for the post-*Crane Bag* era. 'To say "revisionist" should just be another way of saying "historian"'[144] – which is the role of the intellectual in any situation where national identity is being redefined.

An index to the condition of Hugh O'Neill's life both before and after the battle of Kinsale is the fact that Act 1 of *Making History* opens in a room in 'O'Neill's home' but that this room is described as 'comfortless' (*MH* 1). It is described not as a castle, not as a fort, but as a comfortless home. For a man whose life was spent on the run, dodging fate, the oxymoron is an exact expression of the dualities of O'Neill's life: the search for fixity which must always be restless, the 'state' of Ireland which is permanently subjunctive, dependent on 'if'. The divisiveness which in the play is epitomised by the disorderly incursions of Hugh O'Donnell into the events of state underlies the *unheimlich* nature of Ireland on the edge of the unknown. Only O'Neill knows the unknown. Behind him and around him is the gaelic past; ahead of him, and ahead of Ireland, is Elizabethan England, a country which only recently, after internecine centuries, had, under Elizabeth's grandfather, itself become a unitary state. As England emerges from possibility into reality, so its language became more stable and less inclined to deviancy: England was translated into the modern world and began its huge project of translating the rest of the world into its image. Ireland, conversely, resisted this project not out of opposition to its tenets but because it did not have the capacity for such a transformation, was employing translation as a tool of evasion and uncertainty. In both cases, the power of the word, and the role of the translator, is paramount: 'We can make this country – this world – whatever we want it to be by saying so, . . It is the knowledge of this that is the genius and glory of the Gael'.[145]

It would be clear to anyone in England from the mid-sixteenth century that the country, with its internal cohesion and its overseas outreach, was a settled community. No such reference was available to an Irishman. Similarly, on a personal level, where an Englishman might regard monarch and constitution as symbols of at-homeness and of a unified existence, in Ireland those same symbols were instruments of an unsettling destiny.

Characterising 'the gap' or interstitial space occupied by the hapless Hugh O'Neill is the question of affection. It is impossible to understand Hugh O'Neill as a figure of 'History' unless we also regard the private man and his personal 'history'. In both men, the affections, and the affective call, are paramount. When O'Neill asks 'do I . . . or do I?' in his choice of destinies for himself and for Ireland, he also asks whether there is a private fate for this most public of men. He is on the verge of becoming a modern statesman, reminded of his public engagements in the style of a cabinet minister or head of state; he has an official annalist; and he is acutely aware of his precarious position as the leader of his own people who is about to forfeit his status because he is no longer able to lead them.

He is able to claim the respect of international statesmen such as the Earl of Essex because he himself is inter-national in the literal sense of the word, standing between two nations, recognising the power and the distance of each, yet bound to betray both by altering translations between them.

In his poem 'Terminus' Seamus Heaney has referred cryptically to O'Neill as

> the last earl on horseback in midstream
> Still parleying, in earshot of his peers.[146]

The image derives from an historical painting of the mid-river confrontation of O'Neill and Essex, each with his troops at his shoulder, which typifies the meeting between their two civilisations and a climactic moment in European history. In the broadcast to which I referred in Chapter 5, Heaney said 'The marching season is O'Neill and Essex . . . the marching armies confronting one another'.[147] But equally, Hugh O'Neill stands in the centre of a flow of events which expresses Heraclitus' quotidian wisdom 'you cannot step twice into the same river' or παντα 'ρει [everything flows] and this is no less private than public. Every step he takes moves his personal history from past to future. The battle between two civilisations, as emergent modern Ireland was at one stage characterised, takes place within Hugh O'Neill. But it is not only a battle between gael and planter, between Ireland and England, but between Hugh O'Neill the lover of Mabel Bagenal and Hugh O'Neill the Earl of Tyrone and leader of Ireland: 'because of your birth, education and personal attributes, you are the natural leader' (MH 8) says Lombard; but because the shape of History demands that a pattern be imposed on O'Neill, the 'personal attributes' which make him Mabel's lover are excoriated from the ledger together with the education amid the Sidney family to which he allocates so much ambiguous but nonetheless affectionate value.

Almost as if anticipating the Irish short story tradition and its affinity with the seanchaí, Lombard suggests that 'history is . . . a kind of storytelling' (*MH* 8) and that its strategy is to shape events into a narrative. That Lombard speaks of this shaping as an imposition is highly significant. An imposition is of the same order as an eviction in that it invades a space and changes its dispositions. When Lombard signals his reservations about the marriage he does so in the language of the diplomat:

> LOMBARD: We have all got to assess the religious and political implications
> of this association, Hugh.
> O'NEILL: Marriage, Archbishop (*MH* 14).

This is at the opening of the play. By its end, Lombard has not yielded an inch in his allegiance to History. Excluding Mabel from Hugh's life is part of 'making a pattern . . . offering a cohesion to that random catalogue of deliberate achievements and sheer accident that constitutes your life . . . a narrative that people will read and be satisfied by' (*MH* 67).

Making History is the play in which, with the possible exception of *Molly Sweeney*, the idea that unacceptable truths can be manipulated into acceptable fictions is most evident. The public stage has provided Friel with the occasion for bringing home the idea that something may have happened and yet be immaterial, a reversal of the narration of the fishing expedition which did *not* happen and yet is 'true' in the sense that we can regard it as valid even though non-existent. 'I'm not sure that "truth" is a primary ingredient' says Lombard, neatly overturning the historians' criticism of *Translations* by adding 'maybe when the time comes, imagination will be as important as information' (*MH* 8–9). *When the time comes*: thus we arrive at the point where memory becomes affected by events other than those with which it itself can deal – when the private is invaded by the public and is overtaken by the 'greater good'. At the moment of intimacy, a translation between lovers or confederates may contain its grain of truth, and that truth may endure in the memory of each actor. But subsequent 'history' may change each of these perceptions, and may also be diminished by a 'History' which belongs to neither party but which imposes itself at the behest of the community to which they belong.

Thus, as Lombard argues, 'a period of history . . . may contain within it several possible narratives . . . determined by the needs and the demands and the expectations of different people and different eras' (*MH* 15–16). If one is mixed up in 'History', then not only is one's own private history suppressed in the interests of a public narrative, but the way that narrative is told will also change over periods of time.

In the case of Hugh O'Neill, the urgency of creating a narrative encompassing the public fate of his country in the face of English oppression is greater than the compelling love between himself and his English wife. 'Intimations . . . of an emerging nation state' (*MH* 64) are more exacting than intimations of intimacy. Even the crude Hugh O'Donnell is transfigured in the 'life' written of him by Ludhaidh O'Cleary: 'He was a dove in meekness and gentleness and a lion in strength and force. He was a sweet-sounding trumpet' (*MH* 64). 'Maybe you and I remember a different Hugh' says Lombard, adding 'but maybe that's not the point' – the point being that the need for a story is pre-eminent over the need for facts (*MH* 66). A *point* is a place on the map, a punctuation, on the site of which satisfaction and agreement are enabled. It is reached after negotiation, and it is only after several attempts to capture Lombard's agreement that the 'point' is reached. It is this same 'point' at which dramatic secrets are revealed, or truths expressed.

Ironically, it is Lombard who offers to change the narrative – 'I'll rewrite it in any way you want' (*MH* 66) – with all the authority of the writer who is already in command of the ledger. When Hugh suggests that 'the overall thing' should contain his private career, and should reflect all of his character, not merely the public and heroic Hugh, it is the deconstruction of the word 'overall' which brings history and History onto a collision course. Lombard is perfectly willing to rewrite 'history' but not 'History' – 'the big canvas of national events' (*MH* 69) has no place in it for 'a domestic story . . . a love story' which is unhoused as surely as Hugh and Mabel themselves in order top accommodate the arrangement of facts into a pattern which will satisfy the future.

'Which claim would history approve?' (*MH* 28). To give to History the voice of authority is to invest the backward glance with a disabling power. On the personal level it not only negates the love between Hugh and Mabel but impedes the affiliation of the gaelic chieftains. Friel correctly labels the course of History as a 'conflict . . . between two deeply opposed civilizations' (*MH* 28) and thereby grants to History the authority of the backward glance.

In a remarkable fit of self-parody, Friel invents a scene of great beauty which displays memory at its most rampant and its most fictive, demonstrating that 'History' may be more accurate but that 'history' may be more real. Hugh O'Neill never lived at the house of Sir Henry Sidney, but Friel (and O'Faolain) knows better:

> It's the summers I remember and the autumns, in Kent, in the family seat at Penshurst. And the orchards; and the deerpark; and those enormous fields of wheat and barley. A golden and beneficent land . . . Drake was there once, I remember. And Frobisher and his officers on the eve of their first South American voyage. Gross men; vain men. But Sir Henry's grace and tact seemed to transform all that naked brutality and imperial greed into boyish excitement and manly adventure. He was the only father I ever knew (*MH* 34).

To remember Drake and Frobisher as visitors is to allow Casimir
O'Donnell to reincarnate Yeats and John McCormack and Newman as
visitors to Ballybeg Hall in *Aristocrats*. What happens 'when I cast my
mind back'? The Memory Theatre becomes invaded by a desire for what
might have been, and everything becomes golden until a pedant insists 'So
now you know: it never happened!' and the idyll is destroyed.

THE GAP

We are therefore entitled, and obliged, to look at the modern Irish stage
not only as a place of psychiatric divination but also as the arena in
which political discourse is located and its elements exposed. Friel's
approach to this question of political theatre has been characteristically
circumspect and discreet: as we have seen, he has taken a particularist
view of the elements of politics, resulting in a theatre which appears
oblique rather than direct but which is concerned with the psychological
basis of political action.

Friel has said that he and a play move together – as if towards a final
reckoning, a test of strength like the preordained meeting of Hardy and
McGarvey. In the case of *Making History* we can see just how slowly that
approach has been made. The initial impact on the young Friel of
O'Faolain's study of Hugh O'Neill – a study of psychology, of introspection, of the birth and death of civilisations – sets the scene for Friel's
own involvement with the course of Irish history. Furthermore it linked
that history with the question of individual destiny, of loyalty, of filiation
and affiliation.

The agonies that Hugh O'Neill undergoes in *Making History*, and his
eventual defeat by them, are thus the sum of all the doubts Friel has
raised in his preceding work. The fact that he had been approaching this
play for many years, and that his difficulties in doing so largely contributed to his silence as a playwright from 1982 until 1987, explains how
so much of the eventual portrait of Hugh O'Neill finds pre-echoes in
(especially) *Faith Healer* and *Translations*.

Making History is once again a problem play: a problem for audiences
because it lacks dramatic impact, and for critics because it lacks not only
form but, ostensibly, content or matter. There is no story-line as such
because the playwright is concerned with how the future will determine
the stories of the past: the events of O'Neill's greatness and decline, events
which were of significance for the whole imperial world, are interiorised
and made the subject of a monologue on the nature of affection. The
submissions to Elizabeth, the trials of strength and of dignity, the Battle of
Kinsale, and the Flight of the Earls, are all displaced in O'Neill's

continual examination of the ways we use and are used. The boyhood 'recollections' of an Irish princeling in the family homes of Leicester and Sidney, the marriage to Mabel Bagenal (whom the historians, including O'Faolain, largely ignore), the years of lurking between defeat and flight, like Sweeney, in the scrub of his madness, and the dimming years of exile, take the centre of O'Neill's stage in a mesmerism which, in its disregard for the other characters, often takes the form of soliloquy.

But O'Neill also has a public function representing the same sort of history lesson we have been given in *Translations*. He is a man of his time, tortured, like Columba, by 'the enemy within', but also acutely aware of his duplicity in the revolution of the public spheres. If there is a form to *Making History* it grows predominantly from its author's determination to understand, encompass and engross the mind and character of Hugh O'Neill, and the psychic effect on that mind and character of his environment, his personal history and the strophic times in which he lived, thought and acted.

Hugh O'Neill, in Friel's play, embodies the death of Gaelic Ireland, but also predicts the mantic and semantic troubles of *Translations*, the gombeenism of *The Mundy Scheme* and the drawn lines of *The Freedom*. Here, as much as in his own *Translations* or Murphy's *Famine*, is a play for modern Ireland. Friel has implicitly revoked his declaration that the death of God makes modern tragedy impossible. By devising a type of drama which dispenses with both form and content he has come closer to solving the problem of the 'language play'. In *Making History* Friel makes the most serious claims yet for the authority of the playwright in describing the interaction of time and language, as the manipulator of 'history'. In the case of Hugh O'Neill he occupies a *tabula rasa*, firstly because, as O'Faolain observed, 'no intimate details of this great man's character have come down to us . . . we have nothing to go on except his behaviour . . . no real evidence as to [his] mind'.[148] Secondly because Friel himself has cleared the decks for this new phase of action by the necessary writing of *Faith Healer* and *Fathers and Sons*. There is both a literal and an intellectual nihilism in *Making History* which takes tragedy beyond the delineation of man caught between opposing forces, and replaces him with doubt and fear themselves: this moves the story so wholeheartedly from the physical into the metaphysical that it no longer belongs to traditional drama. Friel has thereby succeeded in answering Stanislavsky's predicament about the closure of plays by, in effect, not beginning them. The antiphonal incantation with which *Making History* ends can simply be read, and experienced, as the dimming of lights that will shortly be raised on that with which *Faith Healer* begins.

The reader coming fresh to O'Faolain's *The Great O'Neill* will therefore be struck by the frequency and intensity of what appear to be references to *Faith Healer*. Friel had to learn a great deal about being a twin, about being a bastard and about the fickleness of 'the healing word' as both master and mistress, in order to approach the condition of hopeless apostasy which characterises his Hugh O'Neill. He seizes on the statement in O'Faolain's closing pages:

> his fingers touch the Archbishop's manuscript. . . . This is his life, his mind, his soul. . . . And every word that he reads is untrue. Lombard has translated him into a star . . . He has seen it all as a glorious story that was in every thread a heartbreak. He has made Life into a Myth[149]

and he finally responds to that invitation to make his own 'translation', not merely of the 'facts' woven about Hugh O'Neill and his role in the Irish future, but also about life as a myth: he is answering his own call from *Philadelphia* and *Translations*: 'do your job – translate!'

The 'Ledger' which controls the Butlers in *Living Quarters* has become 'the History', a sinister document which diminishes O'Neill's privacy and inserts him into the public events of his problematic country, and inserts *it* into *him*. Where Frank Butler pleads for the right to object to the harshness of the chronicle, to the limitations to his freedom, O'Neill fights for the bare right to any of those 'intimate details' which the chroniclers have denied him. And whereas 'Sir' is simply the servant and guardian of the Ledger, Peter Lombard is the author of 'the History' which catechetically and inexorably steers O'Neill towards a destiny he is neither able nor willing to encounter.

For those without these *stigmata*, these birth-marks, life can be lived as the simple conflict between siblings and affiliates. As O'Neill acknowledges of one of the Ulster princes:

> Maguire's no fool. Maguire has no choice. Maguire has to rise. History, instinct, his decent passion, the composition of his blood – he has no alternative. So he will fulfil his fate. It's not a tragic fate and it's not a heroic fate. But his open embrace of it has elements of both, I suppose. (*MH* 30)

Heroism need not be tragic, nor tragedy heroic. Fulfilling fate of one kind or another is making history. Most history is private, uncelebrated, unobserved. Maguire is like the Doaltys and the Lanceys, for whom life is black-and-white, where boundaries are clearly drawn. But there is a more cruel fate for those who are unsure, for whom the 'composition of the blood' creates alternatives, demands that choices be made between impossible futures, whose answer resonates, from Columba's dichotomous loyalties to faith and family to Hugh O'Donnell's 'I have no idea at all' (*Tr.* 67). Contemporary Irish drama begins with Gar O'Donnell's 'I don't know. I-I-I-don't know' (*Ph.* 110). Friel has brought it to the point at which the artist, the actor, the pivotal figure of Irish history and the audience are all saying, in O'Neill's closing words, 'Forgive me . . . I'm sorry' (*MH* 71).

Those words express the reluctant side of Friel's work: the admission of a broken, rather than a triumphant, translator or diviner. On our reading of those words, and of the psychological state of mind which the play has been exploring, will depend very largely our view of Friel's divination. We are being asked to go back to the basic questions posed by Friel, albeit subconsciously, when he set out in search of 'concepts of Irishness'; we are still assessing whatever targets have been put up for us after Yeats's images for the affections; we are observing one writer who has been looking for 'a sense of life that will make the end less frightening' and in doing so has written a play that not only sums up his own drama and that of his 'constituency' but also represents many of the concepts exposed and explored in *Double Cross*, *The Morning After Optimism* and *Famine*.

And Friel's particular success in such a difficult play is due to the fact that he locates the tragedy precisely between the public and the private. The 'events' of O'Neill's life are of no more significance than those of Frank Hardy, and the 'liberties' which Friel has taken with the 'facts' of Irish history are necessary liberties if we are to be given a different type of history lesson: one in which the themes of exile and homecoming illustrate *the deep-seated need of the child to be held*. An exile from home is also an exile from meaning, and folktales are all about the search for meaning which we call home. In the whole of Friel's canon, from 'The Child' to Columba, Gar, Frank and Ben Butler, Fox, Frank Hardy and Hugh O'Neill, the story of this search is both a public adult return to the hearth and a private, adolescent flight to the lap, the shoulder, the bosom.

'Sorry' is both an apology and an excuse. It is the codeword of embarrassment between Maire and Yolland. 'Sorry' is at once pleading and yet final, the admission of a measurable failure, the expression of immeasurable hope, and also the extinction of that hope. It drops the speaker into the depths between two types of opposing certainties, the modern version of the tragic birthmark. As Fintan O'Toole has observed, this approximates to 'what Pegeen Mike calls "the great gap between the gallous story and a dirty deed", the gulf that separates heroic talk from vicious action';[150] that 'great gap' is the living space of those who have to live in indecision because, in Antigone's words, 'my choice destroys me'.[151]

We have already seen, in Frank Hardy, faith healer, one man who is not at all sorry, who needs to meet his destruction in a final choice that is made for him. And in the half-brothers of Kilroy's *Double Cross* we have the example of how such choices are made; how loyalties become, like identical egg-cells, divided; how an identity can become trapped between vicious twins. *Making History* locates its 'hero', its sparagmatic victim, in this 'great gap', the interstice between love and hate that we call 'fear'. The gap is between the private and public worlds, between past and future, between illusion and reality.[152] But because 'God is dead, and with him the tragic hero', the remaking of tragedy and of heroism becomes a task entirely of man's own devising: in a godless world we have to dig our own graves. Now we realise that Friel has been saying this all the time – that in Gaelic Ireland, as in Elizabethan England, there was no God; that 'logic', 'myth', 'God' are all versions of the stories that children save up against the darkness, the loneliness and the questions of the night, anything to keep the talk going.

As in *Translations*, we have the prospect of two lives destroyed by exogamy, of two souls thrown into the gap. O'Neill says of Mabel 'She has left her people to join me here'; Mabel herself claims 'this is my home'; whereas her sister Mary insists 'No, it's not. This can never be your home' (*MH* 14, 24). But ultimately Friel, who has played with the received facts[153] in order to create this empathy between O'Neill and Mabel Bagenal, this approximation at an understanding, a translation between cultures, discards her to die, like Yolland, among strangers. He returns to the local, the native who is yet a betrayer, a traducer, an inadequate symbol of his people's predicament, a spokesman who says the wrong, the unexpected, thing, or who speaks too easily in the tongue of the enemy. The hard focus, the cruel anatomical lesson, is the dismemberment, the failure and perdition of O'Neill.

If there is a controlling word in the whole language of *Making History*, a key to the vocabulary of 'the gap', it is: *or*. O'Neill, referring to Maguire's revolt, asks his scout and touchstone, Mabel 'Do I keep faith with my old friend and ally, Maguire, and indeed with the Gaelic civilisation that he personifies? Or do I march alongside the forces of Her Majesty?' (*MH* 27) We have had this already in *Translations*, when, in his turn, the scout asks the invader: 'Do we scrap Tobair Vree altogether . . . or do we keep piety with a man long dead, long forgotten, his name 'eroded' beyond recognition?' (*Tr.* 44) The choice is between extinction of the old pieties or ignorance of the new; between observing old history and making new history; between recognising the fact of erosion, accepting the new language in which it is cast, and turning one's back on the future. Such liminality is the 'or': the choice which destroys. The choice for O'Neill lies between Maguire and his brother-in-law, the 'upstart' Bagenal:

> impulse, instinct, capricious genius, brilliant improvisation – *or* calculation, good order, common sense, the cold pragmatism of the Renaissance mind . . .

Pasture [or] husbandry . . . Do I grasp the Queen's Marshal's hand . . . *or do I grip the hand of the Fermanagh rebel? (MH 28)*

The choice is at once private and public, pertaining both to the single psyche and to his race and culture. Friel with deliberation enforces this with the spectacle of O'Neill relentlessly asking himself a series of private questions ('Do I . . . or do I?) in this most public way. Bagenal is 'a symbol of the new order which every aristocratic instinct in my body disdains but which my intelligence comprehends and indeed grudgingly respects' (MH 28), whereas siding with Maguire would be to 'bear public and imprudent witness to a way of life that my blood comprehends and indeed loves and that is as old as the Book of Ruth' (MH 28). Privately O'Neill is safe because, as O'Faolain observes, we do not know his mind. But publicly, just as it is when Frank Hardy essays the laying on of hands, the noose is immediately put around the neck. Friel in fact moves the discussion away from the public issues explored in *Translations* into the realm that Kilroy has opened up in *Double Cross* (written for Field Day): the way that William Joyce and Brendan Bracken, sourceless Irish adventurers, see with unremitted horror the writing of their past in terms of future history. Like Kilroy's double-crossers, Friel's O'Neill asks 'which hand do I grasp? Because either way I make an enemy. Either way I interfere with that slow sure tide of history. . . . Let's put it another way. Which choice would history approve?' (MH 28) He thus shifts the weight of the discussion onto the nature of history itself. The passage of time, the way that events, and non-events, within that time are recounted, the names that are to be reckoned with, the subjective and objective sides of any discourse, become the results rather than the causes of some indefinable kind of casuistry, a crude definition which replaces the subtle divination of emotions, cultures and rites. Hugh O'Neill sums up for Mabel the 'or' of his public and private dilemma thus:

> I have spent my life trying to do two things. I have attempted to hold together a harassed and a confused people by trying to keep them in touch with the life they knew before they were overrun . . . I have done that by acknowledging and indeed honouring the rituals and ceremonies and beliefs these people have practised *since before history* . . . And at the same time I have tried to open these people to the strange new ways of Europe, to ease them into the new assessment of things, to nudge them towards changing revaluations and beliefs. *Two pursuits that can scarcely be followed simultaneously [my emphasis]. (MH 40)*

Trying to 'keep faith' with something which will expel you if you espouse foreign ideas; admitting that that with which you would keep faith is already the victim of history, however subsequent that history may be; realising that one can make either the impossible attempt to follow both paths simultaneously or the equally impossible attempt to do neither.

O'Neill is destroyed simply because in the outcome he has to satisfy history (and an audience hungry for a tragic victim) by a course – any course – of action, rather than masterly inaction, the device by which he has hitherto defeated, or at least eluded, fate. In addition to referring to O'Neill's 'cautious inaction', O'Faolain says that, of a man who could 'postpone decisions indefinitely . . . knowing how miraculously long the conspiratorial Irishman can refuse to admit consciously that which his soul intends . . . we do right to be especially slow to suspect any decision in this most cautious and secretive man'.[154] O'Neill can satisfy history neither in prospect nor in retrospect. History, inexorable story-telling, defeats him. It uses him. Whichever way he turns, out of the silent safety of his 'or', leaving the terrible security of the gap means meeting a destiny for which he knows he has been chosen: a reluctant volunteer. The only kind of satisfaction is that final silence granted to Frank Hardy. As O'Faolain puts it, 'the only joy that can have been in his heart was that the suspense was at an end'.[155]

'If Hugh O'Neill cannot offer them safety and justice under our Brehon law, they'll have to look for protection under the new English law,' (*MH* 3–4) his secretary tells him. It underlines the shifting nature of temporary, local relationships, affairs which reflect the *ad hoc* and *ad hominem* nature of Irish society. Exogamy, we are hardly surprised to learn, is 'a class of treachery', but only one such: thinking about 'the new assessment of things' can be just as treacherous. Counterpointed against the accusations of his secretary Harry Hoveden (in 'fact', or 'history', his foster-brother) – '*or* are you saying that you're going to take the English side against Maguire? (*MH* 30) – is O'Neill's Ophelian dedication of herbs/flowers: 'Coriander Maguire . . . ripens suddenly and will fall without warning . . . Borage O'Donnell . . . inclined to induce excessive courage, even recklessness' (*MH* 29–30).

Is O'Neill using, or used by, history? Is he the manipulator or the marionette? Friel is in a sense undermining the status of the central character which he has built up in the Hugh O'Donnell of Ballybeg. He is reinforcing the nihilism – even though it is purposeful nihilism – of Bazarov in *Fathers and Sons*. In this play the impetuous Hugh O'Donnell, Earl of Tyrconnell, makes the realistic, post-Kinsale statement we had been expecting from Jimmy Jack: 'This is the end of it all, Hugh, isn't it?'(*MH* 45) Concomitant with that 'end' is the fact that there is no end, only a continuation of the 'ruthless Gaelic logic' contrasted with the 'cold pragmatism of the Renaissance mind' (*MH* 28); and here Friel makes a mistake, because 'logic' is the wrong word – the right gesture, perhaps, but in the wrong language. Sacrifice to the word (logic) which dominates is, in Gaelic terms, quite inferior to sacrifice to the idea (myth) which continues to liberate; as O'Neill expresses more accurately the 'ruthless logic' of Maguire, he is 'trapped in the old Gaelic paradigms of thought' (*MH* 27).

The child who was Brian (or Bernard) Friel (or O'Friel) and who was so apprehensive as to write the story 'The Child' has become, in the rabble-rousing words of Peter Lombard, 'because of your birth, education and personal attributes . . . the natural leader of revolt' (*MH* 8). But he is also the natural traitor, the opposer and traducer of that revolt, the shaman who can see both past and future. He is both 'attack' and 'counter-attack', reformation and counter-reformation, the child of both past *and* history, depending on one's perspective.

As a person, a discrete, single item in history's inventory, O'Neill is wiped out by the gap. Where Synge's active playboy could rise above tragedy to complete a pattern of his own fictive destiny and thereby turn tragedy into comedy, Friel's inactive politician is condemned to become the plaything of other people's fictions. Friel's Archbishop, echoing Doalty, says 'if we can forge ourselves into a cohesive unit . . . we are not warring, we are a united people . . . no longer a casual grouping of tribes but a nation state' (*MH* 11, 64): thus the Gaelic kingdom could come into its own, with Hugh O'Neill as its prince. If only the revenants of Irish history could reform themselves into a cohesive body of acceptable fact, the 'nation state' which continues to bedevil the Irish Constitution[156] would become 'a reality'.

Meanwhile the differences between versions, whether in the Ledger or in the History, or the four gospels which explore the awful privacy of the faith healer, remind us that inflections and nuances can kill. 'Sorry' can be a declaration of war:

O'NEILL: Aw, now, sorry.
MABEL: What does sorry mean?
O'NEILL: That my mistresses stay (*MH* 41).

Or it can be a suing for peace. In the interstices of talk we lose the metaphors:

LOMBARD: I'm no historian, Hugh. I'm not even sure I know what the historian's function is . . .
O'NEILL: But you'll tell the truth?
LOMBARD: My story will be as accurate as possible, if that's what you mean . . . But are truth and falsity the proper criteria? I don't know. Maybe when the time comes my responsibility will be to tell the best possible narrative. Maybe when the time comes imagination will be as important as information. Who's to say at this stage? But I promise you; there'll be nothing written for years and years. History has still to be made before it is remade. (*MH* 8–9)

Within the affect of History writ large is a series of greater and lesser stories. Although O'Neill pleads for the centrality of his relationship with Mabel, the historian, the storyteller, decides that 'all those ladies you chose as your wives – splendid and beautiful and loyal though they undoubtedly were – well, they didn't contribute significantly to . . . the overall thing . . . they didn't re-route the course of history.' (*MH* 68) Lombard argues further: 'I don't believe that a period of history contains within it one 'true' interpretation, one single unambiguous 'meaning' just waiting to be mined. But I do believe that it may contain within it many possible narratives,' (*MH* 15) and that it is his responsibility to tell the best possible narrative, one which in this case disregards Mabel and many other of O'Neill's privacies, simply because it has to satisfy a greater cause, a 'fiction in search of belief'. Friel is once more treading on the corns of his constituency, but for the first time he is seriously (rather than facetiously as in *The Communication Cord*) questioning its shibboleths, not simply its conceits (like the furniture in *Aristocrats*) or its self-deceptions (as in *Cass*), but the very codes by which it discriminates, holds its world together, tells itself stories which are not merely credible but realisable. He asks if a particular 'period of history' – whether it is the sixteenth, nineteenth or twentieth century – is amenable to resolution, to unambiguous interpretation. History has to be both made and remade. Lombard insists 'in the centuries to come the way people live must change – inevitably. As indeed will the modes of writing about how they live. We can't deliberately suppress what we know did happen, can we? – any more than we can foretell how people will live their lives – or what future conventions of writing about those lives may be'.[157]

Making History suggests that in writing Emmet's epitaph we must engage not only in constructing a future narrative for an age of emergence, but also in reconstructing pieties, the biographies of both the princes and the common men; the will must be retrospective too. But the casualties of such a process will be 'truth' and 'falsity' as criteria. In order to be Irish, it is necessary to reject 'either/or' in favour of 'both/and'; it means to suffer the uncertainties of life in the gap, to allow the life sentences of our conflicting and potentially lethal versions of time to run concurrently. The tragedy of this realisation lies in both the rejection of myth and the acceptance of the various narratives which gain their memorability from absolute but uncomprehended and immemorial phenomena. Myth apprehended as life is replaced with life comprehended as myth. Children become citizens who, in Lombard's argument, 'think they believe in some sort of empirical truth. But what they really want is a story' (*MH* 66). Lombard, like the English sappers, is 'making a pattern . . . offering a cohesion to that random catalogue of deliberate achievement and sheer accident that constitutes your life' (*MH* 67). And in so doing he is inventing the life of a nation-state, giving cohesion to a catalogue of fictions or half-truths. This is the answer for 'Fox O'Neill' to the question Crystal has asked Fox Melarkey: 'What are you?' It has made possible, and therefore intelligible, a world of controlled madness; it has placed it within the institutes. And, more unequivocally than before, Friel has shown where 'the enemy within' can be found in the public domain.

Map-making, whether it is a biography or the history of conquest, reduces its subject to an arrangement of affects or concepts. History is forecast as predictable fact and received, in Friel's words, as 'acceptable fiction' or 'performance'.[158] The story of a culture divining its enduring truths becomes a story of nihilism: the inevitable failure of metaphor. If, like analogies and emblems, it is, as Steiner suggests, the thread between mind and world, what use can it be in a world where nothing happens, and happens viciously? In submitting to this situation – one of his own choosing and devising – O'Neill has proved that the middle way is not only a way of staying at home, but a necessary way of exile into time as well as space. The 'so damned constant' of *The Gentle Island* becomes a play on words, damnation and constancy being the definitions of the gap. In O'Faolain's words, O'Neill was

> the first step that his people made towards some sort of intellectual self-criticism . . . In his time the world began that narrowing-in process which has, in our day, finished with the virtual obliteration of all seclusion, removed the word aloofness from the vocabulary of politics, left no corner to the hermit, and condemned to death all the traditions that fail the great modern test of Ubiquity.[159]

Friel, with himself as tympanum, unites the private and public worlds. He shows us the frightened child who, although *doli incapax*, must inevitably break silence and thus, by entering the public world, destroy its integrity. As the child makes itself whole, it betrays the tribe. And Friel's sympathy is with the child. Even when that child is wrong like Manus Sweeney, or as atrocious as Fox Melarkey, Friel mediates its atrocity with compassion and tenderness. And that may be his greatest fault as an artist: O'Neill's soliloquy, in which he recalls, in a Cass-like rhapsody, the 'days without blemish' that he spent in Kent, at Penshurst, in 'a golden and beneficent land' (*MH* 34) (echoes again of 'Mr Sing' and *Faith Healer*) as the house-guest and pupil of the Sidneys, robs O'Neill of some integrity. The soliloquy/rhapsody is about integrity itself, about who makes and who is made:

> I was only a raw boy at the time but I was conscious not only that new ideas and concepts were being explored and fashioned but that I was being explored and fashioned at the same time. (*MH* 34)

Sidney, like Lombard, has told O'Neill that he will 'become a leader of his people' (MH 35). But he characterises O'Neill's duplicity, the dual loyalties that have been ingrained in him by his strange upbringing:

> Those Irishmen who live like subjects play but as the fox which when you have him on a chain will seem tame; but if he ever gets loose, he will be wild again. (MH 35)

Concluding his reverie, 'Fox O'Neill' says that

> that trivial little hurt, that single failure in years of courtesy, has pulsed relentlessly in a corner of my heart. Until now. And now for no reason that pulse is quiet and all my affection for Sir Henry returns without qualification. But all that is of no interest to anybody but myself. (MH 35)[160]

At this most public moment, when he decides to forsake the gap of indecision to wreak his own and his country's fate, O'Neill expresses his love for the colonist and insists on the privacy of his reasons. As a result, Hugh O'Neill is more problematic than Frank Hardy and less heroic than Hugh Mor O'Donnell. But he represents a new version of tragedy because his creator has given him this democratic right to remake 'history'.

Seamus Deane draws attention to Adorno's point that 'art falsifies atrocity (and perhaps all history) by rendering it in forms which afford it a meaning or a spiritual dimension which it does not have'.[161] He adds, 'perhaps it could be said more accurately that such meaningfulness as art gives to experience is always by nature retrospective. Indeed, all our thought and all our art is an interpretation of what is already past, the present is always atrocious'. This study has been addressed consistently to the affective power of memory and the pull of the time dimension on the imagination: this is justified because the trend in modern Irish aesthetics lies toward an examination of that affective past in relation to *will*.

The Irish present *is* atrocious, in its original sense of being fundamentally brutal, hideous, yet perfectly comprehensible in its violence: in its institutions and its culture Ireland today suggests spastic paralysis, involuntary, discommoded, incommunicable. Irish writers have traditionally sought their salvation in ecstasy, standing outside the narrow ground, not only to stamp in their autism on language, but also to reject any emotional possibility at all because of that autism. The ultimate act of despair, therefore, is not the blood-sacrifice of the maniac but a pointless violence bred from absolutely pure rage: the madness of looking, without protection, on the face of a savage god.

Friel's Irishmen are abroad, even when they are at home. This important fact helps us to understand what Kearney calls 'the crisis of cultural ambiguity which so indelibly hallmarks the modern Irish psyche'.[162] To be capable of introspection, but to stand in 'a pained ecstasy' (Tr. 14,65) is to live beyond ambivalence, to have made of oneself the liminal medium which unites otherwise divergent cultures but which is exiled from both. In the sense that Friel's theatre is psychological drama, therefore, it is epic, classical. We are left asking whether we must always kill our father or our brother, in our play, our Eucharist, as we do in our daily lives.

It is therefore quite natural that among the modern Irish dramatists we find men who might want to believe in nothing: to empty their minds of both prejudice and ambition. As Laing says: 'the experience of being the actual medium for a continual process of creation takes one past all depression or persecution or vain glory, past, even, chaos and emptiness, into the very mystery of that continual flip of nonbeing into being, and can be the occasion of that great liberation when one makes the transition from being afraid of nothing to the realization that there is nothing to fear'.[163]

Friel has conferred that kind of nihilism on some of his creations – the winners – and denied it not only to many others but also, one assumes, to himself. As he himself might say at times of weakness, through Fox Melarkey:

> I want a dream I think I've had to come true. I want to live like a child. I want to die and wake up in heaven with Crystal. What do I want? Jaysus, man, if I knew the answer to that, I might be content with what I have. (CF 36)

The child, even he who has abdicated his ecstasy, is enviable because he is the original ignarus, stultus, rusticus, on whom life, in its violence, inflicts a rude eviction. This child needs a code, whether it is the bedtime story or the fireside talk, a private fabula rather than the public historia, to help him meet the dark unknown, to create a language in which he can ask the nighttime visitors to tread softly.

In *Translations* Hugh talks of attempting to fill the unfillable cask of his pupils; but Friel mediates with too great a tenderness because he knows that there are two vessels, the intellectual and the emotional. 'All he had witnessed', says the conclusion to the story 'Aunt Maggie the Strong One', 'could no longer be contained in the intellect alone but was dissolving already and overflowing into the emotions'. The relation between emotion and intellect has been another persistent theme in this book. At times it is hard to tell which is flowing into the other, which is the dominant knowledge.

Magnificence has always seemed in Ireland to reside in pathos. This pseudonym for catastrophe has been the path chosen by most Irish writers. Friel seems prepared to challenge the paradox that in order to be magnificent one must first be pathetic. But such a challenge means that the intellectual cask must be allowed to spill over, back into the emotional. 'I have been educated out of my emotions by my intellectual insight. Now I find it necessary to assert an emotional epiphany out of an intellectual and political grid'.[164] To be filled means to hold the balance between yesterday (when the intellect was distilling the emotional lessons) and tomorrow (when it spills over into time future). In order to be full one must have the courage *to be:* to love, to be free, to communicate, to speak the inexpressible 'I am'. That is a state of homecoming, the *nunc stans*, but further courage is needed for tomorrow, to spill over once again into another exile, a necessary leavetaking.

TRAVESTIES

Even in its baroque appeal to language, *Faith Healer* is a play against language.The language of *Translations* by comparison is lean and spare. Friel uses every word to advantage. He does the same in *The Communication Cord*, the play in which he stands the world on its head to examine it through the spectacles of farce. He took this step for two reasons: to allow himself the freedom of speaking openly and in the vulgate which he had been denying himself in his earlier work; and, with a flood of words, to free his work from the tightness of *Translations* and from the trap of sentimentality; from the danger of being treated as consecrated testament.[165]

In 1980 Friel had written a short parody of the language difficulties in *Translations*, in a playlet entitled *American Welcome*, requested by the Actors' Theater in Louisville, Kentucky. A European playwright arrives in America for the production of one of his plays. He is told by the American director that a revision of the play has been commissioned from an American writer due to language difficulties: 'there is a lot of it we don't understand . . . simply a question of our ignorance of your usage'. The American adaptor 'took all those little confusing words – 5 or 6 thousand approximately – and with wonderful delicacy and skill and *with the utmost respect for the rhythm and tones of your speech* he did this most beautiful job of *translating the play into the language and speech we understand.*'[166] Furthermore the monologal form of the original (which in fact caused *Faith Healer* to flop in New York) is recast because Americans 'talk, we exchange, we communicate'. The irony in Friel's wry humour is that it is impossible to 'translate' from one 'language' to another in the same tongue without completely changing the 'rhythm and tones', the cadences and inflections, of the original, and the meaning which lies between the words themselves – as anyone knows who compares English common speech with Hiberno-English, or English short stories with Irish short stories.

Kearney points out that, like Synge's Christy Mahon, Friel persuades 'by the power of a lie' – asking his audience to make his fiction true.[167] That skill, a word-play that conjures with aural images like an illusionist, is pushed even further in *The Communication Cord*, since Friel uses the farce to highlight the absurdities of the action while continuing to show us a catalogue of mistaken identities, misunderstandings and opposing value systems, all based on a clearly presented semantic theory ('Discourse Analysis', *CC* 18) which summarises and underlines, in a light-hearted way, many of the subtleties and implicit notions of its forerunner. Friel wishes the two plays to be read/seen in tandem.[168] *The Communication Cord* is the mirror image of *Translations*, the key to the author's serious intentions, and thereby qualifying itself as one of the most purposeful and effective applications of farce.

It is also easy to see how well *The Communication Cord* suits Friel's purposes. The same set which in *Translations* was the centre not only of the house but of the entire known world, becomes, in *The Communication Cord*, a travesty of a 'cathedral' but one with a host of side-chapels ('room down', settle bed, loft) in which a Feydeau-type of bedroom farce, including distorted morals, is enacted. By showing us how very nearly serious our misdemeanours can be, Friel persuades us of the proximity of tragedy to comedy, and the ease with which one can be translated from one 'diocese' to the other.

At first it might appear, as some critics have maintained,[169] that the facility of *The Communication Cord* betrays an absence of serious intent; that we expect of Friel not only first-class stagecraft, but also drama of an explicitly intellectual type. Apart from the high quality of the writing, the weakness of the farce lies in the obvious falsity of the sexual relationships, which, unlike the 'high art' of French farce, lack the serious frivolity of *haut bourgeois* misdemeanour. The liaisons of Tim with Susan, and Jack with Evette, are not convincing, nor is the simultaneous affair of Evette with Jack and Senator Donovan, nor the obvious eventual pairing of Jack with Susan and Tim with Claire. However, the keynote to this quite transparent failure is contained in Jack's solemn avowal to both Susan and Claire (a piety as empty as his 'first cathedral'): 'You and I were fortunate enough to experience and share an affection that is still one of my most sustaining memories, and when we broke up . . . a part of me died' (*CC* 72–3).

As Richard Kearney says, 'words have become both the form *and* the content of his drama'.[170] In this sense, also, *Translations* and *The Communication Cord* are twins. In *Translations* the form or 'aboutness' of his intentions, despite its conventional appearance, in fact goes further than his previous plays in promoting its own obsolescence. In *The*

Communication Cord the 'meaning' or content is conversely smothered in a riot of action, all of which in itself is inherently pointless. It thus becomes possible to realise how *Translations* does have a tendency towards farce, so that Jimmy Jack's, Maire's and Doalty's lines in particular can be played for more laughs beyond the stage than they rightly excite upon it. It is almost as if the problem were entirely semantic: discussing the naming of 'Tobair Vree' Owen asks 'do we keep piety with a man long dead, long forgotten, his name 'eroded' beyond recognition?' (*Tr.* 44). It is the same difficulty encountered by the pseudo-archaeologists in *Volunteers* when confronted with the skeletal Leif. If therefore identity *is* inseparably bound up with the ability to utter one's name, or to hear another utter it when one has passed into muteness, the semantic problems become central to the 'meaning of life' as evidenced by the chaotic catalogue of mistakes poured out by the frenetic 'Tim the Thesis': 'You're a German they call Barney Munich and you're married to Claire Harkin whose real name is Evette Giroux' (*CC* 52–3).

Furthermore, lifting some of the conventional limitations of his accustomed genre, Friel is able to allow his characters more anarchy and more space even though the situations he contrives for them are more tightly constructed. So much so that the characters spill over into one another, their identities merge because, due to their lack of common code, they fail to discriminate adequately between what each of them says and does not say and between who says what. Where, in *Translations*, words control the experience of life, in *The Communication Cord* 'life' controls words. But does language have a life of its own? Things fall apart (they literally do at the end of the play); disused agrarian utensils suddenly spring to life; and the fine balance of interpretation on which we depend for the connection between language and meaning is continually upset. In its mockery of the furniture of the cottage, and in the way its inhabitants are trying to erect a tradition upon them, it is also a parody of *Aristocrats*. The time direction also changes in both these plays: whereas previously those who looked into the future were uncertain but articulate about their doubts, the futurists are now in love and unable to communicate; the retrospectives are those with a coherent but incorrect view of where they have come from.

In *The Communication Cord* there is no attempt to summarise past work or to introduce new concepts. Friel indulges in a phenomenal send-up of the ideas which make *Translations* such a valuable play. This involves him in a great deal of simplification; whereas for example the traducer or agent of death has been in a position of trust, ritualised by the community (the revenant son, the faith healer, the pastoral father or *dominus*) here no one trusts him, except the prissy Susan (*CC* 73):

JACK: Just trust me Timothy, will you?
TIM: When someone says that to you, you know you're being betrayed (CC 20)
CLAIRE: Trust you? I never trusted you! (CC 29)

The parody of *Translations* begins with the opening stage directions, indicating that the barn of the hedge-school has been refurbished as a country cottage (*'three wooden posts complete with chains where cows were chained during milking'*, CC 11); a travesty of history, a mythological present, a syntax opulent with *yesterdays*, within which it is quite natural that absurd things should happen. It turns on its head the relation between thinking and experience. In Steiner's words 'analogies, metaphors and emblems are the threads by which the mind holds on to the world even when, absentmindedly, it has lost direct contact with it, and they guarantee the unity of human experience'.[171] But, as in *Aristocrats*, this simply does not happen. All the metaphors seized on by the players in *The Communication Cord* fail to unite experience with thought, and in fact plunge them into deeper communicational difficulties. It is indicative that the only refugees from Friel's earlier work are Senator Donovan and his prissy daughter Susan, who re-enact Senator Doogan and Katie from *Philadelphia*.

Jack invariably refers to this travesty as 'our first cathedral': 'this shaped our souls. This determined our first pieties. Yes. Have reverence for this place' (CC 15). Immediately 'piety', 'soul', 'reverence' become signals not of the deep structures of culture but of doggerel: the fucate travesty, *'an artefact of today making obeisance to a home of yesterday'* (CC 11). We see the museum of pastoral as a product of an imagination 'imprisoned in a contour which no longer matches the landscape of fact' (*Tr.* 43). Nora Dan is 'the quintessential noble peasant obsessed with curiosity and greed and envy' (CC 21): Tim salutes her as 'Mrs Dan', the same error which Lancey makes about 'Mr Doalty' (*Tr.* 63) and thus the series of mistaken identities begins: 'the queer way we have of naming people about here' (CC 22); Barney the Banks: 'but sure, that wouldn't be his real name at all' (CC 23); Nora Dan becomes 'Nora the Scrambler' – but of eggs or motor cycles?; Barney the Banks, because he lives on the edge of the river or because he is very rich? Jack the Cod – a fisherman: 'call a man Jack the Cod and you tell me his name and his profession, and that he's not very good at his profession. Concise, accurate and nicely malicious' (CC 46). Claire becomes Evette:

SUSAN: She has hardly any English.
JACK: She was born and bred in Omagh.
SUSAN: Her name is Evette.
JACK: Her name is Claire Harkin.

SUSAN: She's married to a German.
JACK: She's single (CC 71).

Translations run amok: 'My name is Willie. In English that is Barney . . . just a little bit gallagher' (CC 82, 55). Nicknames are demolished: 'His name isn't Teddy, it's Patrick Mary Pious' (CC 80), or created: Tim becomes 'Tim the Thesis' (CC 91). With the arrival of Senator Donovan the already devalued culture of Ballybeg receives a rude shove in the direction of sacrilege:

> This silence, this peace, the restorative power of that landscape . . . Despite the market place . . . a small voice within me still knows the responses . . . This transcends all those . . . hucksterings. This is the touchstone . . . this is the apotheosis . . . the absolute verity. (CC 32–3)

The parody underlines what has been called 'a willed identification with the Irish-speaking peasantry of the impoverished far west' of cultural nationalism in the era which saw the foundation of bodies such as the Gaelic League and the GAA, but which, instead of achieving cultural revival, involved reinvention.[172]

Later he debases the idea still further, assisted by the half-witted schemer Nora Dan:

DONOVAN: Renewal Nora, Restoration. Fulfilment, back to the true centre.
NORA: The true centre surely. (CC 46)

Tim falls into Nora's Synge-song:

DONOVAN: That is where we kneel to pray. That's where we gather at
          night to tell our folk tales and our ancient sagas. Correct Tim?
TIM: Our ancient sagas surely, Doctor. (CC 59)

Eventually the pretence and the myth are abandoned, exploded in Donovan's outburst, 'This is our native simplicity! Don't give me that shit!' (CC 75). Friel has already indulged in one send-up of this attitude in *The Gentle Island*: 'I envy you, Manus, the sea, the land, fishing, turf-cutting, milking, a house built by your great-grandfather, two strong sons to succeed you – everything's so damned constant. You're part of a permanence. You're a fortunate man' (GI 54).

Tim's 'Discourse Analysis' contains the kernel of the communication theory on which Friel builds a sense of community. Here, however, it can be played for laughs:

> Words, language. An agreed code. I encode my message, I transmit it to you; you receive the message and decode it. If the message sent is clear and distinct, if the code is fully shared and subscribed to, if the message is comprehensively received, then there is a reasonable chance – one, that you will understand what I am trying to tell you – and two, that we will have

established the beginnings of a dialogue. All social behaviour, the entire social order, depends on our communicational structures, on words mutually agreed on, and mutually understood. Without that agreement, without that shared code, you have chaos . . . An extreme example: I speak only English; you speak only German; no common communicational structure. The result? Chaos. (CC 18–19)

There is, however, a serious side to this also: it is only the circumstance of farce that dictates that it should be delivered in a humorous tone. As a commentary spoken by an extraneous 'expert' it would fall nicely into place in *Translations* itself. As Laing says in *The Politics of Experience*:

Two people sit talking. The one (Peter) is making a point to the other (Paul). He puts his point of view in different ways to Paul for some time, but Paul does not understand. . . . The dissociation of each from his phantasy, and the phantasy of the other, betokens the lack of relationship of each to himself and to each other. They are both more or less related to each other 'in phantasy' than each pretends to be to himself and the other.[173]

The process by which private 'phantasy' becomes public reality is an arduous political and cultural struggle; that language is at its centre is the single fact that places on us, as differentiated from the other animals, the twin burdens of tragedy and comedy. The seriousness of Friel's apparent farce is further underlined by the fact that he has employed the example of Erving Goffman's *Forms of Talk* which engages in 'dialogic analysis',[174] but which also explores the idea of 'footing', which Goffman calls 'the dance in talk',[175] something which Friel makes anatomical in the staging of *The Communication Cord*.[176] In the light of this intellectual involvement with the use of words, and the way words use us, which is one of the chief considerations of *Making History*, it is easy to see why Friel wants us to regard *Translations* and *The Communication Cord* as twins, each feeding off the other's dramatic form to impress on us the atrocious dangers of communication of any kind.

So the latter is not simply a farce on the serious theme of 'discourse failure' but an underlining of the lesson of the former, that a whole culture can lose its command over the encoding and decoding of its messages, its commerce with the civilised and barbaric worlds. And within this there is the artist's dilemma, an attempt to find both sense and justice in the situation. The chaos which Friel creates, or allows his characters to indulge in, proceeds directly from the lack of 'communicational structure' – although this is a farce, although it is quite clearly a 'language play' in the same sense as *Translations*, we are nevertheless encouraged to be healthily sceptical of our previous concern for etymologies, our 'means of finding our bearings' (compare the opening of Act Two of *The Communication Cord* with Owen's 'Will you be able to find your way?')

and our particular 'condition of madness', travestied in Claire/Evette's 'I understand perfectly' (*CC* 35). And we see some things more clearly than they are shown in *Translations:* for example the idea of the *omphalos*, the centre of cultural gravity. Donovan says 'You're right Tim, absolutely right. This is the true centre' (*CC* 50), of which Tim observes:

> An interesting discourse phenomenon that. Called statement transference. I never used the phrase 'This is the true centre' but by imputing the phrase to me, as the Doctor has just done, he both seeks confirmation of his own sentiments and suggests to listeners outside the duologue that he and I are unanimous in that sentiment. (*CC* 50)

We might call 'statement transference' a form of wishful thinking. It creates currency for an idea which was originally worthless or spurious and implicates members of the community in a common bond of cultural affiliation to that idea which in itself validates it; one *can* thus repossess that which in fact one never possessed, whether it be called 'dignity', 'freedom' or 'control of the means of production'. Friel thus safely exposes us to the dangers of subverting not only culture but the means of culture – perception, thinking and willing.

The successful formula for this type of exercise is the same as that employed in tragedy: pretence. Pretence as a fictional process runs parallel to history. This cottage is in fact no one's home. The falsity of the spectacle reinforces the inherent falsity of the thing portrayed. No one's culture is being debased because this is no one's 'true centre' – no one actually claims it. I have already used the metaphor of the stage-as-mental-hospital. Here we see the cottage farcically employed as the stage-as-French-hotel; the bedroom capers of that genre help to persuade us, by encapsulating the extra-marital misdemeanours of the bourgeoisie, that mutual deception by husbands and wives is justified because it bestows its own rewards and penalties and thus polices its own morality. In the case of *The Communication Cord* the capers are, as in Alan Ayckbourn's *Taking Steps*, purely directional, rather than occupational, hazards. At the climax of *The Communication Cord* Claire and Tim, like Maire and Yolland, move towards one another talking lovers' nonsense, and realising that the words they are actually uttering have nothing to do with their intentions. Absurdity reinforces the truth of that which is absurd. But they serve the same purpose – to show us how easy it is to mistake our invented culture for a re-invented one. Manus Sweeney tries to do this in *The Gentle Island;* the inmates of 'Eden House' achieve it in some measure in *Cass;* the family in *Living Quarters* rejects it; and in *Aristocrats* they signally fail to find it. In *Translations* we have seen how, through a combination of human and temporal betrayal and obsolescence, a culture may make the journey into the 'dark places of the soul' and begin again to flourish. In this farce, Friel also shows us that chaos can be resolved not by language but by silence.

Daniel Defoe wrote 'The True-Born Englishman' in 1701 to puncture the idea of English racial purity and to assert instead that of a hybrid nation; Charles Macklin adapted the notion in 1761 to suggest the attraction of Englishness for certain types of Irish person who believed that English manners and fashions must be inherently superior to Irish customs and practices. The line between pretence and pretension is very fine, and in *The London Vertigo* Friel slimmed down the Macklin play *The True-Born Irishman* to provide us with a cruel satire of the rage for respectability among the pretentious classes in mid-eighteenth-century Dublin as he had previously shown it among the lower and lower middle classes of his short stories. The pretentious Mrs O'Doherty becomes Mrs Diggerty, a pretender fatefully bound up with the equally pretentious and (eventually) transvestite Count Mushroom.

The fable depicts two worlds – those of 'real' Dublin and 'real' London – and, in between, a make-believe world in which the ambitious Irish squirearchy and the lassitudinous English colonists meet, a world in which anything might happen. London becomes the 'other side' (*LV* 24) of the coin of Irish life. Most people hear of it only through tittle-tattle; Mrs O'Doherty actually travels there, like Alice, and comes back changed: 'among the rest of her madness she has brought back . . . a new language with her' (*LV* 19). Madness is the keynote, the vertigo which distinguishes the Irish creature on the edge of achieving some sort of respectability. Friel satirises this madness with the titles which he gives to these upwardly mobile characters (they have of course bought them for money they could not afford): Lady Kinnegad, Lady Culmore, Lady Belmullet and – predictably – Lady Ballybeg. The transitus – and the change thereby effected – is cruelly expressed:

> No, no, my friend; my wife, your sister, is no longer the plain, modest, good-natured, domestic, obedient Irish Mrs O'Doherty – in other words the perfect wife; but the travelled, rampant, high-lifed, prancing, English . . . Mrs Diggerty (*LV* 19).

Someone whom the English would regard as part of the 'wild Irish' has become disengaged from the domestic Irish hearth and instead has become wild in her attempt at acquired Englishness. Sarcastically, Friel shows us the new Mrs Diggerty falling far short of the target of her acquired mannerisms:

> MRS DIGGERTY: Everything sounds so strange here; everybody talks so peculiar; I scarcely understand them. Even the very dogs when they bark, I swear they bark wit' a brogue (*LV* 26).

Even at the play's conclusion, when Mrs Diggerty is embarrassed into renouncing her new pretence, including her French cook ('back to the frying-pan' – *LV* 36), and her husband declares 'The fine Irish lady's mended' she has the last word: 'For the time being!' (*LV* 45). *The London Vertigo* could be seen as another of Friel's self-deriding commentaries on the fact that when one attempts to jump ship, to exchange culture, language and place, one can end up with no culture, language or place of one's own. Everyone 'here' is 'strange', but the strangest of all is oneself.

We should not overlook the complexities of the master-servant relationship in the play: there are Irish masters and Irish servants, Irish masters who are the servants of the English colonisers and Irish subalterns (such as Mrs O'Doherty) who become slaves to Englishness; Mrs 'Diggerty' thereby nearly takes over the domestic situation because, as an incoming pseudo-colonist herself, that situation is no longer domestic but 'strange'. It is Katty, the O'Dohertys' servant, who, at the beginning of the escapade, aids and abets her mistress in her attempt to smuggle Mushroom into the house and thus cuckold her master, but it is Katty who enacts the 'servant of two masters' in her reversal of the situation in which her master and mistress are saved from embarrassment: *la serva padrona*. And it is Mushroom, the foppish plunderer of Irish affections, who ends up as the servant of the dramatic situation when he exits, dressed as a woman and contained in a trunk, the victim of whatever whim of indignity O'Doherty chooses to inflict on him. Translation thus has its tragi-comic side, indicating what may happen when the possibility of creating two or more *personae* is initiated. Commuting between Dublin and London in thought, word and deed may make one ridiculous; it will certainly make one vulnerable to misunderstanding and exile.

PART IV

Music

On the planet of the blind, no one needs to be cured.
Blindness is another form of music.

Stephen Kuusisto

7

PLAYS OF BEYOND

'Do you believe in the life to come?'
'Mine was always that'.[1]

BEYOND

'Beyond' is otherness, but it is an otherness that we carry within us. The boy who has spent an imagined life fishing in the 'wee lake beyond' comes home to the hearth of Ballybeg, to meet the man who has grown up in what we shall discover is a condition of 'blindsight'. Together, they begin to eliminate the difference that ostensibly sets them apart and instead explore the sameness that binds them together. Public and Private experience a strange intimacy that cannot be known by, or with, outsiders. Memory, to which the outsider cannot be privy, gives them access to some past that is theirs alone, to a world which they carry within them, each holding a fraction of a truth which can only begin to do its work when they discover and speak the same language.

Finding that 'language', and giving voice to it, is the most hazardous occupation for the writer. In titling Part IV of this study 'Music' I have intended to illustrate the ways in which Friel has looked for alternatives to language in order to convey meaning. Music has always been present in his plays, usually very suggestively and purposefully,[2] but in *Lughnasa* the assertion by Michael at the play's conclusion that 'language had surrendered to movement', that language as a form of communication had been superseded by 'this ritual, this wordless ceremony', that 'words were no longer necessary' (*DL* 71) was Friel's first tentative step into the idea of 'dream music'. It is tentative – and highly subjunctive – because it marked a watershed in his writing.

If, in Walter Pater's words, all art aspires to the condition of music,[3] then it may also be postulated that all music aspires to the condition of silence. Such a condition would suit Friel ideally, we might speculate. Add to this Schiller's view that music has the capacity to create meaning without reference to a world beyond itself,[4] and we have an enclosed space with its own language and its own semantic system. If only it were that simple.

The basic fear of homecoming, the danger that Private and Public may continue estranged, is present in *Lughnasa* and its successors. 'Exile', says Friel, 'can be acquired sitting in the same place for the rest of your life'[5] and this helps us to understand that a project of repatriation or irredentism need not involve much movement – simply the restoration of, and to, a *patria* in the sense that we have seen Seamus Heaney using it.

The absence of Public from Private since the first leave-taking has been a form of suspended animation. For each, in Rimbaud's terms, life has been elsewhere, and each has known that 'I' is 'other'.[6] Each has waited on the other's threshold, and the between-space and between-time have been filled with the events or 'realities' of strangers, while their own has been a place of play, an imaginary time.

In the exchange from *Endgame* which stands at the head of this chapter the 'life to come' is the life that takes place in the mind, that is anticipated but never lived. It is when the 'beyond' enters into the 'here' world that it inserts itself *between* meaning and reality, and the illogical, the magical, takes over and becomes potentially very creative or very destructive. As Homi Bhabha says, 'to dwell "in the beyond" is . . . *to touch the future on its hither side*'.[7]

In this chapter we shall explore the idea of life that is lived in, and reported from, a far place, beyond normative concepts of space and time, beyond the everyday, yet to which the everyday must ultimately bow its head. In considering *Dancing at Lughnasa*, *Wonderful Tennessee*, *Molly Sweeney* and *Give Me Your Answer, Do!* under this rubric, we shall observe how a split personality can construct, re-construct or re-member an imagined life, putting in place an identity and a set of meanings in which the relations of image, speech and music are examined, sometimes violently. We shall do so largely through the image of the 'child', and the concept of magic or the *merveilleux*. The metaphors which we shall encounter are *ritual*, *storytelling* and *blindness*, and we shall see how, in his most recent plays, Friel has moved towards the visionary, and towards a new reflection on the meaning of love.

In his study of childhood, *Corruption in Paradise*, Reinhard Kuhn describes a form of autism in which 'the child breaks off all communication in order to withdraw into an autonomous universe shaped uniquely by his own imagination . . . [a] terrifying flight into another world'.[8] We have seen the germ of this withdrawal in Gar O'Donnell, its development in Frank Hardy and its impact on history in Hugh O'Neill. It will be found again in the same degrees in the many 'children' whom we encounter in the four plays under discussion here, among whom Molly Sweeney is the most quiet, but also the most dangerous, in her denial of any world except her own inaccessible truth.

Kuhn illustrates his argument by reference to Conrad Aiken's short story 'Silent Snow, Secret Snow', in which the boy, Paul, is 'seduced by the magic realm from which all others are excluded':

> The new world was the profounder and more wonderful of the two. It was irresistible. It was miraculous. Its beauty was simply beyond anything – beyond speech as beyond thought – utterly incommunicable . . . Its beauty was paralyzing – beyond all words, all experience, all dream.[9]

The repetition of 'beyond' serves to remind us that what is being described, or alluded to, is outside the boundaries of our experience, even the boundaries of civilised thought, as we shall see in the cases of Oileán Draíochta (Wonderful Tennessee) and of Molly Sweeney. All the antinomies delineated in Chapter 1 come into play: those within are abandoned, while those without suddenly become the reality inside which the new life is to be lived.

But this should not blind us to the fact that this is not a 'new world' – it is the reverse image of our perception, the image which has been carried inside but unknown. The fact that it is 'utterly incommunicable' is only a temporary phenomenon, because we know that, in the drama enveloping the child, the incommunicable must be communicated in some form in order for the truth to be known, for the secret to be told, the art of storytelling in this instance being the ability to recount the 'beauty . . . beyond anything' in images which are affective but which allow the dream to remain dream. There is of course a spatial dynamic also: 'the back hills', 'the wee lake beyond' and the energies that are generated there, are removed in a knowable, physical sense. But to go beyond, or to have the beyond enter one's own *foyer*, is to enter an unmeasurable and indefinable space that is also beyond *time*.

The autistic or 'autonomous' world is the liminal time and space where, as Wilhelm Dilthey puts it, 'life discloses itself at a depth inaccessible to observation, reflection and theory' – Dilthey calls the time a 'fifth moment' – when the autist 'freely unfolds images beyond the bounds of reality'.[10] The essential condition is that the disclosure should be inaccessible to reality but is, and must be, accessible to the child or the artist. It is not unlike the mystical experiences of Dame Julian of Norwich, St John of the Cross or the unknown author of The Cloud of Unknowing, in that it is a condition of ecstasy (*ekstasis*) in which one stands outside oneself – that is, outside, or beyond, one's everyday self.

In Aiken's story, 'the beauty was paralyzing' – it induces a *stasis* or a state of suspended animation in which magic can occur. As we have seen in the plays of Friel where memory leads back into the past, different kinds of truths emerge because memory is intensely personal and cannot be shared except by making a version of it (history), which is commonly convincing and therefore acceptable. In the exclusively personal world it is possible that one can be put in touch with one's own deep structure in which a language – untranslateable, incommunicable – still exercises an affective power and provides a set of images which the 'child' can employ to speak to him- or herself. What is said in that space we can never know, but we *can* be made aware that something is being said, that something is being heard, that some images of the past are still being recognised as valid, even though we can have no access to them, merely knowing that they are being affirmed, attested – to use a word of which Friel has made much use recently.

Kuhn says that 'the poet can never recapture the magic language of the past, for it is spoken only in the place of his birth, to which he can never return'.[11] In the sense that one can never return, because one can never be the same person, unchanged, who left, this is a valid comment on the always attempted impossibility of revisiting that primal magic. But it does not prevent the re-membering of the magic in images which may not rely solely on language for their meaning. This is the project on which each of the 'children' in these four plays is embarked. That some achieve a partial success by non-linguistic means – through the agency of dance, images or music – is a profound commentary on the limits of language and on the ontology of the writer.

THE CHILD

The obverse of the child's quest for anterior meaning is the spectator's fascination with his dilemma, and the prurient need to gain partial access to its conditions and qualities. In a most complex way, this is allegorical of Irish history and culture. Anthony Roche has characterised the central image of contemporary Irish drama as 'two men waiting', epitomised in *Waiting for Godot*.[12] Not only are they waiting for 'Godot', or for the reappearance of the boy bearing Godot's putative message, but, in their symbiosis, they are waiting for, and on, each other.

Similarly, in the scenario with which I began this chapter, boy and man wait for each other to occupy the liminal position which will initiate their transformative experience of each other and thus of themselves. Kuhn:

'The enigmatic child has a message to deliver . . . The fundamental paradox of the enigmatic child [is that] though a message-bearer, he is inarticulate, or at least incapable of making himself understood . . . a stranger to this world, sufficient unto himself . . . an unanalyzable catalyst that precipitates an analyzable transformation'.[13]

As such, the 'child' is mythic, as I suggested in my Introduction, something incommunicable which must be communicated, something unbelievable in which we must believe. He is a stranger not only to 'this world' but also to himself. And as we identify with him/her, or at least with his/her dilemma, we become alienated from ourselves and enter the interstitial space in which we meet our childhood and our ancient wisdom.

Childhood – or the imagination of the 'child' – is the unmentionable, that which must remain hidden but refuses to hide, that which unhouses all within when it knocks on the door, declares its uncanny presence and demands re-entry so that its story may be told.

In a sense Friel himself is that child, and *Give Me Your Answer, Do!* can be read as the work of an ageing writer asking not only for an appraisal from an objective source, but also for acceptance, both judgement and recognition. The ultimate goal in such a scenario, however, is the right to start again, the recovery of a self existing before the mistakes were made – what we have seen him adverting to in his remarks on Macklin – 'to begin afresh and anonymously'.

Molly Sweeney is the archetypal child in this respect: unable to communicate her true self and equally unable to accept the 'realities' of the sighted world, she occupies the smallest possible place, the 'tiny ivory cell' as Wilde called it, which contains heaven and hell.[14] And in this space, which is space of a different order to that known by sighted people, Molly creates her own kingdom, a Ballybeg of the mind, within which she can examine and judge the whole world.

Looking back on the course of Friel's previous work, we can sense the frightening, menacing presence of 'the child' in Fox Melarkey, in Cass McGuire, in Casimir O'Donnell; in the remembered childhood of Hugh O'Neill in the gardens of Penshurst, and the hurt received by him from Sir Henry Sidney, we see the arcadian vision closed off, and the 'fox' forced to reoccupy his feral self, set against the world, a barbarian whose actions precipitate the cataclysmic by means of the incomprehensible.

In the 'children' whom he depicts in his later plays, Friel is, on the public stage, providing what can be seen as allegories of Irish culture, a culture of anxiety and confusion awaiting resolution, of primal, pre-adolescent energies and emotions not yet ready to cross the threshold or to abandon dreams, with stories waiting to be told but not yet capable of being adequately received. On a more private level, he is revisiting the blindness and the fury that we saw in some of his short stories and earlier, 'unmediated', plays, where the confusion arises from, and fuels, the inability to answer the basic question, 'What do you want?'

The 'child' embodies both a nostalgia for a home or time that can never be regained or revisited, and a longing for transcendence or transfiguration. In this sense he is quintessentially unhoused or 'unhomely' – the complete enigma of one who is rooted in a non-place and a non-time which must become place and time if he is to be made once again whole, to complete the drama. As such, he/she carries within him/her all the sins, as well as all the joys, of the world – heaven and hell.

Kuhn says that the child's autonomous realm is 'contiguous with the adult world'[15] – which we have seen in the approximations of Gar O'Donnell's crazed imagination to the world of his father and his cronies; of Hugh O'Neill's own story to the 'history' which the elders of Ireland are writing on his behalf; of the 'Eden' which Yolland finds in Baile Beag to the map which his colleagues are creating. Like two maps on facing pages which purport to represent the same landscape, the contours of the imagined and the real, the hidden and the exposed, mirror each other in certain fundamental psychic respects. But they shadow each other only in the means of the depiction and in the terrain to be depicted. The reader's or audience's task, as much as that of actors or the characters they imper-sonate, is to understand sufficiently both maps so that they can pass (translate) with some facility from one to the other.

Audience resistance to some of these plays – *Wonderful Tennessee* and *Give Me Your Answer, Do!* in particular – has been due largely to the painfulness of such a task, to the emotional demands that Friel places on us. The basic fear which Stephen Dedalus expresses on a linguistic level – that words can be simultaneously 'so familiar and so foreign' – is here translated onto the level of the affections. The two maps are contiguous, yet at the same time familiar and foreign. Each is familiar to the other and yet foreign to it – both known and unknown at the same time. The key moments at which it is possible to cross the boundary – for example, when Ben and his father are able to embrace in *Living Quarters* (*LQ* 71–2) – are more rare, more precious and more dangerous in the later plays than elsewhere in his work, not least because, his stagecraft having become so much more mature, the technical and emotional skills of his actors must rise to a level higher than he has previously demanded, in order to convince us of the intensity of the psychic charge which he is passing through them.

In a sense, also, Friel is describing a world on which our culture has turned its back. Despite the allegedly 'new' genre of children's fiction which began in the nineteenth century,[16] modern and post-modern culture is largely unconcerned with childhood.[17] If, as we have heard Frances Yates assert, we have no sense of memory, then the sense of childhood is also vulnerable, as linear time abolishes cyclic time in its hasty march to beyond the millennium. The 'memory play' becomes a fascinating exercise which in the minds of the uninitiated audience is rooted more in fantasy than in everyday life – even though it depends on the contiguity of both for its ultimate effectiveness. Audiences are easily seduced by *Dancing at Lughnasa* because it offers us a spectacle of something golden, remote. But it is also possible to be seduced uncomfortably and dangerously, if we recognise the proximity of its themes to our own condition, rather than its distance from them. It is not a play 'about' a late industrial revolution on a minute scale in 1930s Donegal, nor 'about' a deviant priest carrying incomprehensible messages of pagan ritual from a far country. It is nearly these things, but not quite.

Similarly, *Wonderful Tennessee* provides accessible insights into other worlds: Berna's account of the flying house as 'an offence to reason' is sympathetically inserted into our laughter ducts, so much so that when she says 'a flying house . . . marches up to reason and belts it across the gob and says to it "Fuck you, reason" . . . ' (*WT* 57) laughter releases tension – as, of course, it is designed to do. But it can also expose to us how fragile is the membrane between the story and reality, and us to it.

Friel's latest plays in fact not only make these intense demands on their audiences but they also emphasise the intensity which we may have overlooked in their predecessors. I have already indicated the parallel between Frank Butler in *Living Quarters* and Hugh O'Neill in *Making History*, protesting against their treatment at the hands of history, which sets man in an agonistic relationship to time and fate. And we can readily recognise the demands of *Faith Healer* as possibly Friel's most intense play to date, as *Crystal and Fox* is his cruellest. But in plays such as *The Blind Mice*, *Living Quarters*, *Volunteers* and *The Gentle Island*, which have rarely (if ever) been revived since their original productions, and in his four versions of Chekhov and Turgenev, we can see forces at work which bring us to the edge of madness, tenderness and conscience in a single close encounter.

If the 'child' is qualitatively different from the adult, then the project of nostalgia is not merely to recapture a lost innocence, or arcadia, and to live once more within it, but also to re-experience the moment of transitus from childhood to adulthood and to understand what was not understood at the time. Humphrey Carpenter attributes the phenomenon of children's fiction in the nineteenth century to the loss of faith, the advent of uncertainty, among authors whose own lives were unsettled but who also personified a societal shift from settled values to a state of anxiety. Yet the emergence of such fiction – *Alice in Wonderland, Peter Pan, Winnie-the-Pooh* – was a new phase of a literature that is as old as writing and philosophy: that of master and servant, which revolves around the question of the location of authority. In a post-colonial culture, that locus and its toponymy is a key not only to the possible modus vivendi of a future world but also to the sources of the imaginative energies which have brought master and servant, coloniser and colonised, to this transformative point and which stand ready to negotiate the next phase of their being.

The essence of the master-servant relationship is the exchangeability of the two roles. At any moment one is entitled and expected to ask 'which is master and which servant?' At what point does Plato cease to be the subaltern of Socrates and begin to write in his own voice? At what point can it be said that Sancho Panza is merely the antenna of Don Quixote? *Jacques and his Master*, Milan Kundera's version of Diderot's *Jacques le fataliste*, ably demonstrates for a world trembling with authoritarianism the mutual resemblance of master and servant, the capacity of each to *be* the other. Which is the minder and which the minded? The vital point for us in considering the case of Friel is that the two are not contiguous, in the sense in which we have just been considering the worlds of child and adult, but *the same* – not different, but *other*.

Even to separate the worlds of child and adult – to make them into parallel universes – is not going far enough. Father and son have the same need of empathy and the same symbiosis as master and servant, master and pupil, as Friel's work constantly reminds us. If 'the son is father to the man' is to have more than a gentle function in reminding us of the continuity of human experience, we need also to recognise that exchanges between father and son both communicate and create wisdom in both directions and across time.

We have seen the mutual pathos of Gar and his father in *Philadelphia* – each wanting to reach out by means of a story, a memory, and thus embrace the other, to be father and son, no longer kept apart by the *bounds* of authority but united by its *bonds*. Exile robs them of that chance, as death has robbed Casimir of his chance to tell his father that he understands his saving grace. In *Give Me Your Answer, Do!* we have the unusual spectacle of three generations of a family, with both fathers *and* mothers, exploring the meaning of love in a more demanding and searing fashion – I mean of course for the audience – than Friel has previously depicted. The play's ostensible similarity to *Aristocrats*, due chiefly to the physical setting and its reminiscence of a Russian family drama, should not blind us to the mixture of fantasy and everyday life which makes the play thoroughly 'unhomely'. Life as it is, and life as it might be, make an unholy combination when the dramatic energies of each are engaged in a dialogue which could lead either to love-making or to war.

When we examine the actual demands of the stage, and see that the word 'acting' is, as Victor Turner points out, ambiguous – meaning 'doing things in everyday life' and 'performing on the stage or in a temple'[18] – then the complexity of what happens in a 'play' increases. The behaviour – or 'acting' – of all concerned, stage actors, characters, and audience, is transformed not only for the duration of the play but throughout its aftermath, because each brings to the theatre memories and images of 'how it was' which are metamorphosed by the experience of witnessing whatever is trans-acted. If the experience is effective, one becomes 'wise' – acceding to a vision and thereby enriched but changed.

Kuhn reminds us that

> the conjuring up of a lost time is . . . not a rare experience. As long as the adult can recover, through the intellect, the imagination, or the involuntary memory, the mental set of the child and appropriate for himself the schemata within which the child orders the elements of his experiences, then he can relive the profound reality of his erstwhile condition and can even retranslate it into terms comprehensible to other adults.[19]

It is worth reminding ourselves that we have seen George Steiner stipulating that it must be an act of genius that can reach back across fractured experience and its syntax. Friel *may* be acting as a shaman to his former self or selves, offering an example of metamorphosis which is both his own and ours, making of himself the most explicit spectacle of self-examination and catharsis. Certainly my own reaction, when reading *Molly Sweeney* and *Give Me Your Answer, Do!* for the first time, was one of unease at the proximity in which Friel had placed himself to his characters, at the personal risk he seemed to be taking with his own emotional stock, not least because he had decided to direct the plays himself (which I shall address in Chapter 8). In order to succeed, a fiction of this kind must have 'a sense of personal urgency'.[20] By seeing Friel in this light (as god, priest and communicant, or as law-maker, judge and executioner) we can reach a fresh understanding of his thirty-years-old wish for a sense of religion, in the spiritual and anthropological meanings of that term – something which could satisfy the dismay of the child in the face of the unacceptable, unbelievable or incomprehensible, something to make sense of the phenomena which too often arrive unmediated in the consciousness – the maddening, unanswerable questions.

The pastoral calmness of the settings of the later plays should not obscure the fact that violence lurks only slightly beneath their surfaces. It is of a different order to the explicit violence in *The Enemy Within* (internecine strife), *The Gentle Island* (fear and envy), *Living Quarters* (suicide), *The Freedom of the City* (execution), *Faith Healer* (quietus) or *Translations* (eviction). There are in fact two kinds of violence in these plays. Firstly, the reported burning of the Sweeney boy in *Dancing at Lughnasa* and the 'sacrifice' of Seán O'Boyle in *Wonderful Tennessee* belong to a ritual world which is 'beyond' everyday experience and comprehension. Secondly, the implicit violence of these plays, which adds to their author's risk-taking, is a violence of and to the emotions, conceived and carried out in the name of love. This kind of violence is non-negotiable, because it is simultaneously within us and beyond our capacity to understand.

Quite apart from the Lughnasa fires and those on Oileán Draíochta, there is violence smouldering in the way that love and loyalty are dissected in *Give Me Your Answer, Do!*. The hostility is embodied in the 'performance, that ugly, bitter act we put on when we're with people . . . so that we can wound each other as deeply and as viciously as we can' (*GMYAD* 48). Truths such as this, expressed between husband and wife, clarify not only their feelings for each other but also their perceptions of themselves:

> GRAINNE: I wanted to humiliate you . . .
> GARRET: I'm sorry, love. It's altogether my fault.
> GRAINNE: No, it's not. I'm as ugly as you.
> GARRET: I'm such a shit, Grainne. Who knows that better than you? Am I forgiven?
> GRAINNE: When I knew you first I thought your weakness was attractive
>   . . . .
> GARRET: I need you, love. (*GMYAD* 49)

In *Wonderful Tennessee* Berna tells her parable of the flying house which belts reason in the gob, but shortly after this, humming 'O, Mother, I Could Weep', she jumps off the top of the pier into the sea, which Trish tells her 'was a naughty thing to do. It was a cruel thing to do . . . Particularly cruel to Terry' (*WT* 66) – something of which Berna appears to be unaware. Between the three sets of husbands and wives, and between Terry and his sister-in-law Angela, with whom he is having an affair, there are frictions which only avoid the name of violence because the hurt they cause is unconscious rather than deliberate.

Many of the circumstances in the later plays emanate from nonsensical situations, illustrating the increased presence of the illogical. Unlike the everyday world in which most people live, the situations belong to a world beyond our regular perception or comprehension. Five sisters, an illegitimate child and a finished priest; six people on a pier, waiting; a sightless woman, a feckless husband and a defeated surgeon; even two writers jostling their reputations against the background of an autistic child. They belong more to the fantastic than to the real, and from this emanates their violence and their nihilism – their capacity to say 'no' to anything that impedes their own internal logic. As in *Alice in Wonderland*, there are certain avenues down which reason proceeds at its peril. Not for nothing has Friel already introduced us to 'the lame scholar turned violent'. One senses that in the 'lamed' writers, Garret Fitzmaurice and Tom Connolly, in the bankrupt bookie Terry Martin and the depreciated scholar Frank, in the damaged priest Fr Jack or in the failed, tired surgeon Mr Rice, there is a latent violence, whether it is manifested in words, in drunkenness or in ritual slaughter. These victims – strays – are capable of carrying out acts of atrocity which are intimately connected with acts of love.

Cast between the two poles of homeseeking and vagabondage (the curse of the wanderer – in Irish, *seachrán* or shaughraun),[21] they are absent from *our* real world yet carry their own 'real' and strange truths within them. It would be welcome – perhaps – to think of this inner world (Molly Sweeney's world of blindsight especially) as a walled garden, a secret place of beauty which cannot be diminished by contact with the real world. But it is not. The 'song of the child'[22] is not arcadian. It can be as vicious and as cruel as the 'song' of Frank Hardy, and we should not allow ourselves to be seduced by music, such as the ending of *Dancing at Lughnasa*, into the notion that music can be nothing but beautiful and healing, or that its superiority over language necessarily assuages the effect of words. The sisters' dance in *Lughnasa* should disabuse us of that.

The 'song of the child' is, in George Bernanos's expression, a 'forgotten language'[23] and pursuing it makes us aware of a larger truth: as Novalis says, 'We cannot understand language, because language does not understand itself, does not want to understand itself'.[24] The 'nonsense' language of children becomes nonsense in its own right. Ask the child to explain 'I'm donging the tower' and the beauty recreated by those magic words is dissipated, once more hidden and denied. Press the point about the flying house further than Friel permits, and a truth will emerge which not only offends reason but starts to be murderous. It is when we mistake otherness for difference that we reach for the gun.

RITUAL AS DRAMA

Victor Turner makes the explicit connection between his own work and
that of Erving Goffman by saying that

> The basic stuff of social life is performance, 'the presentation of self in
> everyday life' (as Goffman entitled one of his books). Self is presented
> through performance of roles, through performance that breaks roles, and
> through declaring to a given public that one has undergone a transfor-
> mation of state and status, been saved or damned, elevated or released.[25]

The act of communication is thus role-oriented and what is communicated is a 'part', to which other 'parts' relate. In considering the family
saga related in *Dancing at Lughnasa* we shall see that Friel combines
many different reflections of 'ritual' in order to carry us through the
changing 'state and status' of the Mundy household. He shows us the
ancient conditions of Lughnasa; those of the 'Ryangans' which bear such
close affinity to them; and the communion of the sisters in meeting and
releasing their own savage energies. In the play as a whole, a ceremony is
performed as the tale is told of how change overcame the household and
various losses were incurred and accruals were made.

It was Guthrie who said

> The theatre makes its effect not by means of illusion, but by ritual . . . The
> theatre is the direct descendant of fertility rites, war dances, and all the
> corporate, ritual expressions by means of which our primitive ancestors,
> often wiser than we, sought to relate themselves to God, or the gods.[26]

Audiences witnessing *Dancing at Lughnasa* acknowledge the play's role
as ritual, recognising that the 'rites' evident in the festival of Lughnasa –
as present in, or available to, the Mundy household – are, if not current
in modern Irish society, at least accessible. Guthrie's words serve to
underline the sacred nature of what is transacted. As in the Memory
Theatre discussed in the Introduction, there is no illusion, because illusion
requires that the audience is misled. Instead, a *rite de passage* takes place
in which the audience participates in, and fully subscribes to, a
'transformation of state and status' similar to that of the Christian
eucharist.

As such, Friel continues the idea of theatre as sacred drama in the
Yeatsian spirit: 'the theatre began in ritual and cannot come to its
greatness again without recalling words to their ancient sovereignty'.[27]
But words are not enough, because if one is to enter a world of gods, and
if the whole community is to take part in the transitus, as Victor Turner
suggests,[28] then words, as inadequate counters or gatekeepers to understanding, must be emancipated by means of other symbols – images,
music and dance.

In the liminal situation, words become insufficient as symbols of meaning because their power to produce and support magic is weak in comparison with the more primitive rhythms of that 'thudding of ritual drums' (as Turner puts it)[29] which Heaney also experiences at the 'omphalos' of his own back door. A liminal society, a between-place, is neither one thing nor the other, and cannot therefore be defined by any statement. Like the people in the pub in John B. Keane's *The Field*, conversation stops, action is arrested, as the community waits for something to happen, for the defining moment to be reached – in Keane's case, while they wait in collusion for Bull McCabe to kill on the night road and gather them all into a lie which can never be revealed but which is 'true' for them. That suspense of belief, of the means of believing, that admission of the illogical, the *imprévu* to the home which thus becomes unhomely, is the subjunctive. 'Subjunctivity is possibility' says Turner[30] in describing the essence of play. The uncertainty and indeterminable nature of the liminal makes life into a subjunctive state in which language is insecure because it hangs on the question contained in the word 'if'. As a time of exploration, as it enters 'privileged space',[31] the role of the diviner becomes crucial.

'Play' is both innocent and dangerous, both a revel and a risk. The 'if-ness' in Friel's work which acknowledges this double-edged sword becomes more pronounced in his later plays. In the act of writing, he is prepared to ask more probingly 'What would happen *if* . . . ?', while in the script/text he recognises more successfully and more dauntingly than before that everything – people's lives, their reason and their ontology – is contingent on a form of magic. He achieves this by juxtaposing the idea of *ritual*, 'this wordless ceremony . . . to be in touch with some otherness', with *dancing* into 'the very heart of life' (*DL* 71) and thereby provides the audience's transitus from the magic of the stage to the reality of the auditorium.

To this extent, Friel's later work has seen a changing of the ground-rules, because he is no longer concentrating so steadfastly on a single facet of experience, whether we call it 'love', 'freedom' or 'language', so much as creating layers of experience, addressing several of these ideas with equal priority, pouring various kinds of emotion (fear, love, greed), various kinds of association (family, political genres, conscientious objects and objections) and various speeds of action (retrospect, immediacy and divination) into the same dramatic moulds.

When I wrote in 1990 that '*Dancing at Lughnasa* is Friel's most problematic play to date' I clearly could not anticipate its successors. With hindsight I now realise what an extraordinary and increasingly problematic phase of his work was ushered in by that play. Perhaps because of its autobiographical bearing,[32] it throws into doubt all our previous classifications: what *is* family, and when is a family drama necessarily a public as well as a private occasion? When must we overlay a private grief or hilarity with public connotations, and when must we refuse to do so? The access that we are granted to the author's own privacy is at the same time unremittingly public, just as the ruminant address of his faith healer comes from the open confessional: it is at once the exploration of 'the dark and private places of individual souls' and the laying bare of our own, severally and collectively. It hurts us, and yet we tolerate it. For the playwright himself, 'the play provides me with an acceptable fiction for them [his aunts] now'.[33] In the context of a 'memory play', hurt is of extreme importance because, as Friel reminds us in the closing monologue of *Lughnasa*, 'in that memory . . . the air is nostalgic with the music' (*DL* 71); nostalgic, that is, in the sense in which the entire play has been conceived, both publicly and privately, in the meaning of a word that is both intimate and blatant. Memory, therefore, is the painful *transitus* into time past, into the scenes of childhood which, on the evidence of this play, continue to constitute both Friel's personal quest for meaning and identity and his means of setting his audience on their own independent quests. In this light the play is a homecoming not, as we are ostensibly shown, for the disgraced missionary Fr Jack (redolent of Chris Carroll in *The Blind Mice*) but for Michael, the narrator whom the play facilitates in this return journey. In a certain sense Friel wrote *Lughnasa* as a self-imposed exercise, taking stock (as did John McGahern in a novel much admired by Friel,[34] *Amongst Women*) of his compulsions, responsibilities and ghosts.

Dancing at Lughnasa was retrospective – and perhaps retrogressive – in that it provided a summary of the themes of homecoming: nothing in his previous work was allowed to escape scrutiny, and it thus becomes an utterly theatrical play which, like *Aristocrats*, is more self-contained than the 'language' plays. The evidence that his thoughts and emotions as a writer might tend once more towards the short story is very strong, as it was in the 'forgotten' interview with Smith and Hickey in 1972. Thomas Kilroy has noted 'the way in which the anecdote resides at the centre of Irish fiction giving a vocal rhythm to the Irish novel' – a trait he also observes in Friel: 'a superb creator of story-tellers . . . Whole sections of dialogue in the plays appear to be composed of compacted story-telling'.[35] It is a point to which I will revert in the course of this chapter.

The two great 'memories' which dominate Friel's dramatic progress – privately, the story 'The Child' and publicly the ambiguous legend of Hugh O'Neill so provocatively foretold by Sean O'Faolain – continue to be vigorous and demanding presences in his later work, so much so that the playwright's constant revisiting of both the sites of memory and the memories transacted on those sites is partly conscious self-assessment and partly subliminal echoing, in the hope of stirring ghosts to accompany him on the next part of the journey. Immersion in, and engagement with, the public issues and distractions of his age, are still his companions, but they are less frequently or less openly juxtaposed with the reiterative reflection on the loneliness and isolation of the private artist.

The fact that storytelling, as a characteristically Irish genre, becomes a foreign language to non-Irish audiences, may indeed contribute to the success of *Lughnasa* outside Ireland. The inflections of an Irish short story become a dramatic device in its own right, because its rhythms and its inherent voice are articulated in the music of the play to which the narrator makes specific reference. His own cadences, in the form of the opening incantation – 'When I cast my mind back to that summer' – control the subsequent monologue and dialogue. From this point on, Friel has continued to employ a version of it in the episodic structure of the storytelling in *Wonderful Tennessee*, and in the monologal exchanges of *Molly Sweeney*. The fact that the energy, the imagination and the subjunctivity of the play is now a feminine one highlights the periodicity of the short story which Friel has disallowed for so long. It also underpins the concept of music since, as Barthes explains, there is a distinct *timbre* or 'grain' in every musical voice: 'the "grain" is the body in the voice as it sings, the hand as it writes, the limb as it performs'.[36]

In *From Ritual to Theatre* Victor Turner observes that 'a social drama first manifests itself as a breach of a norm, the infraction of a rule of morality, law, custom, or etiquette in some public arena'.[37] In *Lughnasa* the first infraction has been the antecedent birth of the illegitimate child. The return of Fr Jack, carrying into the household Ryangan customs as pagan affirmations of his native Lughnasa, is the second. To these, the presence of the Marconi radio as something voluntarily introduced into the house, and the establishment of the knitwear factory as an external agent, are subordinate actors in its transformation.

The fact that the narration is entrusted to Michael (rather than, for example, his mother Christina) means that this narrative voice, with its images and inflections borrowed from the short story, takes responsibility for the success or failure of the ritual. The play has been criticised for the fact that its 'central' event – the sisters' dance – comes too early (half way through the first Act) for its dramatic impact to be sustained. But there are many kinds of dance in the play: in addition to the sisters' dance, there is Chris's dance with Gerry in Act One (with music), and Michael's memory of a 'ceremony', a 'dance without music' in which Chris 'marries' Gerry; Agnes's and Maggie's dances with Gerry in Act Two; the description of the fire-dancing of Lughnasa and that of the Ryangans; Jack's shuffle-dance to Michael's tattoo at the close of Act One; his careful steps during the identity exchange with Gerry; and the motionless dance or swaying at the play's conclusion.

In that conclusion, Michael refers to dance, rather than music, as the transcendental form of transfigured speech: 'when I remember it, I think of it as dancing . . . Dancing as if language had surrendered to movement' (*DL* 71). What is remembered is non-specific. It might be everything; it might be one tiny incident; it might be nothing – because, he tells us, it is both 'actual and illusory'. He speaks of everybody 'in isolation' being put ritually 'in touch with some otherness'. As such, the dance is a way of gathering disparate energies into that final tableau of stillness. It is the means by which what is 'beyond' time and space is transmitted into the here and now.

In both a technical and an aesthetic sense *Lughnasa* represents a merging of the 'aboutness' of the play with the author's intentions. In singing a threnody for the 'five brave Glenties women' for whom he has the most transparent affection, he was also solving the problem identified by Seamus Deane, of knowing when to develop the dramatic transitus from private to public. Within the acoustic of the Mundy household of Ballybeg, he publishes the daily details of womenfolk as he has never previously: their sexuality, their poverty, their sheer sense of fun and hope in the face of extinction.

This merging of description and intention is, of course, typical of a memory play, and in the sense that *Lughnasa* is a memory play, it is a play 'about' the nature of home and what happens there: it describes the life of a house which becomes, and is recognised as, a 'home' because everything is both rehearsed and enacted there: a place where memory is shaped hourly, weekly, monthly; a place where fear, hope, tragedy and honesty are as essential ingredients for the family mix as the chickenfeed and the cornflour. It concentrates, as did *Making History*, on forms of truth, on different kinds of memory, and it also continues to ask Lévi-Strauss's question, 'what does "to mean" mean?'

The play almost (but not quite) collapses under the weight of remembrance. One critic wrote that 'when Gerard McSorley [who played Michael in the original production] . . . began to address the audience with the words "When I cast my mind back to that summer of 1936" my heart sank'.[38] One must regard this cavil as more than a mere prejudice against the concept of the memory play, and take it as a serious criticism of the numerous occasions on which memory is invoked, however slightly:

'I remember some great harvest dances' (11);
'She has the memory of the two of you . . . ' (19);

'I remember slipping out one Sunday night' (20);
'I remember Mother lifting you up' (38);
'The annual ritual. Of course I remember' (46).

And not only remembrance of things past, but anticipation of the future:

'We must remember how strange everything must be to him after so long'
(11);
'This is Father Jack's home – we must never forget that – ever' (13);
'And she had good reason for being uneasy about Rose – and, had she
known, about Agnes, too. But what she couldn't have foreseen . . . ' (41).

The weight of remembrance is successfully put on the shoulders of
Michael, the narrator, precisely because, in his recall of 'that summer' – *in
illo tempore* – his persona is divided as it had been in *Philadelphia*:

The convention must now be established that the (imaginary) BOY MICHAEL
is working at the kite materials lying on the ground.[39] No dialogue with the
BOY MICHAEL must ever be addressed directly to adult MICHAEL, the
narrator (DL 7).

It enables Friel to carry out that delicate transaction, divining the 'song of
the child' while simultaneously giving us the historical perspective linking
us to that time. The fact that it is autobiographical, in the sense that the
memory is partially the author's own, is really fortuitous, because Friel is
effectively putting us in touch not simply with a *time* but with a *place*.
'The annual ritual. Of course I remember'. The ritual of Lughnasa, which
has been exhaustively chronicled by Máire MacNeill,[40] was conducted in
a far place. Beside the call to memory in *Lughnasa* we must place the
allusions and direct references to that place, which, in its relation to fires
and dancing, is as remote from the Mundy house as is Ryanga. 'That
Sweeney boy from the back hills' (DL 16) is the means of bringing the
Lughnasa ritual into the house. Rose, who is simple but wise, introduces
the element of paganism into what is ostensibly a Christian household:

They were doing what they do every year up there in the back hills . . . First
they light a bonfire beside a spring well. Then they dance around it. Then
they drive their cattle through the flames to banish the devil out of them . . .
(DL 16)

When Kate intervenes

They're savages. I know those people from the back hills! I've taught them!
Savages – that's what they are! (DL 17)

she does not contradict Rose's story, she amplifies it.

And having brought the memory of such a ritual into the home, the
sisters are prepared for their own ritual Lughnasa dance, which is
specifically depicted in Friel's stage direction:

Now she [Maggie] *spreads her fingers (which are covered with flour)*[41] *...*
and patterns her face with an instant mask . . . a white-faced, frantic
dervish . . . Chris, who has been folding Jack's surplice, tosses it quickly
over her head and joins in the dance . . . Agnes, and Rose, Chris and
Maggie are now all doing a dance that is almost recognizable . . . Kate
dances alone, totally concentrated, totally private; a movement that is
simultaneously controlled and frantic . . . a pattern of action that is out of
character and at the same time ominous of some deep and true emotion. . . .
There is a sense of order being consciously subverted, of the women
consciously and crudely caricaturing themselves, indeed of near-hysteria
being induced (DL 21–22).[42]

On the surface of the play, the liminal situation in which the sisters are
placed is caused partly by Fr Jack's return, which signals the family's
ostracisation from normative catholic society (including Kate's dismissal
from the school), and partly by the opening of the knitwear factory,
which completes their financial ruin. But the arrival, on their threshold,
of the Lughnasa dance is the catalyst which, in Michael's closing words,
puts them 'in touch with some otherness'. Kate, the figure of authority
within the house, becomes the bearer of 'some deep and true emotion'
which is a deeper and a greater truth than the emotions of everyday. The
sub-version taking place is the replacement of that everyday decorum
and respectability by the surrender to things beyond definition.[43]

There is a very distinct sense in which, in *Dancing at Lughnasa*, Friel
was completing yet another homecoming: in addition to his strategy in
splitting Michael into boy and remembered boy, he creates strong parallels between this play and *Philadelphia*. Maire, Gar's mother, was 'wild
and young . . . from a place called Bailtefree beyond the mountains' (*Ph.*
25). That absent figure is reinstated in the Mundy household within the
collective, surrogate motherhood of the five sisters. It was inevitable that,
just as order and authority were subverted in *Philadelphia* – '"Behold-
the-handmaid-of-the-Lord-Gut-and-salt-them-fish"' (*Ph.* 17) – the even
tempo of the sisters would be joined to a rhythm which has to do not
with time but with energy.

One of the strongest resonances in *Lughnasa* is the 'confusion' of Fr
Jack, which is only dispelled when he recalls, and is illuminated by, the
notion of ceremony. One would expect 'ceremony' to be sacred and
therefore acceptable as part of the normal pattern of life in Ballybeg.
But with Jack's return, it becomes a dual embarrassment: the Ryangan
ritual which he describes and the disturbing idea that he might celebrate
Mass in his native village. As with *Philadelphia*, the family discovers that
'we embarrass one another'. To his sisters – especially the prim and proper
Kate – the revelation of the pagan rituals of the Ryangans is an embarrassment. It is clear from the reported reaction of parish priest and school

manager to Jack's career as an Irish missionary who has 'gone native', accepting and recognising the validity of local custom, that there is also a severe embarrassment between the Mundy household and the town. *Embarrassment* is explicitly written into the stage directions (*DL* 18, 22).

Elmer Andrews observes that the dance in *Lughnasa* 'opens up a lyrical space which presses back against history'.[44] Fintan O'Toole has also remarked that 'the drive is not towards history, but towards a collapse of past and present into the eternal suspension of memory'.[45] As such, the dance is not the sole cause of this space, but represents the causes. The dance as described in the stage directions is not a *replica* of an elsewhere dance or, in the use of the surplice, a parody of a Christian ceremony; it *is* an elsewhere dance which takes over a house in which it has always resided. It is 'almost unrecognizable' and it is 'out of character' – on one side contiguous with a known dance, and on the other a standing outside oneself – *ek-stasis*. It is the hidden unknown thing within ourselves which visits us from beyond.

And the dance also presses back against language, which is both the master and the handmaid of history. In *Dancing at Lughnasa*, after the exploration of language, history and translation which we have seen in *Translations* and *Making History*, Friel took the most significant step away from the 'language' play towards the gestural and the affective.

In this respect Friel has moved closer to the balletic, non-lingual 'theatre of images' practised for many years by Tom MacIntyre (*The Great Hunger*, 1983; *Rise Up Lovely Sweeney*, 1985; *Dance for Your Daddy*, 1987) and Michael Harding (*Strawboys*, 1987; *Una Pooka*, 1989) but not, one supposes, out of any sense of affinity with their stage techniques, however much his themes may be contiguous with theirs, or indeed Marina Carr's *The Mai* (1994) which has been seen by one critic as 'a feminist riposte to Brian Friel'.[46]

Lughnasa is a 'play for dancers' as we might call it in Yeatsian terms, and we should recall that Yeats referred to his plays of that title as 'the struggle of the dream with the world'.[47] It is partly for this reason that we find Friel consciously echoing his previous work. In both *Lughnasa* and *Give Me Your Answer, Do!*, characters and themes from the short stories and the plays coalesce to provide a tapestry against which this new departure can be attempted. By putting in place serious echoes of previous work, Friel seems to be bringing forward stated themes and characteristics to underpin the dramatic experiment which he is conducting, in what Elmer Andrews calls 'a dramatic synthesis'.[48] If this is so, then he is doing it in order to show that these are the concerns which the playwright cannot escape – loyalty and conscience, dignity and respectability, truth and untruth – which are to be subjected to a new form of magic. As

Fintan O'Toole observed, 'this kind of obsessive return to the same themes and images is an essential part of Friel's greatness'.[49]

There is in fact a sense in which the text of *Lughnasa*, provided by and through the narrator, resembles a short story, or even the kind of prose poem which Sean O'Faolain had in mind when he wrote to Bryan MacMahon: 'You have done something that very few other writers of fiction have done . . . You have written short stories based on common life in the mood of a prose poet'.[50] This is also partly true of Friel because what he writes is *not* entirely fictional. As Michael tells us at the mesmeric closure of *Lughnasa*, 'everything is simultaneously actual and illusory . . . a dream music that is both heard and imagined; that seems to be both itself and its own echo' (*DL* 71).

If *Dancing at Lughnasa* is 'both itself and its own echo' – and particularly if it is read as both an original play by Friel 'and its own echo' – it runs the risk of being declared structurally unsound in the same way that a musical work obeys no laws other than those of musical structure: it claims to be self-supporting by containing both the actual and the illusory, by obliging each to live beside, and endanger, the other.

Indeed, by resolutely continuing to place language at the centre of a drama which is nevertheless exploring non-verbal possibilities, Friel has refracted the optic in which his verbal images are seen. He is presenting language in a more literary mode, and in this respect his recent work on *Fathers and Sons*, *A Month in the Country* and *Uncle Vanya* is very relevant and will be considered in Chapter 8.

In *Dancing at Lughnasa* woman is restored to the central place in the home, while man is either made the focus of pity and concern (the child and the priest) or marginalised and reduced to a figure of scorn (Gerry Evans). Among the five sisters, Kate becomes the authoritative mother figure, to whom all others in the play submit in some degree, including Chris, the real mother of the child. And yet Kate herself, at the moment she joins in the dance, becomes a 'child' and acknowledges 'the song of the child'.

The reinstatement of the woman is vital to our understanding of how Friel's drama develops from the male-oriented plays which preceded *Lughnasa*. In *Faith Healer* Grace admits in the final lines of her speech: 'Oh my God, I'm one of his fictions too' (*FH* 32); so, leaving aside the Russian adaptations and the arguable exception of Maire in *Translations*, it is not since *Living Quarters* (1977) that a woman has spoken in her own right on his stage.

Kate's recognition of the impending change in the household is the fulcrum on which the play focuses, insofar as it is a play in the liminal mode: when she declares 'Control is slipping away . . . The whole thing is so fragile it can't be held together much longer; it's all about to collapse' (*DL* 35) we witness the first occasion in Friel's work that a woman is capable of announcing the transitus.

This is not, of course, a regression to the short story, although the coincidental use of the boy-narrator does suggest that Friel has chosen to re-integrate woman and child as vital elements in the way he tells a story.[51] The portrayal of Berna, Angela and Trish (two of them actual sisters, three of them potentially so) in *Wonderful Tennessee*, the central figure of Molly in *Molly Sweeney* and the three wives Daisy, Maggie and Grainne in *Give Me Your Answer, Do!*, confirm that by turning from the public to the more intimate, the internal domestic world, Friel has brought home not only the revenant rogue males but also the women who have been cruelly absent since he began writing for the stage.

The dance belongs to the women, in the sense that a similar action among five men would be inconceivable. The fact that they are thus put in touch with their deeper emotions, and that subsequently they will be unable to deny those emotions – Kate in acknowledging Jack's moral imperatives, Rose in her assignation with Danny Bradley – is a completely womanly fact. A similar revelation in a male environment would demand a more argued, more loquacious and perhaps more explicitly violent scene – one thinks of Frank McGuinness's *Someone Who'll Watch Over Me* (1992). Certainly nothing like the Bacchantic suddenness of the moment could be contemplated by men. It is a perfect example of what Peter Brook calls 'the "happening" effect – the moment when the illogical breaks through our everyday understanding'.[52] It is also an example – again, Peter Brook's description – 'of how a metaphysical play can find a natural idiom that is holy, comic and rough'.[53]

As Martine Pelletier observes (my translation): 'The house of the five sisters functions as a point of contact, or at least an intermediate space, between civilians and barbarians, town and country, Christianity and paganism'.[54] It is both a 'rough' space and a 'holy' space in which that communion with 'otherness' can occur, and therefore it is both a home and 'unhomely'. Because language is a traditional means of convincing ourselves of this ritual, we tend to forget that whereas in the Christian eucharist words determine the transubstantiation of wine into blood, of bread into body, in most pagan ceremonies the same effect is accomplished through gesture. It is this barrier to comprehension, this logical obstruction, that Friel seeks, by way of the experiment of *Lughnasa*, to set aside.

'Music facilitates the expression of irrational memory' says Elmer Andrews – speaking specifically of the use of music in *Philadelphia* – and makes the connection between irrational memory and the 'construction of "truth" and identity'.[55] In *Philadelphia* Gar says 'D'you know what the music says? It says that once upon a time a boy and his father sat in a blue boat on a lake, on an afternoon in May. . .' (*Ph.* 98). At first sight, there might seem to be a contradiction between music as a wordless medium and music which 'says'. But all music, whether the 'thudding of ritual drums' or Irish folk music (such as the tune 'The Mason's Apron' which precipitates the sisters' dance) is first of all derived from primal rhythms and secondly linked by way of language to people's direct experience.

It has been said that Václav Havel's plays are 'a sort of musical reflection on the burden of being'.[56] In Havel's case this enables music to be employed in a quasi-political fashion, and this too, quite apart from its mesmeric effect, has its relevance for Friel. Frantz Fanon also says in *The Wretched of the Earth*,

> Any study of the colonial world should take into consideration the pheno-mena of the dance and of possession. The native's relaxation takes precisely the form of a muscular orgy in which the most acute aggressivity and the most impelling violence are canalized, transformed and conjured away. The circle of the dance is a permissive circle: it protects and permits.[57]

This is of course a political strategy to insist on the need for a colonial subject's energies to be expressed and recognised in ways unfamiliar and even unacceptable to the colonist. But it is much more than that: an offering to the imperial world of a healing process which is beyond its own ritual resources, and a warning that to suppress such powers is to encourage their emergence in more violent ways. The sisters' dance contains violence; the ground on which Jack and Gerry exchange identities in the hat ceremony could become a killing field if either misunderstands or misdirects the other.

Ultimately, the test of whether or not *Dancing at Lughnasa* is a 'true' play or an illusion, an irresponsibility, is one of memory. If there is a seduction, are we seduced merely by and into 'dream music' without issue, or into a state of mind wherein we find our 'otherness'?[58] As Heaney says

> Friel's plays ultimately recognise this modern solitude of the person within the universe . . . Memory and its transformations are sometimes the guide, sometimes the misguider. . . . False memory sends the quester into the kind of self-deception, into the limbo of meaningless invention, but true memory gives access to the dancing place.[59]

To the extent that *Dancing at Lughnasa* is autobiographical, Heaney's further comment that 'by telling stories Brian Friel has made a triumph out of the telling of his personal myth'[60] is cardinal. But to the extent that it has disappointed some critics it is clear that the play has sometimes failed to touch that 'modern solitude', perhaps in the same way that Synge failed to make a connection in the mind of his first audience with 'the rich joy found only in what is superb and wild in reality'.[61]

The dominant presence or personality in *Lughnasa* is an indefinable *atmosphere*, and it is this element which most likely has prevented the play from being recognised as political. Friel specifically says at the play's closure that 'atmosphere is more real than incident' (*DL* 71) and to minds expectant of action in order to depict the affairs of state (as in *The Mundy Scheme*) *Lughnasa* would be bereft of development. But (as I have argued elsewhere)[62] to write political drama takes great courage: *Dancing at Lughnasa* and, as we shall see, *Wonderful Tennessee* and *Molly Sweeney* even more so, is political, not in the sense of militant assertions or ideological attitudes but in the sense of discussing, however subliminally, how society is ordered, how different perceptions permit and necessitate different persuasions and perspectives, different versions of events to be written up as 'history', literature, autobiography. In this sense, these plays are like Friel's versions of the Russian, in which there is always smouldering a need to exercise topics in a fashion that can be declamatory one day and whispered the next.

STORYTELLING

If, as I suggested at the outset, Irish drama is 'conversations in images', then in *Wonderful Tennessee* the exchange of stories and the truths within them, and the imaginary landscape of Oileán Draíochta (literally, island of magic or enchantment), become a unifying atmosphere, in the same sense as I have argued in respect of *Dancing at Lughnasa*. Thematically, too, it is closely related to *Lughnasa*, in the pilgrimage on which the six travellers are embarked, or are attempting to embark. This form of ritual, which isolates the characters and enables each to tell a story which in turn facilitates the telling of their own truths, creates a sense – although a false one – of *communitas*, an eternal 'now'.[63] It is emphasised by the fact that *Wonderful Tennessee* starts where *Lughnasa* finished, with minimal sound and movement: it requires that the play passes from '*silence and complete stillness*' to '*silence and complete stillness*' (*WT* 11, 90).

Again, the play may offend some with its over-use of the title word, 'wonderful'. But an analysis of the uses to which it is put shows immediately that it serves two purposes: firstly, to express genuine appreciation of what is happening, the attempted comprehension of Terry's island, 'Island of Otherness; Island of Mystery' (*WT* 28), which enables the pier on which they are situated to be, in Eliade's terms, a 'time of marvels'[64] but also a *place* of marvels. The second use of the word is ironic – to express sarcastic disbelief in the adventure, to subvert the piety of the experience.

Friel has explicitly referred to the play as a 'Canterbury Tales'[65] and, as a form of pilgrimage, it places the travellers in a liminal situation. The pier on which they spend the night truly matches Joyce's definition – 'a disappointed bridge'[66] – which both offers and refuses them access to Oileán Draíochta. The boatman Carlin who, like Godot, never comes, but of whom there are signals and reported speech, has been likened by many commentators to Charon, the ferryman of the Styx in Greek mythology, and many classical references have been detected, including a similarity in the 'maenadic' dance in the play to Euripides' *The Bacchae*. The enactment – or reported enactment – of any ritual of a pagan nature will create resonances with a disappeared world which has perhaps simply taken up a new position behind the real world, but certain elements, such as Frank's vision of the dolphin, have a more direct appeal to our atavistic senses, with its invitation to another kind of dance:

> Just as the last wisp of the veil was melting away, suddenly – as if it had been waiting for a sign – suddenly a dolphin rose up out of the sea. And for thirty seconds, maybe a minute, it danced for me like a faun, a satyr; with its manic, leering face. Danced with a deliberate, controlled, exquisite abandon. Leaping, twisting, tumbling, gyrating in wild and intricate contortions. And for that thirty seconds, maybe a minute, I could swear it never once touched the water – was free of it – had nothing to do with water. A performance – that's what it was. A performance so considered, so aware, that you knew it knew it was being witnessed, wanted to be witnessed. Thrilling; and wonderful; and at the same time – I don't know why – at the same time . . . with that manic, leering face . . . somehow very disturbing. (*WT* 70)

Friel has been described as 'a playwright at the end of the world',[67] and as the author of *Wonderful Tennessee* he has created both a temporal and a spatial finality. Pilgrimages are generally noted for the choice of remote places rather than known centres as the point of arrival for pilgrims. The pier in Ballybeg is remote because Ballybeg is Friel's point not of departure but of arrival. And even then, it is only a resting-place on the journey, because the island lies beyond. It may be that the 'beyond' is to be found not so readily in centres of civic power but in those of more ancient forces, as if what controls our psychic energies resides in an alterity of place and time to that which controls our daily behaviour. This would account for the use of irony in the play as the unifying atmosphere, since it establishes tensions which *do* affect at least three households but which *could* affect the whole world and the way it is organised.

Victor Turner has written of pilgrimages that they exhibit both voluntariness and obligation, 'an amplified symbol of the dilemma of choice versus obligation in the midst of social order where status prevails'.[68] At first, the party, which is in fact a 'birthday party' for Terry, is divided as to whether to go on or to stay, but all defer to Terry's leadership, even though they do not know his reason for choosing the pier as the place of celebration.

The use of irony in the play is in fact very demanding for both players and audience. The relationship between each husband and wife is both a condition of love and one of betrayal, an occasion of wounding, in each of which there is pretence. Terry both loves, and pretends to love, Berna; Terry supports Frank and Angela financially, but pretends not to; he is secretly having an affair with Angela (his sister-in-law); they all pretend not to know that George is dying. As the ritual is enacted, as we see irony-as-atmosphere taking hold of the play as its central character, the 'magic' or 'wonder' of the place and the time is dispelled, and the spectator is drawn into one of Friel's bleakest plays in a way that not even the exposed cruelty of *Faith Healer* could accommodate. Indeed, it recalls Hardy's closing words, the explanation that there was nothing there, that the end had been reached and that it was a necessary end, the defeat of the diviner: 'we had ceased to be physical and existed only in spirit, only in the need which we had for each other' (*FH* 54).

Revelations and admissions abound, as we will find in *Give Me Your Answer, Do!* Of the men, Terry is broke, Frank is a pitiful writer and a cuckold, and George, the best of them, is about to die. Of the women, Berna is mentally broken, Angela cannot acknowledge the deception of her adultery with Frank, and Trish is confused and can only find her bearings by means of classical mythology. In a sense, each of them is saved, and in a sense each of them is damned. It is a disarming play, a cruel play, most likely a conscious decision on Friel's part to deconstruct the surface beauty and tranquillity which he had achieved in *Lughnasa* – as if he intended once more to cast the people of Ballybeg loose on the tide of uncertainty, ambivalence and irony. In its claustrophobia, it is a play set in a confessional and not at all unlike *The Iceman Cometh*.

Criticism of *Wonderful Tennessee* has addressed the fact that, as Fintan O'Toole puts it, allusions both to classical mythology and to Friel's previous work leave the characters 'crushed and gasping beneath the weight . . . There is . . . no dramatic yeast to make all these heavy ingredients rise'.[69] O'Toole does, however, grant Friel the freedom to make the attempt and 'we should respect his right to fail'.

To the extent that O'Toole is suggesting that *Wonderful Tennessee* is not a play, not a drama, this judgement is compelling, since it asks us to consider what other literary label might be applied to it. 'Allegory' seems to be the most apt, since its pilgrimage aspect connects with the mediaeval genres. So too does the idea of staying up all night, for the triple purpose of celebration, storytelling and in the hope of miracles. (That the chief storyteller, Terry, recounts that at the age of seven he had sat up all night with his father on a previous pilgrimage to Oileán Draíochta is sufficiently autobiographical for us to take both a real and a fictional meaning from his statement 'The first time I ever saw the dawn' – *WT* 31.)[70]

The liminality which Friel has created is certainly extreme: the pier is the archetypal 'in and out of time' situation, as it is 'in and out of place'. There is no physical scope for the players. Berna jumps off the pier into the sea at the end of Act One, but at the opening of Act Two she is sitting back on the pier. Frank goes to interview Carlin, but he must return because it is from the pier that the boat will, or may, depart. None of the players can make the choice to leave, because it is from the pier that they will be collected in the morning by the bus-driver. Somewhere out to sea (perhaps) is Oileán Draíochta, but they can move neither towards nor away from it for the duration of their pilgrimage. Perhaps the deepest inaction into which Friel plunges his characters is the fact that what does not happen happens in the course of the night, thus giving literal meaning to the 'dark night of the soul' which each experiences – a long night's journey into day, a feature which the play shares with Frank McGuinness's *Carthaginians* and Stewart Parker's *Pentecost*, both written for Field Day.

In such a Beckettian scenario, there is no scope whatsoever for action or interaction except on a metaphysical level, no possibility of any redemption other than what may be generated within the verbal exchanges. Language in fact ceases to be communication in the accepted sense in which we expect it in the theatre, and becomes a different form of signification, a fabular symbolism in which the meaning lies behind the spoken. If Friel is testing his previous accomplishments by re-introducing a wild dance in August, he fails to relieve any tension or to create any beauty by so doing. In turning his back on the physical possibilities, Friel is in fact taking possession of the metaphysical dimension of the play. This, it seems to me, the critics have refused to acknowledge, and in general audiences have been too intimidated by the author's invitation, or challenge, to follow these characters into the darkness. But if, as a dramatic spectacle, the play lacks sufficient drive, the text does give, to those interested in the direction taken by Friel's mind in recent years, a rich lode of speculative material.

Like the Canterbury Tales, which are intensely moral, as well as highly political for their time and place, *Wonderful Tennessee* in its storytelling is allegorical: it creates a sacred space in which the spectator – or reader, if we leave the theatre and confine ourselves to the printed page – accepts the 'other' logic of the *merveilleux*.[71] There are at least three kinds of allegory at work in the play: the 'stories' such as that of the flying house which constitutes an offence to reason, which is allegorical of the way the illogical can become real; the way that the storytelling organically creates the space within which those more personal admissions can be made; and the admissions each character makes, which are allegorical of the wider world occupied by the audience.

The fact that there are two kinds of story – the fable and the personal truth – thus increases the power of storytelling on one hand and of irony on the other. In particular, it amplifies the resonances between the true and the untrue. In the following exchange, the original statement by Friel about the 'particular veracity' of something which remains a 'vivid memory in the storehouse of the mind'[72] – that it doesn't matter whether it is fact or fiction – is given further exercise (they are asking Trish for a story):

FRANK: Any kind of fiction will do us.
ANGELA: Myth – fantasy –
TERRY: A funny story –
ANGELA: A good lie –
FRANK: Even a bad lie. Look at us for God's sake – we'll accept anything! (*WT* 59)

(The imprecation: 'Look at us for God's sake', however humdrum and colloquial it may be, cannot escape the sacral tone.)

Friel says 'The fact is a fiction', thus laying equal claim to the statement 'the fiction is a fact'. This is an enabling strategy which permits him to set aside the choice of either/or and instead to follow the magic. *Wonderful Tennessee* is wonder-ful because it affirms, or attests to, the magic moment and to the magic itself, without insisting on proofs or definitions. As with *Dancing at Lughnasa*, the 'atmosphere' *is* the magic. Here, too, there is an undeniably political dimension, which Václav Havel exposes in his essay 'Politics and Conscience':

Mediaeval peasant and . . . small boy . . . are still rooted in a world which knows the dividing line between all that is intimately familiar and . . . that which lies beyond its horizon, that before which we should bow down humbly because of the mystery about it. Our 'I' primordially attests to that world and personally certifies it.[73]

It will be immediately apparent that the context in which Havel speaks is that of the disappearance of the world beyond the familiar. It is the same context in which Frances Yates wrote of the disappearance of memory and its affective call on the past on which magic depends. Any world which banishes magic by forbidding memory or by claiming authority over the beyond world, risks the collision between the familiar and the foreign which makes life unhomely. We are back with, and among, the phenomena which prudence tells us must be mediated and separated. Society's task is to find the lost children by giving them a culture within which they can be at home, while maintaining the sense of otherness, of something beyond, to which they can attest and towards which their imagination will turn at moments of uncertainty or insecurity.

Both *Dancing at Lughnasa* and *Wonderful Tennessee* seem to me to be allegories of a society which has lost its memory, its imaginative hinterland. The fact that both plays employ the same features – the 'maenadic' dance (*WT* 17) and the ritual sacrifice – emphasises their common purpose. If *Tennessee* had not been written, the supposition could have been made (wrongly, however) that Friel's intention in *Lughnasa* was merely to refer back to a 'hidden Ireland', to an atavistic memory which can be invoked when things become less than wonderful, that by making that connection to a far place and time, the validity of ancient custom can be affirmed. But *Tennessee* denies that intention. The six lost children on the pier at Ballybeg need to be rescued from a world that is less than perfect. In post-colonial terms, they are 'missing persons' whose identity is migrant and whose being is transitive.[74]

This point has also been disputed by critics Fintan O'Toole and Martine Pelletier. O'Toole believes that 'the final irony of *Wonderful Tennessee* is that the joyous throwing off of political responsibility which Friel accomplished in *Dancing at Lughnasa* may also account for the weakness of [the] play . . . the ultimate attempt to throw off the shackles of Irish complication', and opines: 'for good or ill, it seems, Friel cannot escape the messy social world of modern Ireland'.[75] Pelletier says: 'Friel has exaggerated the separation of the characters from their socio-historical context but does not provide them with sufficiently strong individual identities to sustain the dramatic action [my translation]'.[76] She thinks that *Tennessee* lacks 'the weight of History and stories' and that consequently Friel's excursion into 'mythic space' is unsatisfactory.

As we have seen, Pelletier has most arrestingly argued the commutation between public and private concerns as that between *l'Histoire* (history) and *histoires* (stories), which, as we have seen, Friel exemplifies most eloquently in *Making History*. In *Wonderful Tennessee* it would be possible to see merely the smaller *histoires* occupying centre stage to the exclusion of temporal history, were it not for the fact that the characters themselves commute between the storytelling mode and that of telling truths about themselves. The more serious issue is whether or not, by removing them from the 'real' world, Friel thereby banishes the real world from them.

A further insight into the resistance of critics to *Wonderful Tennessee* is provided by Roland Barthes's essay on 'The Death of the Author':

As soon as a fact is *narrated* no longer with a view to acting directly on
reality but intransitively, that is to say, finally outside of any function other
than that of the very practice of the symbol itself . . . disconnection occurs,
the voice loses its origin, the author enters into his own death, writing
begins. . . . In ethnographic societies the responsibility for a narrative is
never assumed by a person but by a mediator, shaman or relator whose
'performance' – the mastery of the narrative code – may possible be
admired but never his 'genius'. The author is a modern figure, a product of
our society.[77]

To reconcile the authorial power of the modern writer with the function
of the shamanistic storyteller where the story tells itself, would seem to be
one of the tasks of the playwright as the medium of the voices which will
emerge through the characters he creates for them. Barthes speaks of
'the necessity to substitute language itself for the person who . . . had
been supposed to be its owner'[78] – which is in addition a post-colonial
project and echoes what we have seen of Friel's affinity with Heidegger. In
Translations, in other words, Friel, in collaboration with Steiner, was
speaking with an authorial voice. In *Living Quarters, The Loves of Cass
McGuire, Making History* and the plays under scrutiny here, he is not.

The story or stories are thus polyvalent as music is polyphonic. If it is
not the author who 'says', it may well be the music. It is not accidental
that in *Wonderful Tennessee* Friel employs a wide range of musical genres,
from the classical fury of the Beethoven sonata to the hymn 'Regina
Coeli' and 'Knees-up, Mother Brown', or that he directs that the playing
of 'Down by the Cane-brake' should at one point 'sound almost sacred'.
The story stands behind, or beyond, the narration. It is always anterior to
whatever reality is being evoked because it itself resides not in reality but
in the pre-real, the pre-intellectual, which is dream.

It is, of course, valid to say that the characterisation is weak – that the
six are flat rather than dramatically rounded – but, as I have already
argued, the allegorical nature of the story permits this. Are a rounded
personality and a dramatic action the only criteria by which the drama is
to be judged? By contrast, designer Joe Vanek considered that the text is
'all glancing blows, accidental insights and confrontations. It never gets
heavy or ponderous, yet the power and force of it is astonishing, coming
from simple, basic words and phrases'.[79] As with the 'Russian' plays,
the constant exchange of ordinaries is what puts order on sensation,
meaning on perceptions, sharedness on isolation.

As with the Canterbury Tales, *Tennessee* is suggestive of worlds
beyond our own in a way that makes it clear that those worlds are within
us. If a flying house is an offence to reason, so too is the singing corpse in
the Prioress's Tale. But much more important is the fact that the corpse is
what Reinhard Kuhn calls 'an enigmatic child' or a *puer senex*[80] who has

innocently learned and sung a hymn without understanding it, for which he is sacrificed by those who find it offensive: one can suffer the ultimate penalty merely for reciting in an uncomprehending fashion a hymn learned purely because it was beautiful. Was the ritual slaughter of Seán O'Boyle on Oileán Draíochta in 1932 another example of accidental anarchy or of the preordained death of innocence? This 'child' is in both the real world and the world of the bizarre, in the between-place where anything can happen, joyful or deadly, or, in this case, both. The 'children' of *Tennessee* are in a similar position and it would be churlish and unwise of us to assume that there is no dynamic energy between them. In fact, this is denied by documentary evidence of the actors' experience during the inaugural production.

If we have lost memory, then we have lost not merely part of ourselves, but the vital connection to meaning which ensures that we are a part of the world. The cast of the first production of *Wonderful Tennessee* discovered jointly, under the direction of Patrick Mason and with the active participation of Brian Friel, that 'we need to believe', and that the island is an embodiment of hope.[81] In rehearsal, as demonstrated in Donald Taylor Black's television documentary 'From Ballybeg to Broadway', in order to enter into the ceremonial dimension of the play, the cast, author and director participated in the ritual which eventually becomes the stone-laying ritual at the play's conclusion. In the play itself, the device by which this communitas of belief is established is the simple refrain of the song 'Down by the Cane-brake':

> Come, my love, come, my boat lies low,
> She lies high and dry on the O-hi-o.
> Come, my love, come, and come along with me
> And I'll take you back to Tennessee (*WT* 45)

– where 'Tennessee' becomes the code-word for the island, the shared imagined place, the middle ground where each can recognise the other. As Patrick Mason expresses it, the play moves between two poles – the natural desire, among people who bear great hurt, to be happy ('I want to be happy/But I won't be happy/Till I make you happy too') and the need to get on with life, knowing it is hurtful. They both hurt, and are very protective of, each other.[82] Thus they bear witness to the mythology of heaven and hell, the island of mystery and wonder, where beauty resides in the company of the cruel. Affirming the existence of the island, which of necessity must be indeterminate, is the characteristic way of acknowledging the need for a church. It is a place beyond, because ancient time may not be at an end there.

Friel's working title for *Wonderful Tennessee* was 'The Imagined Place' and he conceived the play as dealing with 'the necessity for mystery'.[83]

Oileán Draíochta is not, perhaps, a 'real' island, but an imagined place. In the play, no one exactly locates it or describes its appearance accurately. The only 'sightings' we have are a piece of mediaeval folklore, recounted by Terry, and Terry's own memory of his visit there as a seven-year-old with his father: the autobiographical link with the seven-year-old Michael/Friel in *Lughnasa* will be obvious, as will the fact that Terry's childhood memory may be a fiction, as was Friel's own fishing trip which became the central episode of *Philadelphia*.

> There *is* a legend that it was once a spectral, floating island that appeared out of the fog every seven years and that fishermen who sighted it saw a beautiful country of hills and valleys, with sheep browsing on the slopes, and cattle in green pastures, and clothes drying on the hedges. And they saw leaves of apple and oak, and heard a bell and the song of coloured birds. Then, as they watched it, the fog devoured it and nothing was seen but the foam swirling on the billow and the tumbling of the dolphins. (*WT* 29)[84]

Even the question 'Has it a name, our destination?' (*WT* 28) suggests that the quest is without a map, without bearings of any kind other than those of the imagination. Previously, in *The Gentle Island*, we saw how a name can be completely false, as the violent traditions of Inishkeen, the 'gentle' island, are repeated. In *Wonderful Tennessee* we see that the 'isle of the blessed' can become the isle of the damned, as one pilgrimage, to the Eucharistic Congress, in which the transubstantiation of Christ's body and blood is celebrated, was followed by a pilgrimage to the island, where Seán O'Boyle is sacrificed.

The island is, like the 'tiny ivory cell' that contains heaven and hell, within us. Trying to find it is like trying to describe the journey taken by the *puer senex*; as Kuhn puts it:

> the cartographers of these fictional countries are of necessity adults, and thus there is always a residue of doubt . . . concerning the authenticity of their geographies.[85]

The imagined place, because it is within each of them, and because it is shared in a communal fashion during the night, becomes a sacred space by virtue of the ritual of storytelling and its consequences. At the beginning of the storytelling, Angela insists that George, an accordionist, begin by telling his 'story' – to which he responds by playing the opening of the finale of Beethoven's 'Moonlight' sonata. It is his expression of rage – rage for life, rage against his impending death.[86] At its end, when the stories have been told and the truths have been admitted, George asks Angela to return to the place another time 'in memory of me'. The eucharistic resonance is telling – do this in memory of me.

BLINDNESS

Despite its seductiveness and humour, *Molly Sweeney* is not an easy play, but it is utterly rewarding. Never has Friel written with such lucidity; never have his voices spoken so clearly. Never has he allowed magic so much latitude in demonstrating the capacity for play. It is thoroughly seamless. Peter Brook, who has said 'Of all contemporary authors, there is no one I admire more highly than Brian Friel', has especially praised *Molly Sweeney*,[87] and Brook's appreciation reflects both the beauty of the script and the fact that at its core is a bitter argument or *agon* about the nature of internal and external vision, and its relation to belief, understanding and expression – passionate and political, it places woman and her freedoms at the centre of the world and yet lures her through an opaque field to the border country where 'beyond' is to be negotiated.

Under the heading of 'blindness' I shall discuss *Molly Sweeney* as a narrative having close relations to the short stories; as an allegory of colonisation; as a feminist fable; and as a visitation by Friel on his previous work.

There are, Friel says,[88] deliberate echoes of *Faith Healer* – not only in the re-entry of three characters and not so much in the structure of the play, which in this case consists of thirty-seven monologues intercut in a filmic way, out of which the spectator must compose his own drama and his own truths. The similarity with *Faith Healer* consists more in the resurrection of the 'maddening questions' which each player – Molly, Frank and Paddy Rice – is trying to answer and to silence. *Faith Healer* revolved on the question of 'performance' – whether a healing act can also be a deception, a charade with its own religious forms. In *Molly Sweeney* Mr Rice tells us that during the operation 'The darkness miraculously lifted, and I performed – I watched myself do it . . . Miraculously all the gifts were mine again' (*MS* 47–8). He is an actor. He is a star. He is a healer. In each performance he relocates and regains his gift. *Faith Healer* presented a blurring of subjective and objective as the players groped towards personal truth. In *Molly Sweeney* we find the same blurred sense of innocence debauched by experience, both in Molly herself and in the two men by whom her world is colonised – husband and doctor – who, in disparate but cognate ways, come to represent different aspects of 'father' and therefore 'home'.

In this play, Friel looks not out of the window, but in through the window from the outside. Each player enters the interior looking for miracles ('a phantom desire, a fantasy in my head' – *MS* 18 [Rice], 41 [Molly]). Each is seeking a vision which could answer the question 'What do you want?': Molly, between the thin light of childhood and that of her last autism, looks for a 'brief excursion to this land of vision . . . then to return home to my own world with all that rare understanding within me for ever' (MS 41); Frank, who cannot bear reality and whose life consists of too many brief excursions into the unreal world, for a passion which will endure; Rice, for the restoration of his reputation as one of the world's leading eye surgeons, for escape from a too long excursion into despairing drunkenness.

The interior into which Molly enters is the smallest place imaginable – so much better known by woman than by man. Here, the 'child' makes its peace with a world that the world does not know. Whatever negotiation she makes there will, however, enable her to cross all of the thresholds in the external world. It is this peace and stillness which the colonists – husband and doctor – come to disrupt, with their intention of restoring Molly's sight – a condition she has never known and does not wish to enjoy, in order to restore themselves.

The play is Friel's most risky because it depends on nothing other than words – there is no music, no dance, no gesture, no set – just words on which he relies to create images and connections with the world, by means of which the spectator will himself enter the inner space and compose the drama which the words undoubtedly contain. When Molly tells us that 'In a rage of anger and defiance I danced a wild and furious dance . . . Mad and wild and frenzied' (MS 31) we are of course reminded of the sisters' dance in *Lughnasa* – but it is only approximate or contiguous to that previous dance, and in imagining, or imaging, it we may be able to share with Molly not only the elation of her blindness and 'complete assurance' (MS 32) but also the reason for the madness, the anger and the defiance: her fear of her impending exile from *her* world as the colonists take her into theirs.

Many critics in both Europe and the USA have remarked on the fact that the play is 'anti-theatrical' in the sense that it resembles a novella rather than a drama. In its stasis – considerably more so than in *Faith Healer* – it has a remarkable affinity with the genre of the radio play, and in its internal music it is more cameral than symphonic. If indeed Friel is a 'playwright at the end of the world', then this work resembles Messiaen's *Quatuor pour le fin du temps*. But the individual monologues take the form of highly crafted short stories, each of which summons to the mind's eye an image, and each of which takes its place in a mosaic which is completed with the chilling vision of the border country which Molly finally puts in place at the conclusion. The miniature genre of the address, and its clarity, matches the intimacy of the small place in which the 'action' – the action of words on our imaginations – occurs. (Stephen Kuusisto reminds us that 'everywhere in the world's legends one finds blind sorcerers. Blindness is a coefficient of magic' and adds storytelling to the genres of communication at which the blind are naturally adept.)[89]

The case history which prompted Friel to address the topic of blindness is Oliver Sacks's 'To See and Not See' which documents a case of *retinitis pigmentosa*, 'a hereditary condition that slowly but implacably eats away at the retinas'.[90] The patient, who also had thick cataracts, was able to distinguish light from dark and to 'see' the shadow of a hand before his face. When one cataract was removed, Sacks tells us 'miraculously, the operation had worked' and the patient's fiancée had recorded in her diary that he was 'trying to adjust to being sighted . . . unsure of what seeing means'.[91] Molyneux, Locke and Berkeley all appear in the case history as the first to stipulate that if a blind man received sight, he could not, by means of vision alone, distinguish a sphere from a cube. One of the earliest proofs of this thesis, in 1788, showed that such a patient 'encountered profound difficulties with the simplest visual perceptions . . . had no idea of distance . . . no idea of space or size . . . was bizarrely confused by drawings and paintings'.[92]

To Lévi-Strauss the question 'what does "to mean" mean?' was a basic problem of human ontology. To those working in the field of blindness, 'what does seeing mean?' is the differential calculus of such a question. The concept of perspective in painting was developed in the early Renaissance as a political tool[93] – a strategy of three-dimensional mapping by which we not only make sense of our perceptions but order them, prioritise them, according to the way we wish to organise the world. Thus, the idea that someone coming new to sight and to sight-experience could be 'confused by drawings and paintings', could regard the ordered world as confusing, as having no order, not only alienates that person from other people's perceptions but alienates society from the bewildered.

In the case of Sacks's patient, the fiancée believed 'there was nothing to lose' – the starting position of both Frank Sweeney and Paddy Rice in their argument in favour of Molly's operation. The following is Sacks's account of 'the moment of truth':

> No cry ('I can see!') burst from Virgil's lips. He seemed to be staring blankly, bewildered, without focusing, at the surgeon, who stood before him, still holding the bandages. Only when the surgeon spoke – saying 'Well?' – did a look of recognition cross Virgil's face.
> Virgil told me later that in this first moment he had no idea what he was seeing. There was light, there was movement, there was colour, all mixed up, all meaningless, a blur. Then out of the blur came a voice that said, 'Well?' Then, and only then, he said, did he finally realize that this chaos of light and shadow was a face – and, indeed, the face of his surgeon. . . .
> When Virgil opened his eye, after being blind for forty-five years – having had little more than an infant's visual experience, and this long

forgotten – there were no visual memories to support a perception; there was no world of experience and meaning awaiting him. He saw, but what he saw had no coherence. His retina and optic nerve were active, transmitting impulses, but his brain could make no sense of them; he was, as neurologists say, agnosic.[94]

A reading of *Molly Sweeney* shows instantly how extensively Friel plundered the history (or story) for the background facts to that of Molly herself.

> When Mr Rice did arrive, even before he touched me, I knew by his quick, shallow breathing that he was far more nervous than I was. And then as he took off the bandages his hands trembled and fumbled.
>
> 'There we are', he said. 'All off. How does that feel?'
>
> 'Fine', I said. Even though I felt nothing. Were all the bandages off?
>
> 'Now, Molly. In your own time. Tell me what you see.'
>
> Nothing. Nothing at all. Then out of the void a blur; a haze; a body of mist; a confusion of light, colour, movement. *It had no meaning.*
>
> 'Well?' he said. 'Anything? Anything at all?'
>
> I thought: Don't panic; a voice comes from a face; that blur is his face; look at him.
>
> 'Well? Anything?'
>
> Something moving; large; white; the nurse? And lines, black lines, vertical lines. The bed? The door?
>
> 'Anything, Molly?' A bright light that hurt. The window maybe?
>
> 'I'm holding my hand before your eyes, Molly. Can you see it?'
>
> A reddish blob in front of my face; rotating; liquefying; pulsating. Keep calm. Concentrate.
>
> 'Can you see my hand, Molly?'
>
> 'I think so . . . I'm not sure. . .' (*MS* 41–2, *my emphasis*)

Rice has already explained to Frank that 'neurologists had a word for people in that condition – seeing but not knowing, not recognising, what it is they see . . . agnosic'. 'Strange' Frank tells us, 'because I always thought that word had to do with believing or not believing' (*MS* 22) – a point to which the narrative will return. Molly's 'I think so . . . I'm not sure' is the cruellest instance of the uncertainty that bedevils Friel's characters. And as with Sacks, Rice will explain to Frank that the blind know their world by means of tactile 'engrams', which imprint impressions or perceptions on the memory, whereas sighted people work on visual 'engrams'. When that burden proves too heavy, the newly sighted behave in a manner which is neither that of sighted nor of blind persons: they follow the logic of neither sight nor blindness. Such a between-space allows no mindscape whatsoever. This condition is known as 'blindsight' and resembles a 'demoralized, defeated state' in which patients see but do not see.[95]

Fortuitously, in addition to the case study by Sacks, a correlative text, *Planet of the Blind*, appeared subsequent to *Molly Sweeney*, describing the life experiences of Stephen Kuusisto, a fractionally sighted American whose story has a remarkable affinity with Molly's, not least because it is spoken in the first person. 'Blindness is often perceived by the sighted as an either/or condition: one sees or one does not see. But often a blind person experiences a series of veils: I stare at the world through smeared and broken windowpanes'.[96] Immediately, the resemblance to Molly and to Friel's own creative process is 'uncanny' in the Freudian sense, because the analogy with the window (Chekhov) has everything to do with the way we create a web of stories which satisfactorily describe the world. Because Kuusisto's parents would not accept his blindness, he was as a child obliged (or did he choose?) to act like a sighted person. 'This will be a nearly lifelong puzzle for me: Am I not a sighted boy? Am I not attempting bravely to see? What must I do?'[97] That final question converts 'what do I want?' into 'what do you want of me?' The answer, with which the child concurs, is 'Raised to know I was blind but taught to disavow it'.[98] He not only walks without a stick but he cycles, he even drives the family power boat in 'my hunger for normalcy'.[99] 'I move in a solitude fuelled by secrecy . . . I'm addicted to being independent. Every step is a lie. Step, lie. Step, lie'.[100] Molly, too, walks without a stick, cycles, and in one clifftop incident dives eighty feet into the sea.

The 'unhomely' or unhoused condition is common to Molly and Kuusisto. 'My borderline country is where I live now. I'm at home there. Well . . . at ease there' Molly tells us (*MS* 67). 'Even today I live in the "customs house" between the land of the blind and those who possess some minor capacity to see' says Kuusisto.[101] This state of dispossession, of being in-between, is a classic case of what Homi Bhabha calls 'less than one and double' which we noted in the Introduction. 'I remain ashamed of my blind self' says Kuusisto,[102] thus disclosing that while he is not a whole person, he is aware of an other self. And it is the classic state of being, in Steiner's phrase, 'linguistically "unhoused" or displaced or hesitant at the frontier' which we also noted. These simultaneous equations are the template from which the nomads, the strays, derive their existence, but not their meaning.

Again, the country of the blind offers us analogies with other worlds where people are groping towards truth: 'the sensorium of the blind who possess some marginal vision is by turns magical and disturbing . . . It's a mad, holy vision, the repeated appearance and disappearance of the physical world'.[103] The pilgrims at the end of the world on the pier at Ballybeg share that mad, holy vision, enact their own visions in a mad and holy theatre, as they project onto the appearing/disappearing Oileán Draíochta their ideas of wonder and mystery.

Esse est percipi. 'A disabled child is without a category: one simply does not see them' says Kuusisto.[104] In order to exist one must be seen. 'My little body . . . is something uncanny – a thing that belongs in darkness and that has been brought to daylight'.[105] But if strays are blind, groping, they are straying *inside* their own cartography, feeling their way towards their own interpretation, their own meaning. Kuusisto: 'I find a lighted room inside my head, a place for self-affiliation'. As we have seen in discussing affiliation, to turn away from family and society is to go into exile; here, however, the ground rules have changed radically, since it is by such turning away from the world, from the 'gnosic', that we learn to ask not only 'what does seeing mean?' but 'what does *not* seeing mean?' Molly tells us that Mr Rice

> was the only one who never quizzed me about what it felt like to be blind . . . the others kept asking me what the idea of colour meant to me, or the idea of space, or the notion of distance . . . 'Tell us' (*MS* 23).

Rice doesn't: 'I suppose because he knew everything about it'. Molly's supposition is correct, but only since Rice himself 'knows' the meaning of blindsight, because in a metaphysical way it had caused him to lose his wife to another man who was able to 'see' her beauty as he himself could not.

Further aspects of Sacks's and Kuusisto's accounts make striking parallels with other locations in Friel's work. Thus, the intentness with which the newly sighted man in Sacks's case studied objects and animals – confusing cat and dog because both were black and white. 'The new ideas, the visual recognitions, kept slipping from his mind'[106] recalls Fr Jack's difficulty with the names both of objects and of processes and concepts – 'layout', 'photograph', 'ceremony'. This reminds us that the essence of memory, as of ritual, is naming things, creating spaces within which recognition, acknowledgement, takes place. Jack's sisters contemplate placing a name-tag on a vase of roses 'so that the poor man's head won't be demented looking for the word' (*DL* 37) – a strategy adopted by the inhabitants of *One Hundred Years of Solitude* as a guard against their collective amnesia.[107]

A further point of recollection occurs here: to 'act' as a sighted person, Kuusisto tells us, 'requires a capacious memory . . . every inch of terrain had to be acutely remembered'.[108] The 'strays' who have lost – or are about to lose – their way in *Translations* are like those deprived of sight: the tactile engrams by which they decoded the contours of Baile Beag are no longer available, as if memory had been lost because they had lost the sense of vision rather than the capacity for speech.

As we saw in Chapter 1, the Berkeleyan concept *'esse est percipi'* relies on both partners in the act of recognition, the act of creation, recognising each other as 'not extraneous, but self' – ourselves within. Not just identity, but our very being itself, is at stake. This is at once the most basic, simple concept and the most complex imposition put on us by existence – to have relevance, to 'matter'. The quest not to be immaterial is at the heart of love, the core of 'what do you want?'

For Oliver Sacks, this problem is 'to form a complex perception at a glance'[109] – that is, to synthesise sequential images so as to form a world view which will enable us to live with the phenomena. Frank Sweeney tells us:

> Molly's world isn't perceived instantly, comprehensively. She composes a world from a sequence of impressions; one after another, in time. For example, she knows that this is a carving knife because first she can feel the handle; then she can feel this long blade; then this sharp edge. In sequence. In time. What is this object? These are ears. This is a furry body. Those are paws. That is a long tail. Ah, a cat! (*MS* 35–6)

Frank is (probably) ill-equipped to realise just how vital is this gathering of perceptions to Molly's very sense of being. He is aware that when she failed to make the connection between her own tactile engrams and the visual engrams that the new world demands of her, she 'withdrew' – but has no idea what this *means*.

The *rite de passage* undertaken by Molly, which is so destructive of her entire identity and personality, is described in the original account by Sacks as 'bringing his [Virgil's] own life story – his particular dispositions and needs and expectations – to this critical passage . . . We look not merely at his eyes and perceptual powers but at the whole tenor and pattern of his life'.[110]

On a visit to the zoo, Sacks's patient has difficulty recognising real animals, but exults when he finds a statue of a gorilla which he can examine:

> how skilful and self-sufficient he had been as a blind man, how naturally and easily he had experienced his world with his hands, and how much we were now, so to speak, pushing him against the grain: demanding that he renounce all that came easily to him, that he sense the world in a way incredibly difficult for him, and alien.[111]

(*Against the grain*: let us recall Barthes's insistence on the irreducible quality of the 'grain of the voice', the core of personal song.)

When Molly is submitted to a similar test with flowers, she fails to identify them by visual means and reverts to her own way of knowing things – in this instance not only tactile but olfactory:

> 'Well, Molly? Do you know what they are?'
> We waited. Another long silence. Then suddenly she closed her eyes tight

shut. She brought the flowers right up against her face and inhaled in quick gulps and at the same time, with her free hand, swiftly, deftly felt the stems and the leaves and the blossoms. Then with her eyes still shut tight she called out desperately, defiantly,
    'They're cornflowers!' (*MS* 45)

The place to which Molly is brought is the place of refusal, and her withdrawal from the attributes of sight can be read as an allegory of those who refuse to accept the world as it is. Mr Rice describes this to Frank as 'gnosis'; Frank finds the word defined in the dictionary as 'a mystical knowledge , a knowledge of spiritual things' (*MS* 54) and seems to think that Rice's judgement has slipped, as he can see no connection between the two definitions. Here we meet an unresolved feature of *Molly Sweeney*: gnosis (in Greek, literally 'knowledge') is not explained further in the play. But gnosticism, a philosophy which developed in the second century AD and which had several manifestations in mediaeval Europe such as the Cathar 'heresy', is based on the belief that we must refuse to participate in a world which we know to be less than perfect, and to which death is preferable because we die into the real world of which this one is merely a false copy. 'I am *in* the world but not *of* the world'.[112] (And there is a history alternate to History, in which there is a second son of God, Christ's twin brother – giving a twist to the idea of an *alter Christus*.) Molly's flight from knowledge of the sighted world, the renaissance world of order and normative behaviour, is her second, more real and more harrowing *rite de passage*, as she attempts to regain the inner equilibrium from which she had hoped to make but a brief excursion.[113] The irony is that it must be expressed in the language of the theatre since, Steiner reminds us, 'Language is the main instrument of man's refusal to accept the world as it is'.[114]

The situation is a clear reversal of Berna's story of the flying house in *Wonderful Tennessee*: there, the flying house was so illogical, so improbable, that it constituted an 'offence to reason'. Making what Sacks calls 'a radical switch from a sequential to a visual-spatial mode' of seeing 'flies in the face of the experience of an entire lifetime'[115] – that is, it flies in the face of reason insofar as Molly's life experiences have constituted a set of logical rules by which her life is lived. Where Berna's outburst, 'fuck off, reason', is an act of rhetoric, made out of the struggle with others, Molly's final quiet 'Why should I?' (*MS* 67) is an act of poetry, made out of the struggle with herself.

Sacks employs the explanation by Denis Diderot which Friel also places at the top of his text: 'learning to see is not like learning another language; it is like learning language for the first time'.[116] To this epigraph Friel has attached well-known lines from Emily Dickinson:

> Tell all the Truth but tell it slant –
> Success in circuit lies
> Too bright for our infirm Delight
> The Truth's superb surprise
> As Lightning to the Children eased
> With explanation kind
> The Truth must dazzle gradually
> Or every man be blind.

I take this to be a signal from Friel that we may, if we wish, read *Molly Sweeney* as a feminist fable, as an equivalent to the madness, rage and blindness of Lear, as a riposte to the 'Trust me' that she hears from her father, from Frank and, by implication, from Mr Rice. Dickinson's lines indicate that the circularity, the periodicity of feminine vision, the need to see things, and to report them, lies (my pun is intentional) at an oblique angle to the way they are seen by men. Echoes and allusions are as important as direct, unequivocal statements, and the world of the child, or 'child', deserves protection as well as an explanation.

Faced with the difficulty of learning the visual language for the first time, some patients develop 'blindsight' – a retreat into blindness. Sacks's patient was *'blinder than he had been before his operations'*.[117] Some have 'found the "gift" transformed to a curse, become deeply depressed, and soon after died'.[118] In this case, the patient 'has been shattered', exhibiting

> rage at his helplessness . . . rage at the smashing of a promise and a dream
> . . . rage at being thrust into a battle he could neither renounce nor win . . .
> Now, at last, Virgil is allowed to not see, allowed to escape from the
> glaring, confusing world of sight and space, and to return to his own true
> being, the intimate, concentrated world of the other senses that had been
> his home for almost fifty years.[119]

Kuusisto bears personal witness to this: 'I am about to begin an impossible contest with the sighted world'.[120]

This is a dispensation Friel does not accord to Molly in her own *agon*. Hers is a frightening plunge into a form of madness alternating with despair, which we can only guess at: to have made that 'brief excursion' and to have encountered total failure, to have retreated not into the previous world but into a new world of denial, of blindsight, is something unknowable:

> The world that I now saw – half-saw, peered at really – it was a world of
> wonder and surprise and delight. Oh, yes; wonderful, surprising, delightful.
> And joy – such joy, small unexpected joys that came in such profusion
> and passed so quickly that there was never enough time to savour them.
> But it was a very foreign world, too. And disquieting; even alarming.
> Every colour dazzled. Every light blazed. Every shape an apparition, a
> spectre that appeared suddenly from nowhere and challenged you. And all

that movement – nothing ever still – everything in motion all the time; and every movement unexpected, somehow threatening. Even the sudden sparrows in the garden, they seemed aggressive, dangerous.

So that after a time the mind could absorb no more sensation. Just one more colour – light – movement – ghostly shape – and suddenly the head imploded and the hands shook and the heart melted with panic. And the only escape – the only way to live – was to sit absolutely still; and shut the eyes tight; and immerse yourself in darkness; and wait. Then when the hands were still and the heart quiet, slowly open the eyes again. And emerge. And try to find the courage to face it all once more. (MS 50)

Molly's predicament is similar to that of Irina in Friel's version of *Three Sisters*:

Every day that races past I feel – I *know* I'm losing touch with everything else that has even the smell of hope about it – no, no, even worse than losing touch – sinking, being sucked down into an abyss. I am despairing, Olga. Do you understand what I'm saying? I am desperate. *I see no reason* to go on living. I see no reason why I shouldn't end it now (*Sisters* 81, *my emphasis*).

Mr Rice tells us

In those last few months a new condition appeared. She began showing symptoms of a condition known as blindsight. This is a physiological condition, not psychological. On those occasions she claimed she could see nothing, absolutely nothing at all. And indeed she was telling the truth. But even as she said this, she behaved as if she could see . . . She *was* indeed receiving visual signals and she *was* indeed responding to them. But because of a malfunction in part of the cerebral cortex none of this perception reached her consciousness. She was totally unconscious of seeing anything at all.

In other words she *had* vision – but a vision that was utterly useless to her. (MS 56)

'In those last few months . . .' – nothing has prepared us for the shock of Molly's end. We suddenly realise that as with *Living Quarters* and *Faith Healer*, the central character is speaking to us from the dead. When Rice visits her in the psychiatric hospital to which she has been transferred he is told 'She could last for ever or she could slip away tonight' (MS 64). No one (except Oliver Sacks) has told us that the end of blindness is death. But we are never sure how Molly ends, locked into her autistic knowledge: she is 'at the end of the world' and will always be there, on the fulcrum of meaning.

I think I see nothing at all now. But I'm not absolutely sure of that. Anyhow my borderline country is where I live now. I'm at home there. Well . . . at ease there. It certainly doesn't worry me anymore that what I think I see may be fantasy or indeed what I take to be imagined may very well be real – what's Frank's term? – external reality. Real – imagined – fact – fiction – fantasy – reality – there it seems to be. And it seems to be alright. And why should I question it anymore? (MS 67)

These last words of *Molly Sweeney* alert us to many possibilities because, as we saw earlier in this chapter, 'subjunctivity is possibility'. Does Molly see spectres? Does she meet apparitions? Stephen Kuusisto can help us here: he tells us 'Apparitions only become ghosts when no one can explain them . . . I have no ghosts in my head. . . . Ghosts are possibility seen backward'.[121] In the subjunctive world, where anything can (and will) happen because nothing can ever be the same again, because, as Molly has discovered (with Heraclitus) everything is in motion, the stillness can never be recovered, and music and birdsong will always be harsh because of that.

Fintan O'Toole makes the surprising point that 'as you would expect from Friel, the narrative . . . is buttressed with philosophy'.[122] With the exception of specific references to Heidegger in the programme notes for the original production of *Translations*, there is in fact little recourse to explicit philosophical thought in any of Friel's work, although after writing *Molly Sweeney* he did briefly contemplate a play about Wittgenstein in Ireland.[123] In the sense that all Friel's work could be said to be philosophical, O'Toole's point is valid and perhaps superfluous for that reason, but the references to Molyneux, Locke and Berkeley in the text of *Molly Sweeney* are not of the same order as the use of Lewis, Goffman or Steiner in previous plays or, indeed, of Sacks in this one. In those instances he employed texts as 'case histories' of conditions which were germane to his own preoccupations, which gave him a ready-made key to open, if not to explore, the dark and private places of individual souls.

The philosophy in *Molly Sweeney* is not a buttress but an organic part of the whole. The intensely political implications of what Molyneux and Berkeley were developing, especially in contradistinction to Locke's work, and the implicitly (sometimes explicitly) Irish context in which they were working, make their contribution to the literature of perception a crucial part of the colonial and post-colonial discussion about the 'location of authority' and the 'location of culture'.[124] O'Toole has made a perhaps over-eager case for Friel as the chronicler of collapse – as the diviner of imploding or tottering worlds and sees *Molly Sweeney* as one such allegory.[125] I would hesitate to see Molly as any kind of emblematic Cathleen, blinded by her menfolk as she is dragged into the modern world, but the simple fact that Molly does lose her 'field of vision' allows us to look at her dilemma as that of the subaltern.

In *Translations*, Yolland 'missed the boat' for India and ended up in Dublin. By analogy, Macaulay's minute on Indian education (which we discussed in Chapter 6), which denied the possibility of a native history 'abounding with kings thirty feet high . . . and geography made up of seas of treacle and seas of butter',[126] might have been applied to negating the fantasies of Irish geography (such as those of the *navigatio Brendani* or the concept of 'twilight'). The tenor of his Indian project was not only simultaneous with the mapping of Ireland and the establishment of the national school system, but went back to the time of the 'flight of the earls', when the civilising process really started, and against which Molyneux, Berkeley and Swift reacted so notably. But by a curious irony Surgeon Rice hopes, indeed, that in the Biblical, imagistic sense, Molly will 'see men walking as if like trees' (*MS* 28); Stephen Kuusisto graphically asks: 'Picture this: A darkness rises. Is it a tree or a shadow? A shadow or a truck? . . . There is, at the center of our skulls, a terrible glittering, a requiem of light'.[127] It is to this light that Berkeley's insistence on an 'Irish' vision is curiously pertinent, because his approach to the question of 'seeing is believing' is determined by *how we see.*

Molly's world is an inner place. Because it cannot be seen, it cannot be known by a sighted person, yet it is known to her. Kuusisto tells us 'in every blind person's imagination there are landscapes'.[128] To steal that landscape makes the victim rage not against the dark but against the light. When Fanon writes 'what is often called the black soul is a white man's artefact'[129] he also describes the difficulty of the sighted in comprehending the darkness within which the blind live. It was the project of the coloniser to appreciate, in order to improve on, the qualities of the native.

When Molly danced on the eve of the operation, it was in anger and defiance. Not yet refusal, because she still could not know what the new world would be. But she does already know that it is an exile: 'How can they know what they are taking away from me? How do they know what they are offering me? They don't. They can't. And have I anything to gain? Anything? Anything? I knew, suddenly I knew why I was so desolate. It was the dread of exile, of being sent away. It was the desolation of homesickness' (*MS* 31). The stock expression 'something gets lost in the translation' could never be more apt: what is lost is not only 'home' but memory, meaning, identity, raison d'être.

As Bhabha puts it:

> To exist is to be called into being in relation to an otherness, its look or locus . . . This process is visible in the exchange of looks between native and settler that structures their psychic relation in the paranoid fantasy of boundless possession and its familiar language of reversal . . . It is always in relation to the place of the Other that colonial desire is articulated: the phantasmic space of possession that no one subject can singly or fixedly occupy, and therefore permits the dream of the inversion of roles.[130]

In Molly's case, both Rice and Frank Sweeney are trying to tear the veil from the face of the Other as they persuade Molly to yield her cataracts.

Her inner landscape must be known to them – she must trade it in exchange for theirs, in order to put an end to mystery. And thus we return to the dual role of the trader as the carrier and the traitor of tradition.

To understand the blind world is impossible because we try to do so from an intellectual standpoint: 'Tell us: how do you think your world compares with the world the rest of us know, the world you would share with us if you had visual perception as well?' (MS 23–4). We recall Kuusisto: his parents 'know some necessary vocabulary, *retinal detachment, legal blindness*, and the like, but the emotional language – they don't have that'.[131] Friel does not attempt to find that emotional language; instead he tries to give us access to Molly's predicament as well as her sense of freedom through a medium familiar to the blind – swimming – from which we might 'compose' an idea of her world:

> Oh I can't tell you the joy I got from swimming. I used to think – and I know this sounds silly – but I really did believe I got more pleasure, more delight, from swimming than sighted people can ever get. Just offering yourself to the experience – every pore open and eager for that world of pure sensation, of sensation alone – sensation that could not have been enhanced by sight – experience that existed only by touch and feel; and moving swiftly and rhythmically through that enfolding world; and the sense of such assurance, such liberation, such concordance with it . . . Oh I can't tell you the joy swimming gave me. I used to think that the other people in the pool with me, the sighted people, that in some way their pleasure was actually diminished because they could see, because seeing in some way qualified the sensation; and that if they only knew how full, how total my pleasure was, I used to tell myself that they must, they really must envy me. (MS 24)

Most of us do not understand the concept of freedom, and certainly have never experienced it in its ultimate persuasions. We are too ringed round by the inhibitions of class, culture and even creed. We would entertain a sneaking admiration for the artist's irresponsibility in Frank Hardy, who is able, like Joyce, to fly by the nets of belief and affiliation, but our conventional *mores* would call us away from too close an encounter with such a brilliant but dangerous mind. But we envy the world of the child and perhaps even that of the mad, because we think that somehow they enjoy an internalised state of harmless freedom, of grace. Molly, as the ultimate child whose vision has been stolen from her, who has been cast into a non-place, excites both our sympathy and our jealousy.

Molly as enigma embodies all the unknowable conditions – we cannot know or recover childhood, we cannot appreciate blindness, we cannot, ultimately, apprehend the other. If it were merely difference, the condition could be defined in relation to what it is not, like and unlike; but because it is other, it is contiguous; like Private and Public Gar, it cannot be seen. She is a missing person. If she stood in the place of the actor/spectator in the Memory Theatre, all hell would break loose because a reversal of roles takes place when the blind, capable of knowing images without recourse to external stimulus, set their own memory in train: the process by which memory is created and restored is stood on its head and meaning becomes mercurial.

The echoes of, and allusions to, Friel's previous work in *Molly Sweeney* are quite striking, even alarming. They are due to two factors: firstly, the fact that because he cannot describe Molly's interior landscape he must call on hints from earlier visions of a similar map; the second factor derives from the first, that many aspects of Friel's craft as a writer, of which the vocabulary itself is the most prominent, are converging acceleratedly to a point where some attempt at finality, at making a satisfactory statement, might be possible.

In the passage in which Molly describes the sensation of swimming, there is a direct restatement of the conclusion of *Lughnasa*: 'moving swiftly and rhythmically through that enfolding world' (*MS* 24) not only echoes 'moving rhythmically, languorously, in complete isolation' (*DL* 71) but linguistically it recreates an echoing *image*. My oxymoron is deliberate: as the final image of *Lughnasa* is a shimmering tableau – '*the movement is so minimal that we cannot be quite certain if it is happening or if we imagine it*' (*DL* 71) – so the relationship between the two texts is made to oscillate, both in the eye of the mind *and* in the mind of the eye.

The convergence to which I refer (and again my allusion is deliberate) is of the Yeatsian variety: as in his later plays Yeats became increasingly terse and imagistic, the drama deriving – as in *Purgatory* – from the mental pictures created between man and boy, so in Friel's recent theatre the literary has predominated over the dramatic, but not at the expense of drama: in Yeats's terms, it has become a place of intellectual excitement. It creates a different kind of dramatic effect in which the transaction between characters is achieved covertly, behind the eyelids; as in the short stories, it is made manifest through divination rather than exhibition.

In *Molly Sweeney* Friel echoes much more than *Faith Healer*. There are explicit re-entries, such as that of Gerry Evans (*Lughnasa*) in the guise of Frank Sweeney – the former's fads for working as a dancing master or a travelling gramophone salesman and going to the Spanish civil war as a dispatch-rider, are translated into goat-farming, bee-keeping, saving the whale and famine relief in Ethiopia. The distant figure of authority – the judge/father in *Aristocrats* and Grace's judge/father in *Faith Healer* – reappears as Molly's father, while Grace's mother – 'mother in her headscarf and wellingtons was a strange woman who went in and out of the mental hospital (*FH* 26) – is replicated here.

Where, in *Lughnasa*, Kate has recognised that Jack has 'his own distinctive spiritual search' (*DL* 60), Molly has her 'special knowledge' and 'distinctive sense' (*MS* 31); where, in *Philadelphia*, Gar is bewildered by his leavetaking, Frank fails to understand his need to step outside reality: 'why don't you stay where you are, for Christ's sake? What are you looking for?' (*MS* 62). And in the tropes and cadences of Mr Rice and of Molly we detect the unmistakable voice of their author and of the voices that stand behind him: 'And suddenly and passionately and with utter selflessness I wanted nothing more in the world than that *their* inordinate hopes would be fulfilled, that I could give them their miracle (*MS* 39) . . . And what was strange was that there were times when I didn't know if the things I did see were real or was I imagining them. I seemed to be living on the borderline between fantasy and reality (*MS* 58)'.

But much more significantly, and less tangibly, Friel recreates the atmosphere and the processes through which he revisits his own memories and meanings. Sometimes – but rarely – these are situational, such as Molly's childhood memory of her parents: 'late at night, listening to Mother and himself fighting their weary war downstairs' (*MS* 15), a recall of the core memory in the story 'The Child'. At others, it is associational: 'we'd perform the same ritual of naming' (*MS* 14) which connects us directly with the *caerimonia nominationis* of *Translations* and indirectly with all the *topoi* in his work where bestowing a name has been a sacred moment of calling a person or a place or a thing into existence.

The *conditions* which Friel recalls commute, as usual, between the cruel and the joyful. Not only is the connection made between Paddy Rice and Frank Hardy as 'performers', but their function, it is suggested, is more definitive of failure than suggestive of hope: Molly is brought to Rice 'just to give an opinion, if only to confirm that nothing could be done for her' (*MS* 15) – which summons Frank Hardy's potential victims, too: 'that they came to me, a mountebank, was a measure of their despair . . . They knew in their hearts they had come not to be cured but for confirmation that they were incurable' (*FH* 16). And at the same time the idea of the miraculous is also held out as a bleak but possible prospect, both for healer and healed: 'If that opportunity were being offered to me and if after all these years I could pull myself together and measure up to it, and if, oh my God if by some miracle pull it off perhaps' (*MS* 18).

In *Molly Sweeney* the characterisation is such that what we know of Frank and Paddy Rice in particular must be inferred rather than told to us directly. The echoes of Frank Hardy in Paddy Rice especially suggest that one needs to know the canon of Friel's work in order to derive the strongest resonance from any single play. But the tangential nature of his references means that one character can relate to several others. Thus, Friel immediately follows Rice's prayer for the miracle with a killing line which summons not Frank Hardy but Hugh Mor O'Donnell: 'People who live alone frequently enjoy an opulent fantasy life' (*MS* 18). The associations here are multiple. Not only does this belong primarily to Chekhov – 'When people have no real life, they live on their illusions' stands at the head of Chapter 4 – but it has been taken up by Friel, *via* Steiner, in *Translations*: 'yes, it is a rich language . . . full of the mythologies of fantasy and hope and self-deception – a syntax opulent with tomorrows' (*Tr.* 42). It thus asks us to think about hope deferred not only in the individual soul but also in the collective will and consciousness. It applies principally to Mr Rice but also to Frank Sweeney in his restless quest for something with meaning and outcome, a 'personal sense of urgency' for fulfilment, and to Molly in what becomes increasingly a mindscape opulent with yesterdays – the reversal that is done to all those who have gone willingly or unwillingly into exile. And by extension it not only reconvenes the cast of *Translations* but it speaks on its own ground to the relationship between individual and society, author and audience, about what happens in the imagination when we contemplate the miraculous.

There are also further references to *Translations* which relate directly to the matter in hand, so to speak, in *Molly Sweeney* – the equation or lack of it between seeing and thinking, seeing and believing. Frank explains in his naïve lingo the nature of the engram:

> It accounts for the mind's strange ability to recognise instantly somebody we haven't seen for maybe thirty years. Then he appears. The sight of him connects with the imprint, the engram. And bingo – instant recognition! (*MS* 20)

The reference is once again two-directional. First it recalls Steiner's explanation of congruence in the deep structures of language:

> The Ur-Sprache had a congruence with reality . . . Words and objects dovetailed perfectly. As the modern epistemologist might put it, there was a complete, point-to-point mapping of language onto the true substance and shape of things. Each man, each proposition was an equation, with uniquely and perfectly defined roots, between human perception and the facts of the case.[132]

And secondly it repeats the exchange between Yolland and Owen in *Translations*:

> OWEN: A christening!
> YOLLAND: A baptism!
> OWEN: A hundred christenings!

YOLLAND: A thousand baptisms! Welcome to Eden!
OWEN: Eden's right! We name a thing and – bang! – it leaps into
           existence!
YOLLAND: Each name a perfect equation with its roots.
OWEN: A perfect congruence with reality. (*Tr.* 45)

In Molly's personal Eden there has been a congruence with one
particular reality but there is no longer such a 'perfect equation' or any
equation at all. Equation, as I have written elsewhere,[133] is metaphor –
the point where language enables two qualities or conditions to become
equal, so that a carrying over becomes possible of the entire self to the
otherness beyond. In Molly's case, this possibility may never have been
very strong, but because her world has been invaded by Frank and Paddy
Rice, it is now out of reach for ever.

LOVE

At the close of *Aristocrats*, as Alice O'Donnell prepares to leave Ballybeg
Hall, perhaps for the last time, she tells her husband, Eamon, 'I'm not
unhappy that this is all over – because love is possible only in certain
contexts', to which Eamon replies 'Have we a context?' 'Let's wait and
see' (*Ar.* 84). Friel keeps his audiences in the wait-and-see, anticipating a
context, a home where love can be both enabling and ennabled. In the
thirty years before and after *Aristocrats* he has pursued love through the
contexts of family, duty, artistry and history. The nature of these affections
was explored in Chapter 3, in which I discussed love as an *agon*, where
the lifelines of *eros* and *agape*, sexual and familial loves, between lover
and beloved, son and father, brother and sister, husband and wife, man
and tribe, self and other, are submitted to tests which most people would
prefer to pass them by.

In considering the exchange between Alice and Eamon, Terence Brown
has asked 'Do any of the O'Donnells and those associated with them have
a context where they can experience the meaningful social existence
without which love cannot blossom in innovative and creative life [?].'[134]
In *Give Me Your Answer, Do!* the 'context' is a disordered form of family
life for three couples; the 'pretext' is the impending decision of an American
university to buy or not to buy a writer's personal archive; and the text is
as near to a 'Russian' play as Friel has yet come. It is little coincidence
that the work which followed this was a version of *Uncle Vanya*.

The three conditions – text, context, pretext – coalesce so closely in
Give Me Your Answer, Do! as to make it another seamless garment in the
Chekhovian frame, although a couple of hesitancies in the inaugural
production seemed to detract from that. The theme of love both binds the

play together and lurks within it as a destructive force which can tear its constituents apart. This is the 'meaningful social existence' sought by Terence Brown, in which the 'innovative and creative life' becomes the time of the writer. Thomas Kilroy has said that Friel's work illustrates 'the, at times, dreadful cost of love':

> It is this love-hunger which drives through the plays, burning away at indifference, at social and political stupidity, at the seductive clutch of family bonds . . . Friel, finally, is writing about the effects of process, of time, of growth, upon love.[135]

This judgement (1979) remains valid, but we can add to it: in 1970 Friel said that he had viewed love from the romantic, the Christian and the 'practical' aspects and that that phase of his work was ended.[136] By 1979 his view of love had expanded to accommodate the psychological war-and-peace that we find in *Aristocrats* and *Faith Healer* – the 'love-hunger' which Kilroy sees as the motive force of these plays. By the late 1980s he had ventured into the even more painful territory where the ultimately private play of the emotions is confronted tragically with the ultimately public diktats of history. He has prowled around the foothills of public meaning but since he has moved toward higher ground he has invariably looked more closely at the contours of privacy. *Give Me Your Answer, Do!* is high ground in this respect, but it is also a foothills play in that it exemplifies how, since 1990, he has more fully explored that public, or political, role of love as a commodity to be bartered in the marketplace because it is part of identity, part of regaining 'the imagined place'.

It would at first seem that Friel has returned to simpler, more intimate pastures. But he has returned not to any particular phase or aspect of his work but to *all* his work. The self-assessment of Tom Connolly and the assessment of him by David Knight are both autobiographical, in the sense, firstly, that Friel himself was visited by the representative of an American university with an offer to purchase his personal archive; and, secondly, that the play in which this is shown to us is a personal revisiting and rewriting of all his previous work. It is in the fullest sense of the term a total *retour sur soi-même* (above, p. 113), but it is no longer '*secret*', it is exposed and made apparent – or, as Mic Moroney put it in reviewing the first production, 'something of a serpent with its tail in its mouth . . . curiously self-conscious'.[137]

It would be too easy to see *Give Me Your Answer, Do!* as a reflection on *Aristocrats* – 'decaying country houses filled with dilapidated lives' as Fintan O'Toole calls them. O'Toole also recognises that 'the uses of lies, the relationship between memory and invention, the fear of silence that forces us to keep talking'[138] are also rehearsed. In particular, that fear of silence takes us back to *Philadelphia*, and in the 'monologue that might be a dialogue'[139] between Tom and his mute daughter with which *Give Me Your Answer, Do!* opens, we witness the final version of an attempted homecoming, restrained physically within an asylum, but unrestrained in the avenues of nonsense and self-deception into which the perverse imagination of the father can wander in its attempt to escape reality and despair and to keep open the routes to hope. (We recall that in discussing children's literature we noted the fact that 'nonsense' speech can become nihilistic, and the way that Tom's nonsense talk to, or with, Bridget spills over into the play proper threatens the world of that play with a profound nihilism.) Where *Aristocrats* is a play about a house breaking up, *Give Me Your Answer, Do!* is about people permanently in transit, always at the threshold of some confrontation, strays from all the previous work putting down imaginary roots that are not even temporary because they find no ground to which they can relate.

Two modern notions of love suggest themselves here as referents for the Connollys, Fitzmaurices and Donovans: D. H. Lawrence's concept of marriage as 'a fight to the death' and, once again, the way that the family deals with the affections in O'Neill's *Long Day's Journey into Night* – people displaced by history and disoriented, alienated, defeated by the reality of family life. Lawrence's concept is an *agon*, in which death is the ultimate milestone towards which we each move at the speed of loneliness. 'Between now and [our] death', to paraphrase Friel, we encounter, in varying orders, faith, or lack of it, love or lack of it, affiliation and disaffection – 'life' *in toto* – and we try to make sense of it as far as it inflicts itself on us and as far as we involve ourselves in it. The *agon* of marriage is the struggle of self with other, and of self with self, within the hyphenation of man and woman, and the *agon* of family, as O'Neill shows it to us, is the wider struggle of the affections in a community which is at once the smallest and the largest world. In *Give Me Your Answer, Do!* Friel has thus pared down his domestic situation to the most elementary, and at the same time opened up *the* question to the widest possible range of answers. As we have noted above, the presiding word in this scenario is *danger*.

The binary and symbiotic nature of love underscores the question of identity – 'I need you, love' spells out the fact that each requires the other's acknowledgement and identification in order to exist, for the *agon* to continue. And it is also an admission addressed to love itself. But when we take into the equation the 'blindsight' so recently explored by Friel in *Molly Sweeney*, we realise that if we have sight but are not able to see (to be 'in the world but not of it') not only are we 'blind' to the truth but the world may be 'blind' to us – denying us our identity. And furthermore, if we are blind then we may be unable to see love, or to be seen by one who might love us.

When I first read the script of *Give Me Your Answer, Do!*, I wrote to Brian Friel, feeling that for once I had, like the playwright himself, a 'right to fail' as a critic:

> I am bewildered at what you are saying here. Even the title is pitched so ambiguously as to make everyone wonder what you want to know. What is the question to which you are begging/soliciting/enticing an answer? . . .
>
> Is this familiar territory or is it not? What I am experiencing here is a very anguished and anguishing play (which *Tennessee* also was for anyone brave enough to admit it) and one which goes to the depths of pretence and subterfuge and intense cruelty, and yet I want to know what is it that is new here, what new departure does it signal?. . .
>
> When you sent me *Molly Sweeney* I immediately greeted it as your most transparent play to date. I said I was certain of *its* certainty, its sure-footedness, its difference from, and affinities with, what had gone before. In the present case, I can't talk about transparency – the harmony and counterpoint in the text are extremely subtle and it has the same density and opacity as that of *Aristocrats* or *Translations*. But its sure-footedness is without question. There is a new voice here, a new departure which, for the first time since *Making History*, appears to offer no point of arrival. Like most of your plays it is ruthless, cruel, takes tremendous risks and justifies everything it sets out to do.
>
> But WHAT does it set out to do? This is where the bewilderment sets in. I would be a hopeless and undeserving critic if I thought for a moment that the play could not be explained in critical terms. It can. Everything you have written can be related to everything else, and this is no exception. But this play has been written out of a hurt and perhaps also an anger which has not been present in your work since the early days – since *Philadelphia*, perhaps. . .
>
> Is it just a stock-taking? (I don't think so.) Is it a lament for abandoned work? Is it a threnody for the idea of home and family? Is it simply a joke at the expense of the man from ---?[140] From the audience's point of view, the unease caused by the kind of soul-searching occasioned by *Tennessee* will be more acute this time round. It is vintage Friel in the sense that it starts all over again, goes back to the old wounds and re-examines them, makes an honest assessment and tries to find a *requiescat* without demanding such a thing. Your sureness of touch – that signature which as a recidivist you cannot help leaving on a play – lies in the fact that although you set out for pastures new, you cannot do so without bringing with you all your accumulated wisdom/scars/tears/echoes. This time the previous voices are resonating in a different way – the maddening questions are not quite the same, not quite what we had imagined.
>
> The play is magnificent – magnificent in its honesty, its courage and its singing. It is strong, more so than usual because it needs to be. More demanding on the audience, because you have decided that this is the way you find it necessary to go. More risk-taking, because you are becoming

more and more of a gambler, more willing to put your own life and
reputation on the chopping-block. You don't seem to need a quiet end or a
pretty one.[141]

To this, Friel replied:

> I think you found the play just that bit too mercurial, or at least difficult to
> locate in the 'canon' (I put that in commas because, I suppose, I find it
> embarrassing). You ask me where it came from. And of course the easy &
> immediate answer is the visit of the -- man. But that, I'm sure, was merely
> the casual trigger. The play surely – well, I strongly suspect – is the play of
> an elderly/old writer who has got to that selfish and boring, but
> nevertheless painful, stage where he tells himself he wants an overall
> assessment of what he has done – a judgement, a final verdict. He feels
> uncertainty can't be kept at bay any longer. In this fiction one aspect of that
> older writer (Garret) gets that public assessment – and is astute enough to
> know how worthless it is. The other aspect of that old writer (Tom),
> although he desperately wants that assessment – and meets that need by
> insisting Daisy and he are so broke they must have the money – finally
> turns his back on it on Daisy's insistence and chooses Necessary
> Uncertainty instead. And presumably goes on writing/living.
>   So – wonderfully creative as ever – amn't I back with the old threadbare
> dualities?
>   (Each of the other characters, too, is looking for a verdict, an answer to
> his/her dilemma. And settles for the Beckettian going on.)
>   And of course now that I offer this blunt summary I must withdraw it
> instantly, partly because it deprives the uncertainty of its necessariness, but
> also because – again I suspect – the play is not at all about Careers or
> Death or Judgement Day but about love continuing and its persistence in
> even hostile conditions and its final *necessity* in life. (And again each of the
> characters wrestles with that problem, that addiction.)[142]

Friel's use of the word 'threadbare' is telling – as is his repeated 'I
suspect'. The dualities are worn – not in the sense of being exhausted but
because the warp and the woof are left bare, without any consoling nap.
'Threadbare' emphasises that, for a playwright, the dualities are the
subject and the object of constant iteration, a perpetual return which is,
in Eliade's terms, mythic, an arrival which is also a departure.

But the fact that Friel offers two scenarios – one, the palpable reality of
the writer seeking a valuation, a finality, the other the intangible love-
hunger – demonstrates that the 'dualities' are in fact a pair of simultaneous equations, neither of which can be resolved without the other. If
'to be' means 'to be loved' and if, in Lawrentian terms,[143] all meaning is
derived from the equation <man=woman>, then the only place where our
affections can safely and successfully reside is in the fulcrum of the
equation. The necessary uncertainty means that there can be no 'either/
or', no opting for one or the other, but only a continuing unknown, where
one is left in the 'uncertainties, mysteries, doubts' of Keats's Negative

Capability.[144] But it also means that we continue to be uncertain about love, that the necessary context in which it persists and hungers is indefinite, 'without any irritable reaching after fact and reason'.[145]

That the play is 'difficult to locate' might surprise us, since the evidence of the 'canon' is littered throughout the text – the writer split into two (Tom and Garret), the mute child, the identification of the music. Even the word 'quagmire' recalls Gar's outburst about Ballybeg, where 'everybody . . . goes crazy sooner or later'. But it is 'difficult' in the sense that the 'addiction' to which Friel refers is more pronounced than anywhere in his work since *Crystal and Fox*. Where Crystal had said in utter despair 'I don't know you', we now witness Maggie recognising and confronting 'that shabby little swindler . . . that petty little thief' in the knowledge that 'there's something eternal about people like that' (*GMYAD* 67). 'I suppose he'll go on playing and dancing and stealing forever, won't he?'. Like Friel's own 'I suspect', Maggie's 'I suppose' contains its uncertainty, in this case a hope against hope that Jack will stop being Jack. But that would be 'against the grain' of what Jack is, and we must take him, like Frank Hardy, as 'playing and dancing and stealing' – the artist and performer and the petty thief of love all in one unholy trinity, from which none of the elements can be disengaged. What remains fascinating in Friel's work, and thus a source of renewal, is that the failure of love is never due to disloyalty, but that it is always brought about by betrayal – the seeming paradox being explained by the fact that we are always most loyal to those we are about to betray. We remain faithful to the beloved even when questioning or destroying love.

The 'dualities' are discussed in *Give Me Your Answer, Do!* as in a Russian or Greek play. The play is mythic in the sense that action is pared down to the minimum and the central question under discussion is that of identity, of the very essence of being. The question is no longer 'what do you want?' but 'how do I live?'

> I used to ask God: how do I live with that? Give me your answer, God. But he never told me (*GMYAD* 67).

The interface with the absolute remains inscrutable. The failure of communication between woman and god in this instance, or between man and 'Mr God' in the case of Tom and David Knight, turns the solitary human being once more towards the forsaken hearth. Tom and Daisy interrogate each other. Garret and Grainne excoriate each other. Maggie and Jack torment each other. Tom searches for meaning as he speaks to his ghostly absent daughter; David Knight, as he riffles through the life stories of others. Each – other.

'Give me your answer'. But what is the question? My own question to Brian Friel was 'what does it set out to do?', which was a naïve way of saying that at the time I could not discern the purpose of the play – a view which was shared by at least one drama critic, Mic Moroney, who commented 'no matter how closely you follow the will-o'-the-wisp of Friel's substantial intelligence, it's very difficult to run the more disturbing elements to ground . . . a deliberately inconclusive piece of writing'.[146] And it may be that there was no purpose, in the sense that for once Friel may have 'set out' from base with nothing in mind other than the 'aboutness' of the play, with no map, no trajectory and no place of arrival in mind – indeed, 'inconclusive' insofar as he may have had no intention of returning.

But, as we should know from our encounter with *Faith Healer*, it is not necessary for a play to have a purpose in order for a play to have an effect. Moroney concludes that 'Friel's fetishistic attention to his own text does worm its way uncomfortably into some private recess of your mind';[147] one leaves Brian Friel's theatre of memory bruised and perhaps restored, but certainly aware that one has travelled a long and punishing road and not simply in the company of his 'intelligence'. Put 'in touch with some otherness', it is not essential that we identify the source or nature of the other. When we reach 'home' after such an evening, 'home' has changed and so have we. In any case, therefore, the question will be different as soon as it is asked, because a proposition once uttered can never be the same again. 'I need you, love' is more a question than an answer, always subjunctive, provisional.

Walter Heisenberg formulated his 'principle of uncertainty' in 1927: 'the more precisely we determine the position, the more imprecise is the determination of velocity and *vice versa*'.[148] Quantum mechanics, poetry, passion – in all of them, the need for uncertainty, the inevitable doubt. To create: to attempt to still, even for a moment, the state of flux, to hold the elements in the balance, whether they be electrons, philosophies or the vowels and consonants of love, is to enter the shadowlands, to become an exile from science and art, reality and fiction, to encounter the pretences of science and the truth of art. As soon as it is said, the object – the quark, the loved one, the nightingale – has flown on, has become other again.

One question which I posed in this context when writing a programme note for *Give Me Your Answer, Do!* is: 'what is a writer?'[149] In previous plays Friel had put in front of his audience versions of the writer: map-makers, translators, historians, do-it-yourself philosophers, priests, politicians, schoolteachers, charlatans – all those whose skill depends on the pre-existence of *the word*, those who live by the book and are lived by the book; all those who submit to the idea of myth, of language which becomes fabular as soon as it is spoken. To define *myth* as 'a purely fictitious narrative', as does the *Oxford English Dictionary*, is to limit the word to its popular and traditional role as the antonym of *legend*, as the lurking place of unreal monsters. Myth, for the Greeks, was making words alive. To live with myth is to employ words as a metaphor of the imagined place – 'faithful to more than the measurable'. The paradigms of the absolute phenomena are translated into bearable meaning, but they are still imprecise on the side of the wonderful, the unknown which can be apprehended but not comprehended.

When we see Garret and Grainne tearing each other to pieces, or Maggie exposing the despicable side of her husband, we are privy to intimacies which are petty in their significance to the rest of the world but of overwhelming proportions within the ambit of their own hearth. And it is this naked truth that can kill. Friel brings us face to face with this nakedness in an uncompromising fashion. It has been hinted at in *Wonderful Tennessee* and *Molly Sweeney*. He has been moving towards it resolutely and at the same time hesitantly. Perhaps the most alarming aspect of the audience's confrontation with this 'new voice' is that the play carries within it a contradiction. 'Audiences impose limits on how far we can go' says Grainne – the idea being that fictional characters can go only so far in portraying the emotional guerilla warfare in which 'real' people engage. But we do not in fact set such limits or expect them to be set for us. Medea, Eugene O'Neill and Samuel Beckett have proved that. If they do not exceed the limits in this particular play, Friel has shown us that it is quite possible to do so. It is a return to the barbarous love of *Crystal and Fox*, where no limits can contain the violence of emotions, whether in dreams or waking life. It is a return to the emotive life of *A Month in the Country*, where passion is nicely contained only because we are made aware of how very easily it can spill over into the auditorium.

Maggie Donovan speaks of the 'deformed contour' of her life shaped by her husband. But contours are not boundaries: they are the sinews and musculature and nervous system of change. To put the map of Maggie's psyche with its deformed contours beside that of her husband is to lay bare the privacies of more than two simple souls. It exposes the hurt that is the companion of love, and it makes it clear that the family and the hearth are the starting place of politics.

Many elements of the play are first-time occurrences in Friel's work – a sign not necessarily of the continuing fertility of his invention but more of the fact that this is a more blunt and explicit play than its predecessors. Although there have been 'asylum cases' in the past, this play shows us a girl *in* an asylum; although we have previously seen various types of wordsmith, for the first time we actually see two novelists in contention; where we have seen the motherless family re-imagining an invisible womanhood, here we see no less than three wives, two of them mothers in the same family. Thus the elements at which Friel has hinted, sometimes subtly, sometimes brutally, are exposed: madness is not discounted or refracted, it is wheeled in, centre stage; the self-sacrificing role of the wife is told in her own words; and the value of a writer – indeed, the ontology of the writer and of writing – is discussed openly rather than obliquely.

And although we have witnessed the telling of truths and the interweaving of improbable fictions, nowhere have so many admissions been made by Friel in a single play. The 'truth' is told of and by each character, 'truth' which eliminates futile pretence and puts in its place unpalatable reality – the trivial in place of the fantastic, the sordid instead of the glamorous, the lived rather than the imagined. Tom and Daisy confront the reality of their daughter's situation; they confront their financial situation; and when Daisy pretends that the telephone line is faulty (rather than cut off), we already know that she is lying. We discover that David Knight has not come unsolicited to Ballybeg – Tom has invited him. Jack's 'boa-constrictor' shoes, made in Italy, are English imitation leather; he is not a great artist, simply 'a cocktail pianist of some modest competence' (31) and a petty thief with the ability to 'summon amnesia' (33) to erase each successive incident. Maggie is a doctor who cannot face the truth about her own illness – 'she left the last man [doctor] because he gave her straight answers' (37). Writers, we learn, are 'shits' (22), 'icy and self-centred and always outside' (36). The most telling fact about these revelations and admissions is not that they are necessarily *the* 'truth', but that they effectively confront the antecedent 'truths' which have lost their validity, their context.[150]

We have met a displaced creature in a bed previously in Friel's work: Cass McGuire. But where Cass is voluble in her mutiny against the role she is asked to play, Bridget Connolly is locked into what we might call the 'perspex cube of [her] unshakable autism'.[151] That she does scream her hurt and her anger is vouchsafed to us only by courtesy of her nurse. As 'the child' she is the ultimate enigma. She is both colonised by the absurd stories told by her father (which are absurd only in the degree to which they exaggerate the 'real' world, not in their kind) and she is banished from home, her exile diminishing if not negating the meaning of 'home'. She is the unexplained shadow which casts itself over the play, her name mentioned solicitously whenever we need to be reminded that the mad are our own fault and our own judgement on ourselves, that they are beautiful and sacred and terrible.

Bridget is the admonition who warns her parents that there is no such place as home. Her silence can be read as a refusal to acknowledge not merely the laws of the rational but the very tenets of language itself. Molly Sweeney's privacy culminates here. Bridget *is* the 'cost of love'. If we look back over Friel's work we can see how far he has brought his reflection on, and depiction of, that cost: the uncrossable gap between father and son in *Philadelphia*; the shutting out of Cass; the intent wounding by which Fox Melarkey and Frank Hardy display their bewilderment; the fumblings of *Aristocrats*; the elision and reclamation of Mabel Bagenal in *Making History*; and in all Friel's versions of Chekhov and Turgenev, the alternating chill and fire with which love and longing are expressed and retracted, which is signalled early in *Give Me Your Answer, Do!* with the declamatory quotation from Chekhov, 'happiness isn't for us' (*GMYAD* 19).

But Bridget is both symbol and symptom of 'the cost of love'. In herself, she personifies the cata-strophe to the silent figure in Strindberg's *The Stronger* – an unutterable strength in whose shadow lesser beings define themselves. She takes the lines from *Translations* – 'confusion is not an ignoble condition' (*Tr.* 67) and 'uncertainty in meaning is incipient poetry' (*Tr.* 32) – and ennobles them by eliminating the need for translation. One was Hugh's *envoi* to Jimmy Jack, excusing his embarrassment with Athene; the other was Owen's *apologia* for his hesitation in translating Lancey's English. Taken together, in the context in which *Translations* ends, they represent the confusion over the renaming of Baile Beag, the imposition of a new education system, Maire's failed entente with Yolland and her need for English, and the homesickness – 'the *desiderium nostrorum*' – which turned Hugh and Jimmy Jack from heroes into public house patriots on their march to Sligo in 1798. These failures of translation no longer exist because, as Daisy declares,

> uncertainty is necessary. He [Tom] must live with that uncertainty, that necessary uncertainty. Because there can be no verdicts, no answers. Indeed there *must* be no verdicts. Because being alive is the postponement of verdicts (*GMYAD* 79–80).

It is the permanent non-presence of Bridget which provides the 'context' for this loving because 'Bridget is beyond knowing' (79) and it is this which defines the household. Everything else which occurs in the play emanates from Bridget's beyond-ness, her untouchability, her immunity from knowing, *gnosis*. She is both a saving and an annihilating angel. One recalls the character of Sylvie in Lawrence Durrell's *Avignon Quintet*, 'the great question mark',[152] 'frozen into the total madness of insight', of whom it is said 'although there are distinct signs of madness, to call her mad would be to put all ontology to the question'.[153] Durrell also says 'The mad must be people without selves: their whole investment is in the other, the object. They are ruled by the forces of total uncertainty'.[154] The coincidence of this view with the themes we have pursued in the current study suggests that the 'cost of love' is intimately engaged with the nature of the self and its shadow: the I/not-I enigma, the question of existence as dependent on perception, and the master-servant relationship as exhibited in the husband-as-artist, wife-as-subaltern symbiosis, are the stages on which the unstoppable quest for identity always encounters the unmoving fact of uncertainty and can find no way around it.

The most complex set of 'truths' ever unpacked by Friel is that contained in Daisy's speech at the play's conclusion, when she sets out the reasons why Tom should not accept the American offer. All through the play, characters have come up for 'assessment' – Tom himself, Garret, Maggie ('more assessments, more appraisals – spare me' – 29), and Bridget; but all settle for 'ambiguity' (29) or 'uncertainty' (33). 'Don't you remember?' Maggie asks Daisy about her childhood; 'I think I do. I'm not sure' she replies (26). 'Have you any love for him [Tom]?' Maggie asks Daisy.

DAISY: One of Mother's forthright questions.
MAGGIE: Have you?
DAISY: I think I have.
MAGGIE: But you've thought of leaving him?
DAISY: Oh, yes. Many times.
MAGGIE: But will you?
DAISY: I don't know. Perhaps. Ask again tomorrow. (35)

When the time comes for the argument to embrace 'necessary uncertainty', the case for taking the offer is rehearsed: confirmation that Tom's work is 'good', that it is of value, giving him the freedom to '*dare*'; a new comfortable home; 'a better place for Bridget'. But against that, 'Bridget is beyond knowing', discomfort is tolerable, and 'somehow bills will always be met' (96). Life is the subjunctive; definition is death.

This position has been reached, as it always is in Friel, not by the activity of some external agent (and here the presence of David Knight is of no more imperative significance than that of Dodds in *The Freedom* or Tom Hoffnung in *Aristocrats*) but in *isolation*. Bridget is isolated from her 'home' and her parents are isolated from the world. When Daisy says she cannot gauge the importance of Tom's work because 'I have nothing to compare it with' (12) she does not mean that she has no means of comparing Tom's work with that of others such as Garret. She is speaking of 'forty years of Tom's life' which is known only to him and *perhaps* to her – an eternal privacy which has spilled over at certain points into family life and into public life as published and unpublished writing. The judgement which matters is the internalised assessment, and the 'affirmation' so much desired is not that of an external 'Mr God' but of oneself. Even though Daisy recognises that Tom craves acknowledgement to give him 'the courage? – the equilibrium? – the necessary self-esteem? – just to hold on' (21) she also recognises – or makes the judgement – that uncertainty is more necessary than self-esteem, that the critical path of their love is tracked through anxiety and self-contempt.

But at the very end of the play, as Tom resumes his play-acting with Bridget, Bridget herself emerges once more as the powerful non-presence, the 'other' of their life and love. As Tom enters into a rhapsodic love scene with his daughter, Daisy realises that from her recently re-discovered position of strength as helpmeet she has once more retreated to that of handmaiden, as Tom addresses Bridget as 'my silent love, my strange little offspring' and tells her that *if* he could succeed in overcoming his writer's block, 'I would come straight back here and fold you in my arms; and you and I would climb into a golden balloon – just the two of us – only the two of us' . . . (84). Daisy's gesture of despair as she witnesses this next betrayal is the most frightening and disturbing moment in a play so bleak that one wonders in trepidation where Friel might ask us to accompany him after this.

8

MAGIC

If this were played upon a stage now
I could condemn it as an improbable fiction.[1]

A QUESTION OF FORM

In *Give Me Your Answer, Do!* Brian Friel misquotes these lines from
Twelfth Night: 'I would condone it as improbable fiction' (*GMYAD* 52).
To condemn or condone? This chapter examines Friel's stagecraft and his
attitude to stagecraft, principally in the light of his four 'versions' or
'translations' of texts by Chekhov and Turgenev, and in doing so it also
examines his use of the unreal or improbable as a way of bringing people
home to truths – the magic which, whether welcome or not, takes place
in the theatre when the play achieves its effect, the makebelieve or
pretence which we can either condone (because it provides us with an
acceptable fiction) or condemn (because we find it an unacceptable truth).
   Chekhov said

> Let the things that happen on the stage be as complex and yet just as
> simple as they are in life. For instance, people are having a meal at the
> table, just having a meal, but at the same time their happiness is being
> created, or their lives are being smashed up.[2]

Konstantin Stanislavsky, who was one of Chekhov's chief collaborators in
the Moscow Art Theatre, observed that 'his plays are full of action, not in
their external but in their inner development. In the very inactivity of his
characters a complex inner activity is concealed'.[3] And Thomas Kilroy,
writing in the programme for Friel's version of *Three Sisters*, pointed
out that 'there are no heroes in Chekhov because he understood how the
process of history diminishes even the most Napoleonic ego' – instead, we
see a playwright concerned with 'inconsequentiality . . . ordinary helplessness . . . who accepted completely that he was himself subject to the

same life as that of his creations'. In suggesting that 'at this stage of our century [1981] this single fact may appear revolutionary' Kilroy was expressing much of the difficulty encountered by contemporary critics in assessing Friel.

It is more possible than it was in the late 1980s to gain a sense of what Friel's stagecraft involves. Firstly, because he has written more plays and, since they are of variable natures and qualities, more chance of detecting the rises and falls of his artistic temperament and his strategies and skills in construction. Secondly, because there have been new departures in his work which have not necessarily brought a change in these skills or strategies, but have instead highlighted the perennial disregard for form or 'pattern' which becomes evident not in the act of writing but in the act of having written.

The participants in Friel's Russian plays continually and painfully refer to the trivia of their lives because it is from their substratum (or *sublimen*) that an awareness is built up of the meaninglessness of life, of the fact that it is in the trivia themselves that such meaning resides. As Elena says in *Uncle Vanya*: 'You know that it isn't the great battles that cause the most injury. It's all these petty squabbles, these corroding jealousies, these small domestic hatreds that eat away at our lives' (*UV* 34), which echoes Tusenbach's observation in *Three Sisters*:[4]

> Strange thing is that in the end it's never the great passions, the great ambitions that determine the course our lives take, but some trivial, piddling little thing that we dismiss and refuse to take seriously; until it's too late. And then we recognise that the piddling little thing has manipulated us into a situation that is irrevocable and . . . final (*Sisters* 101: *original ellipsis*).

As George Steiner says of Greek tragedy, there is 'a dialectical reciprocity between what is wholly foreseen and yet shatters the mind',[5] and in this respect the work resembles a melodrama in which villain and victim, storyline and outcome are known from the beginning and fate is acknowledged in place of action.

At the heart of the debate as to whether or not plays by Friel such as *Wonderful Tennessee* or *Making History* are in fact plays at all (because they appear to lack dramatic content and development) is the debate about the nature of drama. All drama is pretence, and all ritual is pretence, moving towards that point where the observers become participants and their credulity becomes acceptance and belief.

Here, form and content are one. Christopher Murray has said that 'Form, for Friel, . . . is something to be elicited from the content as it discloses itself in composition, the search for form is a search for meaning'.[6] When that meaning is found, the story will have been given its form, because, as with the memory of the childhood fishing expedition, belief occurs at the point of connection between memory and identity. The Russians are continually telling themselves such stories, believing them to be true even – or especially – when they know them to be untrue.

I have already referred to the fact that Friel's plays often succeed on radio, where argument is allowed to dominate form, in monopolising the 'private conversation'. Conversely, many of his plays, *Faith Healer* in particular, leave themselves open to criticism because they appear to lack dramatic impact. Moreover, in the 'family reunion' plays – especially *Living Quarters* and *Aristocrats* – it might seem that Friel is experimenting with form without involving the audience at all, that he has adopted a self-indulgence which Michael Longley, in his own attempt at poetic freedom, has called 'a fuck off to form'.[7]

The stasis of *Faith Healer* caused it to flop in New York, and yet *Molly Sweeney*, with a similar sequence of monologues, succeeded almost twenty years later, against the playwright's expectations.[8] The failure of *Faith Healer* was not Friel's first lesson in what the American audience would or would not bear, however, nor his last. In 1969 *Lovers* was playing in Los Angeles and Dan Sullivan of the *Los Angeles Times* wrote:

> Blurb-backlash is the only way I can account for the almost palpable air of disappointment that hung around the lobby of the Lindy Opera House during the intermission . . . The audience had come to see Art Carney in what sounded like a smash comic vehicle, and what had Carney done for them so far? Read them a couple of death notices.[9]

Even as perceptive a critic as Anthony Roche has acknowledged that his first response to reading the text was that its form was *not* essentially dramatic and that he now recognises not only that it is 'the most theatrical of Friel's plays' but that 'like Beckett, Friel has increased, not lessened, the dramatic potential by reducing the setting and props to a minimum'.[10] Others, however, insist that what is not shown cannot exist. George Hughes has argued that:

> Seamus Deane says that *Faith Healer* 'shows a man creating his own death by coming home out of exile'. It's not difficult to understand how Deane comes to say this, but in fact the play doesn't show it at all. In so far as it is concerned with the return of an exile, it *tells* what has happened and *shows* nothing.[11]

The difficulty here seems to be in the word 'shows'. We cannot see what Molly Sweeney can see, but lack of physical sight should not deprive us of metaphysical insight. Frank Hardy himself, in the passage I reiterated in Chapter 7, *tells* us what happened even though he doesn't, and in telling he *shows* – he opens a door into the yard that is our way of knowing, our Memory Theatre. To allow anxiety about the form of the play to interfere with that route to knowledge is foolish.

In this respect *Living Quarters* is a play about playwriting, *more text than experience*. It is due particularly to Friel's sense, also evident in *Aristocrats*, of 'the burden of the incommunicable',[12] the problem of finding ways to place, on the narrow back of dramatic conversation and gesture, a family history, a description of social disease, or a political movement, so that his statements might not only address, but also engage, the audience *within* the fiction, a technique he has been pursuing since he wrote 'Fine Day at Glenties' and Cass's exclamations against her author.

However, while Friel uses the possibilities of stagecraft as tools in a clinical analysis of his own trade, he cannot pour out his absolute concepts of freedom and love without employing the nice paradigms and intermediate levels of knowledge which we have noted, or he would drown the stage with the immediacy of what he has to say; the barbarity of his discourse on language itself might be quite incomprehensible if he did not adopt mediating effects such as we find in *Translations*. Of course we cannot know the nature of such unmediated drama because a form has yet to be found to accommodate its content. One can only speculate what might happen if Friel did *not* use drama to put a distance between himself and the rest of the world, and between his conceptions and their ultimate audience.

But there is a further problem associated with this unknown quantity: is Friel using technical experimentation and distancing in order to avoid engaging in that very discourse which his 'community' demands of him? Does he allow his characters too great a freedom, granting them the same dispensation he gives himself, a distance between them and the real world? In the sense that time itself is a device, then the present, in which past play is experienced, is in fact the future of the play itself. Friel the playwright exists in the past of the characters themselves, while audiences exist in the present and future. In *Living Quarters* Friel mediates the concept of absolute being, with its unlimited possibilities, by means of the adjudicator 'Sir', whose ledger or bible represents all possible and apocryphal texts, both those events which actually happen and all those which might happen. Past possibilities (what might have been) become future choices (what might be).

It is also this, rather than the fact that she is an imagined person, which prevents Cass from communicating, establishing shared meaning with the audience. Revenants on the stage are moving through time as well as space. In *Living Quarters* only the fact that the author adopts film technique in switching the flow of action allows him to arrest the time sequence and interpose the audience's 'now' into the otherwise uninterrupted time continuum. The switch means that at one moment the Butler family believes in its own relative present, while the audience regards its individual members as dispersed, dead, past; at the next, the stage becomes an experimental space occupied by the audience as part of the 'mythological present' directed by 'Sir'. The major question is whether, after we have gone home, the Butlers have any existence. Similarly, somewhere in the time continuum, Cass, Trilbe, and Ingram continue to rhapsodise; but they only have meaning each time they are summoned by our reproductive imagination. We are Friel's accomplices in this access to privacy.

In this sense drama is a time-capsule or fifth province in which our problems can be depersonalised and thus solved *without* rancour or acrimony or the penetration of the private by the public world (or *vice versa*) but *with* tenderness, compassion and dignity. As already suggested, Friel has, on occasions, abandoned – superficially at least – those characteristic mediating qualities. Is the stiletto of *Faith Healer*, Frank Hardy's 'killer instinct', mitigated or even transformed, partly by the seduction of the poetry and partly by the inherent finesse of the gesture itself? The medium employed is a simple one, whether it is court of law, court of chivalry, cabinet room or the sacred wood of the senses: the time-capsule in each case mediates between the absolutes of space, time and being, by setting a distance between us and the immediate realities of place, past and person.

If we can for a moment regard Friel's drama as 'ritual' we could profitably consider the 'liminality' of his writing as a special form of communal process; that is, we can see not only how he places himself as tympanum between two worlds or matrices, but how he engages the audience in his liminality, as the drama-ritual translates us from one state to another. As Victor Turner says:

> it is the analysis of culture into factors and their free recombination in any and every possible pattern, however weird, that is most characteristic of liminality, rather than the establishment of implicit syntax . . . like rules or the development of an internal structure of logic in relations of opposition and mediation.[13]

This is exactly what Friel sets out to achieve in *Living Quarters* and *Faith Healer*, and to a lesser extent in *Aristocrats*. The 'ledger' of each play is an infinite number of pre-determined possibilities, and it would not matter if the actors in those dramas were to abandon all convention and address each other or the audience in unprecedented babel. But of course this is impossible. Frank Butler in *Living Quarters* 'has no fluency in love words' (*LQ* 61) and all the characters in these two plays lack fluency in 'freedom' words.

Although, therefore, Friel is almost dismayingly conventional in his view of the playwright's function, and therefore in his pursuit of it through stagecraft, as always (with the exception of *Faith Healer* and *Making History* in which he abandons all convention and returns to the condition of radio drama) he is so *ingénu* in his response to the demands of his characters, that the fusion of form and content is of little moment. In this sense, his greatest innovation, and his greatest potential failing, lies in an originality of which he avows he is only the intermediary, 'a ministry without responsibility'. He occasionally fails because he does not sufficiently warn his audience of the dangers inherent in this, although a good grounding in Chekhov would be an excellent preparation for the demands he makes on us.

We have to accept the 'tricks' which Friel plays on both audience and players in *Living Quarters* in order to see how vitally he needs this distance in order to advance his personal project. Because he has not yet retreated from a position where he claims the primacy of language, these 'tricks', such as sociologist-ex-machina, baby-alarm (Judas-hole), the armchair rhapsody and play-within-play, are less important than they would be if he were more intent on experimenting with silence or with entirely new dramatic structures. The experiment with silence has proceeded as far as the *dance* – a dramatic symbol which, even in, *Dancing at Lughnasa*, cannot be dissociated from the stage device of the intermittent radio delivery – and in *Dancing at Lughnasa* Friel has approached, more resolutely than heretofore, the idea (for that is all it is) of the dance as an alternative to speech: dance assuming (as a visual dramatic device) the role of language. It is, as all Friel's work, risky, and the demands he places on directors through text and stage directions are almost self-defeating. However, there was an indication in *Dancing at Lughnasa* that he was in fact approaching the idea of new dramatic structures, in a manner congruent to that of Tom Murphy but divergent from that of Tom MacIntyre, which, by means of its intellectualism rather than its intuition, could offer a novel challenge to contemporary Irish-English playwriting.

Contrivance tends to interpose itself between the audience/reader and the author's meaning. Like all effective stage design, it should enhance and decorate the play, underlining its subtleties and drawing out its inner meaning, rather than creating them and being their raison d'être. Friel's use of the private/public technique and of the quotation from Burke in *Philadelphia*,[14] for example, *are not the reason for the play*. The various devices Friel employs, especially the variety of 'truths' and 'realities' which he presents to us in *The Freedom*, *Faith Healer* and *Cass*, the shuffling of the cards in *Living Quarters*, the anachronisms in *Aristocrats*, would be doing him ill service if they left us searching for consistency among the ample debris of inconsistency and doubt which he provides.[15] These are put before us as examples of the various perceptions, the ranges of possibility which can be experienced between whatever extremes he establishes, absurd and momentous, known and unknown, private and public.

Friel also sets out to catch a conscience with his plays. To that extent (and in that sense only) he places great importance on his traps. The complexity and sophistication of the traps will vary according to whether he simply wishes to seduce his public audience into a vision of the world, or to map out a private territory of the characters themselves. It is as if in the 'love' plays he has dredged up emotion in buckets, and in the plays of the 1970s he looked more analytically and formulated some tentative replies to the maddening questions. As we have seen in *Faith Healer*, he begins to come home with less catastrophe, and he completes the journey in *Translations*. But in looking at the strategy he adopts in *Living Quarters* and *Aristocrats* we must maintain the distinction between the public drama which peoples the actual world with imagined characters, and the private play-within-play which confuses the imagined world with the actual.

VERSIONS OF THE TRUTH

The art of coming to terms with Friel's 'versions' of his truth is not to seek for an accommodation between 'reality' and the 'perception of reality', but to accept whatever version is offered at the time. Thus in *Aristocrats* the lawn is simultaneously a lawn, a former tennis court, a former croquet lawn, or an actual game of croquet, depending on which character is investing it with memory, perspective or travesty. There is no point trying to rationalise this; to talk of various perspectives as operating on different 'levels' is pointless. The antiphonal monologues of 'The Illusionists' have been stretched out in *Faith Healer*, shuffled in *Living Quarters* and sublimated in *Aristocrats*. And the latter two are works which we can regard as early attempts at his versions of *Three Sisters* and *Fathers and Sons*.[16]

More significant than the physical devices or mechanisms are the linguistic and iconic 'tricks of the trade' by means of which Friel sets certain rhythms and expectations alive in the consciousness of the audience. The iconic strategy is that of the stock characters who carry within them the 'grain of the voice' (as we have seen Barthes call it) – the figures of authority (schoolmaster, priest, tribal chief), those of inhibited or reduced capacity (the simpleton, the mute, the lame); the sullen, the bossy, the bewildered, the fractious, the enervated and the energised. Always subject to surprise, to the unexpected, to the essential change, they nevertheless represent that tarot which we met in Friel's assessment of Glenties – 'hundreds of people behaving naturally' which is 'the real thing, the superb performance'.

The closing directions of *Aristocrats* tell the director: '*One has the impression that this afternoon – easy, relaxed, relaxing – may go on indefinitely*' (*Ar.* 85). The lights which come down slowly on that scene might well come up on the opening of *Dancing at Lughnasa*. When writing *Translations* Friel discussed 'the atmosphere in which the real play lurks',[17] and nowhere does place emerge more strongly as character than in these plays, in which he brings to some sort of resolution the dilemma sub-liminally (or interstitially) expressed by Casimir in *Aristocrats*: I'd really like to talk to you because I think you – I think you understand . . . (*he gestures towards the house*) . . . what it has done to all of us' (*Ar.* 70). As with *Translations, Lughnasa* and *Wonderful Tennessee* (all of them set in an August, which is on the threshold of autumn), the Russian plays take place under a summer sun. And there are other echoes: at the start of the second scene of *A Month in the Country* we hear '*From the distance the sound of Kolya doing five-finger exercises on the piano*' (*MiC* 36) and in *Fathers and Sons* Arkady says: 'I love that piece. I remember Father and Mother playing it together when I was very small' (*FS* 23) – 'I remember', when coupled with an off-stage piano, becomes a potent link to lost childhood.

The linguistic strategy will be evident to any reader of the 'canon': appeals to memory, a sense of laconic urgency, a hinted absence, an emotion triggered by a phrase or an inflection. Thus the anxiety in *Philadelphia* – keep talking – becomes in *Faith Healer* 'I *know* that he *had* to keep talking' (*FH* 44); in *The Mundy Scheme* the 'political canon' of one cabinet minister is '"*When in danger, keep talking*"' (*Mundy* 191); in *The Gentle Island* one of the emigrants '*has decided that by keeping talking this situation can best be handled*' (*GI* 15); always the deferral of embarrassment, the moment when the truth has to be faced: 'anything, anything at all that keeps the occasion going' (*CC* 92).[18] It is always better to look back to a redeemable past than to move forward into unknown territory. Casimir's 'When I think of Ballybeg Hall it's always like this' (*Ar.* 14) becomes Michael's 'When I cast my mind back' (*DL* 1, 71). In *Three Sisters* this reminiscence becomes a series of urgent appeals to a shared memory: 'D'you remember the day . . . D'you remember a birthday party you had. . .?' (*Sisters* 10, 78).

The subjunctive binds all Friel's Russian plays together, with their constant recourse to 'if', 'perhaps' and 'almost'. Arrivals from the future and departures into the past form a provisional present which hovers on its own threshold like a man permanently stammering and in a state of vertigo. Those keynotes of his own plays – such as 'Sorry – sorry' – pour out of the Russian mouth even more cruelly (*Sisters* 70, *FS* 3, 29, *MiC* 23, *UV* 29). In *A Month in the Country*, for example, we have a poignant echo of Ben's difficulty in *Living Quarters*: 'even if I caught her in my arms, as I wanted to, and said Sorry – sorry – sorry – sorry, . . it would be no good, no good at all' (*MiC* 58). But they provide the advent for some of Friel's most carefully crafted cadences – the set-pieces in which he builds the ladders to hope by means of which emotion is poured out and affection is voiced. For example, the use of the word 'and' in Sonya's speech about Astrov in *Uncle Vanya* which on each occasion lifts and speeds her obvious pride and joy, her love for Astrov which cannot yet be spoken:

> He believes that forests make a harsh climate milder. That is a scientific fact, he says. And the milder your climate, the less energy you spend battling with nature. And the less energy you spend battling with nature, the *more* energy you have to pursue gentler, more civilised habits. And the more gentle and more civilised people become, naturally the more sophisticated their thoughts, the more eloquent their speech, the more graceful their movements – indeed the more beautiful they become. Honestly! It all sounds like an incredible leap from planting more trees – I know – I know. But it has a perfect logic, hasn't it? Just encourage that milder climate with your forests and eventually – eventually – a society will evolve where learning will blossom and people will become hopeful again and men will treat women more gently and with a little more consideration (*UV* 23).

Cadence is also the occasion of *cadenza*, the musical freedom to express one's private emotions, of which we have many examples in *A Month in the Country*:

> This house, this style, this grace, this ease, this refinement, this symmetry, this elegance – for a month I pretended that of course I wasn't impressed. But I was overwhelmed – I was in awe, Natalya – mute with awe. And at the centre of all this elegance and grace, there you were – the core, the essence, the very epicentre of it, holding it all in place, releasing, dispensing its wonders. And you noticed me and you spoke to me and you were kind to me – to me! – Aleksey Belyayev, a nobody in shabby clothes holding the delicate hand of this luminous creature (*MiC* 82).

Providing a link between the iconic and the linguistic is a gerundive reference to characterisation. For example, one of Friel's verbal images is that of the fox: we encounter it in Fox Melarkey, the embodiment of hope and despair; Hugh O'Neill is dubbed 'the fox' by his English hosts; in *The Enemy Within* one monk calls another 'a crafty old fox' (*EW* 54) and at the opening of *Living Quarters* 'Sir' explains that the rest of the cast have 'the idea of circumventing me, of foxing me, of outwitting me' (*LQ* 12). Insofar as 'Sir' represents the inescapable truth of the Ledger, the Russian foxes spend their lives trying to avoid releasing the truths which build up in their homes. Just as Sonya and her kin build up linguistic confections to support the weight of hope and endurance, so the men eventually tell truths in order to bring those confections tumbling down. The deflationary effect of Astrov's outburst to Vanya prepares the latter for his own attack on Serebriakov:

> Face up to what *is* man. The life we lead is without hope. Face that. The life we lead is futile. Face that. Maybe future generations will discover a way of living that is full and fulfilling – and with no self-delusions. Good luck to them! As for us – ! (*Laughs*) there must be a positive side, a dip up, as Telegin puts it. Yes, there is. We have lived out our days in a mean-spirited society but to our eternal credit we have held on to an *idea* of other possibilities, of better things. Aren't we magnificent? (*UV* 73)

In *Three Sisters*, the most vicious of the plays as far as the naked revelations of unlived life are concerned, truths come tumbling out with a passion that is otherwise denied to their speakers:

> What are you all staring at me for? Natasha's having an affair with Protopopov – stare at that for a change! But you'd rather not, wouldn't you? You'd rather sit with your eyes closed while Natasha and Protopopov are carrying on in front of your very noses! (*Sisters* 75)

> My wife looks after me well. My wife is a fine woman. My wife is an honest, straight-forward, high-principled woman. Oh dear God . . . May I tell you about my wife, doctor? May I talk to you in confidence as a doctor, as a friend? My wife is an animal – a mean, myopic, gross, grubbing animal. There's not a trace of humanity left in her. And yet – and yet – and yet – having said all that, I still love her, doctor. God-damnit, I love her, *love* her for God's sake, love her despite her vulgarity, despite everything she is, everything she does, despite everything that's despicable in her (*Sisters* 98).

Which leads us to the much wider meaning of betrayal:

> Anybody who betrays a wife or a husband is equally capable of betraying his country as well (*UV* 16).

As I noted in the first edition of this study, Friel subverted the original text of *Fathers and Sons* by introducing an explicit statement on the theme of betrayal which he intended to place in the final scene of the play by gratuitous reference to Leonard McNally, composer of the song 'Sweet Lass of Richmond Hill':

> PAVEL: McNally's story is interesting. He was a key member of a revolutionary group called the United Irishmen. I'm talking about 60 years ago, in Ireland, obviously. Anyhow, years after McNally was dead and buried, his revolutionary friends made a remarkable discovery: that right from the very beginning and all through the revolution [*sic*] McNally had betrayed them – he had been a spy for the English all along. Interesting, isn't it?

ARKADY: What is?

PAVEL: That a man who composed some good songs and wrote a few good plays[19] was also capable of betraying his friends. Maybe the two instincts – for creativity and for betrayal – maybe they're complementary. Maybe they're identical.

....

KATYA: I think I know what he's suggesting. Perhaps that creativity and betrayal are of a piece. Perhaps that loyalty and betrayal are of a piece . . . that freedom, real freedom, cannot co-exist with loyalty or with love . . . And I think he is also asking what happens when revolutionary friends fall out. Which is the more important – loyalty to the friendship or loyalty to the revolution? . . . And that's what's fascinating about Mr McNally. He was faced with neither of those dilemmas – betrayal endowed him with real freedom from all attachments.[20]

There thus exists, in Friel's deliberate connection between eighteenth-century Ireland and nineteenth-century Russia, some evidence that in the silent years after *Three Sisters* he had approached the question of McNally's sense of freedom as a dramatic study equivalent in the public arena to that of Frank Hardy in the private. *Fathers and Sons* gave him the space to go beyond his own society and current preoccupations in order to create parables (similar in their cadence to those of *Wonderful Tennessee*) which tell us less about the society than they do of the pre-occupations, and thereby to attempt a homecoming from the outside.

Criticism of Friel's recent work has concentrated on a perceived lack of development in the dramatic material. A brief examination of this criticism will guide us towards the real significance of his Russian plays. Irving Wardle, for example, complained that in *Dancing at Lughnasa* 'here is that wan figure, the middle-aged narrator, shovelling out information which the writer has not bothered to dramatise'.[21] And he attributed the emergence of the human complexities of the play to the moment when the radio 'Marconi' erupts and the dance happens. But he finished by calling the play 'a masterly piece of story-telling', suggesting that it is possible to provide a story without dramatising it, making it come alive by means of devices. (When Chekhov was writing *The Seagull* he worried that 'it came out like a story . . . I become once more convinced that I am not a playwright at all'.)[22]

For David Krause, the achievement in *Lughnasa* was 'theatrically effective and artistically disappointing', the dance itself being the 'too easily earned symbol of the play, a purely visual symbol of Friel's theme' – Friel's words 'lack the essential and fulsome poetry and rhythm of dramatic speech'[23] – whereas Frank Rich found that the play 'does exactly what theatre was born to do', which is to portray 'the inescapable drama of every life', and to 'uncover that eternal drama in stolen glances, in bursts of unexpected laughter, . . . that is the poetry of this play – its "dream music"'.[24]

In the case of *Molly Sweeney*, one critic observed that Friel was 'making himself into an antitheatrical writer' and that the play 'grows monotonously dirgelike as literature *and* theater' with an emphasis on language alone.[25] Here, Krause said 'it is a "story" more than a drama because Friel made the crucial decision to *narrate* rather than *dramatize* his premise and its unfolding . . . A courageous but static and failed artistic endeavor'.[26] Vincent Canby, for the *New York Times* found it 'less a play than a novella'.[27] Nancy Franklin, for the *New Yorker*, felt that she had attended 'a staged reading of an essay, not a theatrical work of the imagination . . . If it's drama you're looking for, stay home and read Oliver Sacks'.[28] Donald Lyons thought that 'if drama is dialogue, *Molly Sweeney* is not drama' but recognised that the author 'makes us compose the drama ourselves just as Molly must compose her material world, by imagination alone'.[29]

It is precisely the burden which Friel places on his audience – to compose their own drama – that seems to be the sticking point for his critics. That there is a religious implication in this notion – 'work out your own salvation with fear and trembling'[30] – is no accident, since this is a profoundly religious undertaking, not least in the case of the Russian plays, where we experience a particularly direct encounter with the concept of the 'soul'.

There is a sense in which Friel's idea (as we saw it mooted in 'The Theatre of Hope and Despair') of a theatre for the modern world in which 'God is dead' requires playwright, actors and audience to 'compose a drama' by developing new faith in both the individual and the 'constituency' – troubled, conflictual, riddled with doubt and contradiction but nonetheless a consciousness driven by the sense of quest – opening up afresh the idea of the imagination as an aristocratic conscience. While he was composing his most Chekhovian play, *Aristocrats*, Friel wrote: 'The imagination is the only conscience', thinking of both the writer's autonomous nature and the role he plays in 'forg[ing] the 300 imaginations [of the audience] into one perceiving faculty . . . dominat[ing] and condition[ing] them so they become attuned to the tonality of the transmission and consequently to its meaning'.[31] It is colloquially said that to understand one another people must 'speak the same language'. The trick in creating the 'one perceiving faculty' is to invent a language that sounds so natural that we believe it to be our own and thus accept what is said to us by means of it. Thus, to make the personal myth of his imagined voices into a credible myth which can become an acceptable ritual is the challenge to the playwright. And in finding within the Russian mind the coincidence of 'tonality' and 'meaning' Friel increases the psychic charge transmitted.

As Anthony Roche has cogently argued, 'contemporary Irish drama does not so much rely on a plot as on a central situation, whose implications are explored and unfolded in a process which is likelier to be circular and repetitious than straightforward . . .What the audience most often witnesses . . . are damaged people, on the verge of cracking up, lamenting the absence of wholeness in their lives and the people among whom they live, suffering the break-up of traditional forms of belief'[32] – like the Russians who give Friel access to language and emotions unavailable to him in Ireland but whose dilemmas are expressive of the same spirituality and the same spiritual anxieties. Why, after *Fathers and Sons*, did he return to Turgenev and *A Month in the Country*? 'I'm not sure. Maybe because he is 19th century Russian and I don't feel at all distant from that world'.[33]

In these two cases in particular – *Fathers and Sons* and *A Month in the Country* – the exercise of translation allowed Friel to clear away a writer's block which had been impeding him, thus freeing up his imagination for the creation of, respectively, *Making History* and *Wonderful Tennessee*. (Whether the version of *Uncle Vanya* will have had the same effect is yet to be seen.) In my view, this sense of liberation occurred not because Friel was turning away from preoccupations which, for some intangible reason, could not be addressed, but for the opposite reason: that the work of translation brought him to issues which could – and had to – be addressed if the force of the original was to be transferred to its new context. The helplessness of *Three Sisters*, especially coming two years after *Aristocrats*, the rage of *Fathers and Sons* and *Uncle Vanya*, the suppressed and confined passions of *A Month in the Country*, all accord with themes in Friel's own original work and bring him into the presence of cognate spirits which intensify those themes. That those 'spirits' are to be found in the people of the plays *and* in the fabric of the plays themselves – their settings, their timelessness, their lack of resolution – is what makes the process of playwriting in these cases so powerful.

As with the ensemble which is vital to the successful production of any play by Chekhov, so in Friel's work the inner complexity of the text can only be given voice when each player understands his own part and all the others. It is almost as if Friel follows the advice of Tom Connolly in *Give Me Your Answer, Do!*: 'Be faithful to the routine gestures and the bigger thing will come to you' (*GMYAD* 71). *Molly Sweeney* is Friel's most carefully calibrated play, because the voices are brought from the innermost recesses of conscience and memory and made to speak, with honesty and conviction, in a world where they can hold their own, can tell a story that is not only theirs, but ours. Even though the characters never address each other (and, as with the divided Gars in *Philadelphia*, must not look at each other) there is an intimacy between them which requires an exceptional degree of ensemble playing. Every gesture, every nuance, is crucial, because it is all part of an elaborate ceremonial, where any element which does not receive its proper weight and value can shake the fragile image of the first house. What these voices say has everything to do with rhythm, cadence and trope and their participation in the tragedies of everyday life. The plays only come right when those cadences find their real voice from within the text, because that is where the actor engages with the psychological reality of the character.

However compelling the magic may be, audiences leave Friel's theatre not wondering, but knowing that a statement, however intangible, has been made, that a finality of sorts, however brief, has been reached, and that it somehow concerns and affects them deeply.

A simple reading of his two published diaries reveals that for Brian Friel the process of writing a play is auditory: by making himself 'available' he is ready to give shape to the voices that he thinks he has heard. As (or if) the process continues, the articulation and the coherence increases until the playwright is sure of the nature of the presences who are occupying his mind. Then, it becomes necessary to 'brow-beat the material'[34] but this cannot commence until the play in essence is already 'there'.

On several occasions, Friel has referred to the text as a musical score 'composed with infinite care and annotated where necessary with precise directions. . . I look to the director and the actors to interpret that score exactly as it is written'.[35] Friel's insistence on the musical nature of the text was first expressed in 1972 and the presence of music, conceptually, within the text was recognised by Tyrone Guthrie in *Philadelphia* in 1965: 'meaning is implicit "between the lines" of the text; in silences; in what people are thinking and doing far more than in what they are saying; in the music as much as in the meaning of the phrase'.[36] Friel's assuredness concerning the 'finished' nature of his play text would seem arrogant were it not for the fact that directors of his work such as Joe Dowling and Patrick Mason confirm the completeness of the text and the fact that its coherence depends on two elements: the impossibility of changing any part of the script and the essentiality of the actors discovering the inner voice of the characters within the script. 'If you change a word of Friel', says Dowling, 'it sounds wrong. He's always right'.[37] (This was not always the case, however: when Hilton Edwards was preparing to direct

Philadelphia he requested, and achieved, a change in the play's structure which involved cutting a scene. Once this had been done, however, Friel maintained that 'I *know* now that every word of the play is vital'.)[38]

Some may find it ironical that a writer who has questioned the nature and status of authority both in society (*The Freedom of the City*) and in the theatre (*Living Quarters*) should, as an *author*, insist on the immutability of the text. If the playwright is god, then the director is his high priest, but for Friel to have referred to the work of the director as 'a bogus profession'[39] and to his function as 'a lollipop man'[40] – carrying the actors from text to performance in safety and by a recognised route – is to deny the shamanistic or divining role of the director. To have decided to take matters into his own hands in personally directing *Molly Sweeney* and *Give Me Your Answer, Do!* is to see god dispensing with his high priest and taking on that function himself. Friel has been criticised for this decision[41] and there can be no doubt, watching Patrick Mason initiating the actors – and the playwright himself – into the ritualistic nature of the text during early rehearsals of *Wonderful Tennessee*[42] that it is a necessary function closely related to that of the author.

This decision may have been occasioned by what Fintan O'Toole perceives as 'a loss of faith in the theatre' on Friel's part, in particular seeing *Making History* as 'a hesitant move into unknown territory' where the concept of failure was no longer 'counterbalanced by some mysterious faith'.[43] While I would not agree with the latter aspect of his commentary, it is clear that Friel does share at least in part in what O'Toole calls 'a crisis of faith in what the theatre can achieve' – something which has been evident in his work to some critics at least since his early years.

If we look at Friel's 'Russian' plays it is possible to understand both O'Toole's concern and its explanation. O'Toole sees in Friel's insistence on artistic freedom a strategy for 'dealing with the impossibility of ever constructing a narrative which is more than an acceptable fiction'.[44] But in the unreal situation of limbo in which the Russians find themselves, and in their pathetic attempts to resign themselves to that situation, we can see a fictional world that has its own cohesion. Life *is* empty and meaningless, therefore its emptiness and lack of meaning *become* its raison d'être: those who acknowledge this live with some sense of dignity, while those who rage against it become asylum cases, thus reversing the argument expressed in *Philadelphia* that the asylum is for the weak-minded and the passé.

In all Friel's various genres – the direct address to the audience in *Cass*, *Faith Healer* and *Molly Sweeney*, the stage manager of *Living Quarters*, the narrators in *Winners* and *Lughnasa*, the intercut sequences of *The Freedom*, the unnatural naturalism of *Aristocrats*, *Translations*,

Wonderful Tennessee and *Give Me Your Answer, Do!* – his awareness of the profoundly unstable and unsatisfactory nature of the theatre does not inhibit the plays, but allows him to explore the theatrical possibilities emanating from that instability. Risk-taking at its most extreme has thus been punctuated by the 'Russian' plays which suggest the slowly bending arc of a bow as it prepares to loose an arrow – the growth of both passion and the awareness of passion, its means of exploration, its sense of direction, unfold and expand almost painfully until the moment is reached at which the arrow is to be shot and become a spent force.

In particular, these plays provide us with extracurricular examples of how Friel's mind encompasses the ideas of love, of communication between men and women, and of the split or divided mind.

In *Fathers and Sons* Pavel speaks for many if not all of Friel's characters, and particularly those in *Give Me Your Answer, Do!*, when he says: 'we all want to believe in at least the possibility of one great love. And when we cannot achieve it – because it isn't achievable – we waste our lives pursuing surrogates' (*FS* 87). The faith lives both in the possibility and in the absence, and this defines the work as belonging to the literature in the gap, the waiting world where something may change everything for ever – what Friel in the preface to *The Loves of Cass McGuire* calls 'the beauty that might have been' (*Cass* 7).

Nowhere does Friel find more occasion to explore the varieties of love than in the Russian plays. In *Three Sisters*, *A Month in the Country* and *Uncle Vanya* the fragility, the ambivalence, the treacherous nature of love are rehearsed in such a way that the idea of affection between parents and children, between siblings, between master and servant, is unquestioned and yet menaced by something unspeakable that lies at the centre of the play – the lack of purpose, inability to speak of anything except the most trivial elements of everyday life. The impossible loves of an adoring girl for an older, experienced man, or of a middle-aged passé for a beautiful, languorous young woman; the childish adoration of grown men for their nannies; the shape of an entire life 'determined by a single, ridiculous passion' (*FS* 19); the recognition that love between man and woman requires the full gamut of passion – 'if I have never cried because of him, I can't really love him, can I?' (*MiC* 29); the revelation that love 'makes the unreasonable perfectly reasonable' (*MiC* 80); that 'unqualified love' may be perfect for the lover but suffocating for the beloved (*MiC* 106–7); that 'all love is a catastrophe' (*MiC* 94) – all are employed to ask questions about people's place in the world. When Anna's husband finds her embracing Michel, she exits asking 'I would like to know what passion is so magnificent it can justify this' (*MiC* 69). Behind such a question is a lexicon of exchanges between the sexes that will never be exhausted.

Twice in these plays we have the spectacle of what Friel, with an extraordinary syntactical frankness calls 'almost love'. In *Uncle Vanya* the elderly Serebriakov addresses his young wife:

> You looked after me dutifully, indeed given your innate disgust for me you were wonderfully compassionate and really, really *almost* loving. And could an old man ask for more than – almost love? (*UV* 29)

And in *Fathers and Sons* Bazarov, who has declared that he does not believe in falling in love, in 'being in love' (*FS* 37), suddenly discovers that he is 'hopelessly, insanely, passionately, extravagantly, madly in love' with Anna Sergeevna. It is only after his death that she recognises this unrequited passion and wishes – almost – that she had married him – a marriage which would have been 'difficult'. To have lost 'the possibility of one great love' and to pursue what is now an impossibility for the rest of one's life is to confine the energy of love within the emotion of memory.

In Friel's Russian plays, the attempted transmission of meaning between men and women is one of the most compelling focuses, particularly in the explosive and almost melodramatic *A Month in the Country*. In 'Understanding as Translation' George Steiner comments on 'the strong subtle barriers which sexual identity interposes in communication' and suggests that 'women's speech is richer than men's in th[eir] shadings of desire and futurity'.[45] Later, in 'Word Against Object' he says

> when we speak to others we speak 'at the surface' of ourselves . . . beneath which there lies a wealth of subconscious, deliberately concealed or declared associations so extensive and intricate that they probably equal the sum and uniqueness of our status as an individual person.[46]

This idea, when applied to *A Month in the Country* or *Uncle Vanya*, questions the basic ontology of that individual person. So tantalising is the advance towards, and retreat from, expressions of love between Elena and Vanya, between Elena and Astrov, between Sonya and Vanya, that the approximations to understanding which they achieve, the changes which that brings about in their own natures, become a space occupied by some indefinable presence which is, in fact, defined by its non-presence. Again, as I have suggested, ensemble is the key to the changes that take place because everyone becomes aware together of the spirit of the play.

One of the most significantly explicit features of Friel's Russian plays (again, with the exception of *Fathers and Sons*) is that certain characters split in two and talk to themselves. In *Three Sisters* Dr Chebutykin touches his mirror-reflection with his finger-tip: 'Maybe you're the reality. Why not? Maybe this [body] is the image . . . I wish you [reflection] were

the reality, my friend. I wish – oh God, how I wish this [body] didn't exist'
(*Sisters* 73). In *A Month in the Country* Michel '*conducts the following
conversation with himself at a frantic speed*':

> Oh my God.
> Steady, man.
> She's slipping away from you.
> No, she's not.
> You're losing her.
> Shut up.
> And if you lose her –
> *I will not lose her!*
> – you lose whatever happiness you know (*MiC* 46).

In the same play, Natalya (the object of Michael's love) admits to herself
her own passion for Aleksey, who is actually in love with Vera:

> So now you know: they are in love!
> Yes, they are in love.
> Then God bless them.
> Yes, God bless the fools.
> You know you're jealous of her.
> Jealous of a child?
> Oh yes. And for the first time in your life you're in love yourself.
> Don't be stupid!
> ....
>
> Oh God – oh God – listen to yourself, Natalya. If you're not careful you're
> going to end up loathing yourself (*MiC* 45–6).

And in *Uncle Vanya*, Vanya, Sonya and Elena all employ this method of
communicating with themselves (*UV* 35, 44, 52).

The strategy which Friel had employed in *Philadelphia* thus re-emerges
to illustrate the need of his Russian folk to internalise fears and doubts
which they cannot communicate to others, and thereby suggests strong
parallels with their Irish kin. It also underlines Friel's own need to explore
this exotic dimension of his preoccupations as a playwright.

IRELAND AND RUSSIA

The paradox of Russia which is also the paradox of Ireland is expressed
in the following distinction made by Peter Brook:

> In everyday life 'if' is a fiction, in the theatre 'if' is an experiment.
> In everyday life, 'if' is an evasion, in the theatre 'if' is the truth.
> When we are persuaded to believe in the truth, then the theatre and life are
> one.[47]

This is the magic which happens in Chekhov and Friel, and it is possible
because in Russia and Ireland everyday life *is* theatre, because dissembling

and distorting reality are strategies for living an unliveable situation. Seamus Deane's observation on Ireland might equally apply to the Russian situation as we see it on Friel's stage: 'Friel is unique . . . in his recognition that Irish temperament and Irish talk has a deep relationship to Irish desolation and the sense of failure'.[48] Individual, family, nation are analogous. The baby-alarm (or 'judas-hole') or the faulty radio are ways of living with the twin ideas of 'if' which express speculation ('What would happen if. . .?') and frustration ('If only. . .'). The device facilitates what Brook calls 'the "happening" effect, the moment when the illogical breaks through our everyday understanding to make us open our eyes more widely'.[49]

Russia is a place beyond, but it is also 'here'. The striking similarities between Russia and Ireland, and the Russian and Irish characters in and out of the theatre, especially in the nineteenth century, have been examined in some detail:[50] they often appear in a state of limbo, people to whom things happen and who initiate nothing, who surrender to fate and live for tomorrow because to do so is less demanding than to try and live in the present.

As we have seen, Peter Brook, writing in the late 1960s, thought that one of the main questions evident in contemporary theatre was 'why [man] has a life and against what he can measure it'. This liminal questioning, the examination of inaction as much as of action, is what brings together the Irish and the Russian dramas, both the rough and the holy in what Brook calls 'unreconciled opposition'.[51] And it may be that the questions identified by Brook are most evident in Friel's study of nihilism, *Fathers and Sons*, which is a 'translation' not only from Russian to Hiberno-English but also from Turgenev's novel to Friel's play.

Once again, it is ambiguous whether we are supposed to condone or condemn this opposition, principally because the atmosphere itself is a powerfully active character in the events of the plays. Friel's capacity to evoke this character (as we have seen in discussing *Dancing at Lughnasa* and *Wonderful Tennessee*), his creation of a space which moves beyond time and the concrete ('in that memory atmosphere is more real than incident') is enhanced and expanded by his relationship to Chekhov and Turgenev. In all four of his translations, to quote the closing lines of *Lughnasa*, 'everything is simultaneously actual and illusory' (*DL* 71). This is achieved partly by means of the ritualistic or ceremonial process by which the actors move from one position to another by means of revelation; and partly by means of the spirit which stands behind and has evoked that movement: the sense of loss and inertia, the idea that life is elsewhere, that something is about to happen or that something is about to not happen, and that in the absence of living we must endure the dead

weight of time in a state of colloquy in which everything is arrested except
the condition of speech itself. It is explained in Friel's own comment on
Turgenev's work: 'he fashioned a new kind of dramatic situation and a
new kind of dramatic character where for the first time psychological and
poetic elements create a theatre of moods and where the action resides in
internal emotion and secret turmoil and not in external events' (*MiC* 10).

As much as the work of the stage director, the role of the designer is
vital in the presentation of the Russian plays, in the creation of the
atmosphere pervading the text. Lighting, clothing and the siting of the
stock properties (samovar, swing, wicker chairs, a guitar, the suggestion
of trees and, in the near distance, a lake) will all contribute to the life of
that text, to the grain of its voice. We must be able to hear the off-stage
winnowing machine if and when it ever arrives (*MiC* 31, *UV* 31) to
provide what Elena sarcastically calls 'a Greek drama' (*UV* 53).

Haunting all nineteenth-century Russian literature is what Friel calls
'familiar melancholy'[52] – the spirit of absence, the idea that life as we
know it is a tragedy, and that, if one could only move to the 'beyond'
place, 'real' life could commence. As we have seen, Tyrone Guthrie said
that the ritual of drama acknowledges 'age-old formulae'. So too do the
cadences of Turgenev – in novel after novel (*Smoke*, *The Home of the
Gentry*, *Virgin Soil*) and in his play *A Month in the Country* – of Mikhail
Lermontov's *A Hero of Our Time*, even those of the foolishly tragic
Oblomov of Ivan Goncharov; so too does the resident sadness of Pushkin's
poetry, the maddening questions of the major novelists Tolstoy and
Dostoyevsky. In all these we find the notion that intolerable waiting is
actually palpable, that the arrested moment *is* the play. Nowhere
subsequently do we encounter this so powerfully until the age of Beckett.

I would go so far as to identify, if not perhaps equate, this atmospheric
presence with the concept of myth: indefinable but known. A secret
waiting to be told, and a transitus to be undertaken, are transacted against
the background, or in the presence, of what is hidden. In this double helix
of the real and the illusory, the pretence and the pretended, there can be
no home: the play is inherently *unheimlich* and the purpose of the play is
to restore the focus, to return successfully to the hearth.

This is explicitly set before us in *Three Sisters* – 'there is a great void, a
great emptiness in man's life, and he's searching for something to fill it.
He doesn't know yet what it is he wants. But he's seeking and he will find
it' (*Sisters* 108). It is this latter faith which fills the Russian plays with a
form of hope which many find spurious: the will to *endure*. The same
speaker, Vershinin, has previously told us 'We Russians are a people whose
aspirations are magnificent; it's just living we can't handle' (*Sisters* 43)
which directly refers to Hugh's judgement in *Translations* – 'a syntax

opulent with tomorrows'. The bitterness is redoubled in the figure of
Vanya, who declares 'I'm eaten up with fury and frustration because I've
wasted my life, because I'm too old to pursue the things – the real things –
I might have had' (*UV* 19). Not only has his own life been meaningless
but he has spent it supporting his brother-in-law: 'the life *he* was living –
that was real life, life realized, life fulfilled . . . And now we know it was
all a shell. A life-time of chicanery – spurious, fraudulent, empty' (*UV* 36).

In place of 'real' life, the people of these plays are 'bored – bored –
bored – bored' (*UV* 49). 'Oh damn this – this – this bloody, dreary, grinding
life' declares Masha in *Three Sisters* (31). Life grinds against all the
possibilities which can only be guessed at, which exist beyond the horizons
of both hope and despair. Not only Vanya's life, but all lives, all life in the
abstract, is desiccated and empty, colonised only by the knowledge of its
own meaninglessness. The final line of *Three Sisters* is Olga's 'If only we
knew. Oh, if only we knew' (114) – again the echo of Gar's last line in
Philadelphia is obvious.

But throughout the Russian plays there are more subtle and less direct
appeals to a life-that-might-have-been: 'Did you ever wonder what it
would be like if you could begin your life over again?' asks Vershinin
(*Sisters* 28). 'If I could only tell you – how I feel about you' Andrey cries
out to Natasha (*Sisters* 37). 'If I had been beautiful' Sonya wistfully but
realistically wishes and acknowledges in the one phrase (*UV* 51) and
Vanya himself wonders 'If I had had a normal life, God knows what I
might have become' (*UV* 61) – always the appeal to another life, unlived,
that exists *en principe* parallel and contiguous to one's own.

In the face of a fate so austere that people become bored with their
own *ennui*, and where even drunkenness refuses to create suitable
illusions, people question the meaninglessness of life: 'All this unhap-
piness, all this suffering – what is it all for?' (*Sisters* 113). We are waiting
for Gar or any one of the helpless children of Friel's plays to turn to a
figure of authority and demand 'Isn't it your job – to translate?' 'We
have got to go on living' says Masha in blind faith (*Sisters* 113) to which
her sister responds 'Some day we'll understand'.

The absent presence at the heart of a play such as *Uncle Vanya* (as
with Stewart Parker's *Pentecost*) is intimately concerned with the nature
of both home and affection. Beside the Russian 'spirit' or 'soul' of
expectant lassitude which I have already mentioned, we should identify
the need of Chekhov's characters to discover within themselves, with the
help of an agent from a far place, the meaning not only of life but of home.
In *Fathers and Sons* the arrival of Bazarov in the Kirsanov household,
and later at his own parents' house, definitively decentres both homes.
The challenge to the prevailing inaction by a man who repudiates

everything that personifies 'Russia' unsettles not only the house but also the atmosphere, and the fact that in this particular case the original work was a novel rather than a play helps Friel in his task.

Fathers and Sons is the exception which proves the Russian rule: where Friel's three other translations teem with appeals to the affections, *Fathers and Sons* brings the *unheimlich* centre-stage and presents us with the one element which disturbs the inhabitants of the other plays and makes their lives so pointless: the future. No one in *Fathers and Sons* asks 'what's to become of us?' because the options are clear: either Bazarov's nihilism will remake Russian society or it will evaporate and the society will revert to its sombre complacency. Bazarov says of his father 'He'll go on fussing and dabbling and boring until the whole insignificant little episode that was his trivial life is over' (*FS* 44) but because of his own urgent appointment with destiny he will not live to see it, instead over-turning the relationship between father and son. In a speech which does not appear in Turgenev's original Friel writes: 'There's something not right about a father burying his son, isn't there? Some disorder in the proper ordering of things, isn't it? It's not the way things should be, is it?' (*FS* 78)[53]

It was as necessary for Friel to write *Fathers and Sons* as it was to address the homecomings of *Faith Healer* and *Translations*. Without it, the challenges he makes in *Making History* would not have been possible. In this sense *Fathers and Sons* is the vital bridge between the homecoming of *Translations* and the new departures of *Making History*. In a sense it is almost as if he had returned to the short story as a form of conversation in which the family saga can be conducted away from overtly political and social issues. To locate nihilism in such manifestly rustic surroundings is a risky venture at uniting the local and private with the public and distant. Friel approaches this by providing us with echoes, clues, from his previous work. In many ways we can in fact read *Fathers and Sons* as a 'translation' into Russia of the characters and psychologies of Ballybeg. Thus the father and uncle of the revenant Arkady Nikolayevich Kirsanov respond to the exposition of nihilism as if they were Hugh and Jimmy Jack expressing their despair at the English lack of civilisation: to Arkady's assertion 'the most useful thing we can do is repudiate, renounce, reject' Pavel Petrovich replies 'Civilization has just been disposed of' (*FS* 11). Nikolai Petrovich remonstrates: 'surely rejection means destruction; and surely we must construct too?' Arkady retorts, in the accents of Captain Lancey, 'Our first priority is to make a complete clearance. At this point in our evolution we have no right to indulge in the gratification of our own personal whims.' And in the original version of *Fathers and Sons* (which was substantially cut to bring it within a more satisfactory playing time) Pavel Petrovich responds:

Well I'm sure the Russian people will be pleased to know that they are
about to be relieved of all those things they foolishly hold so sacred – their
traditions, their familial pieties, their sense of faith. Oh yes, that will be
welcome news to them'.[54]

The impact of Bazarov in Friel's play, whether in his own words or
through his acolyte Arkady, is as Turgenev intended: blunt, crude and
brutal. But Friel has added a new aspect to his sweeping nihilism: the
awareness that we cannot 'gratify our personal whims' because we, as
personae, do not yet exist: *ex nihilo* we must create both a public and a
private world. Sweeping everything away is the work of a disillusioned
faith healer, a repudiation, renunciation and rejection of past *and* future,
a dramatic act based on the realisation that civilisation, if it is to exist at
all, must be created out of a void. The possibilities are simultaneously
endless and absolutely finite, our assets invaluable and yet worthless.
For Yolland's father, we recall, 'ancient time was at an end' and, out of
this negation, new time, 'the Apocalypse', began; for his alter ego,
Senator Donovan in *The Communication Cord*, ancient time is only just
beginning. For Yevgeny and Arkady, the predictors of revolution, their
nihilism has already produced the apocalypse. Of all Friel's tortured
personalities, only Frank Hardy has found the liminal way to tread
between them: apocalypse *now*.

The fellow who comes home is the same who went away, but changed.[55]
In *Fathers and Sons* Friel gives us graphic evidence which helps us to
understand more fully the homecomings of Owen, Casimir, and indeed
Gareth O'Donnell. Not only do Arkady and Yevgeny, in relation to their
own fathers, return from Moscow changed by the political tenets of
nihilism but they also experience another form of change in the *transitus*,
the crossing of the domestic threshold. Stepping back into the familial
past with its pieties and niceties also involves stepping into a new future.
Macro-civilisation may be at an end, but the Kirsanov and Bazarov
households begin a new relationship with barbarism: who, here, are the
'*civilised* people'?

With characteristic sympathy Friel extends the treatment of Bazarov's
death in describing the determination with which he throws himself
against the typhus epidemic to which he himself succumbs. Yevgeny is
thus not only brought round to a positive, forward-looking attitude by
the selfish device of love (which in Turgenev's novel is somewhat overdone)
but by a social, humanitarian altruism which Turgenev had seriously
underplayed. Nevertheless Bazarov remains brutal, or at least dangerously
cynical, to the end: 'Everything for the bloody peasants, damn them!' (*FS*
76). But it is a brutality or cynicism tinged and mediated by love between
father and son: when Yevgeny is dying he tells his father (at least in the

uncut version of the play): 'I'm glad you and mother have your religion. I hope it is a comfort to you',[56] a sarcastic but affectionate recognition that not all ancient time can come to an end at once, that some time dies more slowly than others.

Bazarov's exemplary death is used as a means of inspiring Arkady's positive motivation for the revolution. He has moved from his original nihilistic stance to embrace his own father's viewpoint that after destruction there must come regeneration, an assertion in fact that without *a project of the will* our attitude to life remains unmotivated, that we are incapable of response. The project of will, however, must be based on freedom, whether it be the freedom of Bazarov to throw himself into death or that of Kirsanov to go on living, with all the rage against order and disorder that that demands. Once again the cutting-room floor provides us with strong evidence of Friel's own determination to effect the revolution in the relations between father and son that he has only hinted at in *Translations*:

> ARKADY: Why must you always be stupidly flippant about things that are vitally important, Father? What are you afraid of? You are all casually tossing about large words like loyalty and betrayal and love –
>
> KATYA: And revolution.
>
> ARKADY: And revolution – yes, and revolution – as if they existed only [in] the abstract. Good. Great. Splendid. Be as cavalier, as flippant, as you wish. Plan the ideal world to your heart's content . . . but sooner or later you have got to acknowledge that the splendid new world you're concocting is inhabited by ordinary people, real people, your friends, your neighbours, your servants, and that they may not share that magnificent vision. And then you have to face up to your real responsibility: because if those people can't share your vision and if you cannot persuade them, are you going to coerce them into acceptance? . . . Yes, I want a new and better order. Yes, I demand the rejection of all that's mean and ugly and corrupt. But rejection alone is merely destruction. And surely we must construct too?[57]

This is the apocalypse for 'the bloody peasants, damn them' of Ballybeg; it is the acceptance by Hugh O'Donnell of Maire's need for English; and it is the recognition that it is not enough for the oppressed masses to stir in their sleep: they must have a reason for waking. No clearer blueprint is needed for the re-reading and rewriting of the nationalist, republican project. That alternative project, to which Field Day directs its energies, is the imperative which Arkady calls 'the primary and enormous task of remaking an entire society . . . not only a social obligation but perhaps even a moral obligation and indeed it is not improbable that the execution of that task may even have elements of *artistic pursuit'* (*FS* 24–5, *my emphasis*). We begin to see how a modern Irish playwright, following the example of Yeats, could accept appointment to the Irish Senate, having asserted the right and ability of artists to participate in government. We see that the antic gesture of a Skinner or a Keeney or a Doalty, has been abandoned in favour of a reasoned and easily accessible exposition which is also free of diatribe.

In *The Mundy Scheme* Friel, the potentially political artist, had spoken out against the fact that 'the enormous task of remaking an entire society' had been funked by a neo-colonialist native administration which still carried within it its old subservience to the larger world, its deviousness in the face of oppression now turned in upon itself, its desperation for a name and an identity leading it into supermarket politics. In *Fathers and Sons* he pushes those crudities aside in the interests of greater issues: 'we know there is starvation and poverty; we know our politicians take bribes; we know the legal system is corrupt' (*FS* 11). But the world does not revolve on political slogans:

> Liberalism, progress, principles, civilization – they have no meaning in Russia. They are imported words. Russia doesn't need them . . . What Russia does need is bread in the mouth. But before you can have bread in the mouth, you have got to plough the land – deep. (*FS* 13)

We have gone beyond *The Freedom of the City*, where individuated dignity was the focus of revolt, to a scenario where the persona, like civilisation itself, is a *res nullius*. Bazarov, as he is dying, asserts: 'I am no loss to Russia. A cobbler would be a loss to Russia. A butcher would be a loss. A tailor would be a loss. I am no loss' (*FS* 79). But at the same time we are left with the absolutely personal claim of the nihilist, as recognised by his father: 'an extraordinary man cannot be judged by ordinary standards. An extraordinary man creates his own standards' (*FS* 42). It is the rock on which the revolutionary friendship founders, because, as Arkady wryly and jealously observes, 'only Bazarov has the courage and the clarity of purpose to live outside ordinary society, without attachments, beyond the consolation of the emotions' (*FS* 45). His exit raises issues in the quiet rhythm of his own home. In his father's exclamation 'Damn you, Almighty Father! I will not stand for it! I certainly will not stand for it!' (*FS* 78) Russia (and Ireland) creates another *deus absconditus*.

In recreating Frank Hardy, Friel is doing more than simply showing us once again the prototype bastard: he is also demonstrating the symbiotic chemical relationship of two half-brothers. As Bazarov says of Arkady:

> He thinks he loves those damned peasants. I know I hate them. But I know, too, that when the time comes I will risk everything, everything for them, and I'm not at all sure that Brother Arkady is prepared to risk anything. (*FS* 44)

One half of the brother remains in civilisation, the other is an out-and-out barbarian. Bazarov tells Arkady:

> We are now into the area of hostilities – of scratching, hurling, biting, mauling, cutting, bruising, spitting. You're not equipped for those indecencies. When it would come to the bit you would retreat into well-bred indignation and well-bred resignation. Your upbringing has provided you with that let-out. Mine didn't. I am committed to the last, mean, savage, glorious shaming extreme! (*FS* 67)

Arkady's resolve to continue the nihilist revolution is fired by the fact – shameful to him – that Bazarov's final act of freedom has carried him off, whereas his own gentility has kept him the prisoner of ambiguous loyalty. Only a similar unequivocal choice of freedom can bring him out of the losers' enclosure.

It is in the changed relations of father and son – in the Kirsanov household – that Friel's Russian field day brings us fully back to the Ballybeg of *Translations*. Bazarov *père* has said:

> There's something not right about a father burying his son, isn't there? Some disorder in the proper ordering of things, isn't it? It's not the way things should be, is it? (*FS* 78)

And after Arkady's resolution, Kirsanov *père* announces in the closing passage of the play:

> Some people might think that there is something inappropriate about a father and a son getting married on the same day, some disorder in the proper ordering of things. But I know that for both of us it will be an occasion of great joy and great fulfilment. And who is to determine what is the proper ordering of things? (*FS* 94)

The son has recognised the wisdom residing in old age, as well as the right of old age to behave youthfully (for example in begetting children and marrying) while the father acknowledges that it is not *necessarily* either the old *or* the young who have the management of society. Maddening questions can rot the life of the hopeful as well as the hopeless, especially when their attempts at communication bring them into conflict; as Kirsanov *père* tells us early in the play, 'You never really know what people are like, do you? We all have our codes. We all have our masks' (*FS* 16).

With the Russian plays, two elements, both future-oriented, compete for the affections of the characters: one is the sense of collapse, that life is about to break up, the other that life *will* improve, will acquire meaning, but not yet. Sonya tells Vanya, in terms which recall Kate Mundy in *Lughnasa*, 'Look around you. The place is falling apart' (*UV* 39). She is referring to the physical condition of the house and estate but, as with Irish references to the spiritual condition of the great house, this is symbolic of desuetude in the psychic fabric of its inhabitants: as Vanya enjoins: 'Somehow it's all slowly crushing me and I don't know if I can go on. And it's not right somehow – something about it is all wrong' (*UV* 40). Similarly in *Three Sisters* Tusenbach predicts 'an avalanche is about to descend on us' (*Sisters* 14) and Irina – 'I'm beginning to disintegrate too' (80). Even the trees are 'waiting for something to happen' (102).

Against this is Sonya's belief (in *Uncle Vanya*) in a possible future – 'I'm not going to give up. I'm going to endure' (*UV* 73) – which gives the play its open-ended conclusion: 'We will be so happy . . . we will be peaceful then . . . For the first time ever we will know what it is to be peaceful and at rest . . . Endure. And peace will come to us' (*UV* 86). Whether one accepts this as a satisfactory conclusion will presumably depend on whether one subscribes to the despairing or the hopeful part of the drama. The empty boast of *Aristocrats* – 'Semper Permanemus' – gives the lie to those who think that they can 'affirm' or 'attest' to some signal quality and that time might be brought to a standstill for a few moments in which that affirmation is witnessed.

It is the presence of characters such as Bazarov which disrupts this polarity between hope and despair, by challenging the 'complacency' in which they are rooted. The moment that Arkady announces 'I've brought a friend with me, Father' (*FS* 5) the household is doomed to change, as the hedge-school is doomed when Owen makes the same announcement. Bazarov and Lancey have this in common, because their stock characteristics cast them as the villain of the piece, the destroyer: '*BAZAROV, a student, dark, lean, intense. He senses that he is an outsider politically and socially in this house – hence the arrogance and curt manner*' (*FS* 8). The Bazarov type enables Friel to step beyond the frustrations of Gar O'Donnell, beyond the father-son nexus of embarrassment, a destroyer whom fate destroys because he can never survive his encounter with the future. Both hope *and* despair are negated in such a figure.

And there is also something of the Faith Healer in Bazarov, something which corresponds to the needle-point between hope and despair which is a willing acceptance of one's fate. It was Chekhov who said 'in my childhood there was no childhood'[58] and in Turgenev we have the spectacle of the constant deferral of joy. Bazarov not only casts away the prospect of joy for himself but imposes it on others. We have met it before, in Frank Hardy: 'Even though they told themselves they were here because of the remote possibility of a cure, they knew in their hearts they had come not to be cured but for confirmation that they were incurable; not in hope but for the elimination of hope, for the removal of that final, impossible chance' (*FH* 16).

'Have we a context?' The question assumes an increasingly central role in Friel's work. A context – a place to which one belongs, a place where one fits in – is increasingly remote and subjunctive. If we examine the word in its literal meaning (*contextus*, woven together) we find that it relates intricately to both the business of speech and that of connection. In any context there is a past which determines meaning, and a present (the context itself) which looks to a future based on what is about to be transacted. If that context is unhoused or decentred, transactions become impossible; life is interrupted, turned upside down; what is indefinable but known becomes definable and unknown.

As we have seen in the case of *Aristocrats*, love demands a context, a past from which it can derive meaning and validity. The outstanding characteristic of the Russian plays is that, in the midst of indecision and indeterminacy, the characters struggle to define, achieve and demonstrate their concepts of love, passion and affection. The need for a context is underlined by the fact that, because the future is so uncertain and unpredictable, the idea of love is tethered to that of memory. In a situation where the constant refrain is 'What's to become of us?' (*Sisters* 83, *MiC* 58, 84, *UV* 67) love cannot thrive, but it still yearns to be expressed.

CONCLUSION

A text's unity lies not in its origin but in its destination[1]
Roland Barthes

I end this study as I began it, with a critique of the idea of authority – in this case, the authority of the playwright and the text. Throughout this study, we have been concerned with the emergence and development of one voice in the Irish and international theatre, but other voices have also been heard, particularly those of Tom Murphy and Thomas Kilroy. When, therefore, we find Murphy saying of the three writers 'We're all re-writing each other's plays'[2] we could be entitled to suspect that modern Irish drama was static, introspective and incestuous. I shall therefore attempt to place Friel's work in another context, in reference to the wider picture of contemporary Irish drama and to the international condition of, and debate about, theatre.

Where does Brian Friel stand in relation to his contemporaries at home? I do not wish to attempt any kind of definition, because it is obvious that, as Elmer Andrews acknowledges, 'I am left finally to admit the impossibility of pinning down this elusive, complex and fascinating talent'.[3] One would hope so: the essential Friel, in Fintan O'Toole's words, is 'a hunger, an absence, a silence' and critics 'can never be adequate to his restlessness'.[4] To place him in the context of contemporary Irish playwriting is in fact to create the context itself. O'Toole has drawn a severe and incisive picture of theatre in Ireland today which explains this problem: 'contemporary Irish dramatists are the orphans of the Irish Literary Renaissance'; he says that Ireland 'has no genuine theatrical tradition' and that 'to go beyond the dominant nationalism' is 'to construct individual solutions in an often unyielding environment'.[5] We have noted the apparent obsession with identity and naming and with the past. Even more obsessive, perhaps, is the fact that the artist seems to be isolated by intelligence: the intellectual, rather than the poet, is marginalised in Irish society because of the political implications of much of his work. Friel himself has, in many ways, been the leader of a generation of playwrights who affiliate to intellectual exercises in other disciplines, moving away from a violent, bitter and alienated description of their cultural identity towards a more suitable, humane and positive pursuit of identity and purpose. It is as if Friel would say with Gandhi[6] – of the unionists, of the southern nationalists, of the British government, of the terrorists – 'I want to change their minds, I don't want to kill them for weaknesses that are in us all'.

In this sense Friel's (and Field Day's) work represents a *Bildungsdrama*, a celebration of the achievement of certain types of freedom, of growth towards wholeness, of the exercise of will, of increasing strength and maturity, which necessarily contains an awareness of struggle. In Ireland, both north and south, drama is still moving towards a possession of the English language, and, with it, a knowledge of its own powers. Ironically English drama, built upon certainties, is today meeting the same challenges of the failure of language, of a search for words to satisfy a condition of wordlessness. The two experiences, however, are separated by differences in perception and realities: one working from the starting point of poverty which ironically provides it with a certain security or rootedness of its own, the other from a position of wealth which has found its security shattered by the implosion of its own strength, the collapse of empire. Much of this irony is written into the bond tentatively established between Owen and Yolland in *Translations*, and the growing awareness and acceptance of Irish drama in Britain may well represent a cultural dimension of the political *entente* between the two countries.

Irish drama at the end of the 1990s is not static, but it is difficult to know in which direction it is moving, or whether it is moving only in a circular fashion. In 1991 Fintan O'Toole (by far the most significant and sustained commentator on the subject) noted that, while there was some evidence of a movement towards 'the physical, the visual, the imagistic' aspects of theatre, it was also true that 'far from fading away, the literary text has become much more literary. That most abused of notions, a poetic theatre, has, all by itself and without manifestos or deliberation, come back into play'.[7] He also noted that the doubleness of Irish experience in the 1960s, which had contributed to the split personality of Gar O'Donnell and his successors, had given way to 'a series of more or less isolated, more or less angular Irelands'. Commenting on four plays current at that time – Murphy's *Too Late for Logic*, Sebastian Barry's *Prayers of Sherkin*, John McGahern's adaptation of Tolstoy's *The Power of Darkness* and Friel's *Dancing at Lughnasa* – he observed: 'we are moving from a theatre of conflict to a theatre of linguistic evocation, one in which things are called up rather than simply acted out'.

Four years later, O'Toole summed up the year 1995 with the fact that it had produced no new work by either Friel or Murphy (in fact Murphy remained silent as a playwright until 1998) but that the two memorable new works had been by Barry – *The Steward of Christendom* and *The Only True History of Lizzie Finn*. He suggested that a new pattern 'of companies looking for writers to fulfil ideas which are already present in some form' might provide a new direction for Irish drama and theatrical activity.[8] This has in fact been symptomatic of the diversification of Irish theatre and Irish theatres in the past decade – a series of 'crises' at the Abbey Theatre calling in question the role of, and indeed the need for, a 'national' theatre, and a large number of new companies and venues with a new generation of writers, actors and directors opening up physical, artistic and intellectual spaces regionally and nationally. It is no longer valid for any writer to think in terms of 'an Abbey play' in the sense of a text ambitious of and amenable to an establishment reception. To say that 'critical words like "memory" and "home" have changed their meaning' (O'Toole's comment on the changing vocabulary of Irish playwriting)[9] could be taken as a wry reference to the writers' historical relationship with 'The Old Lady'.[10] Friel's own 'secessions', firstly from the Abbey to establish Field Day and secondly from Field Day itself, may be seen as a gauge of this wider divergence. The fragmentation of audiences concomitant with this splitting of the dramatic mindset has also raised different expectations and has made more evident expectations which, while existing previously, had been sublimated within the predominating interests.

One of these has been the practical issue of women playwrights who have been notably absent from the Irish stage.[11] The most prominent of the younger women playwrights in Ireland today is Marina Carr, author of *The Mai* (1994), *Portia Coughlan* (1996) and *By the Bog of Cats* (1998). But in many ways she is symptomatic not of the decentralisation of Irish theatre but of its continuing centredness both on the Abbey (where her plays have been staged and where she has been Writer-in-Association) and on language and ritual. She has said of *The Mai* 'it's a ghost play in many ways. The characters are alive and yet they're not'[12] while Breandán Delap commented 'the play explores how history has a habit of repeating itself and it plays a lot on the tyranny of memory'.[13] Meanwhile, Victoria White saw *By the Bog of Cats* as a ritual of initiation which has 'all the "shock of the new"'.[14] We have already seen that *The Mai* has been called a 'feminist riposte' to Friel, which in itself suggests that Carr might have been looking over her shoulder when she ought to have been looking steadily ahead – an accusation which she may well not deserve.

But the 'shock of the new' can nevertheless remind us that what is new today has been new before.

In fact, both *The Mai* and *Portia Coughlan* relate thematically and strategically to the work of Friel, and the 'riposte' notion stands up to a good deal of scrutiny. Conversations with and from the dead; fractured families and the imprecation to 'come home';[15] dreams which echo the rhapsodies of *Cass* ('he'd take me away to a beautiful land never seen or heard of before');[16] the mixture of monologue and reportage; the recitation of folk legend; the equation of mind with landscape ('I read subtext, Mother . . . and I know the topography of your mind as well as I know every inch and ditch and drain of Belmont Farm');[17] the admission that 'everyone is deranged';[18] the loss of a twin and the idea that 'you're aither two people or you're no one';[19] even the happening-that-never-happened: 'And that's why I cannot remember that excursion into town if it ever occurred'[20] – all echo, validate and develop Friel. But most of these symptoms are also present – or can be read into – Chekhov because those who exhibit them are ordinary people with ordinary emotions. What is *extra*ordinary is the way that all those under discussion here continue to investigate them as if collectively, with a common sense of understanding.

In 1997 O'Toole pointed out that the 1990s had seen the emergence of 'many really accomplished playwrights' including Barry, Marina Carr, Billy Roche, Martin McDonagh and Conor McPherson, besides 'at least another dozen new writers who have produced significant plays and seem likely to go on doing so'.[21] Again, that new work was 'more odd, more angular and more oblique . . . but it is also, if anything, more literary . . . a return to highly charged, self-consciously stylised language'.

Theatre – and it seems Irish theatre in particular – retains the capacity to satisfy what O'Toole calls 'an obvious search for forms that will make sense of the broken narratives and discordant voices of an increasingly globalised world . . . a way of testing contemporary experience'.[22] The global acceptance of plays by Friel, which I discussed in my Introduction, has now been extended, in London and New York at least, to work not only by long established writers such as Frank McGuinness but also to relative newcomers like Martin McDonagh.

If the world is increasingly liminal, perhaps fuelled in its trajectory by a sense of millennium, then the kind of Irish drama we have encountered in this study – a drama acutely and profoundly aware of what happens in the gap, of the nature of disorientation, of disconnection – can provide a focus for people who can find no other hearth.

One pillar of this drama is the central place of illusion in Irish life – the need for make-believe in order to make sense of unlivable situations. A second pillar is the double meaning of the imperative to 'keep on talking'

– 'it's the silence that's the enemy' (*Ph*. 102). One meaning is the necessity of avoiding embarrassment: once we say 'we embarrass one another' the next step is violence. The other meaning is the impossibility of keeping silent, the need to tell stories.

Both these facets have come out of Friel, who might in this respect be regarded as Gogol's overcoat. While it is not by any means correct to speak of him as the 'father' or founding figure of contemporary Irish drama, the claim made in my Introduction, that that drama essentially began with *Philadelphia, Here I Come!*, can be sustained: without *Philadelphia* the development of Irish playwriting would have been very different if not impossible.[23] It is now astonishing to find that in 1975 Douglas Dunn, in his introduction to his survey *Two Decades of Irish Writing* could admit: 'there has been no space for discussions of Irish drama [the collection included ten essays on poetry and four on fiction]. Such plays as Brian Friel's *The Freedom of the City* or David Rudkin's play about Casement [*Cries from Casement as his bones are brought to Dublin*] are, I am prepared to admit, unworthy of being ignored'.[24] In the 35 years since *Philadelphia* (half of Friel's lifetime) the dramatic scene has been transformed not once but twice, when Dunn published his collection not only Friel (with, in addition to *Philadelphia* and *The Freedom*, such a marker as *Crystal and Fox*) but also Murphy had established more than a reasonable claim to be addressed. We have seen Kilroy's obeisance toward the play, and we should also recall that the founding of Field Day was largely a matter of a bonding between Friel and Stephen Rea who says: 'Everybody has to make a pilgrimage at some time and I made mine to Brian Friel'.[25] And it was *Faith Healer*, so closely related to *Philadelphia*, which gave Frank McGuinness his own sense of direction.

But there is another strand of writing for the Irish stage which emanates from the unique folk-drama of Synge, and is evident in George Fitzmaurice, M. J. Molloy and John B. Keane and, most recently, Martin McDonagh. And a third strand, contemporaneous with the theatre of Friel, has been the work of Tom Murphy, whose *A Whistle in the Dark* (1961) unleashed savage energies which we have subsequently seen in Heno Magee's *Hatchet* and McGuinness's *Innocence*. While, therefore, Friel should not be credited with the creation of an entire dramatic tradition, it is nevertheless clear that by his example – the assuredness of his approach to language and techniques of storytelling, and his faithfulness, even in the face of personal failure, to the story of which he is the bearer – most modern Irish dramatists have been stimulated and excited.

The case of Frank McGuinness, whose debt to Brian Friel has been publicly acknowledged on several occasions,[26] is especially apposite. Conversation not unlike Friel's forms the principal activity in

Carthaginians, *Innocence* and *Someone Who'll Watch Over Me*; monologue (in *Baglady*) and near monologue in *The Bread Man*; while in
Observe the Sons of Ulster Marching Towards the Somme the bonding
between men derives in part from the 'two men waiting' who inhabit
many Friel plays (*Philadelphia* in particular) as well as those of Beckett.
But it would be absurd to suggest that Friel had had any *specific* influence
on McGuinness. Instead, McGuinness has responded to the example of a
writer prepared to open up ground that is normally unbroken, to explore
issues and emotions for which the confessional is the normal precinct.

For example, when Fintan O'Toole writes of the stagecraft of
Sebastian Barry, it might easily be Friel himself, especially recent Friel,
of whom he treats:

> You are struck by the absences. Where is the drama? Where is the action?
> Where is the psychology? Where is the suspense? And, in particular, since
> he is a modern Irish dramatist, where is the conflict?. . . . He manages it
> through language. What he has managed to do is to construct theatrical
> language that is so assured, so muscular, that it can afford to yoke together
> within its cadences the most heterogeneous images. . . . So shattered by
> history is the world of those plays that only a stringently beautiful and
> strangely abstract language could allow his characters to occupy the same
> stage at all. If the language were not poetic, these people, cut off as they
> are, would have nothing to say to us or to each other . . . [He] does what
> the best theatre does: helps us to look in the face of terror without ourselves
> being turned to stone.[27]

So too could his description of Martin McDonagh as 'a man to whom
stories come, almost as if they did of their own accord'.[28]

The fact that Friel's own style and his approach to playwriting has
evolved over the decades has perhaps encouraged others to experiment
with dramatic forms. Furthermore, the fact that it was his sense of
dramatic style in *Philadelphia* which made such an impact – rather than
any attempt to dispense with the kitchen as the place of discourse – may
have encouraged others to go on using that traditional *locus* for their
own 'memory theatre' – Murphy, Barry and McDonagh, for example.

There are dangers in this traditionalism, however. The man who leaves
home while gazing back over his shoulder never in fact goes away.
McDonagh has been acclaimed for his 'brilliant dialogue'.[29] I personally
find the script of *The Beauty Queen of Leenane* lacking in any distinction
in that regard, but the obvious and extensive success of his work suggests
that I may be unenlightened in my view. But it is likely that a generic
problem will arise if brilliant or noble dialogue is the central or even the
only element in a play.

Dialogue cannot of itself reveal a secret. The essential element in Irish
playwriting is not so much the nobility of the dialogue as the capacity to

tell a story. When *The Beauty Queen of Leenane* won three Tony Awards in New York in 1998 it was said that Anna Manahan, who played the role of Mag Folan (and parts in other McDonagh plays), had 'brought the Irish art of storytelling back to the theatre where it belongs and gave the play back to the audience'.[30] Similarly, Murphy's *Bailegangaire*, the longest and most harrowing story ever told in the Irish theatre, encompasses a long journey home on the part of Mommo, a transitus from silence to the telling of a secret, in which the image in the audience's mind of the road travelled becomes their own access to truth, their own way of moving into the play.

And in *Volunteers* the need to defer fate by continually making up stories which may or may not be apposite underlines the cruel nature which the storytelling function may exhibit, because we tell stories not only to arrive at the truth but in order to escape the truth. As Eileen Battersby has written of Tom Murphy, 'the conversations in his plays tend to be about life situations and about the delusions people invent to hide behind in order to survive'.[31] History does the same thing, and if Friel's work has any continuing resonance on the public stage it is in this ubiquitous demonstration that private spaces, utterances and stories can accumulate into acts of public history.

O'Toole has commented that 'anyone looking at the theatre in Ireland in the 1990s would find more similarities with the theatre of Synge than they would have done even a decade earlier. Neither Synge's language nor his peasant world remain[s] at the heart of Irish theatre, yet the theatre of the last few years shares much with Synge's'.[32] The problem here is the same as that identified by O'Toole in relation to the recent productions of, and revival of interest in, the work of John B. Keane,[33] which sees the Ireland of the 1950s put once more under one microscope made in its own age and image, and simultaneously under another which veers between parody and pastiche. As O'Toole puts it, 'Irish culture is in the peculiar state of having become post-modern before it ever became fully modern'.[34]

I am not at all convinced that the much-prized and -acclaimed *Leenane Trilogy* is an important series of plays, because I think it is caught in the dichotomy between the styles of parody and pastiche. The traditional rural drama of Keane and M. J. Molloy, and the modern, or post-modern, genre established principally by Friel and Murphy, have signalled a departure for Ireland and have made that departure happen. There is a great deal of *Bailegangaire*, as well as Molloy's *The Wood of the Whispering* in the *Leenane Trilogy*, for example, but where the latter has been extended and developed by a newer writer such as Sebastian Barry in *Boss Grady's Boys* (1988 – again, two men waiting, as in Molloy's *The Wood of the Whispering*), McDonagh does not seem to break new ground while observing the old. His *The Cripple of Inishmaan*, by contrast, is a black comedy which merits serious study and pushes our appreciation of the genres of Synge and Molloy to new limits. Black – or at least serious – comedy is something Friel has ignored. It is instructive to note that O'Toole sees Bernard Farrell (a writer totally excluded from, or not included in, the *Field Day Anthology*)[35] as 'essentially a serious writer, one whose true comedy lies not in the mere tittle-tattle of social observation, but at the borders of human identity . . . The laughter is nervous laughter, the comedy a comedy of terrors', citing Farrell's first play, *I Do Not Like Thee Doctor Fell* (1979) and his *Last Apache Reunion* (1993) as evidence, in contrast to 'the shallow sitcom of plays like *All in Favour Said No!* [1981] and *All the Way Back* [1985]'. Farrell himself has said 'You have to sit down at home with a lot of anger in your heart to write a very funny play. Comedy is not about jokes. Comedy is about people who have to tell a lie and then another lie to catch up with the first one because they are angry about being insulted or alienated'.[36] In this sense, perhaps *The Communication Cord* is not so much a farce or a corrective to *Translations* as a serious work of theatre, however much it is intended to make people laugh. (Friel himself has said 'farce is a very serious enterprise'.) This is a direction which might be further explored, even though it does run the risk of being misunderstood, as the experience of McDonagh's *Cripple* failing to com-municate its ironies for an American audience has shown.[37] In his other plays, too, McDonagh uses comedy with serious intent, in what Fintan O'Toole calls 'a final reversal of Romanticism'[38] in which the West is shown not to be the reliquary of pure and natural life for which the rest of industrialised Europe pines. In fact, to see McDonagh's work as serving the purposes of Druid Theatre Company in its project of demythologising the West ('If Martin McDonagh had not existed, Garry Hynes would have had to invent him')[39] is to see the genre of rural tragicomedy as part of a political agenda from which it appears impossible to escape.

Nothing illustrates this more succinctly than *Making History* with its hesitancy and its sense of both time and personality suspended. Fintan O'Toole has said that *Making History* is 'about the impossibility of writing'[40] which seems somewhat abrupt in its judgement but indicates the scope of the problem which has been a central concern of this study. Robert Welch, on the other hand, alerts us to the fact that 'the "truth" the play has revealed is that there are different sets of cultural awareness which are conveyed in different languages' and that 'the end of the play is powerful in its unremitting focus on a man who is distrustful of language'.[41] If this is a justification for the *stasis* in the play then it is also a reminder of how valuable *Making History* is in preparing us for the even more acute monologal structure *of Molly Sweeney.* The fact that, as a successor to *Translations, Making History* comes to a halt, that we are back on a constant treadmill of history which sees the recurrence of absence and failure as a *leitmotif* suggests that Irish history, and its drama, is open-ended because there can be no closure on a situation which refuses to be pushed across the threshold into a new age. Hugh O'Neill's distrust of language gives the lie to the colonial and post-colonial discussions of Fanon, Said and Bhabha, in which 'the narrative of modernity' is forged in the 'caesura or non-place' or 'lag' between ancient and modern time. The Sperrin mountains where O'Neill hides in Act 3 of *Making History* are such a non-place, as is O'Neill's 'comfortless home' in Act 1, but the discourse between O'Neill and Lombard would satisfy none of the criteria of any post-colonial discipline because it refuses to move forward in either submission or revolt. The simultaneous equations with which the play ends – Lombard reciting the history of a tragic hero as the messiah of his people and O'Neill recanting his life and disavowing his leadership – cancel each other, allowing Irish history and History to enjoy their 'both-and' in a most terrible confluence.

The circularity is striking: the figure of authority who appears throughout Friel's earlier work – as father, teacher, priest, policeman or army officer – is related in his own biography to the figure of his father-schoolmaster, and something of the relationship was resolved in *Translations*. The idea that Friel himself might follow in his father's footsteps was doubly evident in his original decision to enter St Patrick's College, Maynooth, in search of a vocation, and once that had proved illusory, to enter the teaching profession and to remain in it for over ten years. But (much later) to attribute his unsuitability for the priesthood to a 'conflict with my belief in paganism'[42] is to point us in the direction of the later work and its tensions between different kinds and styles of authority and between the author, his text and his audience. It brings him back to the question of how we become aware of our own existence – how do we author ourselves? – when 'the child' is manifestly *there*, aware of others, yet unaware of how or why he is there himself. This has become one of the chief predicaments of the drama which Friel has engendered.

The dramatic trick which Friel has played in both *Translations* and *Making History* is to divide both time and people. The 'private' and 'public' *personae* of Gar O'Donnell have by this stage become the past and future aspects of life in whatever particular context he chooses to evoke. There is no person who can be regarded as whole, yet all partici-pants are required to act a role which recognises the future as well as the past; in Bhabha's terms they are thus 'less than one and double'. The centre is void, and Hugh O'Neill and Molly Sweeney become missing persons – lost to their loved ones and to History. What happens in

Volunteers between the internees and Leif – the imagining of his life and the circumstances of his death, his *context* – is now happening between Friel's characters and his audience This is the trick which he has demonstrated, but not fully explained, to his successors.

But generally the circularity in Irish drama has kept some writers silent while others have explored the same themes with alarming repetition. For Pat Kinevane, author of *The Nun's Wood* (1998), to opine that 'I don't think there's been a play about lunatic young people in the country before'[43] is to display an alarming disregard for a generation of plays (*Philadelphia* and Murphy's *On the Outside* [1962] and *A Crucial Week in the Life of a Grocer's Assistant* [1969] among them) which both celebrated and satirised the madness and the dementia of life in rural Ireland from the 1930s. And to suggest that there was an originality in having his characters in touch with the figures of classical mythology underlines the fact that young writers may know about plays like *Translations* (which in Kinevane's case appeared when he was not yet a teenager) but they do not feel they have to care.

This can be both positive and rewarding or negative and damaging. To find London critic Charles Spencer writing that Conor McPherson's *The Weir* 'puts one in mind of an Irish Chekhov'[44] suggests the reinvention of the wheel in more ways than one, not least because the play 'based on a series of conversations in a quiet Leitrim pub'[45] suggests unnecessary echoes of Murphy's *Conversations on a Homecoming* (1972/85). In July 1998 the *Sunday Times* even asked 'Who is the natural heir to Friel and Murphy – Martin McDonagh . . . or Conor McPherson [?]'.[46]

But in a positive sense, it can be regarded as a continuing affirmation not simply of Friel's original role in the same title but of the need for Irish drama to be still questioning the effects of emigration and returned emigrants, the lack of dialogue within the home, the pretentiousness of Irish affluence, and the struggle with honesty on the personal level; and, on the public plane, the matter of history, self-determination and external relations. 'I have rarely been so convinced that I have just seen a modern classic' says Spencer. I will shortly refer to the relation of Irish drama to the English stage, but here I should remind us that the rewards as well as the disabilities in such a commendation have been manifest in the reception of *Translations* and *Dancing at Lughnasa*.

The view of Garry Hynes, Artistic Director of Druid Theatre Company, is perhaps more pragmatically sanguine than that of Charles Spencer: 'while there is a certain legitimacy in looking for a system of meaning in his [McDonagh's] work, I think it's extraordinarily premature . . . To expect somebody like him to be making fundamental statements is to misunderstand the nature of theatre'.[47]

If McDonagh wants to write plays with a western voice, 'to do something with that language that wouldn't be English or American'[48] then he is writing plays in the same spirit in which Friel began to 'translate' from Anglo-Russian into Hiberno-Russian. If he wants to leave 'little things behind that nobody else could' rather than 'saying things in general about human nature which most people can do if they try'[49] then he is *en route* to finding his own Ballybeg. His insistence on stories which are non- or anti-theatrical is part of the mainstream of Irish drama as we have been studying it. Equally, McPherson's monologues in *St Nicholas* (1997), *This Lime Street Bower* (1995) and *The Weir* derive most of their theatrical validity from the precedents of *Faith Healer* and *Molly Sweeney*. And while the situations of both McDonagh's and McPherson's plays may seem to descend more from Synge and Murphy than from Friel, the combination of storytelling and the emphasis on language and stasis suggests that they both owe much to plays such as *Wonderful Tennessee* and *Molly Sweeney*.

McDonagh, described by O'Toole as 'a citizen of an indefinite land that is neither Ireland nor England but that shares borders with both',[50] could be regarded as archetypally Irish in this respect, underlining a continuance of the Irish-English experience which has been most evident in the life and work of Tom Murphy. Christina Mahony reports that 'one Irish director was heard recently to remark that it had occasioned, in Martin McDonagh, the English now producing their *own* Irish play-wright, rather than relying solely on the imported variety'.[51]

The fact that he was unaware of Synge when he wrote plays such as *A Skull in Connemara* means that while he has not consciously pursued any dramatic tradition, that tradition is pursuing *him*, and this is a perennial problem for the Irish writer. Mahony observes that 'We've been here before in the theatre, and McDonagh sees to it that we are always aware that we have been . . . McDonagh's intention is not to shock us, but to subvert theatrical memory, with Synge as his easiest and most frequent target . . . McDonagh's plays have, then, both an historical sense of Irish theatre con-ventions and a contemporary awareness of viewer sensibility'.[52] Themes with which Synge dealt – the pretence, the lie, the play-within-play – are still lurking because, presumably, not enough has yet been written about them. This constant reiteration of identity and the questions it raises is the most disturbing fact about contemporary Irish drama. Why do Irish play-wrights – with some exceptions – feel the compelling need both from within themselves and from external influences, to participate in this reiteration? Why do audiences need to experience the re-presentation of these themes?

The answer may well lie in the Irish dramatic experience in Britain. In 1958, reviewing Behan's *The Hostage*, Kenneth Tynan wrote that 'it seems to be Ireland's function, every 20 years or so, to provide a play-wright who will kick English drama from the past into the present'.[53] But, as Fintan O'Toole has pointed out in quoting this in the course of an article on Irish plays in Britain, 'it is not hard to suspect that Irish plays are not so much an alternative to as a substitute for hard-edged theatrical explorations of contemporary Britain'.[54] Irish theatre, too, looks to English audiences for validation.

At a very simple level, as Billy Roche has said, 'English people are genuinely missing the art of conversation. They are missing the way we used to talk to one another . . . It's a lack of communication that these plays – mine, Friel's – try to redress'.[55] At a slightly deeper level, Roche goes on to speak of 'the absence of language, storytelling' as a sign of cultural poverty. 'After all, it may be the death of us all if we stop talking to one another' – as sure an indication as one could have of the continuing message of *Philadelphia*.

To probe a little deeper, one element of this 'absence' in London theatres (the same could be said in general terms of New York) is the Irish theme of 'home'. Lucy Davis, Literary Manager of the Donmar Warehouse theatre in London, said in 1997 that Irish theatre is 'often elegiac, nostalgic, family-based, often rural and concerned with exile'.[56] Issues and themes unavailable in the experience of many English people can thus rekindle deeper emotions. The facile nature of most new English writing, and the near silence of the major writers in recent years, is only highlighted by exceptions such as Stoppard's *Arcadia* (1994) or *Invention of Love* (1997). It also has an historical dimension. Irish writers have lived within the cultural umbrella of London for over two hundred years. From Sheridan and Macklin to Wilde and Shaw, there has been a tradition of Irishness inserting itself into, and discomforting, the English dramatic space.

A further reason for the international acceptance of Irish drama is related to this need to talk or to experience talk: it is the fact that Irish people have something to talk *about* which is lacking in many other cultures. One would hesitate to ascribe it to a sense of the spiritual, but it could be taken that, if there is indeed a circularity in the Irish mind and the experience which has been replaced in most of western society by a linearity since at least the end of the eighteenth century, then there may be an energy (let us call it social, intellectual or spiritual as we will) which is unavailable to more 'progressive' cultures. *Translations* in this sense touches a memory of what it is like to find one's world decentred. There is a very distinct sense – despite the fact that the signs of disintegration in Baile Beag are as much internal as external – that the hedge-school is at the centre of the world, a sacred space in Eliade's terms, and that its becoming unhoused in the course of the play is analogous to its people being pushed from sacred time and place into profane time and place.[57]

In seeing McDonagh's plays as portraying an Ireland 'in which all authority has collapsed'[58] we can detect the most telling relationship of the younger playwright with the example of Brian Friel. One of the reasons for the changing nature of modern Irish theatre is the reversal of the poles of authority and submission. Ironically, it is also the reason for history continually repeating itself. The gap between authority and submission, between master and servant, has always been very narrow in Irish history, the ability of both master and servant to entertain familiarity as the bearer of both love and contempt being very marked. In fact, master and servant have commuted towards each other in Irish literature along a route extending from *Castle Rackrent* to *Waiting for Godot* and *At Swim-Two-Birds*.

In his preface (1961) to *The Wood of the Whispering* (1953) M. J. Molloy wrote:

> For forty years Ireland has been free, and for forty years it has wandered in the desert under the leadership of men who freed their nation, but who could never free their own souls and minds from the ill-effects of having been born in slavery.[59]

Thus, eight years before Friel wrote *The Mundy Scheme* an Irish playwright was asking 'what happens to an emerging country when it has emerged?' *The Wood of the Whispering* is another play of 'two men waiting' in which the death of the village, the extinction of vitality and meaning, predominates: freedom desiccated into emotional penury seems to be the price of a servant becoming his own master.

We have seen the master-servant relationship evolve throughout the course of Friel's work: in the short stories the father-son axis, the role of the child in regard to parent, teacher, priest; in the radio plays and their successors, the challenge to parental authority by children who are determined to leave home, to pay the price of freedom by forsaking the hearth; in the concept of a people stirring in their sleep, in their insistence that historians – whether they be the fictional 'Sir' of *Living Quarters* or the real-life Lombard of *Making History* – do not possess a monopoly of the 'facts' or the 'truth', that the servants of History can also become the author of their own stories, we find a powerful post-colonial argument for the inclusion of storytelling as a masterful presence in public narrative, for the insertion and inclusion of silent privacies in what is spoken.

The presiding irony that links master to servant, teacher to pupil, coloniser to colonised is the simultaneous presence and absence of each in the other's life and mind. And it is only by pursuing each other imaginatively, by entering into the mind of otherness, that their dilemma can be resolved. As in Yeats's *The Hour-Glass* the authority of the wise man or *dominus* is rooted in the schoolroom but about to go on an unknown journey, while the *servus* or fool is a pauper, footloose, gormless but illuminated by flashes of rich wisdom, a visionary. Between the two is a path of affirmative dissent, commuting between the sacred and the profane, between the cyclic and the linear, between submission and dominance.[60]

In Friel's 'canon' we find all aspects of this *transitus*, this travelling between identities, and within that *transitus* we find the continual critique of authority – its *locus*, its status, its function – which is the matter of modern Ireland's *realpolitik*: whether it is between master and pupil, father and son, husband and wife, god and man, the *topoi* and the lines of affiliation have altered radically yet no one knows how that will reorientate the Irish world and its mind.

Interpretation is of course subjective. If it were not, not only would there be no disagreement (as signalled earlier in Steiner's quotation of Descartes, p. 186) but there would be no critics, or simply one critic. David Krause, in his review of *Molly Sweeney*, quoted my programme note for the play – 'the brief light of childhood and that of her last autism . . . her dance of anger and despair' – and wondered why Friel had not delivered such a 'disturbing contrast' between light and despair.[61] It would, perhaps, have been more appropriate for him to reflect on why I had detected this aspect of the play and he had not. What makes one critic praise a play – or a production – to the skies while another damns it with not even faint praise? Oliver Sacks's title, 'To See and Not See', could hardly be more relevant, nor the fate of Molly Sweeney more evocative of the fact that we comprehend the world by means of more than the six senses.

Have we a context? It is a question which Irish dramatists might ask themselves afresh. The self-absorption with which most of them are occupied will be self-validating only to the extent that their plays provide their own context, that they are referential to what is internal in the play's dynamics and expressive of it in language and movement which tests the range of those dynamics in the most pressing way.

To that extent, all the writers I have mentioned in this conclusion are pursuing the role of the *seanchaí*, the singer of songs, who, in Jung's words (which Heaney says 'could surely be the voice of Brian Friel himself') has

undertaken . . . to tell my personal myth. I can only . . . 'tell stories'. Whether or not the stories are 'true' is not the problem. The only question is whether what I tell is *my* fable, *my* truth.[62]

There is no point in any writer engaging with an external subject until he has found that voice, that myth. The myth comes from within, but it is verified, validated, *on* the outside and *from* the outside. Allowing a dramatist the freedom and the space to fail is perhaps not even the necessary methodology for reaching a judgement on any particular text. Nor is it necessary that there be any engagement with anything external to that myth, provided the writer can find ways of encapsulating that myth in narrative. Molly Sweeney's almost complete lack of reference to anything beyond the contours of her unsighted mindscape is entirely expressive of the myth which Friel has spent his life narrating.

APPENDIX:
GEORGE STEINER
AND BRIAN FRIEL

GEORGE STEINER

After Babel

Without the true fiction of history,
without the unbroken animation of
the chosen past, we become flat
shadows (p.30). . . . Languages are
wholly arbitrary sets of signals and
conventionalized counters . . . In
certain civilisations, there come
epochs in which syntax stiffens, in
which the available resources of live
perception and restatement wither.
Words seem to go dead under the
weight of sanctified usage; the
frequence and sclerotic force of
clichés, of unexamined similes, of
worn tropes increases. Instead of
acting as a living membrane,
grammar and vocabulary become a
barrier to new feeling. A civilisation is
imprisoned in a linguistic contour
which no longer matches, or matches
only at certain ritual, arbitrary points,
the changing landscape of fact. . . .
'Words, those guardians of meaning,
are not immortal, they are not
invulnerable' wrote Adamov (p. 21).

To remember everything is a
condition of madness (p. 29).

Under extreme stress, men and
women declare their absolute being to

BRIAN FRIEL

Translations

We must never cease renewing those
images; because once we do, we
fossilise. . . .
Words are signals, counters. They are
not immortal. And it can happen – to
use an image you'll understand – it
can happen that a civilisation can be
imprisoned in a linguistic contour
which no longer matches the
landscape of . . . fact [*ellipsis original*]
(p. 43).

To remember everything is a form of
madness (p. 67).

'I wish to God you could understand
me' . . . 'Don't stop – I know what

each other, only to discover that their respective experience of eros and language has set them desperately apart (pp. 44-5).

Any model of communication is at the same time a model of translation, of a vertical or horizontal transfer of significance. No two historical epochs, no two social classes, no two localities, use words and syntax to signify exactly the same things, to send identical signals of valuation and inference. Neither do two human beings (p.46) . . . There will be in every complete speech-act a more or less prominent element of translation. All communication 'interprets' between privacies (p.198).

There appears to be no correlation . . . between linguistic wealth and other resources of a community. Idioms of fantastic elaboration and refinement coexist with utterly primitive, economically harsh modes of subsistence. Often, cultures seem to expend on their vocabulary and syntax acquisitive energies and ostentations entirely lacking in their material lives. Linguistic riches seem to act as a compensatory mechanism. Starving bands of Amazonian Indians may lavish on their condition more verb tenses than could Plato (p. 55).

The vulgate of Eden contained . . . a divine syntax – powers of statement and designation analogous to God's own diction, in which the mere naming of a thing was the necessary and sufficient cause of its leap into reality . . . The Ur-Sprache had a congruence with reality . . . Words and objects dovetailed perfectly. As the modern epistemologist might put it, there was a complete, point-to-point mapping of language onto the

you're saying' . . . (p. 52) 'Strange sounds, aren't they? But nice sounds; like Jimmy Jack reciting his Homer' (p. 60).

I will provide you with the available words and the the available grammar. But will that help you to interpret between privacies? I have no idea. But it's all we have (p. 67).

Certain cultures expend on their vocabularies and syntax acquisitive energies and ostentations entirely lacking in their material lives (p. 42).

'Welcome to Eden!' 'Eden's right! We name a thing and – bang! – it leaps into existence!' 'Each name a perfect equation with its roots'. 'A perfect congruence with its reality' (p. 45).

Everything seemed to find definition that spring – a congruence, a miraculous matching of hope and past and present and possibility (p. 67)

After Babel   *Translations*

true substance and shape of things.
Each man, each proposition was an
equation, with uniquely and perfectly
defined roots, between human
perception and the facts of the case
(p.58).

The violation of natural order in the
proposition that 'it happened
tomorrow' is immediately sensible,
but awkward to analyse (p.132).

The last thing he said to me – he tried
to speak in Irish – he said 'I'll see you
yesterday' – he meant to say 'I'll see
you tomorrow' (p.59).

What logical validation can be found
for statements of future contingency?
What is the status of 'always'?
(p.145)

'Master, what does the English word
"always" mean?' . . . 'It's not a word
I'd start with. It's a silly word' (p.67).

Two men meet . . . The outcome is an
act of naming. Either the one
combatant names the other . . . or
each of the two discloses his name to
the other – 'I am Roland' . . . Several
primordial themes and initiatory rites
are implicit. But one is the crux of
identity, the perilous gift a man makes
when he gives his true name into the
keeping of another (p.225).

'George! For God's sake! *My name is
not Roland!*' 'What!' 'My name is
Owen'. 'Not Roland?' 'Owen' (p.44).

Human speech matured principally
through its hermetic and creative
functions . . . All developed language
has a private core . . . Mature speech
begins in shared secrecy, in centripetal
storage or inventory, in the mutual
cognizance of a very few. In the
beginning the word was largely a
pass-word, granting admission to a
nucleus of like speakers. 'Linguistic
exogamy' comes later, under
compulsion of hostile or collaborative
contact with other small groups. We
speak first to ourselves, then to those
nearest us in kinship and locale. We
turn only gradually to the outsider,
and we do so with every safeguard of
obliqueness, of reservation, of
conventional flatness or outright
misguidance (p.231).

Even if I did speak Irish, I'd always be
an outsider here, wouldn't I? I may
learn the password, but the language
of the tribe will always elude me,
won't it? The private core will always
be . . . hermetic, won't it? [*ellipsis
original*] (p.40).

After Babel	*Translations*
Uncertainty of meaning is incipient poetry (p.234).	'"Uncertainty in meaning is incipient poetry" – who said that?' (p.32) . . . 'Confusion is not an ignoble condition' (p.67).
Human tongues, with their conspicuous consumption of subjunctive, future, and optative forms are a decisive evolutionary advantage. Through them we proceed in a substantive illusion of freedom . . . We secrete from within ourselves the grammar, the mythologies of hope, of fantasy, of self-deception without which we would have been arrested at some rung of primate behaviour or would, long since, have destroyed ourselves. It is our syntax, not the physiology of the body or the thermodynamics of the planetary system, which is full of tomorrows (p.227).	Yes, it is a rich language, Lieutenant, full of the mythologies of fantasy and hope and self-deception - a syntax opulent with tomorrows (p.42).

In Bluebeard's Castle

It is not the literal past that rules us . . . It is images of the past. These are often as highly structured and selective as myths. Images and symbolic constructs of the past are imprinted, almost in the manner of genetic information, on our sensibility . . . The echoes by which a society seeks to determine the reach, the logic and the authority of its own voice come from the rear (p.13). [cf. *After Babel* p.220: We communicate motivated images, local frameworks of feeling. All descriptions are partial. We speak less than the truth, we fragment in order to reconstruct desired alternatives, we select and elide. It is not 'the things which are' that we say, but those which might be, which we would bring about, which the eye and remembrance compose.]	It is not the literal past, the 'facts' of history, that shape us, but images of the past embodied in language (p.66).

In Bluebeard's Castle	*Translations*
We lack histories of the internal time-sense, of the changing beat in men's experience of the rhythms of perception. But we do have reliable eveidenc that those who lived through the 1790s and the first decade and a half of the nineteenth-century . . . felt that time and the whole enterprise of consciousness had formidably accelerated (p. 18).	1798. Going into battle . . . Striding across the fresh, green land. The rhythms of perception heightened. The whole enterprise of consciousness accelerated (p. 67)
Ancient time was at an end (p.21)	Ancient time was at an end (p.40).
Numerous primitive societies have chosen stasis or mythological circularity over forward motion, and have endured around truths immemorially posited (p.104).	We like to think we endure around truths immemorially posited (p.42).

NOTES

Full references are given at the beginning of each chapter (including those cited in previous chapters). Second citations within chapters are given in abbreviated form.

INTRODUCTION

1 G. Steiner, *Language and Silence* (London: Faber & Faber, 1985), p. 47.
2 B. Friel, 'Extracts from a sporadic diary', in T. P. Coogan (ed.), *Ireland and the Arts* (London: Literary Review, n.d. [1982]) p. 59.
3 H. Arendt, *The Life of the Mind* (New York: Harcourt Brace Jovanovich, 1978) vol. 1, p. 191.
4 Fintan O'Toole, 'The man from God knows where', *In Dublin*, 28 October 1982.
5 B. Friel, 'Plays peasant and unpeasant', *Times Literary Supplement*, 17 March 1972.
6 C. Carty, 'Finding a voice in a language not our own', *Sunday Independent*, 5 October 1980.
7 M. Pelletier, *Le Théâtre de Brian Friel: Histoire et histoires* (Villeneuve d'Ascq: Presses Universitaires de Septentrion, 1997), p. 72.
8 Published in *Everyman*, no. 1, 1968.
9 Published in *Aquarius*, no. 5, 1972.
10 *Times Literary Supplement*, 17 March 1972.
11 C. Murray, *Twentieth-Century Irish Drama: Mirror up to Nation* (Manchester: Manchester University Press, 1996), p. 164.
12 *Sunday Tribune*, 21 October 1990, in a review of R. Pine, *Brian Friel and Ireland's Drama*.
13 Programme note for Red Kettle production of *Translations*, 1991.
14 T. Kilroy, 'Theatrical text and literary text', in Alan Peacock (ed.), *The Achievement of Brian Friel* (Gerrards Cross: Colin Smythe, 1993), p. 33.
15 A. van Gennep, *The Rites of Passage* (Chicago: University of Chicago Press, 1960); first published in French 1909.
16 B. Friel, 'Self-Portrait', *Aquarius*, no. 5, 1972.
17 *A Doubtful Paradise*, typescript p. 31.
18 B. Friel, 'The theatre of hope and despair', *Everyman*, no. 1, 1968.
19 Cf. also Michael Etherton, *Contemporary Irish Dramatists* (Houndmills: Macmillan, 1989), p. 147: 'his work is developed around a central poetic vision which has found, and enhanced, a language of theatre to communicate difficult ideas'.
20 Mel Gussow, 'From Ballybeg to Broadway', *New York Sunday Times*, 29 September 1991. Dowling has most recently said '*Philadelphia* . . . in 1964

persuaded me that I needed to be part of a profession that could produce such intoxicating magic. . . . The real joy in working on a Friel play for actor and director comes in the exploration of character and the development of a subtext to support the surface language' – *Sunday Independent* 3 January 1999.

21 'Sporadic diary', in Coogan (ed.), op. cit., p. 60.

22 This strategy was adopted by Will York, director of a production of *Translations* at the Alabama State Theater, Montgomery in 1987; I believe that my reporting this to Brian Friel may have influenced him in taking the same course with Hugh O'Neill in *Making History*. The same strategy occurs in Thomas Kilroy's *Double Cross* in which Brendan Bracken speaks with both his (native) Tipperary accent and his acquired English speech. *Double Cross* is also emblematic of the split personality in which Bracken and Patrick Joyce ('Lord Haw-Haw') shadow each other, both in their propagandist roles for, respectively, Britain and Germany in the Second World War and in their common pattern of escape from an Irish childhood and adoption of a new persona.

23 E. Andrews, *The Art of Brian Friel: Neither Reality Nor Dreams* (Houndmills: Macmillan, 1995), p. 76.

24 G. Steiner, *After Babel* (Oxford: Oxford University Press, 1975) p. 21: 'a civilisation is imprisoned in a linguistic contour which no longer matches, or matches only at certain ritual, arbitrary points, the changing landscape of fact'.

25 W. B. Yeats, 'Anima Hominis', in Norman A. Jeffares (ed.), *Selected Criticism* (London: Macmillan, 1976), p. 170.

26 G. Steiner, *Errata: An Examined Life* (London: Weidenfeld & Nicolson, 1997), p. 98, 154: '*After Babel* . . . was pillaged and quarried both by those who passed it under silence and by the very journals and academic centres for "translation studies" which it helped initiate'.

27 'Sporadic diary', in Coogan (ed.), op. cit.

28 Cf. R. Kearney, 'Language play: Brian Friel and Ireland's verbal theatre', *Studies*, Spring 1983; and Robert S Smith, 'The hermeneutic motion in Brian Friel's *Translations*', *Modern Drama*, 34 (1991).

29 J. Andrews, *A Paper Landscape: the Ordnance Survey in Nineteenth-Century Ireland* (Oxford: Clarendon Press, 1975).

30 Steiner, *After Babel*, p. 89, quotes Whorf and Wittgenstein to the effect that 'spatialisation, and the space-time matrix in which we locate our lives, are made manifest in and by every element of grammar . . . Different linguistic communities literally inhabit and traverse different landscapes of conscious being'.

31 E. Evans, *The Personality of Ireland: Habitat, Heritage And History* (Belfast: Blackstaff Press, 1981).

32 From 'Poetry, language, thought'.

33 Steiner, *After Babel*, p. 58.

34 'Sporadic diary', in Coogan (ed.), op. cit., p. 60.

35 E. Goffman, *Asylums: Essays on the Social Situation of Mental Patients and Other Inmates* (New York: Doubleday, 1961), pp. 4–5.

36 Peter Brook speaks of psycho-drama sessions in psychiatric wards in *The Empty Space* (London: Penguin, 1968), pp. 148–9, in such a way as to remind us that the arrival of a fantastic or exogenous element in an everyday environment, such as Gerry Evans's intrusion into life in Ballybeg in *Dancing at Lughnasa*, or Jack's description of Ryangan ritual, or, in *Translations*, the conflict provoked by the arrival of the English sappers, can create 'true drama'.

37 Richard Schechner, 'Victor Turner's last adventure', in V. Turner, *The Anthropology of Performance* (New York: PAJ Publications, 1987), p. 1.

38 V. Turner, *From Ritual to Theatre: The Human Seriousness of Play* (New York: PAJ Publications, 1982), p. 55.

39 S. Deane, 'Brian Friel: the Double Stage', in *Celtic Revivals: Essays in Modern Irish Literature, 1880-1980* (London: Faber & Faber, 1985), pp. 167–8.

40 V. Turner, *Anthropology of Performance*, p. 168.

41 'Extracts from a sporadic diary', in A. Carpenter and P. Fallon (eds), *The Writers: A Sense of Ireland* (Dublin: O'Brien Press, 1980), pp. 41–2.

42 W. B. Yeats, *Explorations* (London: Macmillan, 1962), p. 254.

43 Cf. Hal Foster (ed.), *The Anti-Aesthetic: Essays on Postmodern Culture* (Port Townsend, Washington: Bay Press, 1983); H. Foster, *Recodings: Art, Spectacle, Cultural Politics* (Seattle: Bay Press, 1985); Theodore Roszak, *The Making of a Counter-Culture: Reflections on the Technocratic Society and its Youthful Opposition* (London: Faber & Faber, 1970); Fredric Jameson, 'Postmodernism and Consumer Society', in H. Foster (ed.), *Anti-Aesthetic*.

44 F. Fanon, *The Wretched of the Earth* (London: MacGibbon & Kee, 1965), p. 28.

45 I suspect that it was this aspect of Sheridan's career which attracted Fintan O'Toole, author of a study of Tom Murphy's work, *The Politics of Magic*, to write such a vigorous account of Sheridan, *A Traitor's Kiss*, which might be subtitled *The Magic of Politics*.

46 Conversation with the author.

47 'The man from God knows where'.

48 'The man from God knows where'.

49 V. Turner, *Dramas, Fields and Metaphors: Symbolic Action in Human Society* (Ithaca, NY: Cornell University Press, 1974), p. 268.

50 Cf. Lawrence Durrell, *Monsieur* (London: Faber & Faber, 1974), p. 257.

51 J. Joyce, *The Essential James Joyce*, ed. H. Levin (Harmondsworth: Penguin, 1963), p. 200. Cf. M. Pelletier, op. cit., p. 114: 'La fiction chez Friel a souvent pour objet de donner une nouvelle virginité à l'identité. Cette deuxième naissance est proprement linguistique, forçant le raconteur à déployer une habileté certaine dans l'art de la rhétorique et de la persuasion'.

52 T. Kilroy 'The Irish writer: self and society 1950–1980', in P. Connolly (ed.), *Literature and the Changing Ireland* (Gerrards Cross: Colin Smythe, 1982), p. 175.

53 R. Welch, *Changing States: Transformations in Modern Irish Writing* (London: Routledge, 1993), p. 237.

54 B. Graham (ed.), *In Search of Ireland: A Cultural Geography* (London: Routledge, 1997), p. xi.

55. B Graham, 'Ireland and Irishness: place, culture and identity', in B. Graham (ed.), op. cit., p. 9.

56 Patrick Duffy, 'Writing Ireland: literature and art in the representation of Irish place', in B. Graham (ed.), op. cit., p. 66.

57 Quoted in Douglas Dunn (ed.), *Two Decades of Irish Writing: A Critical Survey* (Cheadle: Carcanet, 1975), p. 5.

58 This is discussed further in 'Embarrassment', in my *The Disappointed Bridge* (forthcoming).

59 See Julia Carlson (ed.), *Banned in Ireland: Censorship and the Irish Writer* (London: Routledge, 1990).

60 B. Friel, 'The theatre of hope and despair'.

61 In the late 1980s Christopher FitzSimon, then Literary Manager of the Abbey Theatre, told the author that he had approached Brian Friel, without success, for permission to produce *The Mundy Scheme*.

62 Cf. C. Murray, op. cit., p.223: 'Fittingly enough in some ways, the State of Emergency declared in 1939 was not declared officially over until 1995'.

63 G. Smith and D. Hickey (eds) *A Paler Shade of Green* (London: Frewin, 1972), p. 224.

64 Cf. F. Jameson, *Postmodernism Or, the Cultural Logic of Late Capitalism* (Durham: Duke University Press, 1991).

65 G. Smith and D. Hickey (eds), *A Paler Shade of Green*, p. 224.

66 T. Kilroy, 'The Irish writer', p. 180.

67 In a lecture to the Society for the Study of Nineteenth-Century Ireland, University College Cork, 26 June 1998.

68 Smith and Hickey, op. cit., pp. 224–5. It should be noted that, in conversation with the author, Brian Friel has stated that he has no recollection of the interview taking place on which this chapter of *A Paler Shade of Green* is based.

69 Cf. S. Heaney, *The Government of the Tongue: Selected Prose 1978–1987* (London: Faber & Faber, 1988).

70 In 'A defence of poetry'.

71 S. Heaney quoted in M. Pelletier, op. cit., p. 242.

72 'The man from God knows where'.

73 H. Bhabha, *The Location of Culture* (London: Routledge, 1994), p. 28.

74 'A generation of playwrights' in Christopher Murray (ed.), *Irish University Review*, vol. 22, no. 1, 1992.

75 T. Kilroy, 'Tellers of tales', *Times Literary Supplement*, 17 March 1972.

76 D. Kiberd, *Inventing Ireland* (London: Cape, 1995).

77 A. Roche, 'Ireland's *Antigones*: tragedy north and south', in M. Kenneally (ed), *Cultural Contexts and Literary Idioms in Contemporary Irish Literature* (Gerrards Cross: Colin Smythe, 1988).

78 Martin Mansergh (ed.) *The Spirit of the Nation: The Speeches of Charles J. Haughey* (Cork: Mercier, 1986) pp. 335, 476, 663, 673, 714, 755, 835, 1160.

79 J. Joyce, op. cit., p. 252.

80 H. G. Wells, 'The country of the blind'.

81 V. Havel, *Living in Truth* (London: Faber & Faber, 1987), p. 39.

82 Ibid., p. 50.

83 'The man from God knows where'.

84 J. Andrews, K. Barry and B. Friel, '*Translations* and *A Paper Landscape*: between history and fiction', *Crane Bag*, vol. 7, no. 2, 1983, pp. 123–4.

85 M. Pelletier, op. cit., p. 285. In referring to Friel's approach to art as 'a religious one' Patrick Rafroidi adds the caution: 'Such a remark is not intended to transform Friel into a "catholic" writer in the sense we give the word in France. Only one play would fit the definition, *The Enemy Within* . . . nor is Brian Friel a "catholic" writer in the sense often heard in Ireland of using material connected with religion and usually sneering at it', 'The Worlds of Brian Friel' in J. Genet and R. Cave (eds), *Perspectives of Irish Drama and Theatre* (Gerrards Cross: Colin Smythe, 1991), p. 112.

86 B. Friel, 'Self-Portrait'.

87 Conversation with the author.

88 Conversation with the author.

89 T. Kilroy, 'Theatrical text and literary text', in A. Peacock (ed.), *The Achievement of Brian Friel* (Gerrards Cross: Colin Smythe, 1993), p. 92.

90 F. O'Toole, 'Marking time: from *Making History* to *Dancing at Lughnasa*' in Peacock op. cit., p. 208 : 'in the same sense, and with the same consequences, that [Arthur] Miller and [Tennessee] Williams are post-socialist playwrights, Friel is a post-nationalist one'.

91 Cf. Václav Havel: 'The essential aims of life are present naturally in every person. In everyone there is some longing for humanity's rightful dignity, for moral integrity, for free expression of being and a sense of transcendence over the world of existence. Yet, at the same time, each person is capable, to a greater or lesser degree, of coming to terms with living within the lie' – 'The power of the powerless' in *Living in Truth*, p. 54.

92 E. Andrews, op. cit., p. 161

93 Ibid.

94 N. Witoszek and P. Sheeran, 'The desire for transcendence and funerary culture', in *Talking to the Dead: Irish Funerary Traditions* (Amsterdam: Rodopi), pp. 73, 76, 78, 86

95 M. J. O'Neill, 'Irish poets of the nineteenth century: unpublished lecture notes of Oscar Wilde', *University Review*, vol. i, no. 4, 1955.

96 'The man from God knows where'.

97 Paddy Agnew, 'Talking to ourselves' *Magill*, December 1980.

98 This situation has been significantly altered with the publication of T. P. Dolan's *A Dictionary of Hiberno-English* (Dublin: Gill & Macmillan, 1998).

99 'A new look at the language question' (Derry: Field Day, 1983), pp. 13, 17.

100 C. Achebe, 'The African Writer and the English Language', in *Morning Yet on Creation Day*.

101 In B. Ashcroft, G. Griffiths and H. Tiffin (eds), *The Post-Colonial Studies Reader* (London: Routledge, 1995), p. 430.

102 The title of a study of post-colonial literature edited by B. Ashcroft, G. Griffiths and H Tiffin (London: Routledge, 1989).

103 R. Welch, op. cit., p. 240.

104 As discussed in a lecture by Seamus Deane in Trinity College, Dublin, to mark the bicentenary of Edmund Burke, 9 July 1997.

105 'Heroic Styles: the tradition of an idea' (Derry: Field Day, 1984).

106 Quoted in D. Cairns and S. Richards (eds) *Writing Ireland: Colonialism, Nationalism and Culture* (Manchester: Manchester University Press, 1988), p. 142.

107 Ibid., p. 139.

108 Brendan Purcell, 'In search of Newgrange: long night's journey into day', in R. Kearney (ed.), *The Irish Mind: Exploring Intellectual Traditions* (Dublin: Wolfhound 1984), p. 44.

109 M. P. Hederman, 'Poetry and the Fifth Province' *The Crane Bag*, vol. 9, no. 1, 1985.

110 *After Babel*, p. 30.

111 Bhabha op. cit., p. 1.

112 Ibid., p. 2.

113 Ibid., p.3.

114 Ibid., p. 3.

115 P. Brook, *The Empty Space*, p. 59.

116 *The Irish Times*, 22 May 1991.

117 G. Steiner, *Extraterritorial: Papers on Literature and the Language Revolution* (London, Faber & Faber 1972), pp. 27, 72

118 Bhabha, op. cit., p. 45.

119 Ibid., pp. 98, 124.

120 Ibid., pp. 191, 246.

121 George Steiner, *In Bluebeard's Castle: Some Notes Towards the Re-definition of Culture* (London: Faber & Faber, 1971), p. 21.

122 Quoted in Bhabha, op. cit., p. 246.

123 Ibid.

124 Ibid., p. 120. Cf V. Turner, *Forest of Symbols* p. 99: 'the peculiar unity of the liminal: that which is neither this nor that, and yet is both'.

125 Ibid., pp. 219, 5, 36.

126 Hegel, *Lectures on the Philosophy of Religion*, quoted in G. Steiner, *Antigones* (Oxford: Clarendon Press, 1984), p. 21.

127 Derrida, *Dissemination*, trans. B. Johnson (Chicago: Chicago University Press, 1981), p. 213.

128 Bhabha, op. cit., p. 109.
129 Ibid., p. 89.
130 Lady Gregory, *Our Irish Theatre* (London: Putnam, 1913), p. 8.
131 'Man from God knows where'.
132 V. Havel, *Living in Truth*, p. 57.
133 S. Heaney, *New Selected Poems 1966–1987* (London, Faber & Faber, 1990), p. 32.
134 H. Bloom *The Western Canon: The Books and Schools of the Ages* (London: Macmillan, 1994), p. 3; cf. also F. Kermode, *Shakespeare, Spenser, Donne*, p. 179.
135 Cf. R. Kearney, *Transitions: Narratives in Modern Irish Culture* (Dublin: Wolfhound, 1988), p. 121.
136 Bloom, op. cit., p. 336.
137 Freud, 'The "Uncanny"' in *Art and Literature*, Penguin Freud Library, vol. 14 (London: Penguin, 1985) p. 345; Bhabha would add to this the idea, adapted from Hannah Arendt, that the difference between private and public is 'the distinction between things that should be hidden and things that should be shown': Arendt quoted in Bhabha, op. cit., p. 10.
138 Ibid., p. 364
139 Ibid.
140 Ibid., p. 363.
141 Ibid., p. 342.
142 Ibid., p. 341.
143 Cf. ibid., p. 346.
144 Ibid., p. 356.
145 R. Pine, 'Brian Friel and Contemporary Irish Drama', *Colby Quarterly*, vol. 27, no. 4, 1991.
146 Freud, op. cit., p. 369.
147 *Essential James Joyce*, p. 247. Much of the preceding paragraph is drawn from my chapter '"So familiar and so foreign": Irish literature and the end of the canon' in my *The Disappointed Bridge: Ireland and the Post-Colonial World* (forthcoming).
148 The following analysis of Camillo's Memory Theatre is derived from Frances Yates, *The Art of Memory* (London: Routledge & Kegan Paul, 1966), Chapter 6; Yates also discussed a similar Memory Theatre constructed in London by Robert Fludd, and its connection to Shakespeare's Globe (Chapters 15 and 16, ibid.).
149 *Ad. Herennium de ratione dicend* (Cambridge, Mass.: Loeb Classical Library, 1954).
150 F. Yates, op. cit., p.147.
151 Ibid., p. 159
152 Ibid., p. 161.
153 Ibid., p. 161.
154 P. Brook, op. cit., p. 30.
155 cf *From Ritual to Theatre*, op. cit., pp. 112–13.
156 P. Brook, op. cit., p.47.
157 Ibid., pp. 49, 51, 53.
158 Ibid., pp. 54, 51.
159 Brook has written 'Of all contemporary authors, there is no one I admire more highly than Brian Friel . . . *Molly Sweeney* is magnificent and I read it with great joy' – quoted on the cover of *Molly Sweeney*.
160 P. Brook, op. cit., p.150.
161 Fludd's 'Memory Theatre' in London is also discussed by Frances Yates, op. cit.
162 P. Brook, op. cit., p. 58.
163 F. Yates, op. cit., p. 20.

1 THE LANDSCAPE PAINTER

1 F. Yates, *The Art of Memory* (London: Routledge & Kegan Paul, 1966), pp. 252–3.
2 V. Turner, *The Forest of Symbols: Aspects of Ndembu Ritual* (Ithaca, NY: Cornell University Press, 1967), p. 146.
3 Chekhov, *Plays of Anton Chekhov* (Harmondsworth: Penguin, 1954), pp. 149–50, *The Seagull*, Act 2.
4 Larcom quoted by Kevin Barry, *Crane Bag*, vol. 7, no. 2, p. 119.
5 G. Steiner, *After Babel* (Oxford: Oxford University Press, 1975), p. 91.
6 V. Turner, *The Anthropology of Performance* (New York: PAJ Publications, 1987), p. 122; cf also V. Turner, *From Ritual to Theatre: The Human Seriousness of Play* (New York: *Performing Arts Journal*, 1983), p. 9: 'my training for fieldwork roused the scientist in me – the paternal heritage. My field experience revitalised the maternal gift of theatre. I compromised by inventing a unit of description and analysis which I called "social drama".'
7 In conversation with the author.
8 V. Turner, *Dramas, Fields and Metaphors: Symbolic Action in Human Society* (Ithaca, NY: Cornell University Press, 1974), p. 23.
9 'Extracts from a sporadic diary', in A. Carpenter and P. Fallon (eds.) *The Writers: A Sense of Ireland* (Dublin: O'Brien Press 1980) p. 39.
10 P. Brook, *The Empty Space* (London: Penguin, 1968), pp. 47–109.
11 Mel Gussow, 'From Ballybeg to Broadway', *New York Sunday Times*, 29 September 1991.
12 In *Saucer of Larks*.
13 In *Gold in the Sea*.
14 Cf. D. E. S. Maxwell, 'Beckett and Friel: the honour of naming', *A Critical History of Modern Irish Drama 1891–1980* (Cambridge: Cambridge University Press, 1984).
15 Conversation with the author.
16 M. H. Heslinga, *The Irish Border as a Cultural Divide* (Amsterdam: van Gorcum, 1979), p. 37.
17 *The Irish Times*, report, 11 November 1998.
18 James Forsyth, *Tyrone Guthrie* (London: Hamish Hamilton, 1976), p. 25.
19 A. Roche, *Contemporary Irish Drama* (Dublin: Gill & Macmillan, 1994), p. 75.
20 A fact that is becoming less pressing since the appearance of a wide-ranging series of publications by the Institute of Irish Studies at Queen's University of Belfast.
21 D. Murphy, *A Place Apart* (London: John Murray, 1978), p. 1.
22 Fergus O'Ferrall, *Daniel O'Connell and Catholic Emancipation* (Dublin: Gill & Macmillan, 1985), pp. 97–8.
23 Colm Toibin, *Bad Blood: A Walk Along the Irish Border* (London: Vintage, 1994).
24 G. Steiner, *Extraterritorial: Papers on Literature and the Language Revolution* (London, Faber & Faber 1972), p. 14.
25 Peter Lennon, 'Playwright of the Western World', *Guardian*, 8 October 1964.
26 Letter to the author.
27 In conversation with the author.
28 C. McGlinchey, *The Last of the Name* (Belfast: Blackstaff Press, 1986), pp. 12, 4.
29 Cf. Michel de Certau, *The Writing of History* (New York: Columbia University Press, 1988), p. 91. Homi Bhabha in *The Location of Culture* (London: Routledge, 1994), comments 'This caesura in the narrative of modernity reveals something of what de Certau has famously described as the non-place from which all historiographical operations start, the lag which all histories must encounter in order to make a beginning. For the emergence of modernity . . . the template of this 'non-place' becomes the colonial space. It signifies this in a double way. The colonial

space is the *terra incognita* or the *terra nulla*, the empty or wasted land whose history has to be begun, whose archives must be filled out; whose future must be secured in modernity. But the colonial space also stands for the *despotic* time of the Orient that becomes a great problem for the description of modernity and its inscription of the history of the colonized from the perspective of the West.'

30 H. Bhabha, op. cit., p. 71.
31 Introduction to *The Enemy Within*.
32 E. Andrews, *The Art of Brian Friel: Neither Reality Nor Dreams* (Houndmills: Macmillan, 1995), p. 19.
33 'A fine day in Glenties', *Holiday*, April 1963.
34 V. Turner, *From Ritual to Theatre*, p. 9; Turner also says that 'social life, then, in its apparently quietest moments, is characteristically "pregnant" with social dramas' – ibid., p. 11.
35 *Stories from Carleton*, 1889, p. xvi.
36 W. B. Yeats, *Wheels and Butterflies* (London: Macmillan, 1934), p. 6.
37 S. Fitzgerald, *The Irish Times*, 22 May 1991.
38 P. Brook, op. cit., p. 89.
39 'Extracts from a sporadic diary', in A. Carpenter and P. Fallon (eds), op. cit.
40 Ibid.
41 G. Steiner, *After Babel*, p. 276.
42 Ibid.
43 Gus Smith and Des Hickey (eds), *A Paler Shade of Green* (London: Frewin, 1972), p. 223.
44 Bhabha, op. cit., p. 216.
45 'Sporadic diary', in Carpenter and Fallon (eds), op. cit.; cf. Steiner, *After Babel*, p. 269: 'From the perception of unending inadequacy stems a particular sadness. It haunts the history and theory of translation . . . There is a special *miseria* of translation, a melancholy after Babel'.
46 Fintan O'Toole, 'The man from God knows where', *In Dublin*, 28 October 1982.
47 Ibid.
48 Brian Friel, 'Self-Portrait', *Aquarius*, no. 5, 1972.
49 Ibid.
50 Ibid.
51 Ibid. Cf. F. Yates, op. cit., p. 300, where she describes a walk apparently taken by Giordano Bruno through the streets of London from the Strand to Whitehall to attend an 'Ash Wednesday Supper' but which in all likelihood never took place: 'was the journey through the streets and waterways of London then entirely imaginary? I would put it this way. The journey is something in the nature of an occult memory system through which Bruno remembers the themes of the debate at the "Supper"'.
52 G. Steiner, *Extraterritorial*, p. 156 cf. also *After Babel*, p. 215: 'How may we best handle a category of statements which are assuredly intelligible but which cannot be said in principle to be either verifable or falsifiable?'.
53 *The Times*, 5 December 1988.
54 Sean O'Faolain, *The Great O'Neill* (London: Longman, Green & Co., 1942), p. vi.
55 In conversation with the author.
56 B. Friel, 'Self-Portrait'.
57 In an address to an Arts Council conference, 'Partnership – local authorities and the arts', University College Galway, 18 September 1987.
58 Friel, 'Self-Portrait'.
59 S. Heaney, *Preoccupations: Selected Prose 1968-1978* (London: Faber & Faber, 1980), p. 43.
60 S. Heaney *The Times*, 5 December 1988.

61 Blake Morrison, *Seamus Heaney* (London: Methuen, 1982), p. 15.

62 Heaney *Preoccupations*, p. 20.

63 Morrison, op. cit., p. 27. Heaney has also written: 'I have maintained a notion of myself as Irish in a province that insists that it is British' (*Preoccupations*, p. 35); he sees different characteristics in the two tongues: 'I think of the personal and Irish pieties as vowels and the literary awarenesses nourished on English as consonants' (ibid., p. 37).

64 S. Heaney, *North* (London: Faber & Faber, 1975), p. 57.

65 S. Heaney, *The Times*, 5 December 1988.

66 O'Faolain, op. cit., p. 31.

67 Ibid., p. 30.

68 As Augustine called it: cf. H. Arendt, *The Life of the Mind* (New York: Harcourt Brace Jovanovich, 1978), vol. 2, pp. 99–100: 'The Will tells the memory what to retain and what to forget; it tells the intellect what to choose for its under-standing. Memory and Intellect are both contemplative and, as such, passive; it is the Will that makes them function and eventually "binds them together". And only when by virtue of one of them, namely, the Will, the three are "forced into one do we speak of *thought*" – *cogitatio*, which Augustine, playing with etymology, derives from *cogere* (*coactum*), to force together, to unite forcefully.'

69 Steiner, *After Babel*, p. 220.

70 Ulf Dantanus, *Brian Friel, A Study* (London: Faber & Faber, 1988), p. 67; hereafter referred to as Dantanus (1988).

71 Coogan (ed.), op. cit., p. 60; Friel's diary entry for 6 July 1979.

72 *After Babel* p. 29.

73 The line comes from Ovid, *Tristium Liber* V, Elegia X, a reference to his own exile in Pontus where his Latin and Greek were not understood; cf. S. Beckett, *Trilogy* (London: Picador, 1979), p. 135: 'his accent was that of a foreigner, or of one who had lost the habit of speech'.

74 *Consuetudo nominationum*: 'a figure of speech whereby a thing which has no name, or an unsuitable one, receives an appropriate name': *Rhetorica Ad Cornificius Herennium*, 4.31.

75 Cf. Steiner, *After Babel*, pp. 58–9.

76 Ibid. p. 225.

77 Cf. O'Faolain, op. cit., p. 181. See also J. I. Prattis, 'Industrialisation and minority language loyalty', in J. Hansen et al. (eds), *Core-Periphery Theory and Practice* (Bergen: Institute for the Study of Sparsely Populated Areas, 1983): 'naming practices in Lewis – the use of Gaelic nicknames (Iain Nogaidh) and patronymics (Murchadh ic Niall ic Dhomhnaill) – are traditionally an important linguistic reinforcer of community solidarity . . . The use of Gaelic naming systems has the function of identifying individuals but without a unique cultural style, and as such patronymics are an indicator of speech continuity boundaries' (p. 253).

78 R. D. Laing, *The Politics of Experience* (Harmondsworth: Penguin, 1967), p. 95.

79 Quoted in Ezra Pound (ed.), *Instigations* (Freeport, New York, 1967).

80 André Brink, *Mapmakers: Writing in a State of Siege* (London: Faber & Faber, 1983), p. 169.

81 Tim Robinson, *On Setting Foot on the Shores of Connemara* (Gigginstown: Lilliput Press, 1984), p. 9

82 Brink, op. cit., p. 253.

83 V. Turner, *Dramas, Fields and Metaphors*, pp. 13–14.

84 Ibid., pp. 13–14.

85 V. Crapanzano, 'Liminal recreations', review of V. Turner, *From Ritual to Theatre: The Human Seriousness of Play* (New York: Performing Arts Journal, 1983), in *Times Literary Supplement*, 27 April 1984.

86 Quoted in Dantanus (1988), p. 87.
87 Tyrone Guthrie, *In Various Directions* (London: Joseph, 1966), pp. 32 and 38–9.
88 Samuel Beckett, *Film* in *Collected Shorter Plays* (London: Faber & Faber, 1984), p. 163.
89 W. B. Yeats, *Synge and the Ireland of His Time* (Dublin, Cuala Press, 1911), p. 3.
90 Heaney, *Preoccupations*, p. 135.
91 Richard Kearney, Introduction in R. Kearney (ed.), *The Irish Mind* (Dublin: Wolfhound Press, 1984), p. 9.
92 O'Faolain, op. cit., p. 192.
93 Speaking at the opening of an exhibition of work by John Behan, Kenny Gallery, Galway, 18 September 1987.
94 G. Steiner, *Language and Silence* (London: Faber & Faber, 1985), pp. 12 and 39.
95 Ibid., p. 33.
96 E. Estyn Evans, *The Personality of Ireland* (Belfast: Blackstaff Press, 1973), pp. 26–7.
97 A.T. Q. Stewart, *The Narrow Ground: Aspects of Ulster, 1609–1939* (London: Faber & Faber, 1977), p. 181.
98 F. S. L. Lyons, *Culture and Anarchy in Ireland 1890–1939* (Oxford: Oxford University Press, 1978), p. 145.
99 S. Heaney, *An Open Letter* (Derry: Field Day Pamphlets no. 2, 1983).
100 Heaney, *Preoccupations*, pp. 132, 145.
101 Crapanzano, 'Liminal recreations'.
102 *Butcher's Dozen*, originally published Dublin: Peppercanister Press, 1972; reprinted in Thomas Kinsella, *Fifteen Dead* (Mountrath: Dolmen Press, 1979).
103 Friel in 'The future of Irish drama', *The Irish Times*, 12 February 1970.
104 Cf. Eavan Boland, 'The Northern writer and the Troubles', *The Irish Times*, 13 August 1972.
105 Quoted by D. E. S. Maxwell, *Brian Friel* (Bucknell: Bucknell University Press, 1973), p. 29.
106 Friel, 'Plays peasant and unpeasant'.
107 Brink, op. cit., p. 192.
108 In conversation with the author.
109 Thomas Kilroy, 'The Irish writer, self and society 1950–1980', in Peter Connolly (ed.), *Literature and the Changing Ireland* (Gerrards Cross: Colin Smythe, 1982).
110 A. Brink, *An Instant in the Wind* (London: Flamingo, 1976), p. 138.
111 Carpenter and Fallon (eds), *The Writers*, pp. 40–1.
112 Thomas Kinsella, 'The divided mind', in S. Lucy (ed.), *Irish Poets in English* (Cork: Mercier Press, 1972), pp. 209, 213.
113 O'Toole, 'The man from God knows where'.
114 Cf. also the story 'Kelly's Hall'.
115 *The Irish Times*, 12 August 1972.
116 *Henry V*, Act III, scene 1.
117 Declan Kiberd, 'Inventing Irelands', *The Crane Bag*, vol. 8, no. 1, 1984. It is perhaps ironic that in an increasingly pluralistic society Kiberd should have employed the plural 'Irelands' in his preliminary essay and reverted to the singular for the title of his major study.
118 Francis Peabody Magown, Jr, *Kalevala* (Cambridge, Mass: Harvard University Press, 1963).
119 W. B. Yeats, 'Literature and the living voice', quoted by Denis Donoghue, 'The problem of being Irish', *Times Literary Supplement*, 17 March 1972.
120 Friel's diary entry for 15 May 1979, first published as a preface to the programme for *Translations* and reprinted in Coogan (ed.), op. cit.
121 T. Kilroy, preface to *The Enemy Within*.
122 Beckett, *Trilogy*, pp. 26, 267.

2 THE SHORT STORIES

1 S. Beckett, *Trilogy* (London: Picador, 1979), p. 336.
2 S. Deane, Introduction to *The Diviner* (Dublin: O'Brien Press, 1983), p. 9.
3 A. Roche, lecture on novelists of the 1930s, UCD, February 1995.
4 T. Kilroy, 'Theatrical text and literary text', in A. Peacock (ed.), *The Achievement of Brian Friel* (Gerrards Cross: Colin Smythe, 1993), p. 98.
5 Ulf Dantanus, *Brian Friel, A Study* (London: Faber & Faber, 1988), pp. 84, 128, 132, 152, 202; hereafter referred to as Dantanus (1988).
6 Interview with D. E. S. Maxwell, *Images: Arts and the People in Northern Ireland* (Belfast: Northern Ireland Information Office/Arts Council of Northern Ireland, n.d.).
7 Ibid.
8 Ulf Dantanus, *Brian Friel: The Growth of an Irish Dramatist* (Göteborg: Gothenburg Studies in English 59, Acta Universitatis Gothebergensis, 1985), p. 174; hereafter referred to as Dantanus (1985).
9 A. N. Jeffares, 'Place, space and personality and the Irish writer', in A. Carpenter (ed.), *Place, Personality and the Irish Writer* (Gerrards Cross: Colin Smythe, 1977), p. 167.
10 Quoted in Heaney, *Preoccupations: Selected Prose 1968–1978* (London: Faber & Faber, 1980), p. 139.
11 Friel, 'Plays peasant and unpeasant' *Times Literary Supplement*, 17 March 1972.
12 B. Friel, 'The Child', *The Bell*, vol. 18, no. 4, July 1952.
13 In conversation with the author.
14 Peter Lennon, 'Playwright of the Western World', *Guardian*, 8 October 1964.
15 F. O'Toole, 'The man from God knows where', *In Dublin*, 28 October 1982.
16 'Extracts from a sporadic diary', in T. P. Coogan (ed.), *Ireland and the Arts* (London: Literary Review, n.d. [1982]), p. 61.
17 D. E. S. Maxwell, *Brian Friel* (Bucknell: Bucknell University Press, 1973), p. 47.
18 Dantanus (1988), p. 23.
19 B. Friel, 'A challenge to *Acorn*', *Acorn*, no. 14, 1970.
20 Robert Lacy, *Canadian Journal of Irish Studies*, vol. 7, no. 2, December 1981.
21 S. O'Faolain, *The Irish* (Harmondsworth: Penguin, 1969), p. 143; cf. Brendan Kennelly's remark that 'the Irish town was built by men on the run': R Pine, 'Q & A with Brendan Kennelly', *Irish Literary Supplement*, Spring 1990.
22 S. O'Faolain, *The Great O'Neill* (London: Longman, Green & Co., 1942), p. 143.
23 H. Carpenter, *Secret Gardens: A Study of the Golden Age of Children's Literature* (London: Allen & Unwin, 1985), p. 120.
24 G. Steiner, *After Babel* (Oxford: Oxford University Press, 1975), p. 35.
25 Cf. S. Deane, 'Irish poetry and Irish nationalism', and 'Remembering the Irish future', *The Crane Bag*, vol. 8, no. 1, 1984.
26 Introduction to *Diviner*, pp. 15–16.
27 Meg Enright's mistaken perceptions about time future in 'Winners' provide a similar example of physical sense becoming metaphysically damaging.
28 Introduction to *Diviner*, pp. 9–10.
29 Ibid., p. 13.
30 Dantanus (1988), p. 57.
31 In conversation with the author.
32 Introduction to *Diviner*, pp. 15–16.
33 Ibid. p. 12.
34 Northrop Frye, *Anatomy of Criticism* (Ithaca: Cornell University Press, 1957), p. 151.
35 Chekhov, *The Cherry Orchard*, Act 2, pp. 354, 355; Act 3, p. 375, in *Plays by Anton Chekhov* (Harmondsworth: Penguin, 1954).

36 Maxwell, *Brian Friel*, pp. 38, 46; cf. also Maxwell's comments, pp. 17–18, 31, 46–7.
37 Raymond Williams, *The Country and the City* (London: Chatto & Windus, 1973), p. 62.

3   PLAYS OF LOVE

1 B. Friel, *Living Quarters*, p. 44.
2 In Peter Lewis (ed.), *Radio Drama* (London: Longman, 1981), p. 52.
3 Northrop Frye, *Anatomy of Criticism* (Ithaca: Cornell University Press, 1957), p. 134.
4 Ian Rodger, *Radio Drama* (Basingstoke: Macmillan, 1982), p. 18.
5 Ibid., pp. 18–19.
6 Ronald Mason in conversation with the author. Cf. also Ulf Dantanus, *Brian Friel, A Study* (London: Faber & Faber, 1988), pp. 75–7; hereafter referred to as Dantanus (1988).
7 'A sort of freedom', typescript, p. 48.
8 'To this hard house', typescript, p. 53.
9 'A kind of freedom', typescript, p. 43.
10 'A doubtful paradise', typescript, p. 29.
11 'A doubtful paradise', p. 48. Cf. G. Steiner, *After Babel* (Oxford: Oxford University Press, 1975), p. 60: 'The name of Esperanto has in it, undisguised, the root for an ancient and compelling *hope*'.
12 'A sort of freedom', p. 38; the text of the typescript (from the archives of BBC Northern Ireland), which I have quoted, clearly differs from that read, and quoted, by Ulf Dantanus, *Brian Friel: The Growth of an Irish Dramatist* (Göteborg: Gothenburg Studies in English 59, Acta Universitatis Gotheburgensis, 1985), p. 84; hereafter referred to as Dantanus (1985).
13 Ibid.
14 'To this hard house', p. 22.
15 'A doubtful paradise', p. 38.
16 'A sort of freedom', p. 43.
17 J. M. Synge, *Collected Works ii Prose* (Dublin: Maunsel, 1910), pp. 39–43.
18 RTÉ Central Reference Library, cat. no. 2184, p. 25.
19 Ibid., p. 26.
20 Ibid., p. 45.
21 'A sort of freedom', p. 8.
22 'To this hard house', p. 22.
23 William Molyneux, *Dioptrica Nova* (London: 1692).
24 'A sort of freedom', p. 3.
25 Although, as Ronald Mason pointed out to the author, a radio version of *Philadelphia* depends on *one* voice speaking Gar's *two* roles.
26 Edmund Burke, *Reflections on the Revolution in France*, ed. Conor Cruise O'Brien (Harmondsworth: Penguin, 1968). p. 169.
27 Tyrone Guthrie, *In Various Directions* (London: Joseph, 1966), p. 25.
28 Ibid., pp. 28–9.
29 'The blind mice', typescript, p. 26.
30 Interview in *Guardian*, 8 October 1964. T.C. Murray encountered the same kind of resistance to *Maurice Harte* (1912) which depicted a similar tension between a priest's loss of faith and his family's need to maintain respectability: cf. Richard Allen Cave (ed.), *Selected Plays of T C Murray* (Gerrards Cross: Colin Smythe, 1998), pp. xii–xiii.
31 Ibid.

32 Ibid.
33 'The blind mice', p. 26.
34 Ibid., p. 34.
35 Ibid.; on the Irish proclivity for abandoning God (*deus absconditus*), see R. Pine, *Rough Edges: Commitment in Contemporary Irish Drama* (Dublin: Arts Ireland, 1989).
36 Ibid., p. 37.
37 Ibid., p. 48.
38 W. B. Yeats, *Wheels and Butterflies* (London: Macmillan, 1934), p. 6.
39 Cf. H. Arendt, *The Life of the Mind* (New York: Harcourt Brace Jovanovich, 1978) vol. 1, pp. 202–12.
40 W. B. Yeats, *The Poems*, ed. R. Finneran (Dublin: Gill & Macmillan, 1984), p. 73.
41 Cf. Dantanus (1985), p. 215 and R. Rollins, 'Friel's modern 'Fox and Grapes' fable', *Eire-Ireland*, vol. 21, no. 4, 1986.
42 Arendt, op. cit., vol. 1, p. 74.
43 James Simmons, 'Brian Friel, Catholic playwright', *The Honest Ulsterman*, no. 79, Autumn 1985, p. 52.
44 Cf. Dantanus (1985), p. 215.
45 Christopher Murray, 'The rough and holy theatre of Tom Murphy', *Irish University Review*, vol. 17, no. 1, 1987.
46 I owe this point to Colm Toibin, 'Tom Murphy's volcanic Ireland', *Irish University Review,* vol. 17, no. 1, 1987.
47 Programme note for *Famine*, Druid Theatre, Galway, 1984.
48 Thomas Murphy, *Bailegangaire* (Dublin: Gallery Press, 1986), p. 71.
49 Fintan O'Toole makes the case for Murphy in 'Homo absconditus, the apocalyptic imagination in *The Gigli Concert*', *Irish University Review*, vol. 17, no. 1, 1987.
50 Preface to E. O'Neill, *Long Day's Journey into Night* (London: Cape, 1976).
51 Interview with John Waters, 'The frontiersman', *In Dublin*, 15 May 1986.
52 G. B. Shaw, *John Bull's Other Island*, in *The Bodley Head Bernard Shaw* (London: The Bodley Head, 1971), vol. 2: Act 1, pp. 913, 919.
53 Ibid., Act 4, p. 1016.
54 Steiner, *After Babel*, p. 47.
55 Friel's diary entry for 6 July 1979, in T. P. Coogan (ed.), *Ireland and the Arts* (London: Literary Review, n.d. [1982]).
56 Quoted in Arendt, op. cit., vol. 4, p. 4.
57 Friel also somewhat ineptly attempts the same comparison in 'The blind mice'.
58 Beckett, *Trilogy* (London: Picador, 1979), p. 352.
59 Cf. Arendt, op. cit., vol. 2, pp. 99. 164.
60 Steiner, *In Bluebeard's Castle* (London: Faber & Faber, 1971), p. 13.
61 Quoted by G. Poulet, *Studies in Human Time: Valéry* (Baltimore: Johns Hopkins Press, 1956)
62 Cf. Arendt, op. cit., vol. 1, p. 192.
63 Ibid., vol. 2, p. 193.

4 PLAYS OF FREEDOM

1 Chekhov, *Uncle Vanya*, in *Plays by Anton Chekhov* (Harmondsworth: Penguin, 1954), Act 2, p. 209.
2 Descartes, *Philosophical Works* (Cambridge: Cambridge University Press, 1970), vol. 2, p. 75.
3 Louis MacNeice, *Collected Poems* (London: Faber & Faber, 1979), p. 69.

4 John Hewitt, *The Selected Poems of John Hewitt* (Belfast: Blackstaff Press, 2982), p. 20.
5 Cf. Thomas Kinsella and Sean O'Tuama (eds), Introduction to *An Duanaire: Poems of the Dispossessed* (Mountrath: Dolmen Press, 1981), pp. xxvii–xxix.
6 S. Heaney, *An Open Letter* (Derry: Field Day Pamphlets no. 2, 1983).
7 Kinsella and O'Tuama, op. cit., p. 195. In the first edition of this book I inadvertently attributed these lines to Eoghan Rua Ó Suilleabháin.
8 John Milton, *Paradise Lost*, book 1, lines 1–6.
9 Eugene O'Neill, *Long Day's Journey Into Night* (London: Cape, 1976), p.61.
10 E. Andrews, 'The fifth province', in *The Achievement of Brian Friel*, pp. 31, 33.
11 Cf. S. Beckett, *Trilogy* (London: Picador, 1979), p. 167; 'That is what reason counsels. But reason has not much hold on me just now . . . I intend to take the risk.'
12 S. Beckett, *That Time* (1974–5), in *Collected Shorter Plays* (London: Faber & Faber, 1984), p. 228.
13 S. Beckett, *Endgame* (London: Faber & Faber, 1958), p. 21.
14 T. S. Eliot, *The Family Reunion*, in *The Complete Poems and Plays* (London: Faber & Faber, 1969). p. 307.
15 Oscar Lewis, *La Vida*, p. 100.
16 Ibid., p. xlvi.
17 Quoted in R. D. Laing, *The Politics of Experience* (Harmondsworth: Penguin, 1967), p. 118.
18 Friel, 'The theatre of hope and despair', *Everyman*, no. 1, 1968.
19 Ibid.
20 *The Irish Times*, 14 August 1972.
21 Eamonn McCann, *War and an Irish Town* (London: Pluto Press, 1980, second edition), p. 13.
22 Ibid. p. 9.
23 Ibid., p. 118.
24 O'Neill, op. cit., p. 147.
25 Gus Smith and Des Hickey (eds), *A Paler Shade of Green* (London: Frewin, 1972), p. 221.
26 Ibid.
27 *The Irish Times*, 13 August 1972.
28 C. FitzSimon, 'Time for a reappraisal', *The Irish Times*, 3 January 1992.
29 In conversation with the author.
30 C. Murray, 'The history play today', in M. Kenneally (ed.), *Cultural Contexts and Literary Idioms in Contemporary Irish Literature* (Gerrards Cross: Colin Smythe, 1988), p. 269.
31 Francine Cunningham, *Sunday Business Post*, 11 September 1994.
32 Smith and Hickey, *Paler Shade of Green*, p. 222.
33 In conversation with the author.
34 The late Stewart Parker latterly followed a rather ambivalent path: he wrote a six-part series *Lost Belongings* for BBC Northern Ireland television in which 'the myth of "The Exile of the Sons of Uisliu" or "Deirdre of the Sorrows" tied together with the multi-layered tragedies of ancient and modern Ireland' (Helena Sheehan, *Irish Television Drama: A Society and its Stories*, Dublin, RTÉ, 1987, p. 22). He also wrote a more unequivocal confrontation between Catholic and Protestant beliefs, traditions and communities in *Pentecost* written for Field Day (also 1987). The title of the television series *Lost Belongings* in itself ambiguously draws together the idea of displaced tradition and the fact of present dislocation or dispossession.
35 James Simmons 'Brian Friel, Catholic playwright', *The Honest Ulsterman*, no. 79, Autumn 1985, p. 61.

36 S. Deane, Introduction to *Selected Plays of Brian Friel* (London: Faber & Faber, 1984), p. 16.

37 Cf. Smith and Hickey, *Paler Shade of Green*, p. 224.

38 Joseph Mary Plunkett, 'I see his blood upon the rose', in Desmond Ryan (ed.), *The 1916 Poets* (Dublin: Figgis, 1963), p. 192.

39 Seamus Deane in conversation with the author.

40 In a letter to Seamus Deane, quoted by Deane in conversation with the author.

41 Seamus Deane, 'The writer and the Troubles', *Threshold*, no. 25, Summer 1974.

42 Ibid.

43 Ibid.

44 Conor Cruise O'Brien, *Herod: Reflections on Political Violence* (London: Hutchinson, 1978), p. 19.

45 Thomas Kinsella, *Fifteen Dead* (Mountrath: Dolmen Press, 1979), p. 57.

46 Interview with D. E. S. Maxwell in *Images: Arts and the people in Northern Ireland* (Belfast: Northern Ireland Information Office/Arts Council of Northern Ireland, n.d.).

47 O'Brien, op. cit., p. 20.

48 Simmons, 'Brian Friel, Catholic, playwright', p. 63.

49 Kinsella, *Fifteen Dead*, p. 57.

50 Ibid.

51 *Report of the Tribunal appointed to inquire into the events on Sunday, 30th January 1972 which led to loss of life in connection with the procession in Londonderry on that day by the Rt Hon. Lord Widgery OBE TD* (London: HMSO, 1972).

52 V. Turner, *Dramas, Fields and Metaphors: Symbolic Action in Human Society* (Ithaca, NY: Cornell University Press, 1974), p. 232.

53 Ibid., pp. 243–4.

54 Elizabeth Hale Winkler, 'Reflections of Derry's Bloody Sunday in literature', in Heinz Kosok (ed.), *Studies in Anglo-Irish Literature* (Bonn: Bouvier Verlag Herbert Grundmann, 1982), p. 421.

55 Lewis, op. cit., p. xliii.

56 Ibid.

57 Bernadette Devlin (now Devlin McAliskey), politician, who has stood for election in both Northern Ireland and the Republic. Born 1947, elected MP at the age of 21 in 1969. Founded the Irish Republican Socialist Party in 1972. Author of the autobiography *The Price of My Soul*.

58 Cf. V. Turner, *From Ritual to Theatre: The Human Seriousness of Play* (New York: *Performing Arts Journal*, 1983), p. 110: 'the performative genres of complex, industrial societies, as well as many of their forensic and judicial institutions, the stage and the law court, have their deep roots in the enduring human social drama . . . that has its *direct* source in social structural conflict, but behind which perhaps is an endemic evolutionary restlessness.'

59 Simon Winchester, *In Holy Terror* (London: Faber & Faber, 1974), p. 202.

60 M. Shulman, *Standard*, 28 February 1973.

61 McCann, op. cit., p. 28.

62 Ulick O'Connor, 'Brian Friel: crisis and commitment. The writer and Northern Ireland' (Dublin: Elo Publications, 1989: text of a lecture to Yeats International School, Sligo, 20 August, 1987). Reference in this context should also be made to T. G. Fitzibbon, 'Some overt and covert political implications in Brian Friel's *The Freedom of the City, Volunteers* and *Aristocrats*', paper read to the American Conference of Irish Studies, Boston, 1986.

63 Abbey Theatre programme, 1 February 1988.

64 Sean O'Casey, *Three Plays* (London: Pan, 1980), p. 130.

65 Ibid., p. 107.

66 Turner, *Dramas, Fields and Metaphors*, pp. 259–60.

67 Beckett, *Trilogy*, pp. 166, 274, 295, 379.
68 Heaney, *Preoccupations: Selected Prose 1968-1978* (London: Faber & Faber, 1980), pp. 214–15.
69 Ibid.
70 Ibid.
71 B. Friel, 'The theatre of hope and despair'.
72 *Hamlet*, Act 3, scene 2.
73 In conversation with the author.
74 From a radio broadcast quoted on the dustjacket of the first edition of *Lovers*.
75 T. Kilroy, 'Theatrical text and literary text', in A. Peacock (ed.), *The Achievement of Brian Friel* (Gerrards Cross: Colin Smythe, 1993), p. 102.
76 Cf. R. Kuhn, *Corruption in Paradise: The Child in Western Literature*, (Hanover NH: University Press of New England, 1982), p. 118.
77 S. Deane, 'Brian Friel: the name of the game', in Alan Peacock (ed.), *The Achievement of Brian Friel* (Gerrard's Cross: Colin Smythe, 1993), p. 111.
78 Like the commentators in 'Winners' (*Lovers*) and the Stage Manager in Thornton Wilder's *Our Town*. Ruth Niel also draws attention to Wilder's *Pullman Car Hiawatha* in this respect.
79 T. Kilroy, op. cit.
80 In conversation with the author.
81 Friel's diary entry for 7 December 1976, in A. Carpenter and P. Fallon (eds), *The Writers: A Sense of Ireland* (Dublin: O'Brien Press, 1980), p. 43.
82 Cf. Ulf Dantanus, *Brian Friel, A Study* (London: Faber & Faber, 1988), pp. 85–6.
83 Friel's diary entry for 5 November 1979, in T. P. Coogan (ed.), *Ireland and the Arts* (London: Literary Review, n.d. [1982]), p. 61.
84 Friel's diary entry for 16 December 1977, in Carpenter and Fallon (eds), *The Writers*, p. 43.
85 Tyrone Guthrie, quoted in Sam Hanna Bell, 'Theatre', in Michael Longley (ed.), *Causeway: The Arts in Ulster* (Belfast: Arts Council of Northern Ireland, 1971), p. 89.
86 Friel's diary entry for 8 January 1977, in Carpenter and Fallon (eds), *The Writers*, p. 41.
87 Cf. F. Ormsby, 'Brian Friel's plays', *The Honest Ulsterman*, 1970, no. 23.
88 Vivian Mercer, *Beckett/Beckett* (Oxford: Oxford University Press, 1977), p. xii.
89 I am reminded of the attitude of Nikolai Vasilievich in Gerhardie's *Futility* (1922) which Friel had not read at that time: Nikolai singlemindedly pursues a young girl, whose love offers him a once-in-a-lifetime freedom, to the neglect of his own family. His wife says: 'I had to realize that indeed nothing could shame him. So good and wise and indeed well versed was he in his wickedness, that there could be no crime, no sin, of which we others could accuse him of which he had not already in his goodness and wisdom accused himself', William Gerhardie, *Futility* (New York: St Martin's Press, 1971), pp. 34–5. Once again the similarity between the saintliness of the Russian *staretsi* and the Irish bewitched, both of them disengaged from moral society, is striking.
90 *The Seagull, produced by K. S. Stanislavsky*, edited with an introduction by S. D. Balukhaty, translated by David Magarshack (London: Dobson, 1952).
91 Friel's diary entry for 10 September 1976, *The Writers*, p. 40.
92 Reference should be made to an unpublished monograph, 'Filiation and affiliation in the work of Brian Friel', Anthony Bradley, University of Vermont.
93 W. J. Cloonan, *Racine's Theatre: The Politics of Love* (Mississippi University Press, 1977), pp. 113–16.
94 George Steiner, *Antigones* (Oxford: Oxford University Press, 1986).

95 In conversation with the author.
96 Flann O'Brien, *At Swim-Two-Birds* (Harmondsworth: Penguin, 1967), p. 25: 'it was undemocratic to compel characters to be uniformly good or bad, or poor or rich. Each should be allowed a private life, self-determination and a decent standard of living.' It is ironic to note that in *Making History*, history, fate, or the historian, deny all three to the ailing Hugh O'Neill.
97 G. Steiner, *After Babel* (Oxford: Oxford University Press, 1975), p. 454.
98 C. W. E. Bigsby points out the significant number of plays employing the device of the mental hospital in contemporary drama: Durrenmatt's *The Scientists* (1962); Weiss's *Marat/Sade* (1963); Kesey's *One Flew Over the Cuckoo's Nest* (1963); Albee's *Listening* (1960); Storey's *Home* (1970); Orton's *What the Butler Saw* (1968); Shaffer's *Equus* (1973); Edgar's *Mary Barnes* (1977); Stoppard's *Every Good Boy Deserves Favour* (1977); Mary O'Malley's *Look Out ... Here Comes Trouble* (1970): 'The language of crisis in British theatre', *Contemporary English Drama*, p. 19.
99 Eugene McCabe, in conversation with the author, remarked that he feels considerable pity for S. B. O'Donnell, a point very well drawn out by Joe Dowling's 1986 production of *Philadelphia* at the Gaiety Theatre, Dublin, with Seamus Forde as S. B. In this production, however, the gesture was omitted, and the author's stage directions were ignored; instead, S. B. picked up, and scrutinised, his son's passport.
100 Fergus Linehan, *Hibernia*, September 1967, p. 26.
101 Northrop Frye, *Anatomy of Criticism* (Ithaca: Cornell University Press, 1957), p. 285.

5 A FIELD DAY

1 S. Heaney, *Preoccupations: Selected Prose 1968-1978* (London: Faber & Faber, 1980), p. 56.
2 A. T. Q. Stewart, *The Narrow Ground: Roots of Conflict in Ulster* (London: Faber & Faber 1989), p.180.
3 S. Deane, 'Brian Friel: The name of the game', in A. Peacock (ed.), *The Achievement of Brian Friel* (Gerrards Cross: Colin Smythe, 1993), p. 109.
4 B. Graham (ed.), *In Search of Ireland: A Cultural Geography* (London: Routledge, 1997), p. 4.
5 Cf. M. Richtarik, *Acting Between the Lines: The Field Day Theatre Company and Irish Cultural Politics, 1980–84* (Oxford: Clarendon Press, 1995), p. 13.
6 In a lecture to the Royal Dublin Society, November 1984.
7 *Everyman*, no. 1, 1968.
8 *Times Literary Supplement*, 17 March 1972.
9 'Self-Portrait', *Aquarius*, no. 5, 1972.
10 *Times Literary Supplement*, 17 March 1972.
11 Interview with D. E. S. Maxwell in *Images: Arts and the people in Northern Ireland* (Belfast: Northern Ireland Information Office/Arts Council of Northern Ireland, n.d.).
12 The partnership, and Rea's centrality to the venture, became strained when Frank McGuinness's *Carthaginians* was withdrawn as a Field Day production but it continued, despite reports of a winding down of Field Day activity in 1993, until Friel decided in 1990 that *Dancing at Lughnasa* should be presented by the Abbey Theatre rather than Field Day, a decision which marked the beginning of the end of Friel's involvement with the company.
13 Interview with Mitchell Harris, quoted in M. Pelletier, *Le Théâtre de Brian Friel: Histoire et histoires* (Villeneuve d'Ascq: Presses Universitaires de Septentrion, 1997), p. 212.

14 Quoted in M. Richtarik, op. cit., p. 74.

15 There is, however, an echo of the 1833 Commission established to investigate irregularities in the Municipal Corporations of Ireland, chaired by Louis Perrin, which consisted of six Catholic barristers and six Protestant, many of whom were closely associated with O'Connellite and Young Ireland politics; see R. Pine and C. Acton (eds), *To Talent Alone: The Royal Irish Academy of Music 1848–1998*, Dublin: Gill & Macmillan 1998, p. 39).

16 Several important figures were common to both ventures, in particular philosopher Richard Kearney, founder of *Crane Bag*, and editor of *The Irish Mind*, and Declan Kiberd, author of a *Crane Bag* television lecture and of a Field Day pamphlet. Certainly for those such as myself, not directly involved with Field Day, but contributing to *The Crane Bag* and – to a lesser extent – its successor, *The Irish Review*, there was a sense of participating in a collective enterprise which, by positing the 'fifth province', was creating an intellectual space in which a wide range of issues could be debated, and in which those issues from a variety of perspectives, sociological, political, aesthetic, philosophical, semantic, could be seen to have much in common. It would be quite wrong, however, to suggest that 'l'équipe du *Crane Bag* s'installait chez Field Day' (Pelletier, op. cit., p. 224).

17 Preface to *Nationalism, Colonialism and Literature* (Minneapolis: University of Minnesota Press, 1990) p. 14.

18 Cf. P. Brook, *The Empty Space* (London: Penguin, 1968), p. 66.

19 Cf. V. Havel, *Living in Truth* (London: Faber & Faber, 1987), p. 127.

20 *The Irish Times*, 7 September 1988.

21 *Linen Hall Review*, vol. 2, no. 2, 1985.

22 *Ireland's Field Day*, (London: Hutchinson, 1985), p. viii.

23 Programme note for *Translations*, 1980.

24 Programme note for inaugural production of *The Communication Cord*, 1982.

25 Programme note for *Three Sisters*, 1982.

26 *Observer Magazine*, 30 October 1988.

27 M. Richtarik, op. cit., p. 245.

28 Ibid. Seamus Deane informed the present writer in 1985 that if the Field Day pamphlets served no other purpose, they succeeded in eliciting a formal acknowledgement (of receipt) from No. 10 Downing Street – an exercise similar to that of Doalty in *Translations*, moving the sappers' instruments: 'A gesture . . . to indicate . . . a presence' (*Tr* 18).

29 Dustjacket of *Ireland's Field Day*.

30 Ibid.

31 *The Irish Times*, 5 September 1981.

32 Fintan O'Toole, 'The man from God knows where', *In Dublin*, 28 October 1982.

33 Ibid.

34 M. Richtarik, op. cit., p. 254.

35 Ibid.

36 Programme for *Three Sisters*.

37 Conversation with the author.

38 Margo Harkin (director) 'Clear the Stage', BBC Northern Ireland 10 March 1998; cf. Thomas Whitaker, *Fields of Play in Modern Drama* (Princeton, NJ: Princeton University Press, 1977), p.16: 'our ordinary act of listening includes a virtual speaking: we "hear" another as he becomes a voice in our own continuing dialogue. And our ordinary act of watching includes a virtual gesture, to which we attune ourselves. A play focuses that reciprocity and reflects it further. For those who are discovering their roles and for those who are responding to the actors' gestures of discovery, a play is a collaborative miming that is lifted moment by moment into the light of the attention. We are both "outside" and "inside" its action, in a double "now" that is a mimed present and a present miming.'

39 Conversation with the author.

40 *The Irish Times*, 13 September 1984.

41 D. E. S. Maxwell, '"Figures in a Peepshow": Friel and the Irish Dramatic Tradition', in Peacock, *The Achievement of Brian Friel*, p. 64.

42 *The Times*, 5 December 1988.

43 M. Richtarik, op. cit., p. 86.

44 *Irish News*, 29 September 1982.

45 *The Irish Times*, 5 September 1981.

46 Programme note for *The Communication Cord*.

47 Ibid.

48 S. Heaney, *Sweeney Astray* (Derry: Field Day, 1983).

49 S. Heaney, interview with Mitchell Harris, quoted in M. Pelletier, op. cit., p. 226.

50 S. Heaney, 'Ireland's final frontier: it's all in the mind', *Independent*, 12 September 1995.

51 S. Connolly, 'Dreaming history: Brian Friel's *Translations*', *Theatre Ireland*, 13, Autumn 1987.

52 J. Simmons, 'Brian Friel: Catholic playwright', *Honest Ulsterman*, no. 79, Autumn 1985.

53 Cf. P. Hadfield and L. Henderson, 'Field Day – the magical mystery', *Theatre Ireland*, 2, January–May 1983; for a rebuttal of Henderson's attitude see R. Pine, 'Continuing commitment', *Theatre Ireland*, 18 April–June 1989.

54 *Field Day Anthology*, vol. 1 (Derry: Field Day, 1991) p. xxii.

55 F. McGuinness, *Carthaginians and Baglady* (London: Faber & Faber 1988). In reply to Henderson, McGuinness 'emphasizes that the key word is "possible": "If you look at the core of being Irish, we have needed such inner determination in order to live, in order to overcome the process of victimization, the process of wounding".' R. Pine, 'Frank McGuinness, A Profile', *Irish Literary Supplement*, Spring 1991).

56 J. McGrory, 'Law and the Constitution: present discontents' (Derry: Field Day, 1986).

57 S. Deane, *Reading in the Dark* (London: Cape, 1996), p. 23.

58 Garry Agnew, 'Talking to ourselves', *Magill*, December 1980.

59 Deane illustrates the varieties of modes of storytelling when he says of *Reading in the Dark* : 'Some of the material in the novel as it now stands had already appeared in somewhat cryptic form in poems . . . Some of it had only been part of a standard repertoire of anecdote that I had known since childhood. . . . I realised that this was not, could not be, a memoir; but equally, it was not and could not be very far removed from the autobiographical. The problem then was to find a form that would allow me to negotiate between these competing demands', *The Irish Times*, 19 November 1997.

60 S. Heaney, *Preoccupations*, p. 17.

61 Ibid., p. 20.

62 Ibid.

63 Ibid.

64 Ibid., p. 132.

65 Ibid., p. 20.

66 Ibid., p. 57.

67 S. Heaney, *New Selected Poems 1966-1987* (London: Faber & Faber, 1990), p. 214–15.

68 D. Hammond, director, *Something to Write Home About,* (BBC Northern Ireland, 1998).

69 Cf. Mary McAleese, President of Ireland, speaking at Harvard University, 18 October 1998: prompted by Padraig O'Malley, University of Massachusetts, who said 'both communities . . . used the same language . . . in two very different

ways, she agreed that 'people in the North are educated and taught to have different attitudes to language': 'one of the strengths of the Good Friday agreement is that factored into it is an intuitive understanding of that thing which we did not intuitively know before', *The Irish Times*, 19 October 1998.

70 'Building, dwelling, thinking', quoted by Homi Bhabha in *The Location of Culture* (London: Routledge, 1994), p. 1.
71 S. Heaney, *Preoccupations*, p. 41.
72 Ibid., p.52.
73 *Crane Bag*, vol. 1, no. 1, 1977.
74 S. Heaney, *Selected Poems 1965–1975* (London: Faber & Faber, 1980), p. 68.
75 Cf. Ferguson's 'Mesgedra': 'No rootless colonist of an alien earth./Proud but of patient lungs and pliant limb,/A stranger in the land that gave him birth,/The land a stranger to itself and him'.
76 S. Heaney, *New Selected Poems*, p. 21.
77 Ibid., p. 27.
78 M. Richtarik, op. cit., p. 35.
79 Interview with Christopher Morash, quoted in M. Richtarik, op. cit., p. 35.
80 C. Carty, 'Finding voice in a language not our own', *Sunday Independent*, 5 October 1980.
81 'Man from God knows where'.
82 S. Deane 'Heroic styles: the tradition of an idea' (Deasy: Field Day, 1984), p. 46; cf. also ibid., p. 54: 'In such a confrontation, style is no less than a declaration of war. It is the annunciation of essence in a person, in a mode of behaviour, in a set of beliefs'.
83 James Fenton, *The Sunday Times*, 28 September 1980.
84 The main controversy surrounding the neglect of the contribution of women writers, which resulted in the preparation of a fourth, supplementary, volume.
85 'Canon fodder: literary mythologies in Ireland', *Styles of Belonging*, p. 18.
86 *Evening Press*, 19 September 1980.
87 *The Irish Times*, 20 November 1991.
88 C. Milosz, *Native Realm* (Berkeley, CA: University of California Press, 1987) p. 125; S. Heaney, *Station Island* (London: Faber & Faber, 1984), pp. 16–17.
89 S. Parker, *Dramatis Personae* (Belfast: John Malone Memorial Committee, 1986), p. 19.
90 *Newsweek*, 12 May 1986.
91 S. Parker, 'Me and Jim', *Irish University Review,* vol.12, no. 1, 1982.

6 PLAYS OF LANGUAGE AND TIME

1 G. Steiner, *After Babel* (Oxford: Oxford University Press, 1975), p. 73.
2 M. Pelletier, *Le Théâtre de Brian Friel: Histoire et histoires* (Villeneuve d'Ascq: Presses Universitaires de Septentrion, 1997), p. 15.
3 Ibid., p. 197.
4 G. Steiner, *Extraterritorial: Papers on Literature and the Language Revolution* (London: Faber & Faber, 1972), p. 68.
5 Ibid., p. 69.
6 Ibid., p. 69.
7 G. Steiner, *After Babel*, p. 82.
8 *Field Day Anthology* (Derry: Field Day, 1991), vol. 3, p. 1142.
9 G. Steiner, *After Babel*, p. 7.
10 Ibid., p. 22.
11 V. Havel, *Disturbing the Peace* (London: Faber & Faber, 1990), pp. 10–11.

12 G. Steiner, *Extraterritorial*, p. 79; 'Like most true revolutions, it [the language revolution] had behind it a distinctive failure of nerve. The new linguistics arose from a drastic crisis of language: the mind losing confidence in the act of communication itself', ibid.
13 G. Steiner, *Extraterritorial*, p. 10.
14 Ibid., p. 11.
15 Ibid., p. 26.
16 G. Steiner, *Language and Silence* (London: Faber & Faber, 1985), p. 12.
17 F. Fanon, *The Wretched of the Earth* (London: MacGibbon & Kee, 1965), p. 181.
18 G. Steiner, *Extraterritorial*, p. 66.
19 Cf. G. Steiner, *After Babel*, p. 30 and Appendix above.
20 R. Kearney, 'Myth and motherland' (Derry: Field Day, 1984), p. 24.
21 G. Steiner, *Extraterritorial*, p. 66.
22 Fintan O'Toole, 'Marking time: from *Making History* to *Dancing at Lugnasa*', in A. Peacock (ed.), *The Achievement of Brian Friel* (Gerrards Cross: Colin Smythe, 1993), p. 202.
23 'Extracts from a sporadic diary', in T. P. Coogan (ed.), *Ireland and the Arts* (London: Literary Review, n.d. [1982]), p. 58.
24 *The Irish Times*, 15 January 1981.
25 *The Irish Times*, 31 July 1996.
26 C. McGlinchey, *The Last of the Name* (Belfast: Blackstaff Press, 1986), pp. 10–11.
27 Letter to the author.
28 We think wryly of Bhabha's observation 'The very possibility of cultural contestation, the ability to shift the ground of knowledges, or to engage in the "war of position", marks the establishment of new forms of meaning, and strategies of identification', Homi Bhabha, *The Location of Culture* (London: Routledge, 1994), p. 162.
29 S. Deane, 'Brian Friel: the name of the game', in Peacock (ed.), *The Achievement of Brian Friel*, p. 112.
30 Ibid.
31 G. Steiner, *After Babel*, p. 117.
32 J. Andrews, 'Notes for a Future Edition of Brian Friel's *Translations*', *Irish Review*, 13, Winter, 1992–3, S. Connolly, 'Translating history: Brian Friel and the Irish past', in Peacock (ed.), *The Achievement of Brian Friel*.
33 G. Steiner, *After Babel*, p. 395.
34 E. Andrews, 'The fifth province', in Peacock (ed.), *The Achievement of Brian Friel*, p. 162.
35 Lecture at University College Cork, 26 June 1998.
36 *Gay Science* (New York: Random House, 1974), p. 90.
37 V. Turner, *The Forest of Symbols: Aspects of Ndembu Ritual* (Ithaca, NY: Cornell University Press, 1967), p. 20.
38 H. Bhabha, op. cit., p. 44.
39 Ibid., p. 112.
40 E. Andrews, op. cit., p. 172.
41 C. McGlinchey, *Last of the Name*, p. 20.
42 V. Turner, *From Ritual to Theatre: The Human Seriousness of Play* (New York: Performing Arts Journal, 1983), p. 70.
43 S. Deane, Introduction to B. Friel, *Selected Plays* (London: Faber & Faber, 1984), p. 18.
44 H. Bhabha, op. cit., p. 130.
45 Quoted in Marie McCarthy, 'Music education and the quest for cultural education in Ireland 1831–1989', PhD thesis, University of Michigan, 1990.
46 F. Fanon, op. cit., p. 191.

47　Ibid.

48　It is ironic to note that Elmer Andrews, for his part, gets his facts wrong in suggesting that Friel allocates 1789 as the date of Hugh and Jimmy Jack's mock heroism on 'the road to Sligo', E. Andrews, op. cit., p. 172. Friel himself has been responsible for at least two factual puzzles: in *Translations* Yolland is (in 1833) in his 'late twenties/early thirties' and his father was born　in 1789. If, therefore, Yolland is, say, 28, he would have been born when his father was only 16; if, however, he is, say, 32, his father would have been only　14 at the time of his son's birth. When I pointed this out, Friel responded 'I'm buying a calculator'. The calculator was probably never purchased, since in *Dancing at Lughnasa* Jack is 53, his eldest sister is only 40 and his youngest is 26. The 13-year gap between the two eldest siblings is inexplicable, but it does suggest why some critics have unconsciously referred to the priest as the sisters' 'Uncle Jack', cf. A. Roche, *Contemporary Irish Drama* (Dublin: Gill & Macmillan, 1984).

49　In reality, O'Faolain's pub, owned by relatives of Brian Friel.

50　Cf. R. Kuhn, *Corruption in Paradise: The Child in Western Literature*, (Hanover NH: University Press of New England, 1982), p. 168: 'The well that serves as his grave [Joseph in Mann's *Joseph and his Brothers*] . . . is the eternal locus for the reenactment of an archetypal drama'.

51　In this episode we also find an unconscious echo on Friel's part of Yeats's *At the Hawk's Well*: 'I call to the eye of the mind/A well long choked up and dry': Yeats, *Collected Plays*, p. 208. Friel informs the author that he did not have Yeats's text in mind when he wrote this. Cf. R. Pine, 'Yeats, Friel and the politics of failure', in R. Finneran and J. Flannery (eds), *Yeats: An Annual of Critical and Textual Studies*, vol. x (Ann Arbor: University of Michigan Press, 1992).

52　In a letter to the author he states that he has read very little post-colonial literature with the exception of Edward Said, whose pamphlet 'Yeats and decolonization' was published by Field Day in 1988.

53　M. Cronin, *Translating Ireland: Translation, Languages, Culture* (Cork: Cork University Press), p. 111.

54　Ibid.

55　Tom Paulin, 'A new look at the language question' (Derry: Field Day Theatre Company, 1983, *Field Day Pamphlets*, no. 1).

56　Friel's diary entries for 29 May and 1 June 1979, in Coogan (ed.), op. cit., p. 58.

57　Cf. Ronald Hayman, *British Theatre Since 1955* (Oxford: Oxford University press, 1979), p. 9.

58　Quoted by Hayman, *British Theatre*, p. 8.

59　Friel's diary entry for 22 May 1979, in Coogan (ed.), op. cit., p. 58.

60　D. E. S. Maxwell in Peter Connolly (ed.), *Literature and the Changing Ireland* (Gerrards Cross: Colin Smythe, 1982), p. 173.

61　Information from M. H. Heslinga, *The Irish Border as a Cultural Divide* (Amsterdam: van Gorcum, 1979), p. 194.

62　Ibid., p. 161.

63　T. Davis, 'Our national language' and Heslinga, op. cit., p. 194.

64　Heslinga, op. cit., p. 161.

65　John Andrews, *The Crane Bag*, vol. 7, no. 2, pp. 118–24; just as Baudelaire commented at the Salon of 1846, 'there are two ways of understanding portraiture, either as history or as fiction', Charles Baudelaire, 'The Salon of 1846', in Baudelaire, *Art in Paris 1845–62* (London: Phaidon, 1981), p. 88.

66　Seán Connolly, 'Dreaming history: Brian Friel's *Translations*', *Theatre Ireland*, no. 13, 1987, p. 42.

67　P. J. Dowling, *The Hedge-Schools of Ireland* (Cork: Mercier Press, 1968); John O'Donovan, *Letters Containing Information Relative to the Antiquities Collected during the Progress of the Ordnance Survey* (1927); T. Colby, *Ordnance Survey of the County of Londonderry*, 1837.

68 B. Friel, John Andrews and K. Barry, 'Translations and paper landscape: between fiction and history', *The Crane Bag*, vol. 7, no. 2, p. 122.

69 Ibid., p. 123.

70 Dowling, op. cit., pp. 38, 210.

71 John O'Donovan, in a letter quoted in the programme for *Translations*: 'The men only, who go to markets and fairs, speak a little English.' Cf. also Michael Hartnett, *A Farewell to English* (Dublin: Gallery Press, 1975), p. 67: 'a fit language for selling pigs'.

72 Dowling, op. cit., p. 59.

73 Ibid., p. 82.

74 Ibid., pp. 84–5.

75 Proinnsias MacCana, 'Early Irish ideology and the concept of unity', in R. Kearney (ed.), *The Irish Mind* (Dublin: Wolfhound Press, 1984), p. 60.

76 Ibid.

77 J. Andrews, *The Crane Bag*, loc. cit., p. 121.

78 Ibid., p. 122.

79 Seán Connolly, 'Dreaming history', p. 43.

80 *The Crane Bag*, vol. 7, no. 2, pp. 122–4.

81 Cf. Richard Kearney, 'The creativity of language', *Dialogues with Contemporary Continental Thinkers: The Phenomenological Heritage* (Manchester: Manchester University Press, 1984), pp. 20, 23, 28.

82 Cf. Tom Dunne, 'A polemical introduction', to T. Dunne (ed.), *The Writer as Witness* (Cork, Cork University Press, 1987).

83 Kearney, *Dialogues*, p. 44.

84 *The Sunday Times*, 28 September 1980.

85 H. Carpenter, *Secret Gardens: The Golden Age of Children's Literature*, (London: Allen & Unwin, 1985), p. 181.

86 Cf. *Annals of the Four Masters*, ed. John O'Donovan (Dublin: Figgis, 1856), vol. 6, p. 2285. It is ironic also to note O'Donovan's wry comment about differing chronologies: 'the Irish were defeated at Kinsale on the 24th of December, 1601, according to the old style then observed by the English, but on the 3rd of January 1602, according to the Irish and Spaniards' (ibid., p. 2290).

87 'Making history', typescript, p. 58. The words are omitted in the printed text (*MH* 44).

88 Interview with Paddy Agnew, *Magill*, December 1980.

89 Cf. also S. O'Faolain, *The Great O'Neill* (London: Longman, Green & Co., 1942), p. 12.

90 'The required declaration is not an oath . . . the signing of it implies no contractual obligation, and ... it has no binding significance in conscience or in law . . . It is merely an empty political formula, which Deputies could conscientiously sign without becoming involved, or without involving their nation, in obligations of loyalty to the English Crown', *Speeches and Statements by Éamon de Valera 1917–1973*, ed. M. Moynihan (Dublin: Gill & Macmillan, 1980), p. 150.

91 In a lecture at Trinity College, Dublin, 28 April 1987.

92 Ibid., quoted by Dan H. Laurence.

93 G. Steiner, *After Babel*, p. 161.

94 Richard Kearney, 'Language play: Brian Friel and Ireland's verbal theatre', *Studies*, Spring 1983; reprinted, with additional material, in R. Kearney, *Narratives in Modern Irish Culture* (Dublin: Wolfhound, 1987), p. 29.

95 Claude Lévi-Strauss, *Myth and Meaning* (London: Routledge & Kegan Paul, 1978), p. 12.

96 Cf. Seamus Deane, 'An example of tradition', *Crane Bag Book of Irish Studies* (Dublin: Blackwater Press, 1982), vol. 1, p. 373. Deane also observes, 'the Irish idea of tradition was naturally more inclined towards the notion of community betrayed than of community retained' (ibid., p. 374).

97 Lawrence Durrell, *The Key to Modern Poetry* (London: Peter Nevill, 1952), p. 158.

98 'Sporadic diary', in Coogan (ed.), op. cit., p. 60.

99 Ibid.

100 Cf. F. Yates, op. cit., pp. 11, 22, 31.

101 Ibid., p. 287.

102 As Steiner puts it: 'It is very likely that the internalization of language and languages in the human mind involves phenomena of ordered and ordering space, that temporal and spatially-distributive hierarchies are involved', *After Babel*, p. 293.

103 'Sporadic diary', in Coogan (ed.), op. cit., p. 59.

104 Kearney, 'Language play'. For this reason Kearney has placed considerable emphasis on what I have called Friel's 'dramatisation' of Steiner's text. In the Appendix to his essay he lists the main points in the first chapter of *After Babel* which Friel has 'translated'. For further affinities between Steiner and Friel, see Appendix above.

105 The allusion is to John Montague's poem 'Like Dolmens Round My Childhood, The Old People'; we should also take note of 'A Lost Tradition' in which he speaks of 'The whole landscape a manuscript/We had lost the skill to read,/A part of our past disinherited' which highlights the argument of *Translations* (*The Rough Field* [Dublin: Dolmen Press, 1972], p. 25).

106 Introduction to the programme for *The Communication Cord*.

107 Robert Hogan, *Since O'Casey and Other Essays* (Gerrards Cross: Colin Smythe, 1983), p. 131.

108 Ibid.

109 Friel's diary, 1 June 1979, Coogan (ed.), op. cit., p. 59.

110 S. Beckett, *Trilogy*, (London: Picador, 1979), p. 177.

111 R. D. Laing, *The Politics of Experience* (Harmondsworth: Penguin, 1967), pp. 108–9.

112 Steiner, *After Babel*, p. 223.

113 S. Connolly, 'Translating history', in Peacock (ed.), *Achievement of Brian Friel*, p. 156.

114 Ibid., p. 159.

115 Ibid., p. 160.

116 James Fenton, 'Ireland: destruction of an idyll', *The Sunday Times*, 28 September 1980.

117 S. Connolly, 'Dreaming history'.

118 Eric Slater, *Sunday Telegraph*, 8 August 1981.

119 *The Irish Times*, 13 September 1984.

120 E. Andrews, op. cit., p. 162.

121 J. Fenton, op. cit.

122 M. Pelletier, op. cit., p. 171.

123 V. Turner, *Dramas, Fields and Metaphors: Symbolic Action in Human Society* (Ithaca, NY: Cornell University Press, 1974), pp. 237–8.

124 F. Fanon, op. cit., pp. 168–9.

125 D. Harvey, *The Condition of Postmodernity* (Oxford: Blackwell, 1989), p. 218.

126 Paddy Agnew, 'Talking to ourselves', *Magill*, December 1980.

127 Cf. Friel's diary for 7 January 1977 and 2 June 1977, in A. Carpenter and P. Fallon (eds), *The Writers: A Sense of Ireland* (Dublin: O'Brien Press, 1980), pp. 41–2.

128 Seamus Heaney, *North* (London: Faber & Faber, 1975), p. 60.

129 In conversation with the author.

130 Beckett, *Trilogy*, p. 303.

131 Kearney, 'Language play', p. 34.

132 'Everything unreal . . . all served up in that polite, dead language. No roots. No contact with nature, with people', Thomas Kilroy, *The Seagull* (London: Methuen, 1981), p. 10.

133 M Eliade, *Sacred and Profane* (New York: Harcourt Brace Jovanovich, 1959) p. 89.

134 Ibid., p. 185.

135 Virgil, *Aeneid*, Book 1, line 16.

136 Steiner, *In Bluebeard's Castle*, p. 21.

137 O'Faolain, op. cit., p. 94.

138 Cf. Mahler's pathetic insistence on the permanent in the concluding lines of *Das Lied von der Erde*: 'everywhere and eternally the distance shines bright and blue. Eternally, eternally.'

139 O'Faolain, op. cit., pp. 1, 148.

140 Ibid., p. 15.

141 Friel originally discovered this fragment, attributed to Ovid, in a collection which it has since proved impossible to trace.

142 P. Brook, *The Empty Space* (London: Penguin, 1968), p. 94.

143 C. Murray, 'Friel's "emblems of adversity" and the Yeatsian example', in Peacock (ed.), *The Achievement of Brian Friel*, p. 74.

144 *The Irish Review*, vol. 1, no. 1, 1986.

145 Denis Johnston, *Selected Plays* (Gerrards Cross: Colin Smythe 1983) p. 70.

146 S. Heaney, *New Selected Poems*, pp. 214–15.

147 'Something to Write Home About' D. Hammond, director.

148 O'Faolain, op. cit., pp. vi, 143.

149 Ibid., pp. 280–1. In a critique of *Making History* similar in tenor to Seán Connolly's approach to *Translations* ('*Making History*: a Criticism and a Manifesto', *Text & Context*, Autumn 1990) Hiram Morgan makes several points about the liberties taken by O'Faolain and Friel in relation to the facts of Hugh O'Neill's life, including the fact that Lombard did not actually write a life of Hugh O'Neill.

150 Fintan O'Toole, *The Politics of Magic: The Life and Work of Tom Murphy* (Dublin: Raven Arts Press, 1987), p. 15.

151 Tom Paulin, *The Riot Act* (London: Faber & Faber, 1985), p. 332.

152 Cf. O'Toole, *Politics of Magic*, pp. 97–8, 131, 137.

153 In respect of Mabel Bagenal, particularly the little we know of her, and of her leaving O'Neill, cf. O'Faolain, pp. 62 and 121–2.

154 O'Faolain, op. cit., pp. 85, 128, 129.

155 Ibid., p. 149.

156 Cf. Justice Donal Barrington, Thomas Davis Lecture, 'The North and the Constitution', broadcast by RTÉ, 31 January 1988, published in Brian Farrell (ed.), *De Valera's Constitution and Ours* (Dublin: Gill & Macmillan, 1988).

157 'Making history', typescript draft, p. 84.

158 In conversation with the author.

159 O'Faolain, op. cit., p. 278.

160 Friel has adopted the description of 'Fox O'Neill' from a letter from Andrew Trollope to Walsingham, 12 September 1585, included in *The Life of Hugh O'Donnell* by Luadhaidh [Louis] O'Cleary, trans. D. Murphy, 1893.

161 Discussing Adorno's 'Engagement', in *Crane Bag Book of Irish Studies*, vol. 1, p. 152.

162 Kearney, 'Language play'.

163 Laing, op. cit., p. 36.

164 In conversation with the author.
165 In conversation with the author. The point is also made strongly in an interview with Fintan O'Toole, *In Dublin*, 28 October 1982.
166 Brian Friel, *American Welcome: Best Short Plays of 1981*, ed. Stanley Richards (Radnor, PA: Chiltern, 1982). When Friel was working with Hilton Edwards in Philadelphia on a production of *Philadelphia, Here I Come!* he wrote to Micheál MacLiammóir 'I'm so lucky to have Hilton. His patience and sheer professionalism are our only antidote to American literalness' (20 January 1966; Northwestern University Gate Theatre Archive Box 25 file 2).
167 Kearney, 'Language play'.
168 In conversation with the author, and in the interview with O'Toole, *In Dublin*.
169 See a collection of reviews of *The Communication Cord* in *Theatre Ireland*, no. 2, January–May 1983, by (among others) Gerald Dawe, James Simmons and Emelie Fitzgibbon.
170 Kearney, 'Language play'.
171 Steiner, *Language and Silence*, p. 109.
172 S. J. Connolly, 'Culture, identity and tradition', in B. Graham (ed.), *In Search of Ireland: A Cultural Geography* (London: Routledge, 1997), p. 59.
173 Laing. op. cit., p. 162.
174 E. Goffman, *Asylums: Essays on the Social Situation of Mental Patients and Other Inmates* (New York: Doubleday, 1961), p. 5.
175 Ibid., p. 73.
176 Ibid., pp. 99, 116. It should furthermore be noted that Tim's 'discourse analysis', especially the way he promotes the Steinerian problem of interpersonal and inter-cultural translation, owes something to Denis Donoghue: 'The addresser wants to send a message to the addressee. This message needs a context which both parties can share, a code common to them in encoding and decoding the message … The source selects three sub-acts: reception, decoding and development', Denis Donoghue, 'Communication, communion, conversation', *Ferocious Alphabets* (London: Faber & Faber, 1981), pp. 42–3.

7 PLAYS OF BEYOND

1 S. Beckett, *Endgame* (London: Faber & Faber, 1958), p. 35.
2 Cf. P. Burke, 'Both heard and imagined: music as structuring principle in the plays of Brian Friel' in D. Morse et al., (eds), *A Small Nation's Contribution to the World: Essays on Anglo-Irish Literature and Language* (Gerrards Cross: Colin Smythe, 1993), pp. 43–52.; H. White, 'Brian Friel, Thomas Murphy and the use of music in contemporary Irish drama', *Modern Drama*, vol. 33, no. 4, 1990; R. Pine, 'Music and the Contemporary Theatre', RTÉ Radio, May 1995.
3 W. Pater, *The Renaissance* (London: Macmillan, 1893), p.141.
4 Quoted in J. Flannery, *Dear Harp of my Country: The Irish Melodies of Thomas Moore* (Nashville: Sanders, 1998), p. 98.
5 M. Gussow, 'From Ballybeg to Broadway', *New York Sunday Times*, 29 September 1991.
6 Cf. R. Pine, *Lawrence Durrell: The Mindscape* (Houndmills: Macmillan, 1994), pp. 72, 134–7.
7 Homi Bhabha, *The Location of Culture* (London: Routledge, 1994), p. 7; emphasis original.
8 R. Kuhn, *Corruption in Paradise: The Child in Western Literature*, (Hanover NH: University Press of New England, 1982), p. 126.
9 Ibid., pp. 221, 226.

10 Quoted in V. Turner, *From Ritual to Theatre: The Human Seriousness of Play* (New York: *Performing Arts Journal*, 1983), p.15.

11 R. Kuhn, op. cit., p. 212.

12 A. Roche, *Contemporary Irish Drama* (Dublin: Gill & Macmillan, 1984), discusses this topic extensively in the work of Yeats, Friel, Behan, Murphy and Kilroy.

13 R. Kuhn, op. cit., pp. 60–1.

14 O. Wilde, ' To L.L.', *Complete Works of Oscar Wilde* (London: Collins, 1976), p. 811.

15 R. Kuhn, op. cit., p. 6.

16 H. Carpenter, *Secret Gardens: The Golden Age of Children's Literature*, (London: Allen & Unwin, 1985), p. ix.

17 Except insofar as it acknowledges, inadequately, the condition of infantile autism: see my 'Where is this place? Kate O'Brien, autism and modern literature' in J Logan, (ed.), *With Warmest Love: Lectures for Kate O'Brien 1984–93* (Limerick: Mellick Press, 1994).

18 V. Turner, *From Ritual to Theatre*, p. 102.

19 R. Kuhn, op. cit., p. 11–12.

20 H. Carpenter, op. cit., p. 115.

21 I am indebted to Anthony Roche for this observation.

22 R. Kuhn, op. cit., p. 7.

23 Quoted in R. Kuhn, op. cit., p. 61.

24 Quoted in ibid., p. 201.

25 V. Turner, *The Anthropology of Performance* (New York: PAJ Publications, 1987), p. 81.

26 T. Guthrie, *A Life in the Theatre* (London: Hamish Hamilton, 1961), pp. 313–14.

27 W. B. Yeats, *Essays and Introductions* (London: Macmillan, 1961), p. 170.

28 V. Turner, *From Ritual to Theatre*, p. 31.

29 Quoted by V. Crapanzano, 'Liminal Recreations', review of V. Turner, *From Ritual to Theatre*, *Times Literary Supplement*, 27 April 1984.

30 V. Turner, *Anthropology of Performance*, p. 169.

31 Ibid., p.102.

32 'Late on a summer's evening in London in 1987 Brian Friel walked along the Thames Embankment with Tom Kilroy. The two playwrights had just left Britain's National Theatre, where they had seen Friel's dramatisation of Turgenev's *Fathers and Sons*. As they passed homeless men and women curled up in doorways and trash-filled alleys, the writers speculated about the lives of these unfortunate people. Friel said he had two maiden aunts who ended up like that – destitute and abandoned in London. Just before World War II, they had suddenly left the family home in the tiny village of Glenties in Ireland, and never returned. Caught up by the story, Kilroy suggested Friel write a play about it.' (Mel Gussow, 'From Ballybeg to Broadway').

33 Ibid.

34 Ibid.

35 T. Kilroy, 'Theatrical text and literary text', in A. Peacock (ed.), *The Achievement of Brian Friel* (Gerrards Cross: Colin Smythe, 1993), pp. 97–8.

36 R. Barthes, *Image, Music, Text* (London: Fontana, 1977), p. 189.

37 V. Turner, *From Ritual to Theatre*, p. 70.

38 Charles Osborne, *The Guardian*, 18 October 1990.

39 The kites, with their 'crude, cruel, grinning face[s], primitively drawn, garishly painted' (*DL* 70) have a parallel in the Ndembu masks which are part of the 'liminal *sacra*' with their 'grotesqueness and mostrosity', V. Turner, *The Forest of Symbols: Aspects of Ndembu Ritual* (Ithaca, NY: Cornell University Press, 1967), pp. 103, 105.

40 Maire McNeill, *The Festival of Lughnasa: A Study of the Survival of the Celtic Festival of the Beginning of Harvest* (London: Oxford University Press, 1962).

41 Cf. V. Turner, *Forest of Symbols* (p. 293), describing an Ndembu hunting ritual in which the hunter 'puts some powdered white clay . . . on his temples, down the centre of his brow, . . . that his face should be white or lucky';

42 This has been predicted in *Three Sisters*: '*There is a sense that this moment could blossom, an expectancy that suddenly everybody might join in the chorus – and dance – and that the room might be quickened with music and laughter. Everyone is alert to this expectation; it is almost palpable, if some means of realising it could be found . . . If the moment blossoms, they will certainly dance*' (*Sisters* 50).

43 Precedents for the introduction of the supra- or paranormal in Irish drama occur of course in Yeats, but a more recent example is to be found at the opening of Micheál mac Liammóir's *Where Stars Walk*: 'Do you not remember that country, Etáin? That smiling country that is beyond the end of the world?' (*Selected Plays of Micheál mac Liammóir*, edited by John Barrett, Gerrards Cross: Colin Smythe, 1998, p. 5).

44 E. Andrews, 'The fifth province', in Peacock (ed.), *The Achievement of Brian Friel*, p. 172.

45 F. O'Toole, 'Marking time: from *Making History* to *Dancing at Lugnasa*', in Peacock (ed.), *The Achievement of Brian Friel*', p. 203.

46 M. Coveney, *Guardian*, 9 October 1994.

47 L. Miller, *The Noble Drama of W. B. Yeats* (Dublin: Dolmen Press, 1977), p.195.

48 E. Andrews, op. cit., p. 218.

49 F. O'Toole, *The Irish Times*, 10 July 1993.

50 27 June 1985: quoted on the cover of Bryan MacMahon, *The Storyman* (Dublin: Poolbeg, 1994).

51 David Grant, reviewing the inaugural production of *Lughnasa*, found that the strategy of employing a narrator created a division between 'the narrative sections and the enacted episodes' which 'points up the difficulties attendant on innovative ways of storytelling in the theatre', *Theatre Ireland*, no. 22, Spring 1990.

52 P. Brook, *The Empty Space* (London: Penguin, 1968), p. 101; cf. Brook's observation that '*Sergeant Musgrave's Dance* is a demonstration of how a violent need to project a meaning can suddenly call into existence a wild unpredictable form', ibid., p. 79.

53 Ibid., p. 107. We should recall Fintan O'Toole's observation that 'Friel is a writer in despair at, or in flight from [politics, history, language] . . . *Making History* and *Dancing at Lughnasa* . . . are plays which deny the power of rational analysis', 'Marking time', p. 205.

54 M. Pelletier, *Le Théâtre de Brian Friel: Histoire et histoires* (Villeneuve d'Ascq: Presses Universitaires de Septentrion, 1997), p. 282.

55 E. Andrews op. cit., p. 93

56 V. Havel, *Disturbing the Peace* (London: Faber & Faber, 1990), p. xviii.

57 F. Fanon, *The Wretched of the Earth* (London: MacGibbon & Kee, 1965), p. 44

58 Lynda Henderson had previously criticised *Translations* for a similar fault which she perceived: 'Its seductiveness adroitly disguises its dishonesty' – 'A dangerous translation', *Fortnight*, no. 235, 10–23 March 1986.

59 'For liberation: Brian Friel and the use of memory', in Peacock (ed.), *The Achievement of Brian Friel*, p. 240.

60 Ibid.

61 J. M. Synge, *Works* (Dublin: Maunsel, 1910), vol. 2, p. 5.

62 R. Pine, 'Yeats, Friel and the politics of failure', in R. Finneran and J. Flannery (eds), *Yeats: An Annual of Critical and Textual Studies*, vol. x (Ann Arbor: University of Michigan Press, 1992); R. Pine, 'Brian Friel and Contemporary Irish Drama', *Colby Quarterly*, vol. 27, no. 4, 1991.

63 Cf.V. Turner, *Dramas, Fields and Metaphors: Symbolic Action in Human Society* (Ithaca, NY: Cornell University Press, 1974), p. 238.

64 Quoted in ibid., p. 239.

65 Letter to author.

66 J. Joyce, *Ulysses* (Harmondsworth: Penguin 1968) pp. 30–1.

67 Fintan O'Toole, programme note for London production of *Molly Sweeney*.

68 V. Turner, *Dramas, Fields and Metaphors*, pp. 175, 177.

69 *The Irish Times*, 10 July 1993.

70 We should take into serious account Noel Pearson's view that *Wonderful Tennessee* is a 'more difficult' and a 'more interesting' play than *Dancing at Lughnasa* (as expressed in the television documentary *From Ballybeg to Broadway*, directed by Donald Taylor Black).

71 Cf. M. Pelletier, op. cit., p. 110.

72 Friel, 'Self-Portrait', *Aquarius*, no. 5, 1972.

73 V. Havel, op. cit., pp. 136–7.

74 Cf H. Bhabha, op. cit. pp. 45–7.

75 F. O'Toole, *The Irish Times*, 10 July 1993.

76 M. Pelletier, op. cit., p. 296.

77 R. Barthes, 'The death of the author', *Image, Music, Text* (London: Fontana, 1977), p. 142.

78 Ibid., p. 143.

79 *The Irish Times*, 30 June 1993.

80 R. Kuhn, op. cit., pp. 24–5.

81 Catherine Byrne and John Kavanagh in Donald Taylor Black, director, *From Ballybeg to Broadway*.

82 Ibid.

83 M. Gussow, op. cit.

84 Cf. D. Hogan and M. Gibbons, *Inis Bó Finne: A Guide to the Natural History and Archaeology* (Clifden: Connemara and Islands Heritage Tourism, 1992), p. 1: 'Originally a magical place, a place of mists and mystery . . . Inishbofin was a mythical place constantly shrouded in mists in the western ocean. As with other such places it had no constant location in the seas which we know as the Atlantic'.

85 R. Kuhn, op. cit., p. 65.

86 Patrick Mason in Donald Taylor Black, *From Ballybeg to Broadway*.

87 On the cover of *Molly Sweeney*.

88 In a letter to the author.

89 Stephen Kuusisto, *The Planet of the Blind* (London: Faber & Faber, 1998), p. 49.

90 Oliver Sacks, 'To see and not see', in *An Anthropologist on Mars* (London: Picador, 1995), p. 102.

91 Ibid., pp. 102–3.

92 Ibid., p.104.

93 Cf John Berger, *Ways of Seeing* (London: Penguin, 1972), pp. 16–17.

94 O. Sacks, op. cit., pp. 107–8.

95 Ibid., pp. 139, 141.

96 S. Kuusisto, op. cit., p. 5.

97 Ibid., pp.10–11.

98 Ibid., p. 7.

99 Ibid., p. 42

100 Ibid., p. 11.

101 Ibid., p. 7

102 Ibid., pp. 6–7

103 Ibid., p.13.
104 Ibid., p. 20.
105 Ibid., p. 21.
106 O. Sacks, op. cit., p. 115.
107 Cf. Gabriel Garcia Marquez, *A Hundred Years of Solitude* (London: Cape, 1970), p. 45, 'It was Aureliano who conceived the formula that was to protect them against loss of memory. . . . He discovered that he had trouble remembering almost every object in the laboratory. Then he marked them with their respective names so that all he had to do was read the inscription in order to identify them'.
108 S. Kuusisto, op. cit., p. 11.
109 O. Sacks, op. cit., p. 117.
110 Ibid., p. 110.
111 Ibid., pp. 125-6.
112 J. Lacarriere, *The Gnostics* (San Francisco: City Lights,1989), p. 30.
113 When he makes his own peace with his blindness, and meets his guide-dog, Corky, Stephen Kuusisto tells us that 'Corky and I are prayerful gnostics, who have silently identified the proper secret names for air and sunlight.' p. 183
114 G. Steiner, *After Babel* (Oxford: Oxford University Press, 1975), pp. 217–18
115 O. Sacks, op. cit., pp. 133–4.
116 Ibid.
117 Ibid., p. 141, emphasis original.
118 Ibid., p. 143.
119 Ibid., p. 144.
120 S. Kuusisto, op. cit., p. 15.
121 Ibid., pp. 38–9.
122 *The Irish Times*, 27 September 1994.
123 Letter to the author. Wittgenstein's interest in the relationship between language and reality, between word and fact, would of course engage Friel's imagination; cf. G. Steiner, *Language and Silence* (London: Faber & Faber, 1985), p. 39: 'That which we call fact may well be a veil spun by language to shroud the mind from reality'.
124 Cf. H. Bracken, 'George Berkeley: the Irish Cartesian', and D. Berman 'The Irish Counter-Enlightenment', in R. Kearney (ed.) *The Irish Mind* (Dublin: Wolfhound Press, 1984); R. Pine, *The Thief of Reason: Oscar Wilde and Modern Ireland* (Dublin: Gill & Macmillan, 1995), pp. 24–5, 308.
125 Programme note for Almeida Theatre (London) production of *Molly Sweeney*.
126 T. Macaulay, 'Minute on Indian Education', Ashcroft et al., *The Post-Colonial Studies Reader* (London: Routledge, 1995), p. 428.
127 S. Kuusisto op. cit., p. 8
128 Ibid., p. 63.
129 Quoted in H. Bhabha, op. cit., p. 44.
130 Ibid.
131 S. Kuusisto, op. cit., p. 99.
132 G. Steiner, *After Babel*, p. 58.
133 R. Pine, *Lawrence Durrell: The Mindscape*, pp. 207–22.
134 T. Brown, '"Have we a context?": Transition, self and society in the theatre of Brian Friel', in Peacock (ed.), *The Achievement of Brian Friel*, p. 195.
135 Introduction to *The Enemy Within*, p. 8.
136 BBC Northern Ireland radio interview, quoted in S. H. Bell, *The Theatre in Ulster*, p. 106.
137 *Independent*, 15 March 1997.
138 *The Irish Times*, 18 March 1997.
139 Ibid.

140 The American university referred to above.

141 R. Pine to B. Friel, 14 December 1996.

142 B. Friel to R. Pine, 2 January 1997.

143 'The source of all life and knowledge is in man and woman, and the source of all living is in the interchange and the meeting and mingling of these two', D. H. Lawrence to A. W. McLeod, quoted in Harry T. Moore, *The Priest of Love: A Life of D. H. Lawrence* (London: Heinemann, 1974), p. 253.

144 John Keats, letter to G. and T. Keats, 21 December 1817.

145 Ibid.

146 *Independent*, 15 March 1997.

147 Ibid.

148 Quoted in D. C. Cassidy, *Uncertainty: The Life and Science of Werner Heisenberg* (New York: Freeman, 1992), p. 215.

149 Abbey Theatre, programme for *Give Me Your Answer, Do!*, 12 March 1997.

150 Thomas Whitaker bears out this point (*Fields of Play in Modern Drama*, p. 26): 'Drama, I suspect, always explores our equivocal condition. And the negative way of modern drama is a fresh masking devoted to disclosing among us the inauthenticity of our usual masks – our apparent identity as "persons".'

151 Lawrence Durrell, description of the character Sylvie in *The Avignon Quintet* (London: Faber & Faber, 1992), p. 89.

152 Lawrence Durrell, *Monsieur* (London: Faber & Faber, 1974), p. 19.

153 L. Durrell, *The Avignon Quintet* (London: Faber & Faber, 1992), p. 271.

154 Lawrence Durrell, *Sebastian* (London: Faber & Faber, 1983), p.160.

8 MAGIC

1 Shakespeare, *Twelfth Night*, Act 3, iv, 142.

2 E. Fen, Introduction to *Plays of Anton Chekhov*, (Harmondsworth: Penguin, 1954), p. 19.

3 Ibid., p. 7.

4 Although of course in Chekhov's output *Three Sisters* succeeded *Uncle Vanya* chronologically.

5 G. Steiner, *After Babel* (Oxford: Oxford University Press, 1975), p. 149.

6 C. Murray, 'Friel's "emblems of adversity" and the Yeatsian example', in A. Peacock (ed.), *The Achievement of Brian Friel* (Gerrards Cross: Colin Smythe, 1993), p. 82.

7 Michael Longley, interview with Dillon Johnston, *Irish Literary Supplement*, vol. 5, no. 2, 1986.

8 Letter to the author.

9 *Los Angeles Times*, 13 February 1969.

10 A. Roche, *Contemporary Irish Drama* (Dublin: Gill & Macmillan, 1994), p. 107.

11 G. Hughes, 'Ghosts and ritual in Brian Friel's *Faith Healer*', *Irish University Review*, vol. 24, no. 2, 1994.

12 Friel's diary entry for 10 September 1977, in A. Carpenter and P. Fallon (eds), *The Writers: A Sense of Ireland* (Dublin: O'Brien Press, 1980), p. 42.

13 V. Turner, *Dramas, Fields and Metaphors: Symbolic Action in Human Society* (Ithaca, NY: Cornell University Press, 1974), p. 255.

14 Cf. Ulf Dantanus, *Brian Friel, A Study* (London: Faber & Faber, 1988), p. 99; and Ulf Dantanus, *Brian Friel: The Growth of an Irish Dramatist* (Göteborg: Gothenburg Studies in English 59, Acta Universitatis Gotheburgensis, 1985), p. 221.

15 In *Fathers and Sons* Vassily Bazarov notes that his son 'usually brings someone home with him every holiday' (*FS* 39) despite the fact that this is Bazarov's *first* visit home. And those with a flawless knack for map-reading can indulge in locating the actual 'Ballybeg', using the information supplied by Friel (*Tr.* 67) that by walking from Ballybeg for twenty-three miles in the direction of Sligo one may arrive in Glenties. But this is to indulge too much in the 'how many children had Lady Macbeth' school of criticism.

16 As D. E. S. Maxwell says in respect of *Philadelphia, Cass* and *Crystal and Fox*, 'he looks on these . . . as inspections of the diversities of love, undertaken in the way that a sculptor views his work from different angles', D. E. S. Maxwell, *Brian Friel* (Lewisburg PA: Bucknell University Press, 1973), p. 78.

17 'Extracts from a sporadic diary', in T. P.Coogan (ed.), *Ireland and the Arts* (London: Literary Review, n.d. [1982]), p. 58.

18 Cf. T. Whitaker, *Fields of Play in Modern Drama* (Princeton, NJ: Princeton University Press, 1977), p. 86: 'Stanislavsky . . . knew that the actor must sustain, while "pentrating into the most secret places" of his character's heart, an "unbroken flow" of communion with his stage partners, with objects, and with the audience. Only a style founded upon such communion can enable the cast of *Three Sisters* to present, within and beyond these masks of distraction and self-obsession, out mutual immanence'. Whitaker also quotes Jacques Copeau (ibid., p. 128): 'When the man in the audience murmurs in his heart and with his heart the same words spoken by the man on the stage'.

19 Leonard McNally (1752–1820) was a barrister, duelist, playwright and member of the United Irishmen whose secrets he betrayed to Dublin Castle, including the denunciation of both Lord Edward Fitzgerald in 1797 and Robert Emmet (whose case he defended) in 1803. His plays include *The Apotheosis of Punch, Retaliation, Fashionable Levities, Critic Upon Critic, Cottage Festival* and an adaptation of *Tristram Shandy*.

20 Typescript of original draft of *Fathers and Sons*, pp. 77–9.

21 *Independent*, 21 October 1990.

22 Fen, 'Introduction', op. cit.

23 *The Irish Times*, 16 January 1993.

24 *The Irish Times*, 31 October 1991.

25 *New York Times*, 21 January 1996.

26 *Irish Literary Supplement*, Spring 1995.

27 *New York Times*, 8 January 1996.

28 *New Yorker*, 18 January 1996.

29 *Wall Street Journal*, 11 January 1996.

30 Philippians 2, 12.

31 'Sporadic diary', in Carpenter and Fallon (eds), *The Writers*, p. 43.

32 A. Roche, *Contemporary Irish Drama*, pp. 6, 12.

33 *The Irish Times*, 1 August 1992.

34 'Sporadic diary', in Carpenter and Fallon (eds), *The Writers*, op. cit., p. 43.

35 B. Friel, 'Self-Portrait'. In conversation with Mel Gussow, Friel said: 'I want a director to call rehearsals, to make sure the actors are there on time and to get them to speak their lines clearly and distinctly. I've no interest whatever in his concept or interpretation', M. Gussow, 'From Ballybeg to Broadway', *New York Sunday Times*, 29 September 1991.

36 BBC Northern Ireland, 17 December 1965; the view was repeated by the actress Rosaleen Linehan in 1991: 'Like all Friel's plays it is deceptively musical without seeming to be so', *The Irish Times*, 6 May 1991.

37 *The Irish Times*, 1 August 1992.

38 C. FitzSimon, *The Boys: A Biography of Micheál MacLíammóir and Hilton Edwards* (London: Nick Hern Books, 1994), p. 275.

39 M. Gussow, 'From Ballybeg to Broadway'.
40 Conversation with the author.
41 V. White in *The Irish Times*, 26 February 1998.
42 Donald Taylor Black, director, *From Ballybeg to Broadway*.
43 *The Irish Times*, 24 September 1988.
44 Ibid.
45 G. Steiner, *After Babel*, p. 41.
46 Ibid., pp. 172–3.
47 Peter Brook, *The Empty Space* (London: Penguin, 1968), p. 157.
48 S. Deane, Introduction to *Selected Plays*, p. 12.
49 P. Brook, op. cit., p. 101.
50 Thomas Kilroy has discussed this in relation to his own translation of *The Seagull* and on the occasion of Friel's version of *Uncle Vanya* Fintan O'Toole wrote 'From Russia with words' (*The Irish Times*, 26 September 1998); cf. also Richard York, 'Friel's Russia', in Peacock (ed.), *The Achievement of Brian Friel*.
51 P. Brook, op. cit., p. 96.
52 'Sporadic diary', in Carpenter and Fallon (eds), *The Writers*, p. 42.
53 The disorder is suggested by Turgenev in the elder Bazarov's body language, which is in itself suggestive of S. B. O'Donnell's gesture towards Gar's jacket in *Philadelphia*: 'Occasionally he would go into the garden for a few seconds, stand there like a stone idol, as though stricken with unutterable bewilderment', I. Turgenev, *Fathers and Sons*, trans. Rosemary Edmonds (Harmondsworth: Penguin, 1965), p. 222.
54 'Fathers and Sons', typescript draft, p. 22.
55 Or, as Eliot puts it, 'The man who returns will have to meet/The boy who left', *The Family Reunion*, part 1, scene 1, *Complete Poems and Plays*, (London: Faber & Faber, 1969), p. 288.
56 'Fathers and Sons', typescript draft, p. 152.
57 Ibid., pp. 180–1.
58 Programme note for Friel's version of *Three Sisters*.

CONCLUSION

1 R. Barthes, *Image, Music, Text* (London: Fontana, 1977), p. 148.
2 *The Irish Times*, 15 January 1998.
3 E. Andrews, *The Art of Brian Friel: Neither Reality nor Dreams* (Houndmills: Macmillan, 1995), p. 75.
4 *The Irish Times*, 8 December 1990.
5 'Contemporary Irish theatre: the illusion of tradition', in T. P. Coogan (ed.), *Ireland and the Arts* (London: Literary Review, n.d. [1982]), p. 132.
6 In the filmscript of Richard Attenborough's *Gandhi*.
7 *The Irish Times*, 16 November 1991.
8 *The Irish Times*, 25–27 December, 1995.
9 *The Irish Times*, 28 February 1995.
10 In 1929, when Denis Johnston's play, originally entitled *Shadowdance*, was rejected by the Abbey Theatre, it was alleged that the doorman had returned the script to the author with the remark 'The old lady says no', which was taken to be a reference to Lady Gregory. The remark is thought by some to have given the play its new title, and a nickname to the Abbey Theatre itself.
11 Judy Friel, in 'Rehearsing *Katie Roche*' (*Irish University Review*, vol. 25 no. 1, 1995) makes the point that there have been few women dramatists in modern Ireland; Anthony Roche (*Contemporary Irish Drama*, Dublin: Gill & Macmillan,

1994, p. 11) emphasises that the most significant contemporary presence of women dramatists has been in the Northern context.

12 *The Irish Times*, 15 October 1998.
13 *The Irish Times*, 21 September 1994.
14 *The Irish Times*, 15 October 1998.
15 M. Carr, *The Mai* (Loughcrew: Gallery Press, 1995), p. 14.
16 Ibid., p. 54.
17 M. Carr, *Portia Coughlan* (Loughcrew: Gallery Press, 1998), p. 27.
18 M. Carr, *The Mai*, p. 53.
19 M. Carr, *Portia Coughlan*, p. 56.
20 Ibid.
21 *The Irish Times*, 19 August 1997.
22 Ibid.
23 I am of course aware that Anthony Roche has discussed this argument in the opening pages of his *Contemporary Irish Drama*, and that he points to Tom Murphy's *A Whistle in the Dark* (1961) and Brendan Behan's *The Quare Fellow* as significant milestones in modern Irish drama.
24 D. Dunn (ed.), *Two Decades of Irish Writing* (Cheadle: Carcanet 1975).
25 Quoted in M. Richtarik, op. cit., p. 7.
26 In R. Pine, 'Frank McGuinness, a Profile', *The Irish Literary Supplement*, Spring 1991; and most recently in presenting the Special Tribute Award at the *Irish Times*/ESB Theatre Awards 1999: 'No other man has understood us in this century as he has'; Friel's work had 'tormented me and challenged me' – *Irish Times*, 8 February 1999.
27 *The Irish Times*, 13 June 1992.
28 *The Irish Times*, 26 April 1997.
29 *The Irish Times*, 6 February 1996.
30 In an RTÉ radio news bulletin (*Morning Ireland*), 8 June 1998.
31 *The Irish Times*, 15 January 1998.
32 *The Irish Times*, 21 September 1994.
33 Cf. R. Pine, 'Being Said – Text and Context in the Work of John B Keane', in G Fitzmaurice (ed.), *The Listowel Literary Phenomenon* (Indreabhán: Cló Iar-Chonnacta, 1994).
34 *The Irish Times*, 27 June 1995.
35 *The Irish Times*, 22 March 1994.
36 Irish Writers' Union Seminar, October 1994.
37 Christina Hunt Mahony, 'Barry, McPherson and McDonagh in the States: cops, critics and cripples', *Irish Literary Supplement*, Fall 1998; Mahony also suggests that 'one must either, I think, accept the possibility that not all Irish work goes over equally well with foreign, or even diaspora, audiences *or* that Martin McDonagh, working from his London background, may not be as able to differentiate real from stage Irishman as it is believed he can'.
38 *The Irish Times*, 24 June 1997.
39 Fintan O'Toole, *The Irish Times*, 24 June 1997.
40 *The Irish Times*, 7 May 1998.
41 R. Welch, '"Isn't This Your Job – To Translate?" – Brian Friel's Languages', A. Peacock, (ed.), *The Achievement of Brian Friel* (Gerrards Cross: Colin Smythe, 1993), p. 147.
42 Mel Gussow, 'From Ballybeg to Broadway'.
43 *The Irish Times*, 7 May 1998.
44 *The Sunday Times*, 22 February 1998.
45 Victoria White, *The Irish Times*, 5 March 1998.
46 *The Sunday Times*, 12 July 1998.

47 Ibid.
48 *The Irish Times*, 26 April 1997.
49 Ibid.
50 *The Irish Times*, 26 April 1997.
51 C. H. Mahony, op. cit.
52 C. H. Mahony, ibid.
53 Quoted by Fintan O'Toole, *The Irish Times*, 29 May 1996.
54 Ibid.
55 *The Irish Times*, 5 September 1992.
56 *The Irish Times*, 20 November 1997.
57 M. Eliade, *Sacred and Profane* (New York: Harcourt Brace Jovanovich, 1959), pp. 42–3.
58 Fintan O'Toole, *The Irish Times*, 24 June 1997.
59 M. J. Molloy, *Three Plays* (Newark, Delaware: Proscenium Press, 1975), p. 125.
60 Cf. my 'Turning the hour-glass: the Irish mind since independence', in my forthcoming *The Disappointed Bridge*.
61 *Irish Literary Supplement*, Spring 1995.
62 S. Heaney, 'For liberation: Brian Friel and the use of memory', in Alan Peacock (ed.), *The Achievement of Brian Friel* (Gerrards Cross: Colin Smythe, 1993), p. 234.

INDEX